DEEP
SOUTHS

DEEP SOUTHS

SOUTHS

*Delta, Piedmont, and Sea Island
Society in the Age of Segregation*

J. WILLIAM HARRIS

THE JOHNS HOPKINS UNIVERSITY PRESS

Baltimore and London

Johns Hopkins Paperbacks edition, 2003
2   4   6   8   9   7   5   3   1

The Johns Hopkins University Press
2715 North Charles Street
Baltimore, Maryland 21218-4363
www.press.jhu.edu

Library of Congress Cataloging-in-Publication Data

Harris, J. William, 1946–
Deep souths : Delta, Piedmont, and Sea Island society in the age of
segregation / J. William Harris.
p. cm.
Includes bibliographical references and index.
ISBN 0-8018-6563-8 (alk. paper)
1. Southern States — History — 1865–1951. 2. Southern States — Race
relations. 3. Southern States — Economic conditions. 4. Afro-Americans —
Segregation — Southern States. 5. Afro-Americans — Southern States —
Economic conditions. 6. Afro-Americans — Southern States — Politics and
government. 7. Capitalism — Southern States — History. 8. Agriculture —
Economic aspects — Southern States — History. 9. Agriculture and politics —
Southern States — History. I. Title.
F215 .H29 2001
975 — dc21
00-009558

ISBN 0-8018-7310-X (pbk.)

A catalog record for this book is available from the British Library.

For Terry

CONTENTS

Illustrations follow pages 148 and 256
Maps are on pages 12, 27, and 39

ACKNOWLEDGMENTS

When I began work on this book in 1985, I thought, for reasons that escape me now, that it would be a rather short project. That it took only fifteen years is due in no small part to the support I have received along the way from many institutions and individuals. Much of that has come from administrators and colleagues at the University of New Hampshire. Summer Faculty Fellowships at the beginning and near the end of the project enabled me to devote two summers full-time to research and writing. Grants from the Office of the Vice President for Research and Public Affairs, the Center for Humanities, the Institute for Policy and Social Science Research, the Dean of Liberal Arts, and the Signal Fund of the Department of History covered a multitude of expenses for travel, research assistance, purchase of microfilms, map design, and reproduction of illustrations.

A fellowship from the Warren Center for the Study of American History at Harvard University enabled me to spend a semester in the company of outstanding scholars and work in the magnificent libraries at Harvard. Bernard Bailyn, director of the center that year, made sure we benefited fully from the resources of the center. I wrote the first draft of the first chapter of the book while holding a fellowship at the National Humanities Center in North Carolina, where everything—the building itself, the lunches with wonderful colleagues from many disciplines, the superb library staff, and the support from Robert Connor, Kent Mullikin, and the rest of the administrative staff—conspires to produce an ideal setting for scholarly work. A grant from the American Philosophical Society paid for a trip to Mississippi at a crucial point in the research.

Research for the book has taken me to many archives and libraries, and I must thank the staff members in all of these for unfailingly efficient and courteous assistance: Perkins Library at Duke University; the Southern Historical Collection, Wilson Library, at the University of North Carolina at

Chapel Hill (with special thanks for many kinds of help from David Moltke-Hansen); the Georgia Historical Society; the Museum of Coastal History on St. Simons Island; the Brunswick, Georgia, Regional Library; the Hargrett Rare Book and Manuscript Library at the University of Georgia; the Georgia Department of Archives and History; the Mississippi Department of Archives and History; the Special Collections Department at the Mitchell Memorial Library, Mississippi State University; the Archives at Delta State University; the Schlesinger Library of Radcliffe Institute; the Baker Library at the Harvard Business School; the Manuscript Division and the Prints and Photographs Division at the Library of Congress; and the National Archives and Records Service. At the University of New Hampshire, the interlibrary loan staff at Dimond Library helped me obtain many items, and the Media Services Department photographed many of the illustrations.

    The grants from University of New Hampshire sources enabled me to hire a number of fine research assistants. Jeannine L'Heureux, Ryan Madden, Tom Fraser, Susan Barnard, Barbara Caffery, Stephanie Day, Rob Des-Rochers, Kathryn Scaletti, Loren Bourassa, Molly Igoe, and David Wiley all labored for many hours extracting data from statistical sources. Valerie Dunham Adams and Mary Ann Gunderson both collected data and set up computer files for them. Lynn DuMais and Mary Walling Blackburn did crucial newspaper research related to lynchings. These students, and others in my classes, have listened to me discuss the themes of the project, in class and out, for many years, and their feedback has frequently been helpful. Stewart E. Tolnay and E. M. Beck generously shared with me their database of confirmed lynchings in Mississippi and Georgia. William L. Nelson designed and executed the maps.

    The History Department at the University of New Hampshire is truly collegial, and department members have listened to several presentations based on my research in our Faculty Seminar. Their responses have sharpened and corrected my arguments in many places, and they have supported me in many other ways too numerous to mention. I have benefited from comments at several other presentations of my research, including those at the history departments at North Carolina State University and the University of North Carolina at Chapel Hill; the Interdisciplinary Seminar on the South in the Institute for the Arts and Humanities and the Odum Institute for Research in Social Science, both at UNC–Chapel Hill; the Pittsburgh Seminar in Social History at Carnegie-Mellon University; the Graduate Research Seminar in Southern History at the University of California at San Diego; the

Citadel Conference on the South; and the Plain Folk of the South Symposium at Southeastern Louisiana University. David Blight commented helpfully on a paper presented at a meeting of the Organization of American Historians, and Stanley Engerman provided astute comments on a paper based on my research.

Material in the book has appeared, usually in quite different form, in several journal articles and book chapters. I am grateful for the comments I received from the editors and, in some cases, anonymous readers, and to the publishers for permission to use the material here: "The Question of Peonage in the History of the New South," in *Plain Folk of the South Revisited*, ed. Samuel C. Hyde Jr. (Baton Rouge, La., 1997), 100–25 (© Louisiana State University Press); "Etiquette, Lynching, and Racial Boundaries in Southern History: A Mississippi Example," *American Historical Review* 100 (1995), 387–410; "Crop Choices in the Piedmont before and after the Civil War," *Journal of Economic History* 54 (1994), 526–42 (courtesy Cambridge University Press); "Portrait of a Small Slaveholder: The Journal of Benton H. Miller," *Georgia Historical Quarterly* 74 (1990), 1–20 (courtesy Georgia Historical Society); and "Marx, the Market, and the Freedmen: Land and Labor in Late-Nineteenth-Century Georgia," in *Looking South: Chapters in the Story of an American Region*, ed. Winfred B. Moore Jr. and Joseph F. Tripp (Westport, Conn., 1989), 191–203, and "Plantations and Power: Emancipation on the David Barrow Plantations," in *Towards a New South? Studies in Post–Civil War Communities*, ed. Orville Vernon Burton and Robert C. McMath Jr. (Westport, Conn., 1982) (both courtesy Greenwood Press, an imprint of Greenwood Publishing Group, Inc., Westport, Conn.).

Special thanks go to friends who read all or parts of the manuscript as it evolved and were honest enough to point out mistakes and other shortcomings. Ellen Fitzpatrick read an early version of Chapter 5 and her comments contributed to a significant reshaping of the chapter. Burt Feintuch's comments on Chapter 5 were also useful. Lucy Salyer offered incisive comments on Chapters 2 and 6, where her expertise in legal history was particularly helpful. Three scholar-friends, W. Jeffrey Bolster, Jane Turner Censer, and Joan E. Cashin, took time from their own work to read and comment on the entire manuscript. Their questions, suggestions, and critiques helped me improve the book in many places. Where the final version still falls short, it is my fault and not theirs.

In an era of publishing in which most editors are not allowed actually to edit, I benefited enormously from the work of two whose skills harken back to an earlier age. The attention and advice of Jeannette Hopkins have improved virtually every passage and every argument in the book. Robert J. Brugger at the Johns Hopkins University Press has supported the project for several years in many ways. His intervention when I had just begun to write helped to shape the architecture of the whole, and he continued to insist to the very end that I get things right and make them clear. He also found two anonymous readers who provided the right balance of encouragement and criticism. Marie Blanchard's excellent copyediting made the final version more polished and more accurate.

My three children, Kate, Logan, and Hannah, have patiently observed the unfolding of what must have seemed an interminable project and made sure I continued to enjoy the pleasures of fatherhood along the way. My wife, Terry Kay Rockefeller, has read every page, listened to every argument, and asked dozens of hard questions along the way. She did not complain when I refused to agree with her, and she did not seem to mind that it took me as long to write one book as it did for her to produce several prize-winning documentary films. Through it all she has been my best editor, best critic, and best friend. The dedication is a small thanks in return.

DEEP
SOUTHS

Introduction

DEEP SOUTH IS A TERM OF ALMOST MYTHIC RESONANCE. THE phrase names the lower tier of states in the southeastern United States, but it provokes images that a more neutral geographical term — *the lower South* or *the Gulf States* — cannot. "Still waters run deep," we say; a profound thinker is "deep"; the worst of anything is the "depths." All these connotations are suggested by *Deep South*: a place frozen in time, marked by violent extremes of action and belief, yet, in the hands of its writers and musicians, touched by profundity.

The image of a "Deep South" as a society unto itself and, from the failure of Reconstruction to the civil rights movement, hardly changing received perhaps its definitive shape in books and films from the 1930s and early 1940s: the novels of William Faulkner, the comic portrayals of poor whites as grotesques in Erskine Caldwell's *Tobacco Road,* long-standing romantic conceptions of an "Old South" crystallized in the opening scenes of the immensely popular novel and film *Gone with the Wind,* and even in the sophisticated work of the team of black and white scholars who studied Natchez, Mississippi, and in 1941 published the results in *Deep South: A Social Anthropological Study of Caste and Class.* In fact, although by 1941 *Deep South*, with its connotations of uniformity and stasis, had become a standard description of the lower South, the term itself was barely a decade old.[1]

Readers at that time could have found evidence of a more complex and dynamic lower South in other, less popular books. In *Drums and Shadows,* published in 1940, some 140 black residents along the Georgia coast and on the Sea Islands recounted their religious and folk beliefs, and the authors of the book (members of the Georgia Writers' Project, a New Deal agency), documented the connections between their traditions and customs and similar ones in Africa. A year later, William Alexander Percy, a planter, lawyer, and poet from Greenville, Mississippi, published his autobiography, *Lanterns on the Levee: Recollections of a Planter's Son.* Percy's heroes were his father, LeRoy, and other members of the conservative planting gentry, who had, in Percy's telling, dominated the Delta's politics, supervised the building of its levees, helped to carve new plantations out of wilderness after the Civil War, fought the political rise of ignorant and depraved poor whites, and paternalistically guided inferior blacks. In 1943, sociologist Arthur Raper published *Tenants of the Almighty,* a history of Greene County, in Georgia's eastern Piedmont. Raper offered his readers a liberal's view of the southern past. While Percy pitied blacks and loathed poor whites, Raper saw both as the South's hope of the future. Raper devoted nearly half his book to a hopeful analysis of the impact of New Deal programs in Greene County, programs that Raper himself helped to design and implement.[2]

It is easy to find flaws in all three of these books. Most obviously, in none of them did African Americans emerge *as* southerners — as people who had helped to make southern history, not just react to it or flee from it. Percy could not take African Americans seriously as adults; although he admitted that southern whites, who lived "habitually as a superior among inferiors," faced constant "temptation to dishonesty and hubris," he was unable to recognize the symptoms of both in himself. For Raper, while blacks were real people with normal interests and aspirations, they responded to history made by others. *Drums and Shadows* paid little attention to African Americans' contemporary lives or to the historical struggles that had allowed the people on the Atlantic coast to buy plots of land, build churches, and protect the cultural resources that made it possible for them to preserve the traditions its authors recorded. Still, taken together, the three books offered a sense of the particularities, the variety, and the dynamism of life and of lives in the lower South after the Civil War, a sense missing in images of the "Deep South." They were written, not from the viewpoint of the observer flying high above the landscape, where details fade and only the largest forms stand out, but from ground level.

This study, *Deep Souths,* undertakes the task of bringing to the reader a ground-level view of the social history of the three lower-South regions that Percy, Raper, and the Savannah Writers' Project wrote about: the Mississippi-Yazoo Delta, the eastern Georgia Piedmont, and the Sea Islands and rice coast of Georgia. Its time frame is the entire period between Reconstruction and the Second World War. Such a comparative history captures the common experiences that most places in the lower South shared and that leads us to see them, quite properly for some purposes, as belonging to the *same* "Deep South." All were, before the Civil War, majority-black in population and economically dependent on slaves who produced commercial crops on large plantations — cotton in all three areas, rice along the Atlantic coast. All experienced secession, defeat in war, and, during Reconstruction, northern military occupation and the rise of African Americans to political power. In the decades after the war, all struggled to revive their plantation economies in a new system, capitalist and dependent on free, rather than slave, labor. By the end of Reconstruction, private individuals (nearly all white) owned the best land and competed in a market for labor, most of it provided by black wage hands and tenants.

In all three regions, simultaneously with the creation of a new capitalist system came the consolidation of a new era of white supremacy, an age of segregation. "Segregation" meant the legal separation of people on the basis of race in schools, on systems of transportation, and in places of public accommodation, but it also meant much more than that. In the age of segregation, whites dominated public discourse, whites made the law and controlled the courts, whites disfranchised blacks and thus guaranteed that public policy would systematically favor those in control, and whites subjected blacks in daily life to a thousand forms of petty humiliation and, sometimes, to horrific forms of violence. The consolidation of white supremacy did not take place in an instant or even in a decade after the end of Reconstruction, but, by the early twentieth century, African Americans had lost the full rights of citizenship that had been promised them following the Civil War. It was this institutionalized system of white supremacy that prevented the lower South from developing, despite an essentially free-market economy, what historian Thomas Haskell has called the capitalist "form of life." As Haskell writes, the capitalist marketplace may be "a scene of perpetual struggle," but "contrary to romantic folklore," it is "not a Hobbesian war of all against all. Many holds are barred. Success ordinarily requires not only pugnacity and shrewdness but also restraint." Among those restraints are the "lessons taught (and simultaneously presupposed) by the market," the first being that

people must "keep their promises." In the lower South in the age of segregation, whites who controlled public institutions and owned most of the land
did not, as a rule, have to keep their promises to African Americans.[3]

These broadly similar experiences are an important element in the account that follows, but the comparative and local approach here also allows
us to uncover, through plantation records, county newspapers, census and
tax returns, and dozens of other sources, the particular and often very different histories of the Delta, the Piedmont, and the Atlantic coast. It highlights the importance of both time and place. Time mattered: over the decades between Reconstruction and World War II, cotton prices fell, rose, and
fell again, driving changes in living standards, setting off population movements, and shaping politics differently in each era. The rise of the Populist
Party, the entry of the United States into the First World War, and the coming
of the New Deal all shook established political and social patterns. The
spread of new technologies of communication and new patterns in popular
culture spread new values, reshaped traditions, and spurred creativity. Place
mattered: along the Georgia coast, plantation agriculture was destroyed
within a generation after Reconstruction and thousands of former slaves
became landowning peasant farmers; in the Georgia Piedmont, plantation
agriculture revived with the use of black and white tenant labor, but never
brought true prosperity; and in the Delta, largely a wilderness in 1860, huge
public works and land clearing made possible the creation of new cotton
plantations on a scale never seen under slavery. A local and comparative approach also highlights the complex and varying responses of African Americans to the age of segregation. Along the coast, African Americans conserved
old traditions that had largely disappeared elsewhere. In the Piedmont, they
helped to fuel the Populist uprising of the 1890s. In the Delta, they nurtured
the growth of a radically new musical form, the blues. In cities and towns in
all three regions, members of a new African American middle class repeatedly sought to claim their rights of citizenship even as they built a fragile
prosperity based, ironically, on the opportunities opened up by segregation.

The stories and analyses that follow unfold in three chronological parts,
each covering a single two-decade-long generation. Within each of the three
parts, a chapter focusing primarily on economic developments is followed by
chapters concentrating on culture and on politics. Such divisions are to an extent artificial, to be sure, and I am in sympathy with Joan W. Scott's argument
that historians "have to conceive of processes so interconnected that they
cannot be disentangled"; but the interconnections will, I hope, be clear in the

telling.[4] At the end of each of these twenty-year generations a major national development — the Populist response to agricultural crisis in the 1890s, national mobilization after 1916 for the First World War, and the expansion of national power in response to the Great Depression of the 1930s — raised new challenges to the culture and politics of white supremacy. Each challenge was repelled in turn, but by 1940 all three regions were very different from each other and very different from what they had been in 1876.

In one of the most famous passages in William Faulkner's many novels, Canadian Shreve McCannon implores his Harvard roommate, Quentin Compson, to "tell about the South. What's it like there. What do they do there. Why do they live there. Why do they live at all." In what follows, my burden is to do some of that telling, and, above all, to show readers that there is more than one South to tell about.[5]

PART I
1876–1896

What in the world will a man do with out labor in this country? For one can not work the land with out the Negroes.

— Clive Metcalf, Washington County,
Mississippi, in his diary, 3 January 1890

This is a white man's country, a white man's government, and the white people will and intend to rule it at all hazards and at any cost.

— Greensboro (Georgia)
Herald-Journal, 7 December 1888

The great majority of the negroes of Greene county are a respectable, hard-working, honest race of people . . . ; they know that the populist party is the only party that guarantees equal rights to all, both black and white.

— J. M. Storey, in Greensboro (Georgia)
Herald-Journal, 24 November 1894

I

Land and Labor in New South Countrysides

IN THE LATE FALL OF 1875, FORTY-SEVEN-YEAR-OLD LOUIS Manigault traveled up the Savannah River to resume the role of rice planter, which he had relinquished in 1864. He was headed for Gowrie, a plantation a few miles above the city of Savannah on Argyle Island. For twelve years before and during the Civil War, Louis had managed the plantation, with its nearly one hundred slaves, for his father, Charles. Each November, after the first frost had killed off the mosquitoes, he had made his way up the river to live on the property until the next May. Now, in 1875, the property belonged to him. He had not seen it in more than eight years.[1]

In the decade before the war, Gowrie's land and slaves had together made up a productive property for the Manigault family, returning almost $10,000 a year in profits.[2] In 1864, during a battle between retreating Confederate forces and Sherman's advancing troops, near the end of the famous March to the Sea, Gowrie's big plantation house, expensive steam thresher, and water-powered rice polishing mill had all been destroyed. After the war, Louis's father, Charles Manigault, had rented the plantation to men willing to learn how to raise rice without slave labor. After 1869, Gowrie had been leased, at first for $3,500 per year, later for $3,200, to a neighboring planter, Daniel Heyward. After Charles Manigault died in 1875 and left Gowrie to his son, Louis decided to leave his position as a clerk in a Charleston merchant house to assume active management of the property. He borrowed $8,000 from two sisters and $4,500 from a Charlestonian named W. B. Smith, arranged to buy a used threshing machine on credit from Daniel Heyward, and hired as a year-round manager his own cousin, James B. Heyward. In November he and James Heyward traveled to Gowrie to take command of the operation.[3]

When he stepped off a boat onto Argyle, Manigault later wrote, he was "completely overcome" at what he saw. The "settlement" where most of the slaves had lived before the war was "overgrown, moist, and miry," its houses in tumble-down condition. The old overseer's house, where Manigault himself planned to live with Heyward, was almost uninhabitable, with "hardly a pane of glass sound and nearly every window gone, ceilings down in all directions." In the rice fields, the flood gate was "in a most wretched condition": the ditches, drains, and canals dug to carry water to and from the fields were clogged with debris, the bridges had fallen down, and the trunks that regulated water flow could barely hold water. Manigault retired in gloom to his room in the decaying overseer's house, "almost broken down in spirits, and hesitating over my future career."[4]

But with James Heyward's help, Manigault set out to restore Gowrie to its antebellum condition. Their first order of business was to secure a labor force for the plantation for the coming year. Here Manigault encountered a change even more profound than broken gates or clogged ditches. Getting labor now meant bargaining with free men and women. Managing slave plantations had been a difficult job at best, but the slave master's ability to coerce his workers—to whip them when they worked poorly; to beat or jail them, or worse, when they resisted; to sell them and their families away if they refused to knuckle under—had made possible the elaborate works on which rice cultivation depended.[5] After the war, the element of sheer force in management had diminished to the vanishing point. Manigault was no longer the master of his workers; he was their employer.

As a landowner, Manigault still had plenty of leverage over his work force. He could, and did, force off the plantation anyone who caused too much trouble or worked too poorly—one of the first things he did in 1875 was to clear the plantation settlements, where most of the work force still lived, of "boisterous and turbulent negroes." One of those he sent off was "one 'Riley,'" a black trader who had a wife at Gowrie and who trafficked in liquor. By the spring of 1876 he and Heyward had "sent off every worthless Negro, and caused every house to be filled with quiet, orderly people." He would still have to learn how to get people to stay and work in the new regime of planter and free laborer. To Manigault "all of this free-labor system was perfectly new." He had missed the lessons that other rice planters had been absorbing for a decade.[6]

The New Peasantry in the Rice Coast

While Manigault had been a clerk in Charleston, other planters had been through the new school of free labor. The plantation journal of Frances Butler Leigh gives us a lesson book for the course. Like Louis Manigault, Leigh was the child of a planter. Her father, Pierce Butler, owned a rice plantation on Butler Island in Georgia's Altamaha River and a cotton plantation on St. Simons Island. Pierce Butler rarely lived on his plantations, preferring the cosmopolitan city of Philadelphia. When his daughter Frances visited the properties in 1866, it was the first time she had ever seen them. When she arrived in April of that year, she was, like many before her, struck by the exotic beauty of the river's landscape. The dark colors of the evergreen magnolias and cypress mingled with the spring greens of the orange, laurel, and bay trees, "all wreathed and bound together with the yellow jessamine and fringed with the soft delicate gray moss which floated from every branch and twig." When she traveled down the river, headed for Hampton, Pierce Butler's plantation on St. Simons, she saw the Altamaha spread out into a seemingly endless expanse of marsh grass, teeming with oysters, fish, crabs, and insects. On the far side of the expanse of marsh, St. Simons, too, had its beauties. Leigh could ride her horse on an old shell road past pines and cedars and live oaks which at times met overhead to form a natural cathedral, the sunshine breaking through to light up the red and gray trunks of the trees, the palmettos, and the bay trees underneath. Her mother, the celebrated actress Frances Kemble, had ridden thirty years earlier through these "exquisite thickets of evergreen shrubbery," resounding with the cries of mockingbirds. "If I wanted to paint Paradise I would copy this," Kemble had written. "I sat there on my horse in a sort of dream of enchantment, looking, listening, and inhaling."[7]

The semitropical lushness of the coastal and sea island landscapes had captured the imagination of many travelers. So, too, had their dangers — the snakes and alligators, hurricanes and floods, and malaria-bearing mosquitoes. Yet perhaps the most remarkable aspect of those landscapes was what men and women, rather than nature, had created. On the barrier islands like St. Simons, the soil, temperature, and rainfall patterns had proven ideal for

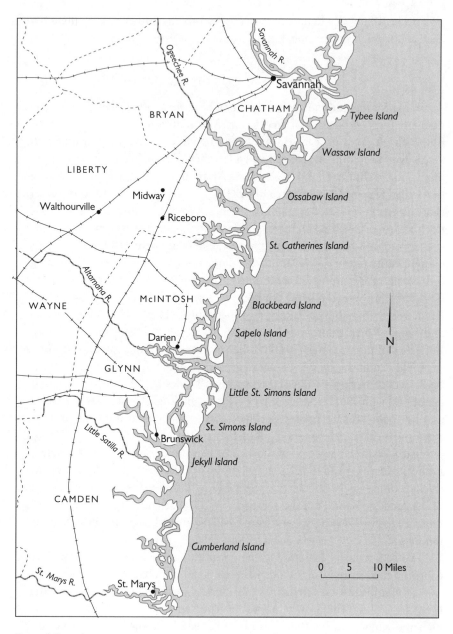

Coastal Georgia

growing the long-staple cotton prized by manufacturers of luxury textiles — cotton so fine that it was ginned by hand and packed in bags, rather than bales, so valuable that it commanded several times the price of the short-staple cotton grown in the upcountry, so particular in its quality that some planters sold their crops year after year directly to English buyers in private bargains, rather than go through normal market channels. The land that made it all possible kept its fertility only through annual applications of mud dug from the swamps and hauled to the fields by the slaves. More remarkable still were the rice plantations on the mainland. There, out of the riverside swamps and lowlands, generations of African and African American slaves had carved, at enormous expense in labor, money, and lives, some of the richest plantations in North America.[8]

Each rice plantation that hugged the swampy lower reaches of the rivers had been built up one section at a time by constructing a system of banks, gates, and trunks; the "rank, intricate wildernesses" at the river's edge had given way to flat, carefully measured quarter-acre fields, set off by drainage ditches. Each big rice plantation — and on the entire coast that stretched from the lower reaches of North Carolina to the southern border of Georgia there were scarcely more than three hundred — was what a contemporary journalist called "a huge hydraulic machine, maintained by constant warring against the rivers." Every spring, the fields were worked and sowed, and then flooded with several inches of water. Rice seeds sprouted under this water, and throughout the spring and summer each field was alternately drained, to allow hoeing and harvesting, and flooded, to kill weeds and support the growing stalks. The rivers provided the fresh water, the tides supplied the motive force, and the elaborate system of banks, ditches, canals, trunks, and floodgates controlled and directed the flow. When the tide rose and pushed the river back upstream, trunks could be opened to let in more water, or as the water level fell with the outgoing tides, they could be opened in the other direction to drain the fields. And so along the lower reaches of South Carolina's and Georgia's rivers — not so high as to be out of reach of the tides nor so low as to expose the land to salt water — slave-owning planters had established immensely productive and profitable holdings.[9]

Rice and Sea Island cotton supported some of the greatest fortunes and largest slaveholdings in the United States. The Manigaults owned several plantations and hundreds of slaves in Georgia and South Carolina. The first Pierce Butler, the great-grandfather of Frances Butler Leigh, left an estate at his death in 1822 with more than six hundred slaves. Lowcountry planters like Butler, his St. Simons neighbor James Hamilton Couper, and Thomas Spalding of nearby Sapelo Island came as close as any to the popular image of the southern planter as a wealthy, leisured, and cosmopolitan aristocrat. Antebellum visitors had marveled at the "perfect ease and politeness" of planter hospitality at its best and the remarkable libraries in the homes of planters like Hamilton Couper, a collector of rare editions. Even a visitor like Frederick Law Olmsted, convinced that slavery blighted everything it touched in the South, had to stop his horse and hold his breath when he turned into the avenue leading to one coastal mansion, lined with live oak trees, their trunks "huge and gnarled"; the dark foliage of their branches was "hung with a delicate fringe of gray moss" and met overhead to form a low, broad arch, with the dappled sunlight filtering through. "I have hardly in all my life seen anything so impressively grand and beautiful," he wrote — no small compliment from the man who would become the country's greatest landscape architect.[10]

This way of life, so delightful for the few at the top, was thrown into turmoil by the Civil War and its aftermath. Gowrie plantation was just one of many to suffer from neglect, military attack, or vandalism. General Sherman, reaching the sea after his march through Georgia, issued orders to set aside the entire area of the coast — the islands and thirty miles inland — as a reservation of land to be distributed to the former slaves. This decree was soon abrogated by President Andrew Johnson, and the plantation owners reclaimed their land — not always without a great deal of difficulty — from the disappointed freedmen who had occupied it. Then, like most of the former slave-owning planters in the South after the war, they tried to rebuild the economic base of their shattered world.[11]

Pierce Butler came to his properties in 1866 to reclaim his land and reestablish the plantations. At first, he tried to operate the plantations much as he had before.[12] Like many other planters he contracted with the freedmen, most of whom had been his slaves, to work for one-half the crop, to be paid out after harvest. The hands and their families received food, shelter, and clothing, the cost of which was debited against their accounts at the end of the year. Many of them ended the year with little or no cash after deductions for supplies and absences from work. Many freedmen quarreled endlessly with Frances, who kept the accounts for her father. As one put it, "Well, well, work for massa two whole years, and only get dis much." Frances complained that "some of them [the freedmen] are working only half a day and some even less. I don't think one does a really honest full day's work. . . . [N]o negro will work if he can help it, and is quite satisfied just to scrape along doing an odd job here and there to earn money enough to buy a little food." She thought that blacks would have to be forced to work; "left to themselves they become idle and useless, and never improve."[13]

Leigh misunderstood traditional work patterns on the rice coast. Elsewhere in the South, plantation slaves worked from sunrise to sunset, either in gangs or alone, while along the coast slaves were assigned a specific "task" fixed by custom. For example, on the coast a daily task for an able-bodied adult male (a "full hand") in harvest season consisted of cutting one-half acre of rice by hand. When the task was finished so was the slave's workday; healthy and able slaves could finish their tasks in mid-afternoon or even earlier. In taking up plantation labor in the era of freedom, the former slaves insisted on sticking to the traditional task system, so what was a "half day's work" to Frances Leigh was, in fact, a full day's labor as traditionally understood.[14]

Leigh also had a poor understanding of freed women, whom she saw as laborers like any other freedmen. As slaves on the Butler plantations, women had suffered grievously from forced labor in the rice fields. Many of their pregnancies ended in miscarriages or stillbirths; many of their children died in infancy; many suffered from chronic poor health caused by their treatment during pregnancy. Now they were determined to labor for themselves and their families. Leigh noted sardonically that Charity and other elderly women were "too old and infirm to work for me, but once let them get a bit of ground of their own given to them, and they became quite young and strong again."[15]

In any case, the "free" time of slaves had never been simply "idle and useless" time. In the afternoon and evening hours, many slaves worked in small garden plots to raise food for their families; others hunted or fished. The Butler slaves, like others, raised chickens, wove baskets, and carved canoes for sale to the master or in nearby towns. In the words of one historian, slaves had "monopolized the local supply" of poultry, eggs, and fish bought by the white residents of places like Darien. Women did much of this work, especially the marketing. Some slaves accumulated substantial amounts of property, held by right of tradition rather than law.[16]

Buying a small plot of land after emancipation was a natural extension of traditional slave activity. For the freedmen, land could become the basis of a more autonomous economic life. After one 1866 payday, some Butler hands who had earned substantial amounts of cash "left me," Leigh wrote, "and bought land of their own, and at one time it seemed doubtful if I should have hands at all left to work." Leigh grumpily attributed this movement to the land to the greed of "small shopkeepers and Jews" in nearby towns, who, she believed, convinced the former slaves to buy overpriced land with dubious titles. ("Gentlemen," she added, were "refusing to sell their land to the negroes.") Nevertheless, "they had got their land, and were building their little log cabins on it, fully believing, that they were to live on their property and incomes the rest of their lives, like gentlemen." "Like gentlemen" was surely Leigh's misconception; "without being hassled by any 'gentlemen'" would probably have been closer to the mark.[17]

Although the coastal ecosystem could be dangerous, especially because of the malaria and other diseases that flourished there, not far from the coast were cheap "pine lands" away from the worst of the mosquitoes. Pine land soil, sandy and acidic, was inhospitable to plantation staple crops, but abounded with deer and other game. So, too, the marshes and the ocean teemed with fish, shrimp, and oysters: "God's pantry," as the freedmen called it. Leigh wrote that "it is a well-known fact that you can't starve a negro," by which she meant that a threat of starvation alone could not force the freed-men to work. "There are about a dozen on Butler's Island who do no work, consequently get no wages and no food, and I see no difference whatever in their condition and those who get twelve dollars a month and full rations. They all raise a little corn and sweet potatoes, and with their facilities for catching fish and oysters, and shooting wild game, they have as much to eat as they want, and now are quite satisfied with that, not yet having learned to want things that money alone can give."[18]

"Not yet having learned to want things that money alone can give." This telling phrase indicates, finally, a truth at the core of Leigh's complaints that blacks were "quite satisfied just to scrape along doing an odd job here and there." It was not that the freedmen did not like and appreciate the power of money—for, indeed, as Leigh herself wrote, they loved to spend their wages in Darien and "it was natural they should like to swagger a little" and spend their money "freely." Money, though, was not everything.[19] Decades before, when Leigh's mother, Frances Kemble, was rowed one day along the Al-tamaha by a crew of Butler slaves, she was struck by their "extraordinarily wild and unaccountable" yet still "very curious and effective" singing. "You can not think . . . how strange some of their words are: in one, they repeatedly chanted the 'sentiment' that 'God made man, and man makes' — what do you think? — 'money'!" This wry comment on the ways of white men is understandable, coming from people liable to be bought and sold for money at the whim of a white master. For the former Butler slaves, money was for the few necessities and a modicum of the comforts that only money could buy, and they did not measure their economic success only in terms of dollars.[20]

Frances Butler married James Leigh, an English clergyman, in 1871, and they spent the next five winter seasons on their Altamaha plantation before moving to England in 1876. They learned to live, and to some extent even prosper, under the new regime of free black labor, but at first they almost despaired of getting the former slaves to work to their satisfaction. The Leighs and other planters even hoped to replace the former slaves with immigrants from Europe or China. One neighbor of Leigh's imported Chinese labor, and Leigh and her husband brought over several English laborers one year. Their experiment with English labor was hardly a success, and it displayed the allegedly poor work habits of the freedmen in a somewhat different light. Within weeks of their arrival, the Englishmen appeared "troublesome, discontented, and constantly drunk," and the African American foreman on the rice plantation begged Leigh to work them in a field by themselves, since they "set so bad an example" for the black workers. Only Irish immigrants were successfully integrated into the rice regime, in the specialized role of ditching and banking; each winter coastal planters hired gangs to clean out the plantation ditches and repair or extend banks. Trained on the canals and railroads of Britain and the United States, these workers were so efficient that they commanded premium wages.[21]

Planters also tried collusion to regulate wages and conditions of labor and to limit workers' mobility. Leigh's husband and his neighbors formed the "Rice Planters Association" in 1876, the object being "to take into consideration a reduction of wages and other matters of mutual interest to the Planters generally." The fourteen members, all owners or managers of large operations, adopted a wage scale with maximum rates for each task or each full day's labor and resolved that whenever a hand under contract "violated his obligations and left the plantation where he was under contract, that the said hand be not allowed to labor, either upon his (the planter's) own land planted, or upon the land planted by any of his contract hands; or upon any land under his control for that year." The association had little effect on the wage rate because, like all cartels, it was no stronger than its weakest member. Within two months of its foundation the members formally resolved that "the Statement of a planter, that a certain party is his contract hand, be regarded as conclusive evidence of the fact," a sure sign that disputes had already arisen among the members. Two of the members had already been "obliged" to pay at least thirty cents for each task, rather than the twenty-five cents called for by the wage scale. It might have been difficult for a big planter to flout the suggested wage openly, but subtle cheating was easier, as evidenced by efforts to prevent it. One of the final meetings, in 1883, passed a new rule to try to prevent employers from evading the wage limitations by promising their workers access to land to grow their own crops, or reducing the number of hours of labor. Even then a certain number of exceptions were allowed for men classified as "expert labor," whose wages were left unregulated.[22]

George Harrison, the white planter who first leased Gowrie from the Manigaults after the war, had tried a different labor arrangement. Harrison divided Gowrie into five parts, each rented to a "foreman." Four of the five foremen in 1867 were former slaves on the plantation. Harrison provided lumber for trunk upkeep, ploughs and other tools, mules, and one-half of the seed; the foremen paid for the other half of the seed, and each foreman selected, hired, and supervised his own hands; hands fed themselves. At the end of the year Harrison kept one-half of the net profits, and the rest was divided up among the workers. This kind of arrangement did not succeed in the long run. Rice plantations, because of their dependence on a system of dykes and trunks, needed centralized management. A decade after the war, Gowrie's managers relied much more on wage labor.[23]

In the winter of 1875–76, James Heyward and Louis Manigault bargained over terms with their hands, who were paid cash wages for daily work on the main rice fields. Those with families received the right to live in a cabin on the plantation, and some received land to grow their own crops. The going rate for a full day's work in the neighborhood was seventy-five cents in cash or fifty cents in cash plus twenty-five cents in rations. Women and children were paid less. The workers were experts at rice cultivation, and Manigault was pleased that the best of these included "many of our old Gowrie Negroes." Specialized workers could earn more. In the summer, Russell, a "very smart negro" who was both carpenter and machinist, was hired at $2 per day to operate the thresher. The available white machinists were, in Heyward's opinion, "very indolent" and not worth hiring, but, like other planters, Manigault and Heyward hired Irish gangs to clean out the ditches and put the banks in good repair. Manigault thought the work of these "quiet and orderly" gangs was "superior to that done by the very best negro men." Manigault spent more than $9,000 on black and white labor for the 1876 crop and $7,000 more on seeds, mules, and other expenses, all paid for with his borrowed money.[24]

"During the entire season labor with us was abundant, and always to be had," Manigault later wrote. The ditches were cleaned, the trunks repaired, and the fields sown. By the end of April rice sprouts covered the fields. As he prepared to leave the plantation in his cousin's hands for the summer, Manigault took his "favorite ride" along the river's edge; in the evening light he could make out the rows of green plants three fields away. It was then, he wrote, that "I pictured to my mind how I expected to recover, and build up, once more by my exertions the property which my kind Father had left me." By the time these words had been written in Manigault's journal, though, his dreams of restoring his antebellum life had been crushed by the harsh realities of working the postwar rice lands.[25]

Nature landed the most serious blow to Gowrie's prospects. In mid-June, "the most critical period to the rice planter," the rice had been in splendid condition; the "long flow," which had protected the young plants, had been drained, and the plants were now exposed for summer hoeings. Then heavy rains along the coast saturated the swamps along the back lands of the Savannah River, while rains in the upcountry, many miles to the north, filled the upper reaches of the Savannah. The rising river washed over the streets of Augusta, some 125 miles upstream from Gowrie. On June 24, six days after the flood peaked at Augusta, the hands hoeing a "finely" stand of rice in Field No. 7 saw water spilling over Gowrie's banks. The water eventually rose until it stood a foot higher than the highest point on the plantation. The rice, in most fields still fragile, lay a full four to five feet beneath the flood. For a full month, water remained on Gowrie's fields.[26]

The result was financial disaster. In some fields the crop was wholly destroyed, in others most plants never reached full maturity, and in only a few fields had the rice plants advanced enough to withstand the flood without major damage. Most of the harvest was of very poor quality and heavily spoiled with "indigo seed," a wild grass brought in on the flood and impossible to separate from the rice itself. On top of everything else, as Heyward pointed out to Manigault shortly after the waters receded, the planters could expect a "heavy toll" from theft by hands whose own rice acreage had been almost completely wiped out. Workers' rice lands were as much a part of their compensation as a daily wage, and a landowner could hardly expect workers to permit their own losses to exceed his in proportion.[27]

The planters along the Savannah hoped to cut their losses by forcing a significant cut in wages. Planters on the South Carolina bank agreed among themselves to reduce the pay for harvesting an acre of rice—a day's task—from ninety cents or $1 down to seventy-five cents. On the Cheves plantation, not far from Gowrie, the wage force refused to work for the lower wage, and they handled roughly some "strange hands" brought in to break their strike. Soon, Heyward wrote to Manigault, "the point having been given up," the Carolina planters had returned to a wage of $1 per acre. A full-scale labor conflict raged for months on the Combahee River, just up the Atlantic coast in South Carolina, and wages there had been pushed to $1.50 or even $2 for a day's task. In Savannah, a white militia company stood ready to break up any such attempts of rice workers to organize a strike in Georgia, but Heyward still had to pay ninety cents per task.[28]

Companies of soldiers, in any case, could not control the price of rice. In early October rice sold for a little over six cents for a pound. At this price, Manigault wrote, "there is money in the article," but it was well above the historic trend of around three cents per pound. Within days the market was glutted with "inferior" rice, and soon it fell to just four cents per pound. By the end of the year Gowrie's nine thousand bushels brought in only $7,568 in sales, less than half the plantation's expenses.[29]

Charleston's factors, who financed and sold most of the rice grown on the Savannah River, grew fearful of the possible effects of unsettled labor and political conditions and refused to advance more credit to rice planters. Manigault faced a deficit of some $4,000 on the year, and he could pay off nothing of the principal on his loans from his sisters and E. B. Smith. In danger of bankruptcy, he gave a lien on the next year's crop to his factor in Charleston, E. H. Frost & Co., in order to raise enough cash to put off the most insistent creditors and save his plantation. In January 1877 he accepted "with relief" a proposal from his cousin James Heyward to lease the plantation, handle all expenses, run the operation, and pay as rent to Manigault half of his net profits. After only a year, Manigault's postwar career as a rice planter had come to an inglorious end.[30]

Louis Manigault's hard lessons in rice growing were common in the rice lands after the Civil War. Still, some learned better than others, and by 1870 planters had partly restored rice plantation agriculture. Overall production along the Georgia coast was just half of what it had been in 1860, but remained steady for the next decade. Manigault's Gowrie, for example, produced over twelve thousand bushels of rice in 1877 and almost fifteen thousand by 1880. Total acreage and production were both well below the 1855–60 average, but the yield per acre was about the same as before the war. While production dropped again during the 1880s, many planters remained hopeful. Whitehall plantation, also on the Savannah River a little below Argyle, by the 1890s produced more than twenty thousand bushels of rice annually, with a yield that sometimes came close to antebellum levels. Frances Butler Leigh, who complained back in 1866 that "no negro will work if he can help it," was honest enough to add a footnote when her letter was published in 1883 admitting, "I was mistaken. In the years 1877 and 1880 upwards of thirty thousand bushels of rice was raised on the place by these same negroes." James Dent, on the Altamaha River, was raising fifteen thousand bushels a year by 1890; in 1895 he raised over twenty-four thousand bushels, about two-thirds of what his plantations had raised in 1859. Dent, like many planters, borrowed heavily over the years to keep his plantation going, but by January of 1894 he was writing hopefully to his lawyer about plans to repay the entire debt and leave the operation in good shape for his children. "Any planter must know," he wrote, "that there is a large margin of profit at [the] present cost of rice planting."[31]

The planters of Sea Island cotton, however, did not survive Reconstruction. The story of the Spalding estate on Sapelo Island is typical. Thomas Spalding was one of the great planters of the antebellum era, as well as a promoter of railroads and canals, founder of a bank, and a prolific writer on agricultural methods and agricultural history. A leading planter as early as 1789, Spalding began acquiring land on Sapelo Island in 1802 and made his holdings there the center of an agricultural empire. He was one of the first during the 1780s to plant the Bahamian seeds that became the basis of the Sea Island cotton industry. Spalding constantly experimented with new techniques and new crops, such as silk and sugarcane. He and others discovered that the sandy Sea Island soil needed regular replenishment to maintain productivity and they found the necessary fertilizer in the swamp grass that separated the islands from the coast. Each winter, Spalding sent his slaves to dig up the swamp mud, enriched by the detritus left by millions of plants and animals that flourished there, and spread it over his cotton fields.[32]

After Spalding's death Sapelo passed into the hands of his daughter Catherine Spalding Kenan and his son Randolph Spalding. During the Civil War the plantation was abandoned and the slaves taken to central Georgia, near Macon. When Randolph died in 1862, his three children, Thomas, Bourke, and Sarah, inherited his share of the property. After the war, Spald-

ing's ex-slaves, encouraged by Sherman's order to distribute land to freedmen, took over much of Sapelo Island. When the Spalding children tried to
take it back, the freed people threatened the family's representatives with
violence and "declared the land was their's [sic]." The Spalding children
appealed to the federal commander in the region, who sent a company of
troops to expel the freed people and return the land to the three Spalding
heirs.[33] They eventually formed a partnership and attempted to revive cotton
planting on the old estate, primarily by renting out land and collecting a
share of the crop as rent. (Upland cotton planters, as we will see, would turn
to the same method.)

In 1871, the first year of their joint operations, the three Spalding grandchildren collected a little under 6,500 pounds of raw cotton from tenants
and experienced most of the problems of dealing with recently emancipated
freedmen, who had their own ideas of how to run their farms and insisted on
their rights as independent operators. The journal kept by Sarah Spalding's
husband, Archibald McKinley, includes a common litany of complaints and
problems in dealing with tenants.

1 January 1872: "All but two of our negroes quit yesterday."

6 February 1872: "The negroes have been annoying me very
much, trying to get money due them for ginning the North end
cotton."

8 March 1872: "We hear today of an underhanded attempt by
Dr. Kenan to entice away our negroes." [Dr. Kenan was married to
Catherine Spalding Kenan, who still owned half of Sapelo.]

9 July 1872: "Tom, Bourke & I rode to the N[orth] end to get our
contract signed, but the negroes all refused to sign, but agree [to]
work up to the same verbal contract."[34]

The census taker in 1870 counted fifty-nine African American families on
Sapelo Island, scattered in settlements they called "hammocks." None owned
any real estate; together they farmed a little more than five hundred acres of
rented land, raising small food crops of corn, peas, and sweet potatoes, along
with seventy-three bales of cotton. But, like other former slaves throughout
the South, their real hope was to own their own farms. In 1871, three of the
former slaves, William Hillery, John Grovner, and Bilally Bell, made a down
payment of $500 toward the purchase of a thousand acres on Sapelo to
"make a black settlement." The three purchasers kept some land for them-

selves and resold the rest to other black families. By 1880 sixteen blacks owned their own farms.[35]

The Spalding heirs (Bourke, Thomas, and Sarah McKinley) continued to rent land for a time, but by the late 1870s, they were trying to sell more land to the tenants. The three were willing to sell their land because they had evolved other plans. Logs from the interior had become a valuable commodity, and Doboy Sound, separating Sapelo Island from the mainland and from the mouth of the Altamaha River, had become crowded with ships from many countries, there to load timber floated down the river. The Spaldings decided to target the ships and their crews as a market for beef. They bought cattle and turned Sapelo Island, with its natural boundaries, into an open range. In 1873, they gave up cotton planting.

The Spaldings did not have a life of leisure and wealth. To be sure, the families enjoyed themselves hunting and fishing; they caught sea bass and turtles, dug clams, netted shrimp, and killed dozens of deer and rabbits, along with an occasional rattlesnake. At the same time, they were their own cowboys, and, though Bourke Spalding's wife, Ella, later remembered her occasional participation in cattle driving as "great fun," her letters at the time tell a different story. In 1872, she wrote, the three partners had "been very busy . . . doing all manner of odd jobs—They have no boy now and are forced to do everything themselves. Their poor hands are dreadfully cut to pieces sometimes." Four years later she reported that Bourke "has been so busy, he is away every day but Sundays. He starts before daylight. I manage to get him breakfast three days out of the six. The other three he is gone from here by five o'clock and he won't let me get up." Bourke Spalding later tried growing potatoes, vegetables, and melons. In 1884, Bourke died in an accident, and large-scale operations on Sapelo virtually ceased.[36]

The final fate of the Spalding cotton fields was shared by all the great Sea Island cotton plantations in Georgia. Whatever wage it might have taken to get freedmen to dig mud in the winter and haul it up to the cotton lands, these planters were unable to pay. By 1879, Sea Island cotton was grown on the islands and nearby coast only by small farmers, some of them white, most of them black; total production was barely one-fifth of the 1859 level (see Chart 4, Appendix). White planters like the Spaldings turned to the most basic exploitation of the land, turning their cattle or hogs out into the woods and old fields and selling the trees themselves for lumber or their sap to a growing turpentine industry. By 1880 white small farmers in Camden and Liberty Counties earned more from the sale of wood products than from their production of rice and cotton combined. The large planters that remained relied on rice alone.[37]

The key to success for rice planters was getting an adequate supply of good labor, which required a continual negotiation with a labor force determined to control as much of their own lives as possible. In 1877, Daniel Heyward wrote to Louis Manigault that he had attracted many hands to Gowrie from nearby plantations on the South Carolina side of the river, because the Carolina rice was full of weeds while "my rice was pretty clean"; "the laborers preferred hoeing a half acre here, [rather] than a quarter of an acre there." In 1881 a localized flood at harvest time put labor at such a premium on the South Carolina bank that wage rates there immediately "boomed up fearfully, at least 50 per ct in some localities." Black workers, well aware of the value of their work, moved from place to place and bargained accordingly.[38]

Rice workers along the coast had a powerful ally in the physical environment. George Dent of the Rice Planters Association noted that "at least 60% percent [sic] of the laborers employed on Rice plantations for wages need them as only supplemental to their support. They are not entirely dependent and have houses outside & pursue other vocations at different times & only work on the plantations at certain seasons & for limited & broken periods as they need money." Planters, forced to adapt, offered access to land as part of the wage bargain. Louis Manigault learned about this labor system from his brother Gabriel, who operated a plantation in South Carolina. Gabriel Manigault rented part of his plantation out as small farms to tenants. Two days a week they worked for wages on the owner's fields, and the rest of the time they worked their own farms. "The wages . . . give them ready money enough to supply themselves with certain necessaries during the week, and each one would have his crop to look forward to at the end of the year." The system "may seem complicated to one accustomed to plant entirely for wages," Gabriel added, but "I have seen it work very satisfactorily where the negroes are industrious and well disposed." He advised Louis to be sure "to give the laborer the same quality of land as you plant yourself," because the plan would not work unless it was "of advantage to both parties." By 1877 this "two-day" system, or variations of it, was widespread along the rice coast. The Altamaha Rice Planters Association, for example, included in its plans to control wages a regulation to set "the amount of land to be given for labour" in order to prevent members from violating the wage scale by manipulating the kinds and amounts of land they offered their workers. For the

1877 season at Gowrie, Heyward set aside one field for day laborers and two fields "to the contract two day hands, so that they may be independent of me by haveing more trunks."[39]

It was only one further step to sell land outright to black farmers, who would then provide wage laborers (either themselves or other family members) to the plantation. To be sure, the land sold to former slaves was not usually the rich muck of the rice fields, but the sandy soil away from the riversides that had never supported commercial farming. On Hofwyl-Broadfield plantation on the Altamaha River, James Troup Dent, in 1890, decided to sell a portion of the plantation uplands — pine land away from the river — "for the purpose of having negroes settle upon the place and furnish labor for it." The next year he sold ten plots to black workers, and, in 1892, three more plots. One Paul Union (a symbolic name, indeed) bought five acres of upland and five acres of lowland in 1891 from Dent for a total of $75 — on credit, at 8 percent per year. Over the next six years he paid off $46 of this amount with cash and rice. After his death, William Union, no doubt a relative, paid off the remainder for Paul's widow. Another hand, Andrew Gadsden, was able to pay for his land — a total of $66 plus $4 interest — by 1894. Some sixteen different purchasers, including two women, are listed in Dent's accounts.[40]

In the pine lands upriver and in scattered settlements on the islands, black farmers increased the rolls of landowners throughout the coastal region. With their cash wages and the money they earned by raising their own small cash crops, they could earn enough to pay their taxes, buy new clothing and tools, and support a local church or school. Their land did not make most of them prosperous, and it provided them with only part of needed food supplies, but it did give them a crucial margin of independence. When conditions on the plantations were bad, as they were in one year when Frances and J. W. Leigh hired a bad overseer, many of the workers "left, not to work for anyone else, but to settle on their own properties in the pine woods."[41]

By 1880, most farms in the coastal region were small family operations with little in the way of commercial production. Many of the farms were rented; still more were owned by former slaves. Few of these black-owned farms raised either cotton or rice — in a sample of about one hundred farms, no black farmer planted as many as ten acres of cotton and only two planted as many as ten acres of rice (the largest rice acreage was twelve).[42] Perhaps the best indicator of the reluctance of black farmers to focus on the market was the amount they spent on cash wages. White small-farm operators along the coast paid out almost $23 per year in wages; black farmers with small farms paid out less than $3. On their small farms, averaging only thirteen improved acres, African Americans concentrated on supplying their families. They planted twice as many acres in corn as in rice and cotton combined; they raised sweet potatoes, gathered honey and fruit, planted gardens, raised chickens and collected eggs, and sold wood. Their farms were not usually big enough to provide self-sufficiency; fewer than one out of four raised enough food for their families and animals. They hunted, fished, gathered oysters, and otherwise got food in ways the census takers did not record. The work lives of most of these black men and women crossed paths with the planters only on the two or three days a week they worked for wages in the rice fields. Twenty years after the Civil War, a precarious balance had been reached in Georgia's rice region. Rice growers, operating in a highly competitive commercial market, depended on black labor to keep their plantations in business. Former slaves owned small plots of land and operated in a peasantlike economy in which autonomy meant more than success. African Americans had won much of the autonomy they wanted, but not all, because they still depended on work in the rice fields to bring in needed cash. Neither former masters nor former slaves had gotten everything they hoped for. The same proved to be true of former masters and former slaves in other regions of the South, although the terms of the final balance would be distinct in each place.[43]

Black and White Labor on Piedmont Plantations and Farms

In the summer of 1876, while Louis Manigault was trying to come to terms with the disastrous flood at Gowrie, David C. Barrow, the owner of another Georgia plantation, was already looking ahead to the next season's operations on Syls Fork, his Oglethorpe County plantation in the rolling hills of Georgia's eastern Piedmont. The Piedmont had been settled later than the coast, and its planters had turned to cotton only after the perfection of the cotton gin in 1793 had made possible the commercial production of the short-staple variety southerners called "upland" cotton. The land of the Piedmont had been much easier to clear than that of the coast. Indeed, before the Civil War some of it had been not only cleared and planted but already abandoned to second-growth trees as the population moved out. Right up to the war, however, the land remained productive enough to support a large population of slaves producing the most famous of the South's crops.[44]

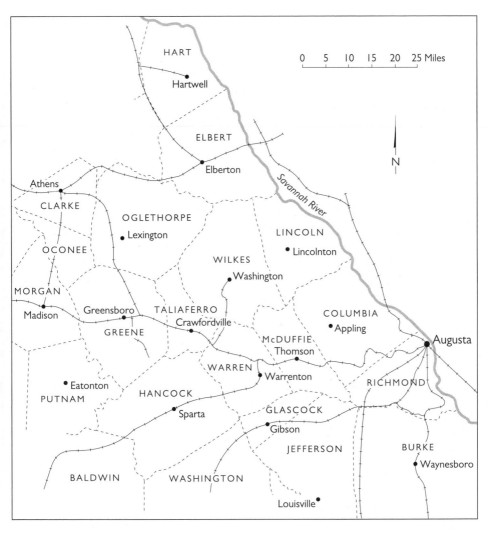

Georgia's Eastern Piedmont

On a trip away from home that summer of 1876, David C. Barrow sat down to write instructions to his son, David Jr., who was looking after Syls Fork in his absence. The cotton gin on the plantation needed repairs, he reminded his son, and it was time to plan for the next year. "I do not think I shall want to hire more than two men for money wages," he told Dave. "I do not expect to plant more crop next year than this, and hire by the day to do any more in the crop than these can do." Two men, of course, could hardly tend a large plantation, and the two wage hands would work only on the small part of Syls Fork that Barrow himself expected to operate. The rest of the plantation's hundreds of acres would be worked under a variety of arrangements with renters. So, for example, Barrow wanted to continue the arrangement with one group of hands who worked "on halves," which meant that Barrow received a fixed rent plus one-half the surplus crop above the rent, the balance going to the workers. Another part of the plantation was worked by "Lewis Watson and his company"; Barrow wanted Watson to add a new man to his work force and plant a larger acreage. Barrow hoped that a neighbor, Mr. Wright, might be willing to rent another section of the plantation for a payment of one-fourth of the crop, but, if not, maybe black tenant Lizzy Dalton would plant that section, or maybe Lewis Watson would "work those farms in addition to the one he currently rented."[45]

Like rice planters on the coast, Barrow was concerned above all with the problem of labor, but, as his letter shows, Syls Fork operated on a fundamentally different basis from Manigault's Gowrie. Nearly all rice grown in the United States was raised on places with irrigation systems owned by wealthy planters, and it would hardly pay a small farmer to build up dikes for a few acres. Cotton, unlike rice, would grow anywhere with decent soil and a growing season, from last frost to first, of two hundred days or more. The plantations of the cotton belt had always been interspersed with small farms operated by men with few or no slaves. Gowrie had to operate as a single unit, so after the war its rice was raised by day laborers working for wages. Syls Fork, instead, evolved into a collection of small tenant farms worked by black families.[46]

In 1881, Barrow's son, David Jr., described this evolution for a national readership. Syls Fork still included about two thousand acres of land, the same as before the war. Before and immediately after the war, the plantation had been "under the absolute rule of an overseer . . . who directed the laborers each day as to their work, and to him the owner looked for the well-being of everything on the place." All the slave houses were close together in "the quarter," where overseer and owner could keep a close watch on the slaves. But "this has all been so changed that the place would now hardly be recognized by one who had not seen it during the past sixteen years."[47]

The plantation had first been divided into halves, each half worked by a "squad" under the direction of a black foreman. A young white man lived on the property and kept the books, according to Barrow Jr., "but was not expected to direct the hands in their work." At the end of the year each large squad was paid a share of the crop, which they divided among themselves. Eventually "even the liberal control of the foreman grew irksome, each man feeling the very natural desire to be his own 'boss,' and to farm to himself." The two squads then split into smaller groups, "still working for part of the crop, and using the owner's teams." This smaller "squad system" seems to have been in effect for parts of Syls Fork in 1876, but four years later David Jr. wrote that this form of renting had come "to involve great trouble and loss. The mules were ill-treated, the crop was frequently badly worked, and in many cases was divided in a way that did not accord with the contract." The squad system was abandoned and the plantation divided into family-sized farms, each rented to a black family. Barrow sold his mules to the tenants on credit. Unlike many Piedmont planters, Barrow preferred to rent for a fixed amount of cotton, rather than a specific share of the crop; in 1880 his typical charge for a "one-horse farm" was 750 pounds of seedless (ginned) cotton. Other than rent, the tenants were responsible only for damage to the farm.[48]

Changes in living arrangements flowed naturally from the changes in farm operations. The former slave families wanted " 'more elbow room' and so, one by one, they moved their houses on to their farms. . . . Wherever there is a spring, there they settle, generally two or three near together, who have farms hard by." There the families built their cabins of logs and mud, usually with small separate kitchens, stables, and corn cribs. Cattle grazed in uncultivated fields on the plantation, and gardens were fenced in to keep the animals out.[49]

Barrow Jr. was writing in 1881 in part to assure his readers — most of whom would have been nonsoutherners — that labor relations in places like Piedmont Georgia were "adjusting themselves" in ways that would solve "the dreaded 'negro problem' in a practical way," that "the colored people, as free laborers, have done well," and that "the negro has adapted himself to his new circumstances, and freedom fits him as if it had been cut out and made for him." One might also read between the lines, "without any help from interfering Yankees."[50] A modern reader needs to accept such statements with caution, but the basic story of Syls Fork can be confirmed in the collection of manuscripts left by the Barrow family. The process by which Syls Fork evolved from a slave plantation "under the absolute rule of an overseer" into a tenant plantation was by no means as smooth as Barrow's article implies, and involved a considerable amount of conflict, though not violence, in the immediate postwar years. In 1865 and 1866 Barrow kept on the same overseer who had run the plantation before emancipation, and the letters from that overseer cry out with his frustrations and exasperation with the former slaves. Like rice planters, upland cotton planters had to learn through trial and error how to deal with free workers, and free workers had to learn how to deal with labor lords turned landlords.[51]

The records of the 1880 census show that the senior Barrow farmed 120 acres himself with the help of two hired hands. Barrow raised 9,000 pounds of cotton on this acreage. He hired extra help for cash wages as needed, for rolling logs, plowing, or cotton picking. He took in another 12,500 pounds of cotton in rent from eighteen tenant families at Syls Fork. The census confirms Barrow Jr.'s judgment that Ben Thomas, the old foreman on the plantation, was "the best farmer among the negroes." Thomas raised six bales of cotton and 150 bushels of corn on his thirty-one-acre farm. David Barrow Sr.'s diary for that year mentions surprisingly few contacts with tenants except when they were doing extra work for wages.[52] By 1880, Barrow had reached a kind of modus vivendi with his tenants. As his son put it, the original plan based on "centralization of power" had changed into one based on "local self-government." The new plan provided Barrow with a substantial, but not high, income from Syls Fork, perhaps a bit over $2,000. The former slaves operated their own small farms with their families, with little supervision or interference, earning modest incomes of perhaps $200 to $500 per family, depending on what they raised and how much outside wage work the family members performed.[53]

A balance had been reached on Syls Fork, as one had been reached in the rice region. On Syls Fork, however, the balance was more favorable to the planter, because the former slaves had not, for the most part, won ownership of the land itself. The same was true elsewhere in the Piedmont. In 1880, most farmland there was still owned by white men, many of them the same planters who had owned slaves before the war, and many others who had operated small farms with few or no slaves. On the old plantations, most of the hard work of raising crops was done by former slaves, working as laborers or tenants.[54]

Although the most common image of white-owned cotton plantations in the late-nineteenth-century lower South is one with black sharecroppers raising the crops, that picture is incorrect for the Piedmont as late as 1880. Most African American family heads were not sharecroppers but farm laborers, who, like the men and women who worked on Barrow's "home place," labored for some combination of cash, rations, and housing. About three-fifths of all black household heads in the Piedmont were classified as laborers by the 1880 census takers, and many other family members of black farmers worked at least some of the time for wages on nearby farms and plantations.[55]

About one-third of black family heads were not wage laborers, but farm operators, men like Ben Thomas and women like Lizzy Dalton. About half of these farm operators were sharecroppers. Sharecroppers, as the name implies, worked on other people's land and split the harvest with the landlord. The share that went to each party varied according to what the tenant brought to the arrangement. Those with nothing to offer but the labor of themselves and their families might receive only one-third of the crop in payment; those with tools and draft animals might claim as much as two-thirds. Wives and children usually contributed a major part of the labor.[56]

The tenants on Syls Fork plantation, like a substantial minority of black farmers, paid a fixed rent, not a share of the yield. The distinction is more important than it might seem, because sharecroppers, like wage laborers, had few economic rights under the law. Indeed, one contemporary observer explained, the sharecropper, when "viewed in the proper light . . . is in reality a day laborer. Instead of receiving weekly or monthly wages, he is paid a share of the crop raised on the tract of land for which he is responsible. Absolute control of the crop remains in the hands of the landlord." By contrast, tenants who paid a fixed rent, like those on the Barrow plantation, exercised much more autonomy. They often received little supervision and the harvest was legally theirs, not the landlord's, to dispose of. The greater autonomy of renters was considered unfortunate by many white planters. N. J. Newsom, a planter in Washington County, Georgia, wrote in one publication that it was "better by far" to let land "lay out and rest" than rent it out, because the renting system "means to sap all the Life out of you[,] Land, Barns, stables, Fencing and everything else."[57]

Some historians have seen sharecropping as not much more than a newer, thinly disguised form of slavery, forced on the former slaves by all-powerful planters.[58] Yet there are good reasons to think that sharecropping became common in the post–Civil War cotton regions because of economic reasons, not coercion. Few planters and farmers could pay cash wages on a regular basis because they had no cash and, without the slaves that had served as collateral on their loans before the war, they had no ready access to credit either. Like the planters on the Altamaha River in Georgia, many white

landlords tried out informal agreements after the war to limit competition
for labor in order to hold wages down; like the Altamaha agreement, these
had little effect on wages and generally fell apart quickly. Freed men and
women would not work like slaves in gangs under close supervision, at least
for the wages that cotton planters could pay, so planters had to concede them
a considerable measure of control over their own day-to-day work patterns.
Given the planters' lack of cash or liquid credit and the freedmen's determination to claim as much autonomy as possible after emancipation, most
planters generally had little choice but to rent out parcels of land to families,
black or white, and to pay these workers with a share of the crop. The same
basic impulse drove rice planters, who could not parcel their plantations out
into small farms, to the "two-day" labor system, which similarly gave black
workers a great deal more control over their own time and labor.[59]

An annual sharecropping contract also addressed one of the biggest headaches of cotton producers: the crop's two distinct and lengthy periods of high
labor demand. In the late spring and early summer, cotton fields had to be
regularly "chopped" to thin the plants and keep down the weeds that sprang
up after each rainfall. Then, in the fall, cotton had to be picked steadily and
promptly over the several weeks it took for the bolls to open in their uneven
fashion—too much sun or rain would stain or rot cotton left in the bolls. A
sharecropping contract, which paid for labor only when the harvest was in,
gave tenant families an incentive to stay with the farm for the entire year, and
usually included the labor of a wife and children as well as the male tenant.[60]

Contemporary observers did not see sharecropping as something forced
on the freedmen. Robert Preston Brooks, who in the early twentieth century
interviewed many planters in Georgia's eastern Piedmont about the evolution of the postwar plantation system, was told by an Oglethorpe County
planter that "the negro became less willing to work in large bodies on the
large plantations, they became harder to manage and many negroes began to
desire to get off to themselves and run one and two horse farms. The large
landowners, finding that they could no longer get the negro low or cheap
enough to allow a margin of profit, began to place their tenant houses all over
their farms and rent to their tenants." A Wilkes County planter made the
same point: "A large part of those renting only wanted more liberty to do as
they felt like and not to improve their condition." Brooks concluded that in
the "unsettled condition" of labor after the war "it was a matter more of
chagrin than of surprise if one's entire plantation force disappeared over
night. The negroes were entirely devoid of any conception of the binding

nature of a contract, and the conduct of the whites in inducing them to break contracts quite naturally did not tend to enlighten them." This "desire for complete emancipation from control," according to Brooks, had been "the most potent factor in bringing about the renting system," and the "fundamentally important fact in the history of the changes that were to come [was] the negroes' control over the situation."[61] In 1877, the editor of Georgia's most widely read agricultural journal wrote that "during the past ten years . . . every one seemed to fear that everybody else would get ahead of him and that he would have no labor at all. Hence a universal rush at the negro — each out bidding the other, the negro in the mean time feeling like a maiden with a dozen suitors at her feet — entire master of the situation."[62]

Lacking not only cash and land but also most other kinds of property, sharecropping freedmen typically went into debt to finance their purchases of food and farm supplies each season. Some of this credit came directly from landlords, but since most landlords, too, owed money, most of the credit came from town and country merchants. In the absence of other collateral, these lenders typically took a lien on the future crop, which could be seized to satisfy the debt at the end of the year; they also insisted that farmers plant cotton in order to ensure that a marketable (and inedible) crop would be harvested to repay the credit purchases. The credit was expensive — both directly, in the form of high interest rates, and indirectly, in the form of higher prices for goods sold on credit. Many contemporary observers deplored this crop lien system as giving control of the countryside to the merchant, who told the farmer what to plant and prevented southern farmers from diversifying their crops. It was also commonly charged that creditors, whether merchants or landlords, manipulated prices and interest charges to make sure that debts were never fully paid off. Farmers were then required to accept the merchant's credit again for the next year, reduced, like Mexican peasants, to virtual "debt peonage."[63] More recent writers have agreed with parts of this indictment and argued that most merchants could get away with this because they held local monopolies on both credit and supplies, so that customers literally had no choice in the matter. Others have claimed that merchants and landlords simply cheated their customers, so that even if a tenant had grown enough cotton to pay his or her debts, "in practice . . . landlords and shopkeepers purloined the tenant's share, no matter how large the crop or high the prices."[64]

Certainly most poorer farmers, white as well as black, and many wealthier ones depended on credit advanced from merchants to run their farms and feed their families. Whether this system amounted to a form of peonage is doubtful, however, especially if peonage is defined as a system that forced tenant farmers to work for the same landlords, year after year, against their will. In the first place, southern agriculture simply could not have functioned without credit. Even Matthew Hammond, one of the severest contemporary critics of the credit system, acknowledged that lien laws should not be blamed for southern farmers' problems, because they did answer a real need for credit. Hundreds of thousands of farmers could have starved without advances of supplies; their growing crops were the only collateral they had. When the South Carolina legislature abolished the crop lien in 1877, farmers clamored to have it restored, as they had no other way to finance their operations. In fact, without the credit system, it is hard to imagine how African Americans could have established any autonomy at all, which was precisely the complaint of writers like Charles Otken, who in 1894 denounced the lien system not only on the grounds that it "enslaved thousands of good people," but also because it "derange[d] negro labor" by making black workers independent of their landlords.[65]

Like farmers, merchants needed credit: "like many good men in these times they are short of money & cant get it without borrowing it at high interest." Also like planters, merchants' prospects depended on the success of the crop. As numerous scholars have pointed out, moreover, for most country and town merchants, monopolies were rare, competition fierce, and business failures frequent. Supply stores typically clustered together in small towns and villages, where they had to compete with one another for customers, as a perusal of advertising in local papers shows. In Georgia's Piedmont in 1881, for example, Hartwell had eighteen stores; Sparta had ten; Crawfordville had eight; even the little village of Linton had three stores. The local reports in the books of the leading credit agency in the United States give a flavor of the difficulties of surviving in the general store business. C. N. Wynne and Co. in Greensboro, Georgia, were in 1875 rated as "clever men" when they opened a store "under favorable auspices"; a year later they were "Broke & Gone." The firm of Corry & Patillo in the same town was, in the fall of 1879, apparently "doing well," but three months later had "Failed." E. A. Young arrived in Crawfordville, Georgia, in 1875 to set up a store; the next year he had to "let some of his creditors take the few goods that he had on hand." The rise of sharecropping and the dependence of sharecroppers on expensive credit seems, on the whole, to be more the product of black poverty than the cause of it.[66]

Cotton on the Yeoman Farm

Cotton could be raised with profit on small farms; from this simple fact much of the social history of the post–Civil War Piedmont can be derived. It meant that David Barrow and other big landowners could turn their plantations into rental properties. It also meant that cotton was as much a crop for white small farmers as for big planters, as it had been before the war, when white small farmers in the Piedmont had participated actively in the cotton market. After the war these small farmers became even more tied to cotton, both in old plantation areas, which had always included a mixture of small farms, and in areas of poor soil or cooler temperatures, inhospitable to the establishment of large plantations.[67] In 1876 one such small farmer, Benton Miller, was growing cotton in Hancock County, Georgia, about forty miles away from Barrow's Syls Fork plantation. Miller had owned three slaves before the Civil War. He served in the 59th Georgia and came out of the war with a rank of captain and with one leg four inches shorter than the other, thanks to a wound at Gettysburg. Miller never really recovered economically from the loss of his slaves, but, after working as a clerk for several years, managed to buy a small farm. On this land, and on a twenty-acre lot in the village of Linton that he partly owned and partly rented, he resumed his career as a farmer after a fifteen-year break.[68]

Hobbled as he was, Miller could do little farmwork himself and, like larger planters, had to patch together a labor force. In 1876 he rented his new farm, called the "Green place," to Bob Taylor, an African American who worked it with the occasional help of his pregnant wife. Their contract called for "halves" on everything — Miller to pay half the costs and get half the cotton and corn at the end of the year, a typical sharecropping arrangement. Miller advanced Taylor food and store credit and charged these against the final accounting at the end of the year. On his second plot, in Linton, Miller hired wage workers. For a time he paid George Speights, a black neighbor, $10 a month to work; then after Speights quit, Miller replaced him with Frank Renfrow, who worked for $8 per month plus board. Miller also hired people by the day. No fewer than twenty men, women, and children worked on Miller's twenty acres in Linton sometime during 1876, with some earning as little as fifty cents a day. Some days Bob Taylor worked on the Linton land; other days Miller and the hired labor helped Taylor out at the Green place. Miller's bad leg meant that he relied on wage labor more than most white small farmers, but in many other ways he was typical of small farmers in the

Piedmont. Even in heavily black counties white small farmers raised a substantial share of the cotton crop, and in majority-white counties, nearly all
small farmers, whether owners or tenants, grew cotton.[69]

Some black farmers in the Piedmont had realized the hopes of most freed
slaves after the war and acquired farms themselves. The percentages are
small, but in one sample more than one out of ten black farmers, or about
one in twenty-five black family heads, owned their farms in 1880 (see Table
4, Appendix). The proportion of "farmers" who owned their acreage is only
one measure of the importance of landholding among blacks, because some
black men and women owned small plots of an acre or so, too small to be
counted as "farms" in the census. They do show up on Georgia's tax records,
however. In Hancock County, for which the records are available, ninety-five
adult black men, about 6 percent of the total, owned land in 1882; thirty-one
black women also owned land. About a third of these holdings were one,
two, or three acres. Small or not, they could be vitally important to the
material and psychological welfare of many black families, providing vegetables and corn for the family table, eggs, chickens, and even a little cotton for
sale to neighbors or in a nearby town. These plots gave black families an
extra margin of autonomy in their choices of landlords and their dealings
with merchants, enough to provide them with the difference between hunger
and satisfaction each summer before wage labor became available in picking
season.[70]

If the economic story of the postwar rice coast is primarily one of struggling plantations based on wage labor and the spread of landownership to the
former slaves, the main story in the postwar Piedmont is one of tenant plantations like David Barrow's together with small white-owned farms like Benton
Miller's. Most large planters, like Barrow, continued to own and operate their
plantations, but they were masters of acres, not of men and women, their
plantations broken up into small farms, rented or sharecropped for the most
part by black families. Small farmers, too, continued to operate many Piedmont farms. Planters, tenants, and owners of small farms alike planted cotton
for the world's markets, and in physical production they succeeded better
than the rice planters in reviving their commercial crop, raising in 1879 more
cotton than they had before the war.[71]

Everywhere in the Piedmont, the trend was toward increased production
of cotton, along with lower production of corn and other crops that farmers
could use to feed their families and their animals. This trend was evident on
the old plantation lands, where black tenants were raising more cotton and

less corn than they had as slaves, and even more so in the upper Piedmont, dominated by white smallholders who, before the war, had grown relatively little cotton. After the war, new railroads brought markets within easy reach for the first time and delivered cheap phosphate fertilizers. One Hart County resident explained, "In this county the cotton crops are cut short by early frosts in the fall, but this is obviated by the use of fertilizers, which causes cotton to open in time to prevent damage." Before the war, about a third of Hart's farmers (all of them white) grew no cotton at all; by 1880, nineteen out of twenty grew cotton. Between 1860 and 1880 cotton production per acre in Hart County multiplied three times while corn production dropped by one-third, a change evident on all sizes of farms, but especially on small farms owned by whites. The same trends show up further south, in the old plantation counties. Before the war, most of the old plantations had raised more than enough food for their white families, slaves, and animals. After the war, few of the black tenants on these old plantation lands were self-sufficient in food.[72]

Unfortunately these small farmers entered the cotton market after the war just when cotton's price was beginning a long, slow decline. Benton Miller's fate in 1876 illustrates the result. Miller tried his best to be a progressive farmer. He belonged to the local Grange, a society devoted to agricultural improvement. He carefully recorded the kinds and amounts of fertilizer he put on each portion of his land, with some left unfertilized, "as an experiment." But in June there was too much rain, in August too little. In early September Miller wrote, "The crops are ruing forever. Cotton, peas, potatoes & turnips are gon up. . . . I am hard run for supplies that I want, such as meat, flour and syrup I got no credit, I am more than sorry that I ever tryed to farm." He concluded that he "would have made as much cotton without the Guano" he had fertilized his crops with. It did not help that cotton in 1876 fetched two cents less than a year before and four cents less than in 1874, when Miller had bought his farm. The $140 for guano, which took a third of his cotton to pay for, was, as far as he was concerned, a total loss. In all, he probably cleared on his farm operations about what the former slave Ben Thomas earned in renting a farm from David Barrow.[73]

No wonder that the next spring Miller tried to sell his "Green place." He found no buyers, and in 1877 he again tried farming, hiring Coy Ezell to work the Green farm for a straight $9 a month. Ezell promised to give Miller "all his time" and not go to his wife's house more than once a month. Not surprisingly, this arrangement only lasted a month, and for the rest of the

year Miller made do with day labor. The results were no better than the year
before. Miller put $35 worth of guano on the Green place and concluded that
he had again lost money on it. For thousands of small farmers like Benton
Miller, the turn to cotton was an economic failure. It was becoming harder
than ever to prosper as a small farmer, and, more often than before the war,
even white farmers might be sharecroppers or renters, rather than farm
owners.[74]

The Delta: Clearing the Wilderness

In Tunica County, Mississippi, about five hundred miles to the west of
Georgia's eastern Piedmont, in January 1876, planter George P. Collins was
trying to perfect his own plans for the coming year. As Collins managed a
plantation for his father-in-law, Paul Cameron of North Carolina, he was,
like Barrow of the Piedmont and Manigault on the Georgia coast, preoccupied with the "first thing," which was getting "a sufficiency of labor." Like
Barrow, Collins operated his cotton plantation with tenants. It "requires a
good deal of thought," Collins wrote to his wife, to match tenants to land. He
was trying to replace some of his "worthless" hands, and he was optimistic:
"I have had a good many applicants. . . . I am trying to make the best
selections I can." But more than getting as much cotton with as little expense
as possible, Collins was also hoping to clear one hundred or more acres of the
wilderness that surrounded the Cameron fields. The land would produce
little rent until it was better developed; once cleared, it would, with a little
luck, begin to produce the fabulous yields of cotton that the Mississippi-
Yazoo Delta was famous for. Collins planned to build three or four more
houses on the fringes of his fields in order to rent out undeveloped parts of the
plantation. "I have fallen in with some that seem anxious to get back there
among the wolves & other wild things." He had "a lot of hands that are
desirous to go back there they have team tools & horse feed & claim to be
able to feed themselves & are willing to pay low rent for some of it."[75]

Throughout the first two months of the year Collins haggled over the
terms of contracts with old and new hands. In addition to weeding out poor
workers, he determined to get rid of one tenant, Robert Flagg, who had a
penchant for "stirring up the other negroes to all sorts of mischief," and
whose "political aspirations" seemed likely in any case to "unfit him for an
agricultural labour[er]." But good tenants he wanted to keep were leaving,
too. Ed Stone went elsewhere in search of a lower rent. Jordan and Henry

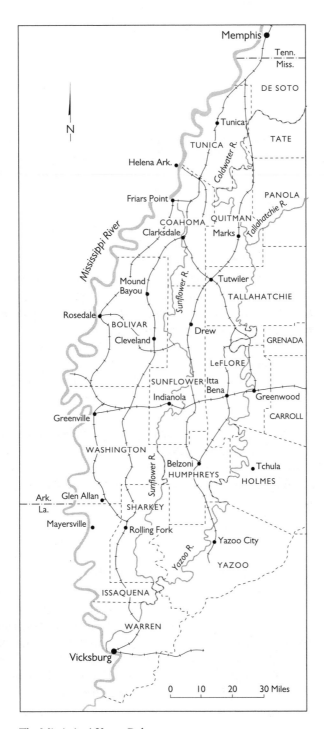

The Mississippi-Yazoo Delta

Willis decided to return to North Carolina. With money so scarce "it is very hard to find tenants able to set themselves up," but "furnishing" them — arranging, that is, to supply them with food, seed, and mules on credit — was a risky business, especially in the case of "strangers." Even after Collins found tenants, he had to be "very particular," as he put it, in drawing up his contracts, "as I find every year more disposition to evade them or to take advantage of me in some little point or other," and so "destroy my whole system, upsetting the control that I exercise & generally demoralizeing the tenants with the idea that they could get the advantage of me in any of the crop." Collins did the best he could — to Gus Brown he rented twenty acres for cash and eighty more for one-third of the crop, and he arranged for Brown to take on one "Duncan" as a farm laborer. He persuaded other tenants to add a few acres to their plots. Later in the spring, as the heat mounted and the mosquitoes arrived, he headed back home to North Carolina.[76]

Like Barrow, Collins had come only gradually to realize that renting out land to tenant families was the best way to operate his plantation. Immediately after the war, Collins had gone to Tunica County to take charge of the plantation. He might have gotten an early inkling of the new problems that came with a free labor system when, in the summer in 1866, a nearby planter had charged another with trying to entice away workers; the dispute escalated into a fight in which one bystander was accidentally shot while trying to break up the row. Collins had scrounged everywhere for wage hands that year to pick his cotton, including Memphis, and even considered a trip to Alabama or Georgia to recruit hands. When a "Mr. Wyant," apparently a labor agent, brought men down from Memphis, one of Collins's neighbors protested that he, not Collins, had first claim to their labor. Many of these hired men left at the end of the year, leaving Collins to lament that "it is so different working now. . . . The negro is so uncertain & it takes such caution & care to avoid continual conflicts with them." The year 1866 was the first of many disappointing years, as Collins struggled to clear debts and build up the plantation. He complained bitterly about black control of local politics and told his mother-in-law in 1872 that a man could expect nothing in Mississippi but "a dog's life & a bare pittance." One time he experimented with German immigrants. They "seem contented & happy," he wrote when they arrived in June 1872. Within a week, the Germans had fallen sick and he was trying to get rid of them; a week later one died. Collins concluded that one source of his problems was trying to run his plantation with gangs of workers under an overseer, and by 1873 he was through with close supervision of gangs. He rented his land to small families or larger groups who worked as "squads," and Collins hoped "to sell them the mules & rent them the land in order that I may go or stay as I choose, & come back & collect my rent."[77]

By 1876 the tenant system was well established at the Tunica plantation, but Collins was still struggling to turn it into a predictable and steady method for supplying himself with labor for his rich soil under the special conditions in the Mississippi-Yazoo Delta, a place of great possibilities and great difficulties. For eons the great Mississippi River had repeatedly changed course as it wended its way between the high bluffs at Memphis and those at Vicksburg. Between the ancient channel of the Mississippi, now occupied chiefly by the Yazoo River, and its current course lay a flat and often-flooded plain. Whenever the rivers inundated it, they dropped their heaviest contents first, so the banks rose as natural levees from which the land then sloped gently away, leaving the rivers themselves higher than most of the Delta's land (thus the frequent flooding). In the interior the rivers and creeks mingled with the solid ground; streams meandered, finding new channels and leaving old ones as long "oxbow" lakes. Some areas, cut off from drainage, became swamps, while others gradually filled with clay deposits. Sluggish creeks — the bayous — were interspersed with higher rises and ridges. In flood times the waters would back from the Mississippi up the Yazoo River, the Sunflower River, and hundreds of smaller streams, covering more or less of the land in between. As they receded they left behind the rich alluvial deposits that, over centuries, built the Delta soil into one of the richest — some said the very richest — in the world.[78]

In that soil thrived a huge variety of trees and other plants. Great cypress trees with huge knobby knees grew in the swamps; higher and drier flatlands supported oaks, elms, and sweetgums; many river banks were covered with cottonwoods. Nearly impenetrable cane fields formed much of the understory. Deer, bears, panthers, wolves, and foxes roamed the forest floors; cormorants, herons, egrets, eagles, woodpeckers, and dozens of other species of birds filled the skies. In 1860, most of the Delta was still a wilderness, isolated from good transportation and often under water. Only the highest land, meaning generally the banks of the rivers, had been put into cultivation, with the interior left to the wolves and the bears. Even well-established towns like Greenville, on the Mississippi in Washington County, were "isolated for a good part of the year, on an island, as it were with mud and water encompassing her in the rear." When a surveying party in the 1870s laid out a line for a short railroad from Greenville east toward Indianola, twenty-five miles away, they went through a "stretch of wilderness for twenty miles with scarcely a break." For miles at a time they did not see a cabin nor any "human face . . . outside of the surveying party."[79]

Economic development depended on the building of artificial levees along the rivers, so the land could be drained, the trees cut, rails laid, and the fabulous soil planted with cotton. In a sense the key to success for Delta farmers was similar to that of the rice planters of the Atlantic coast, but the Mississippi River and its tributaries presented more formidable obstacles than the relatively small rivers in the Southeast. Before the war, plantation slaves built up levees for their own masters' property along the rivers. These provided some protection against overflows, but little against severe floods, as a large flood could easily overflow upstream, or back up from downstream, with a levee for one plantation simply dumping water onto a neighbor's property. In times of high water, one woman recalled, the levees around her family's plantation were patrolled with shotguns to keep people from breaking them in order to relieve the strain elsewhere. In the spring of 1886, two white men in Coahoma County were lynched as levee breakers. Even as late as the twentieth century one planter described levee conflicts as "just like the old range wars in the West. . . . I mean many times there have been cases where men were ready to kill each other."[80]

Early attempts to build levees strong enough to hold back the powerful and unpredictable Mississippi often produced little more than high piles of dirt, mixed with logs, thrown up over the stumps of trees cut down along river banks. Planters soon learned that such levees did not last long. Logs and stumps rotted away underneath, and river crawfish burrowed in to nest in the cavities left behind. When the river rose the water forced itself along the crawfish channels, eventually cutting a path clear through the levee, undermining it until it collapsed and opened a crevasse for floodwaters.[81]

Planters and engineers gradually learned how to do better. They dug up all the stumps and scoured out a depression, then filled it with pure mud and dirt from a ditch dug on the land side of the levee, far enough away so as not to create openings for undermining. (As on the Atlantic coast, much of this digging was done by those specialists with the shovel, Irish work gangs.) In times of high water, men patrolled the tops of the levees, looking for characteristic whirlpool disturbances of the river or for geysers — called "boils" — on the land side of the river, both of which meant water was digging under the base of the levee. Then crews would quickly be summoned to fill the opening with bags of sand. If the river cut into the levee too deeply or too quickly to plug, the only solution was to throw up a new, semicircular dyke surrounding the potential breakpoint, on the land side, a formidable undertaking to be carried out as fast as possible. Nearby plantation hands might be forced to work, and, if there was enough time, convicts would be brought in from camps (or, in later years, from the state prison farm at Parchman). For planters whose land was threatened, this rescue operation was ominous, because the land cut off by the new stretch of dyke might now be "thrown outside the levee," and thus made virtually worthless for planting. The crumbling of the riverbank could require the levees to be moved inland a significant distance, and this, too, meant being "thrown outside the levee." It was a problem too big for individual planters, even wealthy ones. When countywide cooperation proved inadequate to the task, a solution ultimately came from a combination of government regulation and northern capital.[82]

In 1858 the state created the first Levee District, a new entity that collected taxes and built levees along the Mississippi. Neglect and destruction during the war ruined many of these levees, however, and the bonds issued by the district could not be paid off. The state in 1865 established a new Board of Levee Commissioners for Bolivar, Washington, and Issaquena Counties, all on the Mississippi, and in 1867 assigned the bonds issued by the original, antebellum levee district to a new Liquidating Levee Board. The new commission was to build new levees, while the Liquidating Levee Board collected its own taxes to retire the old antebellum bonds.[83] Eventually this scheme served well, but the struggle went on for decades (it is not over yet). New levees would send land values soaring, but before that occurred landowners could scarcely afford the taxes required to build them. Millions of acres — at one time, three-fourths of all Bolivar County — were forfeited to the state for failure to pay. Planters who already had private levees of their own, like George Collins, resisted a large public system "which would make us pay more than our proportion of taxation. . . . [N]ow without our levees those below are worthless & they & not we should bear the heaviest burthen."[84]

Ultimately, however, the fate of the levee system became effectively linked to the fortunes of big land speculators and northern railroad interests. Mississippi's congressmen also played an important role in gaining federal government commitments for the control of flooding on the Mississippi. The combined forces of speculators, levee boards, railroad companies, and government at all levels succeeded in creating a new Delta.[85] Big speculators bought much of the Delta's land from the state agencies that had taken it over for nonpayment of taxes. Thus hundreds of thousands of acres passed in sequence through the hands of local, northern, and British investors before being taken over once again by the state, to be sold yet again. One of the biggest of these speculators was Thomas Watson, who bought 450,000 tax-delinquent acres in 1886 for the equivalent of a single year's taxes. Watson formed the Delta & Pine Land Company (D&PL), which may have owned one-quarter of LeFlore County in the 1890s. D&PL then offered large tracts (ten thousand acres minimum) to buyers as timber lands. Lumber companies that bought the land built temporary rail lines into the swamps, some so rickety that men walked beside them in soft spots carrying poles to keep the cars from tipping over. Rugged crews, both black and white, many of them immigrants, disappeared for months at a time into isolated camps to cut down the wide swaths of trees. The companies would try to sell the cut-over land; if unsuccessful, they let it revert once again to the state for nonpayment of taxes.[86]

Railroad capitalists recognized their own great opportunities in the region. As of 1880 the Delta had only two small local lines. One early resident remembered that, in its first days, the Greenville, Columbus, and Birmingham line was so slow that when a man dropped his hat from the train he could get off, pick it up, and catch up to the train to climb aboard again. Although the line actually went eastward only nine miles from Greenville, it succeeded because it linked together the Mississippi River and Deer Creek, both lined with valuable plantations. A few years later, California capitalist Colis P. Huntington bought up the rights of way to large tracts of land and built a line from Memphis to Vicksburg and, by 1884, on to New Orleans. This line, named the Louisville, New Orleans, and Texas, immediately made large profits shipping cotton. It soon attracted a major competitor, the Illinois Central Railroad, which had begun to buy up local Mississippi companies in 1877 and eventually built its own line from Chicago to New Orleans.[87] In 1884, the fortunes of the railroad builders and the interests of boosters and land speculators came together to make possible further exploitation of the Delta's interior. Inspired by the successes of the levee commission for the Mississippi River counties and chastened by a major flood in 1882, the state authorized a second major levee-building program for the Yazoo River drainage area and named it the Yazoo-Mississippi Delta Levee District. Its commissioners negotiated a complicated arrangement with the construction company that was building the Illinois Central's new railroad. Large planters planned to finance the construction of levees with a land tax. Since the railroad had been granted large tracts of land as an incentive to build, its owners naturally lobbied for a tax on cotton rather than land. The planting interests won the tax battle, but because they needed the clout of the railroad's financiers to help them sell bonds, they promised the construction contract for the levees to the railroad's own construction company. The taxes on land were supplemented by other taxes—$10 per year on insurance agents, $15 on cotton brokers, $25 on pool and billiard owners, and $100 per day for every circus that passed through the district.[88]

And so the levees were built and the new rail line went through. The Illinois Central, to eliminate the messy competition with Huntington's line, bought up the Louisville, New Orleans, and Texas in 1892 and created a new subsidiary, named the Yazoo & Mississippi Valley Railroad, which controlled almost all the important north-south lines through the region. The Y&MVRR was the most profitable section in the Illinois Central system, yielding handsome returns right through the depressed years of the 1890s.[89]

Even before the war dozens of large slave plantations crowded the high ground in Bolivar and Washington Counties. In 1879, Washington County produced more cotton than any other county in the South, in large part because of its alluvial soil—its cotton land ranked fourth in the United States in bales per acre. Most of this postwar cotton continued to be raised on big plantations. Merritt Williams, for example, owned 1,250 improved acres in Washington County in 1880; the previous year he put 1,050 of these in cotton and raised 850 bales. His land, stock, and machinery, he reported, were worth $90,000.[90] Rail connections and effective levees could turn wild swamps into valuable cotton land, opening room for many more operations like Merritt Williams's. Even the first small, narrow-gauge railroad out of Greenville meant that "lands hitherto regarded as of doubtful value . . . became a basis of credit" with bankers and merchants in Memphis and New Orleans. After the levee system protected land in the upper Delta from high water in 1885, property values leaped upward to produce a "great revolution." Owners could now sell off their timber and turn the land to cotton.[91]

The Delta's wilderness, so raw and yet so seductive, attracted not only wealthy investors like Collins's father-in-law. In interior counties like Sunflower, with still-cheap land, farming was more hazardous, but before the levees were built even small farmers could establish themselves. Farms in Sunflower County in 1880 averaged only one-third the size of those in Washington, and few were operated as big plantations.[92] Ruby Sheppeard Hicks, born in the Delta in 1892, has left an evocative portrait of the frontier experience in Sunflower County, where her father rented a farm. She remembered cypress that "grew to unbelievable heights, their bodies straight as arrows and their roots so widely spread it looked as though the trees themselves were set in a framework of roots." In spring the oaks, walnuts, gums, pecans, and cottonwoods sprouted their soft green leaves; flowers covered the dogwood, redbud, and peach trees; iridescent hummingbirds flitted among the flowers. In the uncleared forest were owls, hawks, wild turkeys, possums, raccoons, squirrels, rabbits, mink, and foxes, not to mention wild hogs mean and strong enough to kill dogs. Canebrakes "were so thick one had to cut his way through them. These canebrakes were the last barricade for the bear. . . . Panthers, wolves and wildcats still came out into the open country from time to time, especially during a flood, and there were many floods that drove the wildlife from their haunts." This old forest was gradually cleared as farmers stripped the bark from the trees to let them die. The resulting "deadens" were made even more gaunt when black vultures set down on the now-bare limbs of the trees.[93]

Ruby Hicks only hints at the human cost of all this. The summer heat and humidity made life miserable at times, and the wildlife could be dangerous. In the Delta's waters bred an immense population of flies, biting gnats, and mosquitoes. Mosquitoes, almost all agreed, were the greatest plague; local tradition told of clouds of mosquitoes "so dense that one could run through the swarm and then look back and see the hole that had been made in their ranks." The exaggeration, if it be exaggeration, is pardonable. Mosquitoes were so bad that people would ride outside in the hottest and most humid summer months in thick long-sleeved shirts, with towels wrapped around their heads. When they stopped for midday dinner in the fields they kindled large fires, hoping that the smoke would drive the insects away. The mosquitoes brought malaria and, occasionally and more dangerously, yellow fever, which killed Ruby Hicks's mother. Unsurprisingly, many landowners chose, like Collins, to work in the Delta without their families while they struggled to carve out their plantations. This simply added to the loneliness, a feeling that turned sometimes to desolation, at other times to raw fear.[94]

And yet, when the cotton grew on this cleared land, it was "so tall that a man on horseback would be completely hidden." That is why, despite the hardships, both blacks and whites came to the Delta, and why cotton production soared there after 1870. The Illinois Central advertised its lands as good for ordinary settlers, and when the Southern Railway system completed the first east-west line through the Delta, the editor of the Sunflower *Tocsin* urged the county's citizens to become immigration agents "and solicit settlers in our midst. We want all these woodlands replaced with fields of corn, cotton, and other products. We want men who are willing and able to hew down trees and canebrakes and draw their own water. We can make capitalists of this class of citizens in less than half of a life time. We do not want men who work their thousands of acres with black transient labor and domicile in another clime." Nor was the idea that the Delta could attract small settlers entirely illusory. Even after the big levee systems took shape, large areas of cheaper wetland remained, with plots still affordable for small purchasers willing, as George Collins had put it, "to live among the bears and wolves." Not just white small farmers like Ruby Hicks's father but black families, too, could rent land in the swampy interior. They hoped to make enough money to buy some of their own land, and some did. Some came as communities. One Sunflower settlement was built by blacks from Alabama who first arrived in 1873, when they purchased land at $3 per acre, led by a man who had been a skilled shoemaker as a slave; they heard about the land from the leader's brother, who had been sold away to Mississippi before the war. Although they suffered from the usual hazards of flooding and disease, they prospered enough to attract, eventually, some two hundred more settlers.

The most remarkable group settlement was Mound Bayou, an all-black town in Bolivar County built on land purchased from the Illinois Central. The Mound Bayou settlers were made up mainly of former slaves from the plantations of Jefferson Davis and his brother Joseph and led by Joseph's overseer-manager, a former slave named Isaiah Montgomery. They were able to invest considerable capital in the new town, and Mound Bayou became the most widely known all-black town in the South. Most blacks came as individuals. One came after the war from Alabama to Vicksburg, where "he heard about the richness of the Delta." He went to Sunflower County in 1884, worked as a laborer, plantation manager, and sharecropper, and bought his first land in 1900. By the 1930s he owned enough land to have seven sharecroppers of his own. Another man came to Sunflower because "the land was said to be so fertile that dollar bills sprouted on the cotton plants." He eventually became the leading black businessman in Indianola. These pioneers shared with white settlers the hopes of prospering by growing cotton. Unlike the small owners on the rice coast, black owners in the Delta planted over half their acreage in the main commercial crop, cotton, and, while landownership was certainly not typical for black families, a few owned considerable acreage. Even Robert Flagg, the tenant who bedeviled George Collins because of his politics, became a school teacher and, ultimately, a large landowner as well as the owner of a grocery and dance hall.[95]

But the future of the Delta belonged mainly to those — nearly all of them white — who had the combination of capital, credit, luck, and energy to buy, clear, and plant really big acreages. Will Dockery, after leaving his wife and children back in Memphis, arrived in Sunflower County in 1884 with $1,000, a gift from his father. Within ten years the headquarters of his holdings, Little Dockery, employed six clerks just to keep the records for his plantation, gin, and store. The Heathman plantation on Dogwood Ridge in Sunflower (named for its original owner) included eight thousand acres in the 1890s, producing for its owners, the Crawfords, the kind of wealth that enabled them in 1894 — in the midst of the worst depression in U.S. history to that time and the moment of the lowest cotton prices of the century — to give "the most elegant and elaborate" social affair in the county's history; the Crawfords hired a band and chartered a special train to bring groups of "young, careless, pleasure seeking people" to a dance party, followed by a midnight supper.[96]

These fabulous possibilities required, of course, extraordinary amounts of labor, and the Delta's landowners went to great lengths to get it. They paid premium wages and sent recruiters east in search of workers willing to move. This meant that for most African Americans in the Delta opportunity was defined chiefly in terms of higher wages than easterners could pay and better terms from landlords than easterners could offer. In 1880 wages in the Delta were seventy-five cents per day, a paltry sum except when compared to the fifty cents laborers in Georgia's Piedmont could expect. At cotton picking time good workers could do much better, since they were paid by the pound — at seventy-five cents per hundred pounds, average male pickers in the Delta's rich harvests could earn $3.75 in a day, and outstanding pickers actually hired boys to hold sacks and fetch water so they could pick up to 750 pounds, worth over $5. Merritt Williams of Washington County paid out $6,500 in wages in 1879. When compared with the Piedmont, however, in the Delta African Americans were more likely to be renters or sharecroppers and less likely to be laborers (see Tables 8, 9, Appendix). Merritt Williams's wage bill, for example, would not have covered the cost of raising 850 bales of cotton — picking it alone would have cost over $3,000. No doubt Williams, like Collins, raised most of the crop with sharecroppers and other tenants, even if the census taker recognized that his holding, though worked in part by sharecroppers, was still a true plantation, under the central control of its owner. In newer areas, such as the area where Collins planted, black tenants willing to live with the "bears and the wolves" paid little rent and exercised a good deal of independence. The high demand for black labor ultimately drew many thousands of migrants in the Delta to clear and cultivate the land for its great planters.[97]

As the fate of George Collins shows, however, success was uncertain even for well-capitalized planters. Collins never turned the Cameron land into a source of steady and satisfactory support for himself and his family back in North Carolina. The return of Mississippi to white political control in 1876 was no panacea for him. His fortunes varied from year to year, depending on the price of cotton and the local cost of labor, but even in good years he struggled each fall to pay off the debts he had run up during the year. Collins complained that his hands became "sharper every year," and as soon as he "built up" the good ones, "others offer them inducements that are hard to resist & so now and then one leaves, and it is a hard thing to fill his place with the right material." In 1879 he was desperate enough to suggest that his wife put up her jewels as collateral against a loan. The big flood of 1882 was apparently the last straw, and the next year Collins finally gave up the planter's life and returned for good to North Carolina.[98]

Class in the Countryside: Planter, Farmer, Sharecropper, Laborer

In 1865, soon after capturing Savannah, General William Tecumseh Sherman and Secretary of War Edwin Stanton met with a delegation of African Americans—some born free, others only recently liberated by the Union army—to ask what they needed to "take care of yourselves." They replied "to have land, and turn it and till it by our own labor . . . and we can soon maintain ourselves and have something to spare. . . . We want to be placed on land until we are able to buy it and make it our own." A northern reporter heard the same thing from former slaves in the South Carolina Piedmont. "The sole ambition of the freedman at the present time," he wrote, "appears to be to become the owner of a little piece of land, there to erect a humble home, and to dwell in peace and security at his own free will and pleasure. If he wishes, to cultivate the ground in cotton on his own account, to be able to do so without anyone to dictate to him hours or system of labor, if he wishes instead to plant corn or sorghum or sweet potatoes—to be able to do *that* free from any outside control, in other words to be *free*, to control his own time and efforts without anything that can remind him of past sufferings in bondage. This is their idea, their desire and their hope."[99]

For their part, few planters believed that black men and women would work unless forced, by violence if necessary. As a Louisiana planter put it in 1864, "High wages will not make the Negro industrious. . . . [A]ll he desires is to eat, drink and sleep, and perform the least possible amount of labor." They hoped that the state would give them the legal power to coerce the freedmen, so that they could rebuild their plantations. Neither planters nor freedmen got their way. Planters never received legal power to punish unwilling workers, though they remained owners of the most productive land. Freedpeople got their freedom, but the victorious North never gave them the land they wanted and felt they deserved.[100] The resulting structure of economic wealth and power in the countryside that evolved under these circumstances can be described in a very broad sense as a pyramid. At the top, as before the war, were the relatively few owners of plantations, the 10 percent or so of families who owned half or more of the land. Below that was a larger number of small landowners, and, further down, broad strata of renters and sharecroppers. At the bottom, in the years immediately following Reconstruction, the largest group of all was made up of unskilled laborers working by the month, the day, the hour.

This broad generalization, while accurate enough, conceals the way the local geography — physical, political, and social — could alter the shape of the pyramid and the composition of its layers. Along the Georgia coast, the planter class retained a virtual monopoly of good rice lands. Rice, dependent as it was on the elaborate controls of water flow, simply could not be grown profitably for the market on small, family-sized plots, so big planters raised almost all Georgia's rice.[101] Many freedmen were able to parlay the planters' need for regular labor into something approximating the dream they articulated to Sherman and Stanton. Even as slaves, the task system had allowed them to carve out a larger sphere of autonomous economic activity than was ever possible for slaves in the cotton regions. Slaves on the coast had often provided much of their families' subsistence; some had accumulated small stakes of property. They placed their wage work as freedmen in the context of a continuing search for autonomy, "favoring," as one historian has put it, "production for sale only within the familiar context of an assured production for subsistence. This explains, in large measure, why the freedmen would not forego their hunting and fishing activities for a greater concentration on cash crops, [and] why they aspired to the ownership or rental of land." In this goal they had advantages in the rich natural environment of the coast and the availability of cheap pine lands not too far from the plantations themselves. Already by 1880, most black heads of families along the coast were farmers, not laborers, and more than half of black farmers owned land. Most worked on plantations only part-time. These freed men and women became in effect peasants, centered on their own family farms. Like preindustrial peasants in many parts of the world, they were cautious and conservative rather than risk-taking as farmers, preferring a protected space of autonomy more than the maximum of cash income. Their farms were, for the most part, modest operations indeed. Most could not provide even enough food for the families that lived on them. The average black farm along the coast reported a value of just $156 for its entire annual production. The same features that promoted landownership among the freedmen made the planters' attempts at restoration especially difficult and protracted. This can be seen most obviously and simply in the gross production figures of the coast. In 1879, by which time upland, short-staple cotton production in most places had reached or exceeded the prewar levels, Georgia's rice production was still far below that of 1859.[102]

The pyramid structure more nearly approximates conditions in the Piedmont and Delta cotton regions, but these also differed from each other in important ways. As compared with those in the Piedmont, the Delta's planters were richer, controlled more of the best land, and grew a larger proportion of the cotton (see Table 7, Appendix). Small farmers were relatively few, and nearly all tenants and laborers were black. In the Piedmont, yeoman farm owners formed a larger second layer of the pyramid. A few blacks, and many whites, owned small farms. The Piedmont's broad middling group of small farm owners hoped for prosperity, but feared for good reason that they — or their sons — would fall into the ranks of tenants and sharecroppers, competing directly with black labor. Already by 1880, as they could see, many renters and sharecroppers in the eastern Piedmont were white. To prevent a decline into tenancy, small farm owners in the Piedmont coaxed more and more cotton out of the ground with cheap fertilizers. The long decline of cotton prices that set in during the 1870s eventually caused many agricultural writers, and no doubt many farmers, to regret this turn to cotton. Country newspaper editors pleaded with farmers to "live at home," to return to the presumably better days of their ancestors, who had first provided for basic family needs before risking participation in the market. But, despite declining prices and uncertain yields, an acre of cotton was usually worth far more at the end of the year than an acre of corn or anything else that a Piedmont farmer could grow. Secure, self-sufficient, respectable poverty was not what most farmers, black or white, wanted for themselves or their children. Their families were large — the largest of any group of native-born Americans — which only made subsistence harder to achieve, so most took the gamble on cotton.[103]

Most big planters in the Piedmont divided up their plantations into small farms worked by renters or sharecroppers, and most of these were black men with families. A sharecropper was, legally and economically, not much more than a laborer, but sharecroppers were not slaves. Their family lives were largely their own, and landlords found it very difficult to keep them from moving in search of better deals. A few former slaves were fortunate enough to have white patrons who either gave them land or sold it to them on easy terms. Sometimes these patrons were in fact their fathers or otherwise re-lated. In Hancock County, for example, several wealthy whites who had fathered children with slave women made sure their African American kin got land after the war. But for most black farmers the road to landowner-ship was a long and hard one. With luck and work, they might accumulate enough capital — a mule and some implements — to become true renters, and with more luck and hard work, buy themselves a farm. On the whole, though, such success stories were rare, and more than nine in ten former slaves remained landless and poor.[104]

Some farmers, black and white, went west to the Mississippi Delta. As long as it remained a frontier, the Delta beckoned to those willing to under-take the hard, often dangerous task of clearing and cultivating the land. In the interior, places like Sunflower County began to fill up with both blacks and whites looking for better wages or for rental terms that might yield enough from the rich soil to finance the purchase of a farm. In 1880 Sun-flower had a mixture of plantations and small farms, averaging about sixty-seven improved acres in size. Its neighbor, Washington County, which had been settled along its major rivers and streams well before 1860, was, by contrast, dominated by large plantations. Its typical farm, at 226 improved acres, was three times the size of the average Sunflower farm, and its planters devoted more of their rich acres to cotton. (Washington County's planters and farmers devoted about three-fifths of their land to this crop; in Sunflower farmers planted only about half their acreage in cotton.) Nearly all the biggest planters were white, and nearly all of them depended on a working class of black laborers, sharecroppers, and renters.[105]

The farms operated by African Americans in the Piedmont and the Delta were bigger, and produced more, than black-owned farms along the coast. In the Piedmont, for example, black-operated farms produced crops worth a little over $400 in 1879, so even if a sharecropper received only half the product of the farm, his or her family might have more income than a landowner on the coast. The Delta's black-operated farms were a bit smaller than those in the Piedmont, but more of their acres were planted in cotton, and the Delta's soil was far more productive. Total farm production for the average black farmer in the Delta was more than triple that for the Piedmont, and at the same time Delta farmers could raise more than enough corn to feed their families and stock.[106]

This productivity explains the seeming paradox that, while along the coast freedmen were much more likely to achieve their goal of landownership, the population there stagnated while thousands of black men and women poured into the Delta. It also explains the surprising fact that black farmers had some chance at prosperity in the Delta of the 1880s. In a sample of farms for which both operator status and race could be determined, almost a third of black farms were owned, not rented or sharecropped. In both Washington and Sunflower Counties, black farmers seem to have operated pretty much like their white neighbors, for example planting about the same proportion of their acres in cotton as whites did. The status of the farmer did not matter much; black owners, renters, and sharecroppers all planted a little more than half of their total acreage in cotton.[107]

Fully half of all black household heads in Sunflower and Washington Counties were simple laborers in 1880, and most of the rest were sharecroppers or renters. Still, about 10 percent of all farms in the two counties were owned by black men and women. In Sunflower County, for example, thirty-four-year-old Hawkins Murphy owned an eighty-eight-acre farm in 1880, worth $1,350. Murphy was blessed with eight young children, and in the previous year he had raised, with their help, twelve bales of cotton and 220 bushels of corn. Murphy owned more than a dozen cattle, thirty pigs, fifty chickens, a horse, and a mule; with his three oxen he could clear the sixty-seven acres on the farm that were still unimproved.[108] It was not only the high wages of the Delta but the potential to turn those wages into ownership of a farm like Hawkins Murphy's that drew African American workers there. The Delta's black farmers could make more money than their counterparts in the

Piedmont, and they did not, like farmers in the Sea Island regions, focus most of their efforts on self-sufficiency. Like their richer white neighbors, they wanted their share of the wealth that lay, literally, at their feet. However, black farmers in the Delta faced more than the hazards of a harsh physical environment. In the Delta, along the coast, and in the Piedmont alike, a social and political environment built by and for white men would create the greatest of hazards to their success.

2

"A White Man's Country"

Creating the Age of Segregation

FALL IN THE PIEDMONT WAS COTTON PICKING SEASON, AND that meant it was also settlement time for landlords and tenants. On 27 November 1888, Tom Smith, an African American carpenter who rented a farm in Wilkes County from white landlord James Bramlett, came to Bramlett's cotton shed and began to load his share of the harvest onto his wagon. Bramlett himself was away, and his wife, Jane Bramlett, came to the shed to stop Smith; the cotton had not yet been properly divided between Smith and her husband, she told him. The two argued, and the argument escalated. Smith began "abusing" Mrs. Bramlett, she later claimed, and she took off for the nearby village of Delhi, where she swore out warrants for Smith's arrest. When a constable and a posse arrived back at the Bramlett farm to make their arrests, however, they found that Tom Smith, his brother Jim, and other relatives and friends had armed themselves and seized the Bramletts' cotton storage shed. Threatened with arrest, "they replied with an oath that they would die first." More whites arrived, gunfire erupted, and both Tom and Jim were wounded. "Even after being shot this negro refused to yield, and grabbing a heavy iron wrench retreated into the house and told the negroes to stand by him. He said that d——d scamp Crayton Bufford had shot him, and he would be revenged." The white crowd overpowered and arrested the "ringleaders," including "two negro women who had been instrumental in precipitating the riot," and locked them up in a convict stockade on the property of a white farmer.

That night, reinforced by arrivals from other counties, a mob of white men took Smith, along with a John Coleman, from the stockade, dragged them to the nearby Broad River, tied them to heavy rocks, and threw them into the river alive. The whites then hauled two other prisoners, Hulda Smith and Jim Smith, into nearby woods and gave each a brutal whipping.[1]

The white newspapers described the killing of the two men and the whipping of a man and woman as the outcome of a "Negro Insurrection." The names of the lynchers, the newspapers reported, "will never be known." Blacks had first, they claimed, "grossly insulted" Mrs. Jane Bramlett while her husband was away and then, "armed to the teeth," resisted arrest. "For some time now," one report claimed, "the negroes in that section have been very insulting to the whites, particularly so since the election of [Benjamin] Harrison. They armed themselves and dared any white man to try to arrest them." Now that "quiet" had been restored, the "vigilance committee" was promising to force "the most insolent negroes in that locality" to leave the county. The editor of a paper in a neighboring county assured his readers that "the blacks have been taught a lesson that should last them for years to come," that they must keep in mind "this is a white man's country, a white man's government, and the white people will and intend to rule it at all hazards and at any cost."[2]

The fate of John Coleman and of Jim, Tom, and Hulda Smith gives stark evidence of the ways in which race could make all the difference to African American workers. White tenants quarreled with their landlords and sometimes fought with them, but they were not killed or beaten by revenging mobs. The Civil War destroyed slavery, and in Reconstruction the victorious North tried to build in the South the kind of society they imagined themselves to represent. The former slaves would now become "free" in all the ways that mattered to most northerners — free to marry, to testify in court, to run for office, and perhaps most relevant to the former slaves, free to make contracts, to own property, and to sue in court to protect contracts and property. These rights, the rights of citizens, had been guaranteed to all in the 1866 Civil Rights Act and, at least implicitly, in the Fourteenth Amendment to the Constitution, along with "equal protection of the law." Although reluctantly, the North had also extended the right to vote to black men in the Fifteenth Amendment.

After Reconstruction, whites in the South did not reconcile themselves to genuine racial equality, and they tried, despite constitutional guarantees, to abrogate black rights in practice. They did it by creating new boundaries of race. The metaphors they most often used to describe the results were "color line" and the "place" for black men and women on the other side of that line. In extreme cases, the color line was enforced with brutal lynchings, like the murders of Smith and Coleman. Their killings also illustrate in sharp relief the three arenas of conflict — class (the control of labor), gender (the protection of white women), and politics (the rights of citizenship) — in which battles over the color line and its enforcement would be fought. Tom Smith had disputed his landlord's claim to the harvest, insulted a white woman, and represented, perhaps, the leading edge of African American political organization.

The Wilkes County lynchings also show that the imposition of the color line was difficult, protracted, and ultimately never complete, because whites met resistance at every step. Black individuals, families, and communities fought back, violently or peacefully, openly or stealthily. White landlords did help to reshape the law, but not exactly as they pleased, and ultimately white legal power fell far short of the fully coercive system that many, perhaps most, white landlords wanted. White violence, usually unchecked by law, never cowed all blacks into passivity. African Americans refused to accept the legitimacy of the color line. The result was reported generations later by a scholar observing the Mississippi Delta: a racial system that bred "conflict, deeply felt by every person, black or white."[3]

The Struggle to Control Black Labor

The freedom of contract was the essence of economic rights to the victors in the Civil War, and it was now supposedly guaranteed by federal law. Southern planters could not simply void outright this freedom for African Americans, but they attempted to restrict it as much as possible by writing into law practices that would safeguard their interests and maximize their power. To limit the mobility of black workers, they passed laws designed to restrict or eliminate labor recruiters and to punish those who would "entice" away workers under contract with a planter. To put to work "idle" men and women, they attempted to enforce vagrancy laws, calling for the arrest of unemployed, able-bodied adults who refused jobs. To deter and punish crimes such as theft of agricultural assets, dealt with under slavery by masters rather than by courts, they enacted harsh new criminal codes that could sentence, for example, those convicted of the theft of a pig to long prison terms. Finally, to enforce these laws in a way that would give the maximum benefit to

planters and businessmen and the minimum expense to the state, they authorized both local and state officials to lease out convicts to private companies
and individuals.[4]

For planters, the most important laws would have been those that acted
directly to compel labor from poor blacks and keep them from moving between employers. The restriction on mobility was in some ways the essence
of the antebellum slave labor regime and one key to its economic rationale.[5]
Georgia and Mississippi passed anti-enticement laws making it illegal to hire
workers who were under contract to other employers. Georgia attempted to
drive out labor agents from other states by enacting a prohibitive tax on their
activities. Georgia passed various forms of vagrancy laws in 1876, 1879,
1903, and 1905, and Mississippi did so in 1894 and 1904; these made it
possible, in theory, to arrest African Americans who lacked visible employment. Other laws sought to prevent tenants from selling unginned cotton
without the landlord's permission, by, for example, forbidding the sale of
cotton after dark.[6]

On occasions of sudden, massive out-migration from local areas, these
laws in combination with other pressures could be used with some effectiveness to restrict black mobility. In 1874, in Greene County, Georgia, some
four dozen blacks were prosecuted for either vagrancy or contract violations, and many were sentenced to the chain gang. In 1878 and 1879, when
hundreds, perhaps thousands, of black farm workers in the lower Mississippi valley began moving to Kansas, local planters similarly acted to sup-
press these "exodusters" with economic pressures and violence. In Piedmont
Georgia in the winter of 1899–1900, labor agents led by a white man known
as "Peg-Leg" Williams came from the Mississippi Delta to recruit black farm
workers with free rail tickets and promises of high wages. Many blacks
"responded eagerly," and others "demanded higher wages or less rent." In
the face of this threatened "revolution in the labor circles," local officials
arrested Williams on the charge of failure to pay "licensing" fees, prevented
him from buying tickets for prospective workers, and implicitly threatened
him with mob action. When crowds of the black would-be migrants gathered
expectantly at the Athens train station in March 1900, local whites pressured
the railroad to refuse passage to anyone without a ticket in hand, while police arrested some for disorderly conduct. James Monroe Smith from neighboring Oglethorpe County showed up at the Athens station and had the
police arrest more than a dozen men who, he claimed, had signed contracts
with him.[7]

When white planters dreamed of complete control over their workers, they might have had in mind something like "Smithsonia," Smith's Oglethorpe County plantation. To one contemporary journalist Smith was a "great farmer," perhaps "the most remarkable man in the state." "Smithsonia" encompassed twenty-three thousand acres. Each day, the corpulent Smith sat on the wide veranda of his home, receiving visitors and directing the operations of the huge plantation, receiving "couriers with reports from all parts of the farm," and giving them "his orders to carry back." Smithsonia was, according to this admirer, "a monument to an individual kind of efficiency," with its own railroad, dairy, and cottonseed oil mill; from it Smith cleared an annual profit of $100,000.[8]

The account failed to record that Smith had built his empire on the basis of forced labor. As a federal district attorney later remarked, Smith had "become a multi-millionaire by the employment of convict labor on his vast estate and by some strange process, converting free labor into convict labor." Smith's convict workers were literally chained to their beds, and like slaves of old could still be driven by overseers with whip in hand. A friendly reporter from a neighboring county counted one gang of sixty hands, many in chains, hoeing "faster than we have ever seen before." Supplementing these convicts was a large group of workers signed to five-year "voluntary indentures" requiring them to work faithfully, obey all commands, be "orderly and soberly," and account for any losses of work due to sickness.[9]

The key to Smith's success was his local political power. Smith had launched this political career during Reconstruction as one of fifty "deputy sheriffs" mobilized in 1870 to repress the black vote in Oglethorpe County. He represented the county in the state house of representatives and senate, and by the 1890s "ruled" politics there. Later he served as a member, and frequently as chairman, of the county Democratic Party executive committee. So, too, he was frequently called to serve on the grand jury, at which times he "invariably" was chairman of the jury. He was a member of the county commission that revised the jury lists. Smith personally donated or loaned money to individuals and to local churches and schools, was a director of the local bank, and bought a controlling interest in the largest nearby daily newspaper. The reporter for the county weekly in Oglethorpe, according to Smith's biographer, served, in effect, as his publicity agent. With this combination of wealth and political influence Smith built up his gigantic planting operation, in part by garnering contracts to lease county and state convicts, little different from slaves. Their exploitation was authorized by the

clause of the Thirteenth Amendment that allowed forced labor as "punishment for crime." His political influence was surely also crucial in his effective control of the numerous "free labor" hands and sharecroppers on his
plantation.[10]

In one case that we can trace in the records of the U.S. Department of
Justice, Smith purchased the contract of a man convicted in a neighboring
county of illegally selling liquor. When this man's contracted time was up, in
mid-July, he left Smith's plantation. Within days Smith's bookkeeper swore
before a friendly justice of the peace that the man had been "gambling" and
"carrying a concealed weapon." A month later he had been arrested by an
accommodating sheriff, convicted in an accommodating court, and returned
to Smith's fields. Smith's plantation impressed a young Georgia visitor who
later remembered it, rather fondly, as a model of a well-run plantation based
on coerced labor. The visitor's name was Ulrich B. Phillips, who later became
a leading historian based on his depiction of antebellum slavery as a benign
institution.[11]

The system of convict leasing that allowed Smith's properties to flourish
was often terrible in its consequences for the overwhelmingly black prisoners
who fell under its sway. For the contractors, the incentives to good treatment
were small indeed; the law protected convicts from brutality little more than
it had protected slaves from their masters before the Civil War. Local reporters for their part tended to picture the convict farms in the most benign terms.
In Greene County, Georgia, an editor claimed that "a sleeker, more contented, happier lot of people" than the convicts on one local farm "would be
difficult to find." He found that there were no complaints from the prisoners
except for "one grumbler," a "new-comer — not yet broken into harness."[12]

The editor's comparison to a horse or mule in harness hints at the realities
that occasionally surfaced in brutality so extreme that even certain local
whites were appalled. In 1893, George Culbertson, a convict guard, was
tried for murder in a case "which had excited great interest over Greene
county and the entire country." Culbertson, supervising convicts hired out to
L. J. Boswell, was charged with beating and abusing a prisoner named Barnhart (no first name was given) over a twelve-month period during which the
prisoner had dropped from 200 to 115 pounds. Culbertson, according to
witnesses, had finally knocked Barnhart unconscious with brass knuckles
and then jumped on his chest. Although the prosecutor, a prominent local
attorney named John C. Hart, presented a "powerful and persuasive argu-

ment" that "pictured the sufferings and death of the convict," the jury returned a verdict of not guilty.[13]

A similar case occurred in the Delta in 1902, when "quite a sensation [was] stirred up in Coahoma county over the unmerciful treatment of convicts on Hon. J. W. Eldridge's place." John C. Hardy, a guard employed by Eldredge, had whipped convict Henry Young "so badly from head to foot" that Young was released as useless for work and later died. The grand jury, which called other convicts to testify in the case, "found that Sergeant Hardy has whipped them so often and so brutally that they are in stripes all over their bodies." As for the Hon. J. W. Eldredge, he claimed to "know nothing of the affair."[14]

The horrors of such places may make James M. Smith's convict plantation look benign by comparison, but it is important to remember that even Smith's ability to control his labor was exceptional. Ordinary planters had to deal not with convicts but with free workers, and the laws they designed to control these workers were far less effective in practice than in theory. Anti-enticement statutes and restrictions on sales were intended to restrain landlords themselves as much as laborers, to replace, that is, the failed attempts of planters to regulate themselves. Most migration, however, was not the result of active professional recruitment but of the many individual decisions made by African Americans, as well as many whites, in their kitchens and churches, talking among themselves about the advisability of moving to places where pay might be higher or conditions better. African American laborers continued to pour into the Delta from Georgia and other southeastern states between 1870 and 1910, despite legal restrictions. Moreover, it was difficult and expensive to enforce legal restrictions that had an impact on white employers, not just black workers. As one Georgia editor put it in 1881, "Our landowners need protection from each other in their struggle for labor." Endorsing a proposed bill to "regulate labor" in Georgia, a Piedmont editor in 1888 complained that, by chopping time in late spring, most black workers were "generally well in debt" because of advances of supplies from landlords. Just at this moment, when labor demand was reaching a peak, the "first thing you know your laborer is hard at work in SOMEBODY ELSE'S COTTON PATCH," drawn away by higher wages.[15]

Whites also used vagrancy laws to control black labor. Vagrancy laws had the advantage for planters of affecting black workers without simultaneously restraining white employers. The weight of the evidence, however, suggests that such laws were enforced only sporadically and were no more effective than enticement or labor agent laws in tying African Americans to the land. In Greene County, Georgia, in 1874, the county court prosecuted some four dozen blacks for vagrancy or violations of their contracts with planters, and, in the Georgia "exodus" of 1900, at least one sheriff threatened to use the vagrancy laws to arrest potential emigrants.[16] Yet, surviving court records suggest that the vagrancy statutes were seldom used. Not a single case of vagrancy was among the ninety-three criminal cases brought before a justice of the peace in Columbia County, Georgia, between 1897 and 1902. Vagrancy prosecutions were also rare in the county court of Hancock County, Georgia, between 1896 and 1905, with none in 1896, five in 1897 (with three of the defendants acquitted), and none in 1898. In early 1901 there was a spate of eight vagrancy prosecutions, perhaps related to the "exodus" of the year before; of these, five had the charges dropped and the other three defendants were found not guilty. In 1902 again the Hancock court saw no vagrancy cases. Even in Greene County, where vagrancy was prosecuted in the 1870s, such cases had apparently disappeared by the 1890s.[17] A similar story emerges from state records of prisoners held in county chain gangs. In February and March of 1901 the state received reports from eight camps in the eastern Piedmont, a center of out-migration to the Mississippi Delta. Only one of 187 Piedmont prisoners had been convicted of vagrancy; the others had been found guilty of assault and battery, gambling, disorderly conduct, and other crimes.[18]

Historians have often asserted that planters were able to restrict the mobility of sharecroppers and tenants by getting them into debt and using that debt to keep them from leaving their landlords. Here, too, the evidence shows that indebtedness failed to tie most sharecroppers down to a single plantation or landlord. Indeed, annual turnover of plantation tenants was enormous. In Glascock County, Georgia, for example, from 1868 to 1870, and again from 1878 to 1880, the two-year turnover rate of black tenants was over 50 percent. In Liberty County on the coast, from 1867 to 1869 only 35 percent of black workers were working for the same employer after two years; in Lincoln County, in the Piedmont, the same 35 percent persistence rate prevailed.[19]

The most convincing evidence of the limited power of most planters to control labor mobility lies in the records of planters and farmers themselves. Planters like David Barrow, Benton Miller, and Louis Manigault had to struggle constantly to get and keep labor, to make the best deals they could depending on market conditions. Take, for example, the experience of the overseer on the Newstead plantation in Washington County, Mississippi, in the early 1880s. He notes in his diary resorting to the kind of force that most white workers would not have tolerated. In 1881 he "rattled down several freedmen about their rascality"; the next year he "drove Bill Williams out of the quarter." More often, though, his journal offers a running commentary on the difficulties involved in getting and keeping labor. In early December 1878, many of his workers were "grumbling" about their accounts; two weeks later, the hands were "doing nothing," and the overseer feared he would lose what cotton was still in the fields to be picked. In January, as he settled up with several hands, he wrote, "I shall lose on the majority a small balance," and the next day he heard "a good many of my hands are leaving," which, he thought, would cost him more than $100 in advanced wages and supplies. There is no indication in his journal that he had any way of keeping on hands who were determined to leave at the turn of the year.[20]

In 1880, Newstead's overseer paid labor agents for six hands recruited from the Gulf Coast; the next year he was so short of hands at picking time that he had to hire wage labor, "a most expensive way of gathering a crop." "The freedmen won't work when they can hire [themselves out for day wages]." Later that year more black workers left: Jack Dunlap "goes owing me money. . . . Henry Sanders informed me he intends to leave; I nursed him out of a bed of sickness." In the middle of the next summer, "Macks's wife quit. . . . Negroes quit whenever they feel like it."[21] In these same years, similar labor worries surface constantly in the affairs of the Tunica County plantation run by George Collins. In 1880, Collins wrote to his wife that "there is the greatest commotion in the neighborhood more changes of managers & consequently moves among the laborers themselves everybody trying to secure the best class." At the end of that year the story was the same, and Collins planned to hire a new manager from a neighboring plantation who would, he hoped, bring along new hands as well. "Now in this," he told his wife, "I don't think I am infringing on my neighbours, as both Crews & the hands have declared they will not stay where they are." In 1882 he continued to struggle for the entire crop year to get and keep labor. In April, after losing two tenants just after part of the crop had been planted, Collins had to replace them with wage laborers. One worker, Bedford, left because the manager on the plantation "got after him with a stick," and when local authorities gave him no satisfaction, "B. left." In June Collins was "as busy as it is possible to be & just now am so short of hands that I have to work a good deal myself & unless I am there it seems nothing is done." The state of the neighborhood crops was "obliging the planters to pay high day wages," yet despite this "the weather is so hot that hands don't like such severe labor." A few days later, "the complaint is general wages have gone up all over the neighborhood & labor seems scarce." In the picking season that fall, "cotton pickers are scarce & high & we have more than double what our own hands can pick, I hire all I can get & shall send to M[emphis] tomorrow & try to get more. I wish I had 100 for two or three weeks they would help me out wonderfully." The next week he was off to get cash to pay pickers, as "the crop is opening so fast that it frightens me. . . . [P]rompt payment is the only way to secure pickers."[22]

A decade later, the same constant concerns fill the diary kept by Clive Metcalf, a big Delta planter in Washington County. Sometimes Metcalf's "favored" hands left unexpectedly: "Aaron came to pay me the Bal[ance] due me and he is going away. Well the more you do for a negro the less he will thank you." The end of every year meant a nervous time of settling up and recruiting hands for the next year: "I am worried to death from settling with Negros and getting them satisfied for X mast [Christmas]. been running my Gin all week." "The negroes are very much dissatisfied evry where. They are leaving . . . evry day. Why it is no body knows. They are just like sheep." At times Metcalf benefited from other people's labor troubles. In 1890 a neighbor, Mrs. Urquhart, rented her place to local store owners and almost all her hands left because they were "vary much dissatisfied. A good many have applied to us for situations."[23]

The power of black workers was limited; they had to make accommodations with *some* landholder if they expected to feed themselves and their families. When times were really bad, as after an 1890 flood in the Delta, black workers suffered far more than the big planters, and moving around could help them little: "Every thing's on a stand still. Negroes and white folkes are all poor alike this year and it is the 'Devil' I tell you. . . . Had some hands to come to see me about working on my place. . . . They seem to be crazy to move this year." The plunge in cotton prices in the 1890s meant trouble for everyone, but most of all for African American labor. Clive Metcalf thought his 1892 crop was "the sorriest crop that was ever made on this place. And when the new year comes in it will find me as poor as I was ten years ago." But he could still be "thankful to my Heavenly Father for my health and strength" in the knowledge that his workers were much worse off:

"The Darkies are poorer than I have ever seen then, most of them [have] scarcely nothing."[24]

Still, overstating the power of white planters also distorts the situation. As Metcalf put it, "What in the world will a man do with out labor in this country? For one can not work the land with out the Negroes." Metcalf was struggling not only with African American labor but also with his neighbors, who were equally anxious to get workers. Tenants, especially black tenants, were most certainly poor, but they worked in an economy in which competition for labor was often intense and in which collusion among landowners was anything but easy. African American laborers, even if illiterate, could tell if they were being egregiously cheated, and they knew as well what the competition had to offer, in wages, credit terms, or other working conditions. When the Cameron plantations in the Delta's Tunica County were turned over to the management of local merchants, they told Cameron that his place was in bad shape, with cabins falling down; "of course the Negroes are all very much dissatisfied, and we cant well blaim them. Now if there is not something done and that very soon. [It] will be a very hard matter to get good hands to remain on the place." Clive Metcalf did not feel so powerful when he noted his exasperation in his journal: "A man is a fool for renting his land. The doggone negroes want you to knock off your But. And give them every thing."[25]

In the accounts of planters in both Georgia and Mississippi, debt plays a role that is both smaller and decidedly more ambiguous than in the writings of many historians. Certainly the planter's or merchant's control over credit was a powerful resource in recruiting labor each year, as many workers could not have survived without "furnish" in the early months of the year. It was the planter and merchant, too, who kept the books. But debt was just one of the many factors, ranging from the current price of cotton to a family's ownership of a mule, that affected the labor market. Writing of the eastern Piedmont in the early twentieth century, Robert Brooks noted that "negroes frequently get hopelessly in debt to their landlords. In order to extricate themselves they go to a neighboring planter and borrow enough to square up with the creditor, promising to become tenants to the lender and work out the new debt. So great is the competition for laborers that planters take on hands under such circumstances and are glad to get them." And debts could be a serious problem for the creditor-landlord as well as the debtor-tenant. In 1880, George Collins wrote that "the negroes are falling behind & there are several on the place from whom I can not collect their accounts & will have most probably to loose it, as they are of the trifling class that will never have anything & Nat [his manager] never ought to have kept them on the place nor have allowed them to run up the bills they have made." High debts were a burden and mistake, not a boon, to Collins.[26]

Contract labor laws and the credit system favored the interests of landlords over those of workers and could cause serious problems for black tenants and sharecroppers, but neither laws nor debt gave white landlords the degree of control over labor that they desired. Breaking a contract was a civil rather than a criminal offense in any case; as Harold Woodman has pointed out, "winning a civil suit against a propertyless tenant could be a Pyrrhic victory," and "the courts made criminal suits difficult to sustain." "Criminal surety" laws offered the opportunity to secure labor by paying convicts' fines and requiring labor in recompense. But Georgia's supreme court threw out its statute on criminal surety in 1894. A Georgia law intended to criminalize the violation of a contract by a farm tenant, passed in 1903, was thrown out by the state supreme court in 1911. The Mississippi law of 1900 that "barred a laborer who had broken a contract from entering into a second contract without the permission of the first employer" was struck down in 1913 by Mississippi's courts. The formidable legal challenges faced by southern whites in their attempts to control their labor supply help to explain the continuing high level of mobility by tenants and laborers. They also help to explain why planters at times were so tempted to resort to extralegal violence to enforce their claims to property and labor.[27]

The Great Fear: Protecting White Women

The most visible and deadly instances of this violence were lynchings, such as the killings of Smith and Coleman. Lynchings had appeared in many places and at many times in U.S. history, but in the late 1880s they became a primarily southern and racial phenomenon. Between 1883 and 1900, eighty-three blacks (and two whites) were lynched by mobs in the Delta, the eastern Georgia Piedmont, and Georgia's Atlantic coast. Many thousands of other black men and women, such as Jim and Hulda Smith, were whipped, beaten, or shot. The murders of Smith and Coleman were touched off by a dispute over the crop, and the fundamental economic conflict between white landlords and black laborers was undoubtedly a key factor behind many of the lynchings in the southern countryside.[28]

Other attacks on African Americans were rooted in economic competition with poorer whites, rather than conflict with planters. Sometimes such violence ran directly counter to planters' interests. Indiscriminate terror against blacks might threaten to drive blacks away entirely, something landlords had every reason to resist, since it might reduce competition among laborers and tenants and drive up wages. In southern Mississippi in 1904, an outbreak of such attacks on blacks by white tenants and small farmers broke out. Mississippi's James K. Vardaman, an editor from the Delta, had just become governor after a campaign so viciously racist that even many Mississippians were shocked. Yet, as governor, Vardaman took strong steps to repress the violence, hiring out-of-state detectives to investigate the incidents, convening special grand juries, and prosecuting ringleaders. Had whitecapping, as this kind of violence came to be known, succeeded, it would possibly have raised rural wages and enhanced the bargaining positions of white tenants hoping to rent farms abandoned by blacks. In this case, profits mattered to planters more than white solidarity.[29]

Lynchings of men accused of sexual crimes, however, tapped the deepest emotional wells of whites. A comparison of the reactions to two lynch murders in Oglethorpe County, Georgia, illustrates the point. In 1894 Bob Collins, a black man, was arrested on a charge of "enticing away hands employed in the neighborhood"; he posted bond and went home. A few days later a half-dozen masked white men came to his house, dragged him into the woods, and beat and whipped him so severely that he later died. The coroner's jury made the usual finding — death "from the effects of punishment administered by unknown parties" — but the case did not, as it did in the vast majority of lynchings, end there. Instead, whites protested strongly against "one of the most disgraceful acts of lawlessness that ever occurred" in the county; the local editor wrote that "the crime is too great a stain upon the county's escutcheon to go unpunished." Collins's landlord, D. M. Gaulding, pushed an investigation, and within a week four prominent young white men had been arrested and jailed, charged with the crime.[30] The four men denied their guilt and the prosecution seems to have been dropped. In the same county in July 1887, a mob of whites lynched Ross Griffin, a black man accused of attempting to rape a member of the family he worked for. The editor of the local paper issued a pro forma "regret" at this incidence of "summary justice," but rationalized the lynching as "but the meting out of justice at the hands of an outraged community." He insisted that the mob was not a mob at all "in the real sense of the word." Griffin, the editor added, had

attempted "an act which is . . . a blow directly at every home in the community," and the hanging was more just than the twenty-year maximum sentence for attempted rape, in no way "commensurate with the deserts of the
crime." The lynching would "prove a safe guard to our homes. . . . [W]e, with
all right thinking people, believe that the mob has but furthered the ends of
common justice."[31]

To local white opinion leaders like this rural editor, lynchings on behalf of
"our homes" were different in kind from other forms of violence rife in the
South. Rural newspapers were full of reports of personal quarrels (usually
involving two white men or two black men) that escalated into deadly violence, and many of the white elite deplored society's seeming acceptance of
such behavior. As one judge complained in his charge to a grand jury, "Too
many guilty men have been acquitted by the courts of this State. — This fact
encourages the lawless in the commission of crimes, and discourages the law-
abiding in appealing to the courts. This very thing is the origin and pretext
for mob law, which is always dangerous, and subversive of the best interests
of society."[32] The editor who reported the judge's charge strongly endorsed
his sentiments, and yet the very same editor had defended white mobs who
attacked alleged black criminals just two weeks earlier on the grounds that
"the methods of justice in Georgia have become weak and squeamish. . . .
Summary methods for the protection of the inviolability of property and
home and social purity cannot harm the good; and there is nothing so well
calculated to deter evil doing as the dread of swift vengeance coming like a
whirlwind out of the darkness."[33]

To Victorian-era white southerners, "home and social purity" meant
"white women," and the greatest threat to white women was black men.
Vardaman, in 1893 still an editor in Greenwood, Mississippi, time and again
praised the "exalted virtue, the vestal purity and superlative qualities of
Southern woman" — and did so even when the question at issue was not race
relations at all. White women were — must be — pure, and their place was the
home, where they required the "protection" of their fathers, brothers, and
husbands. From the vantage point of a hundred years' hindsight, we can see
that "protecting" women and the home defined and enforced not only a
"place" for blacks but also a "place" for white women. Such "exalted" and
"superlative" beings were neither independent nor autonomous; their place
was the domestic sphere. For a black man to attack a white woman was to
attack as well the honor of the men who were charged with protecting her.[34]

White women themselves sometimes echoed these fears and endorsed the idea that they needed "protection." Mrs. L. H. Harris, a Piedmont woman, wrote to the *Independent,* a national magazine, to explain the emotions driving a mob that had recently tortured and burned to death a black victim. While the conduct of the mob may have been "atrocious," they had killed a "negro brute," the product of an immoral upbringing that laid only the "cheapest veneering" over his "murderous instincts." The lynched man was a "hideous monster," a "wild beast" driven by the "lust of a fiend." Farmers did not dare to leave their wives and daughters at home to work in the fields; "even in small towns the husband cannot venture to leave his wife alone for an hour at night. At no time, in no place, is the white woman safe from the insults and assaults of these creatures." Such feverish fantasies of the dangers of rape were an important source of the determination to keep blacks in their "place."[35]

Indeed, in many cases a black lynching victim superficially accused of a property crime had actually been accused as well of violating the "purity" of a home. In Thomson, Georgia, not far from Augusta, Allen Sturgis was hanged by a white crowd in 1888, accused of a string of burglaries. The person who reported the lynching stressed that Sturgis had "entered the room of a young lady visitor," "tried to enter the room occupied by two young ladies," and had been discovered hiding under the bed of a Mrs. Burnside, who was visiting her mother at the time. He supposedly confessed to "going to the rooms of several young ladies, and watching them disrobe for the night."[36] The report of the lynching in the state's largest and most respectable newspaper demonstrates how the white elite helped to rationalize such lynchings. The story said that the white mob moved so quietly in taking Sturgis from the jail that "even the night marshall" was unaware of what had happened. The next morning whites and blacks alike found Sturgis hanging from a tree near an African American Baptist church. "Every one seems to be satisfied that Allen has been dealt with as best suited his crime" — even "the colored people approve of the step taken." It editorialized in the body of the account that "his dead body hanging by the public road this Sabbath morning will prove a good warning to both white and black that the men of Thomson and McDuffie [County] know how to act when the emergency arises." The men of the county — "our people" — were normally "conservative and law-abiding," and only the "peculiar" nature of Sturgis's crimes had caused them to "lose their heads." The account captures the way in which whites often treated lynch law *as* law — not law-breaking. It was an alternative form of justice that followed its own set of rules and meted out sentences more just than the regular legal system. Such justifications wholly implicated local elites in the extrajudicial murders of blacks who had stepped out of their "place."

Citizens' Rights in a White Man's Country

White supremacy was a product in part of class advantage, in part of fears about gender relations. It was a product as well of the search for power to control politics and define the meanings of citizenship. Voters chose state and national representatives, governors, and presidents who might conceivably have profound effects on state and national policy. Political power at the local level determined who held office, and some local officials, such as a sheriff, could earn a considerable income. Local politicians controlled the expenditure of taxes, determining, for example, the level of pay for teachers or whether or not to make available anything beyond an elementary public education. Local officials determined whether the constitutional imperative to give all "equal protection of the law" would be followed. Sheriffs decided when and how to enforce laws against gambling and disorderly conduct. Grand juries indicted and petit juries judged the guilt of men and women accused of large and small crimes. Judges and juries decided disputes between tenants and landlords over divisions of the crops. Coroners and coroners' juries decided whether lynching victims had come to their death "by parties unknown." For Tom Smith, the failure of the law lay less in what it said than in what the courts did, or rather failed to do. Some white lawyers, judges, and jury members were honest men, and defended the integrity of their legal system with fair verdicts, if only to reassure themselves that they were, indeed, honest men. Most blacks, however, could expect little from the expensive and cumbersome courts in disputes about weighing the cotton or adding up the interest rates. Planters who juggled the books or resorted to violence faced scant probability of legal liability. In Elbert County, Georgia, in May of 1901, Tom McClanahan, a white planter, went in search of one of his tenants, Robert Smith, who had left him to work on another plantation. When "the negro showed fight," McClanahan shot him. Another planter, in the Mississippi Delta, told the story of a tenant he had caught trying to sneak away. I "whipped him till he couldn't stand up," the planter said. "Thought that would hold him for a while. . . . He couldn't stand up when I got through with him." Like the members of Smith and Coleman's lynch mob, these planters could be confident that they would never have to answer in court for their crimes.[37]

Whites' determination to control the courts was an important impetus behind their repression of black voting during Reconstruction, which had allowed white Democrats to take back power from Republicans. In Greene County, Georgia, the Republican Party took control of local politics in 1868 with the support of black voters plus a few whites. Abram Colby, a former slave (albeit a relatively well off and independent barber) was elected to represent the county in the state legislature.[38] This political revolution was short-lived, however. In part this was because of divisions within the Republican Party itself, but more important was the violent suppression of black leaders and voters by the Democrats through the agency of a new secret organization, the Ku Klux Klan. The KKK there, as in most places throughout the South, focused its attention on the organizers of the Republican Party. Abram Colby was one of the first victims; when he refused a bribe of $5,000 from local merchants to join the Democrats, Klansmen seized him from his bed one night in October 1869, forced him into nearby woods, beat him unmercifully for hours, and left him for dead. Remarkably, Colby survived not only to tell his tale to a congressional committee but to continue to lead Greene County's black voters in future political contests.[39]

Colby was lucky. In nearby Warren County, state senator Joseph Adkins (unlike most Klan victims, a white man) was ambushed and killed. In Hancock, Oglethorpe, and other Piedmont counties, Klan violence and the use of economic pressures reduced the Republican vote and allowed the Democrats to take back control of the state. In Oglethorpe County, for example, the Republican vote was reduced from 1,144 to 116 between the elections for governor and president in 1868; in Hancock the reduction in the same period was from 1,394 to 85.[40]

In the Mississippi Delta, overwhelming black majorities afforded African Americans the opportunity to hold office and exercise a measure of control over their political affairs. The efforts of the Klan there were sporadic and largely ineffective, and it remained for a more subtle and carefully calibrated program of violence and intimidation, the famous "Mississippi Plan," to enable white Democrats to seize control of the state in 1875.[41]

In the Delta, the work of "redemption" (as Democrats called it) was not always subtle, to be sure. The city of Vicksburg and surrounding Warren County had served in December 1874 as the stage for something of a dress rehearsal for the seizure of power by Democrats throughout the state. Democrats organized, first as the "Taxpayers' League" then as the "White Man's Party," with its own informal militia. The White Man's Party won the city elections, then set its sights on the county. An armed mob in Vicksburg forced Republican sheriff Peter Crosby to "resign," then routed a crowd of black men gathered to reinstall Crosby and pursued their black opponents into the countryside, killing at least twenty-five. In Yazoo County in 1875, a vigilante force of more than eight hundred whites took over the county from the Republican organization led by a white carpetbagger, Albert T. Morgan. In Coahoma, at least one hundred whites skirmished with a force of several hundred blacks led by John Brown, an African American carpetbagger.[42]

In extreme cases, a combination of fraud and violence wiped out the Republican vote entirely. In 1872, President U. S. Grant, running for reelection, won 2,433 votes in Yazoo County, and the Republican Party carried the county by a three-to-one margin. In 1876, the Republican vote in the county fell to two. Virtually the same thing happened in Tallahatchie County, where the Republican vote dropped from 891 in 1872 to 1 in 1876. In the Delta as a whole, the Republican vote in these years was cut in half, and a Republican majority of 83 percent was turned into a minority of 38 percent.[43]

Even before the end of the Civil War, African Americans along the Atlantic coast had organized to assert their rights and press their interests, above all their interests in landownership. General William T. Sherman, fresh from his March to the Sea, had given their interests and hopes a tremendous boost by setting aside exclusively for black settlement "the islands from Charleston south, the abandoned rice-fields along the rivers from thirty miles back from the sea," southward all the way to Jacksonville. Newly emancipated slaves, following local grass-roots leaders as well as northern-born African Americans like Aaron A. Bradley and Tunis Campbell, had quickly taken advantage of this "Sherman grant" to seize control of plantation land. Campbell, for example, had organized new black agricultural communities with hundreds of freed men and women on St. Catherines, Ossabaw, and Sapelo Islands.[44]

Although President Andrew Johnson nullified the Sherman grant in 1865, and the freedmen had to give up their land, these grass-roots efforts translated quickly into a strong political organization when Congress ordered blacks to be enrolled as voters in 1867. In 1868, Bradley and Campbell and George Wallace from Hancock in the Piedmont were the only three black men elected to the state senate. Chatham, Liberty, Bryan, and McIntosh Counties all sent

African Americans to the state house of representatives, with McIntosh electing Campbell's son, Tunis Campbell Jr. Later Camden and Glynn Counties also elected black representatives.[45]

Neither threats from the Klan nor the best efforts of Georgia's Democrats managed to destroy this black political power. Although Campbell and his son were, along with other black members, both expelled from the state's general assembly in 1868, he was restored to his seat by federal law and built up a formidable political machine in his home base of McIntosh County. Campbell also served as a justice of the peace and organized a local militia that formed the foundation of his political influence. Frances Butler Leigh, one of many white planters and business people who deplored Campbell's influence in the county, was told by her overseer that if he were too "firm" with her black workers, "I should only get myself into trouble, and have the negro sheriff sent over by Campbell to arrest me."[46]

Whites fought back with considerable success on several levels. The state legislature, with Democrats back in control, created a new board of county commissioners, to be appointed by the general assembly with power to appoint other county officers and even to take over the duties of the justices of the peace. Whites in the county attempted to expel Campbell from his offices on the grounds that he had threatened armed resistance to the new commissioners' law, and when that failed they successfully resorted to fraud to prevent his reelection to the senate in 1872. They managed to convict him on a charge of "false imprisonment" in a trial presided over by a blatantly biased Democratic judge, who sentenced him to the chain gang. After a year as a leased convict, Campbell, then age sixty-four, gave up the political fight in Georgia and moved to Washington, D.C. Black political power survived to some extent in McIntosh and other coastal counties. In the years between 1890 and 1901, McIntosh, Camden, and Liberty Counties all elected African American representatives at one time or another. In McIntosh County, blacks also served in the 1890s as coroner, justice of the peace, constable, and deputy marshall.[47]

While black voters remained especially significant on the Georgia coast, they and the Republican Party were a serious political force in other places well past Reconstruction. In Greene County, because of a strong organization and the courage of leaders like Colby, the Republicans actually captured the legislative elections in 1870, with one seat going to Jack Heard, another African American. As late as 1884 the Republicans carried Greene County in the presidential election, and in the eastern Piedmont as a whole the Republi-

cans continued to draw a third or more of the vote every four years, providing a regular reminder of the potential for a resurgence of black political
power. In the 1888 presidential election, Republican Benjamin Harrison won
38 percent of the vote in the Delta and 54 percent on the Georgia coast. The
importance of the black vote could vary dramatically from one neighborhood or county to another. In 1888, for example, Harrison received only a
single vote in LeFlore County and 1,726 in its Delta neighbor, Bolivar; 12
votes in Bryan County but 673 in McIntosh (both on the Georgia coast); 4 in
Oglethorpe but 714 in Greene (both Piedmont counties). White fear of black
political power was not a fantasy.[48]

Citizenship meant more than an equal chance at political power, however. It was in many ways the essence of equality, implying not only rights but
also dignity and worth. Many whites found it impossible to separate the
pragmatic and the emotional implications of citizenship for African Americans, nor could they draw a sharp line between "political equality" and the
more sexually threatening "social equality." Delta congressman Frank Montgomery wrote in his 1901 *Reminiscences* that he had resigned "in disgust"
from a jury panel shortly after the war when he discovered that Negroes
would serve with him. Although he claimed (quite incorrectly) that "few
southern men regretted the freedom of the negro" and he praised the abilities
of individual African American leaders such as Blanche K. Bruce, who served
as U.S. senator from the state during Reconstruction, and John R. Lynch, the
Reconstruction-era congressman, he stressed in his memoir the utter humiliation he and other whites felt as a result of the "cruel and unnecessary act
by which the former slave was placed upon a political equality with his
master."[49]

The same idea was expressed more crudely in 1890 by the editor of the
Elberton *Star,* in Georgia's Piedmont, to whom the problem of the "insulting
negro" was inseparable from black political power. The very idea of blacks'
holding office was "simply ridiculous"; when "carried beyond the sphere of
an every day laborer" the African American "is a complete failure; he has not
the first instinct of a gentleman, nor has he a virtue." Blacks in office were
"humiliations being placed upon our people. . . . [W]e are in favor of teaching
the negro where he belongs at any cost." More than forty years later northern
observers in the Delta were struck by the emotional force still carried by the
memories of black political power in Reconstruction. One was told that
"Negro supremacy supported by northern force . . . was felt to be . . . a more
terrible humiliation than defeat in war." Another learned that, while "the

war" was a living and powerful memory, "the Reconstruction Period is a memory even more vivid and turbulent. . . . Mere mention of Reconstruction days to the average middle-aged man, whether his family was rich or poor, is enough to release in him a flood of resentment."[50]

The Color Line

In the late nineteenth century the convergence of a white drive for power, of rising fears for white women, and of white desire to gain material advantage motivated white southerners to construct a newer and stronger racial boundary between whites and blacks. The roots of this system lay in slavery and Reconstruction, but some aspects of it were new. Certainly the whites who drew the color line perceived it as new. In the late 1880s, most whites had come to accept black voting as at least a necessary evil, and black voters and, less often, black officeholders were normal parts of political life. Separation of the races was not yet codified into law, and on streetcars and even in city neighborhoods blacks and whites, at times, sat and lived side by side. In the Mississippi Delta, a German visitor complained that, in 1880, he and other "poor victims of white skins given us by Mother Nature" had been "crowded into the corners" of the railroad cars by the "two dozen ladies and gentlemen of the '*couloured race*'" who were already "stretched out on the best seats" of his train. But over the next decade lynchings of blacks would soar. In 1890 Mississippi's new constitution would virtually bar African Americans from voting, and in 1891 Georgia's legislature passed a series of statutes designed to compel segregation in railroad cars, trolleys, and even convict work camps.[51]

The specific events triggering the changes in this period, which one historian has called, with reason, the "crucible of race," are difficult to disentangle, but whites often wrote of the "problem" of the color line in terms of the need to show the new generation of postemancipation African Americans their true "place" in southern society. A letter to the editor of Greene County's newspaper captures this common feeling. "Uncle Peter" wrote to lament the passing away of Porter Turner, one of those "Southern darkies" a white man could be proud of, a "good boy . . . a favorite among the white people — always courteous, affable and polite." Porter, born in 1864, the son of "Uncle Frank" and "Aunt Mary" Turner, was no humble farmhand; he had gone to school, taught in the county, and attended Atlanta University. But what marked him was not his unusual education but his "genuine conservative feeling of respect, and humble obedience to patriotism, as we are apt to portray in the old slave time darkey." "Only a few of the scions that sucker up from the old stumps," wrote Uncle Peter, "can afford to raise their hats to a white lady, and very seldom does a white man even get a handle to the first end of his name. I don't know how those second generations of the negro race will move up, just as they handle etiquet and respect like most of them do now."[52]

The writer's focus on etiquette was no minor point. In their everyday encounters whites often detected a "failure" of blacks to show proper "respect." The litany of complaints about the "second generations" have a counterpart in the rigid system of racial etiquette that hardened into orthodoxy in these years. A generation later, several writers described that system in practice, a system that reinforced the color line in face-to-face contact between whites and blacks: a black man should always remove his hat when speaking to a white or meeting him on a sidewalk or roadway; black people visiting a white house should go to the back door, not the front; blacks had to address whites by titles: "Boss," "Suh," "Mr." or "Mrs."; whites would address blacks with the "first end of his name" only. In one Mississippi town a white postmaster actually defaced the words *Mr.* or *Mrs.* when used on letters addressed to blacks. White people required titles because they were representatives of the entire white race, whatever their personal worth; they were symbols, not just individuals. The use of a title also avoided familiarity, thus protecting the "ideal sphere" of honor that surrounded every white person. Whites denied blacks such a sphere of honor, privacy, and protected space.[53] Rules of etiquette dictated that the racial boundary in the South separate not only the high from the low but also the "pure" from the "impure." The dictate was expressed in such economically irrational beliefs as the conviction that black women could render an item of clothing in a retail store unfit for sale to whites simply by trying it on. Not that trying on a hat or a coat might make the black woman equal to a white; rather contact would defile the clothing. That is, African Americans were not only "inferior" but also "unclean."[54]

The niceties of etiquette and brutality of lynchings fell at either end of a spectrum of controls, with etiquette a daily reminder of blacks' "place" and lynchings as the fatal punishment for the most serious breaches in the color line, especially murder, rape, and other violent attacks, real or imagined, by blacks against whites. Violations of racial etiquette could themselves be fatal. As one country editor crudely put it in 1890, "Almost every day some white person is outraged or subjected to an insult that only a kinky head can offer. . . . [E]very day the Southern man sees a reason why the negro will some time or other have to be taught to know his place, and as matters are going on now the sooner they are taught the better it it [*sic*] will be for all concerned." In the very next issue, the same paper carried an account of the lynching of George Penn for attempted rape. The approving editor issued the usual claim that "we . . . deplore mob violence" but went on to applaud the murder of Penn, on the grounds that "the swift and terrible punishment that was meted out to him cannot but have a salutary effect in detering others from the perpetration of a like crime," that blacks (as well as the "trifling class among the white's [*sic*]") should take notice.[55]

Many lynchings punished black murderers who had been provoked to violence by the accumulated humiliations of day-to-day racism. In Yazoo County, Mississippi, in 1888, Wilks Arnold was lynched after he killed Robert G. Johnson, "one of the most prominent citizens of the county." News reports claimed that Johnson "had had some words with Arnold, but nothing of a serious nature." In LeFlore County in 1896, an unnamed black man was taken and hanged after he shot and killed J. H. Rook, a white man who was "reprimanding a negro woman at her home." Yet another LeFlore County man, Dennis Martin, was hung after he killed Gus Aron, a leading merchant and planter who had "upbraided" him for making a "disturbance" and "lightly" slapped him in the face.[56] Resistance in such cases was suicidal, but for some African Americans death by lynching was not too big a price to pay for refusing to kowtow. Such men often became folk heroes in the black community, even though, not surprisingly, many had used violence against blacks as well. If the price for the violator was all too often death by a lynch mob, the fact of resistance must have given many a pause to a white planter who wanted to batten down on one of his tenants or to a white sheriff ready to arrest a black accused of a crime. A dead white man could get no satisfaction from the subsequent lynching of a black one.

For whites, questions of interest, fear, and power formed a logical whole in the system of white supremacy. One editor blamed what he saw as rising racial conflict on unscrupulous office seekers who were pursuing "venal" voters, by which he meant black voters who supposedly sold their votes to the highest bidder. To this editor, the black "floater" in politics would become "the rapist in fact, and, therefore, he not only corrupts our politics but infests the social fabric." The resulting antagonism, he claimed, threatened "a clash of races that will rival all massacres of the past." In Vardaman's rhetoric, denying education and citizenship to African Americans was proper because "God Almighty created the negro for a menial" and also because "you can scarcely pick up a newspaper whose pages are not blackened with the account of an unmentionable crime committed by a negro brute, and this crime, I want to impress upon you, is but the manifestation of the negro's aspiration for social equality, encouraged largely by the character of free education in vogue."[57]

"Place" and Places: The Geography of Race and Resistance

The color line was a South-wide institution, but its contours varied widely from place to place. Nothing makes this more clear than comparing the raw numbers of lynchings in the Delta, the Piedmont, and the coast (see Charts 7 and 8, Appendix). From 1883 to 1892, the Mississippi Delta witnessed at least forty-nine lynchings of African Americans (plus two of white men); with only a slightly smaller black population, the eastern Piedmont had only one-fifth as many lynchings, and the Atlantic coast, with about one-third the Delta's black population, saw only three lynchings. The Delta was a far more dangerous place for blacks than the Sea Island region, with the eastern Piedmont in between. Multiple factors produced these differences. The coast was long settled, while the Delta was in some places still a raw frontier before 1900, full of single young men on the make. In the Piedmont, and to a lesser extent the Delta, blacks and whites were competing to rent farms. Along the coast, many blacks owned their farms and had no need of regular contact with whites. Another important reason was the strong tradition of black community activism along the coast.

One of the most striking examples of this occurred in Darien, on the Georgia coast, in 1899. In August a prominent black man, Henry Delegale, was accused of rape by a pregnant white woman. Delegale turned himself in to the local jailer, and within hours a large crowd of blacks, many armed, had gathered at the jail to prevent a lynching. They were determined to prevent the sheriff from taking Delegale to Savannah for "safekeeping" because a common tactic of lynch mobs was to seize a prisoner during transport. When the sheriff tried to sneak Delegale away, a signal from the bell of a black Baptist church brought hundreds of people to the jail.[58] In response to this "insurrection," the governor called out the state militia. Blacks, confident now that there would be no lynching, allowed the militia to escort Delegale to Savannah, but conflict continued when some local whites tried to arrest two of his sons on trumped up charges of "rioting." The Delegale sons killed one white deputy and wounded another.

This "insurrection" resembled the conflict that had ended in Wilkes County in 1888 with the lynchings of Tom Smith and John Coleman. In coastal McIntosh County things were different. In 1899, the year of the Darien "insurrection," the county had a black coroner, constable, deputy marshal, and election officer, and at least four blacks served as jurors. As late as 1907 the county was represented in the state legislature by an African American. African American community leaders — including federal appointees, ministers, and an editor — also enjoyed good relationships with local whites and helped to negotiate a resolution which was ultimately peaceful, if not fully just. Henry Delegale, his sons, and several dozen black "rioters" all went to trial, but they received strong representation and the proceedings were serious, not merely pro forma. Delegale himself was acquitted of rape and a majority of the accused rioters also went free. Delegale's two sons, though, were convicted of murder and sentenced to life imprisonment, and nearly two dozen blacks were sentenced to a year on the chain gang for rioting. The contrast with the fates of Tom Smith and John Coleman, tossed into a river tied to a heavy stone, is stark.[59]

At the other extreme was the case of Oglethorpe County, Georgia, with its reputation as a center of coercive labor relations in the Piedmont. As early as 1881, the editor of its weekly paper complained that some planters were reducing blacks to "involuntary servitude" by threatening prosecution for minor offenses, and paying bonds for the accused. By the end of the century the county had begun to attract the attention of federal officials. In January of 1898, H. O. Johnson, an Oglethorpe County resident, sent a letter to Edward Angier of Atlanta, the United States district attorney for the Northern District of Georgia, charging that a nearby farmer, William Eberhart, had been for years conducting "a reign of terror in this community" that made the "rights and liberties of the citizens" impossible to maintain, a situation that was "fast depopulating the settlement." Eberhart, according to Johnson, was holding "farm negroes . . . actually in bondage." Charles Calloway, for example, "was hand-cuffed and beat" until he signed a contract to work for three years and bound his children to Eberhart until they were twenty-one years old. John Robinson had been "beat almost to insensibility and made to sign a contract for three years." Philis Neely and her mother-in-law, Nancy Lovett, were handcuffed together and beaten until they agreed to bind Neely's several children to Eberhart. The district attorney eventually identi-

fied James Monroe Smith as the leader of a local "Convict Ring" in the
county and conducted a vigorous prosecution of Eberhart. Eberhart was
convicted, but the conviction was overturned by an appeals court that ruled
that neither the Thirteenth nor the Fourteenth Amendment authorized prosecutions of private individuals for violations of other individuals' rights.[60]

White supremacy was powerful, but its power was not absolute. Even if
they lacked the advantages of blacks along the Georgia coast, African Americans elsewhere did not passively accept their subordination. After Mississippi disfranchised black voters in 1890, Vicksburg's black veterans continued to lead a solemn parade of African Americans out to the huge national
cemetery on the outskirts of the city each May 30—Union, but not Confederate, Memorial Day—in a pointed reminder of their claims to American citizenship. Blacks also continued to resist politically—voting when possible,
formally protesting the imposition of segregation laws, and boycotting trol-
ley companies.[61]

Despite the received wisdom that blacks would never use the courts or
lawyers, it is clear that many did. A federal investigation of James Monroe
Smith was touched off, for example, by a letter from a convict's wife to none
other than Theodore Roosevelt. Other cases began with complaints to a district attorney from black victims, their wives, or their parents. Local courts
might on occasion be sources of protection for black workers, especially if
they could find white patrons or allies. In Greene County, Georgia, in 1893,
for example, a "prominent" planter named Alec O'Neal was charged with
buying unginned cotton after dark from Jim Armstrong, an African American farmer. After separate trials that "excited considerable interest," both
O'Neal and Armstrong were acquitted.[62] Like Alec O'Neal, African Americans could take advantage of white differences to seek justice in the courts
or rely on white patrons to defend them. The first federal investigation of
peonage in Oglethorpe was triggered by a white man concerned that William
Eberhart's "reign of terror" was "fast depopulating the settlement," which
certainly harmed other farmers trying to keep their labor.

African Americans resisted also with what the anthropologist James Scott
has aptly termed the "weapons of the weak." Their resistance was necessarily
more informal and carefully hidden, as Scott puts it, behind a facade of "calculated conformity." Like slaves of earlier generations, sharecroppers who
felt cheated, or who looked out of their cabins at a failing crop, had their own
ways of trying to even the odds a bit. The complaints of many whites that
black sharecroppers were too "improvident" or "lazy" may not have been

mere racism; why should a tenant convinced he had no chance of breaking even for the year put out extra effort? Why not sneak off to work in "somebody else's cotton patch" when demand and wages were high? By the early years of the twentieth century, James M. Smith of Georgia himself was complaining bitterly about what he called "the new generation of Negroes . . . who had few of the graces and none of the dependability of their forebears." He claimed to see this decline not only in instances of gambling, drinking, and carrying concealed weapons, but also in thefts of tools and hogs and in nighttime thefts from the fields of corn and cotton. Worse still, according to Smith, he had lost $150,000 as a result of suspicious fires. His promises of rewards of $500 had uncovered no culprits.[63]

Moreover, the threat of violence was never a one-way proposition, whatever the fearful price that might be paid by any black man or woman who attacked a white person. In Piedmont Georgia's "exodus" of 1899–1900, one bailiff sent to serve a warrant on a tenant who had allegedly skipped out on his contract was shot to death.[64] A visitor to the Delta from South Carolina wrote in 1905 that "every white man here virtually carries his life in his hands for it is a place where the long arm of the law does not reach. If a white man gets into trouble with a negro he has got to shoot and shoot quick or get shot. Everybody carries a gun however contrary to the laws of the state it may be and is always in a state of preparedness."[65]

Boundaries

The new color line of the age of segregation sought to confine African Americans like the great levees confined the Mississippi River and its tributaries. Although levees had been a feature of life on the river for decades, in the 1880s and 1890s came the consolidation and reconstruction of a scattered, incomplete, often poorly built and ineffective system into a unified, interconnected wall that sought to keep the mighty waters permanently separated from the rich lands of the Delta. So, too, racial boundaries had defined life in the South for generations, but the color line of the late nineteenth century was a new human creation, albeit one built of old materials and sometimes following old plans and ideas.

Having created the boundary, whites liked to stand back and pronounce it as much a part of nature as a mountain range. God himself, whites assured and reassured themselves, had "created the negro for a menial." They drew support and comfort from the new ideas about race and human differences that contemporary social scientists were mistakenly deriving from Darwin's theory of evolution. They argued that attempts to tamper with such a natural force were not only misguided but would inevitably fail with pernicious consequences.[66]

But their actual behavior showed whites knew otherwise: that the color line, like any human construction, could be eroded and swept away. The forces of destruction might start with a small breach or a weakened spot in one place, with the color line silently undermined until it was in danger of collapse whenever the next high water arrived. Hence the southern white obsession with small breaches of etiquette or small steps toward equality. The levee of race had to be constantly patrolled for possible breaches, and when these occurred, the white community had to respond, unified, to meet the threat.[67]

The lynchings of Tom Smith and John Coleman had originated in a dispute over cotton between a landlord and a tenant, but the conflict escalated far beyond that and soon involved the whole range of resistance to white supremacy and violations of the principles of the color line. It threatened the economic privileges of white planters. It involved the "abuse" (in this case purely verbal) of a white woman by a black man. It followed hard upon the election of a Republican to the U.S. presidency, arousing fears of black political organization that escalated into still greater fears of black military organization. Behind whites' terror was a recognition that Tom Smith was not just an isolated man with a grievance but also a symbol for and leader of a larger community of men and women determined to resist what they saw as illegitimate authority. Black resistance had threatened the color line at every point, because these free men and women determined to act as if the South was *their* country, too.

3

The Populist Challenge

IN 1894 THE EDITOR OF A SMALL-TOWN WEEKLY NEWSPAPER IN the Georgia Piedmont, reflecting on the political campaign in his state and county, described it as "the bitterest political contest that has been waged in Georgia since the days of reconstruction. . . . [T]he colored vote is badly divided, and the white Populists are actively canvassing it, as are the Democrats. . . . [H]ow and when will the agitation end? Neighbor against neighbor, brother against brother, and father against son? It is a fearful condition of things, and we greatly fear bitterness is being engendered which will never heal." The "political contest" he referred to was the battle between the Populist and Democratic parties that had begun about three years earlier. A week later, the Democrats repelled the Populist challenge in Georgia, but all offices in the editor's own Greene County were swept by the third party in a "Waterloo for Democracy" there.[1]

This political earthquake was a result of the release of energy caused by a long process of seismic shifts in political forces, fueled by energies released by economic and social change since Reconstruction. The steady rise of cotton production, changes in the organization of farms, the political "redemption" of the South by the Democratic Party, and continuing conflicts over race together created new fissures in the political structure. The Populists had, as this Georgia editor lamented, deeply divided Greene County. And yet, at the same time, the Populist movement caused barely a tremor in the Mississippi Delta or the Georgia rice coast. Populism was not a South-wide phenomenon, despite the political ripples it created, but a locally based movement. Why Populism threatened such profound change in the Georgia Piedmont but had so little impact in other places can be examined through the stories of men like Benton Miller, a farmer in Hancock County. Before the Civil War, Miller had operated a small Piedmont farm with three slaves, growing cotton as did his wealthier neighbors and in-laws. Though many historians have downplayed the commercial orientation of "yeoman" farmers such as Miller, he was firmly committed to the market as the means to achieve prosperity. His subsequent brief career as a merchant confirms his lack of aversion to commerce or markets. As a farmer, Miller kept his slaves hard at work all year, and like his planter neighbors, he kept them mainly at work in his cotton fields. While he raised enough corn to feed his family and stock, about two-thirds of the value of everything he produced came from his cotton harvest.[2]

The Civil War cost Miller his modest wealth in slaves and several inches of his left leg. He struggled after the war, first as a clerk, then, as before the war, a farmer, but his farming experience was so discouraging that he lamented that he "ever tryed to farm." Miller and other Piedmont farmers were growing less corn and more cotton than they had before the war. Railroads lowered transportation costs, making grain and fertilizers cheaper and providing an outlet for cotton. Merchants who sold to farmers on credit wanted the future cotton crop as security. Perhaps most important of all, an acre planted in cotton in 1880 could produce a crop worth perhaps $25; an acre of corn was worth half that. To "live at home" by raising all one's food might put cornbread and hog meat on the table, but it would provide little income to pay for absolute necessities and taxes, not to mention the cost of educating one's children or of purchasing the tempting array of consumer goods that beckoned on every visit to town: hats and boots, dishes, wood stoves, sewing machines.[3]

Farmers had few alternatives to cotton if they sought more than a bare subsistence or if they hoped to save enough cash to buy a farm. As rural population rose, farms got smaller, and farmers turned to fertilizers to try to induce a higher yield from their small plots. Indeed, the rise in the farm population does much to explain the increase in tenancy in the Piedmont. A number of historians have discussed farmers' "decline" into tenancy, and, in the worst of times, no doubt many farmers lost their land to merchants or other mortgage holders. Yet, the number of farm owners in the Piedmont was *increasing*, not decreasing from 1870 to 1890; the problem was that the number of sharecroppers and renters was increasing even faster.[4]

Turning to the market was risky. A farmer had to deal with the potentially fluctuating prices not only of the cotton he grew but also of the grain and fertilizer he had to buy, the labor he might need to hire, and the credit he would need to sustain him each year until the harvest. Benton Miller's experience in 1876 and 1877 shows what happened when the risks did not pay. In an especially telling episode in June 1876, Miller described in his journal how he ran short of corn for himself and his family of tenants. He could get credit neither from crossroads stores nor from town merchants, and finally he borrowed a few bushels from his father-in-law. Soon he was out of corn again. As his searches came up empty, Miller grew desperate; soon he would have literally nothing to eat, with the corn harvest still months away. Finally, a neighbor, Mr. Duggan ("I had no friend to help me but him"), backed up Miller's credit at a local mill so he could acquire thirty-two bushels of corn at $1.25 each. Miller immediately sold a portion of this corn to his tenant Bob Taylor, charging *him* $1.60 a bushel. At next fall's harvest, corn would sell for fifty cents a bushel.[5]

All this might have been at least manageable if the price of cotton had held up, but world demand for cotton, for reasons not entirely clear, failed to rise at the pace of earlier years. This failure translated directly into lower prices and a decade of discouragement for farmers like Miller. The experience led him and others into a search for solutions to their problems, a search that culminated in the founding of a new political party that challenged the ruling powers in Hancock County, Georgia, and beyond. In Hancock itself, the local newspaper editor identified Miller as "the father of the movement in Hancock, and its ablest and most eloquent leader here." A member of the new Populist Party in the county agreed: "When we were groping our way in the darkness and asking relief through the treacherous old Democratic party, who would not even so much as allow us to gather up the crumbs that fall from the table, it was the courageous Capt. Benton H. Miller who, seeing our distress, hoisted the flag of the People [*sic*] party with Relief inscribed thereon and shouted 'follow me, my countrymen.'" The "groping . . . in the darkness" started with a new organization called the Farmers' Alliance.[6]

The Farmers' Alliance

Established in Texas in the early 1880s, the Farmers' Alliance grew sporadically in the southwest for several years, then organized a formal campaign to set up local "suballiances" throughout the South and West. As its recruiters traveled through Georgia, hundreds of county alliances and local suballiances sprang up, like dormant seeds in a desert responding to rainfall. By 1888, Greene County alone had several suballiances with hundreds of members. The Farmers' Alliance attracted some wealthy men, but most members came from the ranks of smaller white farmers. (A loosely allied Colored Farmers' Alliance enrolled African Americans.) In the Bone suballiance in McDuffie County, only one of fourteen founding members owned more than 120 acres of land; about half owned no land at all. Seventeen farmers, most of modest means, founded the suballiance in Crawfordville, in Taliaferro County. Members there owned from 50 to 950 acres of land, and the president, E. T. Anderson, was the only member with property worth more than $5,000. Officers of the eleven suballiances in Greene County were a bit wealthier than that, but not by much. About half of the Greene officers owned less than $1,000 in property, and fewer than 10 percent owned property worth more than $5,000.[7] The Crawfordville suballiance is one of few for which records remain. It was, among other things, a social club that tried to engender a concrete feeling of community. It accepted women as well as men into membership. In their monthly meetings, members sang songs; they organized a dinner at "lay-by" time in August; they contributed money and labor to gather the crop of brother Ed Bentley when he fell sick; they mourned together when member John Henry died.[8]

Like the Grange, an earlier farmers' organization that Benton Miller had joined, the Alliance served as a source of advice and support for the ordinary business of farming. Thus, in January 1890, the members of the Crawfordville Alliance resolved that they should try their best to "raise ample provision crops" during the coming year, and the next fall sent one member to a fertilizer company to check current prices and explore direct purchasing. A perfectly ordinary response to economic problems on the farm, such activities excited no controversy in the community. But the presence of a "lecturer" among the officers selected at the first meeting is a clue to the Alliance's intention to be more than an organization devoted to farm "improvement." The lecturer's job was to teach, and the lessons taught went far beyond standard exhortations to "live at home" by growing more food; they established the study of "principles" from which members might deduce a diagnosis of and solutions for the farmers' problems that were economic and political in the widest sense.[9]

The premise behind the Alliance's program was that control of the U.S. political system had been seized by new forces of "monopoly" from those to whom it belonged by right—the ordinary producers of wealth, such as members of the Alliance. These forces — epitomized in the great corporations of men like Andrew Carnegie and John D. Rockefeller and the great banks of men like J. P. Morgan — were manipulating both politics and the economy to squeeze everyone else in their own interest. Alliancemen harkened back, quite explicitly, to the Jeffersonian ideal of the virtuous yeoman, relying on only himself and God, desiring only to be free of all unnecessary government interference. To such "producers," every man who did not earn his living by the sweat of his own brow — including the ordinary merchant as well as the banker and the capitalist — was suspect on both moral and political grounds. Thus the Alliance excluded from membership bankers, lawyers, brokers, and "anyone who keeps a store, who buys and sells for gain." The Crawfordville local suspended G. H. Mitchell when he took a job as a clerk at a local store.[10]

Monopoly power — what these farmers saw as a new and corrupt form of capitalism — was exemplified in high railroad rates and control over the prices of other vital goods and services, the most vivid example being the decision in the summer of 1888 by a cartel of the manufacturers of jute bagging (used to wrap every bale of cotton) to raise the price from seven to eleven cents a pound. The Alliance responded with a national boycott of jute bagging, and Crawfordville's suballiance was one of thousands that negotiated with local merchants to purchase a substitute bagging made from cotton, provided the merchants promised not to "put on too much profit." Bowing to the pressure, the jute cartel lowered its prices, and the Alliance, its prestige vastly enhanced, harvested new crops of members. A year after its founding, the Crawfordville Alliance had grown from seventeen to forty-five members.[11]

More far-reaching was the attempt by the Alliance to bypass entirely the normal channels of credit and distribution with a set of cooperative "exchanges." Organized at the state level, with local exchanges to serve as a distribution network, these exchanges were to be run by farmers, for farmers. They would negotiate directly with cotton buyers and manufacturers to get the best prices both for selling the farmer's production and for purchasing his consumer goods and farm supplies. The exchanges would rely on the good credit of better-off farmers to subsidize the credit needs of those dependent on the lien system. This was the "cooperative" system — a way for farmers to cooperate with one another to preserve a way of life benefiting all without undermining the fundamentals of private ownership. The Georgia Exchange was at least temporarily successful, reportedly saving members some $200,000 in fertilizer costs alone, but, like those in other states, that exchange finally was forced to close its doors. The reasons for failure were complex; among other things, farmers grossly underestimated both the practical functions of the existing distribution system and the managerial skills needed to run it. Another problem was that the cooperatives, lacking capital, could not get credit of their own, and therefore could not give it.[12]

To the theorists of the Alliance the failure of the cooperative system was more evidence of monopoly control of the nation's financial system. They were convinced that big bankers and their political allies kept the volume of currency too small to serve as an effective medium of circulation and exchange, compelling the country's true producers to rely excessively on credit. In late 1889, led by Charles W. Macune, a Texas physician and editor, the national Farmers' Alliance called for a new government policy, a "subtreasury," designed to wrest control of the rural credit system away from monopolists. The subtreasury scheme would allow farmers to deposit their produce in government-owned warehouses, receiving in return what amounted to open-ended, low-cost loans of paper money, thus freeing themselves from the tentacles of the banks, the merchants, and the crop lien. The loans would work like paper money, the resulting inflation would raise the prices of their crops, and prosperity would be restored to the countryside. The subtreasury plan, added on to earlier Alliance calls for government regulation, or even ownership, of railroads and telegraph companies, marked a profound turning point in the Alliance's history because it necessitated a wholly new strategy for farmers seeking relief. Acknowledging they could no longer control their own destinies by opting out of the market or competing with the gigantic new institutions of industrial capitalism, the Alliance called for countervailing and direct government support and intervention. Only politics, that is, could save them.[13]

The first political strategy of the Alliance in places like the Georgia Piedmont was to seek allies in the local Democratic Party, dominant in the South since Reconstruction. In the spring of 1890, Crawfordville's Alliance, like others across the state, conferred on "the most suitable candidates for the next General Assembly of Georgia." Throughout the state, and through much of the South, the Alliance measured candidates with a "yardstick," the units of which consisted of planks in the Alliance platform — control of railroads, an income tax, and the subtreasury. Some of Georgia's politicians — most notably Democrat Tom Watson, a red-headed firebrand elected to Congress from the Augusta area in 1890 — readily embraced the yardstick; others, less convinced of its wisdom, nevertheless endorsed its principles in order to win votes. Greene County elected Alexander H. Smith and Augustus L. Kimbrough, president and treasurer respectively of the Greene County Farmers' Alliance, to the state legislature.[14]

Indeed, so many candidates backed by the Alliance were elected to the general assembly that it became known as the "Alliance legislature." But the victory was hollow. Most Alliance demands required action at the national, not the state level, and even when the legislature could affect national policy, its members, having given lip service only to the "yardstick," largely ignored Alliance demands. In one of its first orders of business, Georgia's so-called Alliance legislature elected to the U.S. Senate Governor John B. Gordon, who had openly opposed the Alliance's subtreasury plan. In Washington, pro-Alliance representatives, both Republican and Democrat, soon learned that their political influence was severely limited.[15]

The Democratic Party, in fact, was nationally, and often locally, in the hands of men with little sympathy for expanded government aid for farmers. In Greene County the local government in the 1880s was dominated by lawyers, merchants, and wealthy farmers. In Wilkes County the typical local official in the mid-1880s had more than twice the wealth — and the legislators who served the county had more than seven times the wealth — of the average white taxpayer. Before the Civil War, many ambitious but poor young men went into merchandising or the law to make enough money to enter the ranks of planters, but after the war their sons, even while continuing to operate the large plantations they had inherited, turned to the law or merchandising for their true livelihoods. They were in consequence natural allies of the bankers and capitalists whose conservative economic views dominated the policies of the Democratic Party at the national level.[16]

In places like Hancock County, moreover, local elections often turned on purely personal matters or on issues far removed from basic economic problems. In the mid-1880s factions divided into the "friends" of Judge Pottle and those of Colonel Jordan, two men who shared traditional conservative views. The most divisive political issue of the 1880s in Hancock was prohibition, finally enacted in the county in 1887 after what the local editor called "the most unpleasant election . . . ever known in Hancock." The attitudes of the local elite about the economic needs of ordinary folk could be summed up with the comments of that same editor at the beginning of 1887, when "the people generally were never poorer or more heavily in debt than they are at the commencement of the new year." How did he explain this pervasive poverty and indebtedness? "People have failed to be diligent in business, have been unwise in their investments, or have lived wastefully and beyond their means. It would not be amiss to say that many of the financial woes of the people of the whole State are due to idleness and extravagance." Little wonder that men like Benton H. Miller sought to strike out in a new political direction when their hopes of reform from the Democrats were thwarted.[17]

The Alliance's 1890 foray into politics failed, but it led to a stiffening of members' resolve: if the existing parties could not be trusted or changed, perhaps a new one would have to be formed. In November 1891, the national meeting of the Alliance adopted a resolution calling on all congressmen elected with its support to refuse to participate in the caucus of any party that did not embrace its ideas. The only southern congressman to accede to this demand was the man who had pushed for it, Tom Watson of Georgia. Watson had risen from poverty to be a successful lawyer and planter in McDuffie County, just outside of Augusta. His prior history was no indicator of the economic radical he became. Many things contributed to Watson's radicalization. For example, he was incensed when the Richmond Terminal corporation bought up the local railroads and raised shipping charges sharply on the fruit he raised and sent north. His antimonopoly sentiments aroused, he followed these straight into the reform movement embodied in the Farmers' Alliance. A fierce battler by nature, and hardly afraid of a fight, Watson wrote to fellow Georgian Charles W. Crisp in 1891 that, unless Crisp endorsed the Alliance's program, he would refuse to vote for Crisp as speaker in the U.S. House of Representatives, even if Crisp became the choice of the Democrats. This open defiance of the national Democratic Party stirred immense controversy. On June 6, the Crawfordville Alliance, which was in Watson's district, passed its very first resolution in its three years of existence. "The demands embodied in our platform," they said, were far more important than honoring with the speakership someone like Crisp, a man "who will not so much as intimate a willingness to support our cause." They went on to "heartily endorse and appreciate the able and fearless stand that the Hon. Thomas E. Watson has publicly taken in this matter, manifesting a loyalty to his constituents and their demands." The next year, Watson was put up for speaker by a new party caucus consisting of himself and eight western representatives, defectors from the Republican Party. Watson later wrote, "I did not lead the Alliance: I followed the Alliance, and I am proud that I did follow it." He followed it all the way into the new Populist Party, and many ordinary voters could have said the same. As one Greene County

Populist put it in 1893, the Alliance was to a large degree "the cause of the reform movement now in vogue."[18]

Populists

Many Democrats shared the goals and purposes of the Farmers' Alliance. Nearly all could agree on the evils of the money kings, the need for financial reform, and the dangers of railroad monopolies; even the abolition of the national banks and the institution of an income tax received hearty endorsement by local Piedmont editors. The Sparta *Ishmaelite*'s editor agreed in 1889 that the Farmers' Alliance had been "made necessary by the encroachments of monopoly on the rights of the farmers," and the Greensboro *Herald-Journal* even became the official publication of the Alliance in Greene County. When editors thought the Alliance had gone too far, as when its national organization called for government ownership of railroads and the creation of the subtreasury, they complained only that the Alliance had carried the laudable desire for reform too far for practical success. Local Democrats did not, that is, object to the idea of reform, which is why the original Alliances embraced many substantial planters and why newspaper editors throughout rural Georgia had welcomed it, praised its efforts, and cheered on its 1888 boycott of the jute trust.[19]

Yet local elites were suspicious of the Alliance's emphasis on the supposedly distinct interests of "producers." While, one editor wrote, he could agree on the dangers of "monopoly, trusts and combinations," he insisted that farmers and merchants depended on one another; farmers must not be "arraying class against class." The true goal of the Alliance, he suggested, ought to be to get farmers to avoid debt and "live at home." The move toward partisan politics also concerned elites, as well as some Alliance members. The Siloam suballiance in Greene County condemned the idea of using the "yardstick" to endorse candidates for office as "discourteous" to Democrats outside of the Alliance. Above all, the Alliance must be careful lest it cause a split among Democrats and open the way to electoral victory by the Republicans. A Democratic editor wanted to "put the farmers on guard against those enemies of Democracy and good government who seek to make of the Alliance a political tool." Reform might well be needed, but the Democratic Party itself, local Democrats insisted, was the true party of reform.[20]

Not reform itself but a new party as the instrument of reform was what frightened local elites. Thus, when Congressman Tom Watson endorsed the subtreasury and government ownership of railroads, the local editors took issue with some of his stands but praised his abilities and many of his opinions. As late as the end of 1891, the editor of the Greensboro *Herald-Journal* was lauding a stem-winding speech by Watson in the town as "able, strong and temperate."[21] A few months later, however, after Watson had become the local standard bearer of the new Populist Party, the weekly press referred to him as a "clown" who campaigned with "ridiculous antics." "Like an inebriated monkey," one editor wrote, Watson was making "the lowest, most shameless, most degraded appeal to the prejudices and passions of the ignorant" ever heard; Watson was a "sneak," an "apostate," a "Judas." Similarly bitter denunciation and ridicule faced ordinary men who joined the new party.[22]

After Reconstruction, many whites had begun to identify the Democratic Party with the white South itself. It meant rule by white southerners, not by Yankees or black former slaves. It was the party of unabashed white supremacy in a "white man's country." A white voter turning away from the Democrats could be seen not as just a disgruntled voter but as a traitor. Still, the domination of the Democrats was a relatively recent and never uncontested phenomenon in the eastern Piedmont of Georgia. The area had returned Whig majorities in many antebellum years and supported the Republicans in Reconstruction. Many whites there (as well as in other states from Virginia to Mississippi) had, after Reconstruction, voted for "independent" candidates who objected to state tax policies and criticized the Democrats for what they perceived as favoritism toward railroads and the unnecessary growth of bureaucracy. Independents dissented as well on purely local issues. Should the county borrow money to build schools? Pass a law requiring owners of stock to fence in their animals? Prohibit the sale of alcohol? Many such issues pitted older ideas and values against newer ones, and many pitted the inhabitants of the towns against those in the countryside. In some cases dissidents complained that Democrats manipulated nomination and election procedures to make sure they stayed in office. Greene County's voters divided sharply on such issues in the 1880s. They debated the need for a fence law; a requirement to fence in stock could harm the interests of poorer, landless tenants who could otherwise allow their animals to forage in the woods. They differed over local prohibition; in 1885 a referendum on local prohibition lost because a 60 percent majority in Greensboro overcame a smaller majority in the rural districts. They differed also over the passage of bonds to build new schools.[23]

Such issues and divisions helped to make Greene County a center of "Independent" strength. The independent movement in the county was led by old antebellum planters, mostly former Whigs. One, James B. Park Sr., was a longtime politician and planter; another, R. L. McWhorter, was a wealthy former Whig who had temporarily joined the Republican Party during Reconstruction. McWhorter and Park, objecting to such innovations as the stock law and charging the local Democrats with "ring rule" and with "packing" nominating conventions, won election to the general assembly in 1878. The independents carried the county for the next two legislative elections as well. Not until 1884 did the "day of jubilee" (as an editor called it) come to Greene's Democrats. Greene's independents campaigned for and won black votes; they even cut a deal with local Republicans so that their names shared a single ballot with black candidates for office. White independents resisted the frank appeals to white supremacy by supporters of the Democrats, who insisted that "there are but two parties in this country — the Democratic and Radical. Radical rule in the South means negro supremacy. Democratic rule means a government by the white people. This is the issue in a nut shell."[24] This tradition of political dissent combined with Farmers' Alliance agitation and rising economic distress to prepare the way for the new Populist Party. In May 1891, as Greene County's newspaper editor was writing that rain and drought had made "the present year . . . a disastrous one to the farming interests of the country," the new "People's Party," which most people simply called the Populists, was officially formed in Cincinnati.[25]

Populism in Greene County

In Greene County, local Democrats watched with rising alarm as agitation for a new party began to take effect. Yes, we need reform, they said. No, we don't need a new party, because the Democrats are the party of reform. A third party would be nothing but a stalking horse for the Republicans; by splitting the solidly Democratic South, it would place the South "under the rule of the bayonet, the negro, and worse still the scalawag." It was obvious to everyone that the Farmers' Alliance was the driving force behind the new party, but the *Herald-Journal*'s editor predicted hopefully that southern farmers would have nothing to do with the new party, for to abandon the Democrats would "destroy a political and social solidity, which is essential to the safety of their property and institutions." Perhaps hoping to forestall Watson's jump from the Democrats to the Populists, the paper gave respectful coverage to his attacks on railroad monopolies before the state legislature and showered praise on his "Ringing Address to the People of Greene" in November 1891. In his Greene speech, Watson denounced the "Plutocracy" and reiterated the demands of the Southern Farmers' Alliance for an income tax, the subtreasury system, and government takeover of railroads from the "five men on Wall Street" who controlled them. His measures, the editor added, were in reality "Democratic Demands."[26]

The pleas of the editor and other Democratic leaders were in vain. Alliance members were listening not to them, but to Tom Watson and to each other. In one Greene suballiance in this period "Brother Foster" led a discussion of the issues, telling his fellow members that "no true Allianceman can be any other than Third Party," and urging them to look past "sectionalism" and not be frightened by cries of "negro supremacy. . . . The sooner we think for ourselves the Better for us." In early 1892, members of Greenesboro's Farmers' Alliance met to "pass Third Party resolutions." As the national Democratic Party had failed to endorse the Alliance platform, Greene's delegates to the Alliance's upcoming national convention were instructed to "cast our influence" with the new People's Party. The same meeting also endorsed Watson. The local editor somewhat balefully blamed the whole thing on the "outside influence" of "two emissaries of the disruptionists," but the plain fact was that hundreds of disillusioned white men and women in Greene County were prepared to leave the party of the solid South.[27] The president of the county Alliance, J. L. Crossley, indignantly denied in the newspaper that he and his fellow members were "ignorant willing tools" of anyone. They had not abandoned the Democratic Party; rather, the party had abandoned its own heritage, the heritage of Thomas Jefferson and John C. Calhoun. We may not elect a president, Crossley admitted, but "we are studying principles now, not whether we will succeed or not, but we are right in our demands." In the spring local residents formally organized their new party in the county. One of its leaders was R. L. McWhorter, the old Whig, Republican, and independent.[28] A half-decade of fierce political battle began in Greene County. The new People's Party campaigned for candidates for offices from president down to county surveyor. Their platform was based on ideas forged by the Farmers' Alliance—a national income tax, government control or ownership of the railroad and telegraph system, a subtreasury to extend government credit to farmers, a flexible currency based on issues of paper money or extensive coinage of silver. Their enemies, as the first Populist platform rather apocalyptically put it, were part of a "vast conspiracy

against mankind" that was "rapidly taking possession of the world." The
monopolists had utterly corrupted the newspapers and both of the two main
national parties. The Populists only were the true "people's party," their
economic ideas an attempt to ensure that the true "producers" of the country's wealth could control that wealth in a land of equal opportunity for all.[29]

But who, really, belonged to the "all"? By any rational definition, black as
well as white farmers were "producers," and thus real political equality for
producers would mean political equality for black men as well as for whites.
(The Populists in Georgia did not embrace political rights for women.) This
rationale meshed with the purely practical problem of winning elections: African American men were a large majority of the potential voters in Greene
County and they continued to vote in large numbers. Any party that controlled their votes would control the county—and perhaps the South as a
whole. Thus, while the Democrats were eager to denounce the economic platform of the Populists for its "wild, visionary schemes," the cries of "white
supremacy" and "radical rule" were the sharpest arrows in their quiver. G. T.
Norman, a local Democrat, wrote, "Now we begin to hear of that same scum
from the north, which we sent home 20 years ago, nosing around offering
millions if we will walk into their Third party." The Republican Party,
claimed Democratic loyalists, was the true father of Populism. "If the old
party splits in Greene and will not suffer Democrats to rule," wrote one,
"don't complain if you see [African Americans] Timothy T. Jenkins, Winfield
Rhodes or Boston B. Higgins in the [general assembly] seat once occupied
by Abraham Coleby [sic]." A month later the editor of the Herald-Journal
claimed that outsiders were pointing "the finger of righteous scorn" at Greene
County because, in one precinct, Populists "were appointing negroes on their
campaign committees. Our county has always been noted for its prompt
action in meeting and crushing anything resembling negro supremacy and it
is strange that in our midst should the first step be taken to obliterate racial lines." One suballiance in the county formally resolved against the new
party, which would "disrupt the Alliance, break up the solid South, turn the
State over to disorganizers and negroes, elect a Republican administration,
and thus expose the South to a second reconstruction period, than which
there could no worse calamity befall us as a people." How, wrote another
local Democrat, could local whites be denouncing the Democratic Party, in
whose supremacy lay "all their hopes of safety from social and political
degradation?"[30]

Nor did the Populists shrink from courting the African American vote.

The logic of their challenge, both to and about black voters, was laid out in an often-quoted essay by Tom Watson himself, published in 1892. In it he deplored the state of southern politics, with whites and blacks lined up at opposite poles because of distrust going back to the "passions" and "provocations" of Reconstruction. A mere cry of "Negro rule!" was, in consequence, enough to frighten a "Southern white tenant" away from rational consideration of the financial, tax, and transportation policies that kept him in poverty. For their part, poor blacks succumbed to emotional appeals from Republican leaders who claimed that Democrats would put them "back into slavery." As a result, Watson argued,

> here were two distinct races dwelling together, with political equality established between them by law. They lived in the same section; won their livelihood by the same pursuits; cultivated adjoining fields on the same terms; enjoyed together the bounties of a generous climate; suffered together the rigors of cruelly unjust laws; spoke the same language; bought and sold in the same markets; classified themselves into churches under the same denominational teachings; neither race antagonizing the other in any branch of industry; each absolutely dependent on the other in all the avenues of labor and employment; and yet, instead of being allies, as every dictate of reason and prudence and self-interest and justice said they should be, they were kept apart, in dangerous hostility, that the sordid aims of partisan politics might be served![31]

The new third party—the Populists—offered, according to Watson, an opportunity for poor whites and blacks to form a natural alliance, and thereby eliminate "the present status of hostility" between them. Southern whites would never leave the Democratic Party for the Republican, nor would blacks ever join the Democrats, but both might be persuaded to join the People's Party, on the basis of self-interest. The white Democrat will join the Populists "because his industrial condition is pitiably bad; because he struggles against a system of laws which have almost filled him with despair; because he is told that he is without clothing because he produces too much cotton, and without food because corn is too plentiful; because he sees everybody growing rich off the products of labor except the laborer; because the millionaires who manage the Democratic Party have contemptuously ignored his plea for a redress of grievances and have nothing to say to him beyond the cheerful advice to 'work harder and live closer.' " The black man will join when the Populists can show him that "the accident of color can make no possible difference in the interests of farmers, croppers, and laborers." The People's Party would "settle the race question" by appealing to the "*interest*" of both races, by telling both, "You are kept apart that you may be separately fleeced of your earnings. You are made to hate each other because upon that hatred is rested the keystone of the arch of financial despotism which enslaves you both. You are deceived and blinded that you may not see how this race antagonism perpetuates a monetary system which beggars both." And, specifically for the black man, a system of secret balloting (the "Australian" ballot) would protect "his constitutional right to the free exercise of his electoral choice." The Populists, Watson insisted, would provide "a better chance for every citizen to be considered as a *citizen* regardless of color in the making and enforcing of laws."[32]

For the state legislature in 1892, the Populists in Greene County nominated R. E. Davison and J. H. H. Brown, both farmers with moderate land holdings. Davison had been secretary of his suballiance. Both Democrats and Populists courted the black vote. The Democrats managed to win the endorsement of a leading black Republican, W. A. Pledger of Athens. Speaking in Greensboro, Pledger attacked William L. Peek, the Populist candidate for governor, pointing to a bill filed by Peek in the state legislature designed to give landlords more power over their tenants as likely to lead to "re-enslavement of every colored tenant"; it "would put many of the 'croppers' in the chaingang."[33] The election results made it clear how important the black vote had become. While, in the October vote for state offices, Democrats won a "clean sweep" in Greene County, winning about 1,100 votes out of a total of 1,900 cast, in the presidential election in November the Republicans carried the county for only the second time since 1872. The Populist candidate for Congress, with the help of a split in the black vote, defeated his Democratic opponent. In the analysis of the local (pro-Democratic) editor, "the negro vote turned the tide, most of them voting straight through the ticket for Harrison [Republican for president] and Robins [Populist for Congress]. . . . [T]he majority of the negroes came to the polls with tickets in their hands for Harrison and Robins that were grimy and worn from having been carried more than a week in their pockets."[34]

Local politics in Greene County in 1892 thus became an intricate three-way battle for supremacy fought out in every neighborhood. The Democrats' victory in state elections had been too narrow to take future elections for granted, and whatever they felt about "white supremacy," they had to take black voters seriously. They appealed to blacks with claims that Democrats were the strongest supporters of black schools and the strongest opponents of lynching. Meanwhile, their appeal to white voters was undercut by a worsening economy that fell into full-scale depression. Cotton fell to seven cents a pound in 1893 and to an all-time low of four and one-half cents in 1894. Grover Cleveland, the Democrat elected president in 1892, had endorsed the deflationary gold-standard policies favored by big banks in the country. Greene's farmers, in desperate straits, could hardly accept the simplistic accusation that they grew too much cotton and not enough corn. An Alliance-sponsored speaker from nearby Oconee County complained bitterly that "in his own county the condition of the farmers was so desperate that the daughters of the family were compelled to work in the fields, not over thirty families being exceptions."[35]

The most important leader of the party in the Piedmont was, unquestionably, Watson himself. Watson had lost his bid for reelection to Congress in 1892, an election in which Democrats in Augusta had tipped the scales with the help of massive fraud. Two years later he was again campaigning for Congress. Although Greene County was not in his district, he swung through to speak as he opened his 1894 campaign, directing many of his comments to African Americans in the audience. As the *Herald-Journal* described the speech, Watson

> appealed to them not to sell their votes, but to investigate as best they might public questions. If they then thought the Democrats or Republicans were right, for God's sake vote that way. If the Populists were right, vote with them. In any event, their vote ought to be counted. The Populists wanted laws which would give all classes, the rich and the poor, the white and the black man, equal justice. If the whites went down, crushed by a load of oppression, they would manage to keep the blacks below them, so the black man could not afford to vote to perpetuate a bad system.[36]

Although the *Herald-Journal*'s editor, Edward Young (also the mayor of Greensboro) was a strong Democrat, even he was impressed with a Watson speech in May. Young had taken over the editorship when W. B. Patillo had purchased the paper in September 1892. Unlike most local editors, including his predecessor, Young opened his columns to both Populists and Democrats, and his paper is unusual for its balanced reporting of political news. "We have seldom listened to a speech by anyone," he wrote, that "impressed us more favorably than did that of Hon. Thos E. Watson, at White Plains." Watson had made a powerful argument for "Jeffersonian Democratic principles" and decried political corruption. Still, the editor continued, he did not like Watson's "explanation of his position in regard to the negro question." Watson "pleaded guilty to wanting the negro vote, and asked the Democrats if they did not. The question was unanswerable, for as a matter of course they do. Then addressing the negroes, he told them he could understand how they could be Republicans, because they thought the R. party had given them their freedom; he could understand how they could be Populists, for without bread and meat their freedom was not worth anything to them; but the Democratic party had never done anything for the negro, hence the negro must be paid to be a Democrat."[37] Yet, Young challenged Watson, arguing that the southern white Democrat "has been the negro's best friend" and "has spent more money to educate the negro children than the race paid in taxes." To maintain that the Negro is the political enemy of the Democrats is "the strangest and most unnatural spectacle to be found today." True, the Democrats had not appointed blacks to office, but Young argued that "the colored race deserves nothing in that line."[38] Young's comments show how the Democrats, like the Populists, had been forced to compete for black votes. Watson's Democratic opponent in the race openly appealed to blacks to vote for him because the Democrats had taxed themselves to educate black children and because blacks' biggest enemies in the Democratic Party had joined the Populists. In one editorial Young insisted that Georgia needed free and fair balloting even though in some counties "where the negro vote is largely in excess of the white" the results might not be to "our liking."[39]

The Populists, meanwhile, worked hard in the county to attract black votes, citing their economic program and their promise to protect black voting rights. With the help of strong support for Populists from African American voters, the 1894 elections proved to be "A Waterloo For Democracy" in Greene. The turnout was the largest ever seen in the county. The Democrats lost both seats in the state legislature and the Populist candidate for governor easily carried the county. Young lamented that Democrats had failed despite "hard work" "among the colored people to stem their stampede into the ranks of the enemy." In Greensboro, former Democrat J. M. Storey, who had "always heretofore been an effective worker for Democracy, among the negroes," had turned his political talents to helping the Populists.

The most important factor, Young thought, was not the personal influence of people like Storey "but the present low price of cotton" and the "free school book" plank in the Populist platform.[40]

The Populist challenge, Young wrote, had pitted "neighbor against neighbor, brother against brother, and father against son." Politics even invaded the columns of women writers who kept newspaper readers apprised of neighborhood comings and goings. When the White Plains society correspondent wrote that she was in "deepest mourning" because the Populists had carried her village, the author of "Liberty Notes" made clear her own Populist sympathies. The writer of "Woodville Dots," meanwhile, wrote to deplore the fact that "ignorant blacks" were becoming the balance of power in the county and admitted that she herself was "on the fence"; her husband was a Democrat, her friends Populists.[41]

Captain Storey, the Democrat turned Populist, contributed his own analysis of the Populist victory. Pointing out that he had been a county resident for twenty-seven years, had fought for four years with the Confederacy, and had been both a local Democratic Party official and treasurer of Greensboro, he said that people would no longer vote "as a herd of cattle" led by the men "who control." Attempting to skirt the fine line between seeking black votes and endorsing "social equality," he condemned President Grover Cleveland for allegedly endorsing the idea of forcing white children "to attend the same schools with negro children," while attacking the Democrats for trying to buy the black vote with money or liquor. The Populists, Storey wrote, "found that the great majority of the negroes of Greene county are a respectable, hard-working, honest race of people, who scornfully refused to receive money in barter for the greatest privilege a freeman has, to cast his ballot . . . ; they know that the populist party is the only party that guarantees equal rights to all, both black and white."[42] Shortly afterwards the local Democrats made their own deal with Greene's Republican Party leadership, with the Republicans agreeing to endorse Democrats running for reelection. "It was a hopeless fight," the Democrats admitted, "unless the vote of the enemy could be broken into some way." The strategy did not work; in January 1895 the Populists captured all local offices as well.[43]

The Political Geography of Populism

The Populist Party swept over much of the Piedmont with the force of a tidal wave, in 1894 winning control of Greene, Glascock, and Hart Counties, among others. And yet, in other places, the party made scarcely a ripple in the political waters.[44] Not that farmers there were enjoying prosperity — in both the Sea Island region of Georgia and the Mississippi-Yazoo Delta, agriculture suffered through the decade of the 1890s. In the Delta, farmers and planters experienced the same disastrous decline in cotton prices felt by the Piedmont's farmers. Along the Atlantic coast, rice planters staggered from crisis to crisis as they sought to maintain the precarious equilibrium achieved on the postbellum plantations; if anything, agricultural prosperity seemed even more out of reach in the rice regions than in the cotton regions. And yet, in neither the Delta nor the rice coast did the Populist Party attract many voters.

On the Georgia coast, although by 1890 many planting families had given up their attempts to rebuild their antebellum plantations, others, such as James Dent and the Leighs on the Altamaha River, and Louis Manigault and James Heyward on the Savannah, had stabilized and even increased their production of rice. Rice growers in the early 1890s could look back on more than a decade in which the real price of rice in the United States had been, with the help of tariff protection, the highest in a century. In 1894, Dent wrote that "any planter must know that there is a large margin of profit at [the] present cost of rice planting."[45] Already, however, rising production in Louisiana had shown that tariffs on foreign rice were insufficient to protect Atlantic growers. Writing later, Dent recalled that rice lands' prosperity actually "ended in 1892, with the first great crop in the Southwest." This had given him "the first realization of the fact, that what had been for a long time, a recognized menace, was an accomplished fact." The results can be traced through the annual accounts of the Whitehall plantation on the Savannah: in 1890 the owners sold 20,400 bushels at $1.17 per bushel with profits of over $11,000; in 1891, the price was $1.12, and they cleared about $7,500; in 1892, when the price plunged to sixty-three cents, they lost money. Over the next five years, Whitehall's production gradually declined until, by 1898, it was barely a third of the 1892 level.[46]

On top of this catastrophic drop in prices, Georgia's Atlantic coast was hit with a series of destructive hurricanes. Situated at the tidal margin by necessity, rice plantations were extremely vulnerable to flood damage from swollen rivers and coastal storms, and above all from hurricanes. Manigault at Gowrie had suffered tremendously in the 1877 "freshet," as floods caused by upcountry rains were called (see Chapter 1). In the 1880s, Savannah River plantations suffered similar overflows. Still, planters could live with freshets; in fact they fertilized the land with a new layer of rich soil. (This is what made the plantation soil so good to begin with.) But the severe hurricanes of 1893 and 1898 were another matter. The 1893 hurricane struck Savannah and the South Carolina coast especially hard, just as Whitehall and other plantations were trying to cope with the lower prices of the year before, and the storm of 2 October 1898, together with an accompanying tidal wave, swept directly across St. Simons Island to hit Brunswick and the lower Altamaha. Sarah Spalding McKinley wrote a harrowing account of her experience during the hurricane on St. Simons, calling it "the most awful, awful, experience I ever had in my life." She had been lying sick in bed when her husband, Archibald McKinley, came in to tell her the tide was rising rapidly. She rose from her bed to put trunks and other items on tables or chairs to get them off the floor, but within "one second it seemed the water began bursting into the house and was knee deep and in one minute's time it was up to our waist." Out of the window she saw waves sweeping across the old plantation graveyard to "dash to the very tops of our windows." With great difficulty she and her husband maneuvered around floating beds and furniture and nailed shut the front door. "It was hours we stood in that water expecting every breath would be our last. At last Archie said he thought the water was falling, and it went down very slowly, it seemed to us, and such a house I know you never saw in all your life, the dreadful marsh mud was over every thing, the trunks which were unlocked were entirely empty of their contents and all over the house and soaked [with] marsh mud which was ankle deep every where." Many people were drowned. On the mainland, the streets of Brunswick were covered with water, and for the planters it was "the worst, and highest water ever experienced. Not much rice had been removed from the fields and loss was almost total."[47]

During slavery, planters could withstand such blows—they had, in fact, in 1824—because "the large amount of [slave] labor, far the largest per acre of any crop in the South, could be concentrated, for strengthening weak places, repairing breaks in the Levees and for the salvage of crops, under an arbitrary system of control." But "after the war the negro recoiled from putting his foot in cold-water—It did not savor of freedom, and was arduous winter work," while white labor—at $1.50 or $2.25 per day, rather than the sixty cents of the "negro day wage"—was too expensive. Rice plantations could not survive without this kind of maintenance. As Frances Leigh explained it, "Like the inhabitants of Holland, we depend upon our dykes for our livelihood, and the chief expense in connection with such property is keeping up the banks and clearing the canals and drains every year; if this were neglected for two or three years, the plantation would relapse into its original uncivilised state, and become once more a desolate marsh."[48] Thus, while the potential benefits of government intervention might well attract some large cotton planters to the Populist Party, rice planters could see that the competition from Louisiana rice lands, losses from hurricanes, and a transformed labor system were problems quite beyond the reach of such Populist proposals as the subtreasury or the lowering of transportation costs. If anything, the Populist endorsement of lower tariffs promised to make rice planters' conditions even worse.

Nor could the growing ranks of black small farm owners in the region be won over to Populism. Populist proposals took it for granted that small farmers were participating in commodity markets, and that they would therefore benefit from lower railroad rates and government-supported credit. In fact, most of the African American farmers on the coast had no large stake in the market. They did not borrow for food; cotton, rice, and other commercial crops were for them a distinctly secondary concern. When they worked for white planters, they worked for cash wages. Furthermore, in most places along the coast, African Americans saw no need to turn to a new party in search of new guarantees for their rights of citizenship. They were citizens, and they could win elections with their own party—the Republican Party. Democrats had severely reduced but by no means eliminated its influence, and Republicans, many of them African American, continued to win elections to local offices and to the state legislature.[49]

Along the coast, then, small farmers saw the Populist Party as no more relevant to them than it was to the rice planters. In the 1892 presidential race, when Populist candidate James B. Weaver captured almost a third of the vote in the eastern Piedmont, he won a mere 272 votes—less than 3 percent—in the six coastal counties. In the governor's race that year, with no Republican candidate, Populist William Peek took 40 percent of the Piedmont vote, but only 17 percent along the coast.[50]

No place in the South was more dependent on cotton than the Mississippi Delta, and its farmers and laborers suffered accordingly as cotton prices stagnated and then fell. Woes were compounded, as was so often true in the Delta, by repeated flooding. After the severe flood of 1882, George Collins wrote to his father-in-law that "the distress is beyond description & I can't see what the people are to do without stock, food, money, fences or credit." In 1890, a levee on the Mississippi broke through in mid-March. For ten days, planter Clive Metcalf desperately shored up his own levees to keep the flood at bay, only to watch helplessly as the water covered first fifty acres, then one hundred, until "at last it ran over me." "Never in my life," he wrote in his journal, "have I seen such times for poor people. I am very blue."[51]

Walter Sillers, a politically ambitious young lawyer in Bolivar County, agreed with much of the Populist diagnosis of the southern farmers' problems. He joined the Grange in the 1870s because of his opposition to railroad "monopoly," and he was active in organizing the Farmers' Alliance in Bolivar. In 1892, as the cotton crisis deepened, Sillers wrote his wife that it would be all to the good if farmers went down into universal bankruptcy, since that would finally arouse them to "the necessity of action." A man in the poor house "has time then to inquire the reason why he is there. And to ask why others choose to go on getting rich off of his products. The more I read and ponder and think over the condition of the South, the more I drift off with the third party."[52]

In Mississippi as elsewhere in the cotton South, the rise of the new party raised the question of black voting, and the possibility of a powerful enhancement of black political influence. Especially in a place like the Delta, dominated by large plantations worked by propertyless black tenants and sharecroppers, African Americans formed a natural constituency for a party based on the idea of making America once again a democracy run by small producers. But by the Populist era, Mississippi's potential black voters were in a much more precarious position than Georgia's, despite the legacy of black political power during Reconstruction.

After Reconstruction, in the Delta as in Georgia's Piedmont and Sea Island regions, the black vote had been crippled rather than destroyed. Republicans survived and even recovered somewhat, enough to carry the region for James G. Blaine in 1884. At the state level, the black vote was a key part of an 1881 alliance of Republicans, Greenbackers, and independents, who together ran a "fusion" candidate against the Democrats. These dissidents took 40 percent of the state vote and nearly carried the Delta region with 49 percent of the vote.[53]

Throughout the 1880s fusion politics—the strategic alliance of white Democratic factions with African American political leaders and voters— was also important at the local level in the Delta, where, after Reconstruction, politics usually revolved around personal conflicts and immediate concrete issues. In Bolivar County, for example, factions squabbled over location of the county seat—would it remain on the river, at Rosedale, or be moved inland to more centrally located Cleveland? The choice could make all the difference to property values, and thus to property owners.[54] Politics in the Delta revolved above all around the levees — building them, maintaining them, and paying for them. Levee politics formed the foundation of the most powerful political coalitions in the region. The upper Delta was dominated by the machine of Charles Scott, whose only local office was his service as head of the Board of Levee Commissioners. Scott's political faction usually worked with the lower Delta faction, controlled from Washington County by board members William G. Yerger and LeRoy Percy. Percy's father, Colonel William Alexander Percy, had been an antebellum lawyer and planter who, after the war, had become a railroad promoter and been one of the chief organizers of the "Taxpayers" party that had "redeemed" the state from the Republicans; Yerger, his law partner, had organized a rifle company in Washington County to help ensure the victory. Colonel Percy served as speaker of the house of representatives in the state in 1878. Following his death in 1888, his son LeRoy inherited his plantations, his law practice, and his political influence. In addition to his service on the levee board, LeRoy Percy was counsel to the Illinois Central Railroad in the Delta. Charles Scott was married to a Yerger and, like Percy, owned plantations and served as a railroad lawyer.[55]

The levee board made crucial decisions about taxes, controlled powerful resources, and disposed of patronage in various forms, not least of which was legal work. At one point, Scott, Percy, and Yerger combined to thwart another member's proposal to impose a steeper tax on railroad lands. Young Walter Sillers insisted to his wife, Florence, that the issues in these local conflicts involved "independence, manhood & principle," in standing for "honest government for the people against . . . gentlemen who grow rich with the peoples money"; then he added, somewhat more concretely, "There is law practice & everything else involved."[56] Scott parlayed his connections into control of politics in Bolivar County and into major influence in Coahoma and other counties. His brother George served as sheriff and state senator from Bolivar, and another brother, Daniel, was active in Coahoma County. African American voters played a key role in sustaining Scott's power. For example, in return for black support for his brother George's campaign for the state senate, Charles Scott supported the election of African American leaders like Sheriff Joseph E. Ousley and state senator George Washington Gayles, a Baptist minister and former slave. In neighboring Coahoma County, Scott's brother Daniel ran for representative with the support of a black leader, William H. Allen. Among black politicians in

Coahoma were George H. Oliver, elected to the Mississippi House of Representatives, and George Chatters, a justice of the peace and court clerk. Campaigning for black votes required more than simple horse trading of offices.
Local candidates had to make respectful appearances before black crowds to
request their votes. Daniel Scott, while campaigning in Coahoma in 1889,
attended a celebration of the laying of the cornerstone of a new church for
"an old and influential congregation of Colored Baptists," made a "lengthy
and forcible address," and presented to the minister, as his personal gift, "a
large and handsomely bound Holy Bible." These black voters were the potential base for a Populist presence in the Delta, but they had to be pried away
from the influence of big planters like Charles Scott. As Sillers wrote to his
wife, Florence, the Populists might indeed be able to carry the state if they
could "combine with the negro vote."[57]

But, by 1892, when Sillers's letter was written, that possibility had already been destroyed by enactment of a new state constitution that effectively disfranchised most black voters. The impulse behind disfranchisement
did not originate with Delta political leaders, who had learned to live with,
and at times manipulate, the black vote, but with white voters in other parts
of the state. Delta leaders did not resist the move, concentrating instead on
crafting a series of compromises designed to protect their political power at
the state level. In a series of measures that included residency and literacy
requirements for voters, the 1890 Mississippi Constitutional Convention
pioneered techniques to reduce or eliminate the African American vote without violating, at least on the face of things, the Fifteenth Amendment to the
U.S. Constitution.

As late as 1892, Walter Sillers was apparently still not sure how successful
this strategy would prove to be, perhaps because in his own county local
factions continued to court and use black votes well into the 1890s.[58] In any
case, Sillers hedged his bets, perhaps recognizing the inherent weakness of
the Populist cause in his region. He wrote to Frank Burkitt, the state Populist
leader, that he hoped Burkitt's new party would win in 1892; he told his
wife that the Democrats and Republicans had "conspired to impoverish the
South" and that farmers needed a party as much as the bankers, manufacturers, and railroad tycoons. He planned "to cast my lot with the farmers
party"—but not yet. If "I get to be" a corporate lawyer, he added, "I may
change my views."[59] If the comment was meant to be an amusing aside, it
proved prescient. In the ensuing election, the Populists polled about one-
third of the statewide vote, but a mere 287 votes in the Delta, scarcely 5

percent of the total, and the Republican vote in the Delta fell from almost eight thousand in 1888 to just 176 in 1892. The new constitution had done its work, virtually eliminating the black vote, and, in the process, the Populists lost half their potential constituency before even launching themselves as a new party. When, in 1899, the anti-Scott faction finally won control of Bolivar County, Charles Scott issued a statement saying that he would not court black votes in an effort to reverse his defeat since that would involve "the question of White Supremacy, the one supreme issue before which the political fortunes of any man or faction pale into utter and lasting insignificance." In the meantime, Sillers had himself switched to the Scott faction, running for state senator on its ticket in 1893. Perhaps not coincidentally, in 1896 he was retained as an attorney for the board of levee commissioners.[60]

The Populist Dilemma: Class, Race, and the Populist Voter

The negligible vote for the Populists on the Georgia coast and in the Mississippi Delta highlights the difficulties of the new party, even as it was scoring more and more successes at the grass-roots level in places like Greene and Glascock Counties in the Piedmont. Populism's basic appeal in the South was to those who thought of themselves as "the middle class, which is the backbone of the country," the "small landowner," the "artisans and men of small means, who are independent now," but in imminent danger, in the words of a Populist paper, of being "crushed . . . forced to work at the pleasure of the money lords." To this constituency of whites the Populists were trying to add the mass of black voters. As Tom Watson's biographer C. Vann Woodward noted about the Populist crusade, "for the first time in his political history, the Negro was regarded neither as the incompetent ward of White Supremacy, nor as the ward of military intervention, but as an integral part of Southern society with a place in its economy."[61]

The campaign for black votes required a complex and delicate balancing act. On the one hand, the Democrats could respond, as they did at first, with appeals to white supremacy. The editor of the Sparta *Ishmaelite*, in Hancock County, was typical in this regard. He charged, for example, that three-fourths of the crowds that came to Tom Watson's speeches were black (and even worse, "boisterous and fanatical" black women) and that "in so far as Hancock [County] is concerned, the Third party has ceased to be a white man's party and become the organization of the more vicious and ignorant of the negroes." The leaders of the People's Party, he wrote, intended "to destroy white supremacy in the South" and threatened "the social order of the South," founded "on the rock of Anglo-Saxon supremacy."[62] Watson and other Populists had become little more than "pimps and procurers of all the enemies of white supremacy." When this kind of appeal proved insufficient, the Democrats could reverse themselves and compete with the Populists for black votes, focusing on black elites. In Greene County, they bargained with the Republican leadership; in Hancock County, they managed to get a "Sensible Negro," Republican J. H. Rudicile, to endorse the Democratic ticket. Rudicile, in a "Manly Card" in the *Ishmaelite,* told black voters that the Democratic candidate for governor, Hancock County planter William J. Northen, had "always helped and befriended our race" by supporting education and opposing lynch laws, and that J. C. C. Black, Tom Watson's opponent in the congressional race, had contributed to Negro churches. "My colored friends," he concluded, "the only hope for us is to stand by those who stand by us, properly educate ourselves and our children, try to live economically, accumulate property, be loyal and true to our race and country, and be sure that we appreciate and exercise the rights given us."[63]

The Democrats also pointed out, not without justification, that African Americans had some reason to doubt that Tom Watson and other Populists did believe in equal rights for all. Watson's pleas for support, they claimed, merely covered up his "record of bitter and repressive hostility towards the negro," a hostility represented by his votes as a state legislator for expelling black representative Anthony Wilson (from Camden County), against an increase in public school funds, and for a measure to limit the mobility of sharecroppers.[64]

The Democrats could, if necessary, return to some of the methods of Reconstruction and redemption—buying black voters if possible, intimidating them with violence if not. The first strategy was apparently responsible for J. C. C. Black's huge majority in the city of Augusta, a majority which more than overbalanced Watson's victory in most of the rest of his district. The second strategy was resorted to in Hancock County, where Rev. H. S. Doyle, a black minister campaigning for the Populists in 1892, was nearly killed by whites. Two years later, after an altercation at a polling place, black Populist leader Richard Brazille was attacked by a white man, and when Brazille and his brother Emmett resisted the attack they barely escaped arrest and a possible lynching. After the 1892 violence, Hancock County Democrats had the audacity to publish a letter from an African American, J. N. Clay, arguing that his fellow blacks should vote Democratic because, when "some of the most prominent colored men in the Third party narrowly escaped being killed" in the campaign, "not a single Third party white man came to their rescue or interfered in any way, while the attack was being made."[65]

The Populist Party was indeed vulnerable with white voters on the issue of white supremacy, and they responded by trying to draw a line between "equal rights" of citizens, black and white, and "social equality" in informal and formal day-to-day contacts — from encounters on the sidewalk to marriage — between people of different races. One Hancock Populist supporter felt compelled to issue a formal denial that he was "teaching the colored people that they have as much right to go to the hotel in Sparta, and demand meals and rooms as any white man," or that he was "telling the colored people that if Tom Watson is elected that they will be allowed to go into the houses of white people, eat at their tables, sleep in their beds, etc." Watson eventually devoted considerable attention in his speeches to distinguishing the "equal rights" he felt African Americans deserved from the "social equality" he opposed, and to ridiculing the idea that, by appealing to black voters, he was in any way denying "white supremacy."[66]

Such disclaimers by the Populists, as well as evidence that in some counties they may have intimidated black voters as much as any Democrats, demonstrate that many Populists accepted white supremacy. They illustrate also the Populists' difficulties in appealing simultaneously to white and black voters on issues of economic interest. The difficulties were compounded because, despite Populist rhetoric that "the poor white people, with the poor darkies, are in the same boat, floating down the stream without a paddle," that the interests of "the working white man and the working black man . . . are identical," and that "the accident of color can make no possible difference in the interests of farmers, croppers, and laborers," it was not necessarily true that "farmers," "croppers," and "laborers" had the same interests.[67]

Tom Watson himself, for example, was a large planter who raised produce for national markets, and Greene County Populist leader R. L. McWhorter was said to "run 100 plows." J. M. Storey, the Populist who successfully campaigned for black votes in Greene County, had in 1888 backed a law designed to prevent sharecroppers from leaving their employers in midyear. While top political leaders are not necessarily representative of the mass of their voters, many ordinary Populists, small and medium-sized farmers, relied on black laborers and sharecroppers. Walter Wray, a Greene County farmer, a dedicated member of the People's Party who played in a band at party rallies, was, like many others, drawn to the party by economic distress.

In November 1894 Wray wrote in his diary a prayer asking the "Dear Lord" to protect him from the tax collector: "Please sir for Jesus sake help me to pay him up so I can live & help me to [pay] my debts." His last entry for 1894 lamented how "bright expectations" had been "blasted," that "beautiful castles in the air are torn down," that so many "helpless women" and "ruined men and women are to be found in the Land how many Bleeding and Wounded hearts, how many distressed on account of the short crops and the Low Price of all our crops of Every kind." Yet Wray owned what he called a "plantation" worked by both sharecroppers and laborers, and his personal list of possessions was not modest; it included sixteen tables, four wardrobes, a set of china, and twelve "pictures" on his walls, including one of "the village Dance" and another of "the inside of the Pantheon at Rome." Even Benton Miller, the Confederate veteran, small farmer, and "the father of the movement in Hancock," had hired sharecroppers to work his farm and wage laborers to pick his cotton in 1877. When he bought corn at $1.25 in 1876 he sold it to his tenant, Bob Taylor, at a markup of 28 percent.[68]

The interests of owners like Benton Miller and sharecroppers like Bob Taylor were by no means identical, as the Democrats were quick to point out. In the Hancock newspaper, for example, a letter described as being from a farmer in Watson's home county of McDuffie claimed that "the reliability of the farm labor has been almost completely destroyed by Watson's teachings. He has led the ignorant field hands to believe that they are systematically imposed upon and swindled by their employers; and in so doing he has done both the white man and the black man an irreparable damage."[69] Indeed, after Reconstruction, white landlords in the South had fiercely resisted attempts of rural black workers to organize themselves economically. In 1887, Hiram F. Hoover, a Knights of Labor activist, traveled through Georgia's black belt attempting to organize agricultural laborers. The Knights of Labor, whose goal was to combine all "producers," whether on farms or in factories, into a single labor organization, had already organized in Augusta a textile workers' union strong enough to provoke a series of walkouts in 1886 that culminated in a strike followed by an employer lockout of three months. But unions of white workers in cities were one thing; unions of black workers in the countryside were a different matter. While speaking in a black church in Warrenton, Hoover himself was shot and nearly killed. The Colored Farmers' Alliance, a black organization more or less parallel to the all-white Southern Farmers' Alliance, met violent repression whenever its members strayed from noncontroversial matters like how to raise more corn. In

LeFlore County, in the Mississippi Delta, when whites threatened the local organizer, LeFlore's blacks promised to defend him, whereupon whites
raised the cry of "insurrection," and a "posse" reinforced by three companies
of the all-white national guard hunted down and lynched at least four leaders
of the Colored Farmers' Alliance. Across the Mississippi River in Lee County,
Arkansas, a short-lived strike of cotton pickers, also led by the Colored
Alliance, was similarly put down by force.[70]

In the Piedmont, Democrats insisted that Populist agitation would cause
similar unrest. In 1892 the editor of the Sparta *Ishmaelite* charged that "an
anarchist agitator is at work among the farm hands" of Hancock County
urging them "to refuse to work for less than a dollar a day" and promising
that the Populists would assure them of such wages, and that "the party
intended to divide up the land and give them half of it." The editor suggested
that this "anarchist" was an agent of Richard Manning Humphrey, the white
leader of the Colored Farmers' Alliance and the one who apparently had inspired the Arkansas cotton pickers' strike. The outlook in the county, he concluded, was bad enough without "socialistic agitators engaged in organizing
the farm hands and filling their ignorant minds with hopes of impossible
wages and visions of plunder"; such a threat justified "summary methods" or
"violent remedies," since "self preservation is the first law of nature."[71]

Tom Watson and other Populist leaders had to deal with the class differences between the "small landowner," the "artisans and men of small means,
who are independent now," and the black poor who often tilled their acres
and picked their cotton. In the first years of the party, they followed the
precedent of the Knights of Labor in trying to embrace men and women of all
ranks, especially those at the bottom. Ultimately, Georgia Populists virtually
abandoned their attempt to combine "the working white man and the working black man" on any sort of equal basis in their party. Watson and other
leaders sought instead to broaden their base by appealing to the urban middle class, which shared only some of the Populists' resentments of monopoly
practices. Thus the Georgia party in 1895 dropped some of the more contro-
versial goals of the party, including the subtreasury plan, from its platform.
Articles in Watson's newspaper, the *People's Party Paper,* insisted on racially
separate schools, opposed allowing African Americans on juries, supported
Jim Crow transportation laws, and attacked Grover Cleveland for invit-
ing the famous African American leader Frederick Douglass to lunch at the
White House. In 1892, Watson's hasty compilation of campaign documents
for the new Populist Party carried the subtitle "Not a Revolt, It's a Revolu-

tion." Three years later Watson wrote in his own paper that the Georgia party was "for *Reform* and not for *Revolution*."[72]

In the meantime, events on the national political stage doomed the new party to oblivion. The Democratic convention of 1896 nominated William Jennings Bryan for president, adopted a platform that endorsed some of the Populists' milder reforms, and deftly maneuvered the People's Party into giving Bryan their own nomination. The national Populists, attempting to preserve their existence as an independent force, nominated as Bryan's running mate Tom Watson, not the Democrat's own nominee for vice president, Maine banker Arthur Sewell. But neither strategy worked: Bryan lost the election to Republican William McKinley, and the Bryan-Watson ticket received a humiliating 217,000 votes nationwide. Watson wrote afterwards that "our party, as a party, does not exist anymore." And yet its grass-roots appeal was not quite spent. In Greene County, for example, local Populists swept the 1896 elections for both state and county offices even as the party was losing strength elsewhere in Georgia. In later years, when the Populist Party had disappeared, Tom Watson returned to the Democratic Party, but he would still be able to rally voters in the eastern Piedmont to his causes.[73]

Populism, Southern History, and Southern Histories

The contest between the Democrats and Populists was more than one between economic interests or political factions. It was a clash of identities and worldviews, of conflicting visions of southern society and of southern history. This is why the bitterness of the divisions went deep. One woman lamented in 1894, "We long for a reconciliation between our white friends, but it does not seem in sight." It is also why orators sometimes compared party identification to a religious choice. One told his listeners that he had just the other day met a "good brother" who had told him he had got religion and shouted, "Glory hallelujah, I have religion and am going to join the Methodist church and return to the Democratic party."[74]

The vision of the South that was being challenged by the Populists was on display at an event at which partisanship was, on the surface, momentarily put aside. April 26 — the date accepted as the final surrender of Confederate forces — was Confederate Memorial Day in Georgia. Each year on that day in hundreds of little towns, crowds gathered to listen to music and speeches, and to lay flowers on the graves of Confederate veterans. Toward the end of the 1880s it became a significant day of remembrance and reflection on history.[75] In Greensboro, Georgia, in 1893, when local Populist influence was approaching its peak, the Memorial Day address was given by Democratic State Representative James B. Park Jr. Park's theme was "the heroism, the suffering, the noble deeds of the Confederate soldiers." He recounted how "the professional man left his office, the mechanic his shop, the blacksmith his forge, the merchant his store, and the farmer his plow" motivated only by love of country and the goal of "perpetuation of the constitutional government" true to the ideals of Washington and Jefferson. Slavery played no part in Park's account of the Confederacy or of southern history. After the war, Park told his audience, the remnant of "Southern Chivalry" returned home to find devastation, ashes, ruins, and, worse, "our country overrun with a new creature under the sun—a creature worse than the plagues of Egypt, and more detestable than the leper. He had taken possession of our Government, but the unconquerable spirit of the South, remembering its former glory, said to the carpet bagger, my name is Confederate Soldier, and this is our native heath, and he hurled this creature from his throne, and he has never yet stopped descending into Hades." The principles that activated the Confederacy, namely love of liberty and "the doctrine of self-government," Park claimed, had now permeated the governments of Europe and America.[76]

Park concluded with a paean of praise for the southern woman, who was "noble and true at home. Wherever sufferings were to be alleviated, or feverish brows to be soothed, or in the chambers of death she was there. The recollections of her parting words were more enthusing than the martial music of a thousand horns. . . . No one can express the sorrows endured by Southern women—they gave their sons, their husbands, their fathers as a sacrifice to their country's greatness." How appropriate, Park concluded, that we "leave the observance of this sacred day and the graves of our heroes to her keeping."[77]

A number of themes are evident, and others noticeably absent, from Park's version of southern history. Not just slavery but African Americans are irrelevant. Blacks do not even appear as actors in the drama of Reconstruction, which is blamed entirely on white carpetbaggers. Class differences among whites are equally irrelevant—merchant, mechanic, farmer, and professional are united into a single mass of Confederate loyalists. Reconstruction had been a continuation of the war, this time with a victory of the South, and of liberty and self-rule, over the carpetbagging centralizers. This definition of the Confederacy's purpose as the defense of liberty and self-rule made it easy to project that purpose into the present, which would have been impossible if Park had admitted that the Confederacy was created to preserve slavery. The South's women were lavishly praised, but only within the confines of their roles as supporters and helpmeets in the war and as organizers of its remembrance in the present. The occasion of Memorial Day did not allow for partisan comments, but the inescapable, if unspoken, final point was the role of the Democratic Party as defender and preserver of southern women and of liberty and self-rule, understood to mean white rule. Park's oration evoked to his audience a southern identity that was exclusively white. This is who we are, he told them; this is where we came from; this is what we must do to remain who we are.

The Populist Party in 1893 was challenging in almost every particular this definition of community and southernness and Park's conception of the past. The Populists did not, of course, attack the patriotism of Confederate soldiers—like Hancock County's Benton Miller (and unlike James B. Park Jr.) many Populists had fought and suffered for the Confederacy. But the issues of the war itself had, for Populists, faded into insignificance; to the Populists, southern society in 1893 was not unified by loyalty to a cause but deeply divided by class and exploitation. In the Populist past, the story of a battle for self-rule against the carpetbaggers during Reconstruction, ultimately won by white southerners, was replaced by a story of submission to the greedy rule of bankers and monopolists, a submission all the more shameful because it was made willingly by corrupt southern political leaders. The glories of liberty, in the Populist view, were mocked by the frauds at the ballot box as Democrats stole one election after another. Black voters were not the ignorant pawns of outsiders but legitimate—albeit subordinate—members of the body politic; in the words of Captain J. M. Storey, "a respectable, hard-working, honest race of people, who scornfully refused to receive money in barter for the greatest privilege a freeman has, to cast his ballot." And the Democratic Party was not the defender of southern homes and hearths but the subverter of southern prosperity and the betrayer of southerners' hopes.

The Democrats counterattacked. The Populists, they claimed, like the Republicans, represented the wrong side of "the great divide" between those in favor of centralized government and those opposed to it. The Populists also threatened to divide the white race and entice southern whites "to abandon the Democratic ark of safety" and to return to power "that inglorious mass of ignorance and political mockery from whose deadening clutch we rescued Georgia some twenty years ago." The editor of the Sparta *Ishmaelite* told his readers that "Populist supremacy would be an evil equal . . . to the curse of reconstruction" itself. And the Democrats wrapped their party in the Confederate flag. A Greene County editor, reporting on the first mass meeting of Populists in his town, quoted an "old soldier" who compared the Populists' new song "Good bye, Old Party, Good Bye" to the words of deserters during the war who, when they slipped away from the Confederate lines, would turn back to say, "Good bye, boys, good bye; I am going home." Every Populist, the editor implied, was equally "a traitor to our Southern cause."[78]

Whatever the personal feelings and attitudes of Watson and other Populists toward blacks, the Populist embrace of the African American as, in Tom Watson's word, "a *citizen* regardless of color in the making and enforcing of laws" was truly radical because it rejected an essential element of white supremacy, and, by doing so, rejected also an essential element of the sacred history of the "Lost Cause." One critical account of a large Watson crowd described the audience as "about 2,500 or 3,000 people — white, colored and uncolored, principally the latter," suggesting that the Populists had dissolved, at least for a moment, all racial difference.

Even though Populists had not challenged the traditional southern white male's definition of women's place in society, Democrats saw the definitions of gender, too, as under siege. Thus when the Kansas Populist Mary Lease spoke to the Georgia legislature, the *Ishmaelite*'s editor, in fevered alarm and disgust, called her a "watery-eyed, garrulous, ignorant and communistic old female from Kansas," known not for any "womanly offices" but only for her "feeble oratorical imitations" — "the masculine howls of an unsexed female preacher of political diabolism."[79] An old Democratic stalwart like John B. Gordon, a former Confederate general then campaigning for the U.S. Senate and under attack by the Farmers' Alliance for his willingness to go along with national Democratic Party policy, was defended by a Hancock County editor, not in terms of the policy itself but because support for Gordon was "a question of manhood": "He has been a true man to Georgia all his days. . . . He has illustrated the proudest phase of Southern manhood, in both public and private station, through all the years." Thus a vote against Gordon on the basis of monetary policy would be the equivalent of "meek and servile [read womanly] acceptance of the domination of scalawagism in Georgia politics." The editor urged all "true men" in the county to show that their feet were "still planted on the rock of Anglo-Saxon supremacy," that "the white men of our good old county and of our grand old State are yet true to their Democratic heritage and ready, at all times and in all places, to answer every summons which Anglo-Saxon interest and principle may make upon them."[80]

The Populists responded that "no change of law can benefit the white tenant which does not benefit the black one likewise; that no system which now does injustice to one of them can fail to injure both." They insisted that blacks and whites could be brought together by their common desires for "smiling, happy homes." "The colored laborer" deserved a "guaranty for political independence; for a fair return for his work; a better chance to buy a home and keep it; a better chance to educate his children and see them profitably employed." All this implied that white southerners must see their society, their history, and their future in a more honest and inclusive way. The defeat of the Populists removed the most powerful remaining obstacle to white supremacists' determination to make the South, once and for all, a "white man's country."[81]

PART II
1897–1918

The price of cotton and cotton seed read like a Fairy tale.
— Walter Sillers to P. Burrill,

2 November 1909

Got the blues, can't be satisfied
Got the blues, can't be satisfied
Keep the blues I'll catch that train and ride.
— Mississippi John Hurt

I asked Mr. Hennessee as a white man now what would you do if your patriotism at home was crushed as the white people of Vicksburg crush the Negroes. . . . I added I want you to think over what I have said and come back and I will tell you how many bonds I am going to buy.
— Dr. John A. Miller to Walter White,

3 September 1918

4

Capital at Work, Capitalists at Play

OCTOBER 1881 READERS OF *SCRIBNERS MONTHLY* WERE treated to an exciting story of a bear hunt in the Mississippi Delta. Its author, J. Gordon, a Delta planter, had set out with a hunting party that included a friend, Major Duncan; "Old Asa," a professional guide and hunter; "old Hannibal, a negro servant"; and James Rogers, a "fair-haired Northerner" from Long Island, an "enthusiastic sportsman" and "crack shot at pigeons" in his own territory but "almost as helpless as a babe" in the thickets of the Delta. With a pack of two dozen dogs the hunters cornered a large, old, fierce, and wily bear — almost too fierce and wily, as it turned out. A bullet from the Long Islander barely annoyed the bear, and the dogs, bravely attacking, succeeded only in getting in the way of the hunters. At the climactic moment the bear bounded out of a canebreak heading straight for poor Rogers, who shot again, missed, and took to his heels. Old Asa, the "uneducated frontiersman" wise in the way of the woods, stepped between the fleeing northerner and the pursuing bear and wounded the animal with an apparently mortal shot, but the bear fought on and seized Asa's leg. Finally Gordon himself dispatched the bear by plunging a long knife directly into its heart.[1]

The story is unlikely to be literally true; it falls somewhere between the tall tales of the old Southwest and the local color stories just then becoming so popular with readers of magazines like *Scribners*. It serves, however, to show how little cotton culture had spread in the Delta by 1881. Close to the plantation districts, hunters like Old Asa, with "a soul as gay and free as the wild woods he loved so well," could still find an untamed wilderness suitable for a "frontiersman." It was a "hunters paradise," with flocks of thousands of mallard and teal in many acres of open lakes, with cypresses draped with vines trailing into the water, with sycamores and cottonwoods up to ten feet in diameter. Bears could hide in miles of "impenetrable canebreak" and feast on the seasonal harvest of wild grapes, acorns, and hickory nuts, supplemented by the occasional stray pig or ear of corn.[2]

A more famous hunt took place in the Delta twenty years later, including this time a northern hunter of a different stripe, President Theodore Roosevelt, who was down in the Delta to visit friends and get a crack at the Delta's legendary prey. One of his chief hosts was LeRoy Percy, the Washington County planter, lawyer, and political power. The hunting party's version of "Old Asa" was Holt Collier, a former slave and professional hunter. The bear hunt took place in Sunflower County, in the heart of the Delta. By 1902, the year of Roosevelt's visit, much more of the old Delta wilderness had given way to vast, monotonous expanses of cotton fields. It seemed, indeed, that the hunting party might see no bears at all; then, when the dogs finally routed one, TR had moved from his spot of concealment. Someone wounded the bear, and the frustrated Collier clubbed it with his rifle, lashed it to a tree, and invited Roosevelt to get his trophy. TR indignantly refused this unsportsmanlike offer — it was apparently acceptable to shoot a bear treed by a pack of dogs, but not one treed, as it were, by people. It was a gesture so gallant that one New York toy shop proprietor was inspired to create a new stuffed toy that she named, with TR's permission, the Teddy Bear.[3]

Teddy Roosevelt's hunting problems were a mark of the continued development of the Delta, development accelerated by an unexpected and favorable turn in the cotton market. Just after the despair and frustration of cotton farmers had reached new depths in 1896, the market rose. In 1898 cotton sold for 5.73 cents per pound; in 1900 for 9.15 cents; in 1909, for 13.52 cents — the highest price since Reconstruction. Delta planters responded with more cutting, draining, clearing, and planting. Local drainage districts supplemented the work of the big levee commissions by ditching and draining smaller streams and bayous. In the Delta's interior, Sunflower County's cleared acreage shot up from 14,170 in 1880 to 156,906 by 1910.[4] The Delta's planter-entrepreneurs financed this expansion with loans from banks and insurance companies, rationalizing their operations to maximize their profits. Researchers from the U.S. Department of Agriculture's Bureau of Agricultural Economics (BAE) arrived to produce a rich trove of studies of their enterprises. On Runnymede plantation in LeFlore County, an example of these ventures, the first 250 acres had been cleared in 1874; by 1913, the year of a study by the bureau's H. G. Turner, there were 2,600 acres of improved land, "perhaps as good as is to be found in the Delta country." The plantation had its own railroad platform and steam gin and 150 tenant houses. More than one hundred pumps drained water into an elaborate system of ditches, many lined by tiles. (The operator and part owner, Alexander Henderson, was a trained engineer.) An overseer—on the then generous salary of $2,700 per year—supervised the plantation with an assistant; one of his jobs was to take care of two specially designated tenant farms devoted to producing high-quality seed. On Bledsoe plantation, another big operation in LeFlore County, seventy-five black families raised cotton on 2,600 acres. Another 1,400 acres were uncleared. The plantation was divided into two parts, each with its own store, mules, and sawmill. To keep track of profits and costs, every element of the plantation was set up, in accounting terms, as a separate "enterprise." The stores and sawmills were enterprises; the mule enterprise rented out mules to tenants for 20 percent of current value; the feed enterprise bought and sold corn; the hog enterprise raised and "sold" hogs; even the land itself was an "enterprise," charging the tenants rent (one-half the crop for sharecroppers) and an additional fifty cents per acre to cover "what is lost because of use and abuse of wagons and gear borrowed by renters."[5]

Such highly rationalized businesses reaped rewards of large profits with now-higher cotton prices. But profits were harder to come by for smaller farmers without access to credit or capital. As one investigator reported, "While in many sections of the South there has been a tendency for the size of plantations to become smaller . . . the opposite is true of the Delta, and there of recent years plantations are becoming larger rather than smaller. Wealthy owners have been increasing their holdings, and corporations have been purchasing groups of plantations for the purpose of producing cotton on an extensive scale." Thus while more acreage was being cleared, the number of white farm owners in some Delta counties actually fell between 1900 and 1910.[6] The prospects of gain attracted capital from outside Mississippi and even from outside the country. An English syndicate bought Hill House plantation in Washington County for $340,000. The Delta Farms Company included Dutch partners. From headquarters in Memphis the company managed several large plantations in Bolivar County, with over six thousand acres planted in 1914. Stuyvesant Fish, president of the Illinois Central Railroad, headed a group of northern capitalists who bought ten thousand acres in Coahoma County. J. W. Mann of LeFlore County owned one plantation, which was managed by his son-in-law, and managed a separate plantation for a friend from Illinois who bought it "on speculation."[7]

One local player who recognized these possibilities and profited to the maximum was Charles Scott, the 1890s political boss of Bolivar County. Scott was a planter and lawyer, a builder and railroad promoter, a real estate speculator, the president of a bank and of a major levee lobbying association, and an owner of cotton seed mills. In 1911, with cotton prices still high, he bought up options on several plantations, principally in his home county of Bolivar, and hired L. K. Salsbury, a Michigan-born real estate promoter who lived in Memphis, to help him sell the land. Salsbury went to England and convinced members of the Fine Cotton Spinners and Doublers' Association of Manchester that they could profit handsomely from an investment in high-quality cotton land that could, in turn, supply their looms with high-quality cotton. The price was nearly $3 million.[8]

To get around restrictions on the amount of land any one corporation could own in Mississippi (restrictions written into Mississippi's 1890 constitution) the company was set up as a holding company in Memphis, with the Mississippi Delta Planting Company as the largest of a group of actual operating companies. The investors also owned an independent plantation known as the Empire Planting Company. To eliminate the inconveniences of this complicated setup, the company, in 1919, purchased the 1886 charter of the old Delta & Pine Land Company, which had once owned vast acreages throughout the state, though at the time of purchase owned only thirty-seven acres near Greenwood. Since the D&PL charter predated the 1890 constitution, its new purchasers could openly own unlimited amounts of land and operate plantations on any of it. After 1919 the corporation was known under the original charter name of Delta & Pine Land.[9]

Salsbury kept some stock for himself and managed the corporation, with its fourteen separate plantations, from the twelfth floor of the Central Bank Building in Memphis. (It was this kind of arrangement that inspired the 1930s writer David Cohn to describe the Delta as bounded on the north by the lobby of the Peabody Hotel in Memphis.) At Scott, Mississippi, convenient to the plantations themselves, the company ginned cotton, pressed cotton seed oil, and kept track of paperwork, although final accounting occurred in the Memphis headquarters. An agricultural expert, Professor Fox, made the final decisions about "how the land shall be prepared" and "what variety of cotton shall be grown and where." The company developed its own variety of cotton seeds (and today still grows and sells cotton for seed). Against each of the fourteen separate plantation units, the central office kept track of accounts designed to "show the cost of the production of each crop on each plantation."[10] These British absentee owners held Salsbury to a standard of record keeping and reporting considerably more exacting than that of the typical plantation owner. The company's records are correspondingly enlightening. A ledger kept for the Empire Plantation Company shareholders, for example, breaks down the sources of company profits and comments on its strategies. In 1912 the plantation raised 9 bales of cotton with wage labor and another 117 bales on three hundred acres of land worked by sharecroppers. But most of the income came from rentals to cash tenants, who paid the company $11,597 in rent, and who, in addition, sold Empire another 1,109 bales of cotton, on which it earned fees from ginning and profits from resale to the tune of $16,895. Salsbury commented that year that "under normal conditions our Plantation Rents would have shown a much larger figure, but on account of the high water conditions it was necessary for us to make several rebates and concessions to some of our tenants."[11]

The Empire Plantation Company operated a store, as did most big plantations. Then, as now, many observers believed that the plantation store was "often the most profitable part of the plantation business as it produce[d] a double source of income; first, a selling profit on the goods furnished the tenants; and secondly, a high interest charge on the tenant's account." The records of the plantation store are especially interesting. The store in 1912 sold tenants a total of $51,182 worth of goods — $22,330 in cash and $28,821 on credit. The store earned $1,796 in interest on this total, offset by $434 in bad debts. Total net profit was $9,094 — not a trivial sum, but only about one-sixth of its total yearly profit that year of $55,241, a return of about 10 percent on the total investment. In 1914 company profits dropped to $36,299. The store managers had to sell "some old stock at a sacrifice" to reduce inventory and "get it in a salable condition" — which suggests the limits to even monopoly power. The company spent a good deal on wages, in part to clear out new land and clean ditches, but in part to put cash into the tenants' hands so they purchased supplies from the store without resorting to credit; Salsbury wanted to "minimize our chances of loss on accounts." Such losses had ballooned to over $1,600 with low cotton prices, making it impossible for some tenants, who had been "furnished liberally" in anticipation of a big crop, to pay off their debts.[12]

In 1914 Salsbury had raised the rent on a number of farms from six to ten dollars per acre to get rid of as many cash renters as possible, "as we deemed it much more profitable to us to work this land on the half-share plan." Most renters did leave, but this had also caused problems because the renters took with them many subtenants, leaving a shortage of labor "somewhat serious, especially in these times." The following year cotton prices recovered, with profits up to $41,061. On sales of $50,524, the store earned $10,103, a quarter of total company profits, but still lost more in bad accounts than it earned in interest on advances. Despite Salsbury's intention to replace his renters with sharecroppers in 1915, a third of the crops were still planted by renters.[13]

The records of Delta & Pine Land show how a highly rationalized capitalist operation, financed by outside capital and managed in the style of a modern corporation, sought to maximize its profits. The records of LeRoy Percy, who also operated on a big scale with financing from national sources, show how a wealthy, old-time Mississippi paternalist did the same. Percy, born in 1861, traced his Mississippi ancestry to Charles Percy, a British naval officer who planted indigo and other crops before the state was a U.S. territory. LeRoy's father, William Alexander Percy, had inherited and improved rich plantation lands and passed them along to his son. Like other big planters in the Delta, LeRoy Percy could finance his operations in national financial markets, relying, for example, on a credit line from the Bank of America in New York. In addition to large holdings inherited from his father, he managed others in partnership with local and distant businessmen. His correspondence reveals how a reliable labor supply continued to be a key to profitability, and how even the biggest planters operated in a highly competitive labor market.[14]

One of Percy's interests was a share in the Trail Lake Company, which controlled three plantations in the Delta. When Percy and his partners purchased Trail Lake plantation in 1905, labor difficulties immediately arose. The new owners had purchased from the former owner, a Dr. Bizzell, mules and implements, including some sold on credit to tenants. The tenants, Percy learned, "seem to be laboring under the apprehension that we, or Dr. Bizzell, will attempt to collect from them, more than the amounts paid by us to Dr. Bizzel for them." He told the plantation's overseer to assure them that "we do not propose to collect anything from them on their old accounts, except what we paid Dr. Bizzell for such accounts," concerned that otherwise the change-over "will discourage them, and will have a tendency to make them leave the property at the close of the year."[15]

As always, the question of credit for laboring families was important. One tenant, Norman Hasty, left Percy in the spring of 1905, according to Percy, owing him $409, for rent and for a mule purchased on credit. Percy was willing to settle this debt for $300 in cash, or by taking two mules and a wagon belonging to Hasty; or Hasty could come back to Percy's own plantation. At the end of 1905, another tenant, Henry Jones, moved to Percy's plantation; Percy told his former landlord to "please advise me how much he owes." Another tenant, Tobe Williams, moved away, with Percy instructing the overseer to let Williams go with his household goods, promising, "If you have any account against him which you can enforce, I will arrange it." And so it went—a W. L. Hay paid Percy $280 for the debt of "a negro"; in turn Percy paid off John Williams's debt of $27.90 and a debt of $288.96 owed by tenant Archie Jones.[16]

Percy, punctilious about his tenant contracts, did not hesitate to seize their property if they left while indebted to him. When Bill Jones moved away along with his horse, mule, and wagon, Percy filed an affidavit asking the sheriff to seize the property and threatened to have him arrested for theft. Eventually Jones's new landlord settled the debt with Percy and the matter was dropped. But when tenants who owed him more than they owned decided to leave, he let them go. As he told a fellow planter, his rule was that "where a negro leaves without anything, I never expect anyone to take up his account, and have never asked for a payment of the account under these circumstances, and where a negro moves on my place without anything I don't pay his account." All this was in keeping with Percy's own sense of himself as a fair man and paternalistic planter. When Mike Butler, a tenant, complained of being shortchanged by $7.80, Percy instructed his overseer to review the account and check for mistakes. When Percy discovered that Lewis Levi, a tenant with a good deal of influence over other tenants, was considering moving on to a new plantation, possibly taking others with him, he instructed the overseer, "You want to get as many of the hands satisfied as you can, and look around for hands to take the land of those who are going to move. Treat Levi and the other negroes that you think are against you exactly like you do the others. Dont play any favorites at all. Give them an equal chance to do day work, etc. You will certainly be able to win some of them over, and we may be in a position to let the others go."[17]

As Percy's correspondence reveals, violence was always possible in a planter-tenant relationship. J. N. Johnson wrote to Percy's overseer to complain that a black tenant named General Joyce had left him after making a contract and running up a bill of $33. "I'd like to know if there is any chance of my getting what he owes me — and if there is no chance to get it in money, I'd like to know if he is any where in your neighborhood, and I'll take it in the other currency that will be worth something to him." Percy curtly rebuffed Johnson, pointing out that Joyce was working a farm on his plantation "and, of course, now owes us considerable money. . . . We are not willing to take up any indebtedness that he may owe you, nor are we willing for you to come on the place and get the negro. This, of course, would demoralize the labor on the property, and, in addition to this, we would lose the services of the darkey. I do not want to defend a negro who is guilty of a violation of the contract law, but we cannot give the negro up at this season of the year, especially when we are out several hundred dollars on him; and if he is guilty of any crime, you will have to proceed against him in a legal way, or wait until his contract is up with us." The last comment — "until his contract is up with us" — is a reminder of the limits of Percy's power to protect his tenants and of his willingness to enforce what he thought of as rules of fairness.[18]

Percy's protecting General Joyce was a prime example of the kind of paternalist protection a planter could offer tenants in a land with a legal system corrupted by racism. For some planters, this system was quite self-conscious. Alfred H. Stone, a friend of Percy, fellow Delta planter, and amateur scholar, referred to it in 1901 as a relationship of "patron and retainer," one directly descended from that of master and slave. The plantation owner "is called upon to settle family quarrels, to maintain peace and order between neighbours, to arbitrate disputes," as well as "to aid in the erection of churches, to provide for the burial of the dead," and to provide lawyers and bail in the case of a run-in with the courts.[19] But paternalism was part of a system that was highly rational, focused on getting an adequate supply of good labor, a problem that Stone himself called "the most serious problem confronting the plantation management," and one complicated by the "great . . . annual competition among planters for Negro labour." To a planter like LeRoy Percy, violence, whether or not it was morally wrong, was counterproductive. As he warned one overseer, "I just drop you a line to say that I know the report has been circulated among the negroes that you are rather rough with labor, and this is being used for the purpose of keeping hands from going to Tralake. I simply mention this so that you may be on your guard. A difficulty at this time with any of them would be fatal to filling the place up; in other words, you can afford to take now what you would not be willing to do after the hands have begun to know you, and things are in working order. No matter what provocation is given, if you can do so decently, don't have trouble with them at present." Counterproductive at the beginning of contracting season, "rough" practice might be acceptable later on, or it might also be acceptable when it did not involve the crucial problem of labor supply. For example, when Percy learned that "a negro named Toler" (not a tenant) was "doing the place a great deal of injury" on one property, he told the manager, "I do'nt [sic] mind your being rough with Toler if you catch him on the place."[20]

Just as protection from violence was always understood in the context of labor supply and productivity, so were understandings applied to other ways of getting and keeping workers. The paying of debts, for example, was calibrated according to the value of the worker. When Tom Smith asked for an advance of $37.50 for attorney's fees (the reason was not specified), Percy vetoed the request on grounds that the bit of land Smith offered for security was "of small value." But he left the door open to an advance at the end of the season "if his crops justify it." When Aaron Fuller asked for advances of up to $800 to settle litigation, Percy was dubious: "This is entirely too high for Aaron, according to what I know of his value," but under the right circumstances "I might pay it."[21]

Percy did not let his racist assumptions get in the way of his pursuit of Randolph Menefee, an African American farmer who was, in Percy's opinion, an exceptionally talented manager. He told a client named Sarah Compton that Menefee "seems to be a very reliable darkey. He . . . has mules and force enough to work it, and has operated a place larger than this for a number of years, above Greenville." As it turned out Menefee did not rent Compton's land, but Percy pursued him vigorously in hopes that he might manage one of Percy's own properties. "I would like to show you what I think to be the best piece of land in Washington County," he wrote to Menefee in July; "meet me in Greenville Monday morning . . . and I will take you out and show it to you, and you can come back the same day . . . I will pay all of your expenses. Meet me if you can." Three days later he was still trying to persuade the black farmer to deal with him: "I want you to see the piece of land about which I wrote you. I know that it will suit you because there is no better land in the Delta; and the houses are new and good, and I can let you have any amount up to 100 acres, and am willing to make a one year rental, or three to five years. . . . You can go and take a look at it in a day without any trouble . . . and I will pay your expenses, so that if it does not suit you, you will be nothing out."[22]

Percy used all sorts of other angles in his efforts to control labor. Like other planters, he insisted that his tenants get their supplies from his own plantation store. If one man was allowed to be an exception, "the fact of it is, it will lessen your control over him, and then it puts notions in the heads of the other negroes." Christmas money was a useful tool, coming as it did just at annual contracting time, but it, too, had to be calibrated. In 1905 Percy told a manager who passed along several requests for Christmas cash, "We simply can't afford to advance Christmas money on this scale. . . . Here and there it may be necessary to put out a few hundred dollars but a negro like Green Walker ought not think of getting a hundred dollars and should not expect to spend a Hundred Dollars, when he already owes over $400.00. If he can get $25.00 to throw away for Christmas, he ought to be satisfied . . . I know it is hard to satisfy labor and I realize the danger of losing them, but we must take a stand somewhere, and if necessary, I would rather lose him than to give him that much." Day hands were more reliable and predictable if "their women" were also working on the crops; prizes for picking the cleanest cotton each week "should get us cotton picked at least expense and may also get us more pickers."[23]

The voices of black tenants themselves are very rare in these transactions, which makes the correspondence in the Percy papers related to "Arlington" plantation especially interesting. Arlington's five hundred acres were owned by Johanna Reiser, a widow who had leased the plantation to her nephew, L. A. Saunders, for $1,500 per year and moved from the Delta to New York City. In 1907 (a year of brief, but nasty, recession), Saunders abandoned the plantation after subletting it, without his aunt's knowledge, to a W. R. Fleming. Unable to supervise the plantation from New York, Reiser turned to the Percys, LeRoy and his son William Alexander Percy, for legal assistance, hoping simply to break Saunders's lease and pursue other options. They urged her to pursue Saunders in court (he was still liable for the lease) and meanwhile to rent the land to some white man while searching for a buyer. To abandon the land entirely would mean the depreciation of the housing and other improvements. LeRoy Percy advised her to keep the lease with Saunders as "agricultural matters are in an extremely depressed condition. There is great alarm felt about the approach of the boll-weevil, so great that it is practically impossible to make a sale or lease of property in this section."[24]

At the end of the 1908 crop year W. R. Fleming, in turn, abandoned the plantation. Some of the tenants saw a rare opportunity. On December 29 a B. Y. Young wrote to Percy, "I am very much interrested in asking the price per acre of this track of Land that Join the old goldfarb track I was inform that you ar the agen . . . I would Like to rent as much as 25 acres pleas Mr Percy [illegible] this at once as it is very important to me." Percy offered a rental of $6 per acre, and Young immediately agreed: "I do not need eney funishing what ever. all I want is the Land I wright you this becaus I cant come to see you at once tho I Will come on as erly er Date as posoble." So, too, Peter Brown wrote to Percy: "Lawyer Percy sir I one Peter Brown have learned that you are Gardeen [guardian] over the Arlington or Reesier Plant[ation]. Wish to say I would like to see or hear from you as early as posible. . . . we want to know at once so we can have something to depend upon." William Howe told Percy that he "could work between 35 and 45 acres I have bin waiting to here from you in regards of same. I allso asked you for the Old Reiser House and why I did this was that I heard that no white Gentleman was going to live there and though[t] that you would put some good col[ored] family in it as it looks very shabby from the outside and I thought I would speak of it in time in case you had any such ideas as my family was pretty large and it would save the truble of ocupying so many houses. But Hon Sir if this was asking to much of you please for give your most Faithful Servant." These are the letters of ordinary farmers — respectful without being obsequious, considering terms and acreage, living space for their families, and a chance to earn more than an ordinary sharecropper.[25]

Following Percy's suggestion, Johanna Reiser proceeded to rent farms to Howe, Brown, and several other black tenants. But Percy had little faith that the result would be anything other than to limit the depreciation on the property while holding out the option to sue the old leaseholder, L. A. Saunders, for damages. He told Reiser that "the great liklihood [was] that little or none" of the land would be cultivated; she would probably get no rent for the year. In fact, she got just what she had bargained for — from William Howe, $90 of rent (less $16.85, the cost of replacing a chimney on the old house); from Peter Brown, $150 for his twenty-five acres.[26] The experiment worked well enough that the next year Reiser decided again to rent her land directly to black tenants, ignoring offers from a white planter willing to lease the plantation for a mere $2.50 per acre. Reiser herself came to Greenville to work out the terms of the contracts, agreeing to pay Peter Brown a kind of finding fee of fifty cents per acre for any new tenants he could locate. Brown interpreted this as a much broader license to oversee the whole operation, assuming he would receive fifty cents on every acre cultivated. LeRoy Percy's son, William Alexander Percy, wrote to Reiser, "The old negro who is sort of at the head of affairs down at your place, who wears the long plat of hair across his fore-head, was in our office this morning and gave very encouraging reports of the condition that your place is in. He says only about 70 acres are lying out and that the crops are in very good shape. He further quotes Mr. Law as having said that the outlook was as good for your place as almost any place on the lake. . . . [T]he old negro seemed to be sincerely pleased with himself and with the way things were looking from a farmers point of view." In the fall Brown wrote directly to Reiser that he was "doing the verry Best that I can twoards seeing after your property," and he told the Percys that "some of the tenants havnt complied with the agreement yet on the Arlington Place" and that they shouldn't sign any new contracts until "I . . . make my report."[27]

Not surprisingly, not all tenants appreciated Brown's attentions. One tenant, Simon Brantley, wrote that he wanted to stay the next year, "but one thing that has got the people dis sadifid [dissatisfied] and that is Peter Brown is Ridin over the people and got them Dis Sadifide if it was [wasn't?] for that you cood get all the hans you want[.] Peter Brown said . . . we will hafter Leave the plas and we all want stay hear. . . . I am Reddy to tirn over yr Rent to the First Nasnel Bank at Eney day." When another tenant, Charles Thomas, sublet a bit of his land to a neighboring white planter named Skin-ner, who wanted it for an Italian family, Brown told Johanna Reiser that Skinner was "trespassing." Thomas in turn told Reiser that "it seems that Mr. Brown has got offended with me ever since I let Mr. [S]Kiner have that Land." William Howe, Peter Brown's nephew and also a tenant, wrote to Reiser that, while he and his uncle got along "all right," his uncle made "lots of mistakes." Brown wanted to cut down the amount of land his nephew should be allowed to rent because he had not actually planted all of the fifteen acres he had rented, but, so Howe explained, "The rains made me let 3 a[cres] of land go which I had planted in cotton & the weeds . . . out grew the cotton I have not said a word about that and paid my rent for 15 a[cres] just the same. Uncle Peter can't see that Mrs. Rieser. I would like to stay here next year or as long as I can but the people all claim that a man and his wife cannot work over 6 acres of cotton and are liable to not make anything at that price."[28]

Reiser eventually wrote to Percy to clear up the matter of Peter Brown's contract. He was to be paid only for land rented out late in the season, not for supervising others. She had received "any amount of complaint from all the tenants that Peter Brown has been trying to meddle with their affairs." Brown was indignant about being deposed from the position he had assumed, and complained to Reiser that her letter, informing him that he would get fifty cents for only the new tenants, was "not satisfactory." He would like to know her rental terms for the next year when he would be *free from attending to you business.*"[29]

On the whole, though, the year was a financial success for Reiser, and she received nearly all the $1,000 in rent she had contracted for. William Alexander Percy admitted that, although Brown had made himself "unpopular with the other tenants," he had done well, and that "you have every right to be pleased with your experiment this year, but I am free to confess that I never expected you to collect one-half the rent due." Still, Percy thought that Brown, "like all negro's . . . will make what attempt he can to foster his own interest rather than yours" and he advised Reiser to find a "reliable white man" to direct things on the plantation the next year. "It is quite impossible for us to adequately protect your interest," he added, "as long as negro tenants occupy the place, without making repeated trips to the plantation itself, which we cannot do."[30] Reiser's reply was a courteous but firm dissent, reminding Percy of her bad experience of "a white man's honesty," and she suggested that "my experience in Greenville last winter is still fresh in my mind so for the present I will again rent to the colored tenants." This time she made sure to prevent Peter Brown from interfering with the others. Percy's final letter in the preserved correspondence, in the spring of 1911, told Reiser that he was happy not to charge her for his services to date, because "the experience has been an excellent one in human nature, and has given me considerable insight into the methods and characters of the darkies." Planters like the Percys were unable to see Peter Brown, or William Holmes, or Charles Thomas as full individuals, each with his own "character"; to such planters they were still simply representative "darkies."[31]

Labor in the Delta Cotton Fields

The labor in the Delta's cotton fields was, by the early twentieth century, organized with a combination of systems worked out over the generations after emancipation: wage labor, sharecropping, share renting, and cash renting. The vast majority of workers were black, and all four systems were "generally used to a greater or less extent on almost every plantation." On Runnymede plantation nearly all tenants paid a fixed cash rent for each acre. On the Bledsoe plantation sharecroppers worked a little more than half the acreage, share renters about 40 percent, and wage hands the rest. At Delta &

Pine Land, sharecroppers worked 8,000 acres of cotton, share renters 3,800 acres, cash renters about 1,000 acres, and wage laborers 2,000 acres of cotton and 2,500 acres of corn.[32] Some planters still preferred closely supervised wage hands to tenants, but men (and sometimes women) with families "almost invariably" preferred the "greater independence that is accorded to tenants." While many African American adults earned wages at some point during a year, full-time wage laborers were usually young single men making up a "floating and uncertain" force that was on "Monday morning . . . apt to appear rather broken in ranks" because "the single men who comprise such labor are ever on the move." All in all it was "extremely difficult to get the necessary labor to raise the crops attended with wage hands."[33]

Families with no resources but their labor were usually sharecroppers, who split the crop evenly with the plantation owners. A tenant who furnished his own stock, tools, and seeds as well as labor was more often a "share renter" who paid as rent one-fourth or one-third of the crop. A cash renter paid, instead of a share of the crop, a fixed price per acre in either cash or cotton. Within these basic terms, the planter tried to match the number of acres to the size of the tenant's family, while lesser aspects of the contract might vary — whether, for example, a garden was included, whether the tenant had the right to cut wood on the plantation, or whether the tenant's mule could pasture without extra payment. The planter, however, almost always had the exclusive right to buy and market the cotton, and often, in addition, "furnished" the tenant family with food and other supplies, charging whatever prices and interest the market would bear.[34]

Most planters agreed that wage labor would be the best method of running a plantation if only the workers could be tied down for the year, but since that was impossible, sharecropping was next best because sharecroppers could be minutely supervised by owner or overseer. Although croppers, unlike wage laborers, lived and worked on a specific part of a plantation throughout the year, in law croppers were "not considered as tenants at all, but as laborers hired to do the work in return for half the crop and the use of a cabin." On Alfred H. Stone's Dunlieth plantation, for example, croppers were "more directly under the control of the overseers" and were not allowed to go and come freely "as the renter may." Share renters and, especially cash renters, had more autonomy and were less subject to supervision; they were also more likely to be allowed to rent land in "out-of-the-way corners of the plantation, where it is rather difficult for the overseers to get to."[35] Planters tended to rationalize their preference for sharecropping over renting in terms of race. They claimed (and some BAE investigators agreed) that "left to himself, the negro is a poor farmer and lacks judgement," as was proved by the "low yields in land operated by the cash and share renters."[36]

Two BAE economists who surveyed dozens of plantations throughout the Delta in 1914, compiling records on 878 individual tenants, came to a different conclusion. They compared the income of planters and laborers under the three systems of sharecropping, share renting, and cash renting. Their findings are clear and easily summarized — under sharecropping, tenant families earned an average of $463 per year while planters averaged a return on investments of almost 14 percent. With share renting, families earned $562 and planters 11.8 percent; under cash renting tenants averaged $625 per year and planters only a 6.6 percent return. These differences had little to do with crop yields, since sharecroppers and share renters averaged identical yields of cotton per acre, and cash renters only slightly less. Renters operated more acres and produced more measurable "value" than sharecroppers, leading the report's authors to suggest that "cash renters and share renters, as a class, are more industrious than share croppers," exactly the opposite of the planters' received wisdom.[37]

No matter what the rental type, of course, both tenant and owner were better off with higher yields per acre, but the really important difference among the methods was who benefited from the higher yields. A highly productive cropper shared his higher yield equally with the landlord; on the most productive sharecropper farms landlords earned a remarkable 20 percent on their investments. Cash renters paid a fixed amount, no matter what the yield, and captured almost all the benefits of higher productivity. One in twelve cash renters, but only one in two hundred sharecroppers, earned more than $1,000 from their labor.[38]

The reasons planters preferred sharecropping then, are not far to seek, and have little to do with the "native inefficiency" of black tenants or with the alleged fact that blacks were guided by "no logical or reasonable basis," or that "they are controlled far more by their fancies than by their common sense," as planter Alfred Stone wrote. With sharecropping the planters took most of the risk and correspondingly reaped most of the rewards of a good year. With cash renters the opposite was the case: the landlord was fairly assured of a return, even if the crop was a loss, because the renter's property could be seized in payment of the rent, but when crops were good the tenant, and not the landlord, stood to benefit. With a few good years a cash tenant might even be able to save enough to take the much greater step toward independence of buying his or her own farm. No wonder planters preferred sharecroppers, who in 1913 paid twice as well as other types of renters.[39]

Planters' continuing need for more labor as the Delta was cleared led some of the leading planters in the Delta to try to bring in foreign immigrants. As early as the 1880s, some Delta planters had experimented with Chinese laborers, but this short-lived trial had ended quickly, and the few Chinese remaining in the Delta by 1900 were nearly all owners of small stores. New interest was inspired by the massive increase in immigration from southern and eastern Europe to the United States beginning in the late nineteenth century. In 1905, LeRoy Percy arranged for transportation of some twenty Bohemian families from Chicago. (His labor agent in Chicago carefully concealed his commission, which was charged to the immigrants, by counting it as part of the cost of transportation.) Percy settled them on one of his plantations, but almost immediately they complained about the terms and the plantation manager complained that they worked so slowly in building their own houses that "I had to bring in carpenters" and that they were "green & did not know how to plow." At the end of the cotton season Percy conceded to his Chicago agent that the experiment had failed because the Bohemians knew too little about farming and had raised much less cotton than black tenants on adjacent lands.[40]

Percy and planters like Charles Scott were more hopeful about the prospects for importing Italian immigrants to labor in the cotton fields. Italians were coming into the United States in massive numbers, most of them peasant farmers; planters had observed the apparent success of Sunnyside plantation across the Mississippi River, which had been operated with Italian tenants since 1895. Sunnyside was owned by Austin Corbin of New York, but after Corbin's death it had been leased to LeRoy Percy and his partner, O. B. Crittenden. To Percy and other observers of the Sunnyside experiment, Italians seemed to be much more frugal, zealous, and productive farmers than the typical African American renters in the Delta. With the help of the management of the Illinois Central Railroad, Percy and Crittenden courted the support of both U.S. immigration officials and the Italian government for their plans to bring in more Italians. They conducted an official Italian observer, Baron Edmondo Mayou des Planches, through the region and entertained high hopes that they would soon be able to attract many new immigrants to their fields.[41]

These expectations proved illusory. Poor health conditions in the swampy areas along the Mississippi River led the Italian government to be cautious, and, when Italians at Sunnyside later lodged official complaints about their mistreatment with their diplomatic representatives, Italy discouraged further migration to the Delta. The complaints led to an investigation of the Sunnyside operation by Mary Quackenbos of the U.S. Department of Labor, who accused Percy and Crittenden of practicing peonage. Only with difficulty did Percy and Crittenden escape indictment on the charge, with Percy appealing directly to his hunting companion Theodore Roosevelt for support. Even without such complications, Delta planters would have had difficulty attracting a significant number of immigrants who could earn much higher wages in northern factories and mines.[42]

African American farmers, however, continued to pour into the Delta. Although the arrival of the boll weevil slowed production in the Delta temporarily — until planters learned how to apply arsenic compounds to kill these cotton-destroying insects — the arrival of the weevil in areas further south in Mississippi actually made it easier to recruit new labor to the Delta's fields. In 1910 there were some sixty thousand black farmers in the Delta, an increase of 50 percent since 1900. But, though black workers streamed into the region because of its high wages, most found little opportunity to move up to farm ownership. In 1880, a substantial proportion of black farmers in Sunflower County had owned their farms. In 1910 in the same county, among black family heads, sharecroppers and tenants outnumbered farm owners by sixteen to one. Altogether, fewer than 4 percent of black family heads were farm owners that year in Sunflower County (see Tables 9 and 11, Appendix). In the Delta as a whole that year, about 6 percent of African American farmers owned their farms, about 40 percent were cash renters, and the rest were sharecroppers or share renters — the census did not distinguish between these two forms of labor tenancy. Depending on the labor of these tens of thousands of black tenants was the small group of planters who, with their access to capital, had consolidated their control of the Delta's rich land. Altogether, fewer than three thousand whites owned farms and plantations in the region in 1910.[43]

Planters, Farmers, and Laborers in the Piedmont

In Georgia's Piedmont in the early twentieth century, cotton remained the dominant crop, and in many ways the farm economy evolved in a fashion parallel to the Delta's. But if cotton was still king there, the king was no longer a dynamic ruler, even though higher prices, as in the Delta, brought benefits to both planters and small farmers. Enoch Banks, a contemporary analyst of the "economics of land tenure" in Georgia in these years, claimed that the higher price of cotton "has enabled most of the farmers in the state to cancel all debts." He was surely overstating, and even at that was writing mainly of farm owners, but he insisted that croppers and tenants, like owners, were better off and more independent than they had been in 1900.[44] Banks argued that the effects of the credit system had been exaggerated, and he criticized the notion that merchants could use debt to "control" farmers. "Usually there are several merchants in each town competing vigorously for business. In case one merchant, after securing through a mortgage or otherwise the trade of a farmer, makes heavy exactions by means of excessively high credit prices throughout the year, the more alert of his customers, after being so dealt with, will negotiate the following year for lines of credit with other merchants. In this way standard credit percentages to be added to the cash prices are established for the staple commodities." As for the high interest prices, they were required because "to predicate a loan upon a crop is a daring venture. Those who have fallen by the wayside engaged in such an undertaking show that unusual ability is required for success."[45]

Banks thought that, in most cases, the best system was closely supervised wage labor, because the wages would be larger than the cropper's income and the farm owner would produce greater profits. Like researchers in Mississippi, he believed that sharecropping was the least efficient method of labor, "rather a mode of paying wages than a tenancy," but less effective than wage labor because the "typical negro" was "improvident; he does not make plans for the future and organize his present forces for the execution of the plans." He attributed this to a combination of "heredity" and poor training under slavery. Banks thought that in the cotton belt (including the Piedmont) the percentage of farms worked on shares was decreasing in favor of fixed rentals.[46]

Robert Preston Brooks, a Georgia economist writing in 1914, agreed with the fundamentals of Banks's analysis. Since 1900, he said, higher prices and better roads had improved conditions for tenants and everyone else. Landlords were more willing to sell mules on credit to tenants who desired more "freedom." His own sample of twenty-two plantations showed three times as many sharecroppers as renters, but he agreed with Banks that renting by black farmers was on the rise because "the consensus of opinion is that the negro prefers this system, not so much with the view of bettering his condition, as for the purpose of escaping the supervision of the landlord."

And like Banks, Brooks pointed to strong competition among merchants as contributing to greater autonomy for tenants: "Competition among the country merchants is becoming so strong that credit is frequently extended to the average negro without the personal endorsement of the landlord." The merchant would take a second mortgage on the crop or a lien on the tenant's personal property, a risky venture for both parties.[47]

Brooks paid more attention than Banks to what he considered the social significance of changes in the Georgia countryside. Some were worrisome. He quoted an Oglethorpe County planter who complained that "the younger set [of blacks] think of nothing but gadding about, baseball, hot suppers, church fights and the city court. . . . [W]hen they have finished the rounds of the secret orders and the churches, there is no time left for work, and the crop is not worked." To Brooks, as for this anonymous planter, the younger generation of African Americans were becoming "unmanageable" because of their "deep-seated dislike of control and discontent with farming life and conditions. The tendency is strong to wander from plantation to plantation and to the towns." Reinforcing this tendency was the opportunity for "good day wages" in the building of new railroads, streetcar lines, and waterworks in the towns. Yet, like Banks, Brooks wrote favorably of the slow increase of black landowners. He thought that the "mass of the race" were "unfit for economic independence," but the many examples of successful black owners were "a standing refutation of the belief held by many persons that the negro is incapable of advancement. No claim is here made that negroes are not progressing. Such a claim would be idle in the face of the fact that in 1910 they were assessed for taxation in Georgia on $32,234,047 worth of property."[48] Despite this slow increase in black landownership, the overwhelming majority of black farmers in the Piedmont, as in the Delta, were sharecroppers and tenants. In the eastern Piedmont as a whole, about 7.5 percent of all black farmers owned their farms.[49]

Brooks's concern about the influence of town life was not limited to worries about black farmers. More important, in his eyes, was its attraction for white landowners, planters among them. In towns the schools were far better — one Hancock County planter told him that he had moved to town "to educate children"; more important, economic opportunities were far greater. One Warren County planter lived in Athens and visited his plantation only once or twice a year. In his special study of Oglethorpe County, Brooks found that many plantation owners were absentees in Athens or Lexington, "usually engaged in other forms of business."[50] Children of antebellum planters and farmers often abandoned farming altogether. Edward Porter Alexander, who had grown up on the plantation of his father, Adam, in Wilkes County and fought with Lee, never considered planting as a post-war career. Trained as an engineer at West Point, he became president of the Central Railroad & Banking Company. Will Lumpkin was twelve years old when the war began. Though he had expected to take over his father's Ogle-thorpe County plantation, after the war he studied law and worked for a railroad company rather than take up an uncertain planter's life. Clifford C. Farr, born in McDuffie County in 1887, as a teenager decided to take a business course and move to Augusta because he "was keenly interested in advancement." The sons of David C. Barrow of Oglethorpe County, Pope and David Barrow Jr., became lawyers. For such families who retained their plantations, planting ceased to be the dynamic source of the family fortune, as it was in the Delta.[51]

Local boosters and entrepreneurs, recognizing that the land itself would no longer attract capital, turned instead to manufacturing, hoping to emulate the success of Augusta's capitalists and of the small-town manufacturers in North and South Carolina who had built up a formidable textile industry. In Greene County, in 1897, local boosters tried to convince a northern capitalist named Frederick Mosher to buy the site of a grist mill to build a new textile factory and perhaps an electric generating plant. When Mosher arrived for "strong and earnest talks," merchants closed their stores and citizens gath-ered to hear his "stirring" address laying out the benefits of manufacturing employment and promising to invest at least $20,000 of his own money. Local residents at the public meeting pledged at least $37,000 more for the project. The local editor, convinced that the plan would go forward, de-scribed it as "a great day for the people of Greene." When local pledges reached $40,000, Mosher promised another $80,000, outlining plans for a factory with ten thousand spindles and a village with eighty cottages for operatives. "Everybody moves with a lighter and quicker step," the editor wrote. The local investors were led by E. A. Copelan, who had made his wealth in merchandising and then opened the most important bank in the county, and by W. R. Jackson, one of the county's biggest planters. Most of the other investors were local merchants and lawyers.[52]

But by the end of the year, the factory scheme had collapsed and Mosher had withdrawn from the project. Two years later another meeting was called to encourage manufacturing investments and keep Greensboro from "sink-ing into insignificance." This time Copelan and Jackson led a local group who raised enough capital to open in 1900 the "Mary-Leila Cotton Mill," named for the wives of the two chief investors. It opened with a hundred hands working five thousand spindles.[53]

Greene County was exceptional in having such a manufacturing enterprise, and even there, nearly three-fourths of all workers were still employed in agriculture. In the entire eastern Piedmont in 1900, there were fewer than nine thousand manufacturing jobs, and four out of five were in Augusta, the only place that became a significant center for textile production. Textile manufacturers hired blacks for only the most menial tasks. Women and children filled many of the textile jobs, which paid little and required long hours. Such jobs were not a very attractive alternative to farming for most white men. Thus the Malthusian pressure of population on the land continued. In the first decade of the century, white tenants increased in number in the Piedmont by 20 percent, and white owners by only 5 percent. As land prices rose along with the rise in cotton prices, it simply became harder for young men to buy farms. In 1910 there were more white tenants than white owners in the eastern Piedmont.[54]

"Every rice place is practically abandoned"

While furious development was converting the Delta wilderness into plantations, the great rice plantations on the coast were receding into the wilderness from which they had been created. The recollections of a businessman about a duck hunt in the winter of 1899–1900 in the marshes near Darien, Georgia, depict the process. He went with a boyhood companion and with Cain Bradwell, "tall, angular and black, and well known about McIntosh County for his skill as a duck hunter, and his extraordinary knowledge of the abandoned rice fields." They found the best hunting at a "sink hole" pond formed in one old field. Cain guided them through the old ditches and canals, along the mud banks topped by tall grass that hid everything but a narrow strip of sky. Finding the way through the broken trunks "was strictly a job for Cain. He could paddle along a canal, making right angle turns into other canals, until he reached the one he wanted that led to a broken trunk. . . . [B]efore we could see the trunk, but [when we could] feel the water making a swift pace, Cain would say 'hol' fas now we is comin' out in de big ribbuh,' then turn suddenly into the opening of the old trunk and we would be swept through."[55]

The rise in agricultural prices after 1896 was of little help on the Georgia coast, because there was little agriculture left. The overconfident Yankees who had come south after Reconstruction to show southerners how to work with free labor had long since sold out or given up their leases after a few years of losing money. The Sea Island cotton plantations had quickly disappeared, but the rice planters held on for a generation longer. The great hurricane in 1898 was the finishing blow to many planters, although a few struggled on, hoping to rebuild.

Among the last planters was John Girardeau Legare of Darien, who at one time managed the Leighs' place on Butler Island and later ran a plantation owned by a bank that had foreclosed on the owner. This plantation, Champney's Island in the Altamaha River, was inundated by the 1898 hurricane but continued to operate for several years. Each year the problem of securing good labor got worse. In 1900 Legare had "a greater amount of stealing rice by the hands . . . than in all my experience before." Two years later, "the hands on the place" were giving him "trouble" because they claimed his rate of pay was too low. In 1903 he recorded that "all my hoe hands 'struck' me today giving as a reason that the work was bad, and they are afraid I will not pay them for it." Finally, in 1905, the bank sold off the property and rice planting ended on Champney's. Another of the last rice plantations was J. T. Dent's Hofwyl, also on the Altamaha. Dent, in 1894, had written confidently of the future, but by 1900 he hoped merely to leave his estate free of debt. Hofwyl eventually passed to his daughters, Ophelia and Miriam. In the first decades of the new century they managed to fend off banks and other creditors, selling portions of their property from time to time and turning the plantation into a dairy operation. Ironically, even flood-control efforts sometimes destroyed rice plantations. An Army Corps of Engineers dredging project changed the water flow around Argyle Island so greatly that Louis Manigault's Gowrie and the other plantations there could no longer regulate their water supply. In 1892 Gowrie abruptly, and permanently, ceased operating. According to a U.S. Department of Agriculture report, coastal farmers believed that they "must secure a crop that will require less labor than rice."[56]

Charles Spalding Wylly, a descendant of antebellum planters, wrote in 1915 that the rice industry had "entirely disappeared"; the old plantation lands had "already reverted into swamp, or are fast passing into a jungle of marsh, wood and water; great sums of money have been lost by the former owners in the effort to re-establish their prosperity and productiveness, which in every instance known to me have ended in financial disaster . . . [and] at present every rice place on the Savannah, the Ogeechee and the

Altamaha is practically abandoned, and are no longer an asset in their own-ers' ledgers, but rather a charge and incumbrance."[57]

The search for new alternatives to old sources of wealth was frustrating and, for planters, largely fruitless. Charles Spalding's grandchildren had tried to turn the Spalding lands on Sapelo into a cattle ranch. One experiment by several growers to plant olive groves was cut short by an 1886 freeze that killed all the trees. Around Savannah, small farmers turned to growing fruits and vegetables, supplying Savannah itself and also cities in the northeastern United States. But even this enterprise came under pressure from competing sources of supplies in Florida.[58]

Entrepreneurs found their biggest opportunities in sandy pine lands away from the coast, which had never been good for agriculture because of their poor soil, and in upriver swamps too far away from the tidelands to be useful for large-scale rice production. Cheap fertilizer enabled small farmers to grow short-staple cotton in some parts of the pine lands. But the most valu-able crop along the coast was the trees themselves, harvested as lumber and naval stores. The pine forests upland of the coast had attracted timber opera-tors even before the war. The most prominent of these traced its origins to two generations of a Scottish family, the Hiltons, who had moved to Darien in the 1850s. The Hiltons bought logs of long leaf yellow pine that were floated down the Altamaha River by raftsmen and sold them to New En-glanders for ship timber. After the war the business was revived, starting with loose logs and other debris found scattered along the coastal marshes, and by the end of Reconstruction the Hilton Timber & Lumber Company helped turn Darien into a major port for shipments of pine and cypress logs to northern states and to Europe. No fewer than eight countries established consulates there to help deal with shippers, crews, and contract issues, and by 1874 Darien loaded more than a hundred million board feet of lumber. A publisher launched a newspaper in Darien that year named the *Timber Ga-zette* with the boast that "Timber is King here now, and we have christened our paper after him as a perpetual reminder." A new railroad, the Macon and Brunswick, established connections into the interior independent of the wa-ter flows on the river.[59]

Operations on this scale naturally attracted northern capitalists, the most important of whom was William A. Dodge of New York. Dodge and his Georgia Land and Lumber Co., capitalized at $1.5 million, started with a purchase of 300,000 acres in what later became Dodge County, Georgia. Dodge and associates like William Eastman (who had a town named after him) at one time owned most of the land in three Georgia counties. They cut tram railroads into the forests and built new and larger sawmills. The Dodge interests bought land on St. Simons Island in 1876 and built a sawmill that employed three hundred workers. They solved the problem of competition in standard fashion for the era, by merging with the rival Hilton company to form Hilton & Dodge.[60]

The lumber trade gave rise to the colorful local culture of the sort that grew around any substantial river trade, especially if it relied on seasonal work by groups of men who told tall tales, played practical jokes, and frequented the "disreputable houses" in which white raftsmen—most of them farmers looking for seasonal work—slept with their "Negro paramours." Huge rafts of roughly shaped logs floated down the Altamaha and its tributaries; people could walk for a mile on the river without getting their feet wet. Black stevedores working in concert under a leader got the timbers on shore for the sawmills or loaded them on the ships, while the leader "sang a line of a chanty song, the others coming in on the short chorus, then with a 'ho' all heaved together on the big stick in perfect time":

> Call me hangin' Johnny
>   O hang boys hang.
> You call me hangin' Johnny
>   O hang boys hang
> Yes, I never hang nobody
>   O hang boys hang.[61]

As usual, most of the better jobs—better in terms of pay or working conditions—went to white men, but the business was loose enough so that the *Timber Gazette* could point to numerous Negroes "who personally conduct extensive and profitable timber cutting businesses, and who display a surprising degree of skill and shrewdness both as to manufacture or selling to advantage." Typically, the companies stripped the woods as fast as profits would allow, and the inevitable result was the early decline of the major exporting business and its accompanying work culture. After peaking in 1900 at 112 million board feet, shipments from Darien plunged to 17 million board feet by 1910, and the *Timber Gazette* became merely the *Darien Gazette*. The huge sawmill Dodge opened on St. Simons Island in 1876 closed permanently in 1906, and in 1914 Hilton & Dodge went into bankruptcy, its final assets sold off in 1916.[62]

Long leaf pines also provided sap for naval stores — turpentine and rosin. By 1900 these products were used in numerous industrial products, especially in paints. Production of naval stores along the Georgia coast had been trivial before the Civil War, but by 1885 Brunswick was exporting annually over 110,000 barrels. By 1890 Georgia was by far the largest naval-stores-producing state, and by 1910 more than 80 percent of U.S. exports of these products came from Georgia's Atlantic ports.[63]

Turpentine camps in the southeast earned a justified reputation as some of the most repressive workplaces in American history, at times surpassing slave plantations in cruelty and exploitation, especially those camps that relied on convict labor. Convicts could be chained, whipped, and hunted down if they escaped. Gangs of men — nearly all African American — would spend weeks at a time in remote woods, cutting "boxes" into the trees, "chipping" slashes into the bark above, and periodically "dipping" the buckets that gathered the gum. With portable stills they distilled the gum in the forests, filling barrels with turpentine and rosin to ship to Darien, Brunswick, or Savannah. In the 1880s some turpentine companies imported workers from North Carolina who were described as arriving "voluntarily," though in handcuffs. In these rough camps one boss made it a practice to "knock a neggar down whenever I get a new lot of hands" to "give the new ones a good idee of what sort of boss they've got." Yet, even in these camps could be found men "in solemn meditation over a spelling book" and "misers" who saved all their pay and accumulated interest on money lent out for "liquor, musical instruments, brass watches, etc."[64] Such semislavery was far more common in remote camps in Florida and southwest Georgia than those along the coast, which competed for labor with rice plantations, sawmills, and subsistence farming. A careful study of the companies by one historian found that they hired local labor on a wide variety of plans, from very short term to seasonal. Most workers avoided going into debt with their companies and purchased only a few specialized items from the company stores.[65]

A third new postwar industry depended on the fruits of the rivers, swamps, and sea. Oysters and shrimp fed many local families, but they also were caught and packed for national markets. Several companies along the coast relied almost wholly on the labor of black men and women. In the settlement of Warsaw, outside of Savannah in the early 1900s, many families relied on oystering for their primary income. In the strictly gendered division of labor, men "tonged" for oysters in the rich beds in low-lying areas where they flourished, while women shucked and packed in the factories. Some men rented boats from oyster factories, paying one-third of their catch as rent, but four-fifths of the local oyster fleet was owned by black workers themselves. Owners of small oared boats visited nearby beds for a day at a time, earning $5 to $7 a week in season. Larger sailing vessels could stay out for a week or more and travel to the most productive beds; owners of these earned as much as $30 per week. Six of Warsaw's tongers were members of the Georgia Benevolent Fisherman's Association, an African American business group that leased prime oyster beds for their exclusive use. In Monroe Work's 1908 investigation of the African American population in Warsaw, he found only one family that depended entirely on the earnings of the husband and father. In all the rest, wives and children supplemented the family's income. (Work did not discuss families headed by women.) Some women worked as domestic servants, others took in washing, and still others boarded students, but most worked as shuckers in the oyster factories, with unskilled shuckers making as little as $3 a week opening steamed oysters, and skilled shuckers earning up to $3 a day opening raw oysters. Oystering families, like the small subsistence farmers that dominated the black economy, usually owned their own houses.[66]

Work in the forests and on the sea supplemented the living that African Americans could continue to earn from the land. In Camden County in 1910, about half of black household heads operated small farms. About one household head in eight worked in the forests, logging or gathering resin for naval stores. Most of the rest lifted cargoes on the docks, drove wagons, worked for the Carnegies on Cumberland Island, and otherwise got by with the work of their hands. Even those with small farms usually fished and hunted to bring in some of their food, while turpentine, lumber, and stevedore labor helped provide cash for paying taxes and buying cloth, tools, and other necessities, without ever drawing most of these families fully into the market. The large majority of black farmers continued to own and operated their own small farms, which were, as we shall see, much smaller than the ones operated by the successful black owners of the Piedmont or the Delta.[67]

Capitalists at Play in the Sea Islands

Big capitalists eventually came to the Sea Islands, but most came to spend money rather than invest it. The travel writers of the national magazines had publicized the beauties of the coast, and especially of the Sea Islands. Especially influential was Frederick A. Ober's 1880 account in *Lippincott's* of the ruins of Dungeness mansion on Cumberland Island. Dungeness had been built by the wife of Revolutionary War hero Nathanael Greene. Her great nephew, Phineas Nightingale, who had inherited Dungeness, tried like other planters to restore the property as a cotton plantation after the Civil War, and like others, he failed. By the time of Ober's visit, Dungeness had passed to Nightingale's creditors, and then to a former Confederate general, W. G. M. Davis. Cumberland Island was already a local tourist attraction, though most of the permanent residents were former slaves. Ober described Dungeness and Cumberland Island in idyllic terms: April visitors could wake up under an "unclouded sky," watch "great gaudy butterflies" and "gleaming hummingbirds," and then see the vast marshes between the island and mainland turn golden at sunset. In August the air was "heavy with crape-myrtle and orange fragrance." Deserted avenues lined with live oaks passed through ruined fields, and over this "Eden-like retreat" with its "garden of spices and bloom" loomed the ruin of the old mansion, its walls and four chimneys all that survived.[68] Andrew Carnegie's brother Thomas visited Cumberland with his wife Lucy, who fell in love with it; as the wife of one of the wealthiest men in America, she had the wherewithal to turn her dream of living there into reality. In 1881 her husband bought Dungeness itself and 4,000 acres on Cumberland Island for $35,000. The next year he added another estate and its 8,240 acres, and eventually the Carnegies owned 90 percent of the island.[69]

Two years later the Carnegies laid the cornerstone for their new Dungeness, and a year after that it was ready to receive visitors. The entrance at the base of its ninety-foot tower opened into a marbled vestibule that led into the "Great Hall," what one reporter called "a perfect triumph of domestic architecture." There was a gun room, a library, and five hundred gas lights with electric lighters. In the fifty-five-foot-long Great Hall, lit by cathedral-like stained glass windows, was a fireplace with its carved legend, "The Hearth our Altar: Its Flame our Sacred Fire."[70]

Although Thomas Carnegie did not live long enough to enjoy his new mansion—he died in 1886—Lucy made Cumberland her primary residence, expanding it dramatically as the years passed and putting up "cottages" for her children. Here she and they lived on a scale of lavishness beyond the dreams of the greatest of the old antebellum planters. Her manager's summary statement of expenses for 1901, for example, includes almost $32,000 spent on the "Stafford" portion of the property (used principally by the Carnegie children), another $97,000 on the Dungeness "farm," $17,436 on the yacht (Lucy Carnegie was the first female member of the New York Yacht

Club), and more than $200,000 for "household" and "personal expenses," in addition to $85,000 in "allowances" for Lucy's children.[71]

Family tradition remembers the estate as "a feudal fiefdom . . . self-sufficient in almost every respect" and "able to support itself with a minimum of outside help."[72] The manager of the estate did raise some crops, kept dairy cattle, and consulted from time to time with specialists from the Georgia Agricultural Experiment Station about ways to increase food production on the island. The correspondence of one such specialist, C. L. Goodrich, offers a perspective on the Carnegies somewhat different from family tradition. He described the estate in 1911 as "a winter resort and play ground." The new mansion had about one hundred rooms, and each of the six sons had a "cottage" of his own with thirty to forty rooms. There were, in addition, "stables, gardens, tennis courts, spacious lawns, etc." The children, Goodrich said, "have all been taught by tutors or governesses. None of the children are college graduates. Only one son was prevailed upon by his tutor, the present manager of the place, to prepare for Columbia College, which he did and entered, but remained only one year. The family spend their time hunting, fishing, golfing [on their own nine-hole course], playing tennis, boating and traveling, and have not the patience to settle down and study the business." Goodrich conceded that the family had made "an endeavor to find some means of making the plantation productive without effort or labor," with "sporadic attempts" to raise cattle or hogs. "When these cattle congregated on the roadways and interfered with driving and automobiling the business was abandoned with impatience and disgust, the entire herd being sold off the island." The best Goodrich could do by way of advice — obviously he was annoyed at devoting his good time to people he considered pretentious and utterly frivolous — was to suggest ways of raising forage to feed hogs, provided the latter could be kept off the roadways.[73]

Sapelo and Jekyll Islands also passed into the hands of rich northerners. The Scottish-American Mortgage Company took over the old Spalding plantation land on Sapelo and sold it to a group of businessmen from Macon, Georgia, who planned a game preserve for the "benefit, pleasure and use of its members" while keeping an eye on "pecuniary gain and profit." They began to restore the old mansion and clear the land, sinking thousands of dollars into improvements. In 1912 they realized their hopes for "pecuniary gain" by selling their five thousand acres for $45,000, with a two-year profit of $26,289 after all expenses. The buyer was Detroit industrialist Howard Coffin, an engineer by training who had made a huge fortune as an auto manufacturing entrepreneur. Coffin, like Lucy Carnegie, had fallen in love with the area, and like her he was determined to have an island to himself. Eventually he would own virtually all of Sapelo.[74]

Coffin left a more permanent mark on the coast than most other wealthy visitors, but the men who bought Jekyll Island were the most famous of all the contemporary capitalists who came to the Sea Islands. In the early 1880s, John Eugene du Bignon, scion of an antebellum Sea Island planter, spent $8,000 in a series of purchases on Jekyll that united his own family property with large tracts that had been sold to northern would-be planters. With the help of his brother-in-law, Newton Finney, du Bignon then resold the island for $125,000 to a group of Yankees who planned a superexclusive club and resort. The new owners were wealthy financiers and businessmen from New York and Chicago who recruited as owner-members of the club an array of the most famous names in late-nineteenth-century capitalism — J. P. Morgan, William Rockefeller, Vincent Astor, Joseph Pulitzer, and William K. Vanderbilt among them. With few exceptions the members represented both the cream of "society" and the peak of wealth. Du Bignon himself was the only founding member from the South. These men and their families came down each winter in their yachts or private rail cars to hunt, play tennis and golf, or just relax. In a 1910 meeting at the club that later became notorious among conservative midwesterners, Senator Nelson Aldrich and several bankers drew up the outline of what would later become the Federal Reserve System.[75]

Ultimately most of the Sea Islands and many of the old rice plantations were purchased by wealthy northerners. Tybee Island and St. Simons alone among the major islands stayed out of the hands of the rich. Tybee, previously thought to be dangerously unhealthy, was transformed by a rail line completed in 1887 that made it easy to visit from Savannah. It was soon built up with summer cottages and resort hotels for the middle class. One member of the Dodge lumber family moved to St. Simons and rebuilt the ruined church at Frederica. The island's big lumber operations made it both more accessible to ordinary people and perhaps less attractive to wealthy vacationers. Steamers carried visitors to hotels on St. Simons by the 1880s, and Brunswick's businessmen recognized that the coast and the island might attract the kind of middle-class tourists already coming south to Florida for winter vacations. In 1888 a new hotel opened on St. Simons and another, the Oglethorpe, was built "in Brunswick, for Brunswick, and by Brunswick," with crystal chandeliers and carpeting sent all the way from Atlanta. The

Brunswick Street Railway extended a track over a causeway to St. Simons for its mule-drawn wagons. The Methodist Church built a retreat there, "Epworth by Sea," and an Atlanta real estate developer opened "St. Simon's Clubs for Rest and Recreation," promising that any family who purchased the rights to the use of a bedroom in the club would enjoy "every advantage enjoyed by the millionaires on Jekyl [sic] Island," including the important advantage of keeping out "any undesirables" who might try "to force themselves" into membership. The "neighborhood life" and "privacy" of the club allowed families to enjoy "all the benefits and none of the objections to seashore hotel life."[76]

Through all this time, much of the rural African American population was little affected by the new economic developments. In Camden County in 1910, 50 percent of all black family heads were farmers, and most of those farmers still owned their land. They grew corn and garden crops, and they supplemented their incomes, as they had for a generation, with part-time labor on the docks or in the turpentine camps. In that year, about the same number (46 percent) of black family heads in the county were laborers. Without land, they depended more completely on work in the forests or seafood industries. Some worked for the rich northerners who moved in each season, including more than two dozen who worked on the Carnegie estate on Cumberland Island. On other islands, in such small settlements as Hog Hammock on Sapelo and Harrington on St. Simons, cut off from the mainland by the swamps and the sea, lived perhaps the most isolated of African Americans on the coast, controlling their small plots of land, growing their food, catching fish, and making their own way.[77]

The Geography of Wealth in Deep South Regions

The structure of property ownership in the Delta, Piedmont, and coastal regions reflected the nature of the economy of each region as it had evolved in the half century following the war. Patterns of land distribution can be reconstructed from the tax digests of each area, those of Georgia being especially useful because they record the race of each taxpayer and include all taxable property in a single set of returns. These records show the stark difference between the coast and the Piedmont. In Camden County on the coast, land ownership among African Americans was widespread, continuing a trend that developed well before the end of Reconstruction. On the 1910 rolls the tax assessor listed 1,315 African Americans: all men aged twenty-one or

Frances Butler Leigh
worked to revive her
father's rice plantation
on the Georgia coast
after the war.

James Monroe Smith of Oglethorpe
County built up Georgia's largest cotton
plantation by exploiting convict labor.
(Courtesy of Georgia Department of
Archives and History)

LeRoy Percy, lawyer, planter, and
politician in the Mississippi-Yazoo Delta.
(Courtesy of Mississippi Department of
Archives and History)

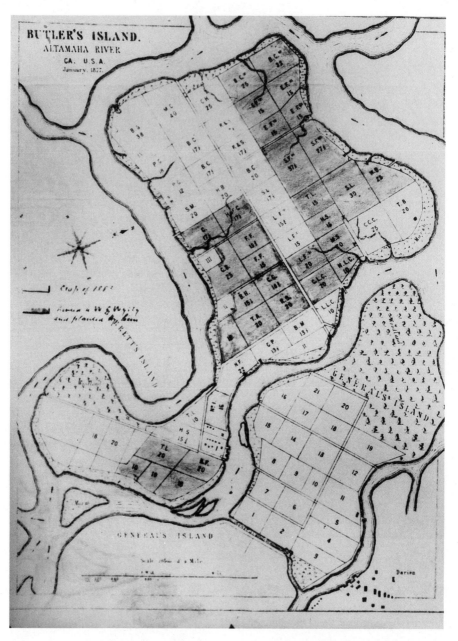

Rice plantations, such as Frances Leigh's Butler's Island, had to be operated as a single unit because of the extensive dikes and ditches necessary to control water flow.

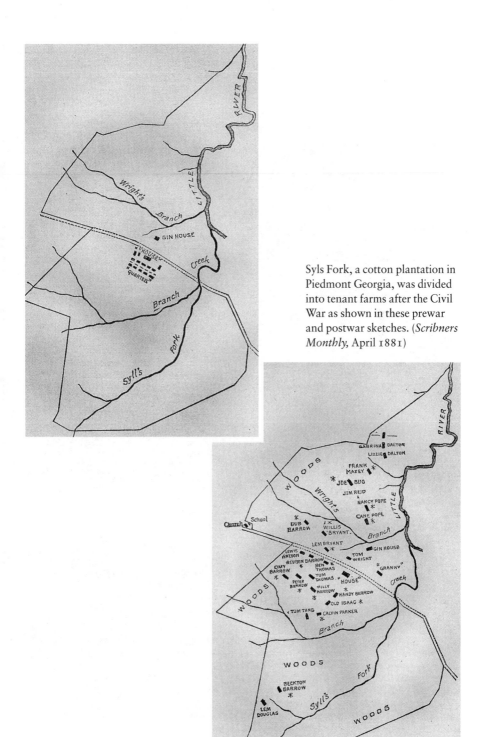

Syls Fork, a cotton plantation in Piedmont Georgia, was divided into tenant farms after the Civil War as shown in these prewar and postwar sketches. (*Scribners Monthly*, April 1881)

African Americans tending to rice fields after the Civil War. (*Harper's Weekly*, 5 January 1867)

Picking season was the highest point of labor demand on cotton plantations. (*Scribners Monthly*, August 1874)

Many African American migrants headed west after the Civil War in search of higher wages. (*Scribners Monthly*, September 1874)

Frequent flooding limited Delta plantations to high ground along the rivers before the leve

...stem was built. (*Scribners Monthly*, July 1881)

The Delta's interior wilderness was famous for bear hunting before it was drained and cleared. (*Scribners Monthly*, October 1881)

Tom Watson was the leader of the Populist Party in the Georgia Piedmont and the candidate for vice president on the party's ticket in 1896. (Courtesy of the Southern Historical Collection, Wilson Library, University of North Carolina at Chapel Hill)

This cartoon in Tom Watson's newspaper shows northern and southern Civil War veterans uniting to bury the past and campaign for reform. (*People's Party Paper*, 25 February 1892)

Women were an essential part of the postwar African American work force. Here women plant rice seed on Hofwyl, one of the last of Georgia's functioning rice plantations. (Courtesy of Georgia Department of Archives and History)

These women are taking produce to market in Augusta, Georgia. (Robert E. Williams Photographic Collection, Hargrett Rare Book and Manuscript Library, University of Georgia Libraries)

Women on the coast still pounded rice for home use in traditional mortars in the early twentieth century. (Courtesy of Georgia Department of Archives and History)

Thomas Carnegie bought most of Cumberland Island, Georgia, and built this mansion, called Dungeness, in the 1880s. (Courtesy of Georgia Department of Archives and History)

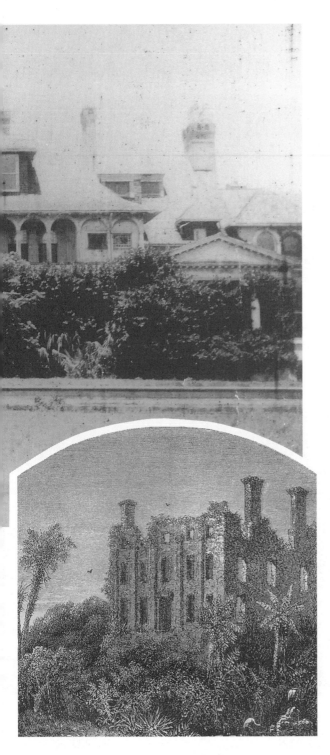

This engraving of the ruins of the original Dungeness on Cumberland Island helped to spark interest in the region among northern tourists. (*Harper's New Monthly Magazine*, November 1878)

Lucy Laney built the Haines Institute in Augusta, which provided a rigorous high school education for African American children. She also helped to found the Augusta branch of the NAACP. (Courtesy of Georgia Department of Archives and History)

Mrs. Mary Harris Armor was active in the Woman's Christian Temperance Union in Greensboro, Georgia, in the early twentieth century. (Courtesy of Georgia Department of Archives and History)

Progressive reformers in both Georgia and Mississippi abolished convict leasing, only to put convicts to work on roads or state-owned properties. (1941 photo by Jack Delano in Oglethorpe County, Georgia, for the Farm Security Administration; courtesy of Library of Congress)

over, plus all women who owned agricultural or town land. Well over half of these African American men and women owned land. Indeed, black tax-payers were more likely to own land than whites; only 42 percent of whites were landowners.[78]

The sizes of these landholdings show clearly the utter destruction of the old plantation regime. In 1878, at the end of Reconstruction, about one in eight white taxpayers owned at least five hundred acres, and the average size of a holding was 586 acres. By 1910 the average white holding had fallen to just 41 acres, and only one white taxpayer in a hundred owned more than five hundred acres. The biggest landowner in the county was Lucy Carnegie, assessed for three thousand acres of her Cumberland Island estate.[79] The average size of black landholdings had also fallen, from fifty-four acres in 1878 to just fifteen acres in 1910, primarily because there were no longer any truly large black landowners; nevertheless, in the same period landownership among African Americans had increased from 40 to 55 percent of all tax-payers. Landowning, however, was not equivalent to farming, since many of these plots were too small to be true farms. The tax assessor found 723 black landowners, but the census counted only 541 black farms (seven-eighths operated by owners). Other black families' land might provide a measure of food, grown in gardens or small cornfields, but these were not "farms" in the census definition, because they did not produce crops for the market. These families supplemented their income with work in the lumber and turpentine camps or on the docks; by fishing; or by day labor on the estates of Lucy Carnegie and other wealthy outsiders. By the 1910 census, black household heads in the county were almost as likely to be listed as laborers as they were farmers.[80]

The structure of property holdings was quite different in Greene County, in the Piedmont, where about the same proportion of white taxpayers owned land as in coastal Camden (42 percent), but where they were much more likely to own true plantations. Forty whites, four of them women, owned more than a thousand acres, and another sixty-three whites owned at least five hundred acres in Greene County. These one hundred or so landowners controlled more than half of all the farm acreage in the county. A few — Edgar and Luther Boswell, or the Kimbro brothers, for example — were mer-chants who may have accumulated land as part of their supply business, perhaps foreclosing on customers from time to time. Other businesses, like the Union Point Improvement Company, Fleetwood Gin and Lumber, or the Griffith Implement Company, also owned large acreages, but most of the big owners were individual planters. Many white extended families included both planters and merchants — there were five Boswell planters who were not merchants. Some planters, including Luther Jackson, the biggest in the county with 4,625 acres, had invested heavily in such commercial enterprises as the Mary-Leila cotton mill.[81]

These plantations were based on tenant labor provided by about 500 white and 1,700 black tenants and their families, and by 1910 there were more white tenant farmers than white farmer-owners in the county. More than 90 percent of blacks on the tax rolls owned no agricultural land at all, and 92 percent of all black farmers reported in the census were tenants. The small percentage of black landowners in Greene presents a stark contrast to Camden County, where landowning was widespread.[82] Greene County's African Americans were more likely to be truly poor than the black petty landholders of the coast. The average total value of assessed wealth per capita among blacks there was about half that in Camden County. But, in Greene's commercial cotton economy, while a black farmer found it difficult to move into the ranks of landowners, once there he had a better chance of accumulating wealth than he would have along the coast. Greene's African American farmers owned bigger and more valuable farms, on average five times the size of Camden's small black farms. Greene had thirty-six black taxpayers worth more than $1,000, Camden seven; Greene had eleven with more than $1,500, Camden only one. Greene's black population owned more town property, enumerated in value rather than acreage, and in total, Greene's African Americans owned more taxable property than did Camden's.

Sunflower County in the Delta was by 1910 a plantation county par excellence. Its farmers, including more than five thousand tenants, raised, in 1909, almost thirty-seven thousand bales of cotton on more than ninety-one thousand acres. In the entire county only 270 whites and 191 blacks owned the farms they operated. Landownership in Sunflower was, nonetheless, distributed far more widely than one might expect based on the number of farmer-owners alone. While the census takers counted 461 owner-operators, over 1,700 individual and married-couple landowners appear on the tax rolls as owners of cleared land. (The Mississippi land tax rolls do not identify taxpayers by race.)[83] Hundreds of owners were therefore either leasing their plots to large operators, renting them out to tenants, or operating them with sharecroppers. Johanna Reiser, the absentee New York plantation owner, was doing this in Washington County. Widows and other heirs held land as a primary source of income, and local or distant investors bought land, hoping to cash in on the early-twentieth-century price boom. Big operators — like LeRoy Percy in Washington County or Sunflower's Will Dockery — assembled plantations by adding such leased properties to their own extensive holdings. With good land so expensive, others worked in partnerships to assemble the necessary capital. Altogether, about one in eleven cleared acres was held by a partnership of some kind. Land speculation was evident also in the holdings of uncleared lands by many companies and partnerships. Fourteen of these owned some sixteen thousand acres of land in the county in 1910.[84]

For most African Americans the first step toward a measure of independence was the ownership of a mule or two. About a quarter of Sunflower's black taxpayers owned mules, which meant that they could move from share-cropping to genuine tenant farming. With hard work and luck — a good marriage, no crippling illnesses or accidents, no encounters with whites out to teach them a lesson or with landlords determined to cheat them out of their property — they might save or borrow enough to buy some land. One possibility was buying cheap uncleared land and slowly clearing it — as Lou Conklin, who owned two mules and eight uncleared acres in 1910, hoped to do. But even if they overcame all the other obstacles to farming success, the rising value of the Delta's land made it increasingly difficult for black farmers to progress to ownership. Just 4 percent of Sunflower's black family heads were farm owners in 1910. These Delta farmers usually owned small plots. Allen Archer owned fifty acres of cleared land, Lou Archer (a relative?), thirty acres; Burt Burton, twenty-five acres; John Clark, twelve acres. Rare indeed were African Americans like B. F. Holmes, who had accumulated a hundred acres, five mules, and personal property assessed at almost $500. For most black farmers, the draining of water from the central Delta's swampy acres had also drained them of the promise of prosperity and independence.[85]

5

Culture, Race, and Class in the Segregation Era

WAYNE COX ARRIVED IN THE DELTA IN THE LATE NINETEENTH century as a poor man and became a rich one. He taught school, saved his money, moved on to become a postal clerk, began to buy land when it was still undeveloped and cheap, and by the turn of the century had moved with his wife Minnie, a former teacher herself, into a fine house in one of the best neighborhoods in Indianola. His story duplicated that of many of Indianola's leading families, with one exception: the Coxes were African American. Cox had been able to pull off the difficult task of making and keeping his fortune, which required constant dealings with white businessmen, through a combination of sharp business acumen and a "humble and polite," but never servile, demeanor, so that whites always felt that he "knew his place." Active in the Republican Party, the Coxes also benefited from political patronage; Minnie served as a postmistress in the town under several Republican presidents.[1]

No one ever questioned Mrs. Cox's competence or efficiency, but neither that nor the high esteem in which her husband was held "by the bankers and business men (white) of that place," saved her job when, in 1902, local whites asked President Theodore Roosevelt to replace her with a white man. Suddenly, Minnie Cox had come to represent a threat of "nigger domination." Whites insisted that an African American postmaster was a "menace to civilization" and an incitement to young black men to rape white women.

They were supported by James K. Vardaman, then campaigning for governor, who chided Indianola's whites for "tolerating a negro wench as postmaster." When Roosevelt refused to replace her, politicians all over the state denounced him, with Indianola's newspaper insisting that continuing Cox as postmistress was tantamount to asking the people of the town "to virtually acknowledge that the negroes are as good as the whites. . . . It is equivalent to saying that it is a heinous crime to oppose negro equality or domination." That Cox was of good character and had served well for six years was irrelevant: "Upon the same principle, all the offices might as well be filled by negroes, and if it is proper that they should rule over us as superiors, they certainly ought to be recognized as social equals." Roosevelt refused to bow to this pressure, but after a mass meeting of whites in the town voted in favor of a resolution ordering Minnie Cox to leave her office by 1 January 1903, she resigned and she and her husband temporarily fled the town. Roosevelt responded by closing the office down rather than appoint a white replacement. In the long run, the incident ironically opened up new opportunities for Wayne and Minnie Cox themselves. Returning to Indianola after the post office controversy subsided, they were instrumental in founding the Delta Penny Savings Bank and the Mississippi Beneficial Insurance Company. The Coxes appealed to black pride and white hostility in selling insurance to their African American customers, succeeding so well that the Cox family was still the richest black family in the area three decades later.[2]

Rising white hostility and new segregation laws more and more separated people like the Coxes from their white fellow townsmen and helped to obscure how much most blacks and whites shared in Georgia and Mississippi — a climate, a landscape, the annual cycle of the cotton plant, and Sunday mornings in Baptist churches. It also obscured how much the lives of both whites and blacks were shaped by local geography, local history, and the powerful effects of class differences among both whites and blacks. Life for African Americans could be very different, depending on whether they sharecropped on a big plantation in Mississippi, taught high school in a city such as Augusta, or owned a small farm on the coast of Georgia. A small but growing number of better-off African Americans like the Coxes had aspirations and styles of life much in common with whites of the same class in the cities and towns, while poor white sharecroppers in the countryside suffered the same hunger and economic frustrations of the mass of blacks in similar circumstances.

Women, Men, and Families on the Farm

For those at the lowest end of the income scale in the rural South, most of them black, life was hard and sometimes brutish and short. The poorest tenants might not even be permitted a garden, and unless they could supplement their incomes with extra labor, their diets were mostly corn and fatty meat. A detailed study of the diets of tenant farmers in the Delta in the 1920s found that nearly three-fifths of families fell below the daily requirements for protein, and more fell short for calcium, phosphorous, and iron. Dietary diseases like pellagra (caused by a lack of vitamin B) were rampant. Infant mortality was high. The typical black woman over forty-five in Sunflower County in 1910 had born seven or eight children, but, on average, only four or five of them were still alive that year.[3]

Labor on a small farm, white or black, involved the whole family. For both blacks and whites, men were seen as "heads" of the family. Men made the most important decisions about what and when to plant and did most of the plowing and other heavy labor. According to Frances Leigh, on the rice coast in the 1870s "the good old law of female submission to the husband's will on all points held good." One woman on her plantation had been expelled from her church because she "refused to obey her husband in a small matter"; she was allowed to return only after a public apology. A black woman who helped raise a family in the Delta told an interviewer, "God intend man to be the head of the family and leader in the community"; according to another, "In order for the community to survive, the men had to be the ones out in front if the family was to be strong." But the labor of women and children was essential to the success of the farm — so essential, indeed, that a man without a wife could seldom expect to rent a farm on his own. If the man was the "head" of the family and community, woman was, as another Delta woman put it, the "backbone out there. . . . Nearly everything was left for them to do and they did it all, from having babies to raising chickens, to running the house and church, and to planting the garden, gathering the crop, and everything else necessary to keep the family together." Whenever they had sufficient land, women planted and maintained large gardens that supplied most of the fresh vegetables — onions, tomatoes, beets, turnips, carrots, cabbage, peas, watermelons — for the family table. They cooked three meals a day, starting sometimes before sunrise, on a wood-burning stove if they could afford one, over an open fireplace if not. They used the ashes to make lye, then made soap from the lye. They hand washed garments in kettles of hot water, then scrubbed them over washboards—carrying the water in from wells or springs. On the Atlantic coast, women pounded rice with big mortars and pestles and fanned the pounded rice to separate the chaff. They sewed clothes and curtains, cleaned house, and took care of the children. In addition, they worked in the fields during much of the year, chopping cotton in spring and summer, and picking it in the fall, since one man could plant more cotton than he could pick. Many women supplemented the family's income by selling chickens, eggs, or vegetables.[4]

In the hard world of the southern farm, communal and shared labor made some tasks easier and more interesting. Ruby Hicks, who was white, remembered white and black families in the Delta getting together for hog-killing. When the weather turned cold, the hogs were killed, scalded in big washpans of boiling water, and cut into hams, shoulders, and bacon to be salted away in family meat boxes. Families wealthy enough to have a smoke-house would cure the meat with the smoke from wet hickory logs. But most communal work was segregated by race, and some tasks were also segregated by gender. African American women quilted together "while the men was in the kitchen talking about farming and business, and the children was outside playing." For Frances Walker, quilting was "long and boring" and "hurt the fingers," but quilting with a group of neighbors "slowed us down and gave us time to collect ourselves."[5]

Births and illnesses were met with a community response. Carrie Gordon, an African American midwife in the Delta—people in her neighborhood called her "mother of all the children"—described the expectation of a new life as "exciting to the whole community. . . . Some women were good at talking the mama through the pain. Some would be standing by heating water, preparing towel and cloth, while others stood by praying. It was always good to have that kind of support so that the mama and her family could see that they didn't have to go through these thing alone." Ruby Hicks recalled that "doctors were few; nurses, as such, were virtually unknown; and hospitals simply did not exist in the Delta of my day." Neighboring women filled the void by "taking turns in caring for victims of malaria, typhoid, and undiagnosed chills and fevers." Estella Thomas, an African American from the Delta, explained that "women visit[ed] people houses and if they was sick, we found a way to get them some medicine or sometime everybody pitch in together to take a sick person to the doctor or have a doctor come out to the farm."[6]

The sharecropping and small-farm economy promoted early marriage and many children. Of married women in 1910, half of both blacks and whites had married by the time they were twenty; a fourth had married before they were seventeen. Farm women younger than forty typically had infants to feed and toddlers to keep track of as they did their heavy chores. "As soon as you wean one from you, there was no rest, 'cause, before you knew it, you was pregnant again, so the children kept coming for me and everybody else out here." By the time they were five or six years old, children shared in important chores; by age ten they were out in the fields picking cotton every fall. "Most people out here" in the Delta, one woman explained, "struggle during the early years, and need the help of children and other family members to survive." In the resulting regime of what demographers call "natural fertility," women with normal fertility bore children every two or three years. In the Delta, the Piedmont, and the Georgia coast, rural black women bore on average seven or eight children. White women had fewer children, but in the Piedmont, where white families, like black families, were likely to be small-farm tenants, they too bore many children.[7]

Most rural black and white southerners were enmeshed in a wider world of kinship that went beyond the boundaries of the nuclear family of parents and children. Often nearby were grandparents, uncles, aunts, and cousins who shared work, visited, and took in children when parents were sick or had died. For black families especially, "kin" was a flexible term encompassing neighbors and friends as well as blood relatives. "There was sisters and brothers all over," is the way one woman described it. Many black and white households included in-laws, cousins, or other relatives.[8]

The economic realities of small-farm life rubbed up against the Victorian family ideals that dominated popular culture, with the father as head and provider and the mother confined to domestic roles. The families of planters and well-to-do farmers drew on cheap domestic labor to put these ideals into practice. Servants cooked their food and cleaned their houses, and hired workers plowed and weeded their family gardens. Washerwomen did the laundry. Wives in these families could focus, as the Victorian ideal would have it, on raising virtuous children, providing gracious homes for their husbands, serving as hostesses for dinners and parties, supervising servants. This was the classic role of the southern "lady" — a wife and mother, an ornament, a symbol of purity; her marriage was her career. Some no doubt accepted and even enjoyed this elevated status, but for many it was stifling and frustrating, especially when husbands were abusive or philanderers or insensitive autocrats like P. L. Mann, a wealthy Glen Allan, Mississippi, planter who insisted that he be served his meals every day promptly at 7:00 A.M., 12 noon, and 6:00 P.M., and that men and women appear in "proper" dress. Mrs. Mann slept in a trundle bed at the foot of her husband's bed.[9]

Middle-class women found it difficult to keep up proper Victorian middle-class standards in the lonely and often frontierlike conditions of rural areas like the Delta. Birdie Abbot Gearhart, the daughter of a Holmes County planter, lived near Itta Bena, Mississippi, where her husband managed a sawmill. Her brother, Nate, had inherited the family plantation. Even when Birdie had help from servants, the cooking, cleaning, and laundry took much time and energy. Birdie was enormously frustrated that Nate, and not she, had been given the use of the family plantation. To add insult to injury, her mother now compared her housekeeping unfavorably to that of Nate's wife, Myra. "I shall never forgive you," she wrote her mother in 1908. It was easy, she said, for Myra to keep house since she did not need to do any sewing and had "*no children* with forty needs at once." Birdie longed for a "modern" home with running water, electric lights, and gas, in a town where she could attend concerts and, especially, somewhere with "no *mosquitos* and *no fleas.*" For such reasons, many women preferred town life to farm life, even when they were freed from most physical labor.[10]

Even in long-settled areas, women in middling rural families had an arduous life. An example is Magnolia Wynn Le Guin, daughter of Dr. J. A. C. Wynn, a physician, farmer, and gristmill owner in the Georgia Piedmont, who lived with her parents, husband, and children in the Wynn family homestead. The diary she kept from 1901 to 1913 gives us a rare view of domestic life in a middle-class rural white family.[11]

Magnolia Le Guin's family was better off than most, with a substantial house, land, and a business. Still, though she had a subscription to *Ladies Home Journal* and, later, a telephone, Magnolia wrote that she did not "crave very expensive things often, because I guess that I know I am not able to have them." When she was visited by wealthier, and more refined, women such as the elegant Mrs. Leola Brown, or Mrs. Horton, who was dressed "in height of fashion — like a beautiful doll," she felt "discouraged or down-hearted concerning my own surroundings." She herself was, by contrast, "a plain hardworking home-concealed woman." Her family duties required almost constant domestic labor. She spent most of every day "ironing, sewing, sweeping, cooking." Though she felt she and her husband, Ghu, had been "richly blessed" with a large family, she admitted that "raising children, working and nursing them is a Herculean task," as she put it. "I *never* catch up with my work and I work all the time someway." Three weeks after her fourth son, Charles Ralph, was born, she lamented the "suffering [and] . . . inexpressible weary, times I've had day and night" since the birth. Two years later came her first daughter, Mary, a "sunbeam" who became the "liveliest, jolliest baby I ever saw," but was also "one of the most nervous, wide-awake babies I ever saw. She worries me to prostration almost every day . . . She allows me no past-time."[12]

Managing such a large household was made more difficult by Magnolia's poor health. For years she had severe headaches; she had to have all her upper teeth pulled before she was thirty-five, and it was two years before she could afford to replace them with false teeth. At the birth of her first child she had suffered a serious back injury — one she blamed on her doctor — and was in pain for much of the rest of her life. When her sixth child was due, she wrote, "The torture [will be] so great I shrink with all my nature from the trying ordeal." When she became pregnant again less than two years after Maggie's birth, she called it a "calamity." The nausea was "so bad! so bad no words can picture my sufferings." At forty-one, she became pregnant for what would prove to be the last time. Again she feared the "dreadful unexpressible suffering that will be my lot to bear." As the due date approached she was "downhearted because of the undescribable physical suffering before me"; yet, she wrote on that same day, "Life is sweeter to me it seems, than ever before. I seem to love my children better and life is richer, more sweet than ever before."[13]

Her domestic labors seldom allowed Magnolia to indulge her simple pleasures of reading, walking in the woods, or talking on the telephone. "How I would love to take a stroll on creak or in woods with my children!" she wrote in 1905, "But work! work! all indoors, except when I'm brushing yards." Even visits from family and friends, a major form of rural sociability that brought her pleasure, added to her work load. After one Sunday with "plentiful" company, she broke down in tears while telling Ghu "how I suffer from daily (almost) cooking for company . . . while I love congenial company, yet *this is like a hotel here.*" She was acutely conscious of failing to keep up her own high middle-class standards to maintain a "clean home, clean premises — good meals, tidy clean children and myself to be so."[14]

The Le Guin family could afford domestic help, although not as consistently as Magnolia would have liked. Over a ten-year period she hired more than a dozen women to help with cleaning, cooking, and nursing. For more than two years she depended on "Aunt Mary," who lived in the household and "relieves me of dishwashing and lots of other steps." Aunt Mary gave small presents to the children and they were "rite fond" of her. Mary and her husband, Monk, both became seriously ill in 1905 and had to leave—" 'twas an unusually sad sight to see two helpless ones carried away in a vehicle." Some servants were scarcely more than children themselves. Fannie, a young teenager, was a "good nurse" and "so much help in many other ways." She worked for a short time after the birth of Magnolia's daughter Maggie in 1906, and was paid $1.40 in advance to buy tobacco and shoes as she was "nearly barefoot." The next year Ada, who was fourteen and a "nice good hand," helped with making beds, washing dishes, and sweeping floors. One of the best of the hired help was Susan Tarpley, an African American woman, very good in the kitchen, but commanding such high wages that Magnolia could not afford her on a regular basis.[15]

By her own lights, Magnolia Le Guin was a good employer who paid well and treated "darkies" with kindness. She nursed Aunt Mary in her illness and brought food and buttermilk to George Griscom, "an old sick negro" in the neighborhood. When a black farmer helped her repair a wagon wheel she wrote that she "felt very grateful for his kindness." Still, her kindness and gratitude remained well within the bounds of southern white racial mores, and were extended only to African Americans who remained firmly in their place. When Dola Tarpley was "a little sassy," Magnolia "slapped her a few times for her wrong doings." When adult African American men and women were not submissive, she became vexed and cross. When Mandy Stewart refused to sweep and iron the day before Thanksgiving, Magnolia was "unsettled, and *nettled,*" prompting her to ask the Lord in her diary to "calm my spirit" and help her to "preserve me gentle in my commands when darkies are insolent." She was shocked when another tenant, Millie High, became "enraged *with me* because I wouldn't let her talk 'sas.' " In 1906, she wrote that she had felt very unpleasant all day because she had had "to reprove a grown negro boy about drinking out of the dipper. . . . Oh, how excited I become over any impudence from darkies." When her twelve-year-old son Askew took his first trip away from home, she learned from his first postcard that "the first thing he did after arriving in Barnesv. was to knock a little negro down; the little negro asked him if he was a *white* boy." Magnolia confessed to herself that "Askew is tolerably dark and there are *white* negroes in cities," but she assumed that "the negro said it with impudence, or at least Askew thought so." "Askew can't bear 'sass' from negroes—neither can I and my Father would not, and did not, bear it. He would do as Askew did first—

'Knock a negro down.' " Magnolia and her husband thought the episode was quite funny and "laughed heartily."[16]

Magnolia occasionally expressed empathy for sick or friendly African Americans, but it apparently never occurred to her that black men and women wanted — as they sometimes demanded — to be treated with respect. Her diary does not suggest that she could imagine that the women who worked in her home might be trying, as she was, to make their homes tidy and pleasant, or that they regretted, as she did, that they had no time to stroll in the woods or play with their children. She was obviously a committed Christian, a devoted daughter, wife, and mother, one who loved her own father in part because he was "bitterly opposed" to whipping his young grandchildren, but none of this affected her perspective on "darkies." It was a measure of the depths of the racism in the heart of rural white culture.[17]

Black and White Families

In most of the ways that can be easily measured, black families and white families were alike. Men married in their mid-twenties, women at around twenty. The average white married couple in 1910 in the Delta, Piedmont, and Sea Island regions had been married about fifteen years, the average black couple, about thirteen years. Rural women bore many children. In the typical black as well as white family, a husband and wife lived with their children — or, from the reverse perspective, the overwhelming majority of children were growing up with parents and step-parents. In part these similarities derived from similar values about family life, and in part from the economic needs of a family farm, which depended on the labor of children.[18]

Death took a heavy toll on family life for both whites and blacks, but especially blacks, most of whom lived in poverty and out of reach of good medical care. Infant mortality was high. The average white woman past childbearing age had seen a child die; the average black woman had seen two or three children die. In the unhealthy Mississippi Delta, the toll was highest of all. The greater mortality among African Americans is one main explanation for the differences between white and black families that are evident in the census statistics. Black families were more likely to be headed by a woman without a husband present. Black children were more likely to be growing up with grandparents or other relatives, rather than with their parents. Black wives and husbands were more likely to be in a second or third marriage.[19]

As a number of recent studies by historians and demographers have indicated, higher mortality alone probably does not explain all the differences between black and white families. The opportunity to earn an income, even a low income, probably gave black women somewhat more independence than white women, and their potential earning power enabled them to support themselves and their children. It is not only that African American women's work was essential to most black families' survival, but also that much of the work of black women was what southerners called "public" work. In addition to laboring on their own family farms and in their own households, they were often paid members of the labor force: laborers in the field, domestics, laundrywomen. In the Piedmont's Greene County in 1910, half of black married women were in the labor force, but just one in fourteen married white women. In Sunflower County, in the Delta, seven out of eight black married women were employed, but just one in fourteen white married women. Hortense Powdermaker, a white anthropologist who interviewed many black women in Indianola in Sunflower County in the 1930s, wrote that the black woman was frequently the chief source of family income and often "head of the house in importance and authority." (She went too far in calling this a "matriarchal" family arrangement.)[20]

One consequence was that black women could support themselves and their children, and this may have made them more willing to leave unhappy marriages. Powdermaker recorded examples of African American marriages cut short by infidelity, or physical abuse, or the husband's unwillingness to work. A young teacher left her husband because he was "mean" to her and refused to work. The wife of a Sunflower farmer left her husband after many happy years because of his affair with someone on a nearby plantation; she "didn't want to work in the fields and keep the household going and him with another woman." The wife moved to town and found a job as a cook and chose to stay single, as she "wasn't going to support any man." Both Powdermaker and John Dollard, another researcher who lived in Indianola in the 1930s, believed that such marital conflict was more common among lower-class blacks than among whites or middle-class blacks, but since neither interviewed poor whites or learned much about poor white families, their evidence is unclear. Other historians have found considerable evidence of difficult, sometimes violent, marriages among southern whites.[21]

It seems to be true, however, that black women were more willing to leave such marriages than were white women, in part because they could support themselves without stigma. Early in the century, attorney Walter Sillers of

Clarksdale, Mississippi, took African American divorce cases often enough
to be able to cite a standard price for an "ordinary negro divorce" of $50 plus
court costs. Because even $50 was a large sum for a poor man or woman, in
most cases marriages ended less formally, when one or the other partner
simply left.[22] Elite whites often pointed to the incidence of family breakup
among blacks as evidence of black inferiority. They similarly pointed to a
more liberal attitude toward sexuality among blacks as evidence of moral
inferiority. What they really meant was that blacks showed less of a double
standard of sexual morality than whites, because black women, like white
men, could have sexual relationships or even bear children out of wedlock
without being ostracized by the community. Although one black woman
from the Delta told an interviewer that "sex outside of marriage was immoral
and unwed pregnancies were a source of shame," other sources describe considerable tolerance for sexual relationships before marriage among young
blacks. When Frances Butler Leigh took over her father's plantations during
Reconstruction, she noticed that for "a girl to have a child before she was
married" was not a reason for condemnation, though, she said, after marriage the freedmen were "severe upon anything like infidelity." Powdermaker
interviewed a number of women in Indianola who had children before marriage, and she believed that, among lower-class blacks, virginity was not
especially prized.[23] A black woman interviewed by Powdermaker in Indianola illustrates this point. Born about 1860, she had children by two different men as a teenager, one with a married man and one with a single man
she did not want to marry. She then married and stayed with her husband for
fifteen years until he died; after three years as a widow she married for a
second time, and this marriage also lasted fifteen years until the husband's
death. "Both her husbands were good men, she says, and treated her right,
and provided food and clothes, although she worked also."[24]

This woman's story illustrates the very important point that sexual activity or childbearing by unmarried women was not at all incompatible with
the belief, shared by both blacks and whites, that the ideal marriage should
be permanent and based on mutual support and fidelity. This is why the
statistical evidence points to fundamental similarities in family structure. The
point must be emphasized because whites, in rationalizing white supremacy,
sometimes argued that differences between black and white family structures
and customs showed that African Americans scarcely had a family life at all.
A Georgia woman writing in 1899 in the magazine *Independent* claimed that
blacks in the South lived in a "cesspool of vice." Another contributor to

the same magazine in 1902 wrote, "I sometimes hear of a virtuous Negro woman, but the idea is absolutely inconceivable to me. . . . I cannot imagine such a creature as a virtuous Negro woman." A white academic wrote in 1903 that among blacks "many matings are consummated without any regular marriage ceremony and with little reference to legal requirements, and divorces are equally informal. . . . The result of it all is that many Negroes do not know their own fathers and so little are the ties of kinship regarded that near relatives are often unknown, and if possible less cared for." To him this was evidence of the "primitive" mental condition of blacks, which had left them "far behind us" — that is, whites — in civilization. In fact, black families were even more likely than white families to take in brothers, sisters, aunts, and other relatives. White observers also preferred to ignore the widespread evidence that many married white men carried on sexual affairs or visited prostitutes, with little stigma. In the Delta, Clarksdale, Greenville, and Indianola were among the towns with African American houses of prostitution catering to white men, and the son of a prominent Greenville man noted that his father was exceptional among his class in that he did not keep a black mistress.[25]

White beliefs about black women not only bolstered white supremacy but also rationalized white men's sexual abuse and exploitation of black women. Black women who worked in white homes were especially vulnerable to such abuse. Writing anonymously in 1912, a "Negro Nurse" from Georgia described her thirty years of domestic service as "as bad as, if not worse than, it was during the days of slavery." In addition to long hours at low pay, she suffered the daily humiliations of segregation and disrespect: "No white person, not even the little children just learning to talk . . . ever thinks of addressing any negro man or woman as *Mr.,* or *Mrs.,* or *Miss.* The women are called, 'Cook,' or 'Nurse,' or 'Mammy,' or 'Mary Jane.'" Worst of all, "a colored woman's virtue in this part of the country has no protection." The author of the article lost her first job when her employer's husband "walked up to me, threw his arms around me, and was in the act of kissing me, when I demanded to know what he meant, and shoved him away. . . . [N]early all white men take undue liberties with their colored female servants — not only the fathers, but in many cases the sons also." One African American woman wrote that there was "no hardship I would not undergo rather than allow my daughters to go in service where they would be thrown constantly in contact with Southern white men, for they consider the colored girl their special prey."[26]

Most black women and men, like most white women and men, hoped for a marriage experience similar to that of Wesley Anthony, an aged African American resident of Washington, Georgia, who was interviewed in 1939. He had married Peggy Booker on Christmas Day in 1877. "I could have married lots more gals if I had wanted to," he told his interviewer, "kase I was black and nice lookin' and have been well brought up and knowed how to work and make a honest livin', but I loved Peggy and I have took good care of her since." Peggy and he were still married sixty-two years and fifteen children later. Now, he said, Peggy was paralyzed and "can't do nothin' to help herself, but she been good to me and took care of me and the children [and] now I takes care of her. I 'members the vows what I took there 'fore Preacher Fortson when he married us, and I 'tends to do all I can for her as long as she lives."[27]

Religion

In their religion, as in their family lives, blacks and whites shared much even while they differed in important ways. In most rural areas of the South the church was the most important community institution, and most people of both races were Baptist or Methodist. Small congregations were often in effect extended kinship groups, gathered around the leadership of a male preacher. Many church buildings were shared by several denominations (though always within racial lines). In Sunflower's Indian Bayou, white Methodists, Baptists, and Presbyterians shared a single building. In Benoit, in Bolivar County, the Community Church was shared among Presbyterian, Methodist, Baptist, and Christian congregations. Not only buildings were shared, but also ministers and services. Warsaw, Georgia, had two black churches but only one minister between them, and he preached twice a month outside the town. "Despite strong denominational preferences," Ruby Hicks recalled, "we regularly attended the service which was being held at the time, regardless of the denomination." In winter there might not be a church service at all: "In that land of muddy roads, unbanistered low bridges, and rough crosslays, there were not many church services held on winter nights. . . . [W]e frequently met in one home in the neighborhood and sang until nearly midnight."[28] Women might take a big pinch of snuff just before entering, while men tucked their tobacco wads in a safe place. According to one perhaps legendary story, Rev. Walter Campbell was heckled by timber workers in the Delta's Sunflower County. The next time he preached in the same place, "he walked up to the upturned barrel, which served as the pulpit in the shed where the meeting was held, laid a pistol down on each side of his Bible, and stated calmly, 'Now, boys, I'm going to preach you a sermon.' He wasn't heckled that time."[29]

Rural ministers — especially black ministers — were typically part-time — farmers six days a week and preachers on the seventh — and they were paid little. Their authority came not from special education or appointment but from experience and conviction. The Reverend Henry Cherry, an African American Baptist minister from Bolivar County in the Delta, had been a sharecropper (along with his mother) all his working life when, in his mid-twenties, as he described it, "The lightning struck me blind one day while I was lying up in the bed in the south side of my room. . . . I heard a voice say, 'Woe be unto you if you preach not the gospel.' " He called to his mother and told her, "Mama I have to go preach." And so preach he did, becoming officially ordained in 1931, supporting himself by farming on shares.[30] His church, like many others, was kept alive with tiny contributions saved from meager incomes. At services attendees were asked to contribute ten cents for the church and twenty-five cents for the pastor. One of the biggest events of rural life, for whites as well as blacks, was the summer "protracted meeting." People would camp out for days or weeks at a time, alternately singing hymns and listening to preaching day and night. Potential converts would be brought to the mourners' bench while the preachers warned them of the fires of hell and beseeched them to be saved "by the blood of Christ." Rev. Cherry remembered that the descriptions of "the fires of hell" were so dramatic — one depicted the devil himself using his fork to turn the sinners over in the coals — that "you could see it." One Sunflower County meeting, the Indianola newspaper editor complained, had become "protracted indeed. It has been going on Sundays and weekdays for two or three months and now still continues, much to the detriment of the crops. . . . We think [religion] elevates and refines, but when it is carried to such an extent, we believe it is contrary to the Good Book and the will of the Lord." But whites like Ruby Hicks also went to "protracted meetings" each summer, when "there always seemed to be a revival in progress."[31]

Blacks and whites both were predominantly evangelical in belief and practice. Both listened to the same kinds of messages from their pulpits about good and bad behavior — work hard, don't sin, don't lie or steal or drink. Both black and white churches mirrored the gendered structure of the family. Men were in control — they were the preachers and headed the Sunday

School boards, even though women filled most of the pews, raised most of the money, and did most of the work. According to one Delta African American woman interviewed in the 1980s, "Men have always occupy the most important leadership position within the church 'cause they was taught to believe that they could do a better job and that it was the men who was 'posed to run the church and not the women 'cause they was 'pose to get behind the men and push them." Preachers' sermons stressed male control and female submissiveness.[32]

There were, however, important differences in black and white worship. As Charles Joyner, one of the most astute students of southern folk culture, has put it, at the "vocabulary level — that is, in its theology — there is little difference between the religion of black and white Christians in the South," despite differences in emphasis, but at the "grammatical level" — the generation of meanings and the worship of God — "the differences . . . are so profound that typically each group thinks nothing very religious is going on in the worship services of the other."[33]

Nearly all observers agreed that black worship was more emotional and spontaneous. Rev. Cherry gives us a vivid picture of black worship, wherein the role of the preacher was primarily not to explain but to exhort. As he put it, the congregation was getting something not so much from "what [the preacher] was saying but the way he was saying it." The church service "was like a great, great Pentecost day. There was shouting all the time and people walking the floor and shouting halleluja you know. And they just — and singing, they didn't have music — we didn't have pianos and organs. . . . [T]hose people would sing from over across there across in the congregation. . . . [W]hen the time come for the preacher to preach, somebody out in the audience would line an old time hymn, Father I Stretch My Hand to Thee, or some kind, you know. . . . And then when they were starting to singing those songs we'd call them 'jump ups', and they'd walk the floor" back and forth "and they'd just rejoice. . . . [O]ne woman when she arrive would shout 'Oh my God, look where I am, I'm in the house of God.'" W. H. Holloway, an educated black minister writing in 1903, who deplored the emotional style of rural churches, admitted that, "while we hate to confess it," the "supreme element" in most black worship was emotionalism. "The church which does not have its shouting, the church which does not measure the abilities of a preacher by the 'rousement' of his sermons and indeed which does not tacitly demand of its minister the shout-producing discourse, is an exception to the rule." By comparison most rural white Baptists and Methodists were, in Ruby Hicks's words, more "dyed-in-the-wool" and "down-to-the-ground," so she never herself experienced the "shouting, trances, and speaking in tongues" that she had heard went on in some services.[34]

Black and white worshipers in the Mississippi Delta were central in one of the most important innovations in American Christianity, the rise of Pentecostalism. The most influential Pentecostal denomination was the African American Church of God in Christ, which had its roots in the work of Charles Mason, a native of Memphis. A committed Baptist, in the 1890s Mason was attracted to the doctrine of "holiness," the belief that people could achieve a "second blessing" of grace, called sanctification, beyond the "first blessing" of conversion. Believers in "holiness" stressed that Christians must go back to the precepts and practices of the original Christians. With like-minded associates, Mason split from the Baptists and in 1897 founded, in Lexington, Mississippi (at the edge of the Delta), the Church of God in Christ, based on holiness principles. Charles Mason later moved on to Pentecostalism. Pentecostals believed that Christians can receive a "third blessing" of the Holy Spirit, and that those so blessed can share powers, such as spiritual healing and speaking in tongues, bestowed by the Spirit on the original apostles. In 1907, Mason led a revival in Memphis and reorganized the Church of God in Christ along Pentecostal lines, with himself as Chief Overseer.[35]

Pentecostalism attracted the poor, both black and white, in the South. The Church of God in Christ, like other Pentecostal denominations, emphasized the spirit above the material world. Its services were highly emotional and expressive, incorporating music and frequently including ecstatic dancing and singing. It had a natural appeal to those with little in life, and nearly all contemporary observers believed that most early adherents came from what Hortense Powdermaker, who observed the church in the 1930s near Indianola, called the "lower middle class, most of them poor and uneducated." With its disdain for worldly life in general, it could at times even erase the distinctions of the color line. Mason and his fellow black ministers converted many whites and ordained white ministers, though the pressures of southern segregationist mores soon led white ministers to found their own, separate organization, known as the Assemblies of God. Although the Church of God in Christ was so new that the U.S. Census of Religious Denominations, taken in 1916, did not take note of its existence, it certainly had already attracted many adherents in the Delta and nearby regions before then.[36]

Progressive Culture in Town and City

Towns in the Delta and in Georgia's coastal and Piedmont regions were usually small, many counties lacking a single place that met the census requirement to be designated "urban," which was a population of at least twenty-five hundred. In each region one or two significant cities on the periphery played important economic roles — Savannah, Augusta or Atlanta, Vicksburg or Memphis — vitally important because of their bankers and real estate brokers, their cotton shippers and railroad connections, their daily newspapers, their political leadership, their specialty shops, hospitals, and schools. Towns, even when too small to count as "urban places," were important far out of proportion to their share in the population. In many small towns scattered through the Piedmont and along the Mississippi River were merchants and lawyers, small banks that financed businessmen and planters, weekly papers, high schools, fancy churches with well-educated ministers, theaters, and concert halls. The big planters of Washington County, Mississippi, who congregated in Greenville made it sophisticated far beyond what its small size (under ten thousand in 1910) would suggest. The wife of Delta planter and political leader LeRoy Percy, who lived in Greenville, told one newspaper reporter, "The fine old mansions from which social life radiated are for the most abandoned or given over for use by managers or tenants. Few of the owners care to live the isolated existence which the plantation now means."[37]

Only a few cities and towns supported a true working class. Even in Greene County, Georgia, home to two textile factories, just 5 percent of employed people worked in the mills. These were not set apart from the rest of the community. While about two-thirds of mill employees in the county lived in households with at least one other mill worker, few of these households were completely dependent on the mills. In one family, the son and daughter (aged eighteen and nineteen) of a carpenter worked in the mill. In another, the daughter of a painter worked as a knitting hand. More than half the employees were male, and many of these were family heads. Except that older children worked in the factory rather than in the field, the mill families were not much different from other families in the county. In most counties manufacturing workers were few, and they worked in small establishments such as sawmills and cotton ginning companies.[38]

In 1900, only the Piedmont city of Augusta, with its large textile mills, had a large, factory-based working class. In that year, Vicksburg, in the

Delta, had about fifteen hundred manufacturing workers, most in small enterprises. Savannah, on the coast of Georgia, had perhaps twice as many, and most of these, too, worked on cotton presses, in sawmills, or in other traditional and relatively small operations. At times, both black and white workers, like their counterparts elsewhere in the nation in this period, organized unions and struck to protect their wages or their jobs. Savannah's dockworkers, 95 percent of them black, were the heart of Savannah's small labor movement, going on strike repeatedly in the 1890s. Augusta's textile mills employed several thousand men and women, nearly all of them white. The Augusta mills were a major center of labor unrest in Georgia. A major textile strike organized by a local of the Knights of Labor lasted four months in 1886 before it collapsed. Again in 1898–99 and in 1902, Augusta's textile workers walked out over pay and working conditions. Still, this urban working class remained closely in touch with its rural roots. In their church services and family life, they would be hard to distinguish from their relatives and friends in the countryside, from which many had only recently arrived.[39]

Although Augusta's textile workers at times made important forays into local politics, by the turn of the century Augusta, like almost all towns and cities in the region, was under the firm control of well-to-do businessmen. In 1897 they succeeded in electing as mayor Patrick Walsh, president of the Augusta *Chronicle* and a director of numerous banks and land development companies. Subsequent mayors included a lawyer, the head of a major plumbing business, a leading textile executive who was head of the board of exchange, and two bank presidents. Businessmen and lawyers dominated the city council; few councilmen came from the ranks of the thousands of textile workers in Augusta. The business elites there, as in other southern cities and towns, shared with their counterparts in the rest of the nation the determination to "modernize" life, and they orchestrated local politics to provide the necessary tax dollars. In Augusta, these leaders pushed the city to build better schools, new parks, and modern utilities, and, in 1912, a big bond issue paid for a new hospital, waterworks, and levee. To men like Walsh, banker Jacob Phinizy, or manufacturer Thomas Barrett Jr., civic boosterism and good business were indistinguishable; they were convinced that what was good for Augusta was good for them as well. They were typical representatives of the "business progressives," who stressed public services and whose byword was improvement — progress — through greater "efficiency."[40]

"Progress" in the form of schools, parks, and hospitals was usually reserved for whites only. In Augusta, for example, city leaders devoted more money to improving white schools, but in 1897 the city school committee abolished seventeen-year-old Ware High School, one of the very few public high schools for blacks in the entire South and the pride of the city's African American middle class. The school committee diverted Ware's budget toward black elementary schools, consistent with white opinion that black students should be educated only for efficient manual labor and that education beyond that level was inappropriate.[41]

The infectious desire for progress reached into the smaller towns, which tried to match the style and the facilities of the cities. In Greensboro, Georgia, voters in 1887 approved a bond issue for new schools; when, two years later, a second bond issue failed, the local editor regretted that Greensboro was falling behind other "progressive" towns. A decade later the editor was admonishing his fellow citizens to follow the example of nearby Madison, which had installed a public electric system. Before the turn of the century Greensboro itself had passed another bond issue to build a new waterworks, one that would guarantee, its backers promised, "Progress" and "Prosperity." In 1913 town leaders considered replacing the elected mayor and council with a city commission form of government, then popular among southern progressives. Nor was "progress" confined to the secular realm. In 1917 Greensboro's Methodists proudly announced the opening of a new church, "Greensboro's Pride," which featured "brilliant lighting," an "elegant carpet," and a "ladies parlor," all at a cost of $21,000. (By comparison, the bond issue for the waterworks had been valued at $22,000.)[42] Similar projects, public and semipublic, were at the center of politics in many small towns. In St. Marys, on the Atlantic coast, citizens debated a bond issue for a bridge to divert tourist traffic headed for Florida. Indianola, in the Delta, awarded its first telephone franchise in 1898 and was wired for electricity in 1901. Dr. Henry Champion bought the first car in Indianola, a Buick, in 1908; eight years later, Indianola had its own auto dealership. (This in a place where, as late as 1912, a driver had to get out to open twenty gates across the road to get to Greenwood, twenty-six miles away.) By 1915 Indianola could boast of a "fine school building," a new Baptist church that cost $30,000, an electric light plant "as good as any in the Delta," and "one of the best and most up-to-date Moving Picture Theatres in the South."[43]

For others, "progress" meant more than physical improvements and greater "efficiency." They wanted, in addition, to purify society and purge it of moral evils, and they believed that government ought to play a part in such reforms. The first and most important of these reforms was prohibition of liquor. As early as 1884 a local temperance group organized in Greensboro and Greene County, Georgia, and began to push for a ban on liquor in the county under the state's local option law. The first referendum, in 1885, bitterly divided the county; the antiliquor forces lost by just 37 votes out of 1,300 cast. The decisive margin was provided by the voters inside the town limits, who opposed prohibition by 218 to 153. The disgruntled temperance voters blamed their failure to outlaw the "whiskey curse" on a corrupt political "ring" in league with the liquor interests. Ten years later the county finally did outlaw the sale of liquor when, in 1895, local ministers led the antiliquor forces. Allied with them were many of "the ladies of Greensboro," who, though unable to vote, shared a "keen desire to rid the county of the whiskey traffic" and rented a soda fountain and dispensed cold drinks at the polling places under the banner "For God, For Home and Native Land."[44]

Involvement of Greene County's women was typical of the prohibition movement nationally and presaged there, as elsewhere, changes that went far beyond the issue of liquor and the drive for social "efficiency," changes that eventually transformed the place of women in the South and the nation. Southern women, according to the Victorian ideal, must be pure and morally superior, rule the home, guide and protect their children, and support and succor their husbands — roles sanctioned by custom and by a conservative interpretation of the Bible that ruled most churches. To step outside of these roles into the "public" sphere of work and politics would court moral and social disaster and violate God's word. When one daughter of a Mississippi planter longed to become a nurse, her father forbade it on the grounds that nurses were "loose women of low class who 'ran around.' " A Georgia editor expressed a common opinion when he called the idea of women's suffrage a "plague" to be held in "supreme contempt and disgust."[45] Southern white men's public stance was that women were, as one Mississippi planter put it, beings "whom man had enthroned." Women like Magnolia Le Guin believed in such ideals even when the realities of their own domestic lives were at odds with enthronement. Augusta's textile mills employed hundreds of white women, many of them mothers, whose choice was to work or let their families starve, yet they accepted the domestic ideals of motherhood even though their poverty made them unable to fulfill them. Participation first in their churches, then in the prohibition campaign, in the long run led many women to conclude that their "throne" bore a strong resemblance to a prison.[46]

Ella Gertrude Clanton Thomas of Augusta followed such a path to the suffrage movement. She was born in 1834 and, even by the standards of the antebellum planter class, had a childhood of extraordinary privilege. Her father, Turner Clanton, owned hundreds of slaves, five plantations, and a mansion in Augusta. She was graduated from Wesleyan Female College in Macon at seventeen, and experienced conversion at that intensely religious institution. In 1852 she married Jefferson Thomas, son of another wealthy planter. Her fascinating diary, which she kept from 1848 to 1889, details a life of material luxury before the war. As a young woman she accepted patriarchal views on marriage, writing at one time that she loved Jefferson Thomas in part because of his "master will," that "true to my sex, I delight in *looking up* and love to feel my woman's weakness protected by man's superior strength." Even in the 1850s, however, her diary hints at what eventually became a commitment to feminism. For example, she denounced as "a *very very* great injustice" the double standard that allowed a woman to be ruined by sexual behavior for "the same offence which in a man, very slightly lowers, and in the estimation of some of his *own sex* rather elevates him." Her indignation at white masters' sexual exploitation of slave women fueled her occasional attacks on slavery itself, which tended to focus on what she perceived as its corrupting influence on the white family rather than its cruelty or injustice to blacks. At times she identified strongly with female slaves as women, writing that if she were a plantation manager, "pregnant women would be highly favored. A woman myself I can sympathise with my sex, whether white or black."[47]

The Civil War and the end of slavery brought a drastic change to Thomas's life. Like all slaveowners, she and her husband suffered from the loss of their slaves, but with farther to fall their landing was all the harder. Gertrude learned to run the house without slaves, doing much of the housework herself, a task she had despised even when she had a houseful of slaves to supervise. The initial shock after the war was a prelude to a long slide into, if not outright poverty, painfully restricted economic circumstances. Her father and husband had invested much of their money in Confederate bonds, and, as she discovered when her father died, her husband had already borrowed from him much of what remained of her inheritance. Jeff Thomas made one foolish business decision after another, losing most of his and his wife's properties to indebtedness. She was humiliated when her teenage son had to leave school to take up the plow, and she saw her husband "broken in fortune, health and spirits." It is clear from the diary, though not explicitly mentioned, that her husband also drank too much, too often.[48]

Gertrude Thomas, unlike her husband, rallied from her postwar despair (she wrote that "for a time I doubted God") to become the emotional and economic mainstay of her family. She managed the household expenses and began to teach school, earning enough to keep her remaining house out of the sheriff's hands. She withstood the heavy blow of the death of her youngest son, Clanton, only seven years old. And she threw herself into a multitude of public activities. She was active in the Wesleyan Alumnae Association, the Grange, and the Ladies Missionary Association of her Methodist church, and an officer of the Ladies Memorial Association, one of the first groups in the South to promote the building of a large public monument to the Confederacy. She was also secretary and vice president of the Woman's Christian Temperance Union in Augusta (her cousin and good friend, Jane Sibley, wife of a wealthy textile executive, was state president). She wrote for newspapers and magazines, crusading for the establishment of a state industrial school for girls and better conditions for women in jails, and denounced wife abuse, noting that "wife beating is not confined to the lower classes." As with so many other southern women of the era, activism through the Methodist Church and the WCTU led her to join the women's suffrage movement, and, in 1899, she was elected the first president of the Georgia Woman Suffrage Association.[49]

One of the South's most important leaders in the campaign for women's suffrage was Nellie Nugent Somerville of Greenville, Mississippi. Somerville, like Thomas, came from a wealthy planter background, though, as a member of a younger generation, born during the Civil War, she followed a less troubled path toward activism. Her father, Lewis Nugent, survived service in the Confederate army and, after the war, practiced law in the state capital of Jackson, where he accumulated a large fortune. Nellie was extraordinarily bright; by seventeen she had graduated at the top of her class from Martha Washington College in Virginia. Her father suggested that she read law in his office, but she preferred to maintain her independence from family patronage. She returned to Greenville, lived with her grandmother, and supported herself by tutoring. In 1880 she married Robert Somerville, with whom she had four children.[50]

Nellie Somerville, like Gertrude Thomas, was a devout Methodist who began her activist career as a church volunteer in the Woman's Board of Home Missions. She also participated in such genteel organizations as the Hypatia Club, at which Delta women met to discuss literary and social topics and listen to lectures like the one on "Woman and her Sphere" given in 1894 by Alfred H. Stone, the prominent planter and writer. That sphere, according to Stone, most certainly did not include suffrage, for "woman should rule by love and kindness and not by force." Nellie Somerville's own later lecture to the club endorsed suffrage for women, acknowledging that, like all improvements in the status of women, it would be "hotly contested by men." She was inspired to join the WCTU by its president, Frances Willard, and, after a visit to Greenville by suffragist Carrie Chapman Catt, she helped organize Mississippi's first suffrage club in 1895. Three years later she was a key organizer of the statewide Mississippi Woman Suffrage Association and the chair of its inaugural meeting. She has been called with good reason "an exotic plant among women in the post-reconstruction south."[51]

Like many other women's suffrage campaigners in the Progressive Era, Somerville accepted the idea that women belonged to a special "sphere" but argued that this was a reason to grant suffrage rights, for it was on the basis of their special qualities *as* women that they deserved full citizenship. As she put it in a speech to the state association in 1898, "there is a growing belief that American institutions cannot be preserved without the infusion in the body politic of a new moral force, and there are not a few who think that only the womanhood of the nation can furnish that moral power. . . . [A]s mothers, we ask for an endowment of rights that shall enable us to rear a generation of truly patriotic citizens." Southern female suffragists, even more than those in the rest of the United States, were facing fierce opposition from religious conservatives who claimed that suffrage for women would violate the word of God. If Divine Providence had indeed "opened the domain of moral leadership to the Christian women of this nation," Somerville wrote, all the more essential that "moral power and political power must be together" if the nation was to have "the blessing of God." The belief that women's suffrage violated Christian precepts and the claim that "political disability is a tribute to their goodness" were among the "wornout theories" that "Christian nations have gradually outgrown."[52]

As Somerville's comments about "outgrown" theories suggest, she placed votes for women firmly within a context of progress in history: "The progress of women is merely a part of the progress of the human family. Christian nations have gradually outgrown the hoary tradition that women are weak, vicious and a necessary evil." Prohibition, better public education, help for poor women, and more general civic improvements also figured in that progress, and women led the way in these areas as well. In 1909, in fact, Somerville's Greenville suffrage club renamed itself the "Civic Improvement Club," and, while continuing to agitate for suffrage, it also campaigned for better garbage removal, gates at railroad crossings, a new public library, and measures to fight tuberculosis.[53]

Women in smaller towns took up similar projects. In many places they took responsibility for preserving the memory of the Civil War, were the main support of church missions, and worked for prohibition and other broad reforms. In 1902, women in Indianola in the Delta formed a club called the "Round Dozen," and many of its members, together with their husbands, organized an Anti-Saloon League in 1903. In 1915 several of the same women established a Women's Civic League to improve sanitary conditions, beautify the town, and, in general, "arouse civic pride."[54] In Greensboro, Georgia, women were active in church, prohibition, and Confederate memorial activity for years, although, as a newspaper exchange in 1899 reveals, many hesitated to take up more extensive reform efforts. When the town served as host for the annual meeting of the Athens District Methodist Woman's Foreign Missionary Society, Anna M. Parks wrote to complain that support for foreign missions was all well and good, but that the money spent on conventions (where women paid too much attention to entertainment and dress) might be better spent to keep Greensboro's boys off the streets. The next week, a letter from Mrs. W. F. Armor defended foreign missions, conventions, and the women who attended them, and cast aspersions on dancing parties, perhaps aimed at Miss Parks herself. Anna Parks, in turn, replied that she was more worried about children at home than in heathen lands and that the town was losing too many of its "best citizens" because it needed better schools. "I have worked on broad lines, the church, educational, the happiness and welfare of the youths of our land, the memorial and many other associations — all tending to the building up and uplifting of our lovely little town. . . . [But] there is need of broader culture, and as I see it, there is nothing here but foreign missions and prohibition that will create even a ripple of excitement."[55]

By the First World War, Greensboro did have its Civic Improvement League, and the town's Woman's Club was "taking a shot" at the mayor and council over the poor state of the town's streets and outhouses and over the failure to enforce laws against spitting. The Woman's Club called for a town-level board of health and a new street cleaning department. The very day that the local paper reported on the women's "shot" at local government, it printed a letter (under the headline "Greensboro Girl Becomes Suffragette") from Marion Morgan, a native of Greensboro then living in San Francisco, and about to vote in the upcoming California election. She was thinking of voting Socialist: "The South doesn't know about socialism," but in a hundred years "everyone will be socialist." She hastened to add, though, "please remember that we are still Georgians and when we return will forget all about voting in California."[56]

The feminist movement for suffrage and for greater equality did not always prompt white women to support similar rights for African Americans — the suffrage campaign, too, was primarily for whites only. One of the strongest antisuffrage arguments in the South was that extending suffrage to women would increase black voting by enlarging the number of African Americans in the electorate. A Georgia editor writing in the *Women's Patriot,* a national antisuffrage magazine, argued that a suffrage amendment would "revitalize the fifteenth amendment, and necessarily bring the Negroes back into politics, creating Negro night meetings again on the plantations" — which would pose a danger to white farm women. At a minimum, white suffragists had to reassure fellow whites that women's suffrage would not weaken white political control; some women assured whites that because white women outnumbered black women in the South, women's votes would make white supremacy all the stronger.[57]

Most white progressives thought about race in terms of a "negro problem," not a white one, and from a perspective of paternalism and moralism. Most condemned lynchings but proposed little in the way of practical steps to prevent them other than to urge blacks to police themselves and refrain from crimes, especially the "unmentionable" crime of rape against white women. In Augusta, Georgia, in 1900, a black passenger shot and killed a prominent white man following an altercation on a streetcar; the black man accused in the killing was lynched outside the city. In response, the city council passed a new segregation law, and a black boycott was unable to break it. Many whites saw such segregation statutes as themselves a "progressive" rationalization of race relations through government action, intended to prevent disorder, especially in towns and cities, where, as C. Vann Woodward has put it, "blacks enjoyed more autonomy and anonymity and rubbed shoulders with whites nearer their own class frequently and in new and unfamiliar circumstances." Progressive support for black attempts at social improvement focused principally on local efforts to train young blacks in industrial schools to take a useful, if permanent, place at the bottom of the South's economy. In Hancock County, Georgia, "local white men of influence" sat on the board of the Sparta Agricultural and Industrial School, where black pupils learned elementary subjects, cooking for the girls and farming for the boys. In Greene County, F. E. Boswell urged the county to hire a farm demonstrator to "stop at every negro house and endeavor to impress upon the negroes the need of looking after their premises, to keep them in a sanitary condition, and to keep their homes better ventilated." Boswell reminded his readers that, "as a laboring class of people we want them strong and healthy." It was the "Christian duty" of whites to teach them that "cleanliness is next to Godliness."[58]

In both Mississippi and Georgia, however, one concrete policy reform involved abolition of the old convict lease system, an institution directly related to race since the great majority of convicts were African Americans. Reformers sought to end the horrific treatment suffered by convicts leased out to private contractors — the cruelties, terrible housing, and other conditions that in some years killed one out of six prisoners — but they also hoped to make the prison system more efficient and useful. The differing paths to reform reflected the differences in the economies of these two states. Georgia did away with leasing in 1908 and put convicts on the chain gang under state control, building new roads which would benefit the merchants in the towns by accommodating the growing number of automobiles. Mississippi also abolished leasing and created a new institution of incarceration, the prison farm. The largest and most notorious was Parchman Farm, a state-owned cotton plantation carved out of the Delta wilderness in Sunflower County. Parchman, which opened in 1904, just a year later turned a profit of $185,000. These new forms of forced labor of prisoners, the large majority of them African American, benefited local and state governments rather than merely private planters and businessmen, as earlier.[59]

The New African American Middle Class

In 1901 W. E. B. Du Bois noted that "the Georgia Negro . . . has steadily acquired property since the war." By 1900 the county tax rolls in the eastern Piedmont counted 136,000 acres owned by blacks, and in the coastal counties almost 100,000 acres — up 27 percent and 14 percent, respectively, over the past decade. African Americans that year also owned over $180,000 in real estate in smaller cities and towns in each region. Such an accumulation of property in a single generation, starting almost from scratch with Emancipation, was a formidable achievement, although it still represented less than 10 percent of all property. Most impressive was the economic success of blacks in the larger cities. By 1900 blacks in Savannah were assessed for almost $700,000 in real property; in Augusta, more than $500,000. This wealth was the material foundation for the new African American middle class in the early twentieth century.[60]

African Americans accumulated property and gradually attained middle-class status in smaller towns, but there were too few to form a truly distinctive group. As late as 1917, Warrenton, Georgia, had only twelve black-owned enterprises, Greensboro only ten; Sparta just nineteen, all with modest revenues and few employees. Few small towns had black physicians or lawyers, and their skilled black artisans faced discrimination that limited opportunities for moving up into independent contracting.[61] Only in the cities were there enough African American professional and business people to form a true middle class, and enough African American customers to support them. Vicksburg, by 1908, had four black physicians, a black dentist, and a black lawyer-banker. Dr. John Miller, a native of Portsmouth, Virginia, had degrees from Williams College and the University of Michigan Medical School. Willis E. Mollison, a lawyer and president of the black-owned Lincoln Savings Bank, attended Fisk University and graduated in 1883 from Oberlin. D. D. Foote, a dentist born in Vicksburg in 1879, attended Straight University in New Orleans before studying dentistry at Howard. Others had succeeded without advanced educations. Rev. Kelly Rucks, of Holly Grove Baptist Church, born a slave in 1848, had never been to school, but he had built up a large church in St. Louis before coming down the river to Vicksburg. A. J. Brown had arrived in Vicksburg in 1886 "practically penniless" and had worked his way up through railroad shops, then selling coal and real estate before establishing a brick factory. W. H. Jefferson had been a Pullman porter before becoming the first black undertaker in Mississippi. The Union Savings Bank, organized by a black physician, was largely run by its cashier, T. G. Ewing, "a brilliant and aggressive young business man." One of the members of this small black elite wrote with considerable pride that "the colored man . . . pursues the path of simple industry and energetic effort to make homes and means of livelihood. He has done this well. He has maintained a number of fraternal insurance orders whose payments have equaled a king's ransom within the past ten years. He has builded homes of beauty and filled them with books whose stories tell of hope and with articles of beauty which make for culture and progress."[62]

By 1900 Augusta and Savannah, too, had a significant black middle class. In Savannah, where some free blacks had built impressive estates even before the Civil War, black artisans, professionals, and small businessmen formed the core of a middle class that supported its own churches, hospital, and newspaper and dominated the remnants of the Republican Party. African Americans in Augusta could be born at the black-owned-and-staffed Burruss Sanitarium, attend elementary and high school at black-run Haines Normal and Industrial Institute, go to all-black Paine College, read the black-owned Georgia *Baptist*, shop in black-owned grocery stores, have a picture taken by a black photographer, save money at the black-owned Workingmen's Loan & Building Association, insure their lives at their choice of black-owned insurance companies, and eventually be buried by a black undertaker.[63]

Many of the older members of the black elite had been helped by white patrons — friends or even relatives. One of the most eminent black leaders in Georgia, Bishop Lucius Henry Holsey of Augusta, was the son of a slave mother and her white master, and had grown up as a slave in Sparta and Athens. He taught himself to read (with the help of a Bible and a copy of *Paradise Lost*), experienced conversion after a sermon by a white evangelical preacher, and, after his marriage to a fifteen-year-old slave, was personally tutored by her master, Methodist Bishop George Foster Pierce. Holsey was one of the relatively small number of emancipated slaves who chose after the war to remain a member of the Methodist Episcopal Church, South; he later became a minister and bishop in the Colored Methodist Episcopal Church that was established and partly supported by white Southern Methodists, and he served as pastor at Trinity C.M.E. Church in Augusta. During his early career as a bishop, Holsey refused to criticize southern whites, even writing that slavery itself had, despite its evils, benefited Africans by exposing them to Christianity. He continued to seek and accept the support of southern whites, most notably for Paine Institute, later Paine College, established in Augusta by the white Southern Methodists.[64]

Holsey was one of a number of light-skinned mulattoes who, in the 1890s, made up most of Augusta's African American elite. Others were Amanda Dickson, heir to the fortune of her white father, Hancock County planter David Dickson; the Ladevezes, who sold pianos and art supplies to a largely white clientele; William J. White, editor of the Georgia *Baptist;* and lawyer Judson Lyons. John Hope, later president of Atlanta University, who grew up in this society, described it as "a rather well organized Negro society, with its social metes and bounds, with its ideals, and a great deal of culture." Many of these families worshiped at Holsey's Trinity Episcopal Church. As late as the 1890s, members of this elite considered Augusta "the garden spot of the country" with respect to race relations, and the black principal of Ware High

School, H. L. Walker, declared that "in Augusta you will find two races of people living together in such accord and sympathy as are nowhere else to be found in all this Southland." After the school committee withdrew support for Ware High School in 1897, some of these people changed their minds.[65]

Although middle-class African American women shared many of the same values as white middle-class women, they were more open to participation in the wider world. Augusta educator Lucy Craft Laney echoed popular middle-class sentiment when she affirmed in 1897 that "the chief joy of home is mother"; that marriage must be a tie till death; and that faithful and loving mothers must teach their children, boys included, to be "pure in life and chaste in conversation." But as one historian has put it, the post–Civil War African American ethos placed great emphasis on "usefulness," and this meant a high value placed on "strength, initiative, and practicality among black women," who were in some respects in advance of whites in their belief that women needed to be educated and that women's work was vital.[66]

When Bishop Holsey was asked by a congressional committee in the 1880s about "virtue" among blacks, he responded that Augusta had "a large circle of young girls who are quite well educated, and as industrious and intelligent as anybody, and that is a circle into which nobody who is in bad repute can enter. . . . I am speaking now especially of the girls." Virtue and education went together: "Most of these educated colored girls are school teachers. Sometimes they marry, and I have known several of them who have kept boarding-houses, some who run washing establishments, and I find those young women to keep their virtue and to stand up for what is right, and I consider them as ornaments of our people."[67] In Vicksburg, Dr. Georgia A. Proctor, a graduate of the Meharry Medical School, practiced with her husband and also owned Proctor's Drugstore. The cashier of Vicksburg's Lincoln Savings Bank in 1908, M. Z. Mollison, was the daughter of the bank's founder and an Oberlin graduate. In Augusta Mary Skinfield, a mortician, held property valued on the tax rolls at almost $8,000. In Greenville, Mississippi, Lizzie Coleman became legendary as the principal of a black school. One teacher in her school recalled that the "big boys didn't give her any trouble" because she would "yank you up and throw you across her knees." According to another portrait, "her physical strength was great, her will indomitable; hence her discipline problems were few. There were those who disliked her, but certainly all respected her." This obviously formidable woman was also famous for her public lecture series in the 1930s on Langston Hughes, Claude McKay, and other black writers.[68]

For many members of the black middle class, the black schoolteacher was key in the uplift of all African Americans, with a heavy responsibility for both the intellectual and moral development of black children. The moral dimension was crucial, and morality generally meant the Victorian standards articulated by Augusta's Lucy Laney—that marriage was sacred and that both boys and girls must be "pure in life and chaste in conversation." Few things infuriated middle-class blacks more than whites' assumption that all black women lacked sexual purity and their refusal to extend the rules of chivalry to African Americans. The principle was important enough that in Vicksburg, on at least two occasions, members of the black elite intervened to try to prevent appointment of black teachers who were reputed to be mistresses of white men, the hypocrisy of the white charges of black immorality of course apparent. In one case they hired a prominent white lawyer to help them, writing him, "We believe we are doing the right thing for our People and the Community and that to overcome the charges of Immorality that are thrown at the race from time to time it is Imperative that we have Teachers in our Public schools who are strong morally as well as intellectually."[69]

No one embodied the ideal of education, "usefulness," and Victorian morality better than Laney herself. Laney was born in Macon, Georgia, in 1854, the seventh child of David and Louisa Laney. Her father was a skilled carpenter and lay preacher who had purchased both his and his wife's freedom. He affiliated with northern Presbyterians after the war and became pastor of a black church in Savannah. Lucy benefited from the unusually liberal attention of her mother's former owner and employer, who encouraged her to learn to read and, after the war, enabled her to attend Atlanta University. She graduated at the top of its first class in 1873.[70]

After teaching in several Georgia cities, Laney opened a private school for African American students in Christ Presbyterian Church in Augusta in 1886, under the auspices of the Presbyterian Board of Missions for Freedmen. She named the school for Francine E. H. Haines, an officer on the women's executive committee of the home mission program. The Haines Normal and Industrial Institute, as it came to be known, received a small amount of financial support from the Presbyterians and managed to survive a fire, a flood, and a typhoid epidemic, as well as complaints from white neighbors about noise. With the support of Augusta's black community and with gifts from Mrs. Haines and other white northern women philanthropists, the school flourished, eventually encompassing most of a city block. It expanded its offerings to include high school and early-college-level classes and nursing training, with concentrated attention to teacher training. Haines, despite the "Industrial" in its name, offered a full liberal arts curriculum and held its students to uncompromisingly high academic standards.

Like many other African American middle-class reformers of the era, Laney shared Victorian standards of morality and behavior, but unlike most white reformers, Laney understood the ways in which the history of slavery, poverty, and economic discrimination could make it almost impossible for many poor blacks to reach the standards she held so dear. She blamed slavery's lack of protection of slave marriages for the "crushing burden of immorality" that, she said, blighted poor black neighborhoods. She deplored "untidy and filthy homes" of poor blacks as breeders of both disease and sin, but she also attacked the injustice and the "burden of prejudice" that fostered those conditions. In an 1896 address to a conference called to discuss the high mortality rates of blacks in cities, she focused on conditions in the homes of the poor. Crowding created health problems, but, she pointed out, low wages and irregular work forced many parents to live with their children in one-room apartments. When "the work of the mother of the family requires that she be away from the home all day," it was inevitable that children would be sometimes unsupervised and cleaning sporadic. Still, she insisted in another address, a good home was within reach of the poor: "I care not how humble may be the house in which two loving hearts may set up their household gods, if blessed with a manly and God-fearing husband, a womanly and god-fearing wife, intelligence and health, that place is a *home*, the nearest approach on earth to heaven."[71]

Laney concluded her 1896 talk with a plea that the conference might be a "Moses come to lead out of the wilderness. . . . That from these meetings may be evolved plans that will bring some relief, is the prayer and aim of all concerned." But Laney was not one to wait for Moses. She belonged to what she called the "class who, by their perseverance, intelligence and economy, have made for themselves better houses, comfortable houses in healthy localities," and whose "hearts ached with alarm at the devastation." She and others in Augusta worked through churches to found the Augusta Woman's Protective Club, which was instrumental in support of the black Old Folks Home and the Shiloh Orphanage. Two African American YWCAs, at Haines Institute and Paine College, were active in social work.[72]

Black women invigorated similar efforts in Vicksburg through the Woman's Christian Union, whose members raised $1,200 for an Old Folks Home and visited rural homes to show "the women of these homes how to improve themselves." In Savannah, African American donations helped the Charity Hospital (an all-black institution) care for poor patients. Elsewhere also, blacks through their churches provided crucial support for black schools, especially for education beyond the elementary grades grudgingly supported by public funds. The Baptists, for example, supported Walker Academy in Augusta, Greenville High School in Mississippi, and an academy and normal school in the little Delta town of Friar's Point.[73]

Sea Island Culture

In an 1899 address at Hampton Institute in Hampton, Virginia, Augusta's Lucy Laney called on black writers to go to the Sea Islands of Georgia and South Carolina to study the Negro in his "original purity," with a culture still close to Africa.[74] Just a generation past slavery, urban middle-class African Americans were aware both of the African roots of much black culture and of their own sense of having traveled a considerable distance from those roots. The Sea Islands' African American culture, if not in some hypothetical state of "original purity," was still, with the possible exception of southern Louisiana, closer to African traditions than any other region in the United States. In 1888, Charles C. Jones Jr., who had grown up on his father's plantation in Liberty County, Georgia, published in *Negro Myths from the Georgia Coast* dozens of African American slave-era tales in the Geechee dialect, the Creole language found only in the Sea Island regions of Georgia and South Carolina.[75] In 1894, white folklorist Abigail Christensen published a vivid description of a Sea Island "shout," the religious celebration that grafted Christian themes onto a dancing and singing ritual with clear African roots. In a cabin or church, a few dancers formed a ring and some celebrants began to sing. The dancers moved in a circle, slowly at first, feet sliding rather than stepping, and the song was picked up by the congregation in call-and-response fashion, accompanied by clapping in complex rhythms. "One after another of the lookers-on who crowded around the sides of the room step into the charmed circle," until "the ring fairly seems to whirl around the room." In response to the invitation of the enthusiastic clappers, "now, brudder!" "Shout, sister!" "Join, shouters!" Christensen could hardly keep herself from joining in.[76]

The African sources for these stories and celebrations, not at first recognized, were explored by Lydia Parrish, wife of the noted illustrator Maxfield

Parrish, who began spending winters on St. Simons Island in 1912. After being introduced to Sea Island spirituals during a visit to friends in Savannah, she became intensely interested in the songs and convinced that they were in danger of dying out because younger blacks in the region considered them old-fashioned. She devoted much of the rest of her life to their preservation, organizing the Sea Island Singers and building a small cabin next to her house as a performance venue, and taking groups of singers to entertain wealthy residents and visitors on the island.[77]

Parrish had a genuine appreciation for the traditional forms not only of African American song but also of the more general culture on the coast. She watched women beating rice, listened to stories, observed grave decorations, and, with the help of wide reading in scholarly literature, found their connections with African practices. Her collection of songs (not published until 1942) included work songs, children's songs, and African chants as well as shout songs and the more conventionally religious spirituals. She scornfully dismissed scholars who had argued that spirituals were derived entirely from white sources, terming them "writers who work in libraries and not in the field." The words were typically adapted from English hymns, but because standard musical notation was wholly inadequate to communicate how the songs worked in actual performance, these "writers from New England" with their "book evidence" did "not appear to realize that their conclusions are valueless without work in the field among the children and grandchildren of native Africans — who are our only authorities." The singers themselves often departed from the standard European scale, and their humming was "not easily transcribed"; above all, African influence was evident in the "complicated rhythms" and the call-and-response style of the song forms. The clearest evidence of the African influence was in the ring shouts Parrish saw for the first time on a night that "I shall never forget." She described Margaret, who "wiggled her hips shamelessly, held her shoulders stiff — at the same time thrusting them forward — kept her feet flat on the floor, and, with the usual rhythmic heel-tapping, progressed with real style around the circle — goodness knows how." Dancer Edith Murphy had her own individual style, "a stylized, angular performance as though copying the poses of the figures in Egyptian decorations." "White folks who attempt the step of the true ring-shout find it difficult," Parrish added, no doubt a considerable understatement.[78]

The polyphonic rhythms and communal, call-and-response style also permeated work songs and children's games. Parrish heard the work songs of women in the oyster factories and men loading ships on the Brunswick docks, usually fitting the task at hand — "it is unlikely that a shanty could be used for rowing, or a rowing song for beating rice." But all tended to follow the classic call-and-response pattern, with a work leader singing solo and the others as chorus.[79] Similar patterns appeared in children's games — often variations on ring-plays — incorporating multiple rhythms of clapping. A later observer wrote of the games taught her by Bessie Jones, one of the Sea Island Singers, "To clap well . . . you must start with your feet," since "the performer finds that his feet and hands are holding a kind of conversation." Handclap, like singing, involved multiple rhythms with each participant changing rhythms and participants following differing but complementary rhythms, with varia-tions in pitch (bass, baritone, and tenor) created by changes in the shape of the hands. The effect, as the writer learned from a gentle rebuke by Bessie Jones, was not that the participants clapped "against" one another, but "with" one another, meaning "to respond to them, to complement and support their silences, to fill in their statements (musical, physical, and verbal) with little showers of comment, to answer their remarks — to clap a *different* pattern."[80]

Many of the tales, ghost stories, songs, and children's games of the Sea Island region were found throughout the rural south. In the early 1940s Alan Lomax observed children's ring games in the Delta similar to the ones Lydia Parrish saw on St. Simons Island. Throughout the South black turpen-tine and railroad gangs sang out in call-and-response form. The ring shout, though, by the early twentieth century was only in the rice and Sea Island re-gions of South Carolina and Georgia, surviving far away from white eyes, in the isolated churches and cabins of Sea Island African Americans. The ring shout was clear evidence of the relative stability and cultural conservatism of African American culture in the area, promoted and protected by the isola-tion of black communities of independent land-owning peasant farmers, who ventured out occasionally to earn cash wages loading ships or shucking oysters. The independence did not translate into prosperity, and the Atlantic coast did not attract black immigrants, who might have brought new cultural practices with them. The landscape itself, with its marshes and snaking wa-terways, added to the relative isolation, so that a ring shout on St. Simons might show subtle differences from one in McIntosh County just a few miles away on the coast. Both blacks like Lucy Laney and whites like Lydia Parrish recognized the islands and the tidal rivers across from them as a distinct cultural region, where legacies of Africa were more clearly visible than any-where else.[81]

Blues Music, Blues Culture

While the settled peasants of the coast served as cultural conservators of African American tradition, the black working class in the cotton plantation regions nurtured, as performers and as audience, an explosion of cultural creativity. Nowhere was this so important as in the Mississippi Delta. In 1901 and 1902, as Charles Peabody of Massachusetts led an archeological dig in the high mounds left by Indians near Clarksdale, he heard the shovel crews singing as they worked, keeping time in the same style described by Lydia Parrish, with a solo leader answered by a chorus. Some of the verses were spontaneous — at one point while Peabody was tossing a knife idly into the ground, the lead worker deep in a ditch sang out, "I'm so tired I'm most dead, / Sittin' up there playing mumbley-peg." Other verses apparently came from a traditional stock; still others from what Peabody called "ragtime" tunes, popular music like "Goo-Goo Eyes" that the workers might have heard in a traveling medicine show. Peabody's subsequent article about the songs for the *Journal of American Folklore* was the first published account of music specific to the Mississippi Delta. He mentioned not only the work songs of his gang but the "autochthonous" music of nearby farm workers: a man following a plow, cursing at his mule while alternately singing hymns and "apparently genuine African music"; a "very old" black worker on nearby Stovall plantation singing in a voice Peabody compared to a bagpipe or Jew's harp: "monotonous but weird"; a mother singing her baby to sleep in a cabin with a lullaby "impossible to copy, weird in interval and strange in rhythm, peculiarly beautiful."[82]

Peabody's account resembles Lydia Parrish's descriptions of Sea Island music. Some of what Peabody heard must have been field "hollers," calls across fields described by Parrish, who called them "peculiar," a "strange form of vocal gymnastics," "something like a Swiss yodel." Peabody's description has become famous among music historians because hindsight allows us to see in it evidence of something more than the continuities of southern black culture; he had been an unknowing witness at the creation of the blues. One work song verse noted by Peabody — "They had me arrested for murder / And I never harmed a man" — resembles one collected by Parrish — "They call me hangin' Johnny / O I never hang nobody." The move from (alleged) hangman to (alleged) murderer has reversed the point of view, and the text thus serves as a symbolic marker for what one writer has called "a sudden and radical turn in African-American music."[83]

By the early twentieth century, many southern African Americans were able to earn a living with their musical talents. As early as 1906, Howard Odum, the most systematic early collector of secular African American songs, recognized the existence of "songsters" or "music physicianers" who traveled around "loafing in general, and working only when compelled to do so, gathering new songs and singing the old ones. Negroes of this type may be called professionals, since their life of wandering is facilitated by the practice of singing."[84] Their songs drew on both popular culture and the African American musical tradition. Blues music, too, drew on traditional forms: field hollers, work songs, spirituals, complex rhythms and "weird" tones, and traditional instrumental styles. But about that time these traditions passed through a cultural magnifying glass that concentrated them down to a bright point of focus in a new form and style of performance. Most notable were the single performer who answered himself with guitar or piano, and the stanza in *aab* sequence:

Got the blues can't be satisfied
Got the blues can't be satisfied
Keep the blues I'll catch that train and ride.[85]

The first blues song was recorded only in 1920, and no one knows just how long the song form had been around by then. Orchestra leader W. C. Handy and vaudeville singer Ma Rainey in later years both claimed to have heard blues songs for the first time around 1902 or 1903 — like Charles Peabody, they thought the music they heard was "weird" or "strange."[86] According to Handy, he was waiting for a train late one night in the little Delta village of Tutwiler when "a lean, loose-jointed Negro" began "plucking a guitar beside me while I slept. His clothes were rags, his feet peeped out of his shoes. His face had on it some of the sadness of the ages. As he played, he pressed a knife blade on the strings of the guitar in a manner popularized by Hawaiian guitarists who used steel bars. His song, too, struck me instantly: 'Goin' where the Southern cross the Dog.' The singer repeated the line three times, accompanying himself on the guitar with the weirdest music I had ever heard." The guitarist was playing what Howard Odum later called a "knife song" — in which the player ran a knife along the strings of a guitar to produce subtle variations in pitch so as to make it " 'sing' and 'talk' with skill" or even to "cuss." The "Southern" and the "Dog" were the Southern Railway and a branch of the Yazoo and Mississippi Valley Railway known as the "Yellow Dog" to Delta blacks, and they crossed at Moorehead, in Sunflower County.[87]

Still, the blues were not, as Handy's story suggests, simply the lonely laments of isolated and poor sharecroppers, but the product, primarily, of the "music physicianers," most of the earliest lost to memory, and some others existing only as names. One who is known well to musical history is Charley Patton, who learned his trade and stamped his genius on American music on Will Dockery's plantation at Drew, also in Sunflower County. Dockery was one of the post–Civil War plantations carved out of the cypress swamps by a driven entrepreneur; by 1910 it was one of the biggest. Will Dockery himself was, as plantation owners went, considered a fair and honest man. He paid up on time, and no one accused him of cheating. When his workers did not cause trouble, they were left pretty much to themselves. Some lived and worked on the plantation for years. Dockery hired black men to manage parts of the plantation, and, as late as the 1930s, when Will's son Joe Rice Dockery had taken over, the *National Negro Digest* reported that "when it comes to giving sharecroppers and all workers a fair chance to earn an honest living, young Mr. Joe Rice Dockery of Dockery, Mississippi, sets a fine example."[88] Charley Patton was probably about ten or twelve years old when he arrived at Dockery's with his parents and four siblings sometime between 1901 and 1904. His father Bill Patton worked hard, saved money, and did so well at Dockery's that he eventually had eight subtenants of his own. He opened his own country store and later bought a three-hundred-acre tract of land. Charley's sisters married well — Katie to Eugene Miller, who had accumulated seven hundred acres, and Viola to John Cannon, who ran one of Dockery's grocery stores. But the farmer's life was not for Charley, who, according to family tradition, was already earning money as a musician at house parties by the time he was ten. By the time he was twenty he was playing at people's houses, at local "juke joints," and at picnics, and may have made more money than his father.[89]

Charley Patton did not, in all likelihood, "invent" the blues, but he brought it to a new kind of perfection, with guitar playing that was extraordinary — he could indeed make it "sing" and "talk" and "cuss" — and a raw voice that Patton used as another instrument. His style almost defies description, but Francis Davis's attempt is probably as good as any:

> The heart of Patton's style was its polyrhythmic complexity — though
> all of the numbers he recorded were in conventional quadruple meter,

he generated tension and ensured variety with high tunings, chimed and choked guitar runs, tapped bass notes, omitted words and spoken asides, and a tricky way of accenting the first beat in the measure with his guitar and the fourth beat with his voice, so that the two would coincide only fleetingly. As many observers have noted, rhythm isn't simply one component of a Charley Patton song — it *is* the song, and it's what pulls you in.

Patton also composed some of the first *personal* blues lyrics — songs not just about "the railroad," but about the Pea Vine Railroad that ran through Dockery's, not just about "the sheriff" but about Sheriff Tom Rushing, who put Patton in jail one night. To all this he added an entertaining stage presence; he would put "his guitar all between his legs, carry it behind his head, lay down on the floor, and never stop playing." Patton's influence was felt directly by many of the best early blues singers who played with him at Dockery's and elsewhere, including Tommy Johnson, Willie Brown, and Son House.[90]

The blues form was not just a group of songs but a "song producing system," flexible enough not only to allow new compositions but also to allow them to be invented more or less spontaneously in performance. Each song might begin with a fairly fixed opening verse or two, but the singer could take traditional "floating" verses from "the air," playing to a dance crowd for a half hour or more. Recorded blues music can easily give a false impression that songs were fixed in melody and verse sequence, but the true unit of music, David Evans has argued, was not the "song" but the performance itself.[91] What they sang about was, of course, *having* the blues:

Took my baby to meet that mornin' train
And the blues come down baby like showers of rain.
(Charley Patton, "Pony Blues")

Got the blues, can't be satisfied
Keep the blues I'll catch that train and ride.
(Mississippi John Hurt, "Got the Blues, Can't Be Satisfied")

I woke up this mornin' blues all round my bed
Had the blues so bad mama till I couldn't raise up my head.
(Tommy Johnson, "Lonesome Home Blues")

The songs were simultaneously personal and collective — personal because they focused on the feelings of the singer (though not necessarily literally on a personal experience), collective because they spoke to the experience of the audience. One musician has said that the blues "relates to a gigantic field of feeling." Bluesman Robert Shaw's words are that "it goes back to feelings. How you feel today. . . . Everybody get the blues. If you wake up in the morning and don't have no money in your pockets, and you can't get a loaf of bread, ain't you blue? And the baby crying too?" To Arthur Lee Williams, "blues actually is around you every day. That's just a feeling within a person, you know. You have a hard time and things happen. Hardships between you and your wife, or maybe you and your girlfriend. Downheartedness, that's all it is, hardship. You express it through your song." Rural black audiences knew what it was like to wake up hungry or have trouble with a wife or husband. Bluesman Henry Townsend described his own feeling about the relationship between the performer and his audience. "There's blues that connects you with public life — I mean you can tell it to the public as a song, *in* a song. . . . Now this particular thing reach others because they have experienced the same condition in life so naturally they feel what you are saying because it happened to them. . . . They feel that maybe I have just hit upon somethin' tha's in their lives, and yet at the same time it was some of the things that went wrong with me too."[92]

Themes of social protest are unusual in the blues. Most blues songs — three quarters of the recorded songs, by the estimate of one historian — focus on the intimate realities of life, and especially relationships between men and women. Men lament when their lovers leave and celebrate when they come back (and marriage is quite irrelevant to love): "Well you see my milkcow tell her t' hurry home / I ain't had no milk since that cow been gone"; "I'm gonna tell you something keep it to yourself baby / You don't tell your husband lord and no one else"; "Bought my gal a great big diamond ring / Come right back home and caught her shakin' that thing. . . . I said baby why did you act this a way / Says I won't miss a thing she gives away." Sadness sometimes turns to anger, and anger sometimes to violence. After Mississippi John Hurt hears his lover tell him he "won't miss a thing she gives away," the next verse is

Took my gun and I broke the bar'l down
Took my gun broke the barrel down
Put my baby six feet under the ground.

But escape was the more common response, and escape, movement, and change are also a central blues theme. "I'm goin' up the country, mama in a few more days"; "Keep the blues I'll catch that train and ride"; "I leave here I'm gonna catch that M. and O. / I'm goin' way down south where I ain't never been before"; "I got up this mornin', feelin' round for my shoes / Know by that I got the walkin' blues."[93]

The blues records the experience of many black men and women in the Delta — movement from plantation to plantation or from town to town, the reality of broken relationships and broken families reflected in the cold statistics collected by the census bureau; that experience was often embodied in the rambling, drinking, womanizing bluesman himself. Charley Patton was constantly on the move, often boasting, Son House remembered, about "his woman yesterday, the day before yesterday, all what he done to the woman. . . . He'd be talkin' about all the time he's 'with' her they goin' to bed and how long they can 'stay,' and all that. . . . Oh I [used to get] *sick* of that son of a bitch." Researchers have found at least four separate marriage licenses for Patton, but he certainly spent a lot of time with more than four women. With drinking, gambling, and sexual tension pervasive at many of the parties, violence was always a threat, and the bluesmen were often part of it. "The experienced bluesman," William Ferris has remarked, "sings near a door or window which provides a quick escape if the crowd becomes too rowdy." Patton's throat was cut by a jealous man at one performance; Robert Johnson, the most famous blues performer of the next generation, died after being poisoned at a party; Son House spent two years in prison after he shot a man to death at a juke joint. In many ways the ethos of the blues with its rejection of Victorian moral standards simply confirmed in white eyes that blacks were incapable of true "civilization."[94]

Commentators have often explained the blues as a response to the general "experience of being black in a white racist society," or, more specifically, as "part of a widespread cultural response to renewed white oppression" at the end of the nineteenth century. In this reading, the blues is a cultural form that "affirms the essential worth of black humanity, even though white people attempted to define blacks as animals," and it "dramatized the cultural vitality and rebelliousness of the participants, evoking race and class solidarity."[95]

This is only partly true. The blues was the creation of a rural, southern, African American working class; no such music could have arisen as part of white folk culture, much less from an optimistic American popular culture.

When Charley Patton sang in his "High Sheriff Blues," "Let me tell you folkses how he treated me / And he put me in a cell lord it was dark as it could be," the context of Delta justice is obvious. Yet Patton's own life scarcely fits a plot of oppression. He came from a stable, relatively successful and prosperous family, and as soon as he could, made sure he never had to follow a mule or pay too much attention to white people. Most of his songs, like most other blues songs, were personal, not statements of social protest. Whites saw no reason to object to the blues on Saturday night, as long as the work got done on Monday.[96]

But the blues encompass celebration as well as oppression, joy as well as sadness. Evolving mainly as party music, the songs found their natural home in the levee and timber camp, the boarding house of the plantation wage hands, the juke joint, the private party in the countryside, the sidewalk of the town, the country picnic. They flourished in the Delta, in part because, despite black poverty there, sometimes the money flowed into and out of workers' hands. On the Dockery plantation the center of blues music was the "quarters" where single men lived, "a group of maybe eight, ten, twelve boardinghouses and some other houses near the barn and the blacksmiths' shops. . . . The boardinghouses were places where some old woman boarded half a dozen or so day hands who were bachelors. They came and went, and that's where the blues was played." Saturday was payday for the wage hands, so "the blues was a Saturday night deal." In the fall the deal would be bigger yet, with lots of work for day hands picking cotton, and with many tenants getting paid cash for their cotton seed as soon as it was ginned.[97]

Bluesman Honeyboy Edwards told one interviewer, "We might hear about where a job was payin' off—a highway crew, a railroad job, a levee camp there along the river, or some place in the country where a lot of people were workin' on a farm." As Roebuck Staples, who lived on the Dockery plantation, remembered it, "on Saturday afternoons everybody would go into town and those fellows like Charley Patton, Robert Johnson, Howlin' Wolf would be playin' on the streets, standin' by the railroad tracks, people pitchin' 'em nickels and dimes." If they struck a deal to play at someone's house that night, they would hang around the train station to tell everyone where the party would be, perhaps in the countryside, perhaps in the black neighborhood in town. "They'd have a plank nailed across the door to the kitchen and be sellin' fish and chitlins, with dancin' in the front room, gamblin' in the side room, and maybe two or three gas or coal-oil lamps on the mantelpiece in front of the mirror." The musicians played mostly for tips, but the money wasn't trivial, especially when compared with the daily wage of a dollar or so. Floyd Jones, from across the river in Arkansas, once made $17 in one day and night at a baseball game and dance. Jake Martin, another Dockery musician who played only occasionally, could earn $10 a night. Patton himself, one biographer has estimated, might take in $50 to $100 a week at a time when the average sharecropper might clear only $200 or $300 a year. They played for white audiences too. Handy told of playing at a white dance in Cleveland and being asked to let a "local colored band" play for a while. He was happy enough to take a break, then watched in amazement as "the dancers went wild" when a group with a guitar, a mandolin, and a bass played an "over-and-over" strain with "no very clear beginning and certainly no ending at all." "A rain of silver dollars began to fall around the outlandish, stomping feet. . . . There before the boys lay more money than my nine musicians were being paid for the entire engagement."[98]

James Baldwin, writing in the 1960s, called blues both "tart and ironic, authoritative and double edged." At parties, he wrote, "perhaps we were, all of us . . . bound together by the nature of our oppression," but "if so, within these limits we sometimes achieved with each other a freedom that was close to love. I remember, anyway, church suppers and outings, and, later, after I left the church, rent and waistline parties where rage and sorrow sat in the darkness and did not stir, and we ate and drank and talked and laughed and danced and forgot all about 'the man.' We had the liquor, the chicken, the music, and each other, and had no need to pretend to be what we were not."[99] To Richard Wright the blues seemed "frankly atheistic," while others have seen the blues as essentially spiritual. But to insist on the religious character of the blues requires an interpretive stretch, because most bluesmen and most country preachers agreed that the blues were *not* religious, that they were the devil's music. Certainly the devil, and not Jesus or Moses or the other central figures of black spirituals, is the only constant "religious" figure in blues lyrics. When preacher Son House took up music he gave up preaching, and when bluesman Robert Wilkins turned to preaching, he gave up the blues. To Wilkins, "In blues it's what you call a felt-inward feeling—of your own self. . . . It's universal, but it don't bring joy in the spirit. . . . The only thing you can get relief from in the spiritual soul is by praising God. . . . It don't say nothing in the Bible about playing any blues." But the very fact that men like Wilkins and House (who composed "Preachin' the Blues") could go from one role to the other is an example of how much the Saturday night dance and the Sunday morning service shared. Patton recorded spirituals, and on one recording he even breaks into a sermon. B. B. King, who grew up in Indianola in the 1930s, explained the connection this way: "I think that in Mississippi you had this combination of believers and non-believers, I mean church-goers and others. Most of the ones—I don't think I really mean they don't believe in God, but a lot of them didn't go the way of the church, but they had the church training. . . . By having the church training, you still have that same feeling that the church people, so to speak, have. The only difference was they were singing about heavenly bodies and we were singing about the others." On the other hand, Arthur Vinson told an interviewer, "The people get happy in church just like they'll get happy at a dance. It's the same thing." Some see this "same feeling" as derived from African communal life, with a style and a feeling that could be expressed in either church or in a more secular setting. Indeed, the "devil" that appears in many blues songs bears a greater resemblance to African trickster gods like the Yoruban god Legba than it does to the Christian tradition of the devil.[100]

Class, Place, and African American Culture

When Lucy Laney died, one of her eulogizers listed among her accom-plishments her "dramatic crusade" to stamp out a popular African American New Year's Eve celebration, one both "sacrilegious" and "unbecoming," known in Augusta as "Egypt Walking." "Egypt Walking," or "Walking Egypt" as it was also termed, was condemned as early as 1878 by the African American Walker Baptist Association in Augusta, which criticized it as nei-ther scriptural nor in good taste. These sources offer no further description of "Egypt Walking," but since the ritual took place on New Year's Eve, in all likelihood it was a variation of the ring shout that Lydia Parrish on St. Simons Island was simultaneously working hard to preserve. Even on the Sea Islands, the shout had become primarily a Christmas and New Year period ritual. This adds an ironic counterpoint to Laney's work, for she was calling for blacks to investigate the "original" African culture on the Sea Islands even while she was trying to eliminate one of its most important legacies in her own city.[101]

It shows also that, sometimes, there was a greater gap between black working-class culture and black middle-class culture than between a uniform "white" culture and a uniform "black" culture, a greater cultural divide between Charley Patton and Lucy Laney than between Lucy Laney and the middle-class white women of her home town of Augusta. Segregation completely obscured this for most whites; Hortense Powdermaker in the 1930s quoted one relatively "liberal" white who, on hearing a northerner refer to an "upper-class Negro," exclaimed in amazement, "What, do the Negroes have classes?" In her addresses to black audiences, Laney glorified motherhood, marriage, and sexual purity. In 1914 she and other middle-class African American reformers met in Atlanta to discuss ways to improve on the "good manners," "cleanliness," "sound morals," and "personal honesty" of African American youth. Her response to white violence, white discrimination, and white disrespect was to demonstrate in her own life that African Americans shared the standards of most white middle-class Americans, and, drawing on her deep resources of energy and commitment, teach to thousands of black girls and boys the lessons of modern American culture, whether in the form of mathematics, or good manners, or sexual mores. Thus armed, they would earn, and could some day demand, equal treatment and equal respect. Charley Patton, who was a hard-drinking womanizer, was in these same years singing his "Pony Blues": "I don't want to marry just want to be your man." He was not trying to reform anyone or anything, but he was also a musical genius whose instinctive response to white oppression was to seek out those spaces that gave rise to a new art form that came to influence music around the world. If he did not fight in an overt way for freedom, he did exemplify Ralph Ellison's later claim that "the art — the blues, the spirituals, the jazz, the dance — was what we had in place of freedom."[102]

6

War's Challenge to Jim Crow Citizenship

ON 23 JULY 1918, A CAR FOLLOWED BY A CROWD OF PEOPLE pulled up to the city hall in Vicksburg, Mississippi. Several men emerged from the car and pulled out Dave Cook, his upper body coated with tar and feathers. They dragged Cook, a small farmer who lived on the outskirts of town, to the top of the stone structure at the front of the building and hung around his neck a sign that read "I am disloyal to the United States government." As a jeering crowd gathered around the building, the car sped off, soon to return with another tarred and feathered victim — this time a physician, John A. Miller. Cook was taken down, and his sign was hung on Dr. Miller. Miller was displayed in this humiliating fashion while the crowd swelled to some two thousand people. County Sheriff Frank Scott finally led Miller away to the "protection" of the jail, and Mayor J. J. Hayes sent the crowd home with the plea that they "be satisfied with work already accomplished."[1]

This spectacle of humiliation in Vicksburg took place in the emotional atmosphere of patriotism prompted by U.S. entry into the First World War in April 1917. In the year after the declaration of war, millions of Americans became determined to enforce "One Hundred Percent Americanism" throughout the country. Cook, according to those who attacked him, had said that "he would see the United States government in hell" before he would allow any of his sons to be drafted. Miller was accused of refusing to buy war bonds and insulting the volunteers who had asked him to do so. But a close look at these events shows that more than patriotism was behind them. Cook was a white man who lived openly with a black woman, and the sons he was allegedly protecting were children of that union. Leaders of the "flying squadron," as the newspapers called the group responsible for the tar-and-feathering, were later quoted as promising to "specialize on both white men and negro women who have been living together, with a view of breaking up this practice entirely." Not just criticisms of war policies but also open violations of racial norms in marriage were signs of something less than the "One Hundred Percent Americanism" demanded by the war.[2]

Dr. Miller's refusal to buy war bonds was also, at bottom, a violation of racial norms, because Miller was African American. When he was approached by John Hennessey, a prominent white member of the volunteer War Savings Committee, he responded with complaints about poor treatment of blacks generally and about bad schools and low pay for black teachers in particular. "After discussing these local conditions," Dr. Miller later wrote, "I asked Mr. Hennessee [*sic*] as a white man now what would you do if your patriotism at home was crushed as the white people of Vicksburg crush the Negroes. . . . I added I want you to think over what I have said and come back and I will tell you how many bonds I am going to buy." As later newspaper reports made clear, even before this meeting with Hennessey, Dr. Miller had begun to earn a reputation as a troublemaker. One paper reported that rumors of his "disloyal" statements had been circulating for months, and according to another, among his "many disloyal statements" about the Liberty Loan and War Savings drives was his claim that "his race got only half a chance in this community anyhow."[3]

It was the color line, then, and not just the war effort, that was being shored up by a tar-and-feather mob on Vicksburg's streets. Yet, if this episode demonstrates some of the power of white supremacy, it also exposes some of white supremacy's limitations and contradictions. White southerners had, in the generation after Reconstruction, attempted to create a uniform and consistent system of racial subordination. In the economy, blacks were expected to be menial laborers in the fields, in the streets, and in the homes of whites; in public life, blacks would remain distinctly second-class citizens, unable to vote, hold office, sit on juries, or otherwise participate in the affairs of a white man's country. Blacks would be relegated to a personal status lacking full honor, known by first name only, required to acknowledge white superiority in everyday etiquette, and forced, by violence if necessary, to stay in their "place." To defend such a system, whites argued (or simply assumed) that

African Americans were intellectually unfit for higher economic positions or genuine citizenship, morally undeserving of the respect due to equals, and on the whole satisfied with their lowly place.

The color line was strong because it meant greater wealth for many whites and greater status for nearly all whites. It was nonetheless vulnerable because white assumptions about African Americans were not rooted in fact. Many African Americans were slowly pulling themselves up into the middle class, buying farms and homes, educating themselves and their children, and moving into prestigious occupations. Virtually all African Americans, middle-class and poor, resented the color line and, when they could or when they dared, resisted it. Dr. John Miller, a physician, superbly educated at Williams College and the University of Michigan, and unwilling to accept second-class treatment quietly, embodied all of this reality.

The color line was vulnerable also because the South was part of a larger national system, and the economic interests and ideological assumptions of other Americans did not necessarily mesh with those of southern whites. For most of the time between the fall of the Populist Party in 1896 and the U.S. entry into the First World War, this national context meant little for race relations in the South, because much of the South's economy, and especially its cotton economy, remained separate from national economic currents, and because most Americans outside the South were willing to ignore the evident contradictions between national ideals and southern realities. The coming of the war changed both the economic and the ideological relationship of the South to the rest of the country. The war set off economic changes that brought the South's black population into the national labor market, touching off a huge black migration to the North. National policies, including conscription, assumed that blacks, like whites, had to share the normal responsibilities of citizens. Official propaganda, which defended U.S. participation in the war on the grounds that it was being fought for "democracy," raised new and urgent questions about the state of democracy in the South. Whites preferred to think that they had already given satisfactory answers to those questions, but events of the war years would prove them wrong.

Unequal Citizens

In 1908 Georgia became the last southern state to put into place a set of comprehensive elections laws designed primarily to disfranchise black voters. The new laws, passed as amendments to the state constitution, came hard on the heels of the election of Governor Hoke Smith, who had made disfranchisement the centerpiece of his campaign. One of Smith's key supporters was the old Populist Tom Watson, who, after a period of retirement from politics, emerged to back Smith, simultaneously denouncing the railroads and the plutocrats who owned them and calling for total disfranchisement of black voters. For Watson, the two were directly related; if blacks and thus the "bugaboo of negro domination" were eliminated from politics, then whites would be free, finally, to vote their economic interests. Smith harped on the alleged connection between political rights and "social equality." The preachers of political equality, according to the newspaper he edited, simply made the black man "more bumptious on the street. More impudent in his dealings with white men; and then, when he cannot achieve social equality as he wishes, with the instinct of the barbarian to destroy what he cannot attain to, he lies in wait . . . and assaults the fair young girlhood of the south." The constitutional amendments Smith championed eliminated the last vestige of black influence in state politics, completing a campaign for disfranchisement throughout the South that had begun in Mississippi in 1890.[4]

The end of full citizenship for African Americans ramified through society, observable, for example, in the schools. Public schools in both Mississippi and Georgia were largely a product of Reconstruction. In the late nineteenth century they were woefully underfinanced in both states. The school board in Greene County, Georgia, in 1876 congratulated itself on the high moral character of the county's schools, high enough, indeed, to "satisfy the demands of a christian people"; it said that every right-minded citizen should be proud that the county was teaching some fifteen hundred pupils, and praised the teachers in the "colored schools . . . who have evinced an efficiency truly remarkable when we consider their surroundings and their early training." Yet the county was spending only $1.98 for each white pupil and seventy-two cents for every black pupil (a ratio of 2.8 to 1), and out of the forty-four schools only two or three could be considered "comfortable." In 1877, Greene's grand jury deemed it "unwise, impolitic, and inexpedient to levy a tax for the support of [the] schools during the present year." As expenditures in the county slowly increased over the next two decades, the ratio of spending on white and black students stayed about the same, with two or three times as much spent on a white student as on a black student. In 1900, for example, total expenditures were $4.24 for each eligible white child in the county and $1.25 for each black child, a ratio of 3.4 to 1. A decade later, after black voting had been decisively and finally ended by

Georgia's disfranchisement law, spending had sharply increased for white schools but barely moved for black ones. Spurred by Progressive Era reformers, in 1910 the county spent $8.81 in teacher salaries for every white child, but just $1.20 for every black one, a ratio of 7.3 to 1.[5]

This kind of disparity was normal throughout the lower South. In the eastern Piedmont, only two counties (one of them urban Richmond) spent more than $2 per black child on teachers' salaries in 1910, while per-pupil spending for whites ranged from $4.41 in Jefferson to $21 in Richmond and Burke. Along the coast, only urban Chatham County spent more than $3 per black child, and in the Delta, salary expenses per black child were between $2 and $3, for white children about $20. In many places, black parents contributed toward teacher salaries so that school terms could be extended. Disparity in salaries was matched by disparity in buildings, class sizes, and books. There were no public high schools in 1910 for African Americans in the eastern Piedmont, none along the Georgia coast, and only a single high school in the entire Delta. For virtually all education beyond the elementary grades, African American parents had to rely on private and religious schools, which, though usually subsidized by white or black churches, still charged tuition that had to be paid from small incomes.[6]

Inequality in the schools was one grievous effect of white supremacy on blacks, but inequality in the courts was perhaps even more glaring. The effects of inequality are brought into sharp profile in the story of a young black man from Vicksburg who was unfortunate enough to be in the wrong place at the wrong time in 1907. In the fall of that year, Jim Lum was standing peacefully on a Vicksburg street corner among a group of black men and women when two white men, Ben Guider and his cousin Charlie Curphey, both drunk, came by carrying a street sign they had just stolen. The white men "pushed [the sign] over on this negro in some way and he protested about it, saying that he would not treat them that way." It was the kind of conflict over public space that "proper" racial etiquette was supposed to prevent, but the white men were too drunk to play their part in the ritual and Lum too insistent on his rights to play his. A fight broke out, and Guider and Curphey — described in one source as "two of the most powerful men in Warren County" — chased Lum until all three were out of sight of other witnesses. A shot rang out, and Ben Guider was felled with a wound to the abdomen. He died the next day. With no witnesses other than Lum and Curphey, the exact circumstances of the shooting could not be proved, but according to a prominent citizen of Vicksburg writing five years later, "a great many believed, and still believe, that Charlie Curphey fired at the negro and missed him, striking Ben Guider." Lum had no gun when he was arrested, and, his lawyer later argued, he would have been fully justified in shooting Guider if he had had one, because he "had every reason to anticipate that [Guider and Curphey] would do him great bodily injury if they should lay their hands on him."[7]

Unfortunately for Lum, this was Mississippi, and Guider, the son of a wealthy businessman, was "a lovable, companiable man, and . . . highly popular." Only by spiriting Lum away to Jackson until the trial did the sheriff prevent a lynching. At the trial at the Vicksburg Court House, a company of militia, rifles loaded, stood guard, and a local man known for his "desperate courage" was sworn in as a special deputy sheriff and ordered to stay at Lum's side, weapon ready. Every seat was filled, and the crowd overflowed into the space beyond the railing at the front of the spectators, right up to the jury box itself, crowding the attorneys so "that there was barely room to rise out of their chairs." When the jury returned with its verdict, the judge cleared the courtroom of all those standing except for a double row of deputies, who lined the aisle down which the prisoner would be hustled when the verdict was announced. According to Carl Fox, Lum's attorney, "every one's nerves, including the jury's, were strung to the highest pitch of excitement," and it was "openly said" that any verdict other than the death penalty would produce a lynching. Indeed, Fox perhaps considered it a triumph when Lum was convicted, sentenced to life imprisonment, and taken away to prison without being killed by the mob. Five years later, Fox and a number of other men, including a member of the jury itself, asked the governor that Lum be pardoned.[8]

The documents produced by the pardon request offer an unusually candid description of the case and the trial, coming as they do from some of Vicksburg's leading lawyers; they illuminate from the inside the nature of Jim Crow justice in places like Vicksburg. An unlucky victim like Jim Lum could hope for no more than avoiding death with a sentence of life in prison . White men like Fox and A. A. Armistead, who later appealed for a pardon, had a certain sense of themselves as fundamentally just, and also as responsible for the fate of a "darkey" like Lum. In this case, they were willing to examine the facts; they concluded that black men who killed white men were sometimes justified. And yet their sense of justice was corrupted by the racial double standard that ruled public institutions. Even a jury of "strong" men (as Fox described them) were, in the face of the menacing atmosphere of the court house, "almost compelled to return some kind of verdict convicting this darkey." Nor did Fox, Armistead, or others of the white elite doubt that justice was, in the end, to be decided among white men — white judges, white juries, white lawyers, white sheriffs, white governors. That was what a "white man's country" meant.

Whites on Race

As Vicksburg's response to Jim Lum's predicament demonstrates, even though white public opinion in the South was united in an insistence on white supremacy, there remained significant differences among white rationalizations and explanations for the subordination of African Americans. Two broad camps emerged, which have been characterized by historian Joel Williamson as "conservatives" and "radicals." Except for dreamy musings about the far distant future, both camps accepted that the African American presence in the South would be permanent and that whites must rule. They differed in their willingness to see African Americans as differentiated by class and as deserving limited rights of citizenship.[9]

Conservatives tended to be either secure and well-educated planters or urban professional and business progressives. The men who appealed for Jim Lum's pardon are representative of the urban progressive type. They believed, or at least they tried to convince themselves and others, that southern justice was real justice. Of the planters, one of the most articulate voices was that of Alfred Stone, Delta planter and writer, who insisted that African Americans received completely fair treatment in the Delta's courts; he knew of instances, he wrote, when blacks accused of murdering whites, or even of assaulting white women, had been acquitted. Such claims reinforced whites' belief that the relationship between planters and their laborers was based on paternalistic kindness. Stone claimed that the typical planter maintained a benign system of plantation justice "to settle family quarrels, to maintain peace and order between neighbors, to arbitrate disputes, to protect wives from the punishment of irate husbands."[10] Another typical conservative voice was that of William J. Northen, one of the biggest planters in Hancock County, Georgia, and governor of the state in the early 1890s. In 1907 Northen outlined for a national audience the white conservative and paternalist defense of Jim Crow. Whites were the strongest and most civilized of races, he argued, and blacks the weakest and most barbarous. It was not the fault of the African that he was brought to America in chains, nor that, in

Reconstruction, "he was untutored and unguarded and allowed to roam the fields and the country at large . . . [and] left to the promptings and instincts of his wild and destructive nature." Because people of African descent were naturally weak and passive, it was up to the (southern) white man to solve the race problem by dint of his "superior wisdom and superior judgement . . . in righteous and just consideration for the inferior race." Those in the North could not legitimately legislate on the subject since they did not have to live with large numbers of blacks, nor had they suffered "the violent shock that came to the white people and the negroes in Georgia immediately after the war."[11]

Northen acknowledged that the "good class" of African Americans was "intelligent, progressive and resourceful," with high ideals and elevated morals. Booker T. Washington was the ideal representative of this class of people who, in cooperation with the "better elements" of the whites, could play a key role in solving the race problem, especially by helping to curb black crime and encouraging blacks to deliver black criminals to officers of the law. Acknowledging that "we have lawless whites as well as lawless negroes," Northen claimed to have set in motion a plan to form committees of the "best white citizens" in several Georgia counties to undertake "the adjustment of the relations of the races and the proper control of the lawless and disorderly of both races." These whites would later "associate" with "numbers of the law-abiding, good negroes" in each community to continue this good work, and, in return for such cooperation from "good negroes," white elites must guarantee certain rights for every black person. First, blacks must receive proper justice in the courts, and be protected from the "riotous savagery" of lynchings, as much condemned in Georgia, Northen claimed, as anywhere. Second, blacks must have full rights to "industrial privileges and business opportunities" and full access to all trades and professions. Third, blacks must have "equal advantages with the white people" to a public-school primary education, though not to the kind of higher education that lifts them "entirely out of [their] place." It added up to a prescription for citizenship of a well-defined second class.[12]

Another well-known racial conservative was LeRoy Percy of the Delta — like Northen, a politician and big planter. At the urging of his friend Theodore Roosevelt, Percy published one of his speeches, wherein he, like Northen, defended the right of African Americans to a public education. He attacked politicians like Mississippi's Governor James K. Vardaman who were arguing that education of any kind spoiled black laborers. Percy insisted that a proper education would improve black workers. Like Northen, he recognized class and cultural distinctions among African Americans and argued that, in the Delta, the "most desirable class of negro farmers" were the land owners and property-owning tenants who did not need credit and who were nearly all literate. To deny such a man an elementary education — an education, that is, that would "enable him to know whether he is being rightfully or wrongfully treated" — was objectionable both practically and morally. Practically, it would drive out the best labor and lead to what Percy in another context called "the burden of a discontented peasantry." Morally, it was "monstrous and intolerable, because of its harshness and cruelty." Although Percy and Northen largely agreed with one another, Percy was far more willing to acknowledge that many white landlords and employers yielded to the great temptation to cheat the "ignorant, trusting" blacks. If blacks were better educated, it would reduce this temptation to dishonesty which, Percy said, was a threat to the manhood, ideals, and character of the (white) south: "It has sapped and undermined, it is sapping and undermining, and it will sap and undermine, and destroy, the character and integrity of our people, your integrity, my integrity, the integrity of your children, and the integrity of my children." The complacent Northen was, by contrast, content to blame "lawless" whites, which he most certainly equated with poor whites. Percy agreed, however, that blacks were not, and never would be, fit for full citizenship; unlike, for example, Italian immigrants, neither they nor their children nor their children's children could "help us bear the burdens, help us solve the problems of government."[13]

Radicals were often politicians who received most of their votes from small farmers and poor whites. In Georgia's Piedmont, Tom Watson pulled his followers into Hoke Smith's racist campaign in 1908. In Mississippi, the most prominent radical voice was that of James Vardaman, a newspaper editor and Democratic Party activist in Greenwood, at the eastern edge of the Delta, who was elected governor in 1903. In his early career, Vardaman did not stand out as a virulent defender of white supremacy; as a member of the state legislature, for example, he supported appropriations for African American colleges. In the complex factional politics of the Delta in the late 1890s he supported the levee board "ring" controlled by LeRoy Percy and his allies in crucial elections for Congress. He ran for governor twice in the 1890s, both times losing the Democratic nomination (tantamount to election) in a convention controlled by Mississippi's conservatives. In these races, he campaigned as a defender of the small farmer against the power of the planters and what he saw as the lust of the Negro. When Mississippi switched to a primary system to nominate candidates in 1903, Vardaman won a huge victory in the polls. Percy's disagreement with Vardaman's race-baiting tactics led him to break decisively with his former ally. Percy helped defeat Vardaman in his 1907 race for the U.S. Senate, then ran against him for a senatorial seat that opened in 1910 because of an incumbent's death. The state legislature chose Percy to fill the remaining years of the term, but in the 1911 primary election for a full term Vardaman won easily while Percy finished a poor third, with less than one-sixth of the statewide vote.[14]

In his characteristic all-white suit and long curls down to his shoulders, Vardaman was a powerful campaigner. At one campaign stop he arrived in a wagon drawn by twenty pairs of white oxen. His denunciations of corrupt railroads stirred his followers' emotions, but the heart of his campaign was his appeal to the racist fears of his constituents. As governor, he would protect black prisoners, he told the crowd, but in the case of black rapists, as a private citizen he "would head the mob to string the brute up." "We would be justified in slaughtering every Ethiop on the earth to preserve unsullied the honor of one Caucasian home." Vardaman complained that education of an African American "only spoils a good field hand and makes a shyster lawyer or a fourth-rate teacher"; even worse, "the unmentionable crime" (by which he meant black rape of white women) was "but a manifestation of the negro's aspiration for social equality, encouraged largely by the character of free education in vogue." Vardaman proposed to segregate poll taxes (the main support of public education) by race, so that black schools would receive only such money as blacks themselves paid. (In fact, such a policy would have had more effect on the white schools than on black schools in heavily black counties such as those in the Delta. Mississippi distributed state funds to counties on the basis of the number of school-age children. The Delta's counties received significant funds because of their large populations, but spent most of the money on their few white students.) As for politics, whites should not, could not, must not share with blacks one iota of "sovereignty and dominion." While history had shown "that the negro was created for some good purpose," God had created the black man or woman "for a menial; he is essentially a servant." In the early years of the century, Vardaman traveled widely through the South and elsewhere in the nation to deliver his lecture on "The Impending Crisis," spreading his views that only repeal of the Reconstruction amendments would stifle among African Americans the ambition that led inevitably to lust for white women.[15]

Radical racist propaganda was not limited to political campaigns. Thomas Norwood of Savannah, a United States senator and candidate for governor as an independent before serving as a Chatham County Superior Court judge, published, on the occasion of his retirement from the bench in 1907, a bitter diatribe against African Americans in general, and against the "calamity" of Reconstruction, which had made them citizens. History demonstrated, according to Norwood, that African Americans were a barbarous race unfit for citizenship. After the disaster of Reconstruction, which Norwood blamed on the "ferocious, implacable Puritan" who had waged a war of abolition on the South, the "negro" had persisted in his "illusion of social, political and mental equality to the white race." The Negro race, he insisted, was "homo in form" only, relegated by ineradicable physical differences to permanent inferiority. No pure black man could rise above savagery. According to Norwood, any African Americans who had done so were invariably mulattoes such as Booker T. Washington, whom he called "the sleekest beggar in America," "the fattest parasite of his race."

Echoing Vardaman, Norwood called all those of African descent "the servant race of the earth," and, like Vardaman, he concluded that "it is neither right, just, nor practicable, for the white race to bear the burden of the entire education of both races." He listed further recommendations for the "reform" of criminal law, originally designed for white men to judge other white men. Such changes would, for example, provide judges like himself wide discretion in imposing sentences, ranging from nominal fines to penitentiary sentences, and also alter laws of evidence so that the state could successfully prosecute solely on evidence like "the character and prior misdeeds of the defendant." Vagrancy laws, which were entirely too lenient, ought to be stiffened so that judges could force into labor the "five to eight thousand vagrants" in Savannah, especially the female vagrants who were "without exception, prostitutes, pickpockets, shop lifters, hall thieves, and nearly all are drunkards." Norwood denounced as "the worst trait of the negro, except his lust," his determination to conceal black criminals. "If the crime be against the white race . . . the criminal always finds with his race shelter, protection, secretion and aid to escape. It is only when the crime is against himself that he will inform and seek the law and the white man's assistance for redress or punishment of the criminal." It seems remarkable that even so obtuse an observer as Norwood could fail to recognize that African Americans would refuse to recognize the legitimacy of law made by judges like him.[16]

Conservatives and radicals both believed in a thoroughgoing white supremacy and insisted that northerners ought to have no say in southern race relations. Conservatives and radicals alike saw white supremacy as a logical derivation from "the elementary principles of the white man's human nature," to use the words of Delta planter Alfred H. Stone. There must be no "social equality" and whites must control politics. Conservatives, who were often planters themselves, differed from popular politicians like Vardaman or Hoke Smith in seeing class issues as complicating the race "problem." Their ideas about race were filtered through a sense of dependence on black labor, rather than a sense of competition with that labor. They often knew the "better classes" of blacks personally, and some of them, like Stone, read widely in black newspapers and other writings. They had considerable knowledge of the differences in class and culture among African Americans as well as a highly developed sense of class differences among whites. Some blacks, they understood, were educated, refined, and moral; some whites (mainly the poor) were lawless and "vicious." Class differences between conservatives and poor whites sometimes loomed larger than racial solidarity. Stone argued that racial conflict was most intense in places where poor whites and African Americans competed with each other economically. Hence, he believed, relations between blacks and whites in the Delta were peaceful because nearly all whites were so superior to nearly all blacks that the latter continued to accept the "absolute obedience" that had characterized antebellum slavery. Whites could give blacks places of "responsibility and trust" as constables, mail carriers, and even cotton buyers and telephone linemen. (Stone blamed the uproar in Indianola over the reappointment of a black woman as postmistress on "outside" interference rather than race prejudice.) Sexual assaults by black men against white women were almost unknown in the Delta, he reported, adding, "We have few midnight assassinations, and fewer lynchings."[17]

But Stone was deluding himself. In the five years before his book was published, nearly thirty black men had been lynched in Delta counties. The lynching rate there was far higher than in the Georgia Piedmont, where white and black tenants competed much more directly with each other than in the Delta. Stone's failure to acknowledge such lynchings was typical of white elites. And the strongest denunciations of lynching by "respectable" citizens were typically tempered with excuses for killing blacks thought to have raped white women. In Bolivar County, Mississippi, in 1904, a public meeting, called to express the public's "deep shame and humiliation" at a particularly brutal lynching of a black woman, denounced lynchers as more dangerous than the criminals they killed, but made an exception for "the crime which in the South, puts its perpertrator [sic] on a level with the beasts of prey, and beyond the pale of human sympathy and protection of the law."[18]

Conservatives like Stone believed that the great mass of southern African Americans were "content with their situation." To Stone they were "model prisoners." A pamphlet put out by Vicksburg's businessmen to attract northern investors assured the readers that "southern labor" — meaning black labor — was not only "cheap and plentiful" but also "docile and obedient . . . easily managed and easily pleased." In contrast to northern labor, which was "headstrong and ofttimes unmanageable," the black worker was "happy, thoughtless, contented. . . . His race indulges in no anarchistic or socialistic ideas. The negro never questions the right of another to take his place when he has been discharged or has voluntarily surrendered it. The idea of a boycott is repugnant to his nature." The wife of a planter, reminiscing about the good old days, described black tenants as "care-free, light-hearted people. The climate suited them, they liked the field work, and they had this wide range for fishing and hunting. They knew they would be cared for in illness or serious trouble." Such fantasies were self-protection against full knowledge of what the South's racial system meant for most blacks and what black men and women really thought.[19]

The first faint stirring of a more liberal view of race among whites, one that rejected radical racism and went far beyond conservative paternalism, appeared among women in the "social Christianity" movement in the South, especially in the Women's Home Missionary Society of the Methodist Episcopal Church, South. Among their leading voices was that of Augusta's Lily Hammond, the daughter of slaveowners and the wife of the white president of Paine College, which had been established by white Southern Methodists for African American students. She and other Methodist women, as early as the 1890s, saw the "negro problem" as an important field for their work. While in early years their concern was heavily moralistic and paternalist, and their "duty" as Christian women focused primarily on the "purifying and uplifting of the negro home," by the turn of the century they turned their attention toward social conditions and white prejudice and discrimination as root causes of the "negro problem."[20]

As early as 1903, Lily Hammond wrote for a national audience in the magazine *Outlook,* pointing to the rise of an educated black middle class as evidence of black progress. Though she deplored the "lack of morals among the mass of the negroes," she argued that whites themselves had been in a similar state a few centuries earlier, and that African Americans were simply somewhat behind on the scale of improvement. In Hammond's 1914 book on race in the South, *In Black and White*, the evolution of her argument and tone is signaled by her deliberate use of the capitalized *Negro* rather than the customary *negro*. Her interpretation of what she saw as black deficiencies was thoroughly environmentalist. "We have mistakenly counted our poverty line and our colour line as one," she wrote, but Negroes were no different from men everywhere who lived in the poor conditions experienced by most Negroes. She condemned the blatant discrimination blacks faced in the courts and the "law-abiding majority" of whites who tolerated lynchings: if the "savage" minority "do the deed, we who could prevent it, permit them." As much as anything, Hammond's contact with Augusta's black middle-class women had altered her understanding of race. Southern whites insisted that they alone truly understood "their negroes," but, Hammond acknowledged, "the truth is, we know nothing about what Negroes were made for or what they are capable of."[21]

One of the first concrete actions of the Women's Home Mission Society concerning black-white relations was its 1901 decision to build an annex at Paine College for industrial training for black girls. A decade later the society's successor, the Women's Missionary Council, sent to Augusta, as their first "home missionary" to blacks, Mary De Bardeleben, who organized a Civic Improvement League that sponsored a kindergarten, a Sunday School, and the first white-run settlement house in a southern black neighborhood. Like Hammond, De Bardeleben, at first, had what she later called "a decided feeling of superiority" to the African Americans she was trying to serve, but she came to an "appreciation of what was good and true and beautiful in the Negro race and to a sense of shame and humility for having been so blind and dumb as not to understand more readily." Like Hammond, she insisted that black problems were rooted in environmental causes and that "we cannot consistently censure the laxness and shiftlessness among many negroes until we have done all we can to better their housing conditions." Women such as Hammond and De Bardeleben represented the still-rare cases of white reformers before 1920 willing to work closely with African Americans to make their lives better, not simply to exhort them to improve their morals.[22]

Blacks on Race

The belief of many whites that southern African Americans were content with their second-class citizenship was bolstered, no doubt, by occasional pronouncements from African Americans themselves, such as the 1908 publication by W. E. Mollison of *The Leading Afro-Americans of Vicksburg,* a compendium of the economic achievements of Vicksburg's black middle class. Mollison was a graduate of Fisk and Oberlin, a lawyer, bank president, and head of a local fraternal organization. Colored people, he wrote, had tried politics after the Civil War only because they "are imitative of the best as well as the worst of their white neighbors," but the black citizen of Vicksburg was not "at his best" in politics, and now "the colored man has no part in the management of local affairs. He has accepted the inevitable and pursues the path of simple industry and energetic effort to make homes and means of livelihood." In these "gentler walks of private and business life," however, the black man has "won for himself a name for integrity as well as ability." A native of Issaquena County in the Delta, Mollison was himself, ironically, a product of the black political activism that survived Reconstruction in Mississippi. He had returned to Issaquena after graduating from Oberlin and, in the 1880s, served there as superintendent of schools and a clerk in both the circuit and chancery courts. In 1892 he had nominated James G. Blaine for president in the Republican National Convention.[23]

Wherever political activism had not been completely crushed by violence, the African American middle class was continuing to organize and protest disfranchisement and segregation. In Georgia in 1906, faced with a rising tide of sentiment in favor of final disfranchisement of black voters and inspired by the "Niagra Movement" organized by black leader W. E. B. Du Bois, African Americans met in Macon at an Equal Rights Convention, led by William J. White of Augusta, publisher of the *Georgia Baptist* and a Reconstruction political activist. The convention's resolutions denounced disfranchisement, Jim Crow transportation laws, lynchings, and the convict lease system, and called upon whites and blacks to live together "as man and man, equal in the sight of God and in the eye of the law." Black grievances were stated in no uncertain terms: "We are too often cheated out of scanty earnings. . . . [T]he laws . . . are cunning with injustice toward us. . . . As long as public and private wealth in Georgia fattens on the sale of black criminals [i.e., convict leasing], so long will crime be encouraged and the outcry against it will ring with hypocrisy." Such sentiments found more concrete expression in the boycotts mounted by blacks in Augusta and Savannah against Jim Crow ordinances. The 1900 boycott in Augusta followed the imposition of segregation in streetcars after a white man was killed by a black passenger (the alleged killer, William Wilson, was lynched before arrest). In Savannah, black leaders aided by streetcar operators who feared that segregation laws would reduce their profits defeated a segregation ordinance in 1902. After a new local Jim Crow streetcar law was passed in 1906, a black boycott that lasted many months cost the streetcar line more than $50,000 in lost revenues.[24]

Neither boycott was, in the end, successful in preventing segregation in the streetcars. Nor could the Equal Rights League prevent passage of disfranchisement laws in Georgia in 1908. Whites had at their command too much political and economic power. They could use economic pressure or outright bribery to divide the black elite. To break the Savannah boycott, whites pressured teachers at Savannah's public black college to ride the cars, and gave money to a black minister, the Reverend Jonathon Nelson, director of the Colored Orphans Home, to persuade him to oppose the boycott. Whites could also resort to violence to limit public protest and organization. In 1900 in Augusta, William J. White was threatened with a lynching himself when he reprinted an article from the Washington *Bee* that referred to lynching victim William Wilson as "a martyr in defense of female virtue." In 1906, he was threatened again with mob violence and compelled to flee the city temporarily in the wake of an editorial in which he suggested that, if Augusta's white families were having difficulty getting good servants, they might hire some of the "white women servants from the North who have been discarded in favor of colored servants" who had gone north to escape Augusta's own Jim Crow laws. In the face of growing opposition, black Georgians cast thousands of ballots against the disfranchising amendments to the constitution in 1908, and along the coast disfranchisement lost by a substantial margin.[25]

Repression could not silence all black voices. White's *Georgia Baptist* and the Savannah *Tribune,* edited by John H. Deveaux and Sol C. Johnson, continued to speak out for black equality. But others in the black elite adopted Booker T. Washington's advice to put aside politics, at least for the time being, to cooperate with the "best white men," and to concentrate on black economic advancement. Vicksburg's W. E. Mollison publicly adopted this line. Another, more private version of such acquiescence appears in the 1904 correspondence of Percy G. Shadd, a "colored lawyer" from Augusta, with Georgia's Governor John M. Slaton. Shadd described himself as a new arrival from Tennessee; "the leading white people" of his county had sent him off with a letter of recommendation. Shadd encouraged the governor to sponsor legislation that would have warmed the heart of many a planter — one new law, he said, should "make it a crime for anyone to encourage any one to leave his job," and another should make a penitentiary sentence mandatory for anyone convicted of stealing. Such laws would eliminate theft and help to solve the "greatest problem that ever confronted my people" by forcing blacks to become reliable laborers. "If we do not become more reliable as a race; in the course of a short time some other race will take our place." Perhaps Shadd identified personally with white paternalist, conservative values, or perhaps he hoped to curry favor with someone who could help him in some way. Rev. Jonathon Nelson of Savannah, who had helped defeat the streetcar boycott, might have calculated that white assistance and white money were more valuable than black solidarity. In the late 1890s, the U.S. district attorney in Atlanta had been thwarted in his investigation of peonage cases in Oglethorpe County by the "interference of interested, officious colored men against a vigorous prosecution by the Government." The white defendants apparently hired a black lawyer from Athens (unnamed in the surviving federal sources) who worked out deals with the alleged victims to compensate them in return for refusal to testify in the case.[26]

Other middle-class blacks turned their backs completely on the white South, advocating racial separatism, even migration to Africa. Perhaps the most revealing such case was that of Lucius Holsey of Augusta, a bishop in the Colored Methodist Episcopal Church. Holsey, who had been fathered by a white man and converted by a white preacher, was trained and ordained by Southern Methodist Bishop George Pierce (a native of Greene County). While insisting on the equality of all races, for most of his life he did not criticize whites or white culture. He wrote in his autobiography that slavery, "however unrighteous or repugnant to a Christian civilization the institution seems to have been," had been a school of Christian training for the Negro race, which "has lost nothing by it, but has gained a thousand pounds sterling where it has lost a penny." Holsey looked to paternalistic whites for "sympathy, aid, and cooperation." He was instrumental in getting white support to establish Paine Institute (later College) in Augusta, where teachers, most of them white, would train African American teachers and ministers. But, by the late 1890s, Holsey had witnessed lynchings and the consequences of new segregation laws in Augusta. In 1896 he endorsed the Populist Party on the grounds that they favored freedom of speech for blacks and because of their opposition to the "shameful, degrading, and disgusting" convict lease system. He moved to Atlanta shortly afterwards, and later admitted that he had been mistaken in his earlier conviction that African Americans would realize full political equality as soon as they had demonstrated the appropriate "culture, wealth, and moral standing." Convinced that white hostility and prejudice were too great for blacks ever to "occupy the same plane of freedom and citizenship" as whites, Holsey proposed a new, all-black state to be established west of the Mississippi, where the African American could rule and judge himself and be "a man among men."[27]

All such expressions of African American opinion — whether favoring acquiescence to the segregated order, separatism, or resistance — originated from the small, educated black middle class. White observers, such as Mississippi's Alfred Stone, who were familiar with these opinions continued to believe that "the Negro masses in the Southern States are content with their situation." The masses of rural laborers and farmers seldom spoke out in ways that whites could hear. Ordinary working-class blacks did not write books or editorials, and even the African American middle class often looked down on the black masses.[28] But ordinary black men and women did express their opinions quite articulately, if not in essays, then in stories, songs, and jokes, none of which were likely to reach the ears of whites. Most of them did not appear in print for a generation or two, when scholars and collectors began to gain the confidence of ordinary African Americans. Alan Lomax, one of the first to do so, heard a lot from the singers he talked to about the blues. Blues singers' songs, as noted earlier (in Chapter 5) could seldom be classified as "protest" songs, but, as Mississippian Big Bill Broonzy told Lomax in 1946, the blues reflected the experiences of everyday labor under white bosses. "I worked on levee camps, extra gangs, road camps and rock camps. . . . I've known guys that wanted to cuss out the boss and was afraid to go up to his face and tell him what he wanted to tell him, and I've heard them sing those things — sing words, you know, back to the boss." Broonzy, Sonny Boy Williamson (from just north of Memphis), and Memphis Slim told Lomax that the Loran brothers, levee contractors, "wouldn't allow a man to quit unless they got tired of him and drove him away." Their workers sang:

I axed Mister Charley
What time of day.
He looked at me
Threw his watch away.

Lomax heard about Broonzy's uncle, who beat up and ran off a white manager who was trying to force his wife to go into the fields and work. A gang of
whites came back that night and lynched him.[29]

One white who recorded some of the songs in which blacks expressed
these feelings and told these stories was Lawrence Gellert, a political radical
who moved to North Carolina in the 1920s and took up residence with
a black woman. Somehow, Gellert won the confidence of both influential
whites and ordinary blacks. He traveled throughout the South with a make-
shift field recording outfit, observing black life and recording more than three
hundred songs. Near Augusta, Georgia, Gellert recounted, "I hung around a
chain-gang for days. One of the Negro convicts somehow aroused the wrath
of the guards. Two of them went for him, pummeled and kicked him until he
lay still and bleeding on the ground. 'Isn't there a law of some kind against a
guard beating a prisoner?' I asked a third guard lolling on the grass beside
me, watching the proceedings. 'Hell,' he answered, 'there ain't no law for
niggers. We has to use our own judgement.' And he showed me the horrible
abrasions and ring sores, brass knuckles had caused in the exercise of 'good
judgement.' 'We ain't allowed to use no whips no more,' he explained."[30]

Gellert later published two dozen of his recordings as "Negro songs
of protest." Some were wry commentaries on black life in a world run by
whites: "I went to Atlanta, Never been dere afo' / White folks eat de apple,
Nigger wait fo' co'." Some complained more directly of exploitation in the
fields: "He work so hahd, jes' fo' gettin' ahead, But he were crosseye, filled
Captain's pockets instead." Others were angry and threatened to answer violence with violence. In "Sistren an' Brethren," about a brother killed "tryin'
to keep what was his all de time," the singers tell blacks to "stand on yo' feet,
Club gripped 'tween yo' hands / Spill dere blood too, show'em yo's is a
man's." A variation on the same theme is "Out in de Rain": "Cap'n Bob
Russell, / meanes' man in town, ef you ast fo' yo' money he shoot you
down. / . . . He better not come mess wit' me no mo' / Ah's all ready dis time
wit mah foh'ty fo'." Summarizing it all is " 'Cause I'm a Nigger":

> You take mah labor, an' steal mah time
> give me ol' dishpan an' a lousy dime
> 'Cause I'm a nigger, dat's why. . . .
> I feel it comin', Cap'n, Goin' see you in Goddamn
> Take mah pick an' shovel, Bury you in Debbil's lan'
> 'Cause I'm a nigger, dat's why.

These songs, or variations of them, no doubt circulated for many years before Gellert began to collect them in the 1930s. They expressed something
much closer to the true sentiments of the "Negro masses" than the happy
contentment many whites imagined, as whites learned in a concrete way
during the First World War.[31]

Markets in War: The Great Migration Begins

The period just before the outbreak of the First World War would be remembered by American farmers as a kind of golden age. Later, in the 1930s,
when new government programs began to prop up agricultural prices, the
period from 1910 to 1914 was selected as the standard for "parity" prices.
Walter Sillers of Bolivar County wrote in 1909 that the prices of cotton and
cotton seed "read like a fairy tale"; they were not much lower in 1913. High
prices had prompted larger and larger cotton plantings, even though the boll
weevil was damaging crops in many places, including in the Delta; the 1914
crop of sixteen million bales was the largest ever grown in the United States
to that time.[32] This bumper crop would probably have lowered cotton prices
in any case, but as it was about to be harvested, war broke out in Europe. The
resulting disruptions and uncertainties battered the markets and drove cotton down to just over seven cents a pound, the lowest in more than a decade.
The resulting financial panic wiped out small banks, including several black-
owned banks in the Delta. In the fall of 1914, Sillers himself was scrambling
to deal with the "gloomy conditions" by selling land to hay and stock farmers
and requiring his own tenants to grow more hay and corn.[33]

Soon, with increased wartime demand and sharp reductions in plantings,
cotton prices bounced back. Prices during the war years soon made the "fairy
tale" prices of 1909 seem low. From eleven-plus cents in 1915 the price went
to seventeen cents, then twenty-seven cents, then over thirty-five cents in
1919. Many white planters and farmers tried to keep as much of this windfall
as they could, and one African American minister and businessman in the
Delta complained to a Baltimore acquaintance that often the crops were
"simply taken from [tenants] at prices to suit the white landlords. If he wants
to allow a Negro from 15 to 20 cents, why that is all there is to it. It matters
not that the colored man can ship his cotton and get 40 and 50 cents for it, if
the cotton is raised on the landlord's place . . . [The tenant] is so cramped to
death but is afraid to say a word for his protection." Even white newspapers
admitted that while "unfair dealing with the Negro is not a custom in the

South . . . here and there the taking of enormous profits from the labor of the Negro is known to exist."[34] Nonetheless, black farmers and tenants throughout the cotton regions of the South did well during the war. In the sharecropping system even the poorest black farmers could make substantial amounts of money when cotton prices were high. By the fall of 1916, one Memphis newspaper applauded a meeting of local black Baptist ministers who criticized the extravagance of "those who find themselves in possession of unexpected money because of the high price of cotton. The purchase of automobiles, pianos, victrolas and other luxuries by those without homes and having nothing but a little cash was condemned as unwise." Delta planter LeRoy Percy told his insurance broker, "I hope you are insuring the colored brethren to a farewell. No possible stone must be left unturned to keep them from becoming unduly opulent and cotton at present prices should make him an 'easy mark.'" If black tenants had become potential "easy marks" for salesmen of insurance, Victrolas, and even automobiles, it was because they had money in their pockets to spend.[35]

Cotton farmers had never been economically isolated from the world; from the beginning of large-scale production in the eighteenth century, they had prospered and suffered with the cycles of world demand, but they had benefited from relative isolation from the rest of the world when it came to the South's huge pool of cheap black labor. Even after the abolition of slavery, the market for unskilled labor in the South was dominated by black men and women. In the Northeast and Midwest, by contrast, the astounding growth of huge new manufacturing industries had been fueled by a new source of labor, immigrants who poured into the country primarily from eastern and southern Europe.[36] Now, as the war was creating a huge new demand for manufactured goods and agricultural products, it simultaneously stanched the influx of immigrants, creating sharp labor shortages. Northern industry turned, for the first time, to southern African Americans as a major source of cheap labor.

The South's relative isolation from the national markets for labor was broken, decisively altering the economic dynamic in both town and country and setting in motion the "Great Migration" of blacks to the North. A turning point, the importance of which is clear only in retrospect, came when the National Urban League, an interracial organization established in New York City in 1910 to provide economic aid to black migrants to the North, in 1915 began to recruit temporary black laborers in the South to help harvest the small tobacco crop in Connecticut.[37] Inspired by this example, the Pennsylvania Railroad sent labor agents down the East Coast to recruit laborers in the summer of 1916, beginning in Jacksonville, Florida, and Savannah. The effect was like a match set to kindling. The railroad's agent arrived in Savannah from Jacksonville in late July, set up shop in a "dingy store" in a black neighborhood, and promised free transportation and food en route to jobs, plus a minimum of $1.80 per day in wages. He promptly signed up three hundred men and sent them on their way. This was enough to get the attention of local employers, who complained to the mayor about an impending "labor shortage," by which they meant a shortage of men willing to work for $1.00 or $1.25 per day. On July 30, the mayor sent the police to arrest the agent for failing to purchase a labor agent's license. The following day, the police arrested two more agents. Readers of the Savannah *Morning News* read the headlines: "Fear Industries Will Be Crippled"; "City Determined to Prevent Emigration of Negroes." The next day twenty-five hundred black men and women—as many as a thousand of them from outside Savannah— swarmed to the train station.[38]

The seeming suddenness of the black out-migration and its quick spread across the South to the Mississippi Delta and beyond created an impression of an utterly spontaneous and almost irrational mass movement. One investigator described the movement as a "fever," with blacks selling everything they had "or in a manner giving it away; selling their homes, mules, horses, cows, and everything about them but their trunks." Another wrote that, when labor agents first arrived in Mississippi, "their offers created unprecedented commotion. Drivers and teamsters left their wagons standing in the street. Workers, returning home, scrambled aboard the trains for the North without notifying either their employers or their families."[39]

A commotion there certainly was, but the migration of African Americans from the South was an eminently rational enterprise, and, in the vast majority of cases, was based on information and planning. The first information came from labor agents, and it was persuasive—jobs were available that might pay double the going southern wage for unskilled labor. An abundance of evidence from migrants and would-be migrants shows this economic motivation. From Savannah, prospective migrants wrote that "jobs are very hard to find down here," that "the reason why I wanted to come up there [to Chicago] is for more wages, I am a man with a family and works hard, but don't get sufficient wages to support my family." From Augusta, a man who had worked twenty years in a lumber mill wrote, "I would like to make some of the good pay for God knows we need it in Augusta." A Vicksburg man making $1.25 per day moved to Chicago, where he earned thirty cents an hour.[40] Many similar letters appeared in the pages of the Chicago *Defender,* a crusading African American paper edited by Robert Abbott, who had come to Chicago after growing up in Georgia's Sea Island region. The *Defender,* a significant source of information for potential migrants, especially in the Delta, was secretly carried by train porters and others down the tracks of the Illinois Central. The *Defender* carried news of the migration, descriptions of the high wages in the North, and exhortations to leave the benighted South. The paper became so notorious among whites that when Abbott visited his Georgia relatives he traveled in disguise. In 1917, two black men were arrested in Savannah for "inciting to riot" after distributing poetry ("doggerel" as the white newspaper put it) on the migration from the *Defender.*[41]

The most important "agents" of the migration, though, were African American migrants themselves. The Pennsylvania Railroad's agent understood quite well that he could not create a movement out of nothing or keep one going by himself. "If we can only get these men North and give them time to get settled and get letters back to their friends here we will get all we want of them," he explained. This pattern of chain migration, with one relative or friend contacting and sometimes subsidizing another, made the migration a great social movement rather than a temporary "commotion." Letters sent home would, in turn, circulate among others. "The migration became the theme of discussion in pulpits, lodges, barbershops, pool rooms, on the street; in fact, everywhere."[42]

The Urban League launched a project to document the reasons for the sudden massive increase in migration. Among the places they studied in detail was the Delta, and their reports contain some of the most candid assessments of what African Americans thought about their lives and why they wanted to leave. Everywhere the league's investigators heard the same litany of complaint, only the details and examples varying. Higher wages in the North were the most important motivating factor, but right behind that were the South's poor schools, injustice in the courts, insecurity of property and person, and the pervasive indignities that marked the lives of almost all black men and women. In Vicksburg blacks complained that the schools were "old and dangerously crowded," that the curriculum was a year behind that of white schools, and that good teachers were difficult to keep because the pay was less than one-third of that for white teachers. They told stories of a white man who, with the help of a deputy, killed the black lover of his

"Negro mistress," of a preacher who was arrested on the road and beaten so badly that he died, of a white man who used a revolver to beat senseless a black buggy driver who had bumped into him (for this the white was fined $5 for carrying a concealed pistol). In Greenville, a researcher heard that Dr. E. P. Brown, a black physician who had practiced there for more than forty-five years, was dragged from his buggy and arrested when he did not move out of the way of a white man's buggy. In Greenwood, Vardaman's home, the constables thrived on fees paid by blacks arrested "indiscriminately on trivial charges." In Clarksdale there was "complete and universal dissatisfaction" with schools — in a recent year black schools had received just $2,000 from the town, white schools $28,000; the "colored principal" was "a tool. Unpopular with Negroes." Outside Clarksdale black tenants felt cheated when planters paid them less than market prices for their cotton. In the courts "Negro witnesses count for nothing" against a white person, but "the testimony of a white woman is conclusive in every instance." Even spending their newly won incomes could be dangerous, for in Clarksdale, as in many other places, a black man in a car might be stopped for trivial reasons, given large fines for any accident, or even beaten for showing off his prosperity. In Indianola and Leland the same complaints were heard: cheating on settlements, poor schools, lack of justice in the courts.[43]

The initial response of whites in power was surprise, alarm, and repression. The surprise was a result of whites' tendency to be taken in by their own propaganda about black satisfaction with life in the South. As one black Mississippi educator explained, "Many white men of high intellectual ability and keen discernment have mistaken the negroes' silence for contentment, his facial expression for satisfaction at prevailing conditions, and his songs and jovial air for happiness. But this is not always so." The alarm was that the South would suffer "labor shortages." In Savannah the *Morning News* editors insisted that "this section is unwilling for its Negro labor supply to be so depleted that when the time comes to harvest the cotton crop, pickers will be scarce." Repression came in formal and "popular" varieties. The police in Savannah tried not only to drive out labor agents but also to intimidate potential migrants. In one day at the train depot more than one hundred African Americans were arrested and, since the jail would not hold them, sent to a local barracks. Seventeen college graduates, waiting to board a steamer for New York City, were arrested on charges of "loitering." J. H. Butler, manager of the black-owned Savannah *Tribune*, while covering the story at the depot, was arrested and charged with "sending labor out of the city." In Greenville, Mississippi, police and other whites assaulted black men at the station, and whites boarded trains to remove suspected migrants.[44]

White elites also turned to black leaders — or, at any rate, black men whom they considered to be leaders — to try to convince would-be migrants to stay. In truth, many members of the black elite had good reason to counsel against migration. Ministers stood in danger of losing their congregations, professionals their clients, businessmen their customers. Whites turned, therefore, to businessmen such as Vicksburg's Mollison or Mound Bayou's Charles Banks, and to ministers such as Savannah's Boliver Davis. Some of these men did, indeed, work hard to stem the outflow, but in many cases whites got both less and more than they bargained for from the black elite. Less, because many refused to help whites and because those who did were largely ineffectual. Several ministers in the vicinity of Greenwood, in the Delta, told an Urban League investigator that they had refused large sums of money offered by local white bankers to discourage the movement. Mollison was asked to come to Greenville and speak out against the migration, but his reception by local blacks was so hostile that he spoke on something else. Rev. Davis urged members of his congregation to stay in the South but admitted, "I have not had smooth sailing in preaching this doctrine to our people." A study of the eastern Piedmont of Georgia, published in 1920, noted that local black leaders "did not oppose but rather encouraged the migration of 1916–17. Although their personal interest is in seeing their race stay in the South, the conditions from which they were moving were so patently undesirable that the leaders either did not discourage or actively encouraged the movement."[45]

Black spokesmen also told whites a good deal more than they really wanted to hear. In Savannah, just as the migration was getting under way, the mayor met with a delegation of blacks led by a professor at Savannah's Georgia State Industrial College. The delegation told the mayor that Savannah did not suffer from any kind of labor "shortage"; on the contrary, many blacks were unemployed. The real problem was low wages and job discrimination. All a black man wanted was an opportunity to work to "provide for his wife and children, pay his rent or his installment on his home, meet his obligations to his society and his church." Under the circumstances, they told the mayor, they could not advise blacks to stay. Baptist ministers meeting in Memphis did urge blacks to stay in the South, but in their discussions they pointed out that emigration from the Delta was caused by the crop lien system, mob violence, and inadequate schools. Charles Banks of Bayou, Mississippi, wrote to the Jackson *News* that "it would be the veriest hypocrisy to pretend easiness and satisfaction when charred remains are brought and displayed on the principal street of a Negro business." On 1 January 1917—in a ceremony commemorating the Emancipation Proclamation—Rev. J. A. Martin, pastor at St. Paul's Colored Methodist Church in Savannah, did urge African Americans to stay in the South but on the grounds that "we must cast our lot in the South or Africa for rights, and protest every inch. The change from Savannah to Pennsylvania will not solve the problem as regards race. It is not the change of home we need, but the change of sentiment. Let us remain in the South and fight manfully for what is right." He spelled out what he meant by "what is right": "The honest colored man cannot be satisfied with anything less than a man's chance, going up or down on his merit. . . . We are satisfied to go apart and be distinct as a race, but to us government, when and where voting, for the purpose of settling moral problems, is colorless and . . . should be wielded without fear or favor." Two days later, a letter from R. R. Wright to the Savannah *Morning News* summarized the sources of the migration in terms that were surprisingly frank, considering the fact that Wright, president of black Savannah State College, was a state employee:

Our white friends should know that not only in the lynchings, and in the courts and in the unwholesome conditions on the southern railway common carriers (as vital as these are), but that in the general attitude of many of our southern white people, there is exhibited a contempt for the negro which makes the best of the negroes feel that they are only tolerated in the South. . . . In the face of our [white] friends it is hard to explain this discounting and this contemptuous attitude, and yet everybody understands that it exists. "You are only a negro and are not entitled to the courteous treatment accorded to members of other races." Another cause is the feeling of insecurity. The lack of legal protection in the country is a constant nightmare to the colored people who are trying to accumulate a comfortable little home and farm.

There is scarcely a negro mother in the country who does not live in dread and fear that her husband or son may come in unfriendly contact with some white person so as to bring the lynchers or the arresting officers to her door, which may result in the wiping out of her entire family.[46]

Blacks spoke, and some whites listened. One Savannah editor admitted that southern whites needed "to extend to the Negroes such treatment only as is fair and just" and to refuse to countenance "wholesale" arrests of Negroes "because they are Negroes." The editor of the Memphis *Commercial-Appeal* agreed. "The South needs every able-bodied Negro," but in order to keep blacks in the South "the Negro should be protected in all his legal rights." A public meeting in the Delta's Bolivar County heard a report from a committee of twelve whites and five blacks that the migration was due to the insecurity of blacks before the law, mob violence, unfair settlements, and inadequate schools. Whites pledged to raise $25,000 for a new agricultural high school for African Americans and promised to "make unpopular the practice among farmers of robbing Negroes of cotton values." A Vicksburg paper reprinted a letter describing the case of a ten-year-old black boy who was convicted for stealing beer bottles and sentenced to a year in the penitentiary, calling it an obvious injustice and appealing to (white) citizens to "thoughtfully consider what is here set forth." The paper also gave column space to African Americans, under such designations as "Colored Citizens" and "A Taxpayer," to explain to whites why so many were leaving. A prominent Vicksburg businessman, Frank Andrews, wrote to Governor Theodore Bilbo to complain that much of the "unrest" of blacks had its sources in unfair treatment by landlords and in the courts. He claimed that, as a member of the grand jury, he had frequently "been impressed with the fact that often a negro is indicted on evidence that would be utterly ignored in the case of a white man." Andrews also claimed to be "as fully a believer in the theory that this is a white man's country" as anyone, but he argued that Mississippi's prosperity was being put in danger by "the evils I have mentioned, and others that exist." In Senatobia at the eastern edge of the Delta, a white speaker told a conference of the African Methodist Episcopal Church that "the time has come when the Negro must be given more consideration." In Greenwood police were told to "stop beating up Negroes." In a more concrete response, wages rose sharply in many places.[47]

"The enforced equality and solidarity of citizenship"

The sudden opening of national labor markets to African Americans would have placed great strain on southern race and class relations in any case. But the entry of the United States into the Great War added an entirely new dimension to societies in the Deep South. The war brought a nationalization of policy, power, and sentiment unknown in the South since Reconstruction and reinforced in many ways the dynamic forces at work in town and countryside. The U.S. entry into war, first, increased the pressure on labor markets dramatically. The armed forces drafted some 367,000 black men, the great majority from the South. It also meant the further ratcheting up of industrial production, which required still more black men and women. Planters and farmers naturally worried about the cost of farm labor, but employers in the towns were even more affected. The high price of cotton meant that farmers could outbid townspeople for unskilled labor, and thousands of potential porters and domestics returned to work in the cotton fields. In Greenville, Urban League investigators found, stores were employing white porters for the first time, and even employing girls as porters. Druggists were delivering their own packages. Local factories found ways to hire black workers to do things formerly limited to whites. A month after the formal declaration of war, the Delta's LeRoy Percy wrote to his congressman to urge that farm laborers be exempted from the draft, noting that "at the rate they are leaving there will be no town darkies much left."[48]

But it would soon be clear to whites that the labor problem was in some ways the least threatening development, and it would be equally clear to blacks that their new economic opportunities might be less important than the ideological implications of the war. The war led to a nationalization of patriotism, unprecedented in the way that it swept through the entire country and through so many different social groups. The upsurge in emotional commitment to the war and the ideals it was said to embody was partly spontaneous, partly the result of propaganda campaigns controlled from Washington. For those whose patriotic emotions were not properly stimulated, coercion could help to ensure that their behavior, at least, would be "truly" patriotic. Senator Vardaman, racist that he was, recognized the threats that might arise from what he called the "melting pot of war." Among the "brutalizing" and "stupefying" influences of the war, he told the Senate, would be an enforced "equality and solidarity of citizenship."[49]

By raising new definitions for the obligations of citizenship, with everyone expected to be a "patriot," the war created an opening not only for men but also for women, not only for whites but also for blacks, to serve their country in new ways. The Council of National Defense set up the Committee on Women's Defense Work to stimulate appropriate patriotism, from the smallest towns to the largest. Marvin Williams, chairman of the Greene County, Georgia, Food Conservation Committee, told county women that the job of conservation must be "largely a women's task." He appealed to local women on behalf of the women in Belgium, who had allegedly been abused by German invaders. Mrs. E. G. Adams became head of the Women's Liberty Loan Committee in the county. Work for the Red Cross was considered to be especially appropriate for women, and local organizations across the South set up canteens to entertain soldiers in nearby camps and provide services to those in transit.[50] War work quickly expanded to take in other long-time progressive aims, often led by women with long experience in progressive causes. "War service," broadly defined, would soon be used by women to press for passage of the Nineteenth Amendment to the Constitution, finally giving women the vote. In Washington County, Mississippi, suffragist leader Nellie Nugent Somerville became a retail price reporter for the U.S. Food Administration, an active member of the Red Cross, and an organizer for efforts of the YWCA in Mississippi to serve soldiers. She was the first chair of the county's Woman's Committee of the Council for Defense; her daughter Lucy was its secretary. Somerville and her committee sold liberty bonds, raised donations for the Red Cross, and taught local families proper methods of conserving food. Mrs. George F. Maynard, chair for child welfare in the Coahoma County Woman's Committee, proudly reported to the national committee of a Baby Welfare Campaign that her group had in one week weighed and measured four hundred children under the age of five, and not just white children; their goal was to weigh and measure every black child in the county, and African American women were appointed in each of the county's fifteen towns as local chairmen. "I think this is the first movement of that kind in Mississippi," Mrs. Maynard wrote. "We have a great many negroes in our county & we must look after their welfare as well as our own."[51]

The ambiguous relationship between the white and black women in this Coahoma County effort was typical. Blacks were the objects of paternalist concern, but they also gained positions of some responsibility. Mrs. Edward McGehee, Coahoma's county chair and the head of Mississippi's State Woman's Committee, wrote that she was glad to learn that the National Council would be sending a "colored woman organizer" to organize African American women, as "in many counties they are trying to put on Public Health nurses as a result of the Baby Welfare Campaign, and there are such large negro districts all over the State, that we need one of their own race to instruct them." Mrs. McGehee noted black women's great enthusiasm for working with the Red Cross, food conservation, war stamps, "or any form of

War service — and they feel slighted, all over the State, if I do not call on them for service."[52] When the council's national organizer for black women, Alice Dunbar Nelson, arrived in Mississippi, she was genuinely impressed with Mrs. McGehee, who, she wrote "has the state splendidly organized and is financing the salary and expenses of the colored organizer out of her own pocket." McGehee arranged for Nelson to share the platform at a "big patriotic meeting" for blacks in Vicksburg, and, in the presence of the entire board of trade and a prominent white judge, Nelson explained the purposes of the Woman's Committee and urged black women to cooperate in the state effort. One Vicksburg paper even referred to her as "Mrs." Nelson in a story that welcomed her as a "Prominent Colored Woman," an extremely rare use of a polite title for an African American in Mississippi.[53]

Still, Alice Dunbar Nelson's own observations show how black women were far from welcomed at all levels of the war effort. Throughout most of the state, black ministers had not been allowed to distribute food conservation pledges to their congregations, because if blacks signed it would be "too much like social equality." In Vicksburg, the local Red Cross refused to allow African American women to work at the canteen while wearing the Red Cross uniform. When Nelson visited Georgia, the redoubtable Lucy Laney, head of Haines Institute in Augusta (whom Nelson called the "strongest colored woman in Georgia . . . whose veracity is unquestioned and whose influence is far reaching") told her there was no support of any kind in her county for war work by black women; in fact, Laney did not even know there was a state Woman's Committee. Colonel William Peel, manager of the southern division of the Red Cross, asserted that no black women would be permitted to join any white chapter, and, indeed, that members in his division resented "the suggestion from any one that we should put them on a footing with us socially." Such ambivalence about the place of African Americans that arose in the course of women's war work — with black women's work both welcomed and feared — ran through all of whites' responses to the war.[54]

Many whites hoped to use the new powers of the national government to increase the reach and effectiveness of racial control. White southerners especially saw an opportunity to coerce black workers by taking advantage of pronouncements from the Selective Service director, Enoch Crowder, that Americans must either "work or fight" in the war. Crowder's directive calling for unemployed men to be drafted into the armed forces — aimed in a general way against war "slackers" and, labor unions feared, at workers who dared to go on strike during the war — was used in the South to try to force black laborers to work under white direction, for white-determined wages. State and local governments there went well beyond Crowder's intent in their attempts to slow emigration and keep African Americans in the fields. Georgia's Defense Council, for example, concluded that it would be a legitimate use of national war powers in effect to draft workers to grow food.[55]

Some whites hoped to use "work or fight" laws to force black women into domestic labor and relieve the growing "servant problem" of white women. When the state of Georgia passed a "Work or Fight" law, some legislators tried to amend it to include women specifically. Such laws could not discriminate against black women as such, but it was obvious to all that no white women who spent their days at home as unpaid housekeepers and mothers would be forced to work. Instead, police and sheriffs could use their new powers with their old discretion to try to force black women who were either self-employed or, in the case of middle-class women, not in the labor market at all, to work in the homes of white families unable to secure cheap domestic workers. Only lobbying by blacks at the statehouse in Atlanta defeated the amendment.[56] Some cities and towns passed their own ordinances, including one in Vicksburg requiring every citizen to carry a card showing that he or she was employed in some "essential" work. It declared to be a vagrant "any person, male or female, who wanders or strolls about in idleness, or who lives in idleness, or who loafs, loiters or idles, or remains in the City of Vicksburg . . . without any regular employment." The burden of proof was placed on a defendant caught "idle" on a workday. No middle-class white women at home with their children would ever be considered "vagrants," but all black women not working for whites might well be. In Greenville, Mississippi, one policeman cruised a black neighborhood until he found a black woman sitting on a porch, took her into custody, drove her to the house of his friend who was looking for a cook, and told her to go to work. (The next day she left for the North.) In Augusta "a respectable colored woman" was arrested for not "working." Protests from "some of the better class of colored men" prevented her from being convicted.[57]

If the war offered new resources for repression and labor control, it also raised unexpected opportunities for black men and women to challenge the meanings of race. By calling all Americans, especially men but also women, to meet the patriotic obligations of citizens in a democracy, it encouraged them to insist, as well, on the rights of citizens in a democracy. The potential contradictions in having black men fight for a "white man's country" were clear from the beginning, especially to those who opposed, for one or another reason, U.S. entry into the war. Mississippi's Vardaman had been the only southern senator to oppose the declaration of war. Vardaman feared the centralization of power that would accompany the war, and he opposed conscription on the same grounds, but also because, as he explained to the Senate, "Millions of Negroes who will come under the measure will be armed." A Vicksburg paper put the point more generally, arguing that "drafting Negroes as soldiers is a gross travesty and contradiction of the color line creed." As African Americans were denied suffrage so they should be exempt from the draft—a position that would also, of course, warm the hearts of many white employers. At the national level, however, appeals to exempt blacks, or at least black farm workers, from the draft met with little sympathy. Southern employers found themselves faced not only with a new source of competition for labor in the form of the U.S. Army, but also with national policies that in some cases favored the shifting of labor away from agriculture to important war industries.[58]

Whites now found themselves literally face to face with black men wearing the uniform of the U.S. Army. The story of the resistance of whites to blacks in uniform has been often told. The sight of black men in official uniforms bothered many, and the fear that black soldiers might meet white women in France as social equals bothered some even more. In Vicksburg some whites sometimes drove black soldiers off the streets and out of town, and white soldiers in the city beat up black women. When Vicksburg blacks complained to the board of trade about the violence, this influential organization of white businessmen responded simply that black soldiers should not wear their uniforms in Vicksburg.[59] Yet, the war called for men and money, including black men and black money. Blacks who opposed the draft were considered treasonous. In Holmes County, Mississippi, Rev. C. H. Mason, the African American founder and head of the Church of God in Christ, was arrested for "preaching pro-German sermons." Witnesses alleged that he preached that black men "did not have to go to war, or did not have to register," and local whites thought these subversive sermons explained why more than half of Holmes's registrants had failed to appear for induction. In Vicksburg the leading white businessmen, clergy, political leaders, and editors joined together to foster and encourage black participation in the war effort, and with every draft of African American soldiers, the city organized an elaborate ceremony. White and black speakers alike praised the civic contributions of newly enrolled black soldiers, who then paraded to the train station for a send-off with bands blaring. A local judge, in his "patriotic charge" to a grand jury, paid "tribute to the colored soldiers" and "stated that regardless of race prejudice or expressions that when the time came the negro soldiers would cover themselves with glory and would be found giving just as valiant service in the defense of their flag as their white brothers."[60]

In the Piedmont town of Greensboro, white elites celebrated "loyal" African Americans. A front-page article in the local paper there covered a banquet for a group of black draftees at the Colored Red Cross Auxiliary. "Artistic" flower arrangements, designed by local black women, decorated the tables, and "well known colored citizens" urged the new soldiers to be faithful and obedient. The editor of the *Herald-Journal* added his own congratulations and commendations to these "colored citizens." When Ben Brookfield, a young black draftee, told the draft board that he wanted to kill a lot of Germans, a front page article lauded him as "a fine specimen of colored manhood."

Meanwhile, both of Georgia's U.S. senators, Hoke Smith and Thomas Hardwick, came in for heavy criticism for being "disloyal to the government." With Tom Watson, they had been the architects of Georgia's disfranchisement legislation a decade before, riding their antiblack rhetoric to high office. Now all three were condemned for their lukewarm support of the war. Greensboro's newspaper editor hoped that Georgia would replace "Herr Hardwick," who was "in league with the Kaiser." He also suggested that Leavenworth prison would be the appropriate place for fellow editor Jim Boykin of Lincoln County, who had led a public protest against conscription. Boykin's stance would simply lead to draft evasion, he declared, and freedom of speech does not protect "fool speech."[61]

If white attitudes and behavior were profoundly contradictory, black attitudes and behavior were not. To be sure, to many African Americans the Great War presented a "damnable dilemma," as they found themselves expected to fight in a "War for Democracy" while facing a lack of democracy in their own country. Still, most decided that the war offered a clear opportunity to re-stake their claims to full citizenship. If the Vardamans and Hardwicks were tainted by opposing the war, blacks could show that they were patriots in every sense of the term.[62] Thus black women, as the head of Mississippi's Woman's Committee had found, were "enthusiastic in their efforts to assist me." In Augusta, Lucy Laney threw herself with her usual energy into a whirl of war-related activities, organizing thrift clubs and campaigning to sell war savings stamps. Many of her students enlisted, and four became lieutenants. In Savannah, R. R. Wright, president of the local black college, told an African Methodist Episcopal Church conference that blacks would do their share for the "rights of mankind." The conference adopted resolutions of loyalty to municipal, state, and national governments. A month later, a mass meeting of African Americans in the city subscribed more than $2,000 for Liberty Loan Bonds. In the fall of that year, a parade of six thousand — described by the *Morning News* as "by far the largest event" of its kind ever held in Savannah — was organized to encourage further Liberty Loan subscriptions; yet more demonstrations marked the next Liberty Loan drive in the spring of 1918. The *Morning News* devoted an entire back page to coverage of an African American parade in May 1918, which it called the largest parade in the city's history. The mayor himself reviewed the "dignified and orderly" procession of marchers, including groups of barbers, members of the bricklayers union, elderly Civil War veterans, and members of the local black branch of the Red Cross, named for none other than Toussaint L'Ouverture, the hero of the great slave rebellion in Haiti in the 1790s.[63]

One of the clearest demonstrations of African American determination to reclaim their full rights as citizens was the establishment of new chapters of the NAACP. Founded in 1910 by northern blacks such as W. E. B. Du Bois and sympathetic white progressives like Mary White Ovington, the NAACP had quickly established itself as the most authoritative national organization campaigning for full civil rights for African Americans. Before the war, its presence in the South had been negligible, with a single branch in Virginia. By 1916 this number had risen to just six, but by 1919 there were more than 150 southern branches, including several in Georgia and Mississippi.[64]

The core of the membership from these new branches came from men and women of the urban middle class. Some branches did come from smaller towns, but the NAACP requirement of fifty members for a permanent charter was a stumbling block. One small town in the Piedmont submitted a charter after the war with the required fifty names. Among them were fourteen farmers and ten laborers. Mound Bayou, Mississippi, an all-black town in the Delta, organized a branch right after the war with more than one hundred members. The leadership came from the ranks of professionals, including president W. P. Kyle, a physician, and vice president J. R. Powe, a minister, but thirty-seven farmers also joined.[65]

Most branches came from the larger cities, including Brunswick, Savannah, and Augusta, in Georgia, and Vicksburg in Mississippi. The Brunswick branch had sixty members at its charter meeting in September 1918. Several were housewives, and most others were professionals and business people — three physicians, two contractors, a pharmacist, and a hairdresser among them. The Savannah branch was organized by James Lemon, a lawyer; its first treasurer was A. B. Singfield, head of the Savannah Negro Business League. The branch immediately plunged into action. They pushed an investigation of the death of a black convict and forced the dismissal of a guard in the case. They sponsored a banquet for black draftees. They carried on a successful campaign to prevent the city from designating a black neighborhood with many black homeowners as an official red light district.[66]

The branch in Augusta was organized before the United States entered the war. The first officers included a post office clerk, a physician, a teacher at Paine College, and a housewife; among the other twenty-four members were eleven professionals and four mail clerks. Lucy Laney was one of the most active members. At a mass meeting on March 5, James Weldon Johnson, executive secretary of the national organization, spoke to an enthusiastic crowd of one thousand people in Augusta. Wilson Jefferson, president of the Augusta branch, wrote to the national office later that spring to report his plans to increase membership to at least two hundred with a house-to-house canvass, although the organizers faced many obstacles. The exodus to the North carried away actual and potential members, and several local black ministers were hostile to the NAACP, "their manhood bartered away" in return for the support of white "friends" for their building projects. But Jefferson's enthusiasm in these early months of the war was strong. "Did you ever know a race to awake as our race has awakened in the last year or so?" he wrote to Johnson. "Augusta is almost another town. The old spirit of humble satisfaction, of let-well-enough alone, is fast dying out. Negroes are leaving by the hundreds. They know where they are going; they know what they are up against." Wilson Jefferson's statement that "Augusta is almost another town" could have been made about hundreds of cities and towns across the South. The war had challenged Jim Crow's economic foundations by opening up new alternatives to black workers and challenged its ideological foundations by assuming that African Americans owed the same obligations to the larger community as all citizens. But those African Americans, like Dr. John Miller of Vicksburg, Mississippi, who followed up on those challenges, would find that the color line did not yield easily.[67]

One Hundred Percent Americans

Blacks in Vicksburg founded a new NAACP branch in 1918. T. G. Ewing, a lawyer, made the initial contact with the national office. The charter application listed D. D. Foote, a dentist, as president, J. H. Handricks, a carpenter, as vice president, T. G. Pinson, a minister, as secretary, and Everett Harris, fish dealer, as treasurer. As in other cities, most of the new members belonged to the small African American professional and business elite. One of them was physician John A. Miller.[68]

Dr. Miller in 1918 was forty-seven years old and had lived in Vicksburg for almost two decades. A native of Virginia, he attended the preparatory school at Howard University and earned degrees from Williams College in 1896 and the University of Michigan's medical school in 1900. Dr. Miller was at the turn of the century probably the best-educated black man in Vicksburg; he may have been the best-educated person, period. As a professional black man, highly educated in elite northern institutions, a native southerner yet not a native of the city or state, Miller epitomized the difficulty of defining racial boundaries. During his nearly twenty years in the city, Miller later wrote, he had "never meddled in the white man's affairs and did not dare murmur or complain at the many acts of lawlessness against my race." On two occasions, however, he had "meddled." In 1909, Miller had helped to prevent the appointment as a public school teacher of a black woman who was "a public woman for white men," and, in 1916, he unsuccessfully opposed the hiring of a black teacher who "was the proud mistress of a white man." Both times, Miller hired white lawyers to help lobby the school board, and in 1916 he collected an affidavit from "a reputable White Lady" to support his case.[69]

White Vicksburg residents may have seen this kind of action as showing that blacks, too, endorsed the color line. But to Miller and other middle-class blacks, this action was more protest than accommodation. The black authors of a letter to white lawyer John Brunini about the 1916 teacher's case explained that they were trying to "overcome the charges of Immorality that are thrown at the race from time to time." Like middle-class blacks elsewhere in the South, they deeply resented white assumptions that all blacks were by nature too sexualized and "immoral" to be able to meet the Victorian standards of behavior that whites identified with civilization itself. In insisting that whites hire only respectable black teachers, Dr. Miller and other blacks were also insisting that respectability knew no color line.[70]

During the war, middle-class blacks like Miller were soon being called upon to buy war bonds and savings stamps. Vicksburg's War Stamp Savings Committee organized a sales campaign led by George Williamson, cashier of the city's largest bank. The committee resorted to highly coercive tactics, promising that anyone who refused to pledge the amount determined by an "Allotment Committee" would put themselves "in line for a yellow card" — a public display reserved for "pledge slackers." When the campaign lagged, Williamson blamed those without "the proper amount of patriotism" and threatened to close (on whose authority is an unanswered question) "every store and place of business in the city" until the full amount had been raised. The campaign came to a climax on "War Savings Day," 28 June 1918, and in the week leading up to that date, local police arrested and fined a British citizen for "acting in a discourteous manner" to members of the stamp committee who had demanded "that he tell something about himself," and they charged a black man, Sam Gaithers, with "interfering with a government loan" for telling his nephew "that he did not have to buy any of the stamps if he didn't want to." Chairman Williamson took out a full-page newspaper ad warning that if any citizens refused to do their duty, "the Government will see to it that their movements will be watched and their actions will be recorded in Washington."[71]

It was in this charged atmosphere that, sometime in the spring or early summer of 1918, John Hennessey of the War Savings Committee visited Dr. Miller and asked him to subscribe to war bonds. His tart reply, that whites had "crushed" the patriotism of African Americans, and that Hennessey should "think over what I have said and come back and I will tell you how many bonds I am going to buy," set off the chain of events that led eventually to Miller's being tarred and feathered on the city's streets on July 23.[72] We do not know just what Hennessey said to Miller in reply, but the plain fact was that he and other white citizens of Vicksburg had been put in a bind. The war had thrown the color line into confusion, as signified by events as various as parades in the streets and appeals to black patriotism. With the line between black and white no longer so obviously the line between citizen and non-citizen, the white elite had begun to approach some black residents as if they had typical patriotic feelings and normal patriotic duties, exactly the kind of "solidarity of citizenship" James Vardaman had warned against. Dr. Miller had accepted their unintended invitation to act like a citizen. It was they, and not he, who had first stepped over the proper racial boundaries. It is telling that the stamp committee did not immediately call out a mob or even visit Miller more discreetly to try to convince him to change his mind. Instead, a member of the committee called him up and insisted that he buy the extraordinary amount of $1,000 in war bonds — borrowing from a bank to do so, if necessary. Another phone call came on June 28 — War Savings Day —

insisting that Miller subscribe to $1,000 in bonds and threatening to arrest
him for sedition if he refused. As he later learned from a white friend, the
War Savings Committee was trying to trap him "into saying I had advised
Negroes not to buy Govt. securities." The Vicksburg elite was going to extraordinary lengths to discredit him, not simply as an uppity black man, but
as a disloyal American.[73]

Dr. Miller, convinced that the city's white leadership had provoked the
July 23 events, accused the stamp savings committee chairman George Williamson of giving a "direct or indirect" order to attack him. The incident, he
declared, could not be blamed simply on "mob spirit." Yet, the response of
the white elite suggests a more complex picture and points toward a significant division among whites themselves. The day after the attacks on Cook
and Miller, Williamson, Mayor Hayes, and several other prominent whites
published a statement "deeply deplor[ing] the unfortunate incident that took
place yesterday afternoon, when a few of our citizens tarred and feathered a
WHITE man and a NEGRO, for disloyal acts and utterances." The signers urged
"all good citizens, white and black, to avoid every utterance and every act
that might lead to a repetition of the outbreak of yesterday" and assured all
"citizens, white and black, that loyalty and proper living will be as highly
approved and heartily defended as disloyalty is condemned."

Perhaps these gentlemen were simply looking away while other people
did their dirty work. But when the "flying squadron" that tarred and feathered Dr. Miller went on to attack two poor black women, Ethel Barrett and
Ellen Brooks, on the night following the tar-and-feathering of Cook and
Miller, the response of elite whites went well beyond denunciation. Mob
members justified the attacks on Barrett and Brooks on the grounds that
"neither of the negro women would work," and they promised to rid Vicksburg of "all loafers and idlers, whether white or black, male or female." It
was soon discovered, however, that Ethel Barrett was a hard-working laun-
dress, and, perhaps most embarrassing for city leaders, both women had
husbands serving in the army. One editor branded the assault on the women
as "one of the most cowardly that could possibly have been committed," and
a reporter suggested that the real motive was that one of the women had
refused to work for one of the mob's leaders. The entire incident, one reporter wrote, had "humiliated" the city. A public meeting on July 26 explicitly condemned the attack on the two women, and, within a week, seven
men, now labeled "whitecappers," were successfully prosecuted in the city
court at the behest of a "citizens committee." The meeting on the 26th was

attended by many leading businessmen and lawyers, including most of the same men who had published the statement condemning the violence against Cook and Miller.[74]

Of the seven men convicted and fined for attacking the women, five can be identified in local records. Four were partners in the Home Taxi Company in 1918, and the fifth identifiable participant was a maintenance supervisor in the local electric company where one of the taxi drivers had formerly worked. The "mob leaders" were a small group of men who knew each other well, not at the bottom of the white occupational hierarchy yet far removed from the world of the city's business elite. Elite leaders who labeled these attackers "whitecappers" were identifying them with the kind of attacks by white small farmers on rural blacks that had plagued parts of Mississippi earlier in the century. Their brutality alarmed the white elite, with its conservative and paternalistic style of preserving racial boundaries. Here, as in the case of the conviction of Jim Lum a dozen years earlier, divisions of both class and culture within white society were laid bare.[75]

Dr. Miller's tarring and feathering was itself ironic evidence of the contradictions within white racist culture, contradictions exposed and, to some extent, created by the war. This was a ritual of shaming, and not, as in lynching, of death. As such, the attack implied that white Vicksburg was judging him as a potentially honorable patriot. It was perhaps the shock of recognition that they had done so, as much as Miller's own actions, that confounded Vicksburg's white leaders, for they, as well as he, had thereby bent if not broken the hierarchical boundaries of race. The city's elite had then allowed lesser white men to punish Miller in a way that violated the ideals of "civilization" and democracy for which the war was supposedly being fought. Only three days after the attack, both Vicksburg newspapers gave front-page coverage to President Woodrow Wilson's denunciation of the lynching of a German immigrant in Illinois, putting "lynchers squarely on the side of Germany." By prosecuting and punishing the crowd leaders for their attacks on the women, Vicksburg's white leaders resolved their dilemma in a way. The court action allowed the city's elite to vindicate the "honor" of Vicksburg without entirely repudiating the punishment of the black physician who had insisted on his own right to the honor of citizenship.[76]

THE FIRST WORLD WAR forced the contradictions of segregation into the open because it pushed the South fully into a national economy and a national definition of citizenship and worth, as southern employers suddenly found themselves competing with northern industrialists for labor, and as the national draft and Liberty Loan drives assumed that blacks as well as whites had the normal obligations of citizenship. A black man in uniform was a walking contradiction of the idea that only whites could enjoy full honor. Whites like Senator Vardaman could see how war might become a "melting pot," as he put it, for segregation. These threats to the "white man's country" were recognized by whites at the popular level, including the whites who attacked Dr. Miller in Vicksburg. The long-term consequences of these conflicts between whites and blacks in the fields, on the streets, and in the nation's legislative halls we can never know, because, as it turned out, American participation in the war was too short to change the culture of segregation dramatically or permanently. It ended just when the massive commitments of money and arms were beginning to have their most profound effects. Segregation survived largely intact, but the nationalization of the economy continued, with migration from South to North reaching unprecedented levels in the 1920s. At the same time, national culture would continue to spread in the South with the aid of new technologies like the radio and the expanded use of others, like the motion picture, the phonograph, and the automobile. In August 1918, Alice Dunbar Nelson, then visiting Vicksburg just after the tar-and-feathering of John Miller, Ethel Barrett, and Ellen Brooks, wrote that "the colored brass band will not lead the colored draftees to the station, seeing no cause for making music." Her report captures well the disappointment of African Americans and their turn from public claims to full honor and recognition. Without the potential alliance with the nation as a whole, based on a national conception of citizenship, blacks in the South would return again to the "weapons of the weak," taking their protests, like their music, into their own spaces. Not until a new kind of economic crisis came in the 1930s would the inherent conflicts built into the segregation era again force their way to public recognition.[77]

PART III

1919–1939

It is a certainty beyond question that our labor situation must be entirely revamped.

— L. K. Salsbury, president of
Delta & Pine Land Co., 1923

We have our eyes on you, and we are many; we are everywhere, and you will not escape.

— Ku Klux Klan statement, Leland
(Miss.) *Enterprise*, 18 March 1922

You Are a Citizen!

— Title of a pamphlet issued by the
Augusta, Georgia, NAACP, 1935

They had assumed that if I used titles for Negroes, I might want to overthrow the government.

— Arthur Raper, referring to an
investigation by the Greene County,
Georgia, grand jury, 1941

7

Twilight in Cotton's Kingdom

FOR COTTON FARMERS AND PLANTERS, THE FIRST WORLD WAR was the best of times, and the years after it the worst of times. Profits during the war reached unprecedented heights, but losses from market fluctuations, boll weevil infestation, and natural disaster brought unprecedented losses. Cotton farmers could be forgiven if, in 1929, they failed to notice the arrival of the Great Depression.

The roller coaster fate of cotton producers can be followed in the annual reports of the Delta & Pine Land Company in the Mississippi Delta, then the largest cotton plantation in the world. In January 1920, L. K. Salsbury, director of operations for the British-owned D&PL and its smaller sister, Empire Plantation, could look back on the past five years with considerable satisfaction. Shareholders had divided more than $600,000 in profits in the last year alone, a step down from the fabulous years of the war, but still a handsome return.[1] The surviving financial records of the Empire Plantation show a rich wartime bounty for Delta planters despite the migration of thousands of black workers to the North and yearly onslaughts by the boll weevil. In 1912, the first year for which reports are extant, the Empire earned $55,000. In 1914, a year of plunging cotton prices, profits fell to $36,000 partly because of "a very serious loss on accounts [of the tenants], much larger than it ordinarily should have been." By 1916 there was a record profit of $56,000 despite a severe boll weevil infestation, with the plantation store contributing only $7,104 toward the profit; tenant accounts were "in a most excellent condition, better than they have been for several years."[2]

In 1917, with cotton prices surging, earnings reached a fabulous $176,580. Facing stiff wartime income taxes (almost $71,000), the company's accountants figured a way to defer another $64,000 in profits to a later year, and the shareholders were rewarded with a dividend of 30 percent. The plantation earned money on its share of tenants' cotton and on its sales of corn and rental of mules to tenants. The company had bought tenants' own shares of cotton for nineteen cents a pound but sold it for thirty cents a pound, the sort of profit on which an African American folk tale provides a commentary. As the story goes, a black man and a white man simultaneously come across two boxes at a crossroads. The black man runs to the biggest one, which turns out to be filled with hoes and shovels. The white man claims the smaller one, full of the pencils and paper that whites used ever after to calculate and collect the wealth produced by the men with the hoes. Still, even tenants did well in comparison with earlier years, receiving for their cotton about $60,000 in 1916 and $136,000 in 1917. Sales at the company store added over $20,000 to the plantation's bottom line.[3]

In 1918 cotton declined a bit in price just after the harvest; as Salsbury noted, "there is a very great difference in purchasing cotton from your tenants on an advancing market and purchasing it from them on a declining market." Still, with record store profits, net earnings reached $115,000 and the dividend was 20 percent. In 1919 prices recovered, but a wet spring and summer produced better conditions for boll weevils than for cotton, and profit fell to a still handsome $82,000, though Salsbury, apparently considering 1917 and 1918 the normal standard, found that unsatisfactory. Shareholders were probably cheered to learn that the deferred profits from 1917, when added in, again allowed a 30 percent dividend. In its eight years of existence, Empire Plantation had earned some 210 percent on its capital stock and paid out 104 percent in dividends. High cotton prices were reflected in a "terrific advance" in real estate prices, making the plantations themselves much more valuable properties.[4]

The war years proved to be a high water mark for cotton, not to be reached again for a generation. The run-up in prices was over. A pound of cotton harvested in 1920 sold for less than half the price of the year before. Low prices affected cotton growers everywhere, but the Delta was hit hard by bad weather as well. Heavy rains (eight feet between August 1919 and August 1920) damaged the cotton plants, wiped out much of the corn the plantation grew for its own purposes, and, once again, allowed boll weevils to flourish. Low prices and poor crops combined to cut gross cotton income by two-thirds. As the season progressed, the plantation store started selling stock below cost, then shut down for the year with a loss on bad debts of $23,000, "far in excess of anything we have ever had." The bottom line for the year showed a $108,000 loss.[5]

Empire Plantation (and its bigger sister, the Delta & Pine Land Co.) spent much of the rest of the decade trying to recover from this postwar slump without ever truly succeeding. Like other planters, its operators learned to poison their crops with arsenic to kill the weevil—adding to the wages of many tenant families, but also, no doubt, to their health problems. Because the land had been purchased before the war, the operation was in better shape than those of planters who had bought or borrowed against their properties in the heady days of the war, many of whom had gone bankrupt, dragging down with them many of the Delta's banks. Empire took out a large mortgage to help with operating costs, adding interest payments to its annual expenses; dividends disappeared, and Salsbury deferred much of his own salary to hoped-for better days. Empire earned a minuscule $8,640 in 1921; in 1922 cotton again went over twenty cents and profits shot up to $105,000. But 1923 was again disastrous, with a loss of $47,000. The bigger D&PL, operator of sixteen separate plantations, rode the same roller coaster of profits and losses. In 1919 it had a profit of a half million dollars; in 1920 a loss of over $340,000; in 1921, a loss of $213,000. After profits in 1924 and 1925, a 1926 price slump produced a record loss of almost $800,000. In some of these years, profits on the plantations themselves were wiped out by carrying charges on the crops and charges against inventories, as a crop held over in hope of a price rise had to be sold off instead at a loss. The Delta could still produce huge cotton crops, and, indeed, productivity per acre on D&PL plantations was actually increasing, but cotton in the boll did not translate into money in the pocket, even for the wealthiest planters.[6]

"Our labor situation must be entirely revamped"

High cotton prices during the war had helped to stem the outward tide of farm labor despite northward migration and conscription, but as prices dropped after the war, and as tenants ran up big, unpayable debts at plantation stores, the labor situation worsened. Planters in the 1920s continued to resort to all sorts of methods to get and keep good workers. On Empire

Plantation, this meant giving favorable terms to tenants willing to work on the poorly drained "back part," which was more likely to suffer from boll weevil infestation. As a consequence, despite the manager's determination to "do everything in our power to get this entire property" on the most-profitable half-share plan, the "back part" was rented out to tenants who owned their own mules and paid either cash or one-fourth of the crop as rent. After the war, the plantation continued to work this back section on any terms it could get.[7]

In early 1920, L. K. Salsbury wrote that he had enough tenants for the time being. A year later he complained that labor had been "high and difficult to handle, and doing as little work as possible, and we were doubtful at all times whether we received one hundred cents worth of work for every dollar paid out." Two years later, the labor situation was "one of the most serious conditions facing us." He had "filled up fairly well with labor," but feared that in the coming year, as in the previous one, tenants would "winter on us" and then "run off North this Summer, leaving us very short."[8]

"We cannot make a big crop without plenty of labor," Salsbury told his plantation managers. "You have a 'full house' now [1925], and if you are diplomatic and smart you will keep a full house; if you are undiplomatic, you will lose it, and somebody else will get them. Without labor, it is impossible for you [to] make a crop of cotton." Nor was force an option: "Negroes are like children and must be treated as such and in this day and time you cannot resort to harsh treatment. We cannot handle this problem for you; it is up to the individual manager as to whether he keeps his labor or loses it." Worse, bad economic times had driven many planters to the edge of bankruptcy. As Salsbury put it, "If we had to contend and compete with men who were solvent and good business men — men who make money and prosper — it would not be so hard, but when we have got to compete with concerns that are grabbing the last straw — paying as much as $200.00 for a single family, we have got to be *quick on our feet* and *on our toes* every single minute. These are the kind of men who are setting the example in the Delta and they are the ones we have to follow and compete with for labor. It is not the man who is solvent . . . that sets the price on a family. It is the man who is 'broke' and making his last kick."[9]

Force might be used effectively to put down formal attempts to organize unions or other collective actions, but it could also drive away prospective tenants to the local competition, if not to Chicago or Detroit. The D&PL's response was in some ways an extension of the old paternalism, long common in the Delta, and in some ways a version of the "welfare capitalism" that was becoming popular with many big corporations in the twenties. In 1920, for example, the company built a new hospital for its tenants, which it believed to be "the only one of its kind in the entire Cotton Belt, and is a wonderful asset and adjunct to our operations . . . a great comfort as well as a pleasure and highly thought of by our tenants." The company also built a new schoolhouse and began to put up larger, three-room cabins. Not that such paternalism had as its main goal the welfare of the tenants themselves; on the contrary, Salsbury criticized his managers for thinking too much in terms of " 'well, we have got to take care of the negroes'. — We must take care of our tenants, but on the other hand *we must take care of ourselves*. We are not philanthropists. . . . [W]e must think of the stockholders who have their money invested and haven't realized anything in return."[10]

The D&PL offered more direct financial inducements to tenants. In the fall of 1921, facing a second money-losing season in a row, the company reduced prices in the plantation stores, lowered charges for doctor bills, and eliminated charges for services such as plowing. "We did this," according to Salsbury, "because we had on the books against the tenants all we felt that we had any possibility of getting"; any attempt to squeeze more money out of them would be simply "to lose our money and run our tenants off." Managers might even want to pay the tenants more for their cotton and seed than it was worth to "pull our tenants all out of the hole, make them pay their debts, and put them in position where they can clear a little money and where we know next year that they will all make money." At the end of that year, the company canceled half of all tenant debts and "paid money to practically every tenant on the place" because in the past two years many sharecroppers who had failed to pay out had "run away." Salsbury warned his managers to stay constantly alert to the competition. The tenants would be "moving about more this year than ever before." Now (October 1921) was the time to lay plans for the next season. "Let's don't sit down and wait for the tenants to come in, let's reach out for them. . . . A good manager . . . has got to be looking after his labor until the first of next year and then begin over again without stopping." A manager must be a politician, and "the politician who does not play politics the entire time and keep his fences up is never a success."[11]

Delta planters, for the first time, began to look to whites as a source of tenant labor. To be sure, there had always been white tenants, but, as late as 1910, fewer than one in fifteen tenants were white. The war years, though, saw a 53 percent increase in the number of white tenants, and in the next decade white tenants more than doubled. (See Chart 14, Appendix.) Ruby

Hicks, of Sunflower County, remembered that white families arriving from the hills brought with them music she had never heard. "Hillbilly musicians they were for the most part, but they joined the Delta boys in providing lively music for community dances on Saturday night. Women fiddlers were new to us, but they not only shared their talent but they opened their homes to us." The editor of Sunflower's newspaper reprinted an article from the *Progressive Farmer* on "Helping 'Poor White Trash.' " Even if the parents in these families were "shiftless and careless," the article argued, there was every reason to hope that their children would make good citizens in the future, as they had "in the blood" the "spirit of . . . restraint and spiritual aspiration which make up the body of Caucasian civilization."[12]

"Shiftless and careless" or not, white workers were not easily recruited, and planters found them harder to manage than black ones. Whites could vote and had rights in the courts and in their private interchanges with planters that, in the long run, could only make them more expensive. Salsbury himself wrote in 1923 that "it is a certainty beyond question that our labor situation must be entirely revamped." He complained that "our experience so far this year with native white labor is very unsatisfactory, which convinces me we must look elsewhere, and without a doubt to the foreign field, for labor to solve this question, and unless it is solved at once there is no hope for this Company or any other company or individual in the planting business." His hope that the Delta could attract foreign immigrants was poorly timed, since the U.S. Congress was just about to enact permanent and far-reaching restrictions on immigration.[13]

Salsbury's pessimism about the future of the Delta's labor supply was unfounded, at least in the short run. After falling between 1920 and 1925, the number of black tenants increased in the second half of the decade. Within a few years, a record 77,000 black tenants — about three-fourths of them sharecroppers — were working Delta farms and growing more cotton than ever, many enticed from elsewhere in the South, where the boll weevil was doing even more damage. The increase occurred despite a catastrophic flood that in 1927 destroyed a year's worth of crops on many square miles of the Delta's rich farmland.[14]

"High water everywhere"

"The levee broke on the plantation of this company at Mound's Landing at about 7:30 o'clock A.M., April 21, 1927. Within twelve hours thereafter the entire plantation was submerged to a depth varying from three to fifteen feet, depending upon the topography of the land. The plantation remained under water until well along in the month of July; in fact, the waters did not recede sufficiently to enable the railroad to bring its trains into the station of Scott until the 9th. day of July. . . . [V]irtually no cotton was grown on the plantation in 1927. The total yield from land we attempted to plant to cotton was 44 bales." Thus opened the 1928 annual report to stockholders of the Delta & Pine Land Company. The flood, the biggest by far ever known on the Mississippi River, poured through the levees first in Mississippi, then in Arkansas and Louisiana, eventually covering more than two million acres in the Delta and some fourteen million acres elsewhere.[15]

The 1927 flood was one of those natural disasters made worse by human efforts to prevent it. For decades, first localities, then states, and finally the national government had cooperated to build up a formidable system of levees that lined the river from Missouri to the Gulf of Mexico. The response to each flood year—those of 1912, 1913, and 1922 the most recent before 1927—was to build the levees higher, wider, stronger. The result was to postpone, rather than make impossible, a great flood. Not even the huge levees of the era could contain the massive flow of water that filled the river's basin in early 1927, starting with heavy rains in the upper reaches of the river during the winter. By mid-April, areas of Kentucky, Illinois, Oklahoma, and Kansas had already flooded; for a time the Ohio River itself ran upstream. On the single day of April 15, with the waters already lapping the tops of the levees in the Delta, Greenville, Mississippi, had more than eight inches of rain; Cairo, Illinois, more than ten.[16]

Under the direction of an expert flood fighter who worked for planter LeRoy Percy, ten thousand men, nearly all black, filled sandbags to raise the levee where it was most threatened and repair it wherever it began to give way. Some were volunteers, some were inmates from Parchman prison farm, and still others had been swept up by police patrols in the black neighborhoods of Greenville and other towns. Armed guards, mostly white, kept watch over the workers and shot at anyone who got too close in a boat, lest they be from Arkansas and trying to blow the levees on the Mississippi side to relieve the pressure on their own side of the river.[17]

At Mound's Landing itself, on D&PL property, over four hundred black men under the control of the National Guard worked through the night of April 20 filling and piling sandbags. One black worker, Bill Jones, piling sandbags near Mound's Landing, said the levee "felt like jelly . . . just trembling." Seeing that a big break was bound to come, some tried to run away, but, as a National Guard lieutenant put it, "It became necessary for the civilian foreman and my detachment to force the negroes to the break at the point of guns." Charlie Williams, Percy's flood fighter, arrived on the scene to direct the action in person, but it was too late. In the words of one of the black workers, Moses Mason, "you could see the earth just start boiling. . . . Everybody was hollering to get off." According to Charlie Williams, the whole levee "just seemed to move as if 100 feet of it was *pushed out* by the river." No one knows how many of the black laborers were swept into the boiling waters of the crevasse and drowned; that detail did not make the D&PL's annual report.[18]

At the Mounds Landing crevasse, the water scoured out a lake — still there — at least one hundred feet deep, and buried the three nearest D&PL properties in sand. Away from the river, though, the waters flowed across the rich Delta Land at a steady pace of under a mile an hour, with a sound described by some as that of a "mighty wind." Within a day it wiped out the eight-foot high protection levee behind Greenville, filling first the gutters, then the streets, then the porches, and finally the lower stories of the houses. Thousands fled to rooftops or climbed trees and prayed for rescue.[19] The rescue and reconstruction effort in the flood was directed by the national Red Cross and, in particular, by President Coolidge's secretary of commerce, Herbert Hoover, who would ride the subsequent publicity into the White House the next year. In Greenville itself, the son of LeRoy Percy, William Alexander Percy, headed the emergency response committee, with LeRoy continuing to pull many of the strings himself. The numbers of people drowned after the initial break was small, owing to the efforts of Hoover, Percy, and other organizers, and to the spontaneous responses of hundreds of men and women. For a moment, race and class disappeared as markers. White boat owners took heavy risks to rescue black families from their perches, and blacks helped to save whites. Will Moore, a black lumberyard worker in Greenville, told historian Pete Daniel, "I made myself and a bunch of men, I got a committee, we just built boats, went out and caught locals." The daughter of a white boat owner told her father's story of rescuing a family waiting in a tree: "I don't know whether she was white or black, it wouldn't matter, and two small children and two teenage boys." Mississippi River bootleggers — and there were many — lent their excellent boating skills to the rescue effort.[20]

To the planters who ruled the Delta's economy and politics, the flood was, when all was said and done, more a threat to their labor supply than to their lands. As refugees were gathered into camps, it soon became clear that one overriding goal of the camp organizers was to keep black tenants and families secure from approaches by labor agents from elsewhere and to ensure, if possible, that the plantations would have workers when the waters receded. In Greenville, the riverfront levee itself became the main refugee camp. The local committee in charge of flood operations first decided that refugees should be evacuated to high ground at Vicksburg, a few miles down the river, but then, discreetly prodded by LeRoy Percy, reversed itself and decreed that the refugees should remain. An investigator for the NAACP wrote that the camps were "closely guarded especially from Negroes who might help them go somewhere else." According to an African American investigator for the Red Cross, "the whole question seems to have been whether guards were stationed there to keep the refugees in or to keep the public out"; local planters were allowed in but labor agents were kept away. At Vicksburg, twenty-five black refugees who tried to leave rather than be forced to work on the levees were severely beaten by National Guardsmen. A number of D&PL's workers who managed to get to the Vicksburg camps were brought back to a camp in nearby Deeson because Oscar Johnston "feared losing them." When Mary E. Williams, another Red Cross investigator, tried to get into the Deeson camp, hostile planters who "did not want any outside interference" kept her out. The report of the Red Cross's "Colored Advisory Committee," which criticized conditions in the camps, was suppressed at the time and never published.[21]

In late May, a new rise in the river threatened Greenville. Will and LeRoy Percy and the city's mayor called a mass meeting of both blacks and whites to respond. The city council, announcing that it had exhausted all funds for the crisis, passed a resolution calling on unpaid volunteers to "close the gaps in the protection levee before the coming rise." If, however, the number of volunteers fell short, "then conscription means must be used." Of course only black workers would be conscripted, although the council did not say so. Blacks in attendance, with local black businessmen as their spokesmen, insisted that "we are citizens of Greenville, and we have leaders among our own people" who would organize them. Whites agreed, and a black-run "General Colored Committee" quickly raised a thousand black volunteers who repaired breaks in the protection levee behind the town and prevented a second flood. But the resulting goodwill between whites and blacks in Greenville did not last long; on July 7, a white policeman, assigned to help collect a

work crew, shot and killed James Gooden, a respected black man who refused to go with him (Gooden had just finished a night of work). Blacks in the
city seethed with anger, but agreed to listen to Will Percy, who spoke at a
black church. Percy pledged that the white policeman would be tried for the
killing (he was never indicted); "every white man regrets this [killing] from
his heart and is ashamed," he added. Percy went on, mingling tones of self-
pity, unrequited paternalism, and racist bombast, to denounce the blacks in
the crowd for their "sinful, shameful laziness" in the face of the disaster, at a
time when he and "every white man in this town" had "worried and struggled and done without sleep in order to help you Negroes." He called the
African Americans in the crowd the real murderers of James Gooden, with
their hands "dripping with blood."[22]

The 1927 flood was deeply etched in the memory of all who went through
it. Will Percy devoted a chapter of his memoirs to it. In the 1930s, both
Richard Wright and William Faulkner wrote short stories about it. Charley
Patton, in his "High Water Everywhere," was one of several who memori-
alized it in song:

Lord, the whole round country, lord, River is overflowed
Lord, the whole round country   Man it's overflowed
I would go to the hilly country, But they got me barred.[23]

The Delta & Pine Land Company, where the levee broke, lost its crop for the
entire year, and all its tenant houses were either damaged or destroyed. A
large lake was gouged out of its land, and some eight hundred acres were
thrown outside the new line of levees. Three of its plantation properties were
almost covered with heavy deposits of sand. "Labor was completely demor-
alized and the plantation left almost without labor." Mules, fences, ditches,
store inventory — all in all, the physical damage added up to more than a
million dollars. And yet, in the end, the Mississippi was not as strong as the
markets. The plantation houses were rebuilt, the mules were replaced, the
cotton lands replanted. In a matter of months, "save for the lands covered by
sand every vestige of the disastrous flood has been effaced. The plantation is
fully equipped with an ample supply of labor to work efficiently the available
acreage." Even the sand-covered plantations had been planted in meadows
and feed crops. The operating loss for the year of $912,000 was not that
much more than the loss of 1926. The next year the yield on the remaining
thirteen thousand acres of cotton land was an all-time record of 419 pounds

of lint per acre, and the company cleared more than $200,000. Cotton re-covered elsewhere in the Delta as well. It has been argued that coercion during the 1927 flood prevented the loss of thousands of laborers, but the fact was that, even while thousands of the Delta's workers headed north, the extraordinary yields of its rich soil continued to draw in black workers from elsewhere in the South. Between 1925 and 1930, the number of black tenant farmers in the region increased by more than 20 percent. With the use of pesticides and improved seeds (in part produced by D&PL itself), productiv-ity went up, and the Delta's landowners continued to drain and develop new land. In 1929 they picked over 900,000 bales of cotton—nearly double the production of just a decade before.[24]

"Bo-Weavil Blues"

Piedmont cotton farmers, like those in the Delta, had prospered during the war, and also like those in the Delta, many convinced themselves that the prosperity would be permanent. Incomes soared and land values soared along with them. Farmers and tenants bought new luxuries, paid off old debts, and took on new debts to snap up land, by 1919 up to as much as $200 per acre. Because of the high prices of cotton, many African American ten-ants there, as in the Delta, had resisted the temptation to migrate north. There were more black tenants (and more black farm owners, too) in the Piedmont in 1920 than there had been in 1910. During the war, Greene County's newspaper editor congratulated his white readers on the fact that "there has been no exodus of negroes from this county," a circumstance he attributed to kind white employers. "The South needs the colored man and woman," he wrote, and would have to replace them if they left with "a class of white labor that would prove infinitely worse" and of which "we have no understanding."[25]

The editor's comments betrayed a misplaced complacency. Blacks were staying behind because of good cotton prices, not because of kindly race relations; in 1920 whites would lynch a local black man accused of aiding the getaway of a man charged with a shooting. Actually, an out-migration in Greene County had been under way for some time; even with new births, the black population was virtually the same in 1920 as it had been in 1880. Black tenants had begun to be replaced by whites drifting down from the northern Piedmont regions. But beyond this, the editor had casually dismissed the threat of the boll weevil.[26]

This insect had entered Texas from Mexico in 1892 and gradually eaten its way through the South's cotton plants, working north and east. Weevils drilled into cotton buds before they opened to feed and reproduce; infected plants dropped their buds to the ground in midsummer. The weevil's arrival in the Delta in the early twentieth century had caused much damage and more alarm. Ballads and blues songs about the weevil followed its course from west to east. Texas's Blind Lemon Jefferson, first of the widely recorded country bluesmen, sang a boll weevil song, as did the Delta's Charley Patton. By the war, its arrival in Greene County was imminent, as predictable as the summer heat. Still, Greene's farmers perhaps took comfort from the knowledge that other areas had been hit and recovered. The Delta's farmers had learned to adapt—spreading plants out more, clearing brush where weevils lived in winter seasons, and poisoning them with calcium arsenate. After a small drop in cotton harvests between 1900 and 1910, production of cotton in the Delta again increased. When weevils were sighted for the first time in Greene County, in 1916, the editor assured his readers that there was no cause for alarm; the local farmer should simply grow "all his home supplies and get out of debt and then grow what cotton he can as a surplus crop"—the same ineffectual advice editors had been dispensing to farmers for decades.[27]

The 1916 crop in Greene County was smaller than that of the year before, but production rose again in 1917, and in 1919 reached over twenty-two thousand bales, almost a record. By the fall of 1919, though, the infestation was beginning to be noticeable, with as many as a hundred farms in the county invaded. A special meeting at the courthouse was called to consider the situation. In 1920, production fell by a third, and with a simultaneous price drop of more than 50 percent, the outlook was grim. In February 1921, the local newspaper ran its own advertisement on its front page, urging everyone to "Start Better Times in Greene County"; it condemned what it called "a certain class of calamity howlers and dull time agitators," and encouraged everyone to pull "together in a community spirit." If half the cotton crop was going to be eaten up, farmers should reduce cotton acreage and grow more food. Businessmen, for their part, should "turn on the sunshine" to boost business. However, the county's farmers did what they usually did, planted a big crop of cotton, fertilized it heavily, and tried calcium arsenate. The crop that year was under 1,500 bales. The next year, 1922, the county ginned 333 bales, a drop of 98 percent in three years.[28]

The destruction of the only predictable revenue crop in the Piedmont threatened planters, bankers, and merchants with bankruptcy and threatened tenants with starvation. With no cotton to pick, unattached men left first, followed by sharecroppers who had no hopes of repaying old advances and no prospects of receiving new ones, and by renters who had lost their mules and other property, seized or sold off for debts. Owners held on longer, though many of them also went under, especially those who had bought land with mortgages when values had soared during the war. In Greene County, seven of the eight largest African American farm owners in 1921 had lost their land by 1927. Georgia-born blues singer Kokomo Arnold captured the general devastation and the (as usual) special burdens of black farmers in his "Bo-Weavil Blues":

> Says I went to my captain, and I asked him for a peck of meal
> Says I went to my captain, and I asked him for a peck of meal
> He said, "Leave here Kokomo, you got boll-weevils in yo' field"
> . . . .
> Says the merchant to the doctor, "Don't sell no mo' C. C. Pills"
> Says the merchant to the doctor, "Don't sell no mo' C. C. Pills"
> 'Cause the boll-weevil down here in Georgia done stopped all these cotton mills.[29]

The boll weevil and the price declines of the 1920s reversed the long, slow accumulation of farm land by the county's black population. Black-owned acreage peaked at almost nineteen thousand acres in 1921; by 1927 more than a third of this had been lost. But the weevil and the markets were no respecters of race. Whites as well as blacks fled. Although many white absentee owners in the county kept their land, because they were earning most of their income from other occupations, other owner-operators who depended on their crops were wiped out. Many of the largest plantation tracts were lost to banks or insurance companies and sold off at auction. (In 1934 loan companies owned about eighteen thousand acres in Greene County.) Arthur Raper, who produced a classic case study of the county in the 1930s, told the stories of two planters whose war prosperity turned to dust. One white planter who had flourished during the good times came out of the war with $10,000 in the bank; he broke even in 1920, but his 1921 cotton crop was barely one-eighth of the previous year's. "This one lean year consumed the fat of the previous years: the owner could not finance another crop; the tenants could not live through the winter without an advance; an exodus occurred, all the tenant families leaving the plantation except a mere hand-ful." Within a year the owner had moved on to Alabama, leaving the planta-tion in the hands of the insurance company that had lent him money. The second planter was a prosperous black who leased a large plantation, work-ing part of it himself and subletting the rest to sharecroppers. In early 1921 he owned six mules and had $3,000 in the bank; a year later he had lost his mules and his tenants and was himself a sharecropper on the property. What remained of his savings had been wiped out by the failure of the Union Point Bank.[30]

By comparison with this sweeping devastation, even the catastrophic Mississippi River flood of 1927 was a light and transient event. Within two years after the flood, the Delta had more tenants (black and white) growing more cotton than ever before. In the Piedmont cotton recovered somewhat from the almost total loss of the early part of the decade, but its recovery was never complete. The added burden of expense for labor and pesticides simply could not be borne by the many marginal producers in the Piedmont; also there were not enough black and white hands left to plant, hoe, and pick. Between 1920 and 1925, the number of black tenants in the eastern Pied-mont fell by more than one-third, the number of white tenants by one-eighth. (See Charts 16 and 17, Appendix.) The 1925 crop was less than half that of 1920, itself the lowest since the years of Reconstruction. By the end of the decade a third of the African American population had gone to Atlanta, New York, Detroit, or Cleveland. In 1930 the eastern Piedmont had a majority white population for the first time since the early years of the nineteenth century.[31] Most of the area's farmers who remained continued to plant some cotton; farm owners could at least feed themselves with careful attention to food crops, and most did so, but subsistence farming produced, as it always had, mere subsistence. Prosperity required cash crops. Those with substan-tial land holdings began to cut and saw the second-growth pine on land long out of production, a process that did bring cash, but for a few years at most. The rabbits that flourished in these old fields became a new (if also short-term) source of income. In the winter of 1927-28, more than fifty thousand rabbits were shipped from Greene County alone. One longer-term alterna-tive was livestock and dairy farming, and many farmers began to produce cream for the Atlanta market. A second long-term possibility was orchard crops. Farmers had always grown fruit trees for themselves and for local markets, but in the two decades before the First World War, many tried to make serious money from their orchards, a time-consuming and chancy business in itself. The most promising orchard crop was peaches. But waiting for trees to produce salable fruit required time and capital not easily available. The peach harvest in the eastern Piedmont increased by over 50 percent from 1920 to 1925, but the harvest in the entire region was smaller than that in several counties in other parts of Georgia. Worse, Greene County's farm agent in 1929 warned that an invasion of the Mediterranean fruit fly could destroy the peach crop and that "disaster is staring us in the face."[32]

Cotton was still king, although a much-diminished one. In Greene County, cotton alone was responsible for almost three-fourths of the total value of all crops in 1929. Competition for labor within a market circumscribed by race continued to be the foundation of this system. Sharecroppers and renters continued to move frequently — the median length of residence of sharecroppers in Greene County was just two and one-half years. Most tenants and croppers spent the year in debt and settled up at harvest time. Raper noted that tenants had learned to create space for maneuvering within the credit system by arranging for credits with more than one person — a landlord and a merchant, for example. "The tenant who is in debt to two or more influential people has secured for himself some protection against exorbitant claims." A tenant might not be able to question a landlord's account, but a merchant to whom he owed money might well do so, and a landlord trying to settle up would also try to see that a merchant did not grossly cheat his tenant. The gradual spread of the automobile made it easier for tenants to get to town and compare prices, and most plantation commissaries in Greene County disappeared in the competition with new chain stores. Planters continued to complain about tenants who worked for others at inconvenient times, who insisted on cash payments for every item of labor outside the standard tenant-farming requirements, who had to be watched carefully at the harvest to prevent "seepage" of cotton and corn — "a sort of grim game in which the landlord and tenant get all they can out of each other, the tenant carrying home all the provisions he can and the landlord furnishing him as little as possible."[33]

The Tourists' Islands

Along Georgia's coast, the arrival of the boll weevil was as devastating to cotton production as it had been in the Piedmont, but it had been many years since cotton had been central to the economy. True, the high prices in the first years of the century and the war years had brought a significant increase in total cotton acreage, as fertilizers made up for poor and sandy soil. More than ten thousand acres of cotton had been planted in 1919, more than double the acreage in 1899. Still, this was fewer acres than most individual counties in the Piedmont, and the harvest on these acres was less than half what had been raised in 1909. The boll weevil had begun its work, and cotton acreage plunged by more than 80 percent by 1929. Both black and white farms were small and usually operated by owners. With properties offering little more than a portion of subsistence, black farm owners were squeezed further by the loss of their small cash crops of cotton. Like other blacks in the region, they began to migrate to Savannah and on to the giant metropolises of the North. The number of black-owned farms fell by over a third in the decade after the war. They were not replaced by white farmers or by tenants — hardly anyone could make a living from the land. (See Charts 18 and 19, Appendix.)

Among the tiny number of owners of old plantation lands who continued to farm commercially were Ophelia and Miriam Dent, inheritors of Hofwyl on the Altamaha River. They turned Hofwyl into a dairy farm, and by working hard, minimizing expenses, and selling portions of their land to lumber companies, they staved off creditors and gradually reduced the mortgages that had accumulated on the property in the last years of the rice regime. But other landowners continued to sell their properties off to wealthy buyers, most from the North. One of the biggest northern buyers of the 1920s was Henry Ford, the automobile magnate, who bought thousands of acres along the Ogeechee River in Bryan County, where, with the bricks from an old plantation house, he built himself a Greek Revival mansion. Ford planted goldenrod in hope that it might serve as the base for a new rubber substitute and dabbled in sweet potatoes as a possible source of alcohol fuel for automobiles, but this operation was more a hobby than a serious business enterprise.[34]

Lumbering and turpentine, though in decline, continued to provide jobs, as did the sea. In Camden County in 1920, entrepreneurs built a plant to turn shrimp heads into chicken feed and planned a new pulp mill. In 1930 manufacturing workers on the coast outnumbered farm operators by nearly three to one (in the same year, the ratio of manufacturing workers to farm operators was one to three in the Piedmont, one to eighteen in the Delta). Tourism was to become the main source of dynamism in the economy. A new highway down the coast offered the promise of siphoning off a bit of the tourist money on its way to booming Florida. Indeed, Camden County's weekly newspaper left the old port of St. Marys in 1926 to publish in Kingsland, on the recently paved U.S. Highway 17.[35]

In 1924, Glynn County built a causeway from Brunswick to St. Simons Island, one of the two large Sea Islands that had not been taken over by wealthy northerners. The grand opening was celebrated with a historical pageant, whose climax was a celebration of plantation life on St. Simons before the war, staged by the local chapter of the United Daughters of the Confederacy. The audience saw scenes of Fanny Kemble and Pierce Butler at their Hampton Plantation and listened to renditions of "Swing Low, Sweet Chariot" and other spirituals by the Butler "servants," who were played, the program assured the audience, by "descendants of the servants of the 60's." This happy scene of slavery time was interrupted by the guns of Fort Sumter. The men went off to war, the women stayed home to spin and sew, the men came limping back. But that was all the past; the future was represented by the automobiles that made their way across the causeway to St. Simons after the celebration. The causeway worked. By the end of the decade, over a thousand cars a day, carrying thousands of passengers, crossed over to the island's resorts on a typical midsummer day.[36]

The most ambitious development on St. Simons, and perhaps along the entire Atlantic coast of Georgia in the 1920s, was the new resort, called Sea Island, built by Howard Coffin, a restless entrepreneur. Coffin, an engineer, had worked for the Olds Motor Works (later part of General Motors) and Thomas-Detroit (later Chalmers-Detroit) before helping to found the Hudson Motor Company. Hudson made Coffin a multimillionaire, and he multiplied this large fortune with investments in Detroit's manufacturing enterprises and real estate. While in Georgia in 1910 for an auto race, he saw and fell in love with Sapelo Island, and within a year put together a series of real estate deals to buy the whole thing. By the twenties, despite his continuing interests in northern businesses (he was chairman of the board of the predecessor to United Airlines for two years), he had made Sapelo his permanent home, seeking, in a sense, to re-create the world of the antebellum planter. He rebuilt the ruined mansion of Thomas Spalding, adding an indoor swimming pool and billiard room, leveled newly grown forests, and, like Spalding's heirs, tried raising crops and cattle. Mixing the profit-minded and paternalistic motives of the old planters as he understood them, he opened an oyster-canning plant to provide jobs for the few hundred African Americans who still made their homes on the island. He bought a 124-foot yacht with a crew of seven, named the *Zapala* (the old Spanish name for Sapelo), and built his own private airstrip. Down the coast, in Camden County, he spent more than a half million dollars for sixty thousand acres of pine lands and built a "fabulous" hunting lodge. One of his hunting parties there included the president of NBC, the publisher of *Field and Stream,* and the society editor of the New York *Sun.* Charles Lindbergh landed at Coffin's airstrip while on his way to South America. The Herbert Hoovers visited, as did the Calvin Coolidges. Coolidge enjoyed a "fine hunt" and was entertained with a group singing spirituals and a rodeo on the beach featuring black cowboys in sombreros.[37]

In the 1920s Coffin expanded his real estate holdings in the area. With a partner, he purchased St. Catherines Island to the north of Sapelo, and he bought part of the old Retreat plantation on St. Simons to the south. He was a major promoter of the new causeway from Brunswick. In 1926 Coffin began to plan a more ambitious development and bought, for $350,000, a tract on St. Simons, separated from the main part of the island by a narrow creek and known variously in the past as the Isle of Palms, Long Island, and Glynn Isle. Although a part of Cannon's Point plantation before the Civil War, the tract had never been developed because it was little more than a wide, beautiful beach and intricate tidal wetlands. The combination of the beach and the relative isolation tickled Coffin's entrepreneurial fancy. He imagined a resort exclusive enough to attract well-to-do visitors though not so exclusive as to depend on the trade of the super-rich who controlled Jekyll Island to the south. It would include cottages, a top-quality hotel, golf and tennis, a gorgeous private beach, plus a high level of personal service (from low-paid black workers).[38] Coffin renamed the property Sea Island, appointed his cousin, Bill Jones, to run the project, bought a dredge, and began filling in the wetlands to make room for cottages, which would be the main source of profits for the development. He put in a golf course and, in a furious six-month stretch of construction in 1928, built a Spanish-style hotel, which he called "The Cloisters." The resort required its own electrical plant and telephone company, and Coffin established his own bus line, to run from Savannah, for visitors who came by train and so could not drive over on the new causeway from Brunswick. On 12 October 1928, the Cloisters opened informally with a party for a group of visitors from Brunswick. Two weeks later, politicians and other guests at the formal opening enjoyed an orchestral performance before they sat down to an eleven-course dinner.

Sea Island was a success. The well-to-do could bask, for a brief time, in what some may have imagined was the leisure of the old planter class that had once ruled St. Simons. To complete the illusion, they might get to hear a performance by Lydia Parrish's Spiritual Singers or her Plantation Singers, groups she had organized to help preserve the songs of the slave era. By 1929, the Atlantic coast had turned its back forever on the agriculture that

The ring shout was a religious ritual that fused traditional African and Euro-Christian cultural practices. It survived in its most traditional form in the Sea Island region. (From Lydia Parrish, *Slave Songs of the Georgia Sea Islands* [1942]; courtesy of the University of Georgia Press)

Ring games such as this one in Yazoo County, Mississippi, were characteristic of African American children's play. (Courtesy of Eudora Welty Collection — Mississippi Department of Archives and History)

African American juke joints in the Delta, such as this one outside Clarksdale, provided an autonomous venue for new music and dance styles. (Photo by Marion Post Wolcott for Farm Security Administration; courtesy of Library of Congress)

Pentecostal churches, such as this congregation of the Church of God in Christ in Jackson, Mississippi, flourished in the Delta region. The blackboard at the right shows that this church, like many others, doubled as a school. (Courtesy of Eudora Welty Collection — Mississippi Department of Archives and History)

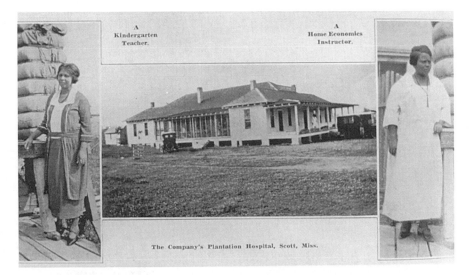

In the 1920s, the Delta & Pine Land Co. in Bolivar County, Mississippi, built a hospital and schools to attract and keep black sharecroppers. (*Manufacturers Record*, 25 October 1923)

Kokomo Arnold of Georgia was one of several blues singers to record a song about the devastation caused by the boll weevil.

Detroit industrialist Howard Coffin bought most of Sapelo Island and rebuilt the antebellum plantation on the property. In the 1920s he entertained President and Mrs. Calvin Coolidge. (Courtesy of Sea Island Company and Georgia Department of Archives and History)

Many descendants of slaves still owned homes and small plots of land on the Georgia coast in the 1930s. Henry Williams's house was in St. Marys, in Camden County. (Courtesy of Malcolm and Muriel Bell and Library of Congress)

Policies of the New Deal's Agricultural Adjustment Administration accelerated already high mobility among African American tenants and laborers. This family is leaving an employer in Morgan County, Georgia. (Photo by Marion Post Wolcott, Farm Security Administration; courtesy of Library of Congress)

New Deal policies gave new protection to labor organizing. These picketers in Greensboro, Georgia, are on strike to gain a union contract at a textile mill in 1941. (Photo by Jack Delano, Farm Security Administration; courtesy of Library of Congress)

The family of a farmer who received a rehabilitation loan from the Farm Security Administration in Greene County, Georgia. (Photo by Jack Delano, Farm Security Administration; courtesy of Library of Congress)

Home of African American Farm Security Administration clients in Greene County. (Photo by Jack Delano, Farm Security Administration; courtesy of the Southern Historical Collection, Wilson Library, University of North Carolina at Chapel Hill)

Films and radio brought national culture to the smallest towns in the South. Segregation laws, like these new technologies of communication, were a modern invention. Blacks had to

climb to the balcony in this theater in Belzoni, Mississippi. (Photo by Marion Post Wolcott, Farm Security Administration; courtesy of Library of Congress)

Howard Coffin lost his fortune in the Great Depression and committed suicide. He was buried next to his first wife in the graveyard of Christ Church on St. Simons Island. (Photo by J. William Harris)

In isolated graveyards in the Sea Islands in the 1930s, African Americans continued to decorate graves, a custom brought from Africa. (Photo by Orrin Sage Wightman from *Early Days of Coastal Georgia* [1955]; courtesy of Fort Frederica Association)

had provided the foundation of its antebellum economy and culture. For the black majority, the tourist industry was the latest in the line of white-controlled economic ventures that might enable them to earn enough cash to continue to enjoy the relative autonomy they had earned for themselves in the generations after the Civil War. The great majority of the dwindling number of black farmers in the area continued to be small landowners. Increasingly, however, it was difficult to support a family on these small plots. The typical black farm owner on the coast in 1930 had harvested fewer than ten acres the year before — less than half of his counterpart in the Delta, and less than a third of the typical Piedmont black owner. Most acreage was devoted to corn; most families needed to supplement their small productions with wage labor, as they always had done. Many gave up and left; around 1925, the six coastal counties of Georgia became, like the Piedmont, a majority-white region for the first time since Georgia had been a young colony.[39]

The Fruits of Their Labor: The Living Standards of African Americans in the 1920s

Less than a month after the levee broke on D&PL property in 1927, the company's chief executive, Oscar Johnston, sent to the Red Cross his estimate of what it would cost to rehabilitate an "average negro family" (parents and two children) who had lost everything in the flood. They would need a cooking stove (cost: $11.35); a few pots and pans for cooking and washing laundry, a knife, fork, spoon, cup, saucer, and plate for each person (all together costing less than $6); a table, four chairs, a dresser, and two beds with mattresses ($38.80); and clothing: for the mother a dress, for the father a pair of overalls, for the children one "suit" each, together with a pair of shoes and socks and two sets of underwear for each person. The grand total for this "rehabilitation," Johnston thought, would be about $75 per family.[40]

Even at the wholesale prices quoted by Johnston, such a calculation stands as a powerful indictment of a system of cotton culture that produced such a low level of wealth (if such meager items deserve the name of wealth) for the "average" family who worked in the fields. Johnston's family is not really "average" for black farmers, though it is close to average for sharecroppers. As a portrait of sharecropping families, Johnston's picture is mirrored by other observers of the period, including a number of researchers who systematically collected data on the material lives of black sharecroppers. In the Delta, for example, Dorothy Dickins of the Mississippi Agricultural Experiment Station made a study of nutrition among black sharecroppers just a month before the great flood. On eight plantations (two in each of four Delta counties) black women researchers visited sharecroppers' homes and helped them keep track of all the foods eaten by the families. Most lived in cabins with two rooms plus a kitchen, whitewashed rather than painted. "The average home has only the furniture they cannot do without, such as beds, chairs (usually not more than four), possibly a dresser and washstand." Decorations were few — most had flowers outside, nearly all had curtains, and walls were often lined with pictures from newspapers and magazines, brightening up the interiors and reducing drafts. Electricity, running water, or sewer connections were "unknown luxuries."[41]

Dickins's researchers estimated the nutrition intake for the families (calories, protein, calcium, phosphorous, and iron) and compared these with the accepted standards for a healthy diet. A majority of families were at least 10 percent "below standard" in protein and in all the minerals, and nearly 40 percent fell short on calories. The value of food eaten by an adult in these poorer families was less than twenty cents per day, and for the poorest this meant real daily hunger: rice, cornbread, and coffee for breakfast, peas and cornbread for dinner, day after day, seven days a week. Even in better-off families real meat (as distinct from the salt pork that, according to Dickins, might better be classed as fat) was a treat reserved for weekends. In some seasons vegetables and fruits were seldom eaten, and over 80 percent of calories came from flour and cornmeal, fats, molasses, and corn syrup. The inadequate protein and shortages of minerals (and, obviously, of vitamins) translated into a high incidence of pellagra, weak constitutions subject to infections and injuries, high infant mortality, and low life expectancy.[42] Dickins blamed some of these poor diets on ignorance of proper nutrition and urged public health officials, schools, and churches to educate and "train" black women in methods to increase and diversify the food supplies, with bigger gardens, more canning, and better care of laying hens. The ownership of a single cow could increase a family's protein intake by 20 percent and double the average calcium intake. But she admitted that at least some planters contributed to the problem by insisting that their croppers use every acre of land for cotton, and, in the end, that poverty was at the heart of these conditions.[43]

A similar picture of poverty among sharecroppers appears in a 1922 study of black farmers in Georgia's Piedmont. The average annual income of thirty-two sharecropping families in the study was $396 per year. Black sharecroppers grew half as much of their food as black farm owners; they drank less milk and consumed only one-third as much meat. Raper's more detailed and comprehensive study of Greene County's black farmers in 1927 came to similar conclusions. The gross income (from crop sales, wages, and home-grown provisions) of sharecropper families was $342, with food consumption paralleling "rather closely" Dickins's findings for the Delta — a diet rich in fat and low in vitamin content, with most calories coming from flour and cornmeal, fatty meats, molasses, and, in season, sweet potatoes. One-third of the families had no cow, and one-fifth few or no chickens. One-seventh of the families "went a whole year without eating a chicken or an egg."[44]

These studies put hard figures on the familiar face of black poverty. But, despite the claims, whether from self-interested planters or academic researchers, that such figures described "average" or "representative" black families, they in fact did not. They described instead the largest single group of rural black families, sharecroppers who made up a majority of rural black families in the Delta in the 1920s and a plurality of the eastern Piedmont's black families. These groups were not "average," but at the bottom of the scale in wealth, income, and living standards. Regular tenants nearly always owned their own stock and were more likely to own cattle and hogs, and in the Piedmont, renters grew considerably more food and ate better. Owners (in the Delta, about 4 percent of black farmers and in the Piedmont about 9 percent of black farmers) were nearly all better off. The 1922 Piedmont study, for example, showed that owner families consumed food worth 45 percent more per capita than did cropper families, they spent 50 percent more on clothing, and "in almost every case the owners' houses were found to be in better condition than those occupied by croppers or tenants." They also spent more than twice as much on "incidentals" — school tuition, doctor's bills, and church donations. Raper found the same in Greene County, where owners' income averaged almost twice that of croppers; owners' houses often had four or five rooms; owners' median length of residence in the same place was over ten years, compared to 3.2 years for renters and 2.5 years for croppers.[45] Black landowning families were a small minority, but important in the African American community out of proportion to their numbers. The black owner, Arthur Raper noted, "is the permanent resident of an otherwise shifting Negro farm population. He provides leadership and much of the support for the local institutions of his race. With an abiding interest in the land he cultivates, in the stock he raises, in the trees he plants, and in the community where he lives, the Negro owner, like the white owner, stands in sharp contrast with the landless farmers who move every two or three years from one barren farm cabin to another."[46]

It must also be remembered that these studies took place in a period of severe economic dislocation. The price declines of the 1920s and the arrival of the boll weevil had ruined the small fortunes of many black families as well as the large fortunes of some whites. The author of the 1922 Georgia study noted that "during 1918-'19, in those sections where the ravages of the boll weevil had not been felt, with the price of cotton high, the farmers [considered in the study] wore good clothes, ate good food, worked high priced work stock, and often rode in automobiles. In 1922 the same negroes, in many cases on the same land as in 1918-'19, wore the clothes of former years, lived on the simplest foods obtainable, worked scrub stock and rode in buggies." Almost half the owners studied still owned automobiles (some of them idle for lack of money for fuel or tires). Even on Oscar Johnston's own plantations (the Delta & Pine Land properties) in 1925 more than 150 tenant families (out of some 1,200 families in all) owned automobiles. Right through the twenties and into the Depression, car ownership continued to grow. In 1934, 45 percent of Greene County's black farmers owned automobiles; even among sharecroppers, nearly 38 percent owned autos.[47]

Many of these generalizations about black farmers apply equally well to whites. The status and incomes of African Americans was determined, as it had been for generations, partly by race, partly by other factors. Most white farmers in both the Delta and Piedmont were landless, and many were also poor (see Charts 14 and 16, Appendix). According to Raper, about half of white farm families in Greene County in the 1920s were landless, and about two-thirds of the owners were small farmers. Only about one-sixth of white farmers, in his estimate, could be considered "planters," with large acreages and many tenants. Patterns of landownership in the county had changed only gradually among whites since the Civil War. The number of really large tracts (over two thousand acres) was about half what it had been in the years of Reconstruction, and the number of tracts between five hundred and two thousand acres had hardly changed since 1900. The number of small farms had gradually increased as bigger tracts had been broken up by inheritance or by sale. As had been true for decades, the number of white tenants had increased much faster than the number of white owners.[48] Some white tenants were young men renting farms from relatives or neighbors until they could save enough to buy a farm. Many, though, filled the ranks of sharecroppers and renters on the big plantations, and their incomes, and thus their living standards, were set in the same labor market as for black tenants. Many white tenants had come down from Georgia's upper Piedmont and mountain counties. As Raper put it, "the increase of white tenants in recent decades has done little to modify the traditional patterns which grew up along the color line in the years following the Civil War. The white and Negro tenants, competing within the system for farms, are now the common heirs to its impositions." In 1934, when Raper compared white and black farmers' incomes in Greene County, whites in each category were somewhat better off than blacks, but a white sharecropper still earned in a year just $385, less than black renters and considerably less than black owners.[49]

Depression

Whites and blacks alike in the Delta, Piedmont, and Sea Island regions, whether raising cotton or catering to tourists, hoped that they had somehow reached a level of stability and predictability in their economic lives. On 4 July 1929, a record number of tourists, riding in a record number of automobiles, visited St. Simons Island's resorts. Wealthy visitors stayed at Howard Coffin's Sea Island resort, while the super-rich visitors at the Jekyll Island Club continued to enjoy their golf and tennis. Buoyed by cotton prices that had stayed over fifteen cents a pound for three years in a row, the Delta harvested record crops that year. The Delta & Pine Land Company had recovered nicely from the 1927 flood to earn over $150,000 in 1929, as in 1928. It benefited from improving yields, which in 1928 reached 419 pounds of cotton per acre, a figure "not heretofore . . . equaled on this plantation," according to Oscar Johnston, "or upon any other large acreage with which I am familiar." In the Piedmont, losses from the boll weevil had been, at least, contained, and cotton harvests were rising again; farmers had begun to experiment with dairy production and other alternatives to cotton monoculture.[50]

No one anticipated the greatest economic crisis in U.S. history. The stock market crash in October 1929 heralded a slump, which turned into the Depression of the 1930s. Cotton, which sold at over sixteen cents in 1929, was at nine and one-half cents in 1930. In the Delta in 1930, the "disastrously low figures for cotton" were compounded again by capricious nature. The Delta & Pine Land Company lost more than a thousand acres of cotton in a severe hailstorm, which was followed by a torrential downpour of over eight inches of rain, then by the most severe drought in a generation. Delta bluesman Son House recorded "Dry Spell Blues" that year:

> The dry spell blues are falling, drove me from door to door
> Dry spell blues are falling, drove me from door to door
> The dry spell blues have put everybody on the killing floor.

From May to September there was no rain at D&PL; yields on the plantation fell by a hundred pounds per acre from the previous five-year average, and the company lost over $350,000. And this was just the beginning. In the 1931 crop year the company cut expenses by 40 percent and yields returned to their previously high levels, but it still lost more than a quarter of a million dollars. Figuring that the price could not stay below ten cents per pound, the company paid its tenants eight cents and gambled on futures in the New York Cotton Exchange. When the price of cotton fell further to six cents, these moves turned into losses of $83,000 on tenants' accounts and $288,000 on the futures contracts. The next year produced another huge loss of over $250,000.[51]

In the Piedmont, where farmers had truly already been suffering from hard times for a decade, the Depression cut short any hopes of permanent recovery as the local economy resumed its downward march. As early as December in 1929, two months after the stock market crash, the Greene County newspaper noted that marriages were being put off and telephone usage had dropped. Later that month a group of local farmers advertised their plan to set up a Georgia Cotton Growers Cooperative Association to halt the slide that had left cotton selling "below cost." The next spring the manager of the local Ford dealership killed himself because of "ill health and business worries."[52] More land passed into the hands of loan companies in Greene County as the Depression deepened, but so many landowners had already lost their land in the 1920s that there was little overall change in landownership patterns. African American farmers owned 11,315 acres in the county in 1927, 11,543 acres in 1934; but in the same period of time, the average cash income of black farm families fell by half, to just $151 per year. Many sharecroppers, black and white, fell to the status of wage hands, as all farmers struggled to survive by reducing cotton acreage and more than doubling the value of home-grown provisions; when the value of these provisions is taken into account, the loss of income was just 18 percent, but this drop was from an income already at poverty levels for most. These income losses no doubt occurred for white farmers, whether owners or tenants. And it must be remembered that the "after" incomes were measured by Arthur Raper in 1934, when the New Deal's agricultural programs had substantially raised cotton prices from their nadir in 1931 and 1932.[53]

Depression-level prices for food could have little impact on the economy of the Atlantic coast, because so few farmers raised crops for the market. But the impact was as great because the Depression dragged down every sector of the economy. The levels of wholesale and retail trade in Savannah fell by half. The managers of the Jekyll Island Club saw its membership fall by half between 1929 and 1932, and they resorted to selling cut-price "associate memberships" to try to stay afloat. The tourists stopped coming to the islands, and Howard Coffin's new Sea Island resort jewel lost its luster. Coffin's losses in his stockholdings and his real estate investments back in Detroit left even him struggling to stave off bankruptcy. He spun off Sea Island into a separate company, practically giving it away to his relative and longtime associate Bill Jones. He turned over St. Catherines Island, which he had added to his holdings in 1927, to a business partner. Unable to keep up his magnificent estate on Sapelo Island, he sold it off to tobacco heir R. J. Reynolds Jr., along with his yacht *Zapala*, thrown into the bargain for an extra $50,000. The Depression had brought down this planter in fantasy as it had brought down so many planters in fact.[54]

8

"Discord, dissension, and hatred"
Cultural Change and Cultural Conflict after World War I

IN THE AFTERMATH OF WAR, A WAVE OF UNEASE ABOUT SOCIAL change swept across the United States, made stronger in the South because of fears about the effects of the war on the color line. Whites feared that military service would embolden black claims to equality. Furthermore, a quickening of technological change, a shaken system of gender relations, and a seeming deterioration in standards of morality all heightened white anxieties that a whole way of life was under siege. The strongest white anxieties sprang from fear that the war might have weakened the color line. Georgia's Senator Thomas Hardwick warned that "tens of thousands of Negroes" returning home "with a record of honorable military service" might well spur "a new agitation . . . as strong and bitter as the agitation for Negro suffrage which swept the North after the Civil War." Editors and letter writers observed "the high tension which seemingly exists . . . about the returning negro soldiers," and cautioned readers to ignore "absurd" stories that the "soldiers who went overseas would come back and expect to marry your sisters." When an Indiana newspaper ran a cartoon of a white man saying, as he orders a crippled black soldier off a sidewalk, "You cain't vote in this state," a Vicksburg editor angrily denounced it. The editor admitted that some people "feared that the returning negro soldier might cause some friction on his return," although he concluded that "so far as we have heard there has not been a single instance of the sort."[1]

Whites in Vicksburg soon demonstrated that they indeed feared breaches in the color line, whether or not they came directly from "the returning negro soldier." On 19 April 1919 the Vicksburg *Evening Post* reported that a black "Midnight Visitor" had "invaded" two homes, frightened ladies, and "attacked" Mrs. F. A. Arnold. Over the next four weeks, more break-ins by "black prowlers" were reported. Several men were arrested on suspicion, but identifications were uncertain and the "epidemic" did not stop. By May 14 white emotions were at a fever pitch. The headline in the *Post* that day screamed "Negro Attempts Rape of Young Working Girl." Bloodhounds had tracked the criminal and authorities had arrested a young black man.[2]

The city's sheriff hustled the suspect, one Lloyd Clay, off to jail, hoping for a quick identification by Mattie Hudson, the victim of the alleged attempted rape, so the city could order a quick trial, get a conviction, and, if possible, avoid a mob scene. The sheriff was no doubt disappointed when Miss Hudson not once, but twice, failed to identify Clay in a lineup. Lloyd Clay's respite was brief, however. The panic in Vicksburg had gone on too long and become too intense. Hundreds of whites, convinced of Clay's guilt, gathered in front of the jail, determined to seize him and administer their own brand of justice. By the evening of the 14th, the crowd had swelled to perhaps one thousand; many in the crowd were drunk. Shortly before 8:00 P.M., they stormed the jail and seized Clay. Some dragged the victim out to the street, others went for Mattie Hudson. Clay strongly denied his guilt. Though she had twice before been unable to identify Clay and remained at first "loathe to identify him," Hudson finally told the crowd "that he was the guilty one." In terror, Clay cried out, "I'm the man. Give me a pistol and I'll blow my brains out." No self-imposed death, however, would satisfy the mob. They stripped Clay, poured oil over his body, roped him and hanged him from a tree at the side of the street. As the rope pulled taut, "the sight of the nude body rising above the crowd increased the excitement." A fire set below his feet lapped at his legs. Without a cry, he "lifted his arms" and "placed his palms together in an attitude of prayer." Many in the crowd fired their guns at him, and "even women were seen to shoot revolvers." In the wild firing a white bystander was mortally wounded by a stray bullet. The flesh of Lloyd Clay continued to burn—described in gory detail in local newspapers—after he was dead. The body was then cut down and the crowd, in a "hubbub of gloating," rushed in to seize souvenirs.[3]

This lynching produced in Vicksburg not a reinforcement of white solidarity but division and discord that exposed deep social and cultural cleavages among whites. A few days after Clay's murder, a group of the wealthiest and most influential men in the city met publicly to denounce it, and in a remarkable inversion of black/white imagery, declared that the lynching had "cast an ineffaceable black shadow upon the fair name of our city" and made Vicksburg "the object of abuse and contempt of people in every section of the civilized world." This language was put into a petition that circulated through the city and soon gained signatures of nearly 10 percent of the adult white male population. The petition called for swift and sure punishment of the lynch mob's leaders.

Some white critics were repelled because the crowd had inflicted "unnecessary" torture and caused the death of a white bystander. The "fiendish gloating" of the crowd reminded one local commentator of the "Bolsheviki" themselves, and a reporter called the mob "an amateur organization," implying that it had lacked proper direction from community leaders. Worse, many soon became convinced that Clay was innocent. Even the strongest champions of southern bloodhounds could doubt that they had correctly tracked Clay from a single scent to a place as public as the railroad station where he had been arrested. So, too, Mattie Hudson had "been loathe to identify" Clay, and she had made her eventual and uncertain identification literally in the face of a howling mob. Clay's brother, furthermore, soon said that Lloyd had spent the entire night of the alleged crime with him. Four days after the lynching, the editor of the Vicksburg *Daily Herald* was lamenting that the "hideous and dehumanizing spectacle" had resulted in the death of an innocent man, "one wholly out of the class of the 'bad negro.'"[4]

Disturbing in its own right was that, in attempting to enforce the boundaries of race, the lynch mob had ignored the proper boundaries of gender. The mob lynched Clay at the doorstep of a home owned by prominent white women, one of whom was so offended that she asked the city to cut down the tree where Clay had been hung. Many white women had witnessed the sadistic torture of the naked black man, with its obvious sexual connotations, and several women had fired revolvers. When local commentators deplored the presence of women at the lynching, a Mrs. Emily P. Shaw responded with a remarkable letter to the *Evening Post*. A witness herself to the lynching, she approved of the "just mob" that had only been "meting out justice." "The day has passed when a woman, 'to be a lady,' must stay behind closed doors. There are times when she should come forth and she is none the less a lady for doing so." Mrs. Shaw, in effect, was denying that white women like herself needed to be protected in their homes. Perhaps her letter raised questions in the minds of some of Vicksburg's white men about the circumstances of

Clay's alleged assault. The crucial break-in had come in the apartment of an unmarried working woman who lived alone. How could such women, living without the "protection" of a man, ever be kept safe? Indeed, such an unattached woman, working as a stenographer in Vicksburg, had just weeks before been accused of poisoning her late husband. One woman replying anonymously to Shaw insisted, "There is an innate feeling in most women that causes them to experience horror at the thought of witnessing such a scene. If I were not sure that this were so with the large majority of women here, I would wish to shake the dust of this city from my feet forever." She vehemently denied that the mob had exhibited a "spirit of chivalry."[5]

These multiple doubts about the lynching led Vicksburg's white elite to repudiate the mob. The language of their condemnation — that the lynching had made Vicksburg "the object of abuse and contempt of people in every section of the civilized world" — suggests a provincial middle class struggling to identify itself with the standards of the "civilized world" of Europe and the North, a civilization that a mighty war had just been fought to preserve. Now, as one letter writer put it, Vicksburg had been witness to a "victory for German ideals." As the petition drawn up by the elite circulated through the city over the next few days, Vicksburg's citizens were asked to identify themselves publicly with these values of civilization, and in effect to reject those of a presumably more primitive cultural ideal. The accumulation of names on the petition offers powerful evidence of the ways in which that cultural divide was also a class divide.[6]

The signers included an array of the most prominent business and professional leaders in the city, among them the mayor, the heads of every bank, the ministers of the major religious denominations, prominent lawyers, owners of important businesses, the supervisor at the main railroad, and the president of the board of trade. Yet the petition contained the names of many men who were not part of that leadership. The great majority of nonelite signers held clerical and similar white-collar jobs in the city. Most were employees of the elite signers themselves. The signature of W. S. Jones, president of the Merchants National Bank, was closely followed by those of C. E. Downing and Preston Wailes, clerks at his bank. The signatures of W. Conway and T. H. Allein, clerks at Warner and Searles Clothing, followed that of C. L. Warner, the president of the company. The pattern is consistent through more than one hundred such signatures from lower white-collar workers. By contrast only three identifiable blue-collar workers signed — one carpenter, one electrician, and one bicycle repairman. Undoubtedly, Vicksburg's white establishment had circulated the petition among themselves, and in each of their businesses had gotten the lower-level employees to sign as well. While it seems reasonable to think that clerical workers might feel intimidated when asked by their employers to sign such a petition, the signatures of contractors were not followed by those of carpenters, nor that of the owner of a boiler works by those of boilermakers. The class divide was not simply a matter of income, but also a matter of culture, as clerks, many of whom were no doubt educated and ambitious to rise in the world of business, chose to identify themselves with the business civilization of Vicksburg's elite.[7]

Despite the efforts of Vicksburg's white elite, Lloyd Clay's killers were never brought to justice, though, when the grand jury met in July 1919, the presiding judge urged them to "bring Clay's slayers to court" and compared the mob to the "lawbreaker and agitator" who would bring about "Bolshevism and anarchy and ruin." The grand jury, dominated by farmers and planters from the rural areas of Warren County, refused to return an indictment. Frank Andrews, the jury foreman, secretary of the Vicksburg Board of Trade, and a signer of the antilynching petition the previous spring, resigned in protest, causing "a considerable sensation about the court house and throughout the city," but the resignation had no effect, and the judge ordered him not to mention publicly the names of any suspected lynchers.[8]

The Radio, the Automobile, and the Bolsheviks

The cleavages evident in Vicksburg, crosscut with conflicts of race, class, gender, and culture, were not always laced with violence. They were evident in a more intimate way in the family of John McRaven, a Yazoo City, Mississippi, businessman in the 1920s. Early in 1922, McRaven received a letter from his son Will Henry (then living in Dallas) about the wonderful experience of listening to the radio. "It must be very interesting to hear over one," McRaven replied; "There is no telling what is going to be the outcome of this invention." In April, when a new station broadcast from Memphis, he thought "the whole country has gone wild over the 'Radio' service, and I presume after a while they will be as common as picture shows; it will no doubt be a great thing for the country people & small towns." By the end of the year McRaven regularly visited his four acquaintances who owned radios so he could listen to "the fad," and in early 1923 he bought his own set.[9]

McRaven embraced this new technology, but he was far less happy with other changes in his world. He worried, especially, about his daughters. He was "awfully put out" that Evie Louise (nicknamed "Easy") succumbed "to the bobbed hair craze," but he kept quiet because her husband, Jack, had consented, "and that was all that was necessary." He worried more about his three younger unmarried daughters—Margaret and Annette at home, and Lucile away at college. His wife had died in a horrifying accident in 1921 (Mrs. McRaven's dress had caught fire on Christmas Day as she backed up to warm herself before the fireplace), and, he wrote to his son, "I realize more & more every day what a responsibility I have on my hands with two grown girls to look after, without the influence of a mother to guide & direct them along the straight & narrow path, because I know there are men who lay just for such cases to try to take advantage of girls in this condition." Exacerbating the situation was the automobile, "a vehicle for immorality into the world that was never equaled before. As long as you kept [your daughters] under the roof of your home at night you could keep them under control but with the night riding, there is no telling what goes on, and the sad feature of it, is that it is getting worse all the time." Countering the threat of moral decline was, he reported, a religious revival sweeping Mississippi. A group of businessmen had organized a "Flying Squadron," traveling about the state to lead noon-hour prayer meetings in the "picture shows." "For a while it seemed that the Christian religion had been forgotten, but now [after the war] since the people have had time to 'take stock of themselves' & whither we were drifting, the layman, seeing the way things were going, no longer felt that, 'Church work' was for the preachers & good women only, but that it is also a large size man's job and have gotten in behind it in a way to arouse the thinking masses of the world as to the duty they owe their God, their country & their neighbor." He hoped to remarry for his girls' sake, although "separations & divorces are . . . so common now that it Makes one shudder who stops to think of the situation."[10]

Despite McRaven's fears about the "vehicle for immorality," he bought a new Ford for Margaret and Annette to drive. His words and actions were at odds with his beliefs about the dangers of moral decline. He certainly did not oppose women's working or in other ways asserting their independence. He went to considerable expense to see Lucile through college, wanting her to get her license to teach, as "we never know when misfortune may overtake us & she may have to earn her living." Nor did McRaven worry that Lucile, who did become a teacher, was still unmarried at the end of the decade. "Keep a stiff upper lip," he advised her, "& so live that you can look any damn man in the face & tell him to go to Hell if necessary."[11]

The conflict between modern and traditional values (to use oversimplified terms), evident in the divisions in Vicksburg after the 1919 lynching, was being fought out not between McRaven as a "traditional" southerner and Yankees from afar, nor between him as a man of the "modern" city and tradition-bound rural men and women, but within his own family and within his own heart. It was a conflict that would be played out in many ways in the next decade — at Delta crossroads, on previously isolated Sea Islands, and in small Piedmont towns. It was brought about in part by the influence of the movies, the radio, and the automobile. Such conflict would, inevitably, intersect in a myriad of ways with the most powerful of southern traditions: gender roles and the color line.

Adoption of the new Nineteenth Amendment in 1920, giving women the right to vote, stirred a chorus of anxieties in the South. Legislatures in both Georgia and Mississippi rejected the amendment, but after its final passage, women in both states promptly acted on their new rights. In the Delta, many prosuffrage women joined the new national League of Women Voters, and one group of them established a newspaper in Clarksdale, *The Woman Voter,* edited by Minnie Brewer, daughter of former governor Earl Brewer.

The new paper was owned, managed, and edited "exclusively by women." It endorsed the old suffrage argument that women's politics was only "housekeeping on a larger scale," and it campaigned for the enforcement of prohibition, passage of child labor laws, and equal access for women to good jobs, to the jury box, and to service on state commissions that dealt with issues directly related to women and children. *The Woman Voter* endorsed female candidates for office, but went beyond politics to praise "flapper" clothing as more comfortable than the long dresses and skirts imposed on women by "fashion propaganda."[12]

Such cultural and social issues as styles of dress seem to have preoccupied public commentators more than women's explicit political activity. John McRaven, for example, wrote in a letter that he had opposed female suffrage, but that the results of the 1922 state elections had convinced him that he was wrong. The passage of the Nineteenth Amendment generated surprisingly little newspaper controversy, and politicians like James K. Vardaman of Mississippi and Tom Watson of Georgia supported women's right to vote. The media frequently sounded the alarm about personal behavior, however. Outside Savannah, at a popular dance pavilion on Tybee Island, the manager forbade women from dancing the "shimmie" — a dance that, in the eyes of one rural editor, "was invented in hell." "Has the womanhood of Savannah," he asked, "sunk itself to the point that it is becoming necessary" to issue these public orders? It was another sign of the declining morality, along with divorce, trashy literature, and the bunny hug. Nor was the moral decay confined to cities like Savannah. The editor's own county had registered five divorces in a single superior court session. Similar laments came from a resident of Camden County on Georgia's coast in 1922, where A. C. Colson blamed the rise in divorce on a decline in character — too many men would rather "play pool and hang out down town" than stay at home to play with their children; too many women would "rather dance, gossip, attend various clubs, go auto riding and take their meals at a restaurant or possibly work in an office or store than keep their house and husband, do the cooking and raise a family like their mother did." In Rolling Fork, Mississippi, a meeting of Methodists denounced Sunday automobiling and condemned modern dancing as "grossly irreligious and damaging to the character."[13]

Most shocking of all to citizens, if headlines are a guide, was the increase in violence by women against their husbands. A sensational trial in February of 1919 of Mrs. Abbott in Atlanta for murder was widely publicized; indeed, the Vicksburg *Evening Post,* hundreds of miles away, carried the most recent details with the help of a "special leased wire." Throughout the spring of 1919 similar stories closer to home dominated the front pages of Vicksburg's papers: a murderess in Selma, Alabama; a "shocking murder" in nearby Indianola, in which a "traveling man" was shot down by a white woman while her husband watched; the arrest of a Vicksburg stenographer, charged with poisoning her husband. At a convention of police chiefs in New Orleans, "women crooks" shared attention with the "spread of Bolshevism" as leading topics of discussion. Such reports became so common that Clarksdale's *Woman Voter* denounced the "rantings" of the newspapers about "the apparent increase in women murderers," pointing out that women were often "mercilessly condemned" for killings inspired by jealousy while husbands were often excused by the "unwritten law" that allowed them to protect their honor with violence.[14]

Such fears of social unrest were exacerbated by the labor conflicts that erupted in 1919 throughout the nation. Most of this unrest was far away, but just across the Mississippi, in Elaine, Arkansas, whites panicked when they discovered black sharecroppers organizing a new labor organization, and they responded with a murderous pogrom. Many connected these labor troubles to the success of the Bolsheviks in Russia, who, in the popular imagination, replaced the Huns as a danger to civilization. Newspaper headlines warned that "Bolshevists Would Contaminate World" or were "Threatening Civilization." Strikes in Seattle and Minneapolis and crime in New York City were seen as extensions of this worldwide threat: "Seattle Thinks that Bolshevism Grips the City"; "Practical Bolshevism in New York. Unprecedented Reign of Crime and Loot." The Bolsheviks seemed to threaten the sexual as well as the class order. Newspapers frightened readers with tales of anarchy, but also titillated them with rumors that Lenin presided over "daily orgies of indulgence . . . at Bolsheviki headquarters," and reported that the Bolsheviks were "nationalizing" Russian women and had "declared war on family life." In Moscow, men were sharing women "and consideration for one another's mother or sister is forbidden. All must be treated alike. The most terrible thing is that the women themselves have accepted their 'nationalization' and very little protest is made."[15] In April 1919 Rev. Charles Criswell, a "militant pastor," told his Vicksburg congregation that the world was "on the edge of a volcano," as demonstrated by the twin eruptions of "bolshevism and infidelity." "Making the world safe for democracy is incidental to making every home safe. The world cannot be safe as long as there is an unprotected country in it, any more than any city can be safe if there is an unprotected home in it."[16]

Such fears about unsafe homes contributed to whites' hysteria over the burglaries in Vicksburg that culminated in Lloyd Clay's lynching, weeks after Criswell's sermon. Clay's was one of three lynchings in the Delta region in 1919, after two years with none. The Piedmont region, with only one lynching in 1917–18, saw six in 1919 alone. Coastal Georgia continued to see much less racial violence, although there was one lynching right after the war in Liberty County, when a mob from an interior county intercepted and murdered a prisoner being transported to Savannah.[17]

The crimes said to have been committed in the aftermath of the war were similar to those that had always provoked lynchers. In some cases a dispute between a landlord and tenant had escalated into violence. In Greene County, Georgia, in 1920, Charles Wright had an argument with prominent planter Robert McWhorter, and, according to white newspaper sources, shot McWhorter after being ordered off the plantation. A massive manhunt failed to catch Wright, who escaped through local swamps, but along the way whites shot and killed Felix Cremer, who was accused of helping Wright get away. In Richmond County, after Walker Smalley was struck by his boss, Smalley shot the boss, then, firing at every white man he saw, fled into the nearest black neighborhood. He was shot down by police, and the city of

Augusta narrowly avoided a major race riot, as crowds of whites burned automobiles of blacks and threatened several with lynchings.[18] In other cases blacks were killed for murdering white men who were symbols of local authority. In Humphreys County, Mississippi, in March 1919, Eugene Green was arrested for shooting and killing the town marshal of Belzoni. A crowd took him from jail, hanged him, and threw his body into the Yazoo River. In Lincolnton, Georgia, six months later, Jack Gordon shot and killed two deputy sheriffs who were trying to arrest him; in retaliation, an "orderly" mob of more than a thousand burned to death both Gordon and an alleged accomplice. In the search for Gordon, according to one report, a group of whites whipped five African Americans, killing one named Moses Martin, until the others told where Gordon was hiding.[19]

As in the case of Lloyd Clay, white men's sexual fears provoked other lynchings. One female "sufferer" asked in a letter about Clay, "Could our fathers, husbᴖnds and brothers take a chance on this man's life?" A white man called the tree on which Clay was hung "a monument to the spirit of manhood of this community who will not tolerate crimes against their women folks." In the Delta county of Humphreys, Robert Truett was lynched in July 1919 for a supposed insult to a white woman. In Oglethorpe County in the Piedmont, Obe Cox was killed that same year in a lynching that caught national attention for its brutality. Cox, accused of the rape and murder of a white farm housewife, was captured in nearby Athens, brought back to the scene of the crime, tied to a stake, riddled with bullets, and burned before a crowd estimated at five thousand.[20]

Many lynch mobs seemed intent on ritualizing the occasion as a way of dramatizing their determination to repair the ruptured color line. As in the past, men accused of attacking white women were especially vulnerable to public burnings. In Yazoo County in 1923, Willie Minnifield, accused of attacking a white woman with an ax, was burned at the stake at midday. But burning rituals were also used in cases not involving sex, even, at times, when the lynch victim was already dead. After Walker Smalley in Augusta and Denny Richards of Warren County, Georgia, were killed in separate incidents while resisting arrest by police or posses, their bodies were taken by crowds and publicly burned. In both cases (and especially that of Richards, whose original crime was killing his former wife) the burnings were motivated less by the original crime than by the desire to eliminate black men's resistance to all white authority.[21]

Many whites convinced themselves that lynchings were preventive. When the Tuskegee Institute published a report indicating that the number of lynchings was lower in 1920 than in 1919, the editor of a Piedmont weekly saw this as gratifying evidence that "the negro is finding out that he will forfeit his life in the most horrible manner devisable by man, if he lets his lust lead him to the rape of a white woman." Shortly after the Obe Cox burning, a nearby daily paper criticized not the lynching but the NAACP's protests against it, which would "contribute much to dissension" because "the negro in the South is satisfied with conditions."[22]

"We have our eyes on you"

The lynchings in Vicksburg, in Greene County, and elsewhere revealed sharp differences within white society. When repression of disorder spawned what seemed to be even more disorder, and when the enforcement of morality resulted in immoral acts, many whites were repelled and disgusted. When, as an investigator in the Delta found in 1932, young whites were being influenced by "what they see in the movies and read about in popular fiction" rather than by religion, when they, like their counterparts elsewhere in the nation went to "petting and drinking parties," parents like John McRaven feared a world seemingly out of joint. Some whites turned to new forms of organization to try to restore a sense of public order ruled by traditional morality. During the war, whites in Greensboro organized their Law and Order League to enforce local prohibition and combat "other forms of vice," and in the summer after the war the league was reinvigorated to fight against gambling, whiskey, and general lawlessness. Illicit whiskey selling — rampant despite state prohibition laws and the recent adoption of the Eighteenth Amendment that established national prohibition — was a special problem. Rev. J. F. Roberts said that he knew of thirty people in the county who were engaged in the sale of whiskey. The local paper printed a coupon for its readers to fill out in order to join the league, which planned to "furnish evidence of lawbreaking to federal officers," and that year a similar league was formed in the little town of White Plains in Greene County. The paper's editor strongly supported this effort; he was especially troubled, he said, that so many violations of the law occurred on Sundays. Women officers of the county's Civic League announced that they would oppose for office anyone who would not work to enforce prohibition.[23]

Such efforts, however, were soon overshadowed by the rise of a new and far larger organization, the second Ku Klux Klan. In 1915, William

Joseph Simmons, inspired in part by his father's stories of membership in the Reconstruction-era Klan, and in part by the success that year of the film *Birth of a Nation*, gathered a few like-minded friends to establish the second Klan on Stone Mountain, outside of Atlanta. The Klan did not become a force, however, until 1920, when Simmons hooked up with Mary Elizabeth Tyler and Edward Young Clarke, partners in a publicity firm, who helped make the Klan a mass organization with branches all across the country (and, in the process, making a small fortune themselves with their cut of membership fees).[24] This second Klan married the trappings of a fraternal organization — with secret membership, rituals, and uniforms to bind members together — to the widespread fears of social and cultural disorder that had prompted formation of a law and order league in Greene County. The Klan was determined to enforce its own version of a "One Hundred Percent Americanism" — an Americanism that was white, Protestant, and ordered along traditional gender lines. The second Klan borrowed from the first an intent to enforce its will politically when possible, and, in some places, violently if necessary.

Because the Klan was secretive, reliable sources tend to be scarce, but we know that in Georgia it was weak along the coast and strong in the Piedmont. In Athens, one of the biggest cities of the upper Piedmont, most Klan members held middle-class or lower-middle-class jobs as clerks, salesmen, skilled tradesmen, or owners of small businesses. In Macon, another Piedmont city further west, known members tended to fall in the lower middle class. But the Klan in both cities attracted professionals as well, among them lawyers, physicians, even a judge. Whether this pattern of membership was typical of rural areas is impossible to say based on the available evidence.[25]

For obvious reasons, African Americans saw the Klan as akin to the lynch mob, but Klansmen themselves claimed that their goal was rather to prevent such violence. The editor of the paper in Greensboro, Georgia — not a Klansman himself — wrote after one black leader criticized the Klan that, as long as the organization was "conducted for 'fair play' to all, we do not see any harm in it." In Indianola, Mississippi, a white writer sympathetic to the Klan replied in similar terms when a Memphis member of the black elite called the Klan a cause of the black exodus to the North. The Klan, the writer replied, was "not the enemy but the friend" of blacks. While the Klan would indeed work to eliminate bootlegging, gambling, and other "contributing causes" of blacks' supposed "moral undoing," it would not "whip, tar and feather or in any other way molest or attack anybody." Indeed, he claimed, the Klan

would strive to ensure that blacks were not "railroaded to prison on frame-
ups" and that their rights were fully protected in court. That such claims
were not entirely bogus is demonstrated by the circumstances surrounding
the 1925 lynching of Lindley Coleman, a black man accused of participating
in a murder in Clarksdale, Mississippi, and, after his acquittal, murdered by a
lynch mob. Coleman's defense attorney in the case was none other than
Thomas S. Ward, identified in one source as the grand dragon of the Ku Klux
Klan in Mississippi. Ward later testified before a grand jury that brought
indictments against four white men, including the sheriff and a local planter,
for their part in Coleman's lynching.[26]

The propaganda and the vigilante actions of the Klan were sometimes
aimed at African Americans who had stepped out of their proper places, but
more often, the Klan targeted whites who had flouted public order or public
morality. Bootleggers were perhaps the single most commonly identified enemy, but husbands who beat their wives or men who threatened the purity of
young white women were also targets for threats or beatings. When the Klan
reached the Mississippi Delta, the Washington County local "klavern" announced its purposes in a public letter on the front page of one weekly paper.
Claiming to speak "in the Name of our venerated dead" and even of George
Washington himself, the Klan pledged that it would stand behind officers of
the law and not take the law into its own hands, and that it would make
Washington County a place where all "flag-loving" citizens would be proud
to raise their children. Belying its promise to assist but not enforce the law,
the letter threatened the Klan's targets: "Bootleggers, gamblers, and all other
law-breakers" should know that "we have our eyes on you, and we are many;
we are everywhere, and you will not escape." Married men "who are not
treating their wives right" must change their ways; the Klan would "know
who you are, too." As for "the boys who take girls out automobile riding,
and park their cars by the roadside," "had you ever thought that what you
do, some other boy is entitled to do with your sister. We suggest to you that
you quit. And let us say to the parents: Join with us and assist us in the
keeping of your daughters at home, for the life of our nation depends on the
purity of womanhood." Finally, the Klan told Negroes, "We are your best
friend, but we wish you to do right."[27]

Members of the Klan, then, shared many values with respectable, even
"progressive" whites. The suffragists who founded *The Woman Voter* in
Mississippi themselves shared many of the concerns of Klan members. Most
suffragists were strong supporters of liquor prohibition; *The Woman Voter*

endorsed prohibition in its first issue, along with "fair play" for women. It defended "flapper" clothing, but denounced jazz, which was, in the editors' opinion, based on "the worst of the negro," and declared that 80 percent of popular songs were "unfit for singing." The paper firmly endorsed segregation. It criticized the Chicago *Tribune* for condemning southern lynchings; Chicago was much worse than the South because white girls there were being "seized" and "sold to negroes in return for political influence." The paper's editors spoke favorably of James Vardaman and Tom Watson, both extreme radicals on race, but attacked Theodore Bilbo, whose record as a governor was progressive, because of his unsavory reputation as a womanizer. He may have been a good governor, but the women of the League of Women Voters were unwilling to have him "HELD UP TO THEIR CHILDREN AS CLEAN AND PURE IN HIS PRIVATE LIFE."[28]

Since many women progressive activists shared some of the Klan's goals in the 1920s, it is not surprising that Mississippi's Nellie Nugent Somerville, one of the South's most influential suffragists, joined with Klan members challenging the power of LeRoy Percy and other leaders of Washington County's Democratic Party "ring." Somerville considered Percy and the rest of his "ring" "wets" on prohibition, and therefore defenders of a corrupt status quo. Somerville was certainly correct about Percy's attitude toward prohibition; he despised it, and, as his correspondence reveals, went to a fair amount of trouble to ensure that his own supply of good liquor would not suffer because of a mere amendment to the U.S. Constitution. More generally, for Percy the Klan itself was not a defender of tradition but a new and intrusive organization of outsiders who threatened not only his own power but also local culture as he understood and treasured it.[29]

The Klan arrived in the Mississippi Delta in 1921, and by 1923 had, in Percy's estimation, come to dominate politics in Bolivar, Coahoma, and other counties. In his own home county of Washington, Percy was an uncompromising foe of the Klan. When the group first declared itself there, it invited Klan orator Joseph G. Camp to speak at the courthouse in Greenville. A number of county officials, including Ray Toombs, the county prosecuting attorney, had already joined. Camp appealed to all right-minded men to join the Klan's fight against the "alien" influences of Jews and Catholics. Even the Negroes, he complained, were better organized than the Anglo-Saxons. Percy replied to Camp in a widely reprinted speech, calling the Klan a "menace to prosperity and welfare of my people." He mocked members for covering themselves "with a clown suit and mask" while claiming to defend southern womanhood. He denounced them as a "gang of sleuths, spies and inquisitors," bigoted against Catholics and Jews, who had "stood shoulder to shoulder" with Protestants through the perils of floods and epidemics: "We have gone through joys and gone through sorrows . . . feasted together at the wedding of our young people . . . struggled on the road to prosperity and happiness."[30]

Percy had many reasons for opposing the Klan. His wife was a Catholic and among his friends and business partners were Jews. Ridiculing the Klan's claim to be the "friend" of the Negro, he recognized it as a potentially serious threat to the Delta's supply of black labor. Citing lynchings in other places that had been blamed on the Klan, he predicted that the Delta could lose its black labor to out-migration within a year if the Klan came to power. Among the dozens of letter writers who congratulated Percy for his stand was an Issaquena planter, Dick Cox, who told him that "every farmer in this delta should feel very grateful to you for what you did." But, perhaps most profoundly, Percy saw the Klan as a threat to his own community of Greenville and Washington County, a community that he identified with, a community over which he presided as a leading political figure, and a community that, he believed, still embodied many of the aristocratic values of the Old South. The true spirit of community, he said, was reflected when, after a serious threat of high water, townspeople had "gathered together in a community service of thanksgiving to return thanks to Almighty God that by His blessing and through our united efforts we had escaped disaster from the great river." Such community love "made me feel when the time should come for me to join the loved ones out yonder, that there was no epitaph I would wish for except, 'He Lies Among His Friends.' " Into this community had now come the Klan, "sowing discord, dissension and hatred where there was gentleness and love and friendship; disrupting churches, threatening civic societies, destroying the spirit of cooperation and making man look with suspicion on man and wonder whether his neighbor is his friend or his secret enemy." Percy's vision, of course, assumed a community to be run by the "best" white men.[31]

Percy's battle required real courage, for klansmen in many places in the South had few qualms about using violence against their enemies. Just sixty miles away, in Mer Rouge, Louisiana, the sons of two prominent planter families were murdered after being warned by the local Klan leader to stop their drinking and sleeping with black women. One night, a stranger knocked at Percy's door and asked him for help with a broken-down auto. The man, as it turned out, probably intended to do him serious harm. The stranger disappeared when the county sheriff fortuitously appeared at Percy's house on a visit. After that incident, Percy's son Will told Ray Toombs, now the Klan's leader in the county, that if his father were hurt, "you will be killed. We won't hunt for the guilty party. So far as we are concerned the guilty party will be you."[32]

Percy succeeded in preventing a Klan takeover of Washington County, but by a narrow margin, and the Klan remained politically influential into the middle of the twenties. In both Georgia and Mississippi, the Klan elected many to local and state offices. But, as the decade wore on, the Klan's influence receded, and in the long run its anti-Jewish and anti-Catholic stance repelled more people than it attracted. The Greene County editor who had written in 1921 that he "was willing to give [the Klan] our endorsement," three years later was denouncing "the Klan or any other secret political order that teaches religious bigotry and intolerance," and declaring that everyone who had ever fought for the United States — including Jews, Catholics, and Negroes — were "as much of a 100 percent American as any Klansman." The Klan discredited itself with widely publicized incidents of violence (including the Louisiana murders) and with money and sex scandals among its top national leadership. By the end of the decade the Klan's influence had declined precipitously and its political influence disappeared in both the region and the nation.[33]

"The days keeps on worryin' me"

The increase in postwar lynchings and the revival of the Klan were the most obvious indications that whites were intent on preventing any serious threats to the color line and would make certain the war years would not permanently change the nature of race relations. African Americans had come out of the war years with just such hopes of change. During the war whites had to pay higher wages, acknowledge some of the honors of citizenship for blacks, and promise better treatment from both public authorities and employers. Blacks had organized in dozens of local chapters of the NAACP. In Savannah, where blacks had paraded in support of Liberty Loans during the war, thousands lined the streets in May 1919 to welcome home twelve hundred black veterans. In Augusta, Lucy Laney and the NAACP, spurred by passage of the Nineteenth Amendment, undertook a drive to register black women. In Vicksburg, a "colored meeting" at the courthouse in

April 1919 condemned lynchings and called for better schools and improved wages for black laborers. Blacks elsewhere throughout Mississippi expressed their grievances in petitions to the state legislature, and some whites took seriously these calls for reform. A white Vicksburg editor praised the organizers of the Vicksburg meeting for their "laudable intentions." Georgia's Governor Hugh M. Dorsey issued a remarkable "Statement... As to the Condition of the Negro" in 1921, summarizing 135 cases of peonage, lynching, and other antiblack crimes, and predicting that if Georgians continued to tolerate such cruelties the result would be "the destruction of our civilization."[34]

The hopes of black reformers would, nonetheless, be largely crushed by white resistance. The dangers of open protest, especially in rural areas, were made clear when black farmers and sharecroppers organized a "Progressive Farmers Union" in the fall of 1919 in Phillips County, Arkansas, just across the Mississippi River from the Delta's Coahoma County. Three men, including a local deputy sheriff, interrupted a meeting of the union at a rural black church; a gunfight left several people dead or wounded. Rumors of a black "revolution" spread among the panicked whites of the county, who then rampaged through rural areas, attacking blacks. Dozens of blacks were apparently killed, and, on the basis of "confessions" elicited by torture, another dozen were convicted and sentenced to die in the electric chair. In the face of such intransigence and resistance, the NAACP chapters in smaller cities and towns shriveled, and attempts to organize rural workers collectively were cut short before they had barely begun.[35]

The church, the lodge, and the juke joint, therefore, rather than the courthouse or the union hall, were the centers of African American community life in the towns and countryside. When sociologist Arthur Raper interviewed black schoolchildren in Greene County, Georgia, in the late 1920s, three in four said that both of their parents belonged to a church; for most of the rest at least one parent, usually the mother, was a member. The great majority were Baptist, and nearly all the rest Methodist. The long-standing patterns of church structure and operation prevailed, with the typical church including about eighty members who worshiped in a building they had erected themselves, sometimes with the financial help of a local white planter. Church governing bodies were usually dominated by a small group of landowners and more prosperous tenants. Rarely did a church have its own preacher, and rarely did a preacher serve a single church. Unlike the prosperous ministers in middle-class urban congregations, the country preachers survived mainly by farming. Few had been educated beyond the early years of high school—

ministers with formal training at a college or seminary were in city churches. Raper estimated that a typical Greene County African American preacher split his duties among three congregations and earned about $150 a year from each one—earnings collected a dime and quarter at a time at the monthly services, a small income but considerably more than the earnings of a typical sharecropper, and much more than black teachers in the public schools.[36] Hortense Powdermaker, an anthropologist who studied black life in the Delta's Sunflower County in the 1930s, found similar patterns. Powdermaker pointed out the special importance of women in the churches. While the preachers and formal officers of the churches were always men, it was "largely the women who run the affairs of the church, and who assume financial responsibility for its maintenance." Nearly every African American church near Indianola had at least one women's club to help maintain and "beautify" the church. She described a meeting of a "Willing Workers" club on a Thursday afternoon in the front room of a "humble" home. The bed was taken out of the room, and twenty-five women crowded in. They had a secretary, a treasurer, and a finance committee, and each week one member prepared and read a short paper (on the day Powdermaker attended, the theme was "God Is Love"). The Willing Workers provided most of the money needed for construction, church debts, and Sunday donations to the preacher, and the club sponsored many social events—suppers, candy pulls, and chicken hunts, which climaxed with a hunt for the head of a chicken, the winner receiving the rest of the chicken as a prize.[37]

Because the church was "the one institution where the Negro enjoys full and undisturbed control," as Powdermaker put it, it was a prime arena for the recruitment and training of leadership and for the accomplishment of community goals. African Americans in their churches could get "the sense of respect and esteem from others which is so essential to the self-respect of most individuals, and which is so consistently refused to Negroes by the white society which dominates most of their lives." Powdermaker concluded that the churches were ultimately a conservative force, led by a cautious middle class of farmers, laundresses, and, in the towns, petty business owners who would not risk loss of their small stakes in life by openly challenging the status quo. Arthur Raper agreed with this assessment. In Greene County the leaders of every important black institution came primarily from the small stratum of landowners, most of whom had acquired their land, and kept it, only with the approval of whites: "The would-be owner must be acceptable to the white community, have a white sponsor, be content with the purchase of acreage least desired by the whites, and pay for it in a very few years." Such men might function as the mediators between the black community and the white elites, when African Americans needed help to repair a school or to deal with a particular miscarriage of justice.[38]

Close by many black churches was a lodge hall, housing the Knights of Pythias, the Masons, the Odd Fellows, Court of Calanthe, United Gospel Aid, the Builders of the Walls of Jerusalem, Travelers Home of Rest, Brothers and Sisters of Charity, Sons and Daughters of Peace, or one of a dozen others, some affiliates of large national organizations, some unique to the community. The lodge buildings often housed a schoolroom on the first floor. Lodge members met monthly to socialize, to inaugurate new members in secret rituals, and to contribute dues to cover the costs of funerals and sick benefits of a dollar or two a week. The Knights and Daughters of Tabor, as much an insurance company as a fraternal order, was one of the largest black-run enterprises in the Mississippi Delta. Sometimes lodges were true mutual aid societies, and a sick member might have his crop planted or harvested by lodge brothers and sisters. In the lodges, as in the churches, the small group of local landowners provided the core of leadership; in larger towns and cities leaders came from the more prosperous middle class of businessmen and women, physicians, insurance agents, and teachers.[39]

The church and the lodge were important along the Atlantic coast as well. Black landowners there enjoyed far more autonomy (though not far more prosperity) than in places like the Piedmont and the Delta, and black culture there continued to be more conservative and traditional than elsewhere. Folklorists like Robert Winslow Gordon in the 1920s and Zora Neale Hurston in the 1930s recorded shouts and observed old-time religious services, as the area became known as a place where some of the oldest traditions of black America survived.[40] Yet, the Georgia coast, too, felt the effects of black migration to the North and the spread of the automobile.

In 1927 the Church of God in Christ arrived on St. Simons Island, following the tourists across the new causeway from Brunswick. A small group of families belonging to the island's First African Baptist Church, attracted by the new doctrines and dissatisfied with the lack of emotion in the Baptist services, split away to found the Harlem Church, affiliated with the Church of God in Christ. Most of the original seven members were women; several had experienced recent personal difficulties, such as sickness or divorce. In the Pentecostal worship of the new Harlem Church, they found, in the words of one writer, "a strong sense of community, inclusion, and acceptance, a periodic exuberance, a temporary feeling of control over circumstances."[41]

It is one of the measures of the relative isolation and traditionalism of coastal African American culture that blues music had barely penetrated by the 1920s. In the Piedmont and Delta, by contrast, blues culture on Saturday nights complemented and competed with the church culture of Sunday morning. At Greene County's black dance parties there were "white as well as Negro bootleggers and white as well as Negro rowdies flourishing guns and seeking the attention of the flashiest dancers." Charley Patton, Tommy Johnson, Son House, and dozens of others entertained in the towns and the plantation barracks of the Delta.[42] Blues, like religion, was being affected by new means of communication and mobility. While radios were still out of reach for the great majority of black families, the Victrola and its many competitors were not. In both the Piedmont and Delta, the humblest sharecropper's shack often had room for one of these hand-cranked, spring-driven machines. Raper found that almost one-fifth of the black families he studied had phonographs.[43] The runaway success of the first blues recording, Mamie Smith's 1920 "Crazy Blues," sent record companies in search of other recording artists who could appeal to the "race" market, as recording companies called it. Although the earliest recorded blues were from such giant talents as Bessie Smith (first recorded in 1923) and other urban, vaudeville performers, their songs were undoubtedly familiar to many black southerners, who could buy records in small local stores, from traveling peddlers, and by mail. In 1926, following the commercial success of several blues recordings by Blind Lemon Jefferson of Texas, a market was discovered for the rougher voices of the rural bluesmen — the kind who still found their principal audiences in Delta towns like Clarksdale and on Delta plantations like Dockery's, in Sunflower County. One of the most successful of the talent scouts for these companies was Henry C. Spier of Jackson, Mississippi, white owner of a record store and a small recording studio who had a good ear for new and unusual work and a good rapport with blacks who patronized his store, recorded auditions with him, and told him about other talent. Charley Patton was one of his "discoveries," and it was thanks to Spier that Patton recorded his first songs in 1929 for Paramount Records.[44]

Singers who recorded made relatively little from the records themselves, but they often became more famous, drew bigger crowds, and commanded higher incomes. Many blues records found their main markets in the localities frequented by the singers. Well-known records often became more important in spreading techniques and lyrics than personal encounters with other musicians. Recording also put a premium on novelty — companies did not want to record multiple versions of the same song — and encouraged singers to write their own new songs; in doing so, they promoted songs with more coherent themes and story lines. With recording studios typically located in northern and larger southern cities, they also promoted wide-ranging travel by the musicians, which further encouraged blending and borrowing of styles and lyrics.

In the hard agricultural economy of the 1920s, the bluesman's life was no doubt especially attractive to many young black men whose alternative was life behind a plow. Georgia's eastern Piedmont was home to many bluesmen, including Blind Willie McTell, born in McDuffie County, Peg Leg Howell, of Morgan County, Buddy Moss of Hancock County, and Robert Fulton of Warrenton. Most of them followed the out-migration from boll weevil country to Atlanta and beyond.[45] The Delta, with its bigger black population and greater flow of dollars in most years, offered more venues for performers on plantations and in towns and small cities. Son House, a failed preacher, played frequently with Patton in the Delta in 1929 and 1930 and accompanied Patton to a 1930 recording session in Wisconsin, where he recorded his own "My Black Mama" and "Preachin' the Blues": "Oh, in my room, I bowed down to pray / Say the blues come 'long and they drove my spirit away."[46]

House in turn became one of the inspirations for Robert Johnson, a guitarist and singer raised in Robinsonville in the Delta. Johnson's hallmark was "the dazzling technique and almost supernatural electricity" of his playing. Relatives later told blues researchers that Johnson had bargained away his soul to the devil at a rural crossroads in return for his talent, a story that had been told about other musicians.[47] Johnson took up the life of the itinerant bluesman, which by now included not just Clarksdale and Memphis but also St. Louis, Chicago, and Detroit. If he did not have a place to stay or play, he would play on the street until a crowd gathered, hoping for an invitation to a party, or, failing that, enough tips to stay well fed. (As one musician who traveled with him remembered, he was ready to play Bing Crosby, if that's what the crowd wanted.) Bluesman Johnny Shines later wrote that Johnson's playing "caused many a woman to weep, and many a man, too." "His guitar seemed to talk — repeat and say words with him like no one else in the world could." Johnson's famous "Walkin' Blues" was based on Son House's "My

Black Mama" and his "Sweet Home Chicago" was a reworking of "Kokomo Blues," recorded in Chicago by Kokomo Arnold of Georgia, but many of his other songs were unique, dark compositions: "Love in Vain," "Crossroad Blues," or the harrowing "Hellhound on My Trail":

I've got to keep movin'
blues fallin' down like hail. . . .
And the days keeps on worryin' me
there's a hellhound on my trail.[48]

By the time Robert Johnson was ready to make musical history, the Depression had arrived and drastically shrunk the record market. Nine different recording units had come to Memphis to record blues between 1927 and 1930; none came between 1930 and 1939. The center of blues recording migrated to Chicago along with the thousands of black men and women who moved there. Johnson himself was not recorded until 1936, when Henry Spier referred him to the American Record Company (giving Spier claim to responsibility for the recording of what most agree are the two greatest of the Delta bluesmen). ARC recorded Johnson in San Antonio and Dallas. His most successful release was "Terraplane Blues" from the first session, appropriately enough for the era, a sexy automobile blues ("And when I mash down on your little starter, then your spark plug will give me fire"). But his later recordings did not sell well, and ARC did not call him back after his Dallas session in June 1937.[49]

The New White Liberalism on Race

While the rise of the second Ku Klux Klan signaled a resurgence of popular white determination to defend the color line as one part of traditional morality, a quiet movement among elite whites began to attack what they saw as the worst and most obviously unjust aspects of Jim Crow. The movement focused at first on antiblack violence, and especially lynching. Some white reformers, like Augusta's pioneering Lily Hammond, were motivated by a religious commitment to social justice. Businessmen sensitive to the North's image of the South as an uncivilized place of lawless violence saw lynchings as a barrier to the South's economic progress. The head of Mississippi's state board of development, for example, complained that every lynching "fortifie[d] those outside in their propaganda against the state." The

NAACP's campaign for a national antilynching law raised the specter of federal officials enforcing law and order in the South for the first time since Reconstruction. At several of the South's universities, especially the University of North Carolina but also the University of Georgia in Athens and Emory University in Atlanta, scholars influenced by modern ideas from sociology and anthropology began to undertake new investigations of social and economic conditions in the rural South, without assuming, as had earlier social scientists, that African Americans were inherently inferior.[50]

In Georgia, the confluence of such impulses led in 1920 to the founding of the Commission on Interracial Cooperation in Atlanta. The guiding force behind the CIC was Will Alexander, a former Methodist minister in Tennessee and a member of the YMCA's War Work Council. The CIC, based on a local Atlanta group organized by businessmen and ministers, was, especially at first, a cautious reform organization, proclaiming its loyalty "to the principle of racial integrity," seeking to bring together black and white elites to explore ways to reduce racial violence, and to undertake research and educational campaigns to improve day-to-day life for African Americans in the South.[51]

The commission tried to set up local branches in cities and towns throughout the South; in reality, most of the branches outside of the Atlanta headquarters included whites only. A major goal was to rally public opinion and exert pressure to prevent racial violence. Outside Georgia, the commission was a presence mainly in the largest cities, but in Georgia it established chapters in smaller communities throughout the state: along the coast in Brunswick and Savannah; in the Piedmont in Greensboro, Madison, and Augusta.[52] At the Atlanta headquarters, Alexander assembled a talented staff of men and women, some veterans of earlier reform movements, others relatively recent products of graduate schools. Jesse Daniel Ames, a suffragist from Texas, headed the "Women's Committee" and later organized the Association of Southern Women for the Prevention of Lynching. Thomas J. Woofter, a Georgia native and graduate of the University of Georgia, had earned his Ph.D. in sociology at Columbia University; he was the commission's first research director, replaced after he left to teach at the University of North Carolina by a doctoral student in sociology at Chapel Hill, Arthur Raper.[53]

Arthur Raper's first significant research project was a two-year study of Greene and Macon Counties in Georgia to pinpoint the causes of the tremendous influx of black migrants into Atlanta and other cities. Raper, raised by a Methodist father and Moravian mother, shared the essentially religious sensibilities of people like Lily Hammond and Will Alexander, but he was also a trained sociologist—in fact, the Macon-Greene project on out-migration served as his Ph.D. dissertation. He knew how to gather economic data from old tax rolls and how to interview schoolchildren about their family lives, but he also learned how to do research by politely listening and chatting around the barbershop and the courthouse.[54] In Greene County, Raper had the advantage of sponsorship by the local affiliate of the Commission on Interracial Cooperation—indeed, he allowed them to review and comment on his report before he submitted it in Atlanta. The local paper described his project, correctly, as a study of the causes of black out-migration, but, quite misleadingly, as part of the overall effort to "lessen the strained relations between the races, caused by the colored soldiers, returning with new ideas in their minds." In fact, Raper's work, later published in 1936 as part of *Preface to Peasantry,* was not on the "negro problem" as seen by complacent whites, but rather a damning indictment of the plantation system upon which Greene County's (and much of the South's) economy and society was based. He documented in detail the enormous racial inequalities in education and public resources, the poverty of most black and many white families, and what Raper called the "rationalizations and defence mechanisms," including the assumptions about black inferiority, "which the controllers of the plantation system have fabricated into a philosophy which justifies and maintains the politically sterile 'Solid South' " and its consequences in "one-crop farming, excessive erosion and depleted soil, low incomes . . . and most devastating of all, human relations built upon the idea that the vast majority of the population—the landless, whether white or Negro—are incapable of self-direction." Raper asserted that the South's racial and class systems had grown out of the demand of the plantations for dependent labor and that the plantation system would have to go if the South were ever to be changed. Raper's analysis was more appropriate for the Piedmont areas of the southeastern states, where the plantation system was in full decline, than for places like the Delta, where plantations remained viable and still supported a wealthy class of owners. He also underestimated the degree to which racist culture had its roots in other than purely economic soil. Nevertheless, his was a powerful critique of society and culture in the lower South.[55]

The Commission on Interracial Cooperation sought to marry important social research to practical reform projects, especially in its campaign to end lynchings. Raper's second big project for the commission was a study of all the lynchings that took place in 1930, published as *The Tragedy of Lynching.*

The commission and its affiliates tried to rally local elites to prevent lynchings and to punish lynchers. Meanwhile, the NAACP, from its headquarters in New York City and aided by its local branches, investigated and publicized lynchings, organized campaigns to pressure public officials to protect their prisoners, and lobbied for a national antilynching law. In combination, this white/black and inside/outside pressure began to have a serious impact on the incidence of lynching.

Perhaps the clearest example of these tactics followed the 1922 lynchings in Liberty County, Georgia, of two men. Joe Jordan and James Harvey, who were hiking through the lower South, worked for a few months in Wayne County, about fifty miles in from the coast. After the two men quarreled with an employer over their pay, the employer's wife charged that they attacked and raped her. Jordan and Harvey were moved to the Savannah jail for safekeeping, and while still in Savannah they were tried in absentia in Wayne County, convicted, and sentenced to death. The NAACP branches in Savannah and Atlanta hired a white lawyer in Wayne County to appeal the case, and a group of white women in the county petitioned for a new trial. Although the appeals were turned down by higher courts, Governor Thomas Hardwick, on the day of their scheduled execution, commuted Jordan's and Harvey's sentences to life imprisonment. However, as the Wayne County sheriff was returning Jordan and Harvey to the relative safety of Savannah's jail, a mob of some fifty men "seized" them in Liberty County and hanged them.[56]

The Savannah NAACP launched an investigation, visiting the site of the murders and gathering evidence from witnesses. They gained support not only from the large local black population but also from prominent local whites — the coastal region had not seen a lynching in over twenty years. Rev. P. T. Holloway of the Midway Methodist Church in Liberty County denounced the killings from his pulpit and, in a widely published letter, accused Wayne County officials of complicity in the lynchings. The Commission on Interracial Cooperation in Atlanta provided legal help for the investigation that followed. Twenty-two men were indicted for the lynching, and four were convicted — an extremely rare occurrence.[57]

With such opposition from both blacks and whites, lynchings almost disappeared for a time in Georgia; at least, none were recorded from 1927 through 1929, and none in the eastern Piedmont from 1925 through 1929. In Mississippi this opposition was less organized and less effective, but even in the Delta lynchings became less common. Twelve were reported in the

1920s, down from fifteen the previous decade. Even in the Delta whites had begun to take a more active role in suppressing lynchings. In 1925 a lynch mob seized Lindley Coleman in broad daylight in Clarksdale after he was acquitted by a jury of participating in the killing of a plantation store manager; they riddled his body with bullets and left it hanging from a tree. Within a week, many of Coahoma County's elite met to denounce the lynching and to bring at least some of the perpetrators to justice. Leading this group was Mrs. Earl Brewer, wife of the former governor and head of the county's League of Women Voters. A local judge immediately called a grand jury to meet, and four men, including the county sheriff and a local planter, were indicted. In the trial a month later the first defendant was acquitted, but only after the jury deliberated for twenty-seven hours. With the loss of acquiescence of local elites, lynchers could no longer take it for granted that they could act with impunity.[58]

"Death by causes unknown"

While the assaults of the NAACP on northern public opinion and the quieter work of southern whites and blacks began to make some practical difference, the white attitudes and beliefs on which the system of segregation depended changed slowly, if at all. The whites in Sunflower County, Mississippi, who responded to a survey by anthropologist Hortense Powdermaker in the early 1930s embodied the combination of paternalism and white supremacy that had long characterized the "better classes" of the white lower South. The whites surveyed denied that Negroes were "abhorrent," admitted that they deserved "civil equality," and agreed that they had made "unique contributions" to music and were "more desirable" than foreigners, in part because (as 73 percent agreed) Negroes had "genial dispositions." In short (with only 2 percent in dissent), "Negroes are all right as long as they stay in their places." That place, said four out of five, was "in manual work."[59] Whites almost unanimously opposed giving Negroes "full political equality" or allowing school integration or racial intermarriage. Only 6 percent of the whites surveyed thought it even somewhat acceptable that "colored people should fight for social equality." Most thought that "inter-racial committees" (such as the CIC) were not improving relations between Negroes and whites, and the vast majority thought that "the older generation of Negroes was more desirable than the present generation" and that African Americans would not and could not "reach the cultural and intellectual level of the

Whites." Even on the question of whether "Christian brotherhood should disregard race lines," the white respondents were evenly divided.

Perhaps the most surprising result of Powdermaker's survey was that a majority of whites agreed, in whole (42 percent) or in part (11 percent), that "there should be a Federal law against lynching," a strong sign of the spread of antilynching ideas in the South. At the same time, nearly two-thirds thought lynching justifiable as punishment for rape. Since Powdermaker had given her questionnaires precisely to those most likely to identify with "progressive" views and most sensitive to national criticisms of the South — students in a junior college, members of the Rotary and Chamber of Commerce, women in Christian missionary societies — the continued strength and persistence of the color line in the Delta in the mid-1930s is apparent.[60]

It was such convictions among even elite and educated whites that made possible the especially brutal lynching of Charles Shepherd in Sunflower County at the end of 1928. Shepherd, a worker on that most famous of Delta plantations, the Parchman prison farm, was serving time for the murder of a fellow black man in Vicksburg. He had become a trusty — an assistant to the sergeant, or overseer, who headed one of the prison's farms, carrying a gun and watching over the regular prisoners in return for better quarters and other modest but cherished freedoms. On 28 December 1928, Charles Shepherd turned on his sergeant, J. D. Duvall, slit his throat, kidnapped Duvall's teenaged daughter, and disappeared into the woods.[61]

Shepherd's crime and escape touched off a massive manhunt, according to a local man, one of only two manhunts he had witnessed that included "pursuers from the big-porched houses in normally quiet little towns." Shepherd, who was illiterate and mentally retarded, let the girl go and turned himself in to a local planter, Miss Laura Mae Keeler, who had once employed him and who promised to protect him. She could not keep her promise; he was taken by one of the search parties, tied up, driven through the countryside, and showed off to the other prisoners at Parchman as a warning. Shepherd was then chained to the roof of a local store, where floodlights illuminated him for passersby, while messengers went into the surrounding countryside to announce the impending execution. One local newspaper story reported that some three thousand automobiles (the line stretched three miles along the road) gathered around the field where Shepherd was to be killed — on the spot where sergeant Duvall had been murdered. According to one report six thousand "enraged farmers" watched as a lynch mob went about their work of torturing Shepherd, according to "a definite plan" that went off "without a hitch." For seven hours, Shepherd was beaten and stabbed. His ears were cut off. The torturers waited for Duvall's sons to arrive before the "actual burning." His nose and mouth were plugged so that he would not die too quickly from fumes when doused with gasoline and set on fire. The Sunflower County coroner's jury met the next day and announced that Charles Shepherd had come to his death "by causes unknown."[62]

9

"Uncle Sam is my shepherd"

The New Deal's Challenge to Deep South Political Economy

IN 1935, THE AUGUSTA, GEORGIA, BRANCH OF THE NAACP published a pamphlet, *You Are a Citizen!*, which was paid for by seven of the city's leading African American businessmen and announced a voter registration drive and "citizenship campaign" for the city's black population. One of the authors, Fred Steely, a teacher at Paine College, reminded readers that the U.S. Constitution guaranteed them citizenship and explained the requirements for voter registration. Another, Rev. I. J. Yancy, summarized what blacks could gain from voting: better police protection, more paved streets and sidewalks in black neighborhoods, more money for schools, better garbage removal and sewage systems. Another section of the pamphlet reported detailed information on African American taxpayers in the city and the surrounding area. More than one thousand black men and more than nine hundred black women paid taxes on real estate in Augusta valued at almost $2 million, and more than seventeen hundred men paid poll taxes. Just 381 men and 109 women were actually registered to vote. The NAACP urged each reader to take a pledge to register, to be active in civic affairs, and to become acquainted "with the issues of the day . . . in order that I may be enabled to vote intelligently."[1]

The 1935 citizenship campaign was just one initiative among many from Augusta's NAACP branch. The branch established there during the First World War had died out in the 1920s, its members disappointed and frustrated by the lack of clear progress toward racial equality. In 1931, Rev.

William Merriwether, apparently inspired in part by the NAACP's defense of seven young black men who had been convicted of raping two white women in Scottsboro, Alabama (the celebrated "Scottsboro Boys"), wrote to the national headquarters about reestablishing the local branch. In October 1931 the new branch had its first full meeting, chose Rev. S. B. Wallace as president, and, ambitiously, set twenty-one goals. These ranged from being treated with more courtesy in the local courts, to establishing a new public high school for blacks, to increasing employment for blacks in both the private and public sectors. Soon Rev. Wallace reported progress: the judge in the police court promised more courteous treatment of blacks in his court-room, and the local A & P had hired two black employees. When Rev. Wallace became ill, the branch struggled, but later B. F. Logan, owner of a local printing shop, took over as president. It was under Logan's leadership that the citizenship campaign was launched.[2]

The reorganization of Augusta's NAACP branch was a signal of revived black protest and activism there and elsewhere in the South, a revival that began even before the election of Franklin D. Roosevelt in 1932. Although FDR's policies, as it turned out, often worked to the detriment of black sharecroppers, his New Deal fueled the new black activism in a myriad of ways. In some places, African Americans for the first time would find important allies among southern whites as they reinvigorated their efforts to claim dignity, economic security, and the rights of citizenship.

The Solid South

As the Augusta NAACP's pamphlet showed, black voting had not en-tirely died out in the city, even after Georgia amended its constitution in 1908 to eliminate the overwhelming majority of black voters. Hundreds of blacks continued to register and participate in Augusta's elections, where they were courted by competing white factions. In Savannah also, several hundred African Americans continued to vote in general and city elections. The mayor there met occasionally with middle-class black leaders to get informal advice on policies. In Darien, Georgia, a local black principal used his control of black votes to curry favor with the school committee and extract a two-room annex to the main school. In Vicksburg, Mississippi, the small number of black voters proved decisive in the victory of Mayor W. J. Holsey in one election in the late 1920s, and he rewarded them with a few more paved streets and street lamps in the black section of town.[3]

In rural areas, however, by 1910 disfranchisement had almost completely eliminated the black vote, cementing into place a one-party political system. In most counties, black voters numbered in the single digits, if there were any at all. Local whites tolerated these few voters, who, in any case, were not allowed to vote in the Democratic primary elections. One local justice of the peace in Greene County, Georgia, told an interviewer in the 1930s that the three or four black voters who showed up in his precinct did not trouble him, because "They're mighty polite . . . Always with their hats in their hands."[4]

In most places politics revolved around personal contests for office and power, sometimes more or less organized along factional lines, always within the Democratic Party. In the 1920s and 1930s, a single political machine knit together by patronage and judicious use of the ballots of dead voters controlled most Savannah elections. In Augusta, a faction known as the "Crackers" won most elections; in Burke and many other rural Georgia counties, a "ring" of local notables controlled politics. In others, like Greene County in the Piedmont, politicians competed as individuals. The poll tax requirement had disfranchised many poorer whites along with blacks. A white warehouse worker in Greene County told an investigator that he and his wife hadn't voted in the most recent county election because "we was behind with our poll taxes. I've been a sick man. Every cent I could get together went for medicine or doctor bills. . . . I got seven mouths to feed." Candidates and "rings" recruited support by paying up poll taxes of voters, then numbering each ballot and checking the tally to make sure they got their money's worth. In Mississippi, too, local politics was personal and factional. One observer wrote, "Local politicians in the Delta have no platforms, no programs, and no issues upon which to run for office." As in Georgia, local contestants paid up the poll taxes of poorer whites who promised to support them.[5]

For the most part local politics ran in familiar ruts, with neighborhood economic issues and personal connections determining political alignments. In Greene County, in Georgia's Piedmont, battles took place over bond issues for a new waterworks for the town of Greensboro and over which sections of the county should get paved roads. In Camden County, on the coast, factions battled for several elections over whether, and where, a new courthouse ought to be built. To be sure, the intense factionalism could bring about nasty personal attacks. Thus a supporter of a new courthouse in Camden, Colonel McElreath, was accused of being short in his accounts as a game warden; in return he called one of his accusers a "low bred Cracker" with a "filthy lecherous private character."[6]

For a time in the 1920s, the moralistic politics exemplified by the Ku Klux Klan intruded into local political contests. The Klan's themes were used by candidates even where the Klan itself was weak. In Camden County, James Vocelle, a candidate for the state legislature in 1920, pledged to support "constructive legislation" that would safeguard the morals of both men and women and "strengthen and uphold a standard of 100% Americanism throughout the land." Vocelle prevailed in the election, but he had to withstand attacks on his Roman Catholic religion. Would "the Protestantism of Camden endorse Roman Catholicism at the Polls?" his opponent asked. Of course not, because Catholicism was "the deadliest menace to American liberties and Christian civilization."[7]

National politics excited little interest in the early 1920s in Georgia or Mississippi. Both were solidly Democratic, and the national administrations were Republican. An exception was the presidential election of 1928, when Herbert Hoover was the Republican candidate. The country was generally prosperous, and Hoover was popular for his role in helping the lower Mississippi valley recover from the great 1927 flood. Hoover's prospects in the South improved when the Democrats nominated New York Governor Al Smith. A Catholic, opposed to prohibition, and a hero of immigrants, Smith represented the antithesis of the Klan's ideals. But to most voters in the lower South, this counted for little against the historic role of the Democrats as the party of white supremacy and southern home rule. In Mississippi, for example, John McRaven of Yazoo City wrote his children that he could scarcely believe that Hoover might run well in Mississippi. "We may not like some things about Al Smith, such as his religion . . . [his] position on the Prohibition & the fact that 'Tammany Hall' of New York is supporting him," McRaven admitted, but how on earth could "a Southern man" support a candidate of the party that had sponsored "the Force Bill, the effect of which was to put the Negro back in the politics of the South at the point of Federal troops?" That the Force Bill had been debated not in 1928 but in 1890 was irrelevant to him. In fact, Smith easily carried Mississippi, and even in the Delta, where Hoover's flood-fighting efforts were centered, Smith won 90 percent of the vote.[8]

In Georgia, too, Democrats appealed to the past to defeat Hoover. In September 1928, Senator Walter George told a Greensboro audience that neither religion nor prohibition should be an issue in the campaign; in any case, even if Smith opposed prohibition, he would be unable to repeal the Eighteenth Amendment. Most important, George said, voters should "not abandon the party which saved the white Anglo-Saxon civilization of the south for the party which sought desperately to destroy it." George recounted that a disabled Confederate soldier "once said that when he came back to Georgia after the war and hobbled down between two lines of federal bayonets to cast his ballot he was voting not for men but for the party; not for his children and grandchildren but for generations then unborn." A Greene County voter, Mrs. Aeola Lee, made a similar plea in the local paper; she was a "country woman," a Methodist, and a strong believer in prohibition, but the most important thing was "to be a southern Democrat and stick to it. . . . My father was a Confederate soldier and fought in that awful war between the states. I have such a reverence for these old soldiers that when I see a group of them or see them marching along together there is such a feeling comes over me that I can not describe." As the election neared, another local writer recounted his boyhood memories of Greene County during Reconstruction, when "Cosby" (he meant the African American Abram Colby) had been elected to the state legislature. Finally, the Klan had arrived and "white supremacy was assured . . . the Democrats took charge, and would count a negro or Republican candidate out of the race." "No sir," he concluded, "I can't see how a southern white man can vote the Republican ticket." On the eve of the election the head of the county Democratic Party reminded whites that "the negro vote is cast in this [general] election," and that as recently as 1908 the black vote had carried the county for the Republican presidential candidate William Howard Taft. Although the number of eligible black voters had been much reduced by Georgia's "stringent registration laws," everyone must still ask, "Am I doing my duty as a Southern man or woman, and as a southern Democrat, if I refuse or fail to vote the national Democratic ticket?"[9]

Voting Republican was so difficult for most white voters that opponents of Al Smith organized a set of non-Republican, "anti-Smith" electors for the November elections. In the eastern Piedmont, the combination of votes for Hoover and for "anti-Smith" was actually a bit higher than the regular Democratic vote for Smith, but Smith gained a large plurality in the region and an absolute majority in the state as a whole. A rural-urban split is obvious in the voting patterns. In Richmond County, including Augusta, Hoover won two-thirds of the votes, but in the rest of the region, under one-seventh. Rural white voters could not bring themselves to vote Republican, no matter how much they were repelled by Smith's Catholicism and opposition to prohibition. Along the coast, traditional Republican strength helped to give Hoover 43 percent of the vote.[10]

When their economic interests were at stake, southerners could find ways to overcome their antipathy to national interference with local affairs. In the Mississippi Delta, Herbert Hoover as the Republican Party candidate might be dangerous, but Herbert Hoover as the key to federal support for rebuilding the levees was another matter. After the 1927 flood, the Delta's planters cooperated closely with Hoover in a lobbying campaign to convince the U.S. Congress that the federal government must take full charge of (and pay all the bills for) rebuilding the devastated levee system. Spearheading the effort was the Delta's LeRoy Percy, secretary of the ad hoc Tri-State Flood Control Committee (the other members represented Arkansas and Louisiana). At a meeting in Arkansas in September 1927, Hoover, together with Percy and other wealthy planter-politicians, drafted plans that became the basis of legislation that President Coolidge signed into law the next May. The new law committed the federal government to the largest peacetime expenditure on a single project in its history, with no money required from local or state sources.[11]

After the Great Depression arrived in 1929 and deepened over the next three years, other rural southerners followed the example of the river lobbyists and, in the face of uncontrollable disaster, decided that it was the duty of the national government to help. Even before the election of Franklin D. Roosevelt in 1932 that help began to arrive. Although President Hoover was loath to have ordinary people corrupted (as he saw it) by direct help from the government, he supported legislation to help farmers through the economic crisis. In Greene County, Georgia, some believed that "scarcely any farm operation could have been carried" on without loans from the Emergency Crop Loan Department and other federal programs.[12] By 1932 desperate farmers were demanding more massive government intervention, sometimes in rhetoric that echoed the Populist appeals of the 1890s. Not surprisingly, these echoes were especially evident in the Piedmont, the heart of Tom Watson's old district. In Greene County, the newspaper editor in 1932 attacked the "big Atlanta dairies," dependent on "eastern capital," for unfair pricing. The marketing of dairy products, he claimed, was "a racket, dominated by a few all-powerful corporations." He reprinted an editorial from a south Georgia newspaper that threatened that, unless "the blindly stubborn men who have managed to corral most of the wealth of the nation see a great light, something most unpleasant probably will happen. . . . [H]istory teaches . . . that when a great class finds itself facing a hopeless situation; when its struggles to improve its condition are vain and all proposals for relief are rejected as impractical, then there is danger of revolution."[13]

Greene's editor supported the "cotton holiday" proposed by Louisiana's Governor Huey Long—to let an entire season go by without planting cotton in order to curtail supply and force the price up. The paper printed several letters in the fall of 1931 from J. W. Whitely of neighboring Warren County in support of Long's plan. "Farmers are hungry," he wrote on one occasion, "they are bankrupt, they are on the ragged edge of slavery and it is high time they were demanding recognition and help." The only people opposed, he claimed, were the fertilizer companies, the cotton oil producers, and the big bankers. The cotton holiday plan went nowhere because there was no authority powerful enough to enforce it. However, the next year voters throughout the South helped to put into office a new president, Franklin D. Roosevelt, who was willing to try policies based on such ideas.[14]

The New Deal: Work and Relief along the Color Line

Within months of Roosevelt's inauguration in March 1933, the federal government had taken on the responsibility of supporting, or at least feeding, the most destitute Americans, and many of these could be found in the lower South. Conditions were terrible even by the low standards of the previous ten years. Planters, themselves forced to the wall, had limited their support of sharecroppers and laborers to as low a level as possible. In May 1933, sociologist Arthur Raper reported that throughout black belt Georgia, many "planters literally cleaned out [tenants'] corn cribs, potato hills, pig pens, gardens, and houses to secure saleable produce with which to settle the tenants' debt." In LeFlore County, Mississippi, a local relief worker wrote confidentially to the state's governor in August 1933, asking him to prevent abuses by certain planters who "take the entire crop for the food furnished, and never let the tenant see his account. The tenant leaves the plantation without food or funds. . . . For the past three years this condition and practice has been so intense that today we have in the Delta hundreds of cases in whose homes you will find no sheets, pillow cases, towels, etc." Along the coast of Georgia, where tenant farming was rare, small independent farmers and laborers suffered because day labor jobs had dried up.[15]

For such desperate cases, a series of new relief programs often provided the margin of survival. The first of these was the Federal Emergency Relief Administration (FERA), established in the spring of 1933, which was followed by the Civil Works Administration (CWA), established fall 1933, and the Works Progress Administration (WPA), in 1935. Although FERA sometimes simply provided emergency aid with no strings attached (known as "direct relief"), all three programs were designed to put the unemployed and destitute to work on government-sponsored projects. A year after Roosevelt's inauguration, about one in seven of the people living in the rural eastern Piedmont of Georgia were on relief of some kind. The numbers were similar in the Delta and along the Georgia coast. In urban counties over one-fifth of the population depended in part on federal relief. (The total numbers receiving relief at some time during the year would of course be much higher than this snapshot shows.) In Morgan County in the Piedmont, more than six hundred people received payments, because of low cotton prices, the "planned restriction of acreage," the lack of construction work, and "general dismissal of domestic help." About three-fourths of black women on relief were widowed, divorced, or separated and supporting families by themselves. Many people were simply too old to work. In McDuffie and Greene Counties in the Piedmont, those on relief were mostly unemployed laborers. In the Delta's LeFlore County, "the refusal of many landlords to 'furnish' certain unproductive members of the households of their tenants" had thrown many people on relief. Along Georgia's coast, there was little work available to anyone without land or to farm families who needed extra money — just two hundred jobs in shrimp factories and ninety more working for small naval stores operations. "The school teachers, ministers, relief officials, and recipients alike," a relief worker on the coast wrote, "stated that . . . if emergency aid had not been provided a revolution would have resulted."[16]

When possible, able-bodied men and, often, black women were put to work by the new government agencies. The pay in many cases was barely enough for a family to survive. Greene County workers earned fifteen cents an hour on their relief jobs; since many worked part-time, the average monthly earnings were just $9. In McDuffie County, workers made about $8 per month on emergency work projects. McDuffie's relief worker, concerned about the low payments, quoted one recipient as saying, "They's ten of us in the family, and this here check ain't near enough." Another asked her for an extra week's work, as "I already owes the check to the man down at the grocery store." In the coastal counties unemployed laborers averaged about $10 per month on emergency jobs.[17]

Despite the low pay, planters and landlords themselves often complained, as did one LeFlore planter, that the programs "were ruining these people, that they should be made to get out and go to work as there were plenty of jobs." The largest landowner in Morgan County, in the Piedmont, told a relief worker that "there is more food thrown out the back doors every day than it would take to feed those on relief," and when he had tried to hire day laborers, they replied, " 'No, suh, boss, I'se can't work 'cause that 'ud take me off de relief.' " In Greene County, Georgia, some local employers argued "on general principles" that it was "a mistake to attempt relief at the expense of the Government," but especially complained because the best relief work, such as that provided by the WPA, paid better and required shorter hours than ordinary farm labor in the county. Indeed, in LeFlore County in November 1934, there were no emergency projects under way at all because relief wages were higher than wages for cotton pickers.[18]

Each county had its own relief administrator and a local advisory committee. The administrators were usually trained social workers (in Georgia, nearly all women), but the advisory committees were largely made up of local politicians, planters, and business people who did their best to influence decisions at the local level. As one of the administrators wrote to Mississippi's governor, "Monied pressure is strong." In LeFlore County, Mississippi, leading local planters and businessmen pressured relief officials to set relief policies according to the agricultural seasons. Traditionally, planters had "furnished" their tenants through the lean winter months to ensure that they would be there when planting season came around. Now the federal government could provide the "furnish" in the lean months, and then, if planters had their way, force workers off the relief rolls when labor was in demand. In January 1934, more than 9,000 of LeFlore's population was on relief, but by the next May that number had fallen to 3,508. Federal investigators likened this to a system of "peonage . . . whereby the farm laborer, cropper, and tenant are thrown on relief agencies for support between cropping seasons." Planters also insisted that the old, the young, and the sick in workers' families go on relief. The same pattern appears in Georgia's eastern Piedmont, where numbers on relief were just 7 percent of the population at harvest time in 1933, but twice that in the following winter.[19]

Relief efforts, not surprisingly, were shaped by the color line, though not always in the direction one might expect. Welfare workers in Mississippi criticized local planters for discriminating against white tenants, often recent arrivals who were, as one comment put it, "poorly adjusted to the local farming situation." The welfare worker who wrote to Mississippi's governor said that when planters were asked to give work to poor whites, "invariably the answer is 'Starve them out. They are not worth feeding. We do not want them in our county.'" White laborers and tenants who had migrated into Washington County in the late 1920s, a report insisted, "proved unsatisfactory due to their lack of training, general shiftlessness, and low standards of living. The plantation owners have gotten rid of this type of tenant, but they're still living in the larger communities. They are untrained, unskilled laborers and not in demand for any kind of work." A LeFlore investigator had a different explanation, writing that "the white croppers and tenants were too shrewd traders and bargainers to suit the planters and they always had arguments over 'trades' and accounts. They also would not 'crop' the land as ordered by their landlords. This type of 'settling of accounts' did not rest well with the landlords and they put the white croppers off their holdings and substituted Negro croppers whom they could more readily handle and 'settle with.'"[20]

Still, racial discrimination in the distribution of relief was much more likely to penalize black workers. Only whites served on the local advisory committees of the rural relief agencies, and nearly all local professional case workers were white. Whites were more likely to get relief, even though they were certainly, as a group, less likely to need it. In ten of fifteen rural Piedmont counties, a higher proportion of the white than of the black population was on direct relief in March 1934, and whites got $2.81 per month per person, compared with only $1.80 for blacks. One investigator pointed out that, while "it has been insisted in all counties studied so far that racial differences are not considered in determining the amount of relief given, and yet in every instance the average for whites has been nearly double that of the Negroes." Although the investigator thought that, for the most part, Negroes required less support because they were used to a lower standard of living, "the white families on relief do not have a sufficiently high standard to warrant the large discrepancy."[21]

Racial discrimination affected access to the best relief jobs, as well. In LeFlore County in 1934, all the members of the Civilian Conservation Corps, an agency set up to give jobs to young men, were white. Funds from the Civil Works Administration supported the salaries of 104 white teachers, but only 17 black teachers, in the eastern Piedmont. In Greene County in 1933 and 1934, CWA projects hired twice as many whites as blacks and paid each, on average, 75 percent more. Arthur Raper estimated that about $44,000 was spent in Georgia's Greene County work-relief projects in the first two years of the New Deal, and of this, some $15,800 went to projects that benefited both blacks and whites, more than $25,000 to white schools or other purposes that benefited only the white population, and just $2,200 to projects that primarily helped the county's African Americans.[22]

The New Deal: Regulating the Cotton Fields

Relief and emergency work programs helped put food on the tables of desperately poor families and provided decent employment to some, but they were not intended to be permanent. Plans for permanent repairs to the cotton economy (and to the rest of commercial agriculture in the U.S.) were embodied rather in the Agricultural Adjustment Act of 1933 and its successors. The Agricultural Adjustment Administration created by the act had, at its heart, a simple strategy and a straightforward goal: reduce production and raise prices. Since the act was not passed until the summer, well after cotton had been planted, the only way to restrict production for the 1933 crop year was literally to plow up the sprouting plants. Quotas for crop reduction were set for each county and administered by local committees, headed by the county agent from the U.S. Department of Agriculture and usually made up of leading planters. Mules trained their entire lives to walk between rows now had to be forced to trample them in front of the plow. Black tenants sometimes were dismayed by the idea of destroying good cotton before it had fairly ripened, and, as Arthur Raper reported, some made deals with neighbors: "Let's swap work that day; you plow up mine, and I'll plow up yours." But the incentives were great. Farmers were guaranteed federal payments of at least six cents a pound for the (estimated) plowed-under harvest, with prospects for a much higher price in the fall. In fact, the harvest price came in at around ten cents per pound, and the government further obliged the farmers by paying them the extra four cents on the plowed-up portion.[23]

The success of the program in increasing prices over the short term encouraged further legislation. A new Commodity Credit Corporation provided government loans directly to farmers, bypassing traditional sources of long-term credit and helping to support prices at "parity," meaning equal (in relative terms) to prices in the golden era of 1909–14. The Bankhead Cotton Control Act of 1934 placed even more rigid controls on production. A national quota of ten million bales in 1934 was apportioned by state, county, and individual farm; the federal government would "rent" from farmers their unneeded land, and tax any production over quota at a prohibitive 50 percent. That year cotton sold for over twelve cents a pound.[24]

The plow-up and price supports of the AAA and the Bankhead program worked to raise prices and profits of growers. In 1932, the Delta's D&PL Company had planted over sixteen thousand acres in cotton and suffered an operating loss of over $50,000. The next year the company plowed up more than four thousand acres, but the remaining twelve thousand acres earned operating profits of over $400,000, $80,000 of which came from government payments for the plow-up. For the rest of the decade the company continued to make large operating profits, and in some years government payments amounted to almost half of those profits.[25] The payments to the D&PL were not typical, since the company was so large; they do, however, show how the benefits of the new system tended to flow to the largest and wealthiest planters. Thus in 1933 D&PL received some $83,000 in federal payments, while all the farmers in Greene County, in the Piedmont, received a total of about $42,000, or about $32 per farmer. Farmers benefited from the higher cotton prices, but this, too, primarily worked to the advantage of the planters. Planters were supposed to share the government benefits with their renters and sharecroppers on a proportional basis. Some did so; others did not. Some landlords seized the tenants' shares in payment of old debts, whether justified or not; others drove away tenants they no longer needed to work land now taken out of production.[26]

In some places in the South, tenants responded by organizing themselves into unions. The best-known examples are the Southern Tenant Farmers' Union in northeastern Arkansas and the Share Croppers' Union in Alabama. Both were ultimately suppressed by local whites, but the publicity surrounding them, especially the STFU, placed pressure on AAA administrators to provide more protection for tenants and to encourage planters who participated in the crop reduction programs to retain the same number of tenants. Eventually also, the huge payments to big operations like D&PL stirred opposition, and legislation limited payments to any one grower. These modest adjustments to the cotton program hardly changed the basic thrust of the AAA, which continued to focus on the narrow economic issue of raising prices paid to farmers.[27] The vast expansion of the federal government's role did, however, create new possibilities for regulation and, perhaps, for forcing more fundamental change in the southern countryside. Many of the new bureaucrats in Washington held quite different ideas about race and class than those of the white southern elite — among them, staff in the legal office of the AAA itself. Led by chief counsel Jerome Frank, these liberal lawyers saw the AAA as a means to social reform, not just to higher prices for farmers. In opposition to Frank and his allies were those with narrow ideas of proper government goals, the most important of whom was Oscar Johnston, head of the AAA's finance section and also the head of the Delta & Pine Land Company. Spurred by the battle in Arkansas around the STFU, where planters were expelling union members from their plantations, the Legal Division proposed a regulation (or, more precisely, a new interpretation of an existing regulation) that would prevent landlords from forcing out any current tenants. Oscar Johnston and the other "pragmatists" in the department mightily resisted the liberals; the battle between the two factions came to a head in February 1935, when Secretary of Agriculture Henry Wallace forced Frank and several other members of the Legal Division to resign.[28] The victory of the pragmatists over the liberals was probably inevitable, because the AAA's success depended on cooperation from large producers. As Johnston had written to Wallace in 1935, big producers would simply drop out of the system if "our agricultural program should be distorted into or used as a weapon to bring about so-called 'social reform', or to revolutionize the social and economic life of the cotton belt." Without planters' cooperation, the crop control efforts of the AAA would collapse.[29]

Johnston's approach should not be confused with an endorsement of the kind of cheating of tenants that often went on under AAA programs, as had gone on for decades in the South. Johnston, as head of D&PL, had no truck with violence or other gross violations of the law that marked the repression of the STFU in Arkansas, nor did he approve of the "dishonest practices" that, he privately admitted, were "widespread" — indeed, perhaps "the rule rather than the exception" in the Delta. When Dr. William Amberson of Memphis, a socialist and STFU supporter, sent an investigator, Buck Jones, to dig up information on D&PL's treatment of tenants, Jones was arrested by the sheriff and brought to Johnston at company headquarters. Jones told Amberson that he refused, in language that "wont be put down in the Bibal," to let anyone search him without a warrant. Johnston's response was to give Jones free access to D&PL's records of its transactions with tenants. He was supremely confident of his position because he knew that his company's profits derived not from cheating or other illegal practices but from his efficient management of an enterprise that competed well in markets within rules that favored him and other employers over their sharecroppers.[30]

The AAA Revolution

The AAA did help to revolutionize the structure of the rural countryside in the cotton South, but not in ways planned or intended; it did so by changing not the legal terms of the landlord-tenant relationship but the financial incentives in that relationship. To begin with, the crop reduction plan almost immediately decreased the demand for labor. In the Piedmont, a Morgan County report in 1934 estimated that two-thirds of the farm families on relief were day laborers affected by government acreage controls; a 1935 report for Greene County noted that "while the AAA crop reduction plan has perhaps been a help to the farmers as a whole, yet doubtless this has caused a decline in the use of farm labor." More profound changes followed. Federal payments to landowners did not have to be shared with wage hands, an incentive to convert their farms from sharecropping to wage labor. Although AAA regulations called for producers to "endeavor in good faith" to maintain "insofar as possible . . . the normal number of tenants," the good intentions of such language counted for little in the long run against the substantial financial incentives working in the opposite direction. The result as measured by an analysis of plantation agriculture in the Delta was, between 1935 and 1940, a "drastic reduction" in cotton acres and a switch to grains, soybeans, and hay, all of which required less labor; a "rapid" trend toward mechanization; and a general move away from tenant labor to wage labor.[31]

Sharecropping and other forms of tenancy had been attractive to planters in part because they ensured that workers who planted cotton in the spring would still be around to pick it in the fall. During the Depression, massive unemployment in northern industries sharply reduced out-migration from the South, and, together with acreage reduction programs, made it much easier than it had perhaps ever been to secure labor for the picking. Annual turnover of tenants dropped sharply to 15 percent annually in the Delta, and planters there found they could replace those leaving simply by choosing from among applicants who showed up to ask for places; they had no need now for labor agents or other recruitment methods.[32] Planters who had always rented out or sharecropped their acres began to convert them to wage labor. The number of tenant farmers in the Piedmont, which had stabilized after the sharp plunge of the early 1920s, again turned downward, falling by 29 percent in the 1930s. In the Delta, the number of tenants declined by 22 percent over the decade. The biggest drops in the Delta came in cash or standing renters, rather than sharecroppers, and, as observers had claimed, the number of white croppers declined faster than the number of blacks, dropping by 34 percent. In both regions, the number of farms and plantations operated by their owners increased — by 7 percent in the Piedmont and 45 percent in the Delta. Most of this increase came because owners of land were working their plantations directly with wage hands, rather than renting them out to tenants.[33]

The New Deal and Race at the Grass Roots

The reach of the New Deal into the countryside had other unintended effects. For the first time since Reconstruction, thousands of employees of the federal government were collecting and analyzing information and providing direct assistance to ordinary black and white citizens in the South. As had occurred during the First World War, these new connections between individuals and the nation stirred new ideas among white southerners and brought into the open claims of black southerners to their rights as citizens. By the end of the 1930s, some whites and many blacks had begun to challenge the economic, ideological, and customary foundations of segregation itself. A 1934 incident in the Piedmont town of Eatonton, Georgia, seat of Putnam County, illustrates how the New Deal's relief and reform programs could threaten the color line. Arthur Raper, then doing research in neighboring Greene County for the Commission on Interracial Cooperation, was asked by an official of Georgia's Federal Emergency Relief Administration to undertake a survey of Putnam families that FERA was planning to relocate because of a reforestation project. Raper hired three African Americans (all college educated) and two whites as interviewers to collect information about the health, education, and skills of the families. The staff members were paid equally and were expected to address one another with polite titles. The whites, both from Greene County, agreed to this, although, Raper noted, "This was new to them, as was also the arrangement for the Negro workers to get equal pay."[34]

Problems began as soon as Raper and his staff arrived in Eatonton. The FERA county administrator was away and his temporary replacement, a Mr. Johns, knew nothing about the project or the survey. Raper soon discovered that the survey had been opposed all along by the Land Utilization Office, one of the bureaucracies in charge of the reforestation project. He later learned that some local whites who had, on the first morning, seen the arrival of Clyde Williams, one of the black survey workers, had "asked each other who this dressed-up 'Nigger' was, in a shiny car"; their grumblings increased when "two other well-dressed Negroes, one of them a woman, appeared in good automobiles." The survey work nevertheless began and proceeded uneventfully for two days, all five staff members working comfortably with each other. On the third day, Raper remembered, Ethel Cochran, an African American staff member, said that she hoped the names of the neighborhood she was headed for — Lynch, down below Murder Creek — did not mean bad luck. That day the real trouble began. After the five interviewers left the office, three local white men came to Raper "to inquire who these 'dressed-up Niggers' were, where I [Raper] was born, and how it was that each one was driving a good car when there were so many white people needing work." Later that day a crowd — described to Raper as farmers and cotton mill workers — gathered outside the office and called Raper out, demanding again to know what the black staff members were doing. As Raper tried to bring the questioning to a quiet conclusion, an Arthur Carpenter, whom Raper described as drunk and "a member of one of the leading families," announced that he "didn't like the idea of 'dressed-up Niggers' being here in good automobiles, being paid by the government, and that as *one* of the taxpayers he didn't mean to tolerate it." Raper's account of the interchange with Carpenter went like this:

"Now, why is it you say you are using these here Niggers? Did you say it was because they were trained?"

"Yes, that's the reason we are using them."

"Does that mean they've got a lot of education?"

"That means they're well educated."

"Do you mean to tell me that any 'Nigger,' however much education he has, can do a better job than a white man can do, even if he didn't have no training?"

"Yes, with the right training Negroes can do a better job than white people can do without training."

"Young man, do you mean to tell me that these educated 'Niggers' of yours can do a better job than I could do?"

Raper tried to answer indirectly, but finally admitted, "Yes, I'm sure they can." The crowd now became unruly and Raper broke off the conversation to look for the mayor, who told him that local dissatisfaction had begun the first morning when he had introduced Ethel Cochran to Mr. Johns as "Miss Cochran" — a fact that Johns had quickly spread. That afternoon the city council, in a special meeting, advised Raper to replace the three black surveyors with local whites. When, much to their surprise, he refused, they told him they could not vouch for the ability of the local police to protect his black staff members; indeed, a mob led by Carpenter gathered in the streets that evening. It took all of Raper's considerable skills and instincts in dealing with fellow white southerners to get both himself and his staff safely out of town.

An investigation of the incident by Taylor Miller, an official of the Land Policy Section of the AAA, confirms Raper's account in nearly all respects, if from the viewpoint of local whites. To Miller, the "primary cause was not the use of Negro investigators, but the method of using them"; Raper "introduced them as Professor, Mrs., Mr., gave them an office and otherwise treated them as if they were white investigators." This was not only entirely contrary to the "local custom and tradition towards Negroes" but also suggested that "if a few Negroes were being brought in by the Government now on such a basis, the local attitude was that it would not be long until more would be brought in." If the government hired only blacks to deal with the majority-black population, it would "thereby give the biggest part of the work to Negroes."[35]

As Raper's experience demonstrates, polite titles were still a major marker of the color line. Putnam's whites thought that blacks did not deserve to be called "Miss" or "Mr." because they should be reminded of their inferiority always and everywhere; that blacks should be poor and look it, not "dressed up" and riding in nice automobiles; that they should be ignorant and act it, not "educated." Above all, they must be controlled by the whites who knew them best — and in Putnam County, that meant Putnam County's white men. Raper's interview project violated all of these expectations and assumptions, which united, for somewhat different reasons, both poorer whites (the mill workers) and members of the local elite (Arthur Carpenter). Any violence, even if mainly the work of the mill workers and other poorer whites, would also have taken place with the sanction of the mayor and the city council. If an outsider, even one as southern as Arthur Raper, could control jobs and terms of address, the whole structure of segregation was threatened. As Raper wrote in another context, local whites believed that "if I used titles for Negroes, I might want to overthrow the government."[36]

For blacks — whether highly educated members of the middle class, like Ethel Cochran, or the very poor families she was interviewing — a new and direct link to the national government that, in theory, granted them full equality as citizens brought with it transforming possibilities. Despite the formidable obstacles placed before black voters, by the end of the 1930s a new political restlessness stirred blacks, especially in cities. The NAACP branch in Augusta, Georgia, which had been revived even before the election of Roosevelt, pushed a broad agenda, agitating in behalf of a young black man convicted, they believed wrongly, of rape, launching their citizenship campaign, petitioning the city council to pave a street in a black neighborhood, and lobbying for a new junior high school. They also helped to start a student branch at Paine College. The Paine branch sponsored an evening of one-act plays on the campus, both on the theme of lynching. The Savannah branch, which had become moribund by the late 1920s, by 1932 reported more than four hundred members and a dozen cooperating clubs and organizations. In both Augusta and Savannah the main organizers came from the business and professional men and women of the black middle class. In Vicksburg, the NAACP was revived in the 1930s by black employees of the local railroad companies seeking to "look after the wellfairs of Railrode Men such as Locomotive Firemen . . . to see after [the] condition of thar jobs and see that they get thar rights."[37]

Political activism among blacks went well beyond the NAACP, however. In Savannah, George Smith organized a Young Man's Civic Club and began a voter registration drive in 1938. The black longshoremen's union provided the key backing for the drive; the club put out handbills and organized meetings in the churches. The local registrar, who had not objected when black voters numbered in the hundreds but now feared they would register in the thousands, began to enforce the requirement in Georgia's law that potential voters be able to write down a paragraph of the state constitution as it was dictated. As the registrar told one white interviewer, "If I read a long paragraph as fast as I can read, I bet you can't write it." When the American Legion sponsored a "citizenship day" to encourage twenty-one-year-old whites to register, the black Civic Club in Savannah sponsored a similar day for African Americans. In Augusta, in 1940, the Negro Civic and Business League formed a new "Committee on Negro Franchise" to organize a registration campaign through the churches and black businesses. In Vicksburg, middle-class black women organized a political club and in 1939 arranged to arrive en masse at the courthouse, where seventy-five of them registered to vote. While most of this formal organizing came from the middle class, a change in political consciousness was evident among ordinary African Americans as well. Blues guitarist and singer Memphis Minnie, in 1935 recorded "Sylvester and His Mule Blues," based on the story of a black Mississippi farmer who called the White House because he was afraid "the white folks down here" would take his farm and mule; the Home Owners Loan Corporation gave him enough financing to save his farm:

> He called the president, on the telephone,
> "I wanna talk to you, I'm 'bout to lose my farm. . . ."
> He said, "Now Sylvester, you can rest in ease,
> Catch that big, black jackass, and go on by your fields."

In Greene County, Georgia, Arthur Raper discovered a folk poet, Louisiana Dunn Thomas, wife of a black tenant farmer. One of her poems, "A Brighter Day Has Dawned," praised Roosevelt in biblical terms: "God has sent a Moses / To lead his people free."[38]

Southern whites, too, began to see new possibilities for change. Many young whites employed in New Deal programs confronted, for the first time, the deep poverty of both races in rural areas. The two young white men from prominent Greene County families whom Raper hired to work on his Putnam County survey became "very much interested in what they were finding. They didn't know there were any people anywhere who had so near nothing as the ones they had been investigating, most of them white people." They had not seen the same kind of poverty on their own families' plantations. Raper wondered, "Did the pencil and a schedule make the difference? Or was it the fact of being away from home, and being paid to do it?" A white relief worker in LeFlore County, Mississippi, condemned "purely selfish" local planters who tried to deny relief to families they disliked, to try to force them out of the county "through a process of starvation."[39]

The work of scholars who launched unprecedented studies of conditions in the South helped, in turn, to spur liberal reform efforts. Arthur Raper's *The Tragedy of Lynching* was a deeply researched study of every southern lynching in 1930, and his *Preface to Peasantry* was based on his research in the late 1920s and in 1933–34 in Macon and Greene Counties in Georgia. Both projects were sponsored by the Commission on Interracial Cooperation. The first part of Raper's research in Greene and Macon Counties explored the reasons for the massive migration from the countryside in the 1920s. Raper then returned to both counties to see how New Deal programs were affecting their people, measuring and describing in detail living conditions, religious life, and patterns of local government. He carefully compared blacks and whites and analyzed class differences among both races. Raper was acutely aware of the effects of race on every aspect of social and cultural life in the black belt, but at bottom he attributed the widespread poverty that he had documented to economic sources rather than racial ones. The plantation system, with its "reckless exploitation of natural resources" and its use of cheap, dependent labor, had left in its wake, he said, "depleted soil, shoddy livestock, inadequate farm equipment, crude agricultural practices, crippled institutions, a defeated and impoverished people." Poverty in the countryside brought down wages in the towns and cities, and by setting "the white worker over against the black worker," planters were able to dominate local and state politics. The plantation economy, Raper argued, "prepares the land and the man for the emergence of a peasant rather than for the appearance of the traditional independent American farmer" (hence the title of his book). His analysis was intended to reform as much as to inform, and it had a major influence on the Roosevelt administration. Secretary of Agriculture Henry Wallace carried with him a copy of Raper's just-published book on a tour of the South in 1936; he commented that to call Raper's poorest farmers peasants "really offends the peasantry of Europe."[40]

While Raper was doing research and promoting New Deal programs in Georgia's Greene County, two other scholars, Hortense Powdermaker and John Dollard, lived and worked successively in Indianola, in the heart of the Mississippi Delta. The fruits of their research also appeared in the late 1930s, in Dollard's *Caste and Class in a Southern Town* (1937) and Powdermaker's *After Freedom: A Cultural Study in the Deep South* (1939). Neither was a political activist like Raper, nor were they, like him, southerners. Raper's principal methods were those of the sociologist — systematic gathering and analysis of measurable data; Dollard and Powdermaker were participant-observers following the methods of cultural anthropology. Powdermaker, an anthropologist, had already spent two years studying the people of the Melanesian island of Lesu before coming to Indianola in 1932; Dollard was a Yale University scholar whose work crossed disciplinary boundaries and was heavily informed by his training in psychoanalysis. Unlike Raper, they made race central to their observations and to their analyses of Delta society and culture.[41]

American scholars had long been concerned with "race," but to the vast majority of white scholars before the 1920s this meant the study of the "Negro problem." Powdermaker and Dollard broke with this tradition in their assumption that they were investigating not a "problem" but a "culture" — a distinct pattern of beliefs, behaviors, and values that together made a functional whole, to be understood in scholarly and objective, rather than moral, terms. Also setting them apart, even from contemporaries like Raper, was their attempt to see this culture from an African American point of view. To be sure, both gathered a good deal of information about white behavior and attitudes, Powdermaker even administering a lengthy questionnaire to over 250 whites, but their main informants were African Americans. Powdermaker interviewed some ninety-seven black women, including most of what she called the "leading" women of the town, and Dollard, who was more interested in psychological issues, interviewed six men and three women, all from the middle class, repeatedly and in great depth.[42]

The "caste and class" in the title of Dollard's book is as good a summary as any of what both scholars found. "Caste" referred to the division of society into a superior and inferior group, with rules regulating the behavior of each, and with the most essential dividing line "a barrier to legitimate descent. A union of members of the two castes may not have a legitimate child." Within each caste, economic and behavioral criteria divided people into classes. The class system was less rigid and the class barriers much more permeable than caste lines, but the divisions were still powerful social determinants. The town of Indianola itself was ruled by a fairly homogeneous white middle class made up of businessmen, professionals, and nearby planters and farmers. A local white "aristocracy" existed more "as memory, as tradition" than as fact. A white lower class consisted of white tenants and sharecroppers in the countryside and poorly paid workers in town. Powdermaker and Dollard disagreed on how and where to draw the line between African American classes. Powdermaker, focusing mainly on values and beliefs, assigned the great majority of blacks to her middle class, while Dollard, using mainly economic criteria, placed 80 percent of blacks in the lower class. They agreed that the black upper class was very small, consisting of a few professionals and the most successful businessmen and planters.[43]

Powdermaker accepted the white middle class view that poor whites, because they were despised by both blacks and higher-class whites, were the most vicious racists and shared a "burning resentment" against blacks. Dollard argued, on the other hand, that "poorer whites show less than the predicted resentment of Negroes and the middle class whites much more." On the central issue of race they largely agreed. In Indianola whites dominated overwhelmingly, reaping great economic and psychological rewards from their domination; they were determined to keep and enforce that domination under any and all circumstances. Both writers laid out in comprehensive detail the meanings of race in a segregated society — from the symbolic superiority implied by the omission of "Mr." and "Mrs." when whites spoke to blacks, to the many forms of daily humiliation and intimidation, to the violence of lynching, which, as Dollard wrote, created a sense of threat "likely to be in the mind of the Negro child from earliest days." Both he and Powdermaker found that whites lived in constant, if unacknowledged, fear that somehow things would get out of control. Dollard experienced "Southerntown" (as he called Indianola) as "a veritable Cheka in its vigilance on caste matters," with "white men guarding the border line of their caste, belligerent and suspicious, repelling every overture of a Negro man across the caste line," but also applying "constant and potent pressures to compel every white person to act his caste role correctly."[44]

African Americans, Powdermaker and Dollard also found, deeply resented the lack of respect inherent in almost every interaction with whites — the refusal to use "Mrs.," the need to wait in an office until every white person was attended to, the casual assumptions of whites that African Americans were all ignorant, sexually promiscuous, potentially violent, simultaneously childlike and animal-like. The deference that whites enjoyed and interpreted as evidence of acquiescence was often a "social mask." The situation bred, in Powdermaker's words, "conflict, deeply felt by every person, black or white, in [Indianola]: conflict of race against race, of class against class, of individual against individual, and of each individual within himself." If Dollard and Powdermaker focused much more than Raper on racial divisions and hostilities, this was partly because the Delta, more than the eastern Piedmont, still had an overwhelming black majority, and big cotton plantations dependent on black labor flourished there as nowhere else. But it was also in part because Raper believed that any direct challenge to segregation would undermine his hopes for economic and social reform. As outsiders with no immediate political agenda, Powdermaker and Dollard could say what Raper could not afford to say.[45]

Works of popular fiction also contributed to the reform impulse, none more so than Erskine Caldwell's *Tobacco Road,* a novel based on Caldwell's experiences growing up in Wrens, Georgia, about thirty miles from Augusta in Jefferson County. Caldwell's father, Ira, a minister of the Associated Reform Presbyterian Church, was well-known for his thundering denunciations of social injustice, whether in the form of poverty or of lynching. Ira

Caldwell spent much of his time traveling through Jefferson County's back roads, offering spiritual and material consolations to poor families. Erskine had often gone with him, and, while he rebelled against his parents' religiosity and Victorian morality, he inherited much of his father's social concern.[46]

Tobacco Road told the story of the Lesters, a family of white sharecroppers. Jeeter Lester, the patriarch, had inherited land from his father but lost it to his father's creditors. Now, neither his landlord, Captain John, who has moved to Augusta, nor the merchants in nearby Fuller (a fictionalized Wrens) will advance him credit to make a crop. Jeeter earns his only income by selling an occasional load of cheap wood in Augusta, and he and his family are "slowly starving." But "there was an inherited love of the land in Jeeter" and he would rather starve than work in a cotton mill: "It wasn't intended for a man with the smell of the land in him to live in a mill in Augusta." In the spring, the first smell of newly turned earth wafting from nearby farms set him off with renewed determination to find a creditor and start farming again.[47]

It was Caldwell's sexual sensationalism and grotesque comedy that captured his readers' attention, yet Tobacco Road also embraced social reforms. Caldwell editorializes that "an intelligent employment of his land, stocks, and implements would have enabled Jeeter, and scores of others who had become dependent upon Captain John, to raise crops for food, and crops to be sold at a profit. Co-operative and corporate farming could have saved them all." One contemporary wrote that by "dramatizing social decay" Caldwell was "touching men's minds with fire," as books like Preface to Peasantry "fill men's minds with facts."[48] The immediate reaction in Georgia's Piedmont to Tobacco Road was surprisingly mild, perhaps because at first it did not sell many copies. A reviewer in the Augusta Chronicle wrote that half of Caldwell's readers would think the story "perfidy," and half "great," and he placed himself in the latter category — with the qualification that the novel told the story only of "the lowest element of the white race in this state," "the pitiable small percentage of backwoods people reduced to miserable semi-savagery by malaria, pellagra, and ignorance." After some debate, the directors of Augusta's library decided that the novel deserved a place on their shelves. Controversy grew, however, when a play based on the novel became a Broadway hit in 1934, and the New York Post commissioned Caldwell to write four articles about the Jefferson County neighborhood in which Tobacco Road was set. His articles portrayed an evicted sharecropper whose four-year-old daughter had died of anemia, a man with eleven children trying to feed them by selling wood, an old woman and her daughter working in a field, and, the most sensational of all, a family in which two hungry young children tried to suck the teats of a dog. Angry residents of Jefferson County insisted that "Caldwell's charges have not the slightest vestige of truth," that, while "poverty exists everywhere," including Jefferson, "such poverty as he writes of is not evident in Georgia."[49]

Two reporters assigned by the Augusta *Chronicle* to check Caldwell's stories, with the help of Caldwell's father Ira, found the families on which they were based: one in which a young daughter had died; a penniless family of sixteen living in a two-room house; a sixty-nine-year-old woman and her daughter, dressed in rags and surviving on field labor; a "wretched two-room shack that feebly houses four half-starved people," too sick or malnourished to work. The details did not always match. The girl had died of pneumonia, not anemia; the family of sixteen "seem[ed] in their ignorance fairly satisfied" and were "not starving"; the old woman laborer felt no shame in her condition, telling the reporters, "I was born poor and I'll die poor, but I work for an honest living." No one could confirm the story of the children suckling from a dog. In the end, the *Chronicle*'s reports confirmed the basic point that there were families in Jefferson County—some said a dozen, others up to three times that many—who were "not only poor but wretched, living in want and squalor."[50]

Caldwell's portrayal of southern poverty in *Tobacco Road* and later publications helped create public awareness of conditions that Raper and others were documenting more systematically. All their writings informed reform efforts of southern liberals. Both the Delta and the Piedmont saw serious reform efforts. A coalition of private individuals and foundations led by Christian socialist activists, including Arthur Raper, established Delta Cooperative Farm in Bolivar County, Mississippi, in 1936 as a refuge for members of Arkansas's Southern Tenant Farmers' Union who had been frightened away or evicted from their farms. Both a producers' and consumers' cooperative, Delta Farm was managed as a collective unit; wage scales and the division of profits were to be determined democratically. The farm included both white and black families; the idea was to demonstrate that the races "could work helpfully and happily together on the cooperative principle." In practice, business meetings were integrated, while housing and social events were segregated in deference to local mores (white housing on one side of the road, black on the other).[51]

The Delta Cooperative Farm was an exotic plant in the Delta's soil. It received neither political nor economic support from the big planters and their allies who ruled the Delta, and, though it received widespread publicity, it had little impact on life in the Delta. More fundamental changes would require a major mobilization of political power. Liberal reformers saw the New Deal as the vehicle for such a mobilization. At the national level, southern whites forged new alliances with African Americans, who had already formed such organizations as the Joint Committee on Economic Recovery to conduct research and to press Congress and the Roosevelt administration for equal treatment of blacks and whites in New Deal programs. The black leaders of this effort — many of them educated in elite colleges and universities in the North — recognized that the precedents for their plans and actions "were in the Reconstruction period and that you had to look to the federal government." For their part, liberal whites such as Raper saw federal power and Franklin Roosevelt's popularity as the means to break the hold of conservative planters and businessmen in southern politics and set the region on a new course.[52]

The programs of the Farm Security Administration (FSA) represented the type of intervention that liberals hoped for. Established in 1937, the FSA was administratively a continuation of the Resettlement Administration of the Agricultural Department. Its first head was Will Alexander, one of the founders of the Commission on Interracial Cooperation in Atlanta in the 1920s. The FSA undertook many projects, reclaiming land, establishing health clinics, providing camps for migrant farm laborers, and, most radically, establishing a few large, government-owned, collectively run farms. Its most important goal was to support farm tenants with credit and technical assistance, improving their lives and, if possible, allowing them to become owners.[53]

Southern liberal hopes for the New Deal reached an apex in 1938, when a group of white southerners working in several New Deal agencies drafted a *Report on Economic Conditions of the South*. Released under the auspices of the federal National Emergency Council, the report outlined in fifteen brief sections the major economic problems of the region. The *Report* acknowledged that the South's people and natural resources offered great potential for economic growth, but it focused on the existing poverty of much of the population. The fundamental problem, the *Report* argued, was that southern workers could too rarely "find work that will provide a decent living," that "neither on the farm nor in the factory is there the certainty of a continuing livelihood." The twenty-two members of the advisory committee for the *Report* included union organizers such as H. L. Mitchell of the STFU, several college and university presidents, and a number of businessmen, including a Georgia planter and the head of the American Cotton Association. If the businessmen were not fully aware of the agenda of the writers of the *Report,* they soon learned of the political uses to which it might be put.[54]

The Politics of Reform

In the summer of 1938, as the *Report on Economic Conditions of the South* was delivered, Franklin Roosevelt was smarting from the defeat the previous year of his plan to increase the size of the Supreme Court so that he could appoint judges likely to agree that his New Deal programs were constitutional. One of the senators who had led the opposition to this "court-packing" plan was Walter F. George, who had represented Georgia since 1922. A cautious conservative, George had supported most of the major New Deal programs before 1937, but after the court fight he became an important member of a coalition of Republicans and conservative Democrats who resisted further New Deal reforms. George and like-minded southerners were happy to support legislation, like price supports, that benefited cotton planters, but they opposed laws that would interfere with their control of labor. Their views were articulated by organizations such as the Mississippi Delta's Chamber of Commerce, which lobbied vigorously against minimum wage or maximum hours laws, calling them "destructive pieces of legislation" for the South. Agreeing with the Mississippi newspaper whose editor claimed that "indiscriminate old age pensions for whites and Negroes alike would paralyze labor conditions" and create "a reign of idleness that would make the depth of depression look like an era of boundless prosperity," the Chamber of Commerce lobbied to exempt farm laborers and domestic workers from the provisions of the Fair Labor Standards Act of 1938 and the Social Security system — in other words, the occupations most likely to be filled by African American men and women in the South. The organization professed full support for the work of agencies like the FSA if they focused on helping "ambitious, thrifty, industrious, promising individual" tenants to achieve ownership of their properties — particularly if such individuals were required to follow the advice of their local county agricultural agents — but it denounced attempts to help farmers "not endowed with the qualities necessary to make a success" and, most especially, any attempt to set up "government owned and operated farms for workers," which it called "unsound" and "un-American."[55]

In September 1938, Walter George was up for reelection in Georgia's Democratic primary. One of his opponents was Eugene Talmadge, a former governor of Georgia, who saw himself as the true heir of Tom Watson, the old Populist leader. Like Watson, Talmadge was a lawyer and substantial landowner who pitched his appeal to the state's ordinary farmers; like Watson, also, he was a powerful stump speaker who was able to connect at a visceral level with his rural supporters. He differed from Watson, however, in his almost total lack of substance. Talmadge preached the traditional pieties of conservative religion, low taxes, and hard work; his main promise in his first race for governor was to reduce the cost of automobile tags. Voters liked this, and perhaps liked even more his promise that they could come sit with him on the front porch of the governor's mansion in Atlanta and "piss over the rail on those city bastards." Bankers and other businessmen learned to like him, too, when they realized that his low-tax policies helped them much more than they hurt. Their approval increased when Talmadge quickly turned against the New Deal, denouncing it as a "combination of wet nursin', frenzied finance, downright Communism an' plain dam-foolishness," and did everything he could as governor to thwart its programs. Talmadge might be "lacking in the elegancies," as the head of the state's biggest utility put it, but "he is strong, determined and courageous. . . . I am a great admirer of his." In 1934, Talmadge called out the National Guard and declared martial law to help crush a textile strike, and in 1936 he helped to form an anti–New Deal alliance with national big businessmen, apparently under the fantastic delusion that he could get elected president. Later in 1936, he ran unsuccessfully for the U.S. Senate as an out-and-out opponent of the New Deal.[56]

The third candidate in Georgia's 1938 primary was Lawrence Camp, a former state legislator and federal district attorney who was running as an all-out pro-Roosevelt New Dealer. The colorless Camp was given little chance against his two formidable adversaries, but the president himself decided to try to remake the U.S. Senate by getting men like Camp elected. The *Report on Economic Conditions of the South* gave the president his rationale, and a speech in August 1938 at the dedication of a rural electrification project in Barnesville, Georgia, gave him the occasion. FDR referred explicitly to the *Report,* terming the South "the Nation's No. 1 economic problem." To fix that problem would require "action by the Federal Government in Washington," and, therefore, election of "Senators and Representatives whose constituents are directly concerned with Southern economics and Southern social needs . . . who are willing to stand up and fight night and day for Federal statutes drawn to meet actual needs — not something that serves merely to gloss over the evils of the moment for the time being — but laws with teeth in them which go to the root of the problems; which remove the inequities, raise the standards, and, over a period of years, give constant improvement to the conditions of human life." Roosevelt asked the voters of Georgia to select in the upcoming primary a man "who honestly believes that many things must be done and done now to improve the economic and social conditions of the country, a man who is willing to fight for these objectives." Thus, he concluded (with Walter George himself sitting on the platform behind him), that voters should cast their ballots for Lawrence Camp.[57]

If Roosevelt's candidate Camp were to win this contest in Georgia, it would have to be in places like Greene County. Within living memory, the county had been controlled by the old Populist Party. The county's residents overwhelmingly favored New Deal reforms, its farmers voting in December 1938 by a margin of 1,268 to 87 to endorse the annual AAA crop control plans. The county was also home to two textile mills whose workers had benefited from the New Deal's pro-labor legislation. In a 1934 general strike called by the National Textile Workers of America, workers had closed down both mills. At least 650 workers went out for most of September, with the Mary-Leila Company's employees holding out for several days even after the collapse of the national strike. In Greene County, if anywhere, it should have been possible for a coalition of poor farmers and industrial workers to come together in support of a candidate who was, in FDR's words, "willing to stand up and fight night and day" for their constituents.[58]

Carey Williams, editor of the county newspaper and secretary-treasurer of the county Democratic Party, rallied with other local leaders to George's candidacy. Williams had supported Talmadge in his 1934 governor's race, but Talmadge did not receive a single line of space in his paper during the primary campaign. Williams portrayed the campaign, not as a fight over the economic condition of the county and country, but as a fight over the soul of the Democratic Party and the survival of white supremacy. "The Democratic Party in the South," one of his editorials stated, "has been fostered by Southern white men who desired to exclude the Negro. The New Deal has captured the Negro vote by placing it on relief in the doubtful states. Under New Deal influences, the names of Negroes have been placed in Superior Court jury boxes in Alabama. Under New Deal influence around 8,000 Negroes are to vote in the South Carolina primary." A letter from an Augusta resident called Roosevelt's intervention in the primary a "new and subtle invasion of

Georgia . . . no less dangerous, no less malicious, no less calculated to do us harm than that infamous march of Sherman to the Sea." An editorial copied from another paper argued that FDR wanted to oust George to appease "Negro politicians" in the North who had carried their wards by promising passage of a national antilynching bill. Roosevelt wanted George and other southern senators who had stopped the bill to "be tossed to these negroes even as Nero tossed Christians to the lions."[59]

The anti-George campaign was fatally handicapped by Georgia's registration and election laws. The primary excluded all black voters, and the poll tax requirement further excluded poor white laborers, tenant farmers, and mill workers. Whites like editor Williams liked this because, as he told an interviewer, "Roosevelt's greatest strength is with the lower element. That's why I think he is so dangerous." In the September primary fewer than half of Greene's eligible white voters, and fewer than a quarter of all eligible voters, took part. George carried the county with 529 votes, less than 10 percent of all potential voters. Talmadge ran a close second, and Camp, the New Deal candidate, managed just 385 votes. Camp carried just one precinct—Union Point, home of one of the mills that had struck four years earlier. The results in Greene County echoed those in the rest of the state, as George turned back the challenge from Talmadge and Camp ran a distant third.[60]

Limits of Change

The defeat of Roosevelt's candidate in the 1938 primary was repeated elsewhere in the South. FDR was unable to build a clear majority in the Congress that would support extension and deepening of New Deal reforms. Perhaps the outer limits of change in the rural South were reached in Greene County, which became a showcase for the FSA's programs, thanks to the long-continuing interest in Greene County's people by Arthur Raper and Will Alexander, who helped to launch in the county a coordinated effort, called the "Unified Farm Program," involving several federal agencies. Much of the local county elite supported the Unified Farm Program, recognizing that in the eastern Piedmont, unlike the Delta, the old cotton plantation economy was doomed, in any case, beyond revival. In 1939, FSA raised the number of families on assistance from 146 to 535. Federally financed programs expanded health and dental care for hundreds of people, bought up thirty thousand acres of poor farm land to return it to forest, put the Civilian

Conservation Corps to work terracing eroded fields, and paid for demonstration agents to give advice on everything from canning to plowing. Small loans were provided for purchasing baby chicks and calves to promote more consumption of milk and eggs, for repairing barns, for installing window screens and digging sanitary outdoor privies. On nineteen thousand acres of arable land, the FSA carved out seventy-four farms with new houses and barns to rent out to eligible families; the families would, if all went well, be able to purchase these properties. In a county with just 324 white and 100 black farm owners in 1940, this program promised a substantial impact. Altogether the FSA in three years put over a million dollars into Greene County, more than the value of all the farms in the county in 1940. No wonder that Louisiana Dunn Thomas, taking off from the Twenty-third Psalm, began one of her poems, "Uncle Sam is my shepherd / And I shall not want."[61]

But Greene County was exceptional. In all of Georgia, fewer than six hundred families were being resettled in new housing in 1941. In the South as a whole, the FSA helped some tenants and left an extraordinary photographic record of the 1930s, but, viewed with suspicion from the beginning by southern conservatives, it never received enough funding to have more than a marginal effect in most places. Even in Greene County, the long-term impact of the Unified Farm Program was cut short by the coming of the Second World War, which diverted money and attention from domestic programs. Only twelve tenant families there (eight white, four black) had purchased farms through the FSA by 1942; in 1943 the competing needs of the war gave the FSA's opponents the chance to kill it in Congress.[62]

Thus the forces set in place by the AAA and other New Deal farm programs — the "Southern enclosure," as some historians have called it — continued to work their way through the countryside. In the Delta, although planters were steadily moving toward wage labor, the vast majority of African Americans still worked as sharecroppers in 1940. One survey of Delta plantations found that a third of black family heads were illiterate and that high school attendance was rare. Families dependent on wage labor earned $365 per year; sharecroppers made $483. Sixty percent of black families on the plantations lived in houses with two or three rooms; 44 percent had no screens on windows, 92 percent had no electricity; 100 percent had no running water. Black families were more likely to have things they could buy for themselves — two out of three owned a sewing machine; three out of ten, a radio; one out of four, a car. A small proportion of Mississippi black farmers became landowners during the 1930s, sometimes with help from the New Deal. Hundreds of families, some with help from the U.S. Department of Agriculture, took over land in the "backwater" areas of the Delta that had never been fully protected from flooding. The FSA helped 128 African American tenants buy farms in the Delta during the 1930s — about two-tenths of 1 percent of black farmers there. It is a measure of the continuing racial bias in government programs that, by contrast, the FSA helped 185 white tenants become landowners in the Delta, even though black tenants outnumbered white tenants by six to one.[63]

By the end of the 1930s the Atlantic coast of Georgia had changed the least. Most blacks still on the coast were earning a living in Savannah or smaller cities, laboring on the docks or in the multitude of tasks offered by factories or construction projects, or they were low-level service workers in the tourist industry. Both blacks and whites on the coast benefited from the relief and employment programs of the New Deal. Men and women in Savannah and smaller places got supplies that helped them stave off hunger and sometimes earned good wages on WPA relief projects. Coastal agriculture, though, remained a world apart, with a little more than a thousand black farm owners holding on, eking out a precarious living on their small plots and hardly touched by the AAA. A McIntosh County report pointed out that "most of the negroes are very industrious. . . . They own a plot of land, a house for a home, be it ever so humble, and pay their taxes. They send their children to school, and make good citizens." Arthur Raper received a similar impression from his visit to Burroughs, an African American settlement fifteen miles south of Savannah. Most of the families there owned from five to twenty acres of land; they fished and worked for wages to supplement what they raised. Houses in Burroughs, many made of mud-daubed logs, were scattered individually or in small clusters. Although the houses were small and some in poor condition — Raper called one "the least trustworthy structure I have ever seen people living in" — the people themselves "showed evidence of a reasonable standard of living," with "tidy" beds, tablecloths, and neat, clean yards. While many of the community's men had gone to work in cities, north and south, "the people are by no means psychically pauperized — they take pride in ownership and cleanliness."[64]

Unfortunately, as Raper pointed out, the plots of these small farmers could no longer sustain most families. In 1940 there were 1,109 black-owned farms in the coastal counties averaging about thirty-nine acres in size, but on average only six of those acres had been planted the year before. Here, indeed, were the potential sturdy, independent yeoman farmers that many reformers were trying to create, but New Deal agricultural policy paid them little attention. The programs of the AAA ignored them altogether, because they raised neither cotton nor any other major commercial crops. They were not tenants, so they did not fit into the plans of the Farm Security Administration.[65]

Conclusion

Deep South Histories

In 1938, the Carnegie Foundation of New York hired a Swedish economist, Gunnar Myrdal, to undertake a major research project on African Americans and American race relations. Myrdal, whose work would culminate in his massive 1944 volume *An American Dilemma,* hired a number of black researchers for the project. Myrdal himself traveled through the South with Ralph Bunche, a brilliant young African American political scientist. Other researchers conducted interviews and gathered information all across the South, from Vicksburg to Savannah.[1] Northern and well-educated, these talented professionals were often angered by the daily inconveniences and humiliations of segregation. One, Wilhelmina Jackson, thought that her experience of traveling on the bus from New York, with blacks "packed on the back seat like sardines" and forced to eat in the backs of restaurants during stops for meals, was "indicative of what the Negro in the South has to contend with"; she concluded that "seemingly the South wanted to leave tamped on my consciousness its old cry, 'we haven't changed, despite the Civil War, a nigger is still a nigger!' "[2]

It is understandable that Jackson and her coworkers could think that nothing had changed in the decades since the era of slavery. The words of some of the people they interviewed gave support to such a view. Jackson interviewed one young woman named Sarah as she was picking lettuce in the fields of the old Butler rice plantation, just outside Darien on the Georgia coast. Sarah described working "from sun-up to sun-down" for less than a dollar a day. "There is a few of us who try to make the man pay us more money but it don't mean a thing. The man cuss us out and say 'God damn you, you can take it or leave it, there's plenty more where you come from'. . . . Slavery days done come back." Robb Lewis of Greene County, Georgia, a relatively well-to-do landowner, told Ralph Bunche that he could not afford to forget his "place" — "Saying yessir and nosir to any white from a boy up; don't dare look at or touch any white woman; go around to the back door when you want to call on a white man; work hard and pay your debts." In Vicksburg, Myrdal researcher James Jackson was told by Dr. Owens, the African American physician who served as chairman of the Warren County, Mississippi, Republican Committee, that his committee wielded no real power but was paid enough by the national party "to buy enough liquor to wash the inconveniences of being a nigger out of our brains." Each testimony spoke to the deep continuities in the history of the South after Reconstruction, continuities anchored in the southern white memories of defeat and in the ideology and institutions of white supremacy, which kept so many African Americans in menial jobs, which forced them to suffer the daily humiliations of segregation, and which shut them out of meaningful political power.[3]

But, notwithstanding the continuities, the South had changed since the Civil War. Change could be seen in southern landscapes, it could be measured in the ebbs and flows of capital and labor, and it could be found in the stories of opportunities lost and gained by whites and blacks alike. These changes were caused in part by shocks from the natural world or from distant events — the coming of the boll weevil, the rise and fall of cotton prices, the outbreak of war in Europe. They resulted also from choices made by countless families and individuals, who responded to natural disaster and price changes by moving to nearby cities, or across the South, or out of the South altogether; from investments made, and not made, by thousands of wealthy southerners and nonsoutherners; from the decisions of politicians who called on blacks, as well as whites, to fight and pay for the First World War, and who responded to the emergency of the Depression in the 1930s with unprecedented government intervention. The changes were also shaped at every stage by one of the hidden continuities of southern history, the determination, sometimes visible and other times hidden, of African Americans to claim a rightful place in the South as full citizens.

The changes in the South show in sharp relief when seen comparatively at the local level. Along the Georgia coast, although black workers still toiled for long hours at low pay on the same lands where Frances Butler Leigh had tried to revive her father's rice plantation, Butler Island was unusual in that it was producing crops at all. Most of the old rice plantations had been receding back into the swamps and river banks for more than a generation, the remains of ditches and banks serving as silent reminders of an earlier economy and society. The long-staple cotton plantations on the islands had long ago grown up in scrub, sometimes to be reinvented as golf courses and tennis courts for wealthy northerners. In the back woods of the coast or in isolated island villages, black families had bought small plots of land and built their two- or three-room frame houses and their simple churches in the shadows of the pines and live oaks. These isolated black settlements provided the physical and cultural space needed to preserve long-standing traditions of story, song, and dance.

Plantation agriculture in the Piedmont had survived for a generation past the end of the rice era, but the decay of the plantations in that region was, by the end of the 1930s, evident in the washed fields and decrepit mansions on many properties. In Oglethorpe County, most of David C. Barrow's Syls Fork plantation had been abandoned. In 1881, David C. Barrow Jr. had described its transformation from a slave-based plantation before the Civil War to a tenant-based plantation afterwards, citing that experience as proof that "the dreaded 'negro problem'" had been solved. By 1940, only a few tenant families farmed the best tracts of the Barrow land, while the rest was grown over with weeds and scrub pines. Not long after, the Barrow family sold most of the property to a local lumber company that planted the remaining acres in pine, now a more valuable crop than any other.[4] Arthur Raper and Ira Reid in 1941 described a Greene County plantation that had once produced a hundred bales of cotton a year. Now a single black tenant lived with his wife in a few rooms of the abandoned plantation mansion, scratching out a meager living by growing a bit of cotton and corn. Scattered among the old Piedmont plantations were the farms of black owners like Robb Lewis, the Greene County farmer interviewed by Ralph Bunche. Lewis bought the first acres of his farm in the decade of high cotton prices before the First World War. The white man who had sold it to him claimed the parcel included 140 acres, but when surveyed, it turned out to have just 83. Lewis sued, and despite threats and curses, refused to withdraw his suit, though he eventually settled the case for $225, about one fourth of what he had overpaid. Lewis gradually added more land, and by 1939 he owned 165 acres. Although, as he told Bunche, he had to be careful not to step out of his "place," the farm had earned him a certain amount of respect from local whites, and one neighbor, Lewis said, "comes over to my house with his wife and children and acts just like I was a white man . . . and when my wife goes over she sits right down to the table with them."[5]

The plantation landscapes in the Mississippi Delta, by contrast, were the product of a very different economic transformation. So little of the rich mixture of animal and plant life that had once proliferated in the Delta remained by the 1930s that the land could seem almost as flat and unbroken as a tabletop, a rich, dark brown in plowing season, brilliant white with cotton bolls by September. On the plantations of the Delta & Pine Land Company, cotton was still raised by sharecroppers, and the annual agricultural rhythms would have seemed familiar to George Collins, who had tried, unsuccessfully, to establish himself as a Delta planter in the years during and after Reconstruction. The hospital and schools on the D&PL property, however, would have seemed strange to Collins. More strange still would have been the offices of the giant company, where clerks prepared written accounts for all the tenants, a university-trained scientist kept track of the company's ongoing experiments with seed, fertilizer, and pesticides, and accountants kept the complex set of books required to make sure that the company got the subsidies it was entitled to under the federal government's agricultural programs. Meanwhile, on other Delta plantations, still greater changes were evident. On the Hopson plantation near Clarksdale in 1939, a village of tents signaled the arrival of migrant Mexican cotton pickers, and an experimental mechanical cotton picker from the International Harvester Company rumbled through one of the plantation's fields. Some of the sharecropper shacks in the Delta ranked among the worst of the country's housing, but inside many were the Victrolas and battery-powered radios that brought music and news from far away, and alongside many of them were now automobiles that gave black families new mobility.[6]

The landscapes of plantation and farm had been reshaped by the flows of capital and of people for over sixty years. In the face of western competition and the inexorable deterioration of the dykes and trunks on their plantations, rice and Sea Island planters had one by one abandoned their properties or sold them off to men and women, many from the North, who could afford to use them for mere amusement and leisure. In the Piedmont, the plantation regime, though under powerful stress from the low cotton prices of the late nineteenth century, had recovered in the price rise during the early years of the century and survived for another generation. They could not, however, survive the boll weevil and the crash of prices after the First World War. The always-difficult struggle of Piedmont tenants (white and black) to climb to landownership became ever more difficult, and many of the most ambitious of both races looked for greater opportunities in cities and towns and, after the First World War, in the North. In contrast, the fabulously rich soil of the Mississippi Delta promised enough profit to attract major capital investments even from across the Atlantic. In the Delta, old families like the Percys, in Washington County, and new ones like the Dockerys, in Sunflower County, built a new cotton kingdom. Thousands of African Americans went to the Delta, where they cut the timber, built the levees and the railroads, drained the swamps, and sharecropped on the plantations. In their levee camps and juke joints, they nurtured the growth of the blues.

The economic transformation of the Mississippi Delta was a product not only of capital and labor but also of the intervention of government at every level. Local drainage districts, state-sponsored levee boards, and national aid for "navigation" on the Mississippi River had been crucial to the building and rebuilding of the levees that made Delta agriculture possible. National political developments shaped southern change in many other ways as well. The decision of the national government, including the Supreme Court, to let southern states deal on their own with the issue of race had, in effect, authorized the creation of the legal apparatus of segregation and disfranchisement after 1890. The immense mobilization of men and resources during the First World War had in turn called segregation into question by giving symbolic support to the African American claim to full citizenship. The New Deal response to depression had resulted in dozens of new agencies that regulated agriculture, put blacks and whites to work on government payrolls, protected union organizing, and placed liberal reformers like Arthur Raper in positions of unprecedented authority and influence.

In each generation, blacks had resisted white supremacy in whatever ways made sense. The resistance might be as simple as moving away from a plantation at the end of the year, and as complex as organizing a campaign to register voters. By the 1930s, most organized resistance came from the African American urban middle class. Gunnar Myrdal's researchers heard many stories of both past and present political efforts. In Darien, Georgia, Wilhelmina Jackson learned from a local teacher about the long tradition of political activism in the rice region, including the period of Reconstruction, when Tunis Campbell's political machine had ensured black control of McIntosh County. In Augusta, she learned about the movement to register blacks to vote and collected a copy of the NAACP's pamphlet *You Are a Citizen!* In

Vicksburg, Mississippi, James Jackson spoke with T. G. Ewing, a lawyer, and W. P. Harrison, a pharmacist, who had been charter members of the first NAACP branch in Vicksburg during the World War. Harrison told Jackson how he and his friend, Dr. John Miller, "took a stand that they wouldn't buy any Liberty Bonds," and how he had narrowly escaped the tar-and-feathering administered to Dr. Miller. Jackson also learned about Lydia Turner's contemporary effort to register blacks to vote in Vicksburg.[7]

James Jackson was mainly impressed by the repeated failure of middle-class political efforts, rather than by their struggles. Jackson thought that too many black Mississippians had been "terrorized and their ambitions crushed for so long that their will to a better life has dried up," that the teachers he met were "conservative and cowardly," that black preachers were "among the worst oppressors of the Negro . . . informers and agents of the Planters and landlords."[8] But the failures had more to do with inability than un-willingness, especially the inability to succeed without substantial assistance from white allies, either inside or outside the South. In the 1890s, it appeared that, in places like Georgia's Piedmont, the Populist Party would supply those allies in its search for an electoral majority over the Democrats. During the First World War, blacks hoped that the national crusade to win a war fought for "democracy" would provide the leverage needed to promote fun-damental change. In the 1930s, the New Deal and all that flowed from it gave rise to new hopes for change. But the allies had proved inconstant, like the Populists, or largely failed to follow through, as in World War I, or too weak, as in the 1930s. Nevertheless, from the Progressive Era on, a slowly growing group of whites had come to see white supremacy as the basis of a social system both unjust and unwise, one that produced poverty among whites as well as blacks. One of these was Arthur Raper, who campaigned against lynching and worked to implement New Deal measures intended to bring greater prosperity to both whites and blacks. As he learned the importance of better housing and easier credit for tenant farmers, Raper also learned how important it was to treat blacks, as well as whites, with dignity and respect.

Many southern whites of the era recognized the transformations the South had undergone. Some deplored the changes. William Faulkner, in his great novella "The Bear," brooded over the destruction of the Delta's wild forest, once "profound, sentient, gigantic"; now the Delta had been "de-swamped and denuded and derivered" and the forests replaced by cotton that "is planted and grows man-tall in the very cracks of the sidewalks." To William Alexander Percy, son of the Delta leader LeRoy Percy, change was also decline; he wrote that in his lifetime he had "witnessed a disintegration of that moral cohesion of the South which had given it its strength and its sons their singleness of purpose and simplicity." To Arthur Raper, by contrast, the changes, and especially the programs of the New Deal, gave hope that the South might possibly be rescued from a mistaken past.[9]

Despite the real and visible continuities, then, a closer look shows evidence of profound transformations, and many of these — the decline of the plantation, the rise of an African American middle class, the growth of federal power, the new birth of white liberalism — had eaten away at the foundations of segregation. Like a levee that looked unbroken on the surface but underneath was riddled with rotted wood and crawfish nests, the color line was less strong than it appeared. To many white southerners, the very presence of Ralph Bunche, Wilhelmina Jackson, and James Jackson might have seemed, like a heavy spring rain on the upper Mississippi, a portent of future danger. They would have been right to see it that way. The New Deal, like the First World War, would fall far short of overturning the lower South's racial system, but after another and bigger war, a new civil rights revolt would erupt, sparked by the South's urban black middle class, pursued with great courage by farmers in places like the Mississippi Delta, and aided by white allies in both the North and the South. Then, the mighty flood that most southern whites had always feared would finally come; it would breach the walls of the color line, and finally sweep away the age of segregation.

Coda

Endings

LeRoy Percy died 1929, just as the Great Depression was getting under way. He had been exhausted by the battle against the great 1927 flood and by the intense lobbying effort that followed, which culminated in legislation that called for the federal government to pay for rebuilding the Mississippi's levees. The death of his wife, Camille, and the suicide of his nephew in 1929 sent him into depression. A ruptured appendix sent Percy into the hospital, and he died there on Christmas Eve. Hundreds of people, many of them African Americans, attended his funeral the next day at his home. The local paper called him "the impersonation of those manly virtues that belong to a period almost past, that laid the foundation of the prosperity and the culture of the New South." His son Will commissioned a sculpture of a mailed knight to stand as a marker for LeRoy's grave, intended to represent the virtues of what LeRoy himself had called "the old aristocracy of the South, which with its many faults and weaknesses is yet far in a way of the best thing the South has yet produced." Of course, LeRoy Percy, railroad lawyer, lobbyist, operator of big plantations both owned and leased, was at least as representative of the modern age as he was of the legendary virtues of the past.[1]

No one recorded the burial of Delta bluesman Robert Johnson, whose body was laid to rest in 1938 in an unmarked grave not far from Greenwood, Mississippi. Not long before, in his final recording session, Johnson had recorded some of his most haunting songs — "Hellhound on My Trail,"

"Love in Vain," and "Me and the Devil Blues," with its startling final verse: "You may bury my body, ooh, down by the highway side, / So my old evil spirit can catch a Greyhound bus and ride." Johnson was the last of the great blues singers whose performances, as well as whose life, were rooted in the Delta itself; his death marked the end of an era as much as LeRoy Percy's had ten years before. The manner of his dying suited Johnson's life and art. He was playing at a roadhouse not far from Greenwood, in August 1938. The juke joint's owner suspected him — apparently with good reason — of "messing around with his wife" and gave him poisoned whiskey. Johnson took three days to die. His grave is in a small churchyard near Morgan City, not far from where Greyhound buses passed on Highway 7.[2] William Alexander Percy would surely have been astonished to know that Robert Johnson's art would become among the most celebrated of all the Delta's products.

Robert Johnson had probably never heard of Lucy Laney, but if he had, it isn't likely that he would have mourned her death at the age of seventy-nine. She was busy into her last years with her life's work of educating black children and defending black rights. In the 1920s she served as head of the "colored section" of the Augusta branch of the Commission on Interracial Cooperation and worked to increase public spending on education and sanitation for the city's African Americans. In her seventies, as her health declined, she moved out of a dormitory in the Haines Institute into a house of her own, built on the campus with money donated by graduates. After her death in October 1933, thousands of people filed past her body, and nearly three dozen speakers from around the country paid tribute with praise, prayers, poems, and songs. The obituary in the white-owned Augusta *Chronicle* said that she would "rank among the foremost women of her generation in the service she has rendered for humanity." If she had not succeeded in her life-long battle to claim a full measure of equality in the South, she had at least won a clear acknowledgment of her respectability. She was buried on the campus of her beloved school.[3]

Lucy Laney outlived her Piedmont Georgia contemporary Tom Watson by a decade; they had been born just two years apart in the 1850s. Watson had enjoyed a last hurrah in 1920, when he had won election to the U.S. Senate — his first electoral victory since his days as a congressman in the early 1890s. He carried his old congressional district with a majority in the Democratic primary over two strong opponents. His campaign was based on an amalgam of stands that only a Tom Watson could have put together: all-out opposition to "Wilsonism," whether this meant membership in the League of

Nations or the suppression of civil liberties during the World War; all-out attacks on the "rich young officers" who made up the " '100 per cent' idiots" of the American Legion; warnings about the Catholic "menace." His brief Senate career was noted mainly for his belligerent speeches from the floor. When he died in September 1922, ten thousand people came to his funeral at his home in McDuffie County. The Ku Klux Klan sent a cross of roses eight feet high.[4]

Howard Coffin, the Detroit engineer and businessman who had bought Sapelo Island and rebuilt the old planter's mansion there, also did not survive the Depression. After going broke, selling off Sapelo, and giving up control of his Sea Island resort, he suffered a further blow when his wife of many years died in February 1932. A second marriage quickly broke down, and Coffin, deeply depressed, killed himself in November 1932. He was buried in the graveyard of Christ Church on St. Simons Island, next to his first wife and among the graves of many antebellum planters. Sixty-five years before, Frances Butler Leigh had gone to Christ Church for the burial of James Hamilton Couper, one of the last of the island's great planters. "A most terrible scene of desolation met us," she wrote then. "The steps of the church were broken down. . . . The roof was fallen in, so that the sun streamed down on our heads, while the seats were all cut up and marked with the names of Northern soldiers"; the graveyard was "overgrown with weeds and bushes, and tangled with cobweb like grey moss." After the war, Anson Dodge, who had come south to work in his family's lumber business, rebuilt Christ Church and restored the graveyard. Later Dodge, one of many northerners seduced by the islands, quit business and served as an Episcopal priest at the church.[5]

A few favorite slaves excepted, Christ Church's cemetery was for whites only. African Americans on St. Simons had their own burial grounds, and sometimes their bodies were brought back home from great distances for the funerals. Long-standing traditions of mourning and burial, dating from slavery days and probably back to Africa, still survived in some places. In isolated graveyards, many graves were still decorated with broken pieces of pottery or other items that had belonged to the one dead. "The spirit need these," one woman explained, "jis lak wen they's live." But by the 1930s, many traditional burial customs were eroding under the influence of modern values and technologies. Undertakers discouraged the tradition of " 'settin'-up' with the dead," when friends and relatives would spend the night, singing spirituals, with the body of the deceased. At the funerals witnessed by Lydia

Parrish, mourners no longer walked from the church to the graveyard but instead rode in automobiles, and in one case the undertaker himself led the traditional practice of shoveling dirt in the grave. It is not clear from the surviving evidence whether African Americans on St. Simons still followed the slaves' practice of aligning graves so that bodies lay with their heads to the west, "facing" to the east.[6]

Howard Coffin had the peculiar idea that the rotation of the earth interfered with the proper circulation of blood in the body, and to compensate for this supposed effect, he had always slept with his head toward the north. He made sure that he and his wife would be buried the same way, so that their flat gravestones lay on the diagonal with all the other graves in the Christ Church cemetery, which were headed toward the northwest. It seems just about right: Coffin's grave not quite aligned with those of Couper and the other antebellum planters that had so captured his imagination and that Coffin had sought, in style of life at least, to emulate, and with him quite at right angles to the old graves of the island's slaves, their bodies laid with heads to west, their spirits ready to greet each day's rising sun.[7]

APPENDIX

Charts and Tables

Note on Sources for Charts and Tables; Regional Definitions

The boundaries of the Delta, the rice coast / Sea Islands, and the Mississippi-Yazoo Delta are defined here in terms of counties, since much of political life took place at the county level and since the U.S. Census generally collected and published information by county. The simplest region to define is the Georgia rice coast / Sea Island region. It includes the six counties on the coast: Bryan, Camden, Chatham, Glynn, Liberty, and McIntosh. Only in these counties was there significant production of rice or Sea Island cotton in 1860; they embrace all of the barrier islands of Georgia. The Mississippi-Yazoo Delta proper includes the area between the Yazoo and Mississippi Rivers. Some counties straddle the geographical boundary between the Delta and the higher, drier ground to the east. I chose to include all counties with some Delta land: Bolivar, Coahoma, Humphreys, Issaquena, LeFlore, Quitman, Sharkey, Sunflower, Tallahatchie, Tunica, Warren, Washington, and Yazoo. The definition of the eastern Georgia Piedmont is the most arbitrary, and might well have been either extended or contracted. For the sake of convenience, I used the same counties as in an earlier study of the region for the period 1840–65. In 1860 all these counties used Augusta as their major cotton market; over the next decades, some would reorient toward Atlanta as new rail connections were built. The counties are: Burke, Columbia, Elbert, Glascock, Greene, Hancock, Hart, Jefferson, Lincoln, McDuffie, Morgan, Oglethorpe, Richmond, Taliaferro, Warren, and Wilkes.

Regional information in Tables 14 and 25 and in Charts 1–6 and 14–19 was compiled from the county-level reports published by the decennial United States Census. The amount of information published grew over time, but in all years there were reports on basic demographic, agricultural, and manufacturing data. In 1925 and 1935, separate censuses of agriculture were taken. Table 24 is derived from the U.S. Census's *Census of Religious Bodies* (1916). Election results for president and Congress, as reported in Charts 10–13, were collected from the annual *Tribune Almanac* (New York). Results from local elections in Greene County, Georgia (Chart 9) are based on reports in the Greensboro *Herald-Journal*. Information on lynchings (Charts 7 and 8) is based on data compiled by Stewart E. Tolnay and E. M. Beck for

337

their study of lynchings in the South, published in *A Festival of Violence: An Analysis of Southern Lynchings, 1882–1930* (Urbana, Ill., 1993). Tolnay and Beck generously shared with me their raw database of confirmed lynching reports in Georgia and Mississippi.

Tables (except for 14, 24, and 25) are based on samples from the manuscript census returns of the U.S. Census and on data from local tax records. Census records are available on microfilm from the National Archives and Records Service. Tax records are available on microfilm from the Georgia Department of Archives and History and the Mississippi Department of Archives and History.

Tables 1 through 10 are based on systematic samples of households from the manuscript records of the U.S. censuses of population and agriculture for 1880. Data were collected about the household head (sex, race, age, etc.), about basic characteristics of the household (number of adults; of children, etc.), and of farms (production of every crop, number of acres, value of product, etc.). Although the information about households is for April 1880, the official date of the census, information about farms is based on reports of production for 1879. The data for Georgia's eastern Piedmont were derived from samples of households from Hart, Taliaferro, and Glascock Counties. All household heads in the sample who were farmers were then matched, if possible, with the corresponding farm data in the manuscript census of agriculture for that year. These counties were chosen to make it possible to compare the postwar development of a county that had a plantation economy and a majority of slaves (Taliaferro) with two counties that had a white majority and few plantations in 1860. A detailed analysis of the prewar economy in these three counties can be found in the relevant sections of J. William Harris, *Plain Folk and Gentry in a Slave Society* (Middletown, Conn., 1985).

For the Atlantic coast and Delta regions, the 1880 census samples were collected somewhat differently. From the agricultural census manuscripts, samples were taken for two counties in each region: Camden (109 farms) and Liberty (118 farms) in Georgia, and Sunflower (121 farms) and Washington (117 farms) in Mississippi. The farmer in each case was matched, where possible, with the corresponding household in the population census (that is, the matching process for the coast and the Delta was made in the opposite direction from that for the Piedmont). Since it was not always possible to match a farm with a household, the number of farms used for each type of analysis can vary. When measures of "self-sufficiency" in food production are reported (for example, in Table 2), food crops of all kinds have been converted to their nutritional equivalent in bushels of corn and allowances have been subtracted for feeding stock and saving seed. The procedure followed was that described in Roger L. Ransom and Richard Sutch, *One Kind of Freedom: The Economic Consequences of Emancipation* (New York, 1977), Appendix E. In order to get occupational information in 1880 on a cross-section of all household heads, not just farmers, a separate sample of about two hundred household heads was taken for each county.

Tables 11–13 and 18–23 are based on systematic samples from the manuscript population census of 1910 for one county in each region: Sunflower in the Delta (425 households), Greene in the Piedmont (495 households), and Camden on the Georgia coast (512 households). For 1910, information on every member of every household in each sample was collected. The 1910 census collected important information on family history, including the number of marriages for each married person and the number of children ever born, and number of children still living, for every woman. Although the census collected information as well on every farm, the original manuscript agricultural records were later destroyed. However, the population census records whether the family lives on a farm and, for farmers, whether the farm is owned or rented.

Information in Tables 15 through 17 is based on the tax records for Sunflower, Greene, and Camden Counties for 1910. In this case, information was collected for every person appearing in the rolls. Since Mississippi and Georgia had different tax laws and different ways of recording taxes, it is difficult to compare these two states directly. Georgia recorded white and black taxpayers separately, while Mississippi's land tax records do not indicate the race of the taxpayer. The Georgia records report consolidated landholdings within the county for each landholder, while Mississippi's records often list each person several times, with each surveyed tract a different entry. To consolidate these records, I alphabetized the entries and combined tracts owned by the same person or group.

Additional source information appears as needed with individual charts and tables.

Chart 1
White and Black Population, Georgia Coast, 1860–1940

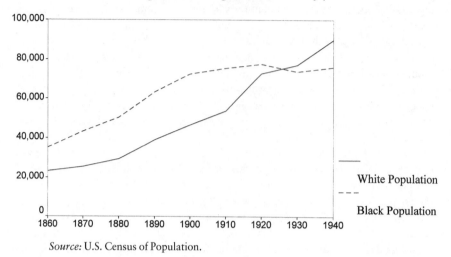

Source: U.S. Census of Population.

Chart 2
White and Black Population, Georgia Eastern Piedmont, 1860–1940

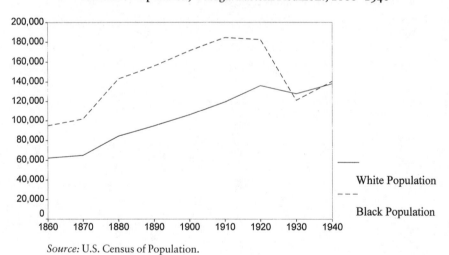

Source: U.S. Census of Population.

Chart 3
White and Black Population, Mississippi Delta, 1860–1940

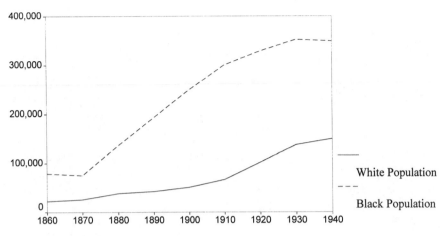

Source: U.S. Census of Population.

Chart 4
Rice and Cotton Production, Georgia Coast, 1860–1940

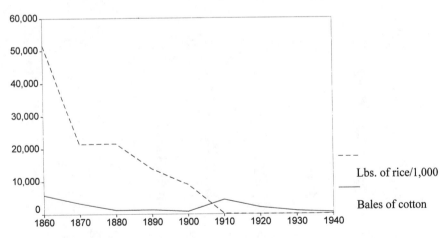

Source: U.S. Census of Agriculture.

Chart 5
Cotton Production in Bales, Delta and Eastern Piedmont, 1860–1940

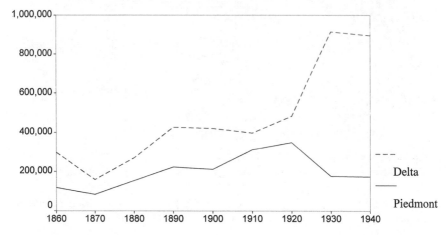

Source: U.S. Census of Agriculture.

Chart 6
Cotton, Corn, and Wheat Production, Georgia Eastern Piedmont, 1860–1900

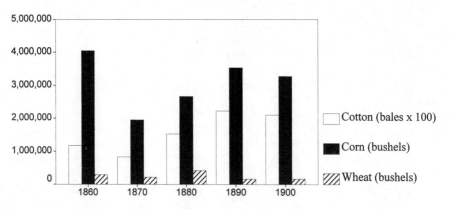

Source: U.S. Census of Agriculture.

Chart 7
Lynchings by Region, 1883–1930

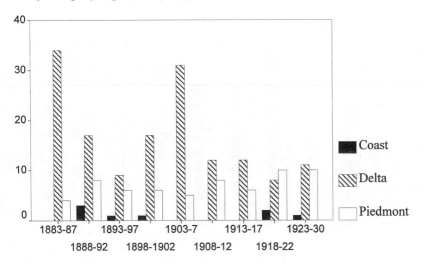

Chart 8
Lynchings per 100,000 Black Population, 1883–1930

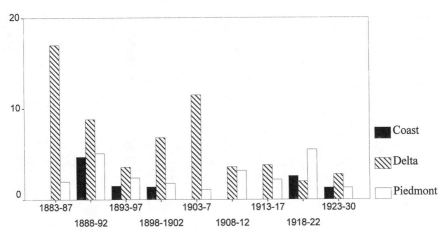

Chart 9
Votes in Local Elections, Greene County, Georgia, 1884–1898

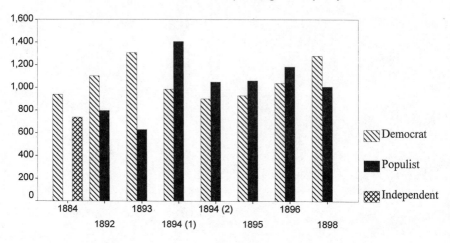

Chart 10
Votes in National Elections, Greene County, Georgia, 1868–1896

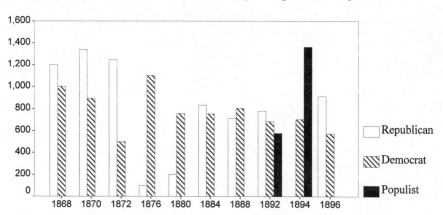

Note: 1870, 1894: congressional; other years: presidential.

Chart 11
Votes for President, Georgia Eastern Piedmont, 1868–1896

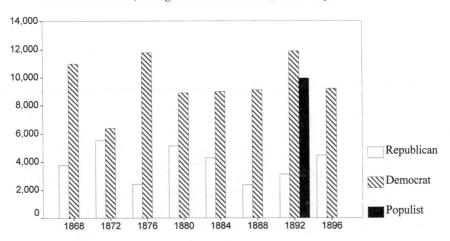

Chart 12
Votes for President, Georgia Coast, 1868–1896

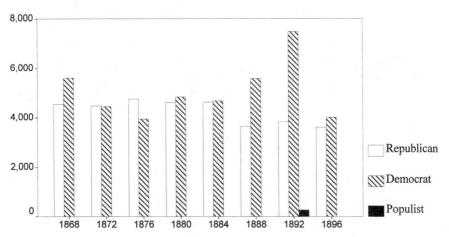

Chart 13
Votes for President, Mississippi Delta, 1872–1896

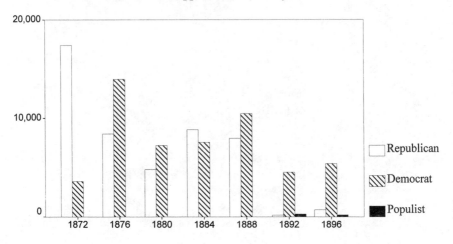

Chart 14
White Farm Owners and Tenants, Mississippi Delta, 1900–1940

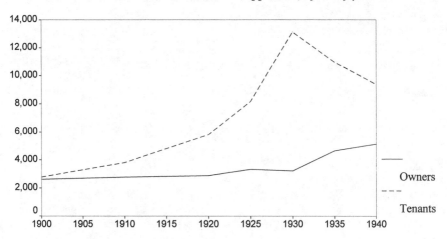

Source: U.S. Census of Agriculture.
Note: 1905 and 1915 interpolated.

Chart 15
Black Farm Owners and Tenants, Mississippi Delta, 1900–1940

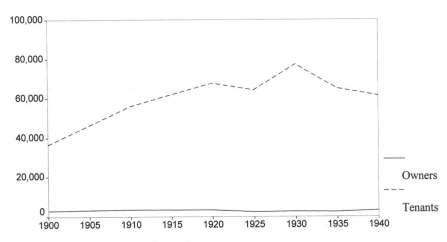

Source: U.S. Census of Agriculture.
Note: 1905 and 1915 interpolated.

Chart 16
White Farm Owners and Tenants, Georgia Eastern Piedmont, 1900–1940

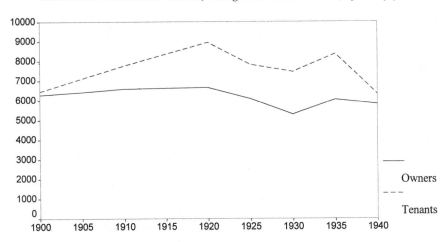

Source: U.S. Census of Agriculture.
Note: 1905 and 1915 interpolated.

Chart 17
Black Farm Owners and Tenants, Georgia Eastern Piedmont, 1900–1940

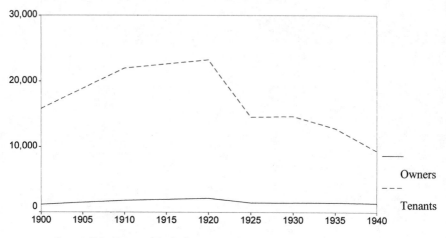

Source: U.S. Census of Agriculture.
Note: 1905 and 1915 interpolated.

Chart 18
White Farm Owners and Tenants, Georgia Coast, 1900–1940

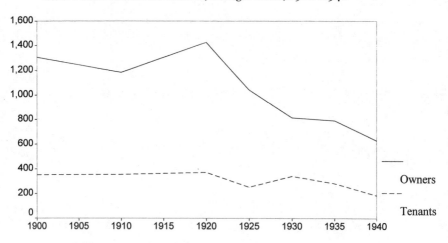

Source: U.S. Census of Agriculture.
Note: 1905 and 1915 interpolated.

Chart 19
Black Farm Owners and Tenants, Georgia Coast, 1900–1940

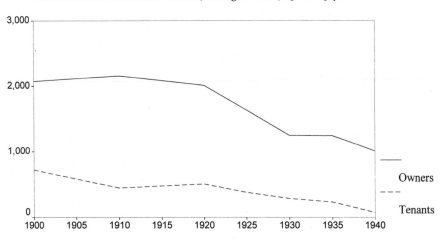

Source: U.S. Census of Agriculture.
Note: 1905 and 1915 interpolated.

Table 1
Farm Production by Race of Farmer, Georgia Coast, 1879

	Black Farmers	White Farmers	All Farmers
Operated by owners	57%	91%	71%
Mean values of:			
Improved acres	13.4	54.3	32.7
Acres planted in cotton	1.0	1.3	1.2
Cotton (bales)	.30	.54	.43
Acres planted in rice	2.4	16.0	8.1
Rice (lbs.)	1,601	20,846	10,229
Acres planted in corn	6.2	10.8	7.7
Corn (bu.)	52	101	70
Wood products	$7	$109	$44
Wages paid	$4	$390	$172
Value of all product	$157	$999	$510
(N)	(104)	(83)	(227*)

Source: Samples from Manuscript Schedules of the U.S. Census of Agriculture, 1880, for Liberty and Camden Counties.
*The race of forty farmers could not be identified.

Table 2
Production Patterns on Farms with Fewer than Fifty Improved Acres,
Georgia Coast, 1879

	Black Farmers	White Farmers	All Farmers
Operated by owners	57%	91%	68%
Mean values of:			
Cotton (bales)	.30	.31	.31
Rice (lbs.)	1,633	558	1,660
Corn (bu.)	51	85	62
Wood products	$7	$98	$36
Wages paid	$3	$23	$16
Value of all product	$155	$249	$201
Food per capita in bu. of corn-equivalents	8.5	−1.5	4.5
Percent self-sufficient in food*	23%	26%	24%
(N)	(102)	(65)	(203**)

Source: Samples from Manuscript Schedules of the U.S. Census of Agriculture, 1880, for Liberty and Camden Counties.

* "Self-sufficiency" defined as the production per person of at least fifteen bushels of corn or their equivalents in foodstuffs after accounting for seed and animal feed.
** The race of forty farmers could not be identified.

Table 3
Cotton Production in Three Piedmont Counties, by Size of Farm
and Race of Farmer, 1879

	White Farmers			Black Farmers		
	All Owners	Owners of Fewer than 50 Acres	Renters	All Owners	Owners of Fewer than 50 Acres	Renters
Glascock County						
Percent growing cotton	95%	88%	95%	—	—	100%
Cotton acres/tilled acres	.29	.32	.34	—	—	.42
(N)	(123)	(51)	(54)	—	—	(19)
Hart County						
Percent growing cotton	98%	96%	94%	92%	89%	91%
Cotton acres/tilled acres	.39	.44	.41	.33	.30	.38
(N)	(173)	(104)	(69)	(12)	(9)	(32)
Taliaferro County						
Percent growing cotton	95%	94%	96%	90%	75%	98%
Cotton acres/tilled acres	.33	.42	.41	.35	.37	.46
(N)	(56)	(18)	(22)	(10)	(4)	(62)
All Three Piedmont Counties						
Percent growing cotton	96%	94%	95%	91%	85%	96%
Cotton acres/tilled acres	.35	.40	.38	.34	.32	.43
(N)	(352)	(173)	(145)	(22)	(13)	(113)

Source: Samples from Manuscript Schedules of the U.S. Census of Agriculture, 1880.

Table 4
Occupations of Household Heads, by Race, Three Piedmont Counties, 1880
(percentages)

	Black HH	White HH	All HH
Farmers			
Owner	4.1	42.1	26.8
Renter (fixed rent)	4.8	5.5	5.2
Share renter	15.4	12.0	13.4
Other/unknown	6.7	7.3	7.1
All farmers	31.0	66.9	52.4
Unskilled labor	60.3	11.7	31.3
Other manual labor	2.3	5.5	4.2
Nonmanual labor	0.2	5.0	3.1
None	1.8	1.9	1.9
Woman at home	4.4	9.0	7.1
Total	100.0	100.0	100.0
(N)	(564)	(836)	(1,400)

Source: Samples from Manuscript Returns for the Census of Population, 1880, for Glascock, Hart, and Taliaferro Counties in Georgia.

Table 5
Farms, by Size, in Sunflower and Washington Counties, Mississippi, 1880

Improved Acreage	Sunflower County	Washington County
Less than 25	66.6%	41.2%
50–99	17.5%	16.7%
100–249	11.4%	13.2%
250–499	1.8%	12.2%
500 and over	2.6%	16.7%
Total	99.9%	100.0%
Mean size (improved acreage)	67	226
(N)	(114)	(114)

Source: Samples from Manuscript Returns for the Census of Agriculture, 1880.
Percentages may not add to 100 due to rounding.

Table 6
Farm Characteristics, by Race of Farmer, Delta, 1879

| | White Farmers | | Black Farmers | |
	All Whites	White Owners	All Blacks	Black Owners
Mean size (improved acreage)	182	209	55	94
Acres in cotton	111	128	30	50
Cotton bales raised	86	98	27	45
Value of product	$3,948	$4,563	$1,546	$2,542
(N)	(110)	(82)	(61)	(21)

Source: Samples from Manuscript Returns for the Census of Agriculture, 1880, for Sunflower and Washington Counties.

Table 7
Shares of Major Commercial Crops, by Region and Size of Farm, 1879

	Coast	Piedmont	Delta
Share raised by:			
Largest 10% of farms	85.5%	36.1%	52.9%
Smallest 50% of farms	3.3%	24.2%	7.4%

Source: Samples from Manuscript Returns for the Census of Agriculture, 1880, for seven counties.

Table 8
Occupations of Black Household Heads in Three Regions, 1880 (percentages)

	Coast	Piedmont	Delta
Farmer	54.0	31.0	42.9
Unskilled labor	35.5	60.3	49.7
Other manual labor	4.2	2.3	2.3
Nonmanual labor	1.7	0.2	1.7
None, at home	4.5	6.2	3.4
Total	99.9	100.0	100.0
(N)	(287)	(564)	(294)

Source: Samples from Manuscript Returns for the Census of Population, 1880, seven counties.

Table 9
Status of Black Farmers in Three Regions, 1880 (percentages)

	Coast	Piedmont	Delta
Owner	57.7	16.4	31.8
Fixed rent	34.6	19.3	54.5
Share rent*	7.7	62.1	13.6
Manager	0.0	2.1	0.0
Total	100.0	99.9	99.9
(N)	(104)	(140)	(66)

Source: Samples from Manuscript Returns for the Census of Agriculture, 1880, for seven counties. Percentages may not add to 100 due to rounding.
*Includes sharecroppers and share renters.

Table 10

Mean Size and Production for Black-operated Farms in Three Regions, 1879

	Coast	Piedmont	Delta*
Improved acres	13	48	44
Acres planted in:			
Rice	2.4	—	—
Cotton	1.0	19.5	26.4
Corn	6.2	14.5	12.0
Annual production			
Rice (lbs.)	1,601	—	—
Cotton (bales)	0.3	6.0	25.0
Corn (bu.)	51	111	265
Total value of product	$157	$273	$1,373
(N)	(104)	(140)	(61)

Source: Samples from Manuscript Returns for the Census of Agriculture, 1880, for seven counties.

*Excludes one farm of 700 acres.

Table 11
Occupations in Sunflower County, Mississippi, by Race, 1910 (percentages)

	Household Heads		Single Men	
	White	Black	White	Black
Farmers:	61.1	81.7	21.1	8.2
Farm owners	17.6	4.0		
Farm renters*	43.5	77.7		
Domestic labor	0.0	1.5	0.0	0.0
Other unskilled labor	5.9	14.1	57.7	89.3
Other manual labor	2.4	0.6	0.0	2.5
Lower white collar	16.5	0.0	17.3	0.0
Proprietors, managers	7.1	0.9	0.0	0.0
Professionals	2.4	0.3	3.8	0.0
None, at home	4.7	0.0	**	**
Total	100.1	100.1	99.9	100.0
(N)	(85)	(327)	(52)	(122)

Source: Samples from Manuscript Returns of the Census of Population, 1910.
Percentages may not add to 100 due to rounding.
*Includes "farmers" not living on a farm or owning a farm.
**Only single males with occupations are included.

Table 12
Occupations in Greene County, Georgia, by Race, 1910 (percentages)

	Household Heads		Single Men	
	White	*Black*	*White*	*Black*
Farmers	56.5	64.4	17.6	4.0
Farm owners	29.2	4.7		
Farm renters*	27.3	59.7		
Domestic labor	0.6	8.4	0.0	7.1
Other unskilled labor	4.3	20.9	48.6	84.9
Other manual labor	11.2	2.8	14.9	1.6
Lower white collar	6.2	0.3	13.5	0.8
Proprietor, managers	6.8	0.3	4.1	0.8
Professionals	2.5	1.3	1.4	0.8
None, at home	11.8	1.6	**	**
Total	99.9	100.0	100.1	100.0
(N)	(161)	(320)	(74)	(126)

Source: Samples from Manuscript Returns of the Census of Population, 1910.
Percentages may not add to 100 due to rounding.
  *Includes "farmers" not living on a farm or owning a farm.
**Only single males with occupations are included.

Table 13
Occupations in Camden County, Georgia, by Race, 1910 (percentages)

	Household Heads		Single Men	
	White	*Black*	*White*	*Black*
Farmers	48.8	49.8	12.5	1.6
Farm owners	43.4	42.2		
Farm renters*	5.4	7.7		
Domestic labor	1.8	1.8	0.0	2.4
Other unskilled labor	13.3	38.1	44.4	84.6
Other manual labor	14.5	5.3	27.8	11.4
Lower white collar	7.2	0.6	12.5	0.0
Proprietors, managers	3.6	0.9	1.4	0.0
Professionals	4.8	1.2	1.4	0.0
None, at home	6.0	2.4	**	**
Total	100.0	100.1	100.0	100.0
(N)	(166)	(339)	(72)	(123)

Source: Samples from Manuscript Returns of the Census of Population, 1910.
*Includes "farmers" not living on a farm or owning a farm.
**Only single males with occupations are included.

Table 14
Status of Farmers, by Race, for Three Regions, 1910 (percentages)

	Georgia Coast	*Georgia Piedmont*	*Mississippi Delta*
Black owners	52.1	4.7	5.3
Black tenants	10.8	57.7	84.8
White owners	28.6	17.3	4.1
White tenants	8.5	20.4	5.7
Total	100.0	100.1	99.9
(N)	(4,141)	(38,141)	(66,015)

Source: U.S. Census, *Thirteenth Census, 1910. Agriculture.* Percentages may not add to 100 due to rounding.

Table 15
Distribution of Taxable Farm Acreage, by Size and Race,
Camden County, Georgia, 1878 and 1910

	1878		1910	
No. Acres	Black Taxpayers	White Taxpayers	Black Taxpayers	White Taxpayers
None	59.2%	56.7%	45.0%	57.6%
1–24	17.8%	2.2%	43.1%	27.8%
25–49	6.8%	2.8%	10.1%	7.9%
50–99	9.5%	3.6%	1.4%	3.5%
100–199	3.9%	7.7%	0.2%	1.6%
200–499	2.9%	14.0%	0.2%	1.0%
500 and over	0.0%	12.9%	0.0%	0.6%
Total	100.1%	99.9%	100.0%	100.0%
Mean acreage	22	254	8	18
Mean acreage (owners only)	54	586	15	41
(N)	(591)	(534)	(1,315)	(686)

Source: Tax Digests, Camden County, 1878 and 1910. Percentages may not add to 100 due to rounding.
Note: Figures for white taxpayers exclude merchants and nonagricultural businesses.

Table 16
Distribution of Taxable Farm Acreage, by Size and Race,
Greene County, Georgia, 1910

No. Acres	Black Taxpayers	White Taxpayers
None	90.6%	57.8%
1–24	3.6%	3.0%
25–49	1.6%	3.2%
50–99	1.6%	7.6%
100–199	1.8%	12.6%
200–499	0.7%	10.7%
500 and over	0.2%	5.1%
Total	101.1%	100.0%
Mean acreage	7	112
Mean acreage (owners only)	76	267
(N)	(1,482)	(1,736)

Source: Tax Digest, Greene County, 1910. Percentages may not add to 100 due to rounding.
Note: Figures for white taxpayers exclude merchants and nonagricultural businesses.

Table 17
Distribution of "Cleared Acres" in Land Tax Rolls, by Size,
Sunflower County, Mississippi, 1910

No. Acres	Individuals and Married Couples	Partnerships
None	14.3%	18.2%
1–24	18.8%	12.5%
25–49	18.6%	8.0%
50–99	20.1%	13.6%
100–199	14.4%	10.2%
200–499	10.3%	20.5%
500 and over	3.6%	17.0%
Total	100.1%	100.0%
Mean acreage	110	237
(N)	(1711)	(88)

Source: Land Tax Rolls, Sunflower County, 1910.
Note: Because personal property and poll taxes were recorded in a separate tax roll, the land tax roll includes *only* owners of either "cleared" or "uncleared" land. Excludes nonagricultural businesses and property companies owning only or mainly large areas of "uncleared" land.

Table 18
Ever-married Women's Mean Fertility, by Race and Region, 1910

	Camden County (Coast)			Greene County (Piedmont)			Sunflower County (Delta)		
	Children Ever Born	Children Living	(N)	Children Ever Born	Children Living	(N)	Children Ever Born	Children Living	(N)
Whites 45+	5.4	4.3	(47)	6.3	5.0	(54)	5.0	3.3	(19)
Blacks 45+	7.4	5.0	(98)	7.0	4.5	(80)	7.7	4.6	(62)
Whites 20+	4.5	3.8	(144)	4.5	3.7	(150)	3.8	2.7	(74)
Blacks 20+	5.2	3.8	(292)	4.4	3.2	(281)	4.4	2.8	(259)

Source: Samples from Manuscript Returns of the Census of Population, 1910.

Table 19
Mean Age at Marriage of Persons in First Marriage, by Race, Gender, and Region, 1910

	Camden County (Coast)	Greene County (Piedmont)	Sunflower County (Delta)
White men	26.3	25.0	24.1
(N)	(104)	(122)	(84)
White women	19.9	20.1	19.9
(N)	(107)	(137)	(90)
Black men	26.8	23.9	24.2
(N)	(173)	(199)	(129)
Black women	19.8	20.1	20.1
(N)	(181)	(229)	(151)

Source: Samples from Manuscript Returns of the Census of Population, 1910.

Table 20
Status of Household Members, by Race and Region, 1910 (percentages)

	Camden County (Coast)		Greene County (Piedmont)		Sunflower County (Delta)	
	Whites	Blacks	Whites	Blacks	Whites	Blacks
Head or spouse	37.1	36.3	37.0	38.9	40.7	44.1
Child of head*	50.6	45.6	52.8	47.2	42.7	41.8
Other relative of head	9.4	13.7	7.6	11.3	11.2	11.1
Nonrelative	2.9	4.4	2.6	2.5	5.3	3.0
Total	100.0	100.0	100.0	99.9	99.9	100.0
(N)	(828)	(1,707)	(811)	(1,466)	(393)	(1,355)

Source: Samples from Manuscript Returns of the Census of Population, 1910.
*Includes stepchildren of head.

Table 21
Household Status of Children under Fifteen Years of Age, by Race and Region, 1910
(percentages)

	Camden County (Coast)		Greene County (Piedmont)		Sunflower County (Delta)	
	White Children	Black Children	White Children	Black Children	White Children	Black Children
Head of household is:						
Parent or stepparent	90.1	80.2	95.4	82.7	91.3	83.7
Grandparent	5.4	11.9	3.3	10.0	3.6	6.7
Self or spouse	0.9	0.1	0.0	0.0	0.0	0.6
Other	3.6	7.7	1.3	7.3	5.1	9.1
Total	100.0	99.9	100.0	100.0	100.0	100.1
(N)	(332)	(738)	(304)	(613)	(138)	(496)

Source: Samples from Manuscript Returns of the Census of Population, 1910.
Percentages may not add to 100 due to rounding.

Table 22
Occupations of Wives, by Race and Region, 1910 (percentages)

| | Camden County (Coast) | | Greene County (Piedmont) | | Sunflower County (Delta) | |
	Whites	Blacks	Whites	Blacks	Whites	Blacks
None*	99.3	76.9	91.3	48.7	93.0	12.5
Farmers	0.0	1.9	0.0	1.1	0.0	0.4
Farm and general labor	0.0	17.2	3.3	41.2	2.8	84.8
Domestic labor	0.0	3.4	0.0	7.9	0.0	1.9
All others with occupations	0.7	0.7	5.3	1.1	4.2	0.4
(Total with occupations)	(0.7)	(23.2)	(8.6)	(51.3)	(7.0)	(87.5)
Total	100.0	100.1	99.9	100.0	100.0	100.0
(N)	(135)	(268)	(150)	(267)	(71)	(257)

Source: Samples from Manuscript Returns of the Census of Population, 1910.
*Includes "At Home," "Housekeeper," and similar entries.

Table 23
Marriage and Household Status of Women, by Race and Region, 1910

| | Camden County (Coast) | | Greene County (Piedmont) | | Sunflower County (Delta) | |
	Whites	Blacks	Whites	Blacks	Whites	Blacks
Households headed by women	7.7%	10.2%	11.2%	18.2%	3.4%	9.5%
(N)	(169)	(342)	(169)	(325)	(89)	(338)
Married women not in first marriage	10.6%	20.4%	4.9%	11.8%	12.8%	30.1%
(N)	(123)	(235)	(143)	(263)	(78)	(266)
Mean number of years in current marriage	16.3	14.5	16.2	12.5	14.3	13.4
(N)	(106)	(182)	(142)	(263)	(67)	(180)

Source: Samples from Manuscript Returns of the Census of Population, 1910.

Table 24
Membership in Religious Denominations, by Region, 1916

	Coast	Piedmont	Delta
Main white denominations			
Southern Baptist	5,790	28,455	7,051
Southern Methodist	6,394	22,503	11,055
Episcopal	3,121	1,188	1,655
Presbyterian	1,268	2,362	2,257
Main black denominations			
Baptist	27,455	76,505	101,792
African Methodist Episcopal	5,252	8,944	13,788
A.M.E. Zion	—	2,479	2,230
Colored Methodist Episcopal	943	9,189	5,394
Methodist (Northern)	1,265	916	5,830
All other denominations*	12,000	8,231	11,111
Total membership	63,488	160,772	162,163

Source: U.S. Census Bureau, Census of Religious Bodies, 1916.
* "Other" includes Catholic, Jewish, smaller Protestant denominations, and "others."

Table 25
Total Farm Acreage by Region and Farmer Status, 1930–1940

	Piedmont			Delta		
	1930	1940	% change	1930	1940	% change
All tenants	22,061	15,674	−29.0	90,343	70,620	−21.8
All croppers	11,897	6,306	−47.0	65,198	59,560	−8.6
White croppers	3,441	2,007	−41.7	8,094	5,350	−33.9
All owners	6,739	7,182	6.6	5,736	8,303	44.8

Source: U.S. Census of Agriculture.

ABBREVIATIONS

AH	*Agricultural History*
BAE	Records of the Bureau of Agricultural Economics, U.S. Department of Agriculture, Record Group 83, National Archives and Records Service
Bunche Papers	Ralph Bunche Papers, Research Library, University of California at Los Angeles
CWDW	Central Correspondence File, Committee on Women's Defense Work, Records of the Council of National Defense, Record Group 62, National Archives and Records Service
DPL	Records of the Delta & Pine Land Company, Special Collections, Mitchell Memorial Library, Mississippi State University
GDAH	Georgia Department of Archives and History
GHJ	Greensboro [Ga.] *Herald-Journal*
GHQ	*Georgia Historical Quarterly*
GHS	Georgia Historical Society
HBP	Hofwyl-Broadfield Papers, Hofwyl Plantation State Park, McIntosh County, Georgia (microfilm copy at Brunswick Regional Library)
Hist. Stat.	U.S. Bureau of the Census, *Historical Statistics of the United States, Colonial Times to 1970* (Washington, 1975)
JAH	*Journal of American History*
JEH	*Journal of Economic History*
JMH	*Journal of Mississippi History*
JSH	*Journal of Southern History*
MDAH	Mississippi Department of Archives and History
MSU	Mitchell Memorial Library, Mississippi State University
NAACP Branch	Series G, Branch Files, in Papers of the National Association for the Advancement of Colored People, Library of Congress
NAACP 7A	*The Papers of the NAACP,* August Meier and John H. Bracey Jr.,

	editorial advisors (Frederick, Md., 1981–), part 7, series A, Anti-Lynching Investigative Files (on microfilm)
NAACP 10	*The Papers of the NAACP,* August Meier and John H. Bracey Jr., editorial advisors (Frederick, Md., 1981–), part 10, Peonage, Labor, and the New Deal (on microfilm)
NARS	National Archives and Records Service
NUL	Papers of the National Urban League, Library of Congress
Peonage Files	The *Peonage Files of the U.S. Department of Justice, 1901–1945,* ed. Pete Daniel (Frederick, Md., 1989) (on microfilm)
Percy Papers	Percy Family Papers, Mississippi Department of Archives and History
R. G. Dun	R. G. Dun & Co. Collection, Baker Library, Harvard Business School
RPA	Survey of Rural Problem Areas, Federal Emergency Relief Administration, filed in entry 155, Bureau of Agricultural Economics, U.S. Department of Agriculture, Record Group 83, National Archives and Records Service
RRR	Rural Relief Reports [1935], in Records of the Division of Farm Population Rural Life and Its Predecessors, entry 156, Bureau of Agricultural Economics, U.S. Department of Agriculture, Record Group 83, National Archives and Records Service
SHC	Southern Historical Collection, Wilson Library, University of North Carolina at Chapel Hill
SI	Sparta [Ga.] *Ishmaelite*
UGA	Hargrett Rare Book and Manuscript Library, University of Georgia
VDH	Vicksburg *Daily Herald*
VEP	Vicksburg *Evening Post*

NOTES

Introduction

1. Erskine Caldwell, *Tobacco Road* (New York, 1932); Margaret Mitchell, *Gone with the Wind* (New York, 1936); Allison Davis, Burleigh B. Gardner, and Mary R. Gardner, *Deep South: A Social Anthropological Study of Caste and Class* (Chicago, 1941). According to the *Oxford English Dictionary*, the earliest use of *deep South* was in Rebecca West's 1936 novel *Thinking Reed*, but it was used in 1932 by Rupert Vance in his *Human Geography of the South: A Study in Regional Resources and Human Adequacy* (Chapel Hill, N.C., 1932). There, Vance applied the term only to the warmest areas of the South, where the growing season was long enough to support profitable rice and sugar cultivation. I have not found earlier instances of the term.

2. Savannah Unit, Georgia Writers' Project, *Drums and Shadows: Survival Studies among the Georgia Coastal Negroes* (1940; reprint, Athens, Ga., 1986); William Alexander Percy, *Lanterns on the Levee: Recollections of a Planter's Son* (New York, 1941; reprint, Baton Rouge, La., 1973); Arthur Raper, *Tenants of the Almighty* (New York, 1943).

3. Thomas L. Haskell, "Capitalism and the Origins of the Humanitarian Sensibility, Part 2," *American Historical Review* 90 (1985), 550–51. There is, of course, a large historical literature on the broad changes described here. I have briefly addressed my many debts to earlier historians, as well as my disagreements with some of them, in the Essay on Sources.

4. Joan W. Scott, "Gender: A Useful Category of Historical Analysis," *American Historical Review* 91 (1986), 1053.

5. William Faulkner, *Absalom, Absalom!*, in *Novels, 1936–1940* (New York, 1990), 145.

Chapter 1   Land and Labor in New South Countrysides

1. Plantation Journal, "Season of 1876 at Gowrie," Manigault Papers, GHS. The Manigault Papers are scattered in several repositories, and the original manuscript journal is in the SHC. Unless otherwise noted, however, I have relied on the typescripts of the papers deposited at the Georgia Historical Society by James Clifton. Much of the material up to 1867 appears in James M. Clifton, ed., *Life and Labor on Argyle Island* (Savannah,

1978). The property was actually a combination of two neighboring plantations. The first, "Gowrie," was purchased by Charles Manigault in 1833; the second, "East Hermitage," was added in 1849.

2. Clifton, ed., *Life and Labor*, xxxviii. This represented about 10 percent on the capital invested. See also William Dusinberre, *Them Dark Days: Slavery in the American Rice Swamps* (New York, 1996), 12-24.

3. Clifton, ed., *Life and Labor*, xliii-xlv. Louis Manigault's grandfather was Nathaniel Heyward, who was James Heyward's great-grandfather.

4. Plantation Journal, "Season of 1876," Manigault Papers, GHS.

5. For examples on Gowrie, see Clifton, ed., *Life and Labor*, passim; for detailed treatments of master-slave relations at Gowrie, see also Dusinberre, *Them Dark Days*, 48-210, and Jeffrey Young, "Ideology and Death on a Savannah River Rice Plantation, 1833-1867: Paternalism amidst 'a Good Supply of Disease and Pain,'" *JSH* 59 (1993), 673-706.

6. Plantation Journal, "Season of 1876," Manigault Papers, GHS.

7. Frances Butler Leigh, *Ten Years on a Georgia Plantation since the War* (London, 1883; reprint, New York, 1969), 29, 63-64; Frances A. Kemble, *Journal of a Residence on a Georgia Plantation in 1838-1839* (London, 1863; reprint, New York, 1969), 186.

8. Lewis Cecil Gray, *History of Agriculture in the Southern United States to 1860* (2 vols., Washington, D.C., 1933; reprint 1958), 1:277-87, 2:675-80; Joyce E. Chaplin, *An Anxious Pursuit: Agricultural Innovation and Modernity in the Lower South, 1730-1815* (Chapel Hill, N.C., 1993); Mart Stewart, *"What Nature Suffers to Groe": Life, Labor, and Landscape on the Georgia Coast, 1680-1920* (Athens, Ga., 1996).

9. Edward King, *The Great South* (1875; reprint, Baton Rouge, La., 1972), 434; Julia Floyd Smith, *Slavery and Rice Culture in Low Country Georgia, 1750-1860* (Knoxville, Tenn., 1985); Clifton, ed., *Life and Labor*, "Introduction"; Stewart, *"What Nature Suffers to Groe,"* 87-151; Sam B. Hilliard, "The Tidewater Rice Plantation: An Ingenious Adaptation to Nature," *Geoscience and Man* 12 (1975), 57-66. Dusinberre, *Them Dark Days*, 395, estimates that about 320 plantations produced most of the rice along the Atlantic coast.

10. Charles Lyell, *A Second Visit to the United States of America* (New York, 1849), and Frederick Law Olmsted, *A Journey in the Seaboard Slave States* (New York, 1856), both excerpted in Mills Lane, ed., *The Rambler in Georgia* (Savannah, 1973), 193, 214-15.

11. Clarence Mohr, *On the Threshold of Freedom: Masters and Slaves in Civil War Georgia* (Athens, Ga., 1986), esp. 99-119; Russell Duncan, *Freedom's Shore: Tunis Campbell and the Georgia Freedmen* (Athens, Ga., 1986), 18-41; Paul Cimbala, "The Freedmen's Bureau, the Freedmen, and Sherman's Grant in Reconstruction Georgia," *JSH* 55 (1989), 597-632.

12. This second Pierce Butler was born Pierce Mease, the grandson of the first Pierce Butler and the son of Sarah Butler Mease. He changed his name to Butler in 1826 in accordance with conditions attached to his inheritance of the Butler properties. He died in 1867. Frances Butler married the Reverend James Wentworth Leigh in 1871, and afterwards operated the plantation properties with her husband; see Malcolm Bell Jr., *Major Butler's Legacy: Five Generations of a Slaveholding Family* (Athens, Ga., 1987), and, on the economics of the Butler plantation under slavery, Dusinberre, *Them Dark Days*, 213-81.

13. Leigh, *Ten Years,* 75, 70–71.

14. Gray, *History of Agriculture,* 1:553–54; Smith, *Slavery and Rice Culture,* 61–62.

15. Leigh, *Ten Years,* 58; Dusinberre, *Them Dark Days,* 235–47.

16. Betty Wood, *Men's Work, Women's Work: The Informal Slave Economies of Lowcountry Georgia* (Athens, Ga., 1995); Phillip D. Morgan, "The Ownership of Property by Slaves in the Mid-Nineteenth-Century Low Country," *JSH* 49 (1983), 399–420; Olmsted in *Rambler in Georgia,* 220; Lyell in *Rambler in Georgia,* 198.

17. Leigh, *Ten Years,* 79.

18. Abbie Fuller Graham, "The History of the St. Simons Mills — 1875–1906," typescript, in folder 100, Hilton Papers, GHS; Leigh, *Ten Years,* 124.

19. Leigh, *Ten Years,* 25, 96.

20. Kemble, *Journal,* 219.

21. Leigh, *Ten Years,* 151, 202–7. James B. Heyward paid Irish ditchers $1.40 per day in 1880 when black ditching labor was going for 90 cents per day, because he found the Irish gangs ended up costing only 5 cents per "running yard" of ditching while blacks cost 7 cents for the same amount of work. Heyward to Charles Manigault, 29 February 1880, Manigault Papers, GHS.

22. "Records of Proceedings of Association of Rice Planters of Altamaha River," 29 April 1876 (1st meeting); 4th meeting (no date); 15 January 1883, in Margaret D. Cate Collection, GHS.

23. "Contract," in Clifton, ed., *Life and Labor,* 364–65. The contract did not specify how the foremen and their crews divided the workers' share of the profits.

24. Plantation Journal, "Season of 1876," and James B. Heyward to Louis Manigault, 30 July 1876, both in Manigault Papers, GHS.

25. "Plantation Journal, 1876," and Louis Manigault to W. Banford Frost, 28 March 1876, both in Manigault Papers, GHS. Late antebellum production and exports are summarized in Dusinberre, *Them Dark Days,* 388–91. On the economics of rice culture, see especially Peter A. Coclanis, *The Shadow of a Dream: Economic Life and Death in the South Carolina Low Country, 1670–1920* (New York, 1988), and Coclanis, "Distant Thunder: The Creation of a World Market for Rice and the Transformations It Wrought," *American Historical Review* 98 (1993), 1050–78.

26. "Plantation Journal, 1876," Manigault Papers, GHS. See Clifton, ed., *Life and Labor,* xxii, for a description of the sequence of water flows on the typical rice plantation.

27. James B. Heyward to Louis Manigault, 8 July 1876, Manigault Papers, GHS.

28. James B. Heyward to Louis Manigault, 1 September, 11 September, and 5 October 1876, and Plantation Journal, "Season of 1876," Manigault Papers, GHS. For a discussion of the South Carolina labor conflicts, see Eric Foner, *Nothing but Freedom: Emancipation and Its Legacy* (Baton Rouge, La., 1983), 74–110.

29. Plantation Journal, "Season of 1876," Manigault Papers, GHS. Total expenses were about $16,000. The prices cited here are for "polished" rice. I have converted the price of "rough" rice, cited by Manigault, to an equivalent in polished rice to provide a consistent measure.

30. For some of the details of Manigault's tangled financial problems, see, for example, Plantation Journal, "Season of 1876"; "Gowrie Plantation Account"; E. H. Frost & Co. to Louis Manigault, 6 December 1876; Louis Manigault to E. H. Frost & Co., 8 January

1877; Louis Manigault to Messrs. Palmer and Deppish, Savannah, 14 May 1877, all in Manigault Papers, GHS.

31. Letters from James B. Heyward to Louis Manigault throughout the 1880s, Manigault Papers, GHS; Whitehall Plantation Accounts, typescript, GHS; Leigh, *Ten Years*, 25; draft of letter by James T. Dent, Account Book, Hofwyl-Broadfield Papers (pp. 94–97). Gray, *History of Agriculture*, 2:730, cites one 1857 source reporting that typical yields on the Savannah River were forty-five to fifty-five bushels per acre of paddy rice. For overall trends, see Chart 4, Appendix.

32. Ellis M. Coulter, *Thomas Spalding of Sapelo* (Baton Rouge, La., 1940).

33. Ella Barrow Spalding to Charles Spalding Wylly, August 1914, printed in Robert L. Humphries, ed., *The Journal of Archibald C. McKinley* (Athens, Ga., 1991), 238–40; William S. McFeely, *Sapelo's People: A Long Walk into Freedom* (New York, 1994), 82–98.

34. Humphries, ed., *Journal of Archibald McKinley*, 91, 94, 97, 107.

35. Bourke Spalding to David C. Barrow, 8 January 1879, Barrow Papers, UGA; McFeely, *Sapelo's People*, 140–43.

36. Clara E. Barrow to David C. Barrow, 29 November 1872, and "Nelly" [Ella McKinley] to Poole, 8 January 1876, Barrow Papers, UGA.

37. In a sample of 186 farmers identified by race in Camden and Liberty Counties in the 1880 Census of Agriculture, 62 of 104 blacks raised cotton; 38 of 84 whites raised cotton. Only four of these farmers planted more than ten acres in cotton; the largest planting was twenty-one acres. The 65 white farms in this sample with fewer than fifty improved acres in 1880 averaged 558 lbs. of rice, or perhaps 300 lbs. of polished rice, worth about $15, plus an average of .3 bales of cotton, or 150 lbs., worth perhaps another $20 to $30 if we assume it was all Sea Island cotton. They averaged $98 in wood products sold. Liberty County, it should be noted, had by far the largest Sea Island cotton crop in Georgia in 1860. See Tables 1 and 2, Appendix.

38. James B. Heyward to Louis Manigault, 22 June 1877, and 15 September 1881, Manigault Papers, GHS.

39. Undated notes, probably about 1886 (pp. 110–13 of the notebook in which the record was kept), and entry for 6 December 1876 in "Record of Proceedings," Cate Papers, GHS; Gabriel Manigault to Louis Manigault, 29 November 1876, and James B. Heyward to Louis Manigault, 6 December 1876 and 25 February 1877, Manigault Papers, GHS. On the background of this system see Phillip Morgan, "Work and Culture: The Task System and the World of the Lowcountry Blacks, 1700 to 1880," *William and Mary Quarterly*, 3d ser., 39 (1982), 563–99.

40. Horace A. Crane to James T. Dent, 22 December 1890, and "Account Book for Hofwyl and Broadfield," 34–35, HBP. Crane was an official of the bank to whom Dent was heavily indebted, and he was writing to approve Dent's plan. I consulted the microfilmed papers; financial correspondence is on reel 4; account books on reel 5.

41. Leigh, *Ten Years*, 156.

42. In the 1880 coastal farm sample, from two of these counties, about half the farmers are identifiable as African American, and over half of these owned their farms. See Table 1, Appendix.

43. Based on the 1880 coastal farm sample; "small farms" means farms with fewer than fifty improved acres. The estimate of self-sufficiency is based on ninety-five farms

operated by African Americans. Only twenty-two of these raised the fifteen bushels of corn-equivalents in food per adult on the farm, which is a conservative measure of self-sufficiency. See Table 2, Appendix.

44. The land "out" of production is described in the county reports included in Eugene Hilgard, Special Agent, Tenth Census [1880], *Report on Cotton Production in the United States*, 2 vols. (Washington, D.C., 1884).

45. David C. Barrow to David C. Barrow Jr., 24 July 1876, David Barrow Papers, UGA.

46. On the unprofitability of rice growing on smaller farms, see Dale Evans Swan, *The Structure and Profitability of the Antebellum Rice Industry, 1859* (New York, 1975).

47. David C. Barrow Jr., "A Georgia Plantation," *Scribners Monthly* 21 (April 1881), 830–36, quotation p. 831.

48. Ibid. On the "squad system" after the Civil War, see Ralph Shlomowitz, "The Squad System on Postbellum Cotton Plantations," in *Toward a New South? Studies in Post–Civil War Southern Communities*, ed. Orville Vernon Burton and Robert C. McMath Jr. (Westport, Conn., 1982), 265–80; Gerald David Jaynes, *Branches without Roots: Genesis of the Black Working Class in the American South* (New York, 1986), 158–90.

49. Barrow, "A Georgia Plantation," 832.

50. Ibid., 830.

51. See J. William Harris, "Plantations and Power: Emancipation on the David C. Barrow Plantations," in *Toward a New South?* ed. Burton and McMath, 246–64. The description of planters as changing from "laborlords" to "landlords" is from Gavin Wright, *Old South, New South: Revolutions in the Cotton Economy* (New York, 1986).

52. U.S. Census, 1880, Manuscript Schedules, Agriculture, Oglethorpe County, Georgia; Diary, 1879, DCB. The 1880 Agricultural Census refers to farms operated in 1879. The two hands are identified in the diary by first name only. Thomas also produced twenty bushels of wheat and seventy-five pounds of butter. There are minor discrepancies among the census reports, Barrow Sr.'s 1879 diary, and Barrow Jr., "Georgia Plantation," but none that would change the basic summary given here. For more details, see Harris, "Plantations and Power."

53. Total cotton income from rental, his own acreage, and small amounts from two other plantations that had been passed on to sons was twenty-six thousand pounds of cotton sold for $2,210. From this we must add the value of grains and cotton seed raised and received in rent, and subtract the costs of hiring labor and the payment of taxes, fertilizer, and other farm expenses. This was on the order of ten times the farm income of the typical tenant family in 1879 according to Roger Ransom and Richard Sutch, *One Kind of Freedom: The Economic Consequences of Emancipation* (New York, 1977), 219. By comparison, the "average money income" of "normal families of workers in 9 basic industries" in 1888–91 was $573: *Hist. Stat.*, 322. Gowrie Plantation rented for $3,200 per year in the 1870s.

54. See Table 4, Appendix, for farm ownership patterns by race in 1880.

55. See Table 4, Appendix. For similar findings that a majority of black household heads worked as laborers, not as sharecroppers, see, for Piedmont Virginia, James R. Irwin, "Farmers and Laborers: A Note on Occupations in the Postbellum South" *AH* 64 (1990), 53–60; James R. Irwin and Anthony P. O'Brien, "Where Have All the Sharecroppers

Gone?: Black Occupations in Postbellum Mississippi," *AH* 72 (1998), 280–97; Robert Tracy McKenzie, *One South or Many? Plantation Belt and Upcountry in Civil War–Era Tennessee* (New York, 1994), 135–41.

56. For a more detailed discussion of the labor of women and children on farms, see Chapter 5.

57. Robert P. Brooks, *The Agrarian Revolution in Georgia, 1865–1912* (Madison, Wis., 1914), 65; Kenneth Coleman, ed., "How to Run a Middle Georgia Cotton Plantation in 1885: A Document," *AH* 42 (1968), 57–58. See also Robert Preston Brooks, "A Local Study of the Race Problem," *Political Science Quarterly* 26 (1911), 193–221; E. M. Banks, *The Economics of Land Tenure in Georgia* (New York, 1905), 80–81. Harold D. Woodman, *New South — New Law* (Baton Rouge, La., 1995), surpasses earlier studies of the legal status of various types of tenants.

58. For example, Jay R. Mandle, *The Roots of Black Poverty: The Southern Plantation Economy after the Civil War* (Durham, N.C., 1977).

59. Richard Holcombe Kilbourne Jr., *Debt, Investment, Slaves: Credit Relations in East Feliciana Parish, Louisiana, 1825–1885* (Tuscaloosa, Ala., 1995); Harold Woodman, *King Cotton and His Retainers: Financing and Marketing the South's Cotton Crop, 1800–1925* (Lexington, Ky., 1968); Jaynes, *Branches without Roots;* Ralph Shlomowitz, "Planter Combinations and Black Labour in the American South, 1865–1880," *Slavery and Abolition* 9 (1988), 72–84.

60. Gavin Wright, "American Agriculture and the Labor Market: What Happened to Proletarianization?" *AH* 62 (1988), 182–209.

61. Brooks, *Agrarian Revolution,* 42, 53, 30. See also W. Fitzhugh Brundage, "A Portrait of Southern Sharecropping: The 1911–1912 Georgia Plantation Survey of Robert Preston Brooks," *GHQ* 77 (1993), 367–81.

62. "Thoughts for the Month," *Southern Cultivator* 35 (1877), 1, quoted in Ralph Shlomowitz, " 'Bound' or 'Free'? Black Labor in Cotton and Sugarcane Farming, 1865–1880," *JSH* 50 (1984), 573.

63. George K. Holmes, "Peons of the South," *Annals of the American Academy of Political and Social Science* 4 (1893), 264–75. For a more comprehensive discussion, including the historiography of southern "peonage," see J. William Harris, "The Question of Peonage in the History of the New South," in *Plain Folk of the New South,* ed. Samuel Hyde (Baton Rouge, La., 1997), 100–125.

64. For an argument that merchants were monopolists, see Ransom and Sutch, *One Kind of Freedom,* 128–32, 237–43; quotation "in practice . . ." is from Nell Irvin Painter, *The Exodusters: Black Migration to Kansas after Reconstruction* (New York, 1977), 58–59. The actual amount of effective interest is a matter of considerable dispute, but could clearly go as high as 50 percent. On the general operations of the lien system, see M. B. Hammond, "The Southern Farmer and the Cotton Question," *Political Science Quarterly* 12 (1897), and C. Vann Woodward, *Origins of the New South: 1877–1913* (Baton Rouge, La., 1951), 180–84, both of which are very critical of the lien system. Woodman, *New South — New Law,* 28–66, and Thomas B. Clark, "The Furnishing and Supply System in Southern Agriculture since 1865," *JSH* 12 (1946), 24–44, are more inclined to see the system as a necessary response to circumstances.

65. Matthew B. Hammond, *The Cotton Industry: An Essay in American Economic*

History (New York, 1897), 143; Lacy K. Ford, "Rednecks and Merchants: Economic Development and Social Tensions in the South Carolina Upcountry, 1865–1900," *JAH* 71 (1984), 294–318; Woodman, *New South — New Law,* 50; Charles Otken, *The Ills of the South* (1894), 24, 36. In a pioneering study of African American farmers in North Carolina, Sharon Holt shows how many of these farmers used credit from local merchants or landlords to finance their slow and painstaking rise to landownership: Sharon Holt, "Making Freedom Pay: Freedpeople Working for Themselves, North Carolina, 1865–1900," *JSH* 60 (May 1994), 229–62. The question of "peonage" is discussed at greater length in Chapter 2.

66. Gill Insong, "Furnishing Merchants and the Rural Credit Market of the American South: Alabama, 1870–1920" (Ph.D. diss., Yale University, 1990); Georgia *Gazetteer and Business Directory* (1881) (including all listings for "general stores"); "Mississippi," 21:118D (Warren and Washington Counties); "Georgia," 15:78, 105 (Greene Co.); "Georgia," 31:107 (Taliaferro Co.), R. G. Dun.

67. An example of a long-time plantation county is Taliaferro; of a county with poorer soil, Glascock; of a county on the northern edge of the antebellum cotton belt, Hart. In 1879, the percentage of white farmers raising cotton in these counties was 95 percent or greater in all three. See Table 3, Appendix. For a general and more technical analysis of agricultural developments in this area, see J. William Harris, "Crop Choices in the Piedmont before and after the Civil War," *JEH* 54 (1994), 526–42.

68. For Miller's story, see J. William Harris, "Portrait of a Yeoman Slaveholder: The Journal of Benton Miller," *GHQ* 74 (1990), 1–19. Most of the account below of Miller's farming activities is based on his journal, on microfilm, GDAH. For the year 1875 Miller apparently simply rented out the new land to another man, and took no active role in operating the farm. The daily entries for the postwar period begin on a regular basis on 1 January 1876.

69. For cotton production on small farms, see Tables 3 and 7, Appendix.

70. Tax Digest, 1882, for Hancock County, on microfilm, GDAH; U.S. Bureau of the Census, *Tenth Census, 1880. Agriculture,* 43. The census definition of a farm required a plot of at least three acres or marketable produce worth at least $100. The 1880 census reported no black-owned farms in the county with less than four acres of improved land.

71. Cotton production in the Piedmont is shown in Chart 5, Appendix. The wealthiest 10 percent of real estate holders owned about the same proportion of all real estate in 1870 (the last year the census reported these figures) as in 1860. For example, in Taliaferro County in 1860, the wealthiest 10 percent of white household heads owned 51 percent of all the real estate value in the county; in 1870, the same proportion of whites owned 46 percent of the real estate. Similar continuities can be found in Glascock County (53 percent of all real property in 1860, 46 percent in 1870) and Hart County (51 percent in 1860, 49 percent in 1870). These figures are based on samples from the 1860 and 1870 U.S. Census manuscripts for the three counties.

72. The trends are summarized in Chart 6, Appendix. The quotation from Hart County is from Hilgard, *Report on Cotton,* 1:348. The change in the upcountry is analyzed in David F. Weiman, "The Economic Emancipation of the Non-Slaveholding Class: Upcountry Farmers in the Georgia Cotton Economy," *JEH* 45 (1985), 71–93; and for the Georgia Piedmont as a whole in Harris, "Crop Choices."

73. Journal of Benton Miller, 19 April, 20 May, 3 September 1876; 3 March 1877; 28 October 1876, GDAH. For an estimate of Miller's farm income, see Harris, "Portrait."

74. Journal of Benton Miller, 7 April, 13 May, 3 November 1877, GDAH. The entries in the diary for the fall of 1877 became shorter and shorter; the final one is for November 11. Thus it is impossible to know with precision what his production or income was for the year. On Benton Miller's political activities, see Chapter 3.

75. George P. Collins to Anne Cameron Collins, 23 and 25 January, 7 and 15 February 1876, Anne (Cameron) Collins Papers, SHC. See also Sidney Nathans, " 'Gotta Mind to Move, a Mind to Settle Down': Afro-Americans and the Plantation Frontier," in *A Master's Due: Essays in Honor of David Herbert Donald*, ed. William J. Cooper Jr., Michael F. Holt, and John McCardell (Baton Rouge, La., 1985), 204–22. Quotation about "sufficiency of labor" is from Coleman, ed., "How to Run a Middle Georgia Cotton Plantation."

76. George Collins to Anne Cameron Collins, 15 February, 27 February 1876, 24 February 1876, Collins Papers, UNC.

77. George Collins to Anne Cameron Collins, 19 August, 28 August, and 30 September 1866, 9 February 1867; George Collins to Mrs. Paul Cameron, 6 January 1872; George Collins to Anne Cameron Collins, 15 June, 22 June, and 27 June 1872, 23 November, 30 November, and 11 December 1873, Collins Papers, SHC; Nathans, "Gotta Mind to Move," 209.

78. Robert L. Brandfon, *Cotton Kingdom of the New South: A History of the Yazoo-Mississippi Delta from Reconstruction to the Twentieth Century* (Cambridge, Mass., 1967), 22–32; Hilgard, *Report on Cotton*, 2:73–76, 241–47. Hilgard's report noted that "taken as whole, the plant-food percentages in this soil are probably unexcelled by any soil in the world thus far examined" (246).

79. Henry T. Ireys, "County Seats and Early Railroads," *Papers of the Washington County Historical Society* (read in 1915), 310, 322. Antebellum planting in the Delta is discussed in John Hebron Moore, *The Emergence of the Cotton Kingdom in the Old Southwest: Mississippi, 1770–1860* (Baton Rouge, La., 1988).

80. "High Water and Low," in Breckenridge Family Reminiscences, SHC; Memphis *Daily Appeal* 30 April 1886 (I am grateful to information provided by E. M. Beck and Stewart E. Tolnay for this citation); Joe Rice Dockery Oral History (OH 80-12), MDAH. In more mundane prose the U.S. Department of Agriculture's *Report of the Commissioner of Agriculture, 1878*, made the same point: "A private citizen can at great expense protect his river front or levee; but suppose his neighbor is unable to protect his equally well, the neglect of his neighbor, yes, neighbors for miles, will visit him with as great a loss as would have resulted from his own neglect." Quoted in Ralph Shlomowitz, "Plantations and Smallholdings: Comparative Perspectives from the World Cotton and Sugar Cane Economies, 1865–1939," *AH* 58 (1984), 11 n. 33. There is a fascinating account of what is probably the same lynching by a black eyewitness in Alan Lomax, *The Land Where the Blues Began* (New York, 1993), 219–21.

81. Walter Sillers, "Flood Control in Bolivar County, 1838–1924," *JMH* 9 (1947), 3–20; Robert W. Harrison, "The Formative Years of the Yazoo-Mississippi Delta Levee District," *JMH* 13 (1951), 236–48.

82. Sillers, "Flood Control"; Brandfon, *Cotton Kingdom*, 22–32. See Christopher

Morris, *Becoming Southern: Warren County and Vicksburg, Mississippi, 1760-1860* (New York, 1994), 140-43, for antebellum attempts to build levees in Warren County.

83. Robert W. Harrison, *Alluvial Empire*. Vol. 1: *A Study of State and Local Efforts Toward Land Development in the Alluvial Valley of the Lower Mississippi River; Including Flood Control, Land Drainage, Land Clearing, Land Forming* (Little Rock, Ark., 1961), 95-112; Harrison, "Formative Years"; Brandfon, *Cotton Kingdom*, 39-64.

84. Sillers, "Flood Control"; Brandfon, *Cotton Kingdom*, chap. 3; George Collins to Anne Cameron Collins, 3 June 1882, Collins Papers, SHC.

85. Brandfon, *Cotton Kingdom*; Harrison, *Alluvial Empire*. The earliest federal efforts came under the guise of aid to "navigation."

86. Brandfon, *Cotton Kingdom*, 39-64; Willie D. Halsell, "Migration into, and Settlement of LeFlore County in the Later Periods, 1876-1920," *JMH* 10 (1948), 250; James W. Silver, "Paul Bunyan Comes to Mississippi," *JMH* 19 (1957), 93-119. Watson should not be confused with the famous Populist politician of the same name.

87. Ireys, "County Seats," 319; Brandfon, *Cotton Kingdom*, 65-90.

88. Harrison, *Alluvial Empire*, 103-6; Harrison, "Early Years."

89. Brandfon, *Cotton Kingdom*, 65-90. The branch to Ruleville was first named the Yazoo Delta; when the locals saw the Y.D. painted on its distinctive yellow engines, they dubbed it the Yellow Dog, a name later made famous by blues singers: Marie M. Hemphill, *Fevers, Floods, and Faith: A History of Sunflower County, Mississippi 1844-1976* (Indianola, Miss., 1980), 253-60.

90. Hilgard, *Report on Cotton*, 1:3; the estimate of the costs of picking cotton is based on information in Hilgard, 1:356-57. Merritt Williams data from Manuscript Returns, Tenth Census, 1880, for Washington County.

91. James Robertshaw, "Greenville in Its Early Days," *Papers of the Washington County Historical Society*, 86-87; Harrison, *Alluvial Empire*, 107.

92. Average farm size in Sunflower was 67 improved acres; in Washington, 226 improved acres; see Table 5, Appendix.

93. Ruby Sheppeard Hicks, *The Song of the Delta* (Jackson, Miss., 1976), 5, 12, 19.

94. Hemphill, *Fevers, Floods*, 141; Hicks, *Song of the Delta*, 33-34. The psychological effects are evident often in George Collins's letters to his wife.

95. Hicks, *Song of the Delta*, 23; Sunflower *Tocsin*, 12 July 1889, quoted in Hemphill, *Fevers, Floods*, 140; Nathans, "Gotta Mind to Move," 211-12; Hortense Powdermaker, *After Freedom: A Cultural Study in the Deep South* (New York, 1939; reprint, Madison, Wis., 1993), 96-106, 111-12 (Powdermaker, who recorded these stories in the 1930s, does not name her informants); and, on Mound Bayou, Janet Sharp Hermann, *The Pursuit of a Dream* (New York, 1981); Kenneth Marvin Hamilton, *Black Towns and Profit: Promotion and Development in the Trans-Appalachian West, 1877-1915* (Urbana, Ill., 1991), 43-98. See Table 6, Appendix, for acreages and commercial crop production on white and black farms in the Delta, and Chart 5, Appendix, for overall trends in cotton production in the Delta.

96. Hemphill, *Fevers, Floods*, 403-5, 407-8; Joe Rice Dockery Oral History, MDAH.

97. William F. Holmes, "Labor Agents and the Georgia Exodus, 1899-1900," *South Atlantic Quarterly* 79 (1980), 436-48. Wages for various places and tasks are reported in Hilgard, *Report on Cotton*, 1:438; 2:355-57. Additional evidence for the existence of

large plantations in Washington County is presented in Irwin and O'Brien, "Where Have All the Sharecroppers Gone?"

98. George Collins to Anne Cameron Collins, 6 March 1877, 15 February 1879, Collins Papers, SHC; Nathans, "Gotta Mind to Move," 207–8.

99. Ira Berlin et al., eds., *The Wartime Genesis of Free Labor: The Lower South,* vol. 3 in *Freedom: A Documentary History of Emancipation, 1861–1867* (New York, 1990), 334; Eric Foner, "The Meaning of Freedom in the Age of Emancipation," *JAH* 81 (1994), 459.

100. James Roark, *Masters without Slaves: Southern Planters in the Civil War and Reconstruction* (New York, 1977), 116; Wright, *Old South, New South.*

101. Swan, *Structure and Profitability of the Antebellum Rice Industry,* found that rice farms with fewer than five slaves consistently lost money, and only those with more than fifteen slaves were consistently profitable. For shares of crops in each region grown by big and small producers, see Table 7, Appendix.

102. Morgan, "Work and Culture," 595; Thomas Armstrong, "From Task Labor to Free Labor: The Transition along Georgia's Rice Coast, 1820–1880," *GHQ* 64 (1980), 432–47. See Chart 4, Appendix, for trends in production levels. The drop in production is sometimes attributed to new competition from western rice lands, but this competition, while real, was still too small before 1880 to account for the drop-off in the South Atlantic. For example, production in Louisiana in 1879 amounted to 21 million pounds, less than one-fifth of national production and little more than a third of Georgia's own production in 1859. Foreign competition had indeed driven U.S. rice from European markets, but this had been true even before the war, and a high tariff protected U.S. producers on the home market.

103. Harris, "Crop Choices"; Gilbert Fite, "The Agricultural Trap in the South," *AH* 60 (1986), 38–50; Brooks, *Agrarian Revolution.*

104. Mark R. Schultz, "The Dream Realized? African American Landownership in Central Georgia between Reconstruction and World War Two," *AH* 72 (1998), 298–312.

105. Tables 8 and 9, Appendix, show occupations and farmer status for African Americans in each region.

106. Delta farms operated by black farmers yielded four times as much cotton as similar Piedmont farms on just one-third more planted acres. The detailed data are displayed in Table 10. The samples are relatively small and based on few counties, so small differences between regions (for example, in farm size in the Delta and the Piedmont) may not reflect realities for all farms in the regions.

107. In samples of African American farmers in Washington and Sunflower Counties, twenty-one owners planted 53.4 percent of improved acres in cotton, thirty-three renters 58.9 percent, and seven sharecroppers 53.6 percent. The sample is described in the Essay on Sources.

108. These examples were taken from the sample of farmers in 1880 described in the Essay on Sources.

Chapter 2   "A White Man's Country"

1. Atlanta *Constitution,* 2 December 1888. More detailed reports appear in local weekly papers, for example, *GHJ,* 7 December 1888, an account that was in turn largely

taken from one in the Elberton *Star.* The details of the *GHJ* account and the one in the Atlanta *Constitution* do not fully agree. According to the *GHJ,* the two men lynched were Tim (not Tom) Smith and his brother Jim Smith. I have followed the attributions given in W. Fitzhugh Brundage, *Lynching in the New South: Georgia and Virginia, 1880–1930* (Urbana, Ill., 1993), 271.

2. Atlanta *Constitution,* 2 December 1888; *GHJ,* quoting Elberton *Star,* 7 December 1888.

3. Hortense Powdermaker, *After Freedom: A Cultural Study in the Deep South* (New York, 1939; reprint, Madison, Wis., 1993), 372.

4. For overviews of the legal issues in the South in general and in Mississippi and Georgia in particular, see William Cohen, *At Freedom's Edge: Black Mobility and the Southern White Quest for Racial Control, 1861–1915* (Baton Rouge, 1991); Jennifer Roback, "Southern Labor Law in the Jim Crow Era: Exploitative or Competitive?" *University of Chicago Law Review* 51 (1984), 1161–92; Harold D. Woodman, *New South, New Law* (Baton Rouge, La., 1995); Steven W. Engerrand, "'Now Scratch or Die': The Genesis of Capitalist Agricultural Labor in Georgia, 1865–1880" (Ph.D. diss., University of Georgia, 1981).

5. Christopher Hanes, "Turnover Costs and the Distribution of Slave Labor in Anglo-America," *JEH* 56 (1996), 307–29.

6. A convenient source for these laws is the appendix to Cohen, *At Freedom's Edge.*

7. For Greene County in 1874, see Jonathon M. Bryant, *How Curious a Land: Conflict and Change in Greene County, Georgia, 1850–1885* (Chapel Hill, N.C., 1996), 157–58, and for Mississippi, see Nell Irvin Painter, *The Exodusters: Black Migration to Kansas after Reconstruction* (New York, 1977). The affected counties in Georgia in 1899–1900 included Oglethorpe, Morgan, and Greene, as well as several further to the west and north. *GHJ,* 12 and 19 January 1900; William F. Holmes, "Labor Agents and the Georgia Exodus, 1899–1900," *South Atlantic Quarterly* 79 (1980), 436–48.

8. Harry Hodgson, "A Great Farmer at Work," *World's Work* 9 (1905), 5723–33.

9. E. A. Angier, Atlanta, to Attorney General, 30 July and 3 December 1903, reel 1, frame 657 ff, *Peonage Files; GHJ,* 14 July 1894; John Dittmer, *Black Georgia in the Progressive Era, 1900–1920* (Urbana, Ill., 1977), 77–80; E. Merton Coulter, *James Monroe Smith, Georgia Planter, before Death and After* (Athens, Ga., 1961). Coulter tries, none too successfully, to defend Smith from charges of peonage.

10. Coulter, *James Monroe Smith,* 93–100, 150–63.

11. Mentha Morrison, "Col.," Lavonia, Ga., to "Mr. President," 22 October 1903, reel 1, frames 610–11; C. D. Camp to E. A. Angier, 28 November 1903, ibid., frames 642–54, both in *Peonage Files;* Ulrich B. Phillips, "Plantations with Slave Labor and Free," *American Historical Review* 30 (1925), 738–53. Phillips's best-known work on slavery is *American Negro Slavery: A Survey of the Supply, Employment, and Control of Negro Labor as Determined by the Plantation Regime* (New York, 1919).

12. *GHJ,* 17 September 1886. The farm had sixty-eight black and four white prisoners. For convict leasing in Mississippi and Georgia, see David M. Oshinsky, *"Worse Than Slavery": Parchman Farm and the Ordeal of Jim Crow Justice* (New York, 1996); Alex Lichtenstein, *Twice the Work of Free Labor: The Political Economy of Convict Labor in the New South* (London, 1996).

13. *GHJ*, 23 August 1893. The next year Louise Barnhart, the dead convict's wife, won $750 in damages from L. J. Boswell in "probably the most noted civil case that has come before the Greene county court for five years past." *GHJ*, 24 February 1894. These reports do not identify Barnhart's race.

14. Indianola *Enterprise*, 19 December 1902.

15. Oglethorpe *Echo*, 13 February 1881; *GHJ*, 9 November 1888.

16. Bryant, *How Curious a Land*, 157–58; Holmes, "Labor Agents," 444.

17. Columbia County Justice of the Peace Minutes, 1897–1902 (129th militia district), microfilmed with the records of the County Ordinary, GDAH; Hancock County, County Court Minutes, 1896–1904, GDAH; Edward L. Ayers, *Vengeance and Justice: Crime and Punishment in the Nineteenth-Century American South* (New York, 1984), 324 n. 7. For similar findings for other Georgia counties, see Engerrand, "Now Scratch or Die," 192–222.

18. Monthly Reports of the Misdemeanor Chain Gangs, 1898–1901, GDAH. The reports are for February 1901, from Burke, Elbert, Greene, Wilkes, and Oglethorpe in the Piedmont, with the latter two reporting two camps each; and for March 1901, from Hancock in the Piedmont. The Elbert and Burke reports did not list crimes of the convicts, but both counties do list crimes on earlier reports, and the pattern is the same. For example, in November of 1899 the Elbert and Burke camps together held fifty-six prisoners, none of whom had been convicted of vagrancy.

19. Georgia's late-nineteenth-century tax records make it possible to trace landlord-tenant relationships on a year-to-year basis because black farmers and farmworkers who did not own their land (that is, the vast majority) are listed according to their employer or landlord. The exact rate for Glascock County depends on how it is measured. Seventy-one percent of black tenants and laborers in 1868 were not working for the same employers in 1870. If we eliminate employers who appear in the 1868 records, but not the 1870 records, 52 percent of 1868 tenants and wage hands were not employed by the same person in 1870. The comparable percentages for the period from 1878 to 1880 are 57 percent and 51 percent. The figures for Liberty and Lincoln Counties are from Engerrand, "Now Scratch or Die," 175–92. Engerrand used the same sources as I used for Glascock County. These turnover rates are quite comparable to estimates of the annual turnover among industrial workers in the Northeast in the same time period: Daniel T. Rodgers, "Tradition, Modernity, and the American Industrial Worker: Reflections and Critique," *JAH* (1977), 663. For a more general discussion, see J. William Harris, "The Question of Peonage in the History of the New South," in *Plain Folk of the South Revisited*, ed. Samuel C. Hyde Jr. (Baton Rouge, La., 1997), 100–125.

20. 30 November 1881, 11 July 1882, 7 December 1878, 20 December 1878, 24 and 25 January 1879, Newstead Plantation Journal, SHC.

21. Newstead Plantation Journal, 14 January 1880, 4 February 1881, 29 December 1881, 11 July 1882.

22. George Collins to Anne Cameron Collins, 10 January 1880, 26 October 1880, 28 April 1882, 27 June 1882, 1 July 1882, 3 November 1882, 7 November 1882, Collins Papers, SHC.

23. Clive Metcalf Diary, SHC, 19, 21, and 31 December 1888; 1 January 1890.

24. Metcalf Diary, 8 and 9 January 1891; 31 December 1892.

25. Metcalf Diary, 3 January 1890; Freeman & Bowdre to Paul Cameron, 13 August 1886, Cameron Papers, SHC; Metcalf Diary, 11 May 1890.

26. Robert Preston Brooks, "A Local Study of the Race Problem," *Political Science Quarterly* 26 (1911), 214; George Collins to Anne Collins, 9 December 1880, Collins Papers.

27. Woodman, *New South, New Law,* 41–42; Cohen, *At Freedom's Edge,* 232; Engerrand, "Now Scratch or Die," 136–37. The Supreme Court invalidated an Alabama statute in *Bailey v. Alabama* in 1911; see Pete Daniel, *Shadow of Slavery: Peonage in the South, 1901–1969* (Urbana, Ill., 1972), chap. 4. See also Pete Daniel, "The Legal Basis of Agrarian Capitalism: The South since 1890," in *Race and Class in the American South since 1890,* ed. Melvyn Stokes and Rick Halpern (Oxford, 1994), 79–102.

28. See Charts 7 and 8, Appendix, for a summary of trends in lynchings in each area. Among the most useful of a growing number of studies of lynching in the New South are Brundage, *Lynching in the New South,* and Stewart E. Tolnay and E. M. Beck, *A Festival of Violence: An Analysis of Southern Lynchings, 1882–1930* (Urbana, Ill., 1995). I am grateful to Beck and Tolnay for sharing with me their comprehensive list of confirmed lynchings in Georgia and Mississippi, which forms the basis for the summary statistics reported here.

29. William F. Holmes, "Whitecapping: Agrarian Violence in Mississippi, 1902–1906," *JSH* 35 (1969), 165–85.

30. Oglethorpe *Echo,* 16 and 23 February 1894. The four included "one of the county's most progressive and prosperous young farmers," a manager in a local mill, and a clerk.

31. Oglethorpe *Echo,* 15 July 1887.

32. *SI,* 14 June 1889. On violence, honor, and the courts, see especially Ayers, *Vengeance and Justice.* Among Ayers's three county case studies is Greene County in the eastern Piedmont.

33. *SI,* 31 May 1889.

34. William F. Holmes, *The White Chief: James Kimble Vardaman* (Baton Rouge, La., 1970), 37. On the connection between sexual fears and racial violence, see Joel Williamson, *The Crucible of Race: Black-White Relations in the American South since Emancipation* (New York, 1984).

35. Mrs. L. H. Harris, "A Southern Woman's View," *Independent,* 18 May 1899, 1354–55. Harris lived in Rockmart, Georgia, in the upper Piedmont, rather than the lower eastern Piedmont, but I have quoted her here because she represents a rare public voice of a white woman. A more prominent voice expressing many of the same ideas was that of Rebecca Latimer Felton, one of the pioneers of Georgia's woman suffrage movement: see Williamson, *Crucible of Race,* 124–30.

36. Atlanta *Constitution,* 4 June 1888. This confession seems so improbable that it was probably, if not a complete fabrication, tortured out of the victim.

37. Elberton *Star,* 2 May 1901 (Robert Smith was apparently not killed); James C. Cobb, *The Most Southern Place on Earth: The Mississippi Delta and the Roots of Regional Identity* (New York, 1992), 104–5. For cases in which blacks received fair treatment in the courts, see instances cited in Woodman, *New South, New Law,* 82–85; Christopher Waldrep, "Substituting Law for the Lash: Emancipation and Legal Formalism in a Mississippi County Court," *JAH* 82 (1996), 1425–51.

38. Bryant, *How Curious a Land,* 90–140.

39. Ibid., 132–33; *Report of the Joint Select Committee to Inquire into the Condition of Affairs in the late Insurrectionary States,* 13 vols. (Washington, D.C., 1872), *House Reports,* 42d Congress, 2d sess., no. 22, Georgia, 696–705.

40. Allen W. Trelease, *White Terror: The Ku Klux Klan Conspiracy and Southern Reconstruction* (New York, 1971), 226–39. From 1868 to 1870 the Republican vote in the eastern Georgia Piedmont fell from 12,118 to 9,081. In Oglethorpe the drop was from 1,144 to 365; in Warren from 1,124 to 462.

41. The political history of Reconstruction in Mississippi is covered in detail in William C. Harris, *The Day of the Carpetbagger: Republican Reconstruction in Mississippi* (Baton Rouge, La., 1979).

42. Harris, *Day of the Carpetbagger,* 634–36, 645–49, 661–62, 671–72.

43. In 1872 in the Delta counties, Grant won by a margin of 17,390 to 3,594; in 1876 the Republican Rutherford Hayes lost by 8,396 to 13,967.

44. Russell Duncan, *Freedom's Shore: Tunis Campbell and the Georgia Freedmen* (Athens, Ga., 1986); Joseph P. Reidy, "Aaron A. Bradley: Voice of Black Labor in the Georgia Lowcountry," in *Southern Black Leaders of the Reconstruction Era,* ed. Howard N. Rabinowitz (Urbana, Ill., 1982), 281–308.

45. Duncan, *Freedom's Shore,* 42–75; lists of representatives and senators for all Georgia counties since their creation are published in the *Georgia Official and Statistical Register,* an annual publication of the Georgia Secretary of State.

46. Duncan, *Freedom's Shore* (quotation p. 88).

47. Ibid., 76–110; Albert Colbey Smith, "Down Freedom's Road: The Contours of Race, Class, and Property Crime in Black-Belt Georgia, 1866–1910" (Ph.D. diss., University of Georgia, 1982), 295.

48. See Chart 11 for voting trends in the eastern Piedmont as a whole, and Charts 9 and 10 for trends in Greene County in national and local elections. On the continuing salience of the Republican vote in the South, see J. Morgan Kousser, *The Shaping of Southern Politics: Suffrage Restriction and the Establishment of the One-Party South, 1880–1920* (New Haven, Conn., 1974), chap. 1.

49. Frank A. Montgomery, *Reminiscences of a Mississippian in Peace and War* (Cincinnati, 1901), 268–69, 264, 279, 292.

50. Elberton *Star,* 6 June 1890; John Dollard, *Caste and Class in a Southern Town* (New Haven, Conn., 1937; reprint, Madison, Wis., 1988), 49; Powdermaker, *After Freedom,* 30.

51. Frederic Trautmann, ed. and trans., *Travels on the Lower Mississippi, 1879–1880. A Memoir by Ernst von Hesse-Wartegg* (Columbia, Mo., 1990), 65. On disfranchisement, see Chapters 3 and 6; on integrated neighborhoods, see Chapter 5; on Georgia's segregation statutes see Kenneth Coleman, ed., *A History of Georgia* (2d ed.; Athens, Ga., 1991), 247–49. Overall trends in lynchings in the South, which reached a peak in 1892, are summarized in Beck and Tolnay, *Festival of Violence,* 30. As Chart 7, Appendix, indicates, lynchings in the Delta were at their highest in the period 1883–87; in the Piedmont they were highest during 1888–92.

52. *GHJ* 30 July 1896; Williamson, *Crucible of Race.*

53. Systematic treatments of racial etiquette in the South date to the 1930s, including Bertram Wilbur Doyle, *The Etiquette of Race Relations in the South* (Chicago, 1937);

Dollard, *Caste and Class;* and Allison Davis, Burleigh Gardner, and Mary Gardner, *Deep South: A Social Anthropological Study of Caste and Class* (Chicago, 1941). A powerful examination by someone who grew up in and near the Delta in the 1920s is Richard Wright, "The Ethics of Living Jim Crow," in his *Uncle Tom's Children* (1940; reprint, New York, 1993), 1–15. The postmaster is cited in Neil R. Mcmillen, *Dark Journey: Black Mississippians in the Age of Jim Crow* (Urbana, Ill., 1989), 24. The quoted remark on the "ideal sphere" of honor is from Georg Simmel, *The Sociology of Georg Simmel,* trans. and ed. Kurt Wolff (Glencoe, Ill., 1950), 321, as quoted in Erving Goffman, "The Nature of Deference and Demeanor," in *Interaction Ritual: Essays in Face-to-Face Behavior* (Garden City, N.Y., 1967), 62–63. I have discussed the role of racial etiquette in somewhat greater depth in J. William Harris, "Etiquette, Lynching, and Racial Boundaries in Southern History: A Mississippi Example," *American Historical Review* 100 (1995), 387–410.

54. "In spite of their widespread uses as nurses and servants, there remains a strong feeling that the color of the Negroes is abhorrent and that contact with them may be contaminating": Davis et al., *Deep South,* 15–16. See also Harris, "Etiquette, Lynching, and Racial Boundaries," esp. 391–93, and, for a general treatment of the relationship between "purity" and social boundaries, Mary Douglas, *Purity and Danger: An Analysis of the Concepts of Pollution and Taboo* (London, 1966) .

55. Elberton *Star,* 6 June and 13 June 1890 (order of the first quotation has been reversed). Of 184 victims lynched in the Delta, eastern Piedmont, and Atlantic coast from 1883 to 1930, the most common accusations were murder (39 percent), rape or other sex-related crimes (24 percent), and other violent crimes (23 percent). The remaining 14 percent involved alleged property crimes (such as arson or burglary) or actions that were not crimes at all, such as violations of proper etiquette.

56. New Orleans *Daily Picayune,* 20 November 1888 (since Arnold had turned himself into the sheriff and claimed self-defense, this description must obviously not be taken literally); ibid., 21 October 1896; ibid., 8 December 1890.

57. *GHJ,* 4 August 1899 (quoting "Two Racial Questions" from the Oglethorpe *Echo*); "Governor Vardaman's Inaugural," *Current Literature* 36 (1904), 271.

58. W. Fitzhugh Brundage, "The Darien 'Insurrection' of 1899: Black Protest during the Nadir of Race Relations," *GHQ* 74 (1990), 234–53.

59. Ibid.; Smith, "Down Freedom's Road," 295. The county's political tradition is discussed in Chapter 3, below.

60. Oglethorpe *Echo,* 18 March 1881; H. O. Johnson to Mr. Ed. Angier, 14 January 1898, in *Peonage Files,* reel 1, frame 1; Atlanta *Journal,* 21 April 1898; Record of Indictment, 19 April 1898, reel 1, frames 10–19; E. A. Angier to Attorney General, 19 April 1898, r. 1 f. 20, *Peonage Files.* The best general treatment of peonage in the South and of the federal efforts to repress it is Daniel, *Shadow of Slavery.* W. E. B. Du Bois, in his well-known 1901 study of black landowners in Georgia, singled out the county as one in which "the system of peonage has been widespread." W. E. B. Du Bois, *The Negro Landholder of Georgia,* U.S. Department of Labor, Bulletin 35 (1901), 750.

61. Evelyn Brooks Higginbotham, *Righteous Discontent: The Women's Movement in the Black Baptist Church, 1880–1920* (Cambridge, Mass., 1993), 114. See Chapters 3 and 6 for discussion of black political activities and protests.

62. The trials are reported in *GHJ,* 28 April 1893. The paper's report did not explicitly

link the two trials, which occurred on the same day. Similarly, Columbia County's superior court in 1902 and 1903 saw a single prosecution for "enticing away a cropper" and one for buying seed (i.e., unginned) cotton; the defendant in the first case was not indicted; in the second, found not guilty. Columbia County Superior Court Minutes, 1897–1908, microfilm in GDAH. For the difficulty of using local courts to repress blacks in Reconstruction Mississippi, see Christopher Waldrep, *Roots of Disorder: Race and Criminal Justice in the American South, 1817–80* (Urbana and Chicago, 1998); Waldrep, "Substituting Law for the Lash." For another example see Bryant, *How Curious a Land,* 158.

63. James Scott, *Weapons of the Weak: Everyday Forms of Peasant Resistance* (New Haven, Conn., 1992); Coulter, *James Monroe Smith,* 48–49. See also Albert C. Smith, "'Southern Violence' Reconsidered: Arson as Protest in Black-Belt Georgia, 1865–1910," *JSH* 51 (1985), 527–64. For an analysis of urban African Americans drawing on Scott's work, see Robin D. G. Kelley, "'We Are Not What We Seem': Rethinking Black Working-Class Opposition in the Jim Crow South," *Journal of American History* 80 (1993), 75–112.

64. Holmes, "Labor Agents," 441.

65. Quoted in Cobb, *Most Southern Place,* 126.

66. "Governor Vardaman's Inaugural," 271.

67. This kind of thinking affected even white "reformers" who recognized some of the terrible injustices suffered by African Americans in the South. One of the most famous of these, Edgar Gardener Murphy of Alabama, once told a northern journalist that he regretted not being able to invite an "exceptional" black man like Booker T. Washington to dinner, even when he was visiting in New Haven, Connecticut. For if he invited Washington to dinner, he would have to invite also Washington's wife, which might lead to a return invitation, which might in turn lead to visits of children back and forth, and so on. "Where do you draw the line? Can you draw it, unless you keep all negroes behind it?" Quoted in Louis Harlan, *Booker T. Washington: The Wizard of Tuskegee* (New York, 1983), 306.

Chapter 3   The Populist Challenge

1. *GHJ,* 29 September, 6 October 1894.

2. On Miller before the war, see J. William Harris, "Portrait of a Small Slaveholder: The Journal of Benton Miller," *GHQ* 74 (1990), 1–19, and J. William Harris, "The Organization of Work on a Yeoman Slaveholder's Farm," *AH* 64 (1990), 39–52; and for Miller's farming experience in the 1870s, see also Chapter 1.

3. This important point is emphasized in Gilbert Fite, "The Agricultural Trap in the South," *AH* 60 (1986), 38–50.

4. In the eastern Piedmont (as defined here) the population increased from 227,263 in 1880 to 250,591 in 1890; the number of farm owners increased from 7,591 to 7,695 in the same period. For comparison with a New England town where out-migration allowed farmers to sustain their operations, see Hal S. Barron, *Those Who Stayed Behind: Rural Society in Nineteenth-Century New England* (New York, 1984).

5. Benton Miller Journal, GDAH, 18, 19, 30 June and 1 July 1876.

6. *SI,* 22 April 1892, 6 May 1892. It is unfortunate that Miller's farm journal does not

extend into the Populist period, so that we could have his own analysis of and commentary on the movement.

7. Figures from McDuffie are from Randolph Dennis Werner, "Hegemony and Conflict: The Political Economy of a Southern Region, Augusta, Georgia, 1865–1895" (Ph.D. diss., University of Virginia, 1977), 242. Members for Taliaferro are recorded in Minutes of the Farmers' Alliance, Crawfordville, microfilm in GDAH, and officers for Greene listed in *GHJ*, 30 November 1888. Wealth values for Taliaferro and Greene are from the *Gazetteer of the State of Georgia*, 1888, which omitted people with less than $1,000 in taxable property and placed the rest in broad categories. See also Charles L. Flynn, *White Land, Black Labor: Caste and Class in Late-Nineteenth-Century Georgia* (Baton Rouge, La., 1983), 177.

8. Minutes of Farmers' Alliance, Crawfordville, 1 March 1890, 5 July 1890, 2 August 1890, 4 July 1891, 1 August 1891.

9. *GHJ*, 19 February 1892. On the history of the alliance, see especially Robert C. McMath Jr., *Populist Vanguard: A History of the Southern Farmers' Alliance* (Chapel Hill, N.C., 1975), and Theodore R. Mitchell, *Political Education in the Southern Farmers' Alliance, 1887–1900* (Madison, Wis., 1987). The Grange, or more formally the Order of the Patrons of Husbandry, was a farmers organization that combined the secret rituals common to fraternal groups such as the Masons with educational and social activities.

10. C. Vann Woodward, *Origins of the New South, 1877–1913* (Baton Rouge, La., 1951), 193; Minutes, Farmers' Alliance, Crawfordville, 31 January and 25 February 1891. For an analysis of alliance and Populist theory see, in addition to works cited previously, Bruce Palmer, *"Man over Money": The Southern Populist Critique of American Capitalism* (Chapel Hill, N.C., 1980).

11. Robert C. McMath Jr., *American Populism: A Social History, 1877–1898* (New York, 1993), 95–97; Farmers' Alliance Minutes, 1 June 1889. Membership in the Crawfordville alliance is reported in the "Quarterly Reports" appearing at the end of the volume with the minutes.

12. McMath, *Populist Vanguard*; Barton C. Shaw, *The Wool-Hat Boys: Georgia's Populist Party* (Baton Rouge, La., 1984), 23–27.

13. McMath, *American Populism*, 108–42.

14. Farmers' Alliance Minutes, Crawfordville, 21 May 1890; *GHJ*, 30 November 1888 and 12 September 1890.

15. William F. Holmes, "The Southern Farmers' Alliance and the Georgia Senatorial Election of 1890," *JSH* 50 (1984), 197–224; Shaw, *Wool-Hat Boys*, 30–42.

16. Jonathon M. Bryant, *How Curious a Land: Conflict and Change in Greene County, Georgia, 1850–1885* (Chapel Hill, N.C., 1996), 166–82, 192; Steven W. Wrigley, "The Triumph of Provincialism: Public Life in Georgia, 1898–1917" (Ph.D. diss., Northwestern University, 1986), 15. On southern Democrats at the state and national level, see Woodward, *Origins of the New South*.

17. *SI*, 8 October 1884, 25 November and 2 December 1887; 7 January 1887.

18. McMath, *American Populism*, 143–51, 157–60, quotation, p. 158; Farmers' Alliance Minutes, Crawfordville, 6 June 1891; C. Vann Woodward, *Tom Watson: Agrarian Rebel* (New York, 1938; reprint, New York, 1970), 169–72; *GHJ*, 30 June 1893.

19. *SI*, 13 September 1889; 4 April 1890.

20. *GHJ*, 7 September 1888, 14 September 1888, 18 July 1890, 11 April 1890. For the South as a whole, see also James Tice Moore, "Redeemers Reconsidered: Change and Continuity in the Democratic South, 1870–1900," *JSH* 44 (1978), 357–78.

21. For mixed praise and critique of Watson, see, e.g., *SI,* 17 July 1891 and 28 August 1891; *GHJ*, 28 August 1891, 13 November 1891 ("able, strong, temperate").

22. *GHJ*, 17 June 1892; *SI,* 2 and 9 September 1892.

23. *GHJ*, 14 July 1881, 19 January 1882, 25 December 1885. In Hancock County as well, three-fourths of the antiprohibition votes in 1886 came from the county seat of Sparta. *SI,* 12 February 1887. On Independents in the South as a whole, see Michael R. Hyman, *The Anti-Redeemers: Hill-Country Political Dissenters in the Lower South from Redemption to Populism* (Baton Rouge, La., 1990); Woodward, *Origins of the New South,* 75–106.

24. *GHJ*, 23 June 1881, 3 October 1884, 12 October 1882, 27 July 1882. See Chart 9, Appendix, for voting patterns in Greene County's local elections.

25. *GHJ*, 15 May 1891; McMath, *American Populism,* 143–47.

26. Such are the themes of numerous editorials and letters in the *GHJ* throughout the summer and fall of 1891, for example, *GHJ*, 21, 28 August, 18 September ("rule of the bayonet"), 29 May ("safety of property," quoting the Atlanta *Constitution*), 6 and 13 November 1891.

27. Diary "July 1, 1893–Aug 31, 1895," Walter Wray Papers, GHS; *GHJ*, 5 February 1892. Walter Wray was a Greene County farmer and Populist Party member. The first four pages of this diary volume include minutes of the Liberty Suballiance No. 1628 in the county. While the minutes are undated, the content of the meetings indicates they cover the period including 1892. Wray apparently used the volume to take up his diary entries starting in 1893. The diary itself for the early 1890s is missing.

28. *GHJ*, 19 February 1892, 8 April 1892. Others who spoke at the organization rally were Luther Young and J. T. Edmondson, both farmers worth between $1,000 and $2,000 in 1888. McWhorter's large planting operations are described in *GHJ*, 17 July 1885; the wealth of the other officers is from the Georgia *Gazetteer* for 1888.

29. McMath, *American Populism,* 160–62.

30. *GHJ*, 22 July 1892, 22 April 1892, 13 May 1892 (quoting the Macon *Telegraph*), 20 May 1892, 1 July 1892.

31. Tom Watson, "The Negro Question in the South," *Arena* 6 (1892), 542. (The essay also appeared in Watson's newspaper, published in Georgia, the *People's Party Paper,* 16 September 1892.)

32. Ibid., 543, 545, 547–49 (emphases in original).

33. *GHJ*, 16 September 1892. Pledger toured the area speaking on behalf of the Democratic Party; see Shaw, *Wool-Hat Boys,* 83.

34. *GHJ*, 11 November 1892. In the presidential race Harrison got 777 votes, Cleveland (Democrat), 684, and Weaver (Populist), 578. The Republicans did not run a candidate for Congress; the Populist candidate won by 250 votes.

35. *GHJ*, 21 July 1893.

36. *GHJ*, 27 January 1894.

37. *GHJ*, 19 May 1894

38. Ibid.

39. *GHJ*, 22 September 1894. See Shaw, *Wool-Hat Boys*, 118–20, for a comparison of Populist and Democratic appeals to black voters.

40. *GHJ*, 6 October 1894. See Charts 9 and 10, Appendix, for votes by party in local and national elections in Greene County.

41. *GHJ*, 29 September 1894, 20 October 1894. The White Plains correspondent replied that, though she was a Democrat, she preferred that, as a woman, she take no part in politics: *GHJ*, 27 October 1894.

42. Storey was writing under the name of "Democrat"; these comments are part of an exchange in the *GHJ* in October and November 1894 with a correspondent calling himself "True Blue." Some of the issues are missing. Quotations come from issues on 27 October, 10 November, and 24 November.

43. *GHJ*, 1 December 1894, 8 December 1894, 5 January 1895.

44. See Chart 11, Appendix, for votes by party in the eastern Piedmont region of Georgia.

45. See Chapter 1. For prices see Peter A. Coclanis, "Distant Thunder: The Creation of a World Market for Rice and the Transformations It Wrought," *American Historical Review* 98 (1993), 1075.

46. "Rice Lands," a typed MS by James T. Dent, apparently prepared for submission to *The Country Gentleman*, in part 5, HBP; Whitehall Plantation Accounts, typescript, GHS; Mart Stewart, *"What Nature Suffers to Groe": Life, Labor, and Landscape on the Georgia Coast, 1680–1920* (Athens, Ga., 1996), 193–97.

47. Mrs. Archibald C. McKinley to My Dear Nellie, 9 November 1898, Spalding Papers, GHS, reprinted in Robert L. Humphries, ed., *The Journal of Archibald C. McKinley* (Athens, Ga., 1991), 233–38; Dent, "Rice Lands."

48. F. B. Leigh, *Ten Years on a Georgia Plantation since the War* (London, 1883; reprint, New York, 1969), 263; Dent, "Rice Lands"; John Scott Strickland, " 'No More Mud Work': The Struggle for the Control of Labor and Production in Low Country South Carolina, 1863–1880," in *The Southern Enigma: Essays on Race, Class, and Folk Culture*, ed. Walter J. Fraser Jr., and Winfred B. Moore Jr. (Westport, Conn., 1983), 43–62.

49. For black officeholders, see Albert Colbey Smith, "Down Freedom's Road: The Contours of Race, Class, and Property Crime in Black-Belt Georgia, 1866–1910" (Ph.D. diss., University of Georgia, 1982), 295.

50. See Chart 12, Appendix, for trends in voting on the Georgia coast.

51. George Collins to Paul C. Cameron, 1 March 1882, Collins Papers, SHC; Clive Metcalf Diary, 18 March through 1 April 1890, microfilm in SHC.

52. Walter Sillers to Florence Sillers, 27 July 1892, quoted in Thomas N. Boschert, "The Politics of Expediency: Fusion in the Mississippi Delta, Late Nineteenth Century" (M.A. thesis, University of Mississippi, 1985), 172–73. On Sillers, see also Ellis Ray Branch, "Walter Sillers, Sr.: The Politics of a Southern Planter, 1890–1931" (M.A. thesis, Delta State University, 1975).

53. The Republicans won the Delta counties in 1884 by a margin of 8,821 to 7,524. The results, compared with 1876, suggest a fairly steady level of Republican turnout, together with greater ability to resist Democratic attempts to force blacks to vote Democratic. The political history of Mississippi in these years is covered well in Albert D. Kirwan, *Revolt of the Rednecks: Mississippi Politics, 1876–1925* (Lexington, Ky., 1951).

54. Boschert, "Politics of Expediency," chap. 3. In Coahoma, a similar battle raged between supporters of Friar's Point and Clarksdale.

55. Lewis Baker, *The Percys of Mississippi: Politics and Literature in the New South* (Baton Rouge, La., 1983), 3–21; Boschert, "Politics of Expediency," chap. 3.

56. R. J. Nugent to Walter Sillers, 22 February 1888, and Walter Sillers to Florence Sillers, 26 August 1890, in Walter Sillers Papers, Special Collections, Delta State University. See also Boschert, "Politics of Expediency," 128–32. One reason that young Walter Sillers was part of the anti-Scott faction in Bolivar was that Nugent was his brother-in-law.

57. Boschert, "Politics of Expediency," 105–44 (quotation p. 143, from the *New Coahomian,* 27 July 1889); Walter Sillers to Florence Sillers, 20 July 1892, Sillers Papers.

58. Boschert, "Politics of Expediency," 160–66. On the Mississippi Constitution of 1890, see J. Morgan Kousser, *The Shaping of Southern Politics: Suffrage Restriction and the Establishment of the One-Party South, 1880–1920* (New Haven, Conn., 1974), 139–45; Kirwan, *Revolt of the Rednecks,* 58–84.

59. Walter Sillers to Florence Sillers, 27 July 1892, Sillers Papers. This letter mentions that he had written to Burkitt.

60. Boschert, "Politics of Expediency," 194 (quoting the Friars Point *Coahomian* 29 July 1899), 174–75; Branch, "Walter Sillers, Sr.," 13. See Chart 13, Appendix, for voting patterns in the Delta.

61. *Wool Hat* (Gracewood, Ga.), 27 July 1892; Woodward, *Tom Watson,* 221.

62. *SI,* 9 September, 11 March, 8 April, and 29 April 1892.

63. *SI,* 16 September 1892. See also Shaw, *Wool-Hat Boys,* 82–83.

64. *SI,* 26 August 1892. See also Shaw, *Wool-Hat Boys,* 78–90; Charles Crowe, "Tom Watson, Populists, and Blacks Reconsidered," *Journal of Negro History* 60 (1970), 99–119.

65. *Wool Hat,* 22 October 1892; *SI,* 5 October 1894; *SI,* 21 October 1892. On voting in Augusta, see Woodward, *Tom Watson,* 241–42, and Shaw, *Wool-Hat Boys,* 75–77. (Shaw points out that in some counties Populists may also have engaged in election frauds.)

66. *SI,* 4 November 1892. In his well-known *Arena* article, Watson argued that "the question of social equality does not enter into the equation at all": Watson, "Negro Question," 550.

67. *Wool Hat,* 13 August 1892 (first quotation is from letter by R. S. Rowe of Burke County; the second is an editorial comment on the letter); Watson, "Negro Question," 549.

68. *GHJ,* 17 July 1885; Werner, "Hegemony and Conflict," 185; *GHJ,* 9 November 1888; entries for 24 February 1894, 18 June 1894, 20 June 1894, 1 August 1894, 12 November 1894, 30 December 1894, in Diary, Walter Wray Papers, GHS.

69. *SI,* 14 October 1892. See also Flynn, *White Land, Black Labor,* 115–49.

70. Flynn, *White Land, Black Labor,* 107–8; Thomas W. Kremm and Diane Neal, "Challenge to Subordination: Organized Black Agricultural Protest in South Carolina, 1886–1895," *South Atlantic Quarterly* 78 (1978), 98–112; Merl E. Reed, "The Augusta Textile Mills and the Strike of 1886," *Labor History* 14 (1973), 228–46; William F. Holmes, "The Leflore County Massacre and the Demise of the Colored Farmer's Alliance," *Phylon* 34 (1973), 267–74; William F. Holmes, "The Demise of the Colored Farmers' Alliance," *JSH* 41 (1975), 187–200. Holmes believes that as many as two dozen men in LeFlore may have been killed.

71. *SI*, 20 May 1892.

72. Robert M. Saunders, "The Transformation of Tom Watson, 1894–95," *GHQ* 54 (1970), 339–56; Shaw, *Wool-Hat Boys*, 149–53.

73. Shaw, *Wool-Hat Boys*, 153–61 (quotation p. 161); McMath, *American Populism*, 200–209. The vote total is that for the Populist ticket of Bryan and Watson. The Bryan-Sewell regular Democratic ticket won over 6.2 million votes. In 1892, the Populist candidate for president, James B. Weaver, had received 1,029,846 votes.

74. *GHJ*, 20 October 1894, 22 September 1894.

75. On the origins and history of these celebrations, which became more common, more important, and more formal in the early 1890s, see Gaines M. Foster, *Ghosts of the Confederacy: Defeat, the Lost Cause, and the Emergence of the New South, 1865 to 1913* (New York, 1987); Charles R. Wilson, *Baptized in Blood: The Religion of the Lost Cause, 1865–1920* (Athens, Ga., 1980); LeeAnn Whites, *The Civil War as a Crisis in Gender: Augusta, Georgia, 1860–1890* (Athens, Ga., 1995).

76. *GHJ*, 28 April 1893.

77. Ibid. For a similar address, see *GHJ*, 30 April 1896.

78. *GHJ*, 8 July 1892, 1 July 1892; *SI*, 6 May 1872 (quoting Senator John B. Gordon), 26 October 1894; *GHJ*, 8 April 1892.

79. Watson, "Negro Question," 550; *SI*, 14 August, 21 August 1891. For similar rhetoric from Senator Gordon in Richmond County, see Woodward, *Tom Watson*, 228.

80. *SI*, 7 November 1890, 29 April 1890.

81. Watson, "Negro Question," 549.

Chapter 4   Capital at Work, Capitalists at Play

1. J. Gordon, "Bear Hunting in the South," *Scribners Monthly*, October 1881, 857–63.

2. If evidence is needed that such hunting stories partook of the fictional, one could cite the diary of Vicksburg journalist Charles Ball, who in 1896 celebrated the acceptance of a story by *Outing* magazine: "Surely if I can write an acceptable account of a bear hunt (never went bear hunting in all my life) I can write as well on some subject I know something about." Charles Ball Diary, 8 October 1896 (microfilm in SHC).

3. Indianola *Enterprise*, 21 November 1902; Lewis Baker, *The Percys of Mississippi: Politics and Literature in the New South* (Baton Rouge, 1983), 25.

4. Cotton prices are from *Hist. Stat.*, table K-555. Improved acreages for each county are reported in the decennial reports of the U.S. Census of Agriculture.

5. H. G. Turner, "An Account of Runnymede Plantations. Leflore Co., Miss. Jan. 1916," and H. G. Turner, "Mississippi. LeFlore Co., Bledsoe plantation, 1913," both in Reports, Speeches, and Articles Relating to Farm Management, 1902–1920, entry 133, BAE.

6. M. A. Crosby, "Present Status of farm management work in Alabama and Mississippi," January 1915, in Reports, Speeches, and Articles Relating to Farm Management, 1902–1920, entry 133, BAE, quotation p. 6. In LeFlore County the number of white owners declined from 114 in 1900 to 110 in 1910; in Washington, from 134 to 127. In the Delta as a whole the number of white-owned farms increased by 6 percent while improved acreage increased by 25 percent. These acreage increases came in the face of the first arrival

of the boll weevil in the region, which led to a slight reduction in cotton production in the Delta during this decade. See Chart 5, Appendix.

7. Greenville *Times,* 29 September 1907; Indianola *Enterprise,* 25 July 1902; M. A. Crosby, "Report on Delta Farms," and H. G. Turner, "Notes on Plantation Partnerships," both in Reports, Speeches, and Articles Relating to Farm Management, 1902–1920, entry 133, BAE.

8. The history of this purchase is outlined in a memo from Minor S. Gray to W. T. Winterbottom, 2 March 1962, and in Minor S. Gray to W. T Winterbottom, 1 November 1962, both in "History. Charter and History of the D&PL: Information compiled by Minor Gray for W. T. Winterbottom, 1962," box 26, DPL. Some of the information is quoted by Minor from letters from Oscar Johnston to Martel McNeely, 16 July 1945, and to Alexander Fitz-Hugh, 30 June 1948; the letters themselves are not included in this file. Information on Scott's economic activities is given in Curt Lamar, ed., *History of Rosedale, Mississippi, 1876–1976* (Spartanburg, S.C., 1976), 31–35; for his political activities, see Chapter 3.

9. Memo from Minor S. Gray to W. T. Winterbottom, 2 March 1962, box 26, DPL. The Empire Company remained separate until 1924.

10. H. G. Turner, "Mississippi Delta Planting Company. Bolivar County, Mississippi," in BAE entry 133: Reports, Speeches, and Articles Relating to Farm Management, 1902–1920. The title page is marked in pencil, "Notes taken November 14, 1913," while the manuscript itself is dated 21 April 1915. Some of the details of Turner's account differ from information in the records of the company (DPL). For example, while Turner writes of fourteen plantations, a list from 1911, the year of the purchase (box 14, folder "Financial Records: Property Acreages and Locations" 1911) lists sixteen different properties, including one apparently devoted to the raising of stock. David Cohn's comment is in David L. Cohn, *Where I Was Born and Raised* (Boston, 1948; part 1 first published as *God Shakes Creation,* 1935), 12.

11. Annual Statement, 1 January 1913, in ledger 67, "Annual Reports Empire Plantation Co. 1913–1924," in box L5, DPL.

12. Crosby, "Present Status of Farm Management"; Annual Statement, 1 January 1913, and Annual Statement for 1914, in ledger 67, box L5, DPL.

13. Annual Statements for 1914 and 1915, in ledger 67, "Annual Reports Empire Plantation Co. 1913–1924," in box L5, DPL. In 1915 the plantation earned $2,284 in interest on tenant advances, and lost $3,945 in bad accounts.

14. For information on Percy's political activities see Chapter 3, above. The family's history is traced in Baker, *The Percys of Mississippi,* and Bertram Wyatt-Brown, *The Literary Percys: Family History, Gender, and the Southern Imagination* (Athens, Ga., 1994). The credit line is mentioned in LeRoy Percy to Wm. H. Perkins, New York City, 14 June 1907, in Percy Papers, MDAH.

15. The firm leased the plantations, although the records are not clear as to whether Bizzell was the owner or the lessee of part of the property before Percy became involved. See LeRoy Percy to Samuel McPeak, 25 April 1905 and 6 October 1905, Percy Papers.

16. LeRoy Percy to A. S. Sinclair, 31 May 1905; LeRoy Percy to J. W. Best, 6 December 1905; LeRoy Percy to Samuel McPeak, 27 December 1905 and 12 February 1906; LeRoy Percy to Herman Wilczinski, 21 December 1906; LeRoy Percy to J. E. Branton, 6 March 1907, Percy Papers.

17. LeRoy Percy to Ike Muckle, 29 January 1907; LeRoy Percy to F. H. Ivy, 31 January 1907; LeRoy Percy to Ike Muckle, 1 March 1907; LeRoy Percy to John L. Hebron, 4 January 1908; LeRoy Percy to Ike Muckle, 22 November 1906; LeRoy Percy to Mr. Hawkins, 17 July 1906, Percy Papers.

18. J. N. Johnson to Samuel McPeak, 27 April 1906 and 2 May 1906; LeRoy Percy to J. N. Johnson, 25 May 1906, Percy Papers. For a similar case see Percy's correspondence about a tenant with planter George Hebron (20 January 1908): "I have learned, I do not know whether correctly or not, that you made some threats against this negro. Of course, I can't protect him against you, but under the circumstances stated, I don't think it would be the right thing for you to carry out the threats. I am sure it would not be a wise thing. You know what my relationship with your people has been, and I write this in all kindness and sincerity." It is unclear whether Percy's more respectful tone with Hebron is because of a personal connection or because Hebron was simply wealthier and more powerful than J. N. Johnson.

19. Alfred H. Stone, *Studies in the American Race Problem* (New York, 1908), 92–93. The chapter quoted was presented at an academic conference in 1901.

20. Stone, *Studies*, 125; LeRoy Percy to J. B. Ray, 26 December 1906; LeRoy Percy to J. B. Ray, 28 December 1906, Percy Papers.

21. LeRoy Percy to Samuel McPeak, 2 February 1906; LeRoy Percy to J. B. Williams, 11 February 1907, Percy Papers. For a theoretical discussion of the economic rationale for paternalism, see Lee J. Alston and Joseph P. Ferrie, "Labor Costs, Paternalism, and Loyalty in Southern Agriculture: A Constraint on the Growth of the Welfare State," *JEH* 45 (1985), 95–117.

22. LeRoy Percy to Sarah Compton [unsigned] 7 July 1906; LeRoy Percy to "Randolph," 14 July 1906; LeRoy Percy to "Menefee," 17 July 1906, Percy Papers. The change in address, from first name to last, suggests a conscious attempt by Percy to ratchet up the measure of respect he was trying to convey to Menefee, even though he clearly could not bring himself to address him as "Mr." Menefee.

23. LeRoy Percy to J. B. Ray, 28 December 1906; to Samuel McPeak, 18 December 1905; to J. B. Ray, 23 March 1907; to J. B. Ray, 10 November 1906.

24. LeRoy Percy to Johanna Reiser, 19 October 1908.

25. B. Y. Young to LeRoy Percy, 29 December 1908 and 1 January 1909; Peter Brown to LeRoy Percy, 29 December 1908; Wm. H. Howe to LeRoy Percy, 1 January 1909.

26. LeRoy Percy to Sophie Reiser, 26 January 1909; to Johanna Reiser, 24 November 1909.

27. William Alexander Percy to Johanna Reiser, 1 June 1910; Peter Brown to Mrs. Reiser, 2 September 1910; Peter Brown to William Alexander Percy, 27 October 1910.

28. Simon Brantley to Johanna Reiser, 23 October 1910; Charles Thomas to Reiser, 20 October 1910; William Alexander Percy to Reiser, 1 June 1910; undated letter from William Howe enclosed in Reiser to W. A. Percy, 5 December 1910, Percy Papers.

29. Johanna Reiser to William Alexander Percy, 4 November 1910; Peter Brown to Reiser, 1 December 1910, Percy Papers (emphasis in original).

30. William Alexander Percy to Johanna Reiser, 10 November 1910, Percy Papers.

31. Johanna Reiser to William Alexander Percy [dated 14 October 1910, but more likely written on 14 November 1910, as it is a reply to the letter cited in note 30]; W. A. Percy to Reiser, 14 March 1911.

32. H. G. Turner, "Labor Management on some Plantations in the Yazoo-Mississippi Delta," Reports, Speeches, and Articles Related to Farm Management, 1902–1920, entry 133, BAE; Turner, "Bledsoe Plantation 1913"; Turner, "Mississippi Delta Planting Company."

33. Turner, "Labor Management," and Turner, "Bledsoe Plantation 1913," 11, 13. See Table 11, Appendix, which reports occupations for household heads and single men in Sunflower County in 1910.

34. Turner, "Bledsoe Plantation"; E. A. Boeger and E. A. Goldenweiser, *A Study of the Tenant Systems of Farming in the Yazoo-Mississippi Delta*, USDA Bulletin 337 (13 January 1916), 6.

35. Turner, "Labor Management," 1–2 (first and last quotations); Boeger and Goldenweiser, *Study of the Tenant Systems*, 6; H. G. Turner, "An Account of Dunlieth Plantation," 17 January 1916, in "Reports, Speeches, and Articles Relating to Farm Management: Mississippi," entry 133, BAE.

36. Turner, "Labor Management," 1.

37. Boeger and Goldenweiser, *Study of the Tenant Systems* (quotation p. 10). The income figures here combine income of the entire tenant family, including a small amount earned each year in wage labor. The authors took into account all the costs and income of the farm enterprise, including such items as depreciation on mules and tools. They excluded any interest or profits earned by the planter (and paid by tenant families) from advances and purchases of food and other consumer items, which means that for many families the incomes reported would be considerably reduced. Also excluded are the value of housing and any food raised by the cropper or wood or other supplies provided by the owner without charge.

38. Ibid., esp. 10–13. On Empire Plantation Co., profits per acre in 1915 were $4.36 on crops worked by wage hands, $12.68 on farms operated by sharecroppers, and $7.96 on farms operated by share renters (who paid one-fourth of the crop as rental). By way of comparison, in 1901 a group of "normal families" of clerical and other wage earners in northern cities averages $651 per year in income. "Annual Reports Empire Plantation Co. 1913–1924," DPL; *Hist. Stat.*, 321.

39. Stone, *Studies*, 144.

40. Robert Soto Quan, *Lotus among the Magnolias: The Mississippi Chinese* (Jackson, Miss., 1982); Robert Rose to LeRoy Percy, 4 March 1905; Rose to Percy, 30 March 1905; Percy to B. L. Lee, 8 March 1905; Rose to Percy, 13 May 1905; Samuel McPeak to Percy, 16 May 1905; Percy to Rose, 29 July 1905, Percy Papers.

41. Robert L. Brandfon, "The End of Immigration to the Cotton Fields," *Mississippi Valley Historical Review* 50 (1964), 591–611; Stone, *Studies*, 180–97.

42. See the issue of the *Arkansas Historical Quarterly* (vol. 50, 1991) devoted to Sunnyside, and especially Willard B. Gatewood, "Sunnyside: The Evolution of an Arkansas Plantation," 5–29; Brandfon, "End of Immigration."

43. In 1910 the census reported for Delta counties 59,465 black farmers, an increase from 39,397 in 1900. Of the 1910 farmers 3,484 were owners. The census did not cross tabulate race and tenancy type in 1910, but since the vast majority of all renters in the Delta were black (55,981 black tenants, 3,791 white tenants) we can estimate the proportions of cash renters with reasonable accuracy. There were 2,759 white farmer owners. On the

failure of the census to distinguish between sharecropping and share renting before 1920, see Lee J. Alston and Kyle D. Kauffman, "Agricultural Chutes and Ladders: New Estimates of Sharecroppers and 'True Tenants' in the South, 1900–1920," *JEH* 57 (1997), 464–75. Alston and Kauffman estimate that in Mississippi as a whole, about half of the "share tenants" reported in the census were true sharecroppers.

44. E. M. Banks, *The Economics of Land Tenure in Georgia* (New York, 1905), 61.

45. Ibid., 54–55.

46. Ibid., 81 (quoting a South Carolina court decision), 74. Because the Census of Agriculture did not report specific forms of tenancy by race, it is impossible to verify Banks's claim about the trend toward fixed rentals.

47. Robert P. Brooks, *The Agrarian Revolution in Georgia, 1865–1912* (Madison, Wis., 1914), 90, 59–62, 88; Robert P. Brooks, "A Local Study of the Race Problem," *Political Science Quarterly* 26 (1911), 208–10 (quotations pp. 210, 209). Brooks's plantation sample data are reported in the appendix to Lee J. Alston and Robert Higgs, "Contractual Mix in Southern Agriculture since the Civil War: Facts, Hypotheses, and Tests," *JEH* 42 (1982), 327–53. On the twenty-two plantations, there were 103 renters, 357 sharecroppers, and 153 wage workers.

48. Brooks, "Local Study," 218–19; Brooks, *Agrarian Revolution*, 62; see also Banks, *Economics of Land Tenure*, p. 77: landowning Negroes "as a usual thing, are respected alike by whites and the members of their own race. They obtain goods from merchants upon as good terms as do white men similarly circumstanced. . . . They live in better constructed and better furnished homes, and on the whole make conservative citizens."

49. See Table 14, Appendix. In the eastern Piedmont there were 1,787 black owners and 22,002 black tenants and sharecroppers.

50. Brooks, *Agrarian Revolution*, 54; Brooks, "Local Study," 211–12.

51. Maury Klein, *Edward Porter Alexander* (Athens, Ga., 1971); Katherine Du Pre Lumpkin, *The Making of a Southerner* (New York, 1947), 99–101; "The Depression Was a Republican Trick," Works Progress Administration Life History of Clifford C. Farr, Augusta Georgia, WPA Life Histories, Library of Congress. Historical geographer Charles S. Aiken has also argued that in the eastern plantation belt talented managers fled the countryside and turned to other fields. Aiken, *The Cotton Plantation South since the Civil War* (Baltimore, Md., 1998), 68–76.

52. *GHJ*, 22 January, 26 March, 2 May, 9 May 1897. Information on these investors comes from a special issue of the *GHJ*, 1 October 1897, and the Greene County Tax Digest for 1910, GDAH.

53. *GHJ*, 3 November 1897; 27 January, 26 May, 30 June 1899, 22 March 1901. Directors, other than Jackson and Copelan, included W. P. Mcwhorter, the biggest landholder in the county, J. O. Boswell, from a prominent family of merchants, and planters A. H. Smith and Luther P. Jernigan.

54. In 1900 there were 8,913 manufacturing workers in the eastern Piedmont, and 7,206 of these were in Richmond County. For occupations in Greene County in 1910, see Table 12, Appendix; for farm owners and tenants in the entire eastern Piedmont, see Table 14, Appendix.

55. "Two Boys on a Duck Hunt," undated typescript, Hilton Papers, GHS.

56. Buddy Sullivan, ed., *The Darien Journal of John Girardeau Legare, Ricegrower,*

1877–1932, entries for 26 October 1900, 18 September 1902, 21 May 1903; draft of letter by James T. Dent, Account Book, Hofwyl-Broadfield Papers (pp. 94–97); James M. Clifton, ed., *Life and Labor on Argyle Island* (Savannah, 1978), xlvi; "Harmon Benton Rice Land Reports 1905–1907," in "Reports, Speeches, and Articles Relating to Farm Management," entry 133, BAE.

57. Charles Spalding Wylly, *These Memories* [1916], pamphlet in local history room, Brunswick Public Library.

58. On the Spalding lands, see Chapter 1, and William S. McFeely, *Sapelo's People: A Long Walk into Freedom* (New York, 1994), 129–45; on truck farming, U.S. Department of Agriculture, *Soil Survey of Glynn County, Georgia* (Washington, D.C., 1912); Savannah *Morning News* 16, 17, and 25 January 1884; Mart Stewart, *"What Nature Suffers to Groe": Life, Labor, and Landscape on the Georgia Coast, 1680–1920* (Athens, Ga., 1996), 225–29.

59. Thomas Hilton, "High Water on the Bar" (Savannah, 1951), pamphlet in Hilton Papers, GHS; Carlton A. Morrison, "Raftsmen of the Altamaha" (M.A. thesis, University of Georgia, 1970), 20–21; Stewart, *"What Nature Suffers to Groe,"* 207. On the antebellum lumber industry, see John A. Eisterhold, "Savannah: Lumber Center of the South Atlantic," *GHQ* 57 (1973), 526–43.

60. Hilton, "High Water on the Bar"; Stewart, *"What Nature Suffers to Groe,"* 207–10.

61. Hilton, "High Water on the Bar," 10; Lydia Parrish, *Slave Songs of the Georgia Sea Islands* (1942; reprint, Athens, Ga., 1992), 203.

62. Darien *Timber Gazette*, 20 February 1886, quoted in Morrison, "Raftsmen of the Altamaha," 38; Margaret Cate, "Epworth by the Sea," typescript in Hilton Papers, GHS. Brunswick and especially Savannah continued to ship timber, brought in by rail from distant sources.

63. A. W. Schorger and H. S. Betts, *The Naval Stores Industry*, USDA Bulletin 229 (1915); Brunswick *Advertiser and Appeal*, 18 April 1885 (reprint from an article in the Atlanta *Constitution*).

64. Brunswick *Daily News*, 2 May 1885, reprinted from New York *Sun*. On conditions in some Florida camps, see Robert N. Lauriault, "From Can't to Can't: The North Florida Turpentine Camp," *Florida Historical Quarterly* 67 (1989), 310–28; Jerrell H. Shofner, "Forced Labor in the Florida Forests: 1880–1950," *Journal of Forest History* 25 (1981).

65. Thomas F. Armstrong, "The Transformation of Work: Turpentine Workers in Coastal Georgia, 1865–1901," *Labor History* 25 (1984), 518–32.

66. Monroe N. Work, "The Negroes of Warsaw, Georgia," *Southern Workman* 37 (1908), 29–40. Work was an African American scholar trained at the University of Chicago and a teacher for a time at Savannah State Industrial College.

67. For occupations in Camden County in 1910, see Table 13, Appendix.

68. Frederick A. Ober, "Dungeness, General Greene's Sea-Island Plantation," *Lippincott's Magazine of Popular Literature and Science* (August 1880), 241–49.

69. Louis Torres, *Historic Resource Study Cumberland Island National Seashore, Georgia and Historical Structure Report, Historical Data Section of the Dungeness Area* (Denver: National Park Service, n.d.), in GDAH, 159–60. See also B. N. Nightingale, "Dungeness," *GHQ* 22 (1938), 369–83.

70. Torres, *Historic Resource Study,* 271–74, quoting *Florida Mirror,* 4 April 1885.

71. Annual Account for 1901, Carnegie Papers, GDAH.

72. Torres, *Historic Resource Study,* 167, 179. For a descendant's view, see also Nancy Carnegie Rockefeller, *The Carnegies and Cumberland Island* (privately published, 1993), in GDAH.

73. Martin Calvin, Director Georgia Experiment Station (Griffin, Ga.) to W. E. Page, 29 May 1911, Carnegie Papers, GDAH; C. L. Goodrich, "Dungeness, Cumberland Island," in folder for "Georgia, Camden County," in Reports, Speeches, and Articles Relating to Farm Management, 1902–1920, entry 133, BAE.

74. Account Book, pp. 2, 9, 12; copy of agreement with Scottish-American Mortgage Company; statement, 24 June 1910; treasurer's report, 29 September 1911; notes of sale, 4 April 1912; David C. Barrow to William E. Harrold, 29 May 1912; deed of sale from Sapelo Island Co. to H. E. Coffin, 6 June 1912, all in Sapelo Island Company Records, GDAH; "Howard Coffin," *Dictionary of American Biography.*

75. William Barton McCash and June Hall McCash, *The Jekyll Island Club: Southern Haven for America's Millionaires* (Athens, Ga., 1989); Stewart, *"What Nature Suffers to Groe,"* 220–23.

76. Brunswick *Daily News,* 14 March 1885, 13 January 1888; Cate, "Epworth by the Sea"; "St. Simons Club for Rest and Recreation" [1914], promotional pamphlet in local history room, Brunswick Public Library; Stewart, *"What Nature Suffers to Groe,"* 216–20. Wealthy purchasers on the coast include the Wanamaker family, Ossabaw Island; the Rauers of Savannah, St. Catherines Island; and, on the coast itself, Henry Ford and William Du Pont. On Ford, see "Henry Ford at Richmond Hill: A Venture in Private Enterprise," in George A. Rogers and R. Frank Saunders, *Swamp Water and Wiregrass: Sketches of Coastal Georgia* (Macon, Ga., 1984); on Du Pont, see William Allister Noble, "Sequent Occupance of Hopeton-Altama, 1816–1956" (M.A. thesis, University of Georgia, 1956), chap. 6.

77. See Table 13, Appendix, for occupations and farm ownership by race in Camden County.

78. These statistics, and those given below for landholding in Camden County, are reported in Table 15, Appendix.

79. These totals do not include "wild land," which means land not suitable for agriculture. Wild lands were assessed at only $1.00 per acre. Because the returns for wild land were not broken down by race, they are not included in the analysis here. See also Peggy G. Hargis, "Beyond the Marginality Thesis: The Acquisition and Loss of Land by African Americans in Georgia, 1880–1930," *AH* 72 (1998), 241–62.

80. For occupations in Camden in 1910, see Table 13, Appendix.

81. Land ownership data is reported in Table 16, Appendix. The Georgia Department of Archives and History has no tax records for Greene County in the Reconstruction era, but it is useful to compare the proportion of large holdings in 1910 with the proportion of large "farms" reported by the 1860 census. In 1860 a total of 96 farms had more than five hundred acres, and these were 24.8 percent of all farms. In 1910 holdings of five hundred acres or more included 103 owners, or 12.8 percent of all white landholding. See U.S. Census Office, *Eighth Census, 1860. Agriculture,* 196.

82. However, there were more owners of agricultural land than farmers. The tax rolls

include 733 white individual or married-couple landholdings. Presumably many of these were entirely rented out to tenants. The number of black farmer-owners reported in the census, 147, is very close to the number of black landowners on the tax rolls, 141. Note that Table 12, Appendix, shows a slightly higher number of white owners than tenants in Greene County. This table is based on a sample of households taken from the census manuscripts. The published census, based on all households, shows 512 white farm tenants and 474 white farm owners.

83. Data on landholding in Sunflower are reported in Table 17, Appendix. Because of differences in the kinds of property taxed and the ways in which values were assessed, the Mississippi and Georgia tax digests are not exactly comparable. Among the more important differences: Mississippi used separate land rolls and personal property rolls; only the latter are identified by race. Therefore the only way to identify the race of landowners in the land rolls is to link the two tax lists. Secondly, each specific plot of land is listed in the Mississippi rolls, while in Georgia all of the land owned by a single taxpayer is listed under a single entry. Total acres owned for Sunflower taxpayers were calculated by alphabetizing the tax rolls and combining the amounts assessed to each name. The somewhat inexact process will tend to overestimate the number of individuals who own land by some small, but indeterminate, amount.

84. "Partnerships" includes those landholdings held under such names as "Williams & Sherman" or "Wilson & Dugan." Land held jointly by married couples are not counted as partnerships. Holdings by recognizable business entities ("Moorhead Mfg. Co.", "Indianola Brick and Tile," etc.) represented about six percent of the county's acreage. The tax assessments do not attempt to provide accurate estimates of land's value. Cleared land was assessed uniformly at $10 per acre; uncleared land at $5 per acre, for the purpose of assessing the land tax, which went to pay for the levee system.

85. Occupations and farm ownership are reported in Table 11, Appendix. The individual examples are taken from the Sunflower tax rolls.

Chapter 5   Culture, Race, and Class in the Segregation Era

1. Neil R. McMillen, *Dark Journey: Black Mississippians in the Age of Jim Crow* (Urbana, Ill., 1989), 184–86; Hortense Powdermaker, *After Freedom: A Cultural Study in the Deep South* (New York, 1939; reprint, Madison, Wis., 1993), 111–13 (where Cox is identified only as "W."); *Economic Co-operation among Negro Americans* (12th Atlanta University Conference, 1907; reprint, New York, 1969), 145–46.

2. Willard B. Gatewood Jr., *Theodore Roosevelt and the Art of Controversy: Episodes of the White House Years* (Baton Rouge, La., 1970), 62–89 (quotations pp. 68, 71); Indianola *Enterprise*, 16 January 1903 (quotations copied from the Memphis *Morning News*); McMillen, *Dark Journey*, 61–62.

3. Dorothy Dickins, *A Nutrition Investigation of Negro Tenants in the Yazoo-Mississippi Delta*, Bulletin 254, Mississippi Agricultural Experiment Station (August 1928); for fertility data see Table 18, Appendix. The most comprehensive treatment of fertility and family structure in the early-twentieth-century rural South is Stewart E. Tolnay, *The Bottom Rung: African American Family Life on Southern Farms* (Urbana, Ill., 1999).

4. Frances Butler Leigh, *Ten Years on a Georgia Plantation since the War* (London,

1883), 164; Valerie Grim, "Black Farm Families in the Yazoo-Mississippi Delta: A Study of the Brooks Farm Community, 1920–1970" (Ph.D. diss., Iowa State University, 1990), 202 (interviews with Mae Liza Williams and C. B. Myes), 142 (Minnie Brown). On rural southern families, see also Jacqueline Jones, *Labor of Love, Labor of Sorrow: Black Women, Work, and the Family from Slavery to the Present* (New York, 1985), 106–7; Jacqueline Jones, *The Dispossessed: America's Underclass from the Civil War to the Present* (New York, 1992), 73–103.

5. Ruby Sheppeard Hicks, *The Song of the Delta* (Jackson, Miss., 1976), 78–85; Grim, "Black Farm Families," 114 (interviews with Frances Walker and Freddie Wiley).

6. Hicks, *Song of the Delta,* 33–34; Grim, "Black Farm Families," 96, 153–54.

7. Grim, "Black Farm Families," 94 (Freddie Wiley), 88 (Margaret Ball). See Tables 18 and 19, Appendix, for data on age at marriage and fertility of women. These data for black women are similar to those reported in earlier studies: for example, Stewart E. Tolnay, "Fertility of Southern Black Farmers in 1900: Evidence and Speculation," *Journal of Family History* (1983), 314–32, and Stewart E. Tolnay, "Black Family Formation and Tenancy in the Farm South, 1900," *American Journal of Sociology* 90 (1984), 305–25.

8. Grim, "Black Farm Families," 90 (Beatrice Collins). See Table 20, Appendix, for data on household relationships.

9. Virginia Estes Causey, "Glen Allan, Mississippi: Change and Continuity in a Delta Community, 1900 to 1950" (Ph.D. diss., Emory University, 1983), 63–66. The basic book on the Southern "lady" is Anne Firor Scott, *The Southern Lady: From Pedestal to Politics, 1830–1930* (Chicago, 1970).

10. Birdie [Abbot Jones Gearhart] to Mama [Mrs. Liberty Abbott], 23 August 1908, Abbott Collection, MSU.

11. Charles A. Le Guin, ed., *A Home-Concealed Woman: The Diaries of Magnolia Wynn Le Guin, 1901–1913* (Athens, Ga., 1990). Le Guin lived in Henry County, Georgia, during the period of her diary. Although Henry is in the central, rather than eastern, Piedmont region of Georgia, her life is undoubtedly typical of many white rural women further east (and elsewhere in the rural South).

12. Ibid., 192, 91, 311, 149, 27, 212, 58, 38–39, 151, 117.

13. Ibid., 113, 167, 323, 324.

14. Ibid., 177, 59, 170.

15. Ibid., 73, 103, 189, 204, 278, 167.

16. Ibid., 96, 17, 103, 183, 314, 255, 299.

17. Ibid., 75.

18. For age at marriage, see Table 19; for mean length of current marriages, see Table 23; for fertility, Table 18; for living arrangements of children, Table 21, all in Appendix.

19. For children's deaths, see Table 18; for the proportions of households headed by females and proportions of married women who have been married more than once, see Table 23; for the household living arrangements of children, see Table 21, all in Appendix. The higher mortality rate for blacks does not necessarily show up in a higher proportion of widows, because remarriage rates were very high. Only in Sunflower County, in the Delta, was there a significant difference between blacks and whites in the proportions of ever-married women who were widows.

20. Powdermaker, *After Freedom,* 145. See Table 22, Appendix, for occupations of

wives by race. Some of the differences, to be sure, may be due to reporting, since white men and women may have been reluctant to acknowledge how much labor women did in the fields. It seems unlikely, for example, that three-fourths of black women in Camden County were engaged only in "keeping house" or had no occupations at all, as reported in the census. For the 1910 census, however, from which these figures derive, the census bureau gave "more specific and comprehensive" instructions to its enumerators to make sure they properly recorded occupations for women: U.S. Census Bureau, *Negro Population*, p. 507 (quoted in Robert Higgs, *Competition and Coercion: Blacks in the American Economy, 1865–1914* [New York, 1977], 63). For the best overall analysis of the higher labor force participation of black than white women, see Claudia Dale Goldin, *Understanding the Gender Gap: An Economic History of American Women* (New York, 1990).

21. Powdermaker, *After Freedom*, 158–59, 164; John Dollard, *Caste and Class in a Southern Town* (New Haven, Conn., 1937; reprint, Madison, Wis., 1988), 276–78, 86. For a sensitive consideration of the evidence and a judgment that for very many southern women, both black and white, "marriage was a cruel trap, motherhood often a mortal burden; husbands were too often obtuse, unfaithful, drunken, and violent," see Jack Temple Kirby, *Rural Worlds Lost: The American South, 1920–1960* (Baton Rouge, La., 1987), 155–94 (quotation pp. 169–70).

22. Walter Sillers to J. W. Sistrunk, 19 November 1918, Sillers Papers, Delta State University; Powdermaker, *After Freedom*, 156–57. The actual number of divorces is difficult to measure, because of the high incidence of remarriage. The percentages of ever-married persons who were currently divorced was very low, typically 1 or 2 percent. See Table 23, Appendix.

23. Grim, "Black Farm Families," 106; Leigh, *Ten Years*, 164; Powdermaker, *After Freedom*, 153, 160. This pattern of acceptance of childbearing before marriage has been documented also in Deanna L. Pagnini and S. Phillip Morgan, "Racial Differences in Marriage and Childbearing: Oral History Evidence from the South in the Early Twentieth Century," *American Journal of Sociology* 101 (1996), 1694–1718. A number of historians have traced this pattern back to slavery. See, e.g., Herbert G. Gutman, *The Black Family in Slavery and Freedom, 1750–1925* (New York, 1976), 45–100; Brenda E. Stevenson, *Life in Black and White: Family and Community Life in the Slave South* (New York, 1996), 206–57. For comparisons of black and white families early in the twentieth century and reviews of the issues, see Tolnay, *Bottom Rung*, and Steven Ruggles, "The Origins of African-American Family Structure," *American Sociological Review* 59 (1994), 136–51.

24. Powdermaker, *After Freedom*, 154–55.

25. Mrs. L. H. Harris, "A Southern Woman's View," *Independent*, 18 May 1899, 1355; *Independent*, 17 March 1904, quoted in Beverly Guy-Sheftall, *Daughters of Sorrow: Attitudes toward Black Women, 1880–1920*, vol. 11 in *Black Women in United States History*, ed. Darlene Clark Hine (Brooklyn, 1990), 46; Carl Kelsey, *The Negro Farmer* (1903), 64–65; McMillen, *Dark Journey*, 16–17. About 12 percent of the members of black households were relatives who were not members of the nuclear group of parents and children: see Table 20, Appendix.

26. "More Slavery at the South. By a Negro Nurse," *Independent*, 25 January 1912, 196–200 (quotations pp. 196, 198); *Independent*, 17 March 1904, quoted in Guy-Sheftall, *Daughters of Sorrow*, 58–59. The polished prose of "More Slavery at the South" suggests a

highly educated author, perhaps an African American woman familiar with the problems of domestic servants, though not one herself. The author claims to live in a city larger than fifty thousand in population, which would have to have been either Savannah or Atlanta.

27. "I Is a Baptist," interview with Wesley Anthony, Washington, Georgia, in *American Life Histories: Manuscripts from the Federal Writers' Project, 1936–1940*, Library of Congress (on Library of Congress website at http://rs6.loc.gov).

28. Marie M. Hemphill, *Fevers, Floods, and Faith: A History of Sunflower County, Mississippi, 1844–1976* (Indianola, Miss., 1980), 468, 487; Lucy Weissenger Oral History, OH 39-74, MSU; Monroe N. Work, "Negroes of Warsaw, Georgia," *Southern Workman* 37 (1908), 38; Hicks, *Song of the Delta*, 57–59. On the overlap of congregations with kinship groups, see, e.g., Rev. W. H. Holloway, "A Black Belt County," in *The Negro Church* (8th Atlanta University Conference, 1903; reprint, New York, 1968), 57–62 (the county was Thomas County in southwest Georgia); and Peter D. Goldsmith, *When I Rise Cryin' Holy: African-American Denominationalism on the Georgia Coast* (New York, 1989). See Table 24, Appendix, for the breakdown by denomination in 1916.

29. Hemphill, *Fevers, Floods,* 476.

30. Rev. Henry Cherry Oral History, OH 9-74, MSU. As late as 1922, two-thirds of white Baptist ministers in the rural south were part-time as well: J. Wayne Flynt, "Southern Baptists: Rural to Urban Transition," *Baptist History and Heritage* 14 (1981), 24.

31. Rev. Henry Cherry Oral History; Hemphill, *Fevers, Floods,* quotation on 506–7; Hicks, *Song of the Delta,* 60.

32. Grim, "Black Farm Families," 176–208, esp. 188–94 (quotation p. 200).

33. Charles Joyner, "A Single Southern Culture: Cultural Interaction in the Old South," in *Black and White: Cultural Interaction in the Antebellum South,* ed. Ted Ownby (Jackson, Miss., 1993), 14. For an enlightening comparison of post–Civil War black and white Baptists, see Paul Harvey, *Redeeming the South: Religious Cultures and Racial Identities among Southern Baptists, 1865–1925* (Chapel Hill, N.C., 1997).

34. Rev. Henry Cherry Oral History; Holloway, "A Black Belt County"; Hicks, *Song of the Delta,* 60. For a general treatment of what he calls the "spirit of worship" in southern black churches, see William E. Montgomery, *Under Their Own Vine and Fig Tree: The African-American Church in the South, 1865–1900* (Baton Rouge, La., 1993), chap. 6.

35. Hans A. Baer, "The Socio-Religious Development of the Church of God in Christ," in *African Americans in the South: Issues of Race, Class and Gender,* ed. Hans A. Baer and Yvonne Jones, Southern Anthropological Society *Proceedings,* no. 25 (Athens, Ga., 1992), 111–22; David M. Tucker, *Black Pastors and Leaders: Memphis 1819–1972* (Memphis, Tenn., 1975), chap. 7.

36. Tucker, *Black Pastors,* 98; Powdermaker, *After Freedom,* 234.

37. St. Louis *Globe-Democrat,* undated clipping, Percy Papers, MDAH.

38. These generalizations about Greene's textile workers are based on forty-seven textile employees included in the sample of households from Greene County in 1910. See the Essay on Sources for more information on the sample.

39. Manufacturing employment is reported by county in the U.S. Census, *Twelfth Census* (1900). The cities themselves were not large enough for detailed individual reports. Strike activity is reported in the *Tenth Annual Report of the Commissioner of Labor, 1894*

(Washington, D.C., 1896), and Dittmer, *Black Georgia*, 28. For strikes in Augusta, see Merl E. Reed, "The Augusta Textile Mills and the Strike of 1886," *Labor History* 14 (1973), 228–46; Melton Alonzo McLaurin, *Paternalism and Protest: Southern Cotton Mill Workers and Organized Labor, 1875–1905* (Westport, Conn. 1971), 93–110, 145–47, 186–92; Julia Mary Walsh, " 'Horny-Handed Sons of Toil': Workers, Politics, and Religion in Augusta, Georgia, 1880–1910" (Ph.D. diss., University of Illinois at Urbana-Champaign, 1999). Walsh, who offers the best analysis of the culture of Augusta's workers, argues that they retained many ties to rural areas.

40. Richard H. L. German, "Queen City of the Savannah: Augusta, Georgia, during the Urban Progressive Era, 1890–1917" (Ph.D. diss., University of Florida, 1971); see German's appendix for a list of mayors and councilmen with their business affiliations and occupations; Randolph D. Werner, "The New South Creed and the Limits of Southern Radicalism," unpublished paper in author's possession.

41. J. Morgan Kousser, "Separate but *not* Equal: The Supreme Court's First Decision on Racial Discrimination in Schools," *JSH* 45 (1980), 17–44; June O. Patton, "The Black Community of Augusta and the Struggle for Ware High School, 1880–1899," in *New Perspectives on Black Educational History*, ed. Vincent P. Franklin and James D. Anderson (Boston, 1978), 45–60.

42. *GHJ*, 17 September 1886, 21 January and 11 February 1887, 8 February and 15 February 1889, 22 July, 5 August, and 12 August 1898, 21 February 1913, 5 January 1917; Dewey W. Grantham, *Southern Progressivism: The Reconciliation of Progress and Tradition* (Knoxville, Tenn., 1983), 284–87.

43. *Southeast Georgian* [St. Marys, then Kingsland], 14 July 1916; Hemphill, *Fevers, Floods*, 144, 147, 149, 151; Sunflower *Tocsin*, 27 May 1915.

44. *GHJ*, 24 October 1884, 11 and 25 December 1885, 14 and 28 September 1895. In the 1895 referendum the antiliquor forces won by 645 to 403.

45. Causey, "Glen Allan, Mississippi," 63–64; *GHJ*, 5 December 1884. However, the editor in the same editorial argued that some kinds of clerical employment "in the different branches of the government is entirely consistent with the modesty and delicacy of a refined lady."

46. Stone quoted in Mary Louise Meredith, "The Mississippi Woman's Rights Movement, 1889–1923: The Leadership Role of Nellie Nugent Somerville and Greenville in Suffrage Reform" (M.A. thesis, Delta State University, 1974), 32–33; LeeAnn Whites, "The De Graffenried Controversy: Class, Race, and Gender in the New South," *JSH* 54 (1988), 449–78; John Patrick McDowell, *The Social Gospel in the South: The Woman's Home Mission Movement in the Methodist Episcopal Church, South, 1886–1939* (Baton Rouge, La., 1982), chap. 5; Marjorie Spruill Wheeler, *New Women of the New South: The Leaders of the Woman Suffrage Movement in the Southern States* (New York, 1993).

47. Virginia I. Burr, "A Woman Made to Suffer and Be Strong: Ella Gertrude Clanton Thomas, 1834–1907," in *In Joy and in Sorrow: Women, Family, and Marriage in the Victorian South, 1830–1900*, ed. Carol Bleser (New York, 1991), 215–32; Virginia Ingraham Burr, ed., *The Secret Eye: The Journal of Ella Gertrude Clanton Thomas, 1848–1889* (Chapel Hill, N.C, 1990), 122, 168–69, 149.

48. Burr, "Woman Made to Suffer," quotation from 224–25.

49. Burr, ed., *Secret Eye*, 277, 447–54; Burr, "Woman Made to Suffer." An excellent

treatment of the role of work in the transformation of elite women's lives after the Civil War in the South is Jane Turner Censer, "A Changing World of Work: North Carolina Elite Women, 1865–1895," *North Carolina Historical Review* 73 (1996), 27–55.

50. Meredith, "The Mississippi Woman's Rights Movement"; Anne Firor Scott, "Nellie Nugent Somerville," in *Notable American Women: The Modern Period*, ed. Barbara Sicherman and Carol Hurd Green (Cambridge, Mass., 1980), 654–56.

51. Meredith, "Mississippi Woman's Rights Movement," 32–34; Scott, "Nellie Nugent Somerville" ("exotic plant"); McDowell, *Social Gospel in the South*, 118, 134–35.

52. Meredith, "Mississippi Woman's Rights Movement," 39; Nellie Nugent Somerville, "Moral Leadership: The True Basis of Woman Suffrage," undated pamphlet, and Somerville, in undated clipping, both in notebook 9, "Scrapbooks," Somerville-Howorth Papers, Schlesinger Library. For a good treatment of the leadership of the southern suffragist movement as a whole see Wheeler, *New Women of the New South*; Somerville is one of the leaders that Wheeler's book examines. For opposition to suffrage (some from women), see Elna Green, "'Ideals of Government, of Home, and of Women': The Ideology of Southern White Antisuffragism," in *Hidden Histories of Women*, ed. Virginia Bernhard et al. (Columbia, Mo., 1994), 96–113. For religious opposition to increased rights for women within the confines of Thomas's and Somerville's Methodist denomination, see McDowell, *Social Gospel in the South*, 132–34.

53. Meredith, "Mississippi Woman's Suffrage," 49; Nellie Nugent Somerville, "The Civic Improvement Club and Equal Suffrage Work in Greenville," clipping dated 24 March 1915, and undated clipping, both in notebook 9, "Scrapbooks," Somerville-Howorth Papers.

54. Hemphill, *Fevers, Floods,* 565; Sunflower *Enterprise,* 20 February 1903; Sunflower *Tocsin,* 3 June 1915.

55. *GHJ,* 23 and 30 July, 7 October 1899.

56. *GHJ,* 15 December 1911, 20 September 1912.

57. James Callaway, "The White Woman's Problem," in *Woman's Patriot,* 26 June 1920, quoted in Elna C. Green, *Southern Strategies: Southern Women and the Woman Suffrage Question* (Chapel Hill, N.C., 1997), 87. Antisuffragists were much more likely to stress racist themes than prosuffragists. For white suffragists and race, see Green, *Southern Strategies,* 80–98; Wheeler, *New Women,* 100–132.

58. Dittmer, *Black Georgia,* 17; Augusta *Chronicle,* 14 and 15 May 1900; August Meier and Elliot Rudwick, "The Boycott Movement against Jim Crow Streetcars in the South, 1900–1906," *Journal of American History* 55 (1969), 756; C. Vann Woodward, "*Strange Career* Critics: Long May They Persevere," *JAH* 75 (1988), 858; U.S. Department of the Interior, Bureau of Education, *Negro Education: A Study of the Private and Higher Schools for Colored People in the United States,* 2 vols., Bulletin 38 (1916; reprint 1969), 2:228; *GHJ,* 27 February 1914.

59. David M. Oshinsky, "*Worse Than Slavery*": *The Parchman Farm and the Ordeal of Jim Crow Justice* (New York, 1996), 31–54, 109–34; Alex Lichtenstein, *Twice the Work of Free Labor: The Political Economy of Convict Labor in the New South* (London, 1996), 152–85.

60. These figures are based on local tax assessments, and so must be considered approximations only. They are reported in W. E. B. Du Bois, *The Negro Landholder of*

Georgia, U.S. Department of Labor, Bulletin 35 (1901), 647–777 (quotation p. 777). The State of Mississippi did not, like Georgia, publish figures separately for whites and blacks. See also Loren Schweninger, *Black Property Owners in the South, 1790–1915* (Urbana, Ill., 1990).

61. *Economic Co-operation among the Negroes of Georgia* (22d Atlanta University Conference, 1917; reprint, New York, 1969), 50.

62. Willis E. Mollison, *The Leading Afro-Americans of Vicksburg, Miss., Their Enterprises, Churches, Schools, Lodges, and Societies* (Vicksburg, 1908) (quotation p. 6); McMillen, *Dark Journey,* 166–86.

63. Robert E. Perdue, *The Negro in Savannah, 1865–1900* (Hicksville, N.Y., 1973), 105–36; *Economic Co-operation among Negro Americans,* 86, 99, 128–31; *Economic Co-operation among the Negroes of Georgia,* 46, 50; Dittmer, *Black Georgia,* 36.

64. The Methodist Episcopal Church, South had broken away from the national Methodist organization in 1844 over the issue of slavery. Most black Methodists in the South joined the African Methodist Episcopal Church or the African Methodist Episcopal Zion Church. On Holsey, see Glenn T. Eskew, "Black Elitism and the Failure of Paternalism in Postbellum Georgia: The Case of Bishop Lucius Henry Holsey," *JSH* 58 (1992), 637–66.

65. Kent Anderson Leslie, *Woman of Color, Daughter of Privilege: Amanda America Dickson, 1849–1893* (Athens, Ga., 1995); Willard B. Gatewood, *Aristocrats of Color: The Black Elite, 1880–1920* (Bloomington, Ind., 1990), 90–91; Ridgely Torrence, *The Story of John Hope* (New York, 1948), 54; Eskew, "Black Elitism," 654. In 1883 William J. White, editor of the Georgia *Baptist,* former official of the Freedmen's Bureau and certainly no apologist for whites, told a visiting congressional committee that in Augusta "the colored people are certainly friendly with the white people, and the white people are friendly with the colored people. Augusta is an exceptional city in that respect. The relations between the white and colored people in Augusta are really more cordial than in any other place that I know of, and I am pretty well acquainted throughout the whole South." U.S. Congress, Senate, *Report of the Committee of the Senate upon the Relations between Labor and Capital,* 5 vols. (Washington, D.C, 1885), 2:787.

66. Lucy Laney, "Address before the Women's Meeting," in *Social and Physical Condition of Negroes in Cities* (2d Atlanta University Conference, 1897; reprint, New York, 1968), 55–57; Glenda Gilmore, *Gender and Jim Crow* (Chapel Hill, N.C., 1996), 36.

67. *Report of the Committee upon the Relations between Labor and Capital,* 776 (where Holsey's name is misspelled as "Halsey").

68. Mollison, *Leading Afro-Americans of Vicksburg,* 45, 49; Daisy Miller Greene Oral History, MDAH; *History of Blacks in Greenville, Mississippi, 1868–1975* (Greenville, Miss., 1975) (pamphlet in MDAH).

69. Letter to John Brunini, typescript in folder "Migration Study. Negro Migrants, Letters From 1916–17," series 6, box 86, NUL. The writers of the letter are not identified on the typescript but some of them, including Williams and Michigan graduate Dr. John Miller, can be identified from other sources. See J. William Harris, "Etiquette, Lynching, and Racial Boundaries: A Mississippi Example," *American Historical Review* 100 (1995), esp. 395–99.

70. Sadie Daniel St. Clair, "Lucy Craft Laney," in *Notable American Women,* ed. Sicherman and Green, 2:365–66; A. C. Griggs, "Lucy Craft Laney," *Journal of Negro*

NOTES TO PAGES 182–184

History 19 (1934), 96–102. On African American education in this era, see especially James D. Anderson, *The Education of Blacks in the South, 1860–1935* (Chapel Hill, N.C., 1988).

71. Griggs, "Lucy Craft Laney"; Lucy Laney, "The Burden of the Educated Colored Woman," paper read at the Hampton Negro Conference no. 3, 1899; reprinted in *Black Women in Nineteenth-Century American Life: Their Words, Their Thoughts, Their Feelings,* ed. Bert James Loewenberg and Ruth Bogin (University Park, Penn., 1976), 296–301, quotations p. 298; Lucy Laney, "General Conditions of Mortality," in *Mortality among Negroes in Cities* (1st Atlanta University Conference, 1896; reprint, New York, 1968), 35–37; Laney, "Address before the Women's Meeting," 55. Laney is a representative of what Evelyn Brooks Higginbotham has called the "politics of respectability": *Righteous Discontent: The Women's Movement in the Black Baptist Church, 1880–1920* (Cambridge, Mass., 1993), 14, 185–229.

72. Laney, "General Conditions of Mortality," 37.

73. *Some Efforts of Negro Americans for their Own Social Betterment* (3d Atlanta University Conference, 1898; reprint, New York, 1969), 8–9, 19; *Economic Co-operation among Negro Americans,* 82–83, 128–31; *Efforts for Social Betterment among Negro Americans* (14th Atlanta University Conference, 1909; reprint, New York, 1968), 53–54, 59, 82–83, 89, 92, 99, 105; Elizabeth Lindsay Davis, *Lifting as They Climb 1933* (1933; reprint, New York, 1996), 336–38. On African American women's voluntary activism see Dorothy Salem, *To Better Our World: Black Women in Organized Reform, 1890–1920,* vol. 11 of *Black Women in United States History,* ed. Darlene Clark Hine (Brooklyn, N.Y., 1990); Gilmore, *Gender and Jim Crow;* Kathleen C. Berkeley, "'Colored Ladies Also Contributed': Black Women's Activities from Benevolence to Social Welfare, 1866–1896," in *The Web of Southern Social Relations: Women, Family, and Education,* ed. Walter J. Fraser Jr., R. Frank Saunders Jr., and John L. Wakelyn (Athens, Ga., 1985), 181–85.

74. Quoted in August Meier, *Negro Thought in America, 1880–1915: Racial Ideologies in the Age of Booker T. Washington* (Ann Arbor, Mich., 1963), 266.

75. Charles C. Jones Jr., *Negro Myths from the Georgia Coast, Told in the Vernacular* (1888; reprinted Detroit, 1969). The dialect known as Geechee in Georgia was called Gullah in South Carolina.

76. Abigail M. Holmes Christensen, "Spirituals and 'Shouts' of Southern Negroes," *Journal of American Folklore* 7 (1984), 154–55. Christensen wrote that the circle moved first in one direction and then "without a second's pause, start[ed] again in the opposite direction." Since virtually all observers of the ring shout saw movement in counterclockwise direction only, this alleged detail suggests that Christensen may not have observed shouts as closely as her short article suggests. The importance of the ring shout to African American culture, and its roots in African cosmology and ritual, is emphasized in Sterling Stuckey, *Slave Culture: Nationalist Theory and the Foundations of Black America* (New York, 1987), 3–97.

77. Lydia Parrish, *Slave Songs of the Georgia Sea Islands* (1942; reprint, Athens, Ga., 1992).

78. Ibid., 9, xxx, xxxii, 4, 55. See also Art Rosenbaum, *Shout Because You're Free: The African American Ring Shout Tradition in Coastal Georgia* (Athens, Ga., 1998); Robert Winslow Gordon, "Negro 'Shouts' from Georgia," *New York Times Magazine,* 24 April

1927, reprinted in Alan Dundes, ed., *Mother Wit from the Laughing Barrel: Readings in the Interpretation of Afro-American Folklore* (Berkeley, 1973), 445–51, and Gordon's recordings from Darien, Georgia, in the 1920s, in the Library of Congress recording "The Robert Winslow Gordon Collection, 1922–1932" (LC AAFS L68).

79. Ibid., 197–200 (quotation p. 199). See Chapter 4 for a song used by lumber loaders.

80. Bessie Jones and Bess Lomax Hawes, *Step It Down: Games, Plays, Songs, and Stories from the Afro-American Heritage* (New York, 1972; reprint, Athens, Ga., 1987), 19–24 (quotation p. 24).

81. Alan Lomax, *The Land Where the Blues Began* (New York, 1993), 84–91. Lomax also later recorded religious and secular songs on St. Simons in 1961, some of which appeared on "Georgia Sea Island Songs" (New World Records 278).

82. Charles Peabody, "Notes on Negro Music," *Journal of American Folklore* 16 (1903), 1–4.

83. Ibid.; Parrish, *Slave Songs,* 197, 203; Robert Palmer, *Deep Blues* (New York, 1981), 23–25; Luc Sante, "The Genius of the Blues," *New York Review of Books,* 11 August 1994, 46.

84. Howard Odum, "Folk Song and Folk Poetry as Found in the Secular Songs of the Southern Negroes," *Journal of American Folklore* 24 (1911), 258–59. For suggestive accounts of blues origins, see Jeff Todd Titon, *Early Downhome Blues: A Musical and Cultural Analysis* (Urbana, Ill., 1977; 2d ed., Chapel Hill, N.C., 1994), 22–29; David Evans, *Big Road Blues* (1982; reprint, New York, 1987), 41–44; and William Barlow, *"Looking Up at Down": The Emergence of Blues Culture* (Philadelphia, 1989), 7–24.

85. Other typical aspects of the blues form include the twelve-bar verse, with four bars to a line, most often with lines having five stressed syllables, with room for an instrumental reply. The form, while standardized, was not rigidly fixed, and individual singers and songs often varied from the standard in one detail or another. See Titon, *Early Downhome Blues,* 22–25. The verse quoted is from the transcription of Mississippi John Hurt, "Got the Blues, Can't Be Satisfied," in Titon, 76–77. Unless otherwise noted, all verses cited in this chapter are from songs recorded by Mississippi Delta blues performers.

86. Palmer, *Deep Blues,* 44–47. The blues discussed here is the "rural" or "downhome" blues, rather than what musical historians call the "urban" or "vaudeville" blues. The latter was the province of touring vaudeville female singers like Mamie Smith, whose 1920 "Crazy Blues" was the first commercial recording of a blues song (it sold an astonishing seventy-five thousand copies in its first month, thus opening the eyes of record producers to the African American market). In addition to Mamie Smith, they included Ida Cox, Lucille Bogan, and the two most successful, Ma Rainey and Bessie Smith. Many of their most popular songs were composed by Tin Pan Alley professionals. The "downhome" blues circulated in the Mississippi Delta, probably in East Texas, and possibly in other places as well, at least a generation before Mamie Smith's breakthrough 1920 recording. Country blues singers themselves were not recorded until 1926, after the commercial success of Texan Blind Lemon Jefferson's "That Black Snake Moan." Francis Davis, *The History of the Blues* (New York, 1995), 60–64; Titon, *Early Downhome Blues,* 193–217.

87. W. C. Handy, *Father of the Blues: An Autobiography* (1941), quoted in Barlow, *"Looking Up at Down,"* 31; Odum, "Folk Song," 261.

88. Joe Rice Dockery Oral History, MDAH; *National Negro Digest*, September 1938, quoted in Hemphill, *Fevers, Floods*, 405; Palmer, *Deep Blues*, 49–54; Stephen Calt and Gayle Wardlow, *King of the Delta Blues: The Life and Music of Charlie Patton* (Newton, N.J., 1988).

89. Calt and Wardlow, *King of the Delta Blues*, 40–84; Palmer, *Deep Blues*, 48–54; David Evans, "Charley Patton — The Conscience of the Delta," in *The Voice of the Delta: Charley Patton and the Mississippi Blues Traditions: Influences and Comparisons*, ed. Robert Sacre (Liege, Belgium, 1987), 143–50.

90. Davis, *History of the Blues*, 99, 102 (quoting Sam Chatmon, who also complained that Patton could "clown better than he could pick"); Evans, *Big Road Blues*, 167–264.

91. Titon, *Early Downhome Blues*, 137–74 (which uses the phrase "song-producing system"); Evans, *Big Road Blues*, 106–15; William Ferris, *Blues from the Delta* (Garden City, N.Y., 1978), esp. 101–5.

92. Titon, *Early Downhome Blues*, 64, 76, 92; Palmer, *Deep Blues*, 276 (quoting Leo Smith); Ferris, *Blues from the Delta*, xii, 42; Bruce Bastin, *Red River Blues* (Urbana, Ill., 1986), 23 (quoting from Paul Oliver, *Conversation with the Blues* [1965], 164–65). Townsend was not from the Delta.

93. Verses are quoted from Son House, "My Black Mama" (from Titon, *Early Downhome Blues*, 118); Charley Patton, "It Won't Be Long" (from Palmer, *Deep Blues*, 70); Mississippi John Hurt, "Got the Blues, Can't Be Satisfied" (from Titon, 76–77); Charlie Patton, "Pea Vine Blues" (from Palmer, 53); Willie Brown, "M and O Blues" (from Titon, 91); Son House, "Walking Blues" (from Lomax, *Land Where the Blues Began*, 19). It should be noted that such common verses as "I'm goin' up the country, baby, don't you want to go" could be sung by different performers, or by the same performer at different performances and in different recordings, with different combinations of other verses.

94. Calt and Wardlow, *King of the Delta Blues*, 36–39, 135–51 (House quotation from pp. 150–51); Evans, "Charley Patton"; Ferris, *Blues from the Delta*, 101; Peter Guralnick, *Searching for Robert Johnson* (New York, 1989); Palmer, *Deep Blues*, 81–82. For measures of the relatively high level of family instability in the Delta, see Table 23, Appendix. Alan Lomax suggests that the literal danger of the job of blues performer is one reason that women rarely became country blues performers: Lomax, *Land Where the Blues Began*, 361.

95. James H. Cone, *The Spirituals and the Blues: An Interpretation* (New York, 1972), 115, 117 (first and third quotations); Barlow, *"Looking Up at Down,"* 7, 5 (second and fourth quotations).

96. See Chapter 6 for a discussion of protest themes in (nonblues) black music.

97. Joe Rice Dockery quoted in Palmer, *Deep Blues*, 55–56.

98. Palmer, *Deep Blues*, 61–62, 120; Evans, "Charley Patton," 148–49; Davis, *History of the Blues*, 27 (quoting Handy). Sam Chatmon and Big Bill Broonzy were among Delta musicians who performed frequently for whites: Lomax, *Land Where the Blues Began*, 384, 432.

99. James Baldwin, *The Fire Next Time* (1963), reprinted in *James Baldwin: Collected Essays* (New York, 1998), 310–11. Baldwin included jazz in this assessment. He was specifically writing this passage about Big Bill Broonzy, who was born in the Delta.

100. Richard Wright, "Forward," in Paul Oliver, *Blues Fell This Morning: Meaning in the Blues* (2d ed.; New York, 1990), xiv; Cone, *Spirituals and the Blues;* Jon Michael

Spencer, *Blues and Evil* (Knoxville, Tenn., 1993); Wilkins quoted in Titon, *Early Down-home Blues,* 32–33; B. B. King Oral History, MDAH; Vinson quoted in Ferris, *Blues from the Delta,* 83; Barlow, *"Looking Up at Down,"* 49–50.

101. Griggs, "Lucy Craft Laney"; Walker Baptist Association cited in Walsh, "Horny-Handed Sons of Toil," 82.

102. *Morals and Manners among Negro Americans* (18th Atlanta University Conference, 1914 [where Laney spoke]; reprint, New York, 1968); Laney, "Address before the Women's Meeting," 55; Patton, "Pony Blues" (Titon, *Early Downhome Blues,* 64); Ralph Ellison, *Shadow and Act* (New York, 1964), 247.

Chapter 6   War's Challenge to Jim Crow Citizenship

1. *VDH,* 24 July 1918; *VEP,* 24 July 1918. The incident is also documented in NAACP 7A, reel 14, frames 1 ff, 120–97. See also Neil R. McMillen, *Dark Journey: Black Mississippians in the Age of Jim Crow* (Urbana, Ill., 1989), 31, 171, 304–5, and J. William Harris, "Etiquette, Lynching, and Racial Boundaries in Southern History: A Mississippi Example," *American Historical Review* 100 (1995), 387–410.

2. *VDH,* 24 July 1918. Less plausibly, Cook was also accused of saying "there would be no race distinction after the war is won by Germany and the negro and white children will be sent to the same schools." *VDH,* July 25, 1918. Cook also told one reporter that he suspected the attack was motivated by men who were angry that he had refused to sell them his farm. There is no way to confirm his suspicion, but if true, it illustrates the ways in which cultural and economic issues and motives are inextricably intertwined. *VEP,* 25 and 26 July 1918; *VDH,* 25 July 1918.

3. Miller to Walter White, 3 September 1918, NAACP 7A, reel 14, frame 36. Miller wrote that he could "sell $1500 worth of bonds myself if Negroes are given a taste of better treatment." *VDH,* 24 July 1918; *VEP,* 24 July 1918. This newspaper report apparently referred to a different incident; when Miller was asked for a contribution of $10 to the Red Cross, he had given only $5, he wrote, because he "had only half [his] rights." Miller's correspondence refers only to "Mr. Hennessee," and the actual visitor could have been one of two lawyers, apparently brothers, who served on the war savings committee. I have used John in the text.

4. Atlanta *Journal,* 1 August 1906, quoted in C. Vann Woodward, *Tom Watson: Agrarian Rebel* (New York, 1938; reprint, New York, 1970), 379.

5. Records of the Greene County School Board, 7 November 1876, 9 January 1900, microfilm in GDAH; Arthur F. Raper, *Tenants of the Almighty* (New York, 1943), 106.

6. U.S. Department of the Interior, Bureau of Education, *Negro Education: A Study of the Private and Higher Schools for Colored People in the United States,* by Thomas Jesse Jones (2 vols.; Washington, D.C., 1916), 2:185–258 (reports for Georgia counties), and 333–78 (reports for Mississippi counties). Reports are included only for counties with either a private school or a public college for Negroes. However, for each of those counties, the report includes total spending in 1910 by the public schools for white and black teachers, together with spending per child age 6–14. For a summary of public high school education, see pp. 190, 336–38. Georgia had one public high school for Negroes in Athens, in the upper Piedmont county of Clarke.

7. The account here is based on a series of documents related to a request for Lum's pardon. A. A. Armistead to Governor Earl Brewer, 23 January 1913; Carl Fox to Governor Earl Brewer, 5 December 1912, Governor's Correspondence, Earl Brewer, MDAH.

8. Fox to Brewer, 5 December 1912, ibid.

9. The distinction between "radical" and "conservative" racial thought was made in Joel Williamson, *The Crucible of Race: Black-White Relations in the American South since Emancipation* (New York, 1984).

10. Alfred H. Stone, *Studies in the American Race Problem* (New York, 1908), 73, 91–92.

11. W. J. Northen, "The Negro Situation — One Way Out," *The World To-Day* 13 (1907), 893–96 (quotations pp. 894, 896).

12. Ibid., 895, 896.

13. LeRoy Percy, "A Southern View of Negro Education," *Outlook*, 3 August 1907, 730–32 (quotations pp. 731, 732); *Speeches of Senator LeRoy Percy before the Mississippi Legislature and Resolutions Adopted by the Legislature in Regard to the Senatorial Election* (n.p., [1910?]), Percy Papers; LeRoy Percy to Theodore Roosevelt, 10 August 1907, Percy Papers.

14. The best sources for Vardaman's career and thought are William F. Holmes, *The White Chief: James Kimble Vardaman* (Baton Rouge, La., 1970), and Albert D. Kirwan, *Revolt of the Rednecks: Mississippi Politics, 1876–1925* (Lexington, Ky., 1951). In the Delta, Vardaman won 47 percent of the vote, Percy 38 percent, and C. H. Alexander 15 percent.

15. Kirwan, *Revolt of the Rednecks*, 152, 146–47; Holmes, *White Chief*, 77–78, 198–99; "Governor Vardaman's Inaugural," *Current Literature* 36 (1904), 271.

16. Thomas M. Norwood, *Address on the Negro* (1908), reprinted in John David Smith, ed., *Anti-Black Thought 1863–1925. Vol. 8: Racial Determinism and the Fear of Miscegenation Post 1900* (New York, 1993), 319–47. Quotations (using original pagination) 1, 3, 5, 6, 24, 7, 19, 21, 22.

17. Alfred H. Stone, *Studies in the American Race Problem* (New York, 1908), 52, 86, 88, 94, 112, 309.

18. Copy of resolutions from Bolivar County *Democrat*, 30 April 1904, in Sillers Papers, Delta State College. The resolutions are in a folder dated "1909." It is not clear what lynching these resolutions referred to. It may have been the killing of a "Mrs. L. Holbert," who was lynched along with her husband in Sunflower County in February: New Orleans *Daily Picayune*, 8 February 1904. For lynchings see Charts 7 and 8, Appendix.

19. Stone, *Studies in the American Race Problem*, 235; H. P. Chapman and J. F. Battaile, *Picturesque Vicksburg: A Description of the Resources and Prospects of that City and the Famous Yazoo Delta, Its Agricultural and Commercial Interests, to Which Is Attached a Series of Sketches of Representative Industries* (Vicksburg, Miss., 1895), 27–28 (pamphlet in MDAH); Frances Bowman Carson Memoir in Breckenridge Family Reminiscences, microfilm at SHC, 1–3. This memoir refers to the period from 1892 to 1903 in Coahoma County.

20. John Patrick McDowell, *The Social Gospel in the South: The Woman's Home Mission Movement in the Methodist Episcopal Church, South, 1886–1939* (Baton Rouge, 1982), 84–115, quotation p. 99.

21. Ibid., 99–103; Jacqueline Dowd Hall, *Revolt against Chivalry: Jesse Daniel Ames and the Women's Campaign against Lynching* (New York, 1979), 65–74; Lily Hammond, "A Southern View of the Negro," *Outlook* 73 (1903), 619–23; L[ily] H. Hammond, *In Black and White: An Interpretation of Southern Life* (1914; reprint, New York, 1972), 30, 39, 64, 41.

22. McDowell, *Social Gospel in the South*, 85–86, 107–8, 106; Grantham, *Southern Progressivism*, 238; Coleman, ed., *History of Georgia*, 307.

23. Willis E. Mollison, *The Leading Afro-Americans of Vicksburg, Miss., Their Enterprises, Churches, Schools, Lodges, and Societies* (Vicksburg, 1908), 5, 6, 15.

24. John Dittmer, *Black Georgia in the Progressive Era, 1900–1920* (Urbana, Ill., 1977), 16–19, 173–74; "What the Southern Negroes Think of Themselves," *Public Opinion*, 10 March 1906, 305. See also August Meier and Elliot Rudwick, "The Boycott Movement against Jim Crow Streetcars in the South, 1900–1906," JAH, 55 (1969), 756–75.

25. Walter E. Campbell, "Profit, Prejudice, and Protest: Utility Competition and the Generation of Jim Crow Streetcars in Savannah, 1905–1907," GHQ 70 (1986), 197–231; Dittmer, *Black Georgia*, 164–65, 18–19 (quotation p. 165). The vote on the coast in the 1908 referendum on disfranchisement was 2,571 for and 3,944 against. In the Piedmont it was 8,237 for and 3,251 against.

26. Percy G. Shadd to Gov. John M. Slaton, 9 and 12 February 1914, Executive Department, Governors' Incoming Correspondence, John M. Slaton, GDAH; E. A. Angier to Attorney General, 30 January 1904, in *Peonage Files*, reel 1, frame 722.

27. Glenn T. Eskew, "Black Elitism and the Failure of Paternalism in Postbellum Georgia: The Case of Bishop Lucius Henry Holsey," *JSH* 58 (1992), 637–66 (quotations pp. 646, 649, 655, 658, 659). See also Clarence Bacote, "Negro Proscriptions, Protests, and Proposed Solutions in Georgia, 1886–1908," *JSH* 25 (1959), 471–98.

28. Stone, *Studies in the American Race Problem*, 235.

29. Alan Lomax, *The Land Where the Blues Began* (New York, 1993), 460, 462, 467–68.

30. Gellert quoted in Bruce Bastin, *Red River Blues* (Urbana, Ill., 1986), 65; Lawrence Gellert (collector) and Elie Siegmeister (arranger), *Negro Songs of Protest* (New York, 1936), 1–2.

31. The songs quoted are "I Went to Atlanta," "Pickin' Off De Cotton," "Sistren an' Brethren," "Out in de Rain," and "'Cause I'm a Nigger," all in Gellert and Siegmeister, *Negro Songs of Protest*.

32. Walter Sillers to P. Burrill, 2 November 1909, Sillers Papers, Delta State University. Prices and production of cotton are reported in *Hist. Stat.*, 517.

33. Walter Sillers to Thomas Poor, 11 September 1914; Sillers to H. F. Wheeler, 20 October 1914; Sillers to A. G. Paxton, 11 November 1914; Sillers Papers, Delta State University. On plans to raise prices, see George B. Tindall, *The Emergence of the New South, 1913–1945* (Baton Rouge, La., 1967), 33–37; Gilbert C. Fite, "Voluntary Attempts to Reduce Cotton Acreage in the South, 1914–1933," *JSH* 14 (1948), 481–99.

34. Letter from an unnamed source to Dean William Pickens, Morgan College, reprinted in the Baltimore *Afro-American*, 26 January 1916; Memphis *Commercial-Appeal*, 5 October 1916, both transcribed in "Migration Study Newspaper Extracts 1916–17," series 6, box 86, NUL.

35. Memphis *Commercial-Appeal,* 29 December 1916, "Migration Study Newspaper Extracts"; LeRoy Percy to A. D. Pace, 29 November 1916, Percy Papers.

36. Gavin Wright, *Old South, New South: Revolutions in the Southern Economy Since the Civil War* (New York, 1986).

37. Emmett J. Scott, *Negro Migration during the War* (Oxford, 1920), 53–54.

38. Ibid., 61–62; Savannah *Morning News,* 30 July–1 August 1916.

39. Scott, *Negro Migration,* 41; "Migration Study Mississippi Summary," series 6, box 86, NUL.

40. Letters to Chicago *Defender,* typescripts in folder "Migration Study. Negro Migrants, Letter From 1916–17," and folder "Migration Study Chicago Interviews," both series 6, box 86, NUL.

41. Savannah *Morning News,* 13 May 1917; Scott, *Negro Migration,* 37. On the *Defender*'s role, see esp. James R. Grossman, *Land of Hope: Chicago, Black Southerners, and the Great Migration* (Chicago, 1989), chap. 3.

42. Savannah *Morning News,* 30 July 1916; "Migration Study Mississippi Summary," NUL.

43. These quotations are from typescript drafts of reports of investigators for the National Urban League. Each town or community has a separate report filed in series 6, box 86, NUL.

44. Savannah *Morning News,* 31 July 1916; Scott, *Negro Migration,* 23 (Mississippi educator), 72–73; Report on Greenville, typescript in "Migration Study," NUL.

45. "Migration Study" reports on Greenwood and Greenville; extract from Columbia (S.C.) *State,* 1 November 1916, in "Migration Study Newspaper Extracts," NUL; Thomas J. Woofter, *Negro Migration: Changes in Rural Organization and Population of the Cotton Belt* (New York, 1920), 138.

46. Savannah *Morning News,* 2 August 1916; Savannah *Tribune,* 5 August 1916, Memphis *Commercial-Appeal,* 29 December 1917, and Jackson *News,* 12 June 1917 from "Migration Study Newspaper Extracts," NUL; Savannah *Morning News,* 2 January 1917; Wright, quoted from Savannah *Morning News,* 3 January 1917, in Scott, *Negro Migration,* 172.

47. Savannah *Morning News,* no date, and Memphis *Commercial-Appeal,* 5 October 1916, both in "Migration Study Newspaper Extracts"; Correspondence between Alexander Fitzhugh and James D. Thomas in Vicksburg *Herald,* 26 June 1917, and Frank Andrews to Gov. Theodore Bilbo, 26 June 1917, typescripts in folder "Migration Study. Negro Migrants, Letters From 1916–17"; typescript reports on Greenwood and "Mound Bayou and Boliver [*sic*] Co.," "Migration Study," all NUL.

48. Walter F. White, draft for report on "Work or Fight" laws for the NAACP, NAACP 10, reel 23, frame 338; typescript report on Greenville, in "Migration Study," NUL; LeRoy Percy to Hon. B. G. Humphreys, 26 May 1917, Percy Papers.

49. Quoted in Holmes, *White Chief,* 326.

50. *GHJ,* 19 October 1917.

51. Copy of minutes of executive committee of the Woman's Committee [for Washington County, Mississippi], 28 July 1918; Mrs. George F. Maynard to Dr. Jessica B. Peixotto, 12 August 1918, and Sallie J. Metcalfe (Mrs. Harley Metcalfe) to Press Service,

Children's Bureau, both in folder for "Mississippi" in box 509, CWDW. See also the records in folder 67, Somerville-Howorth Papers, Schlesinger Library.

52. Mrs. Edward McGehee to Mrs. Joseph Lamar, 15 July 1918, folder for "Mississippi," box 509, CWDW.

53. Alice Dunbar Nelson to Hannah Jane Patterson, 20 August, 21 August, 23 August 1918, folder 131, box 516, CWDW; *VEP,* 22 August 1918. See also William J. Breen, "Black Women and the Great War: Mobilization and Reform in the South," *JSH* 45 (1978), 421–40.

54. Alice Dunbar Nelson to Hannah Jane Patterson, 21 August, 23 August, 4 September 1918, folder 131, box 516, CWDW; Peel quoted in Suzanne Wones, " 'Unreconciled Strivings': A Study of the Effects of Race and Gender on the Identities of African American Women, 1895–1924" (M.A. thesis, University of New Hampshire, 1997), 30–31.

55. Savannah *Morning News,* 16 May 1917.

56. Walter F. White, draft report on Georgia, for report on "Work or Fight" laws, NAACP 10, reel 23, frames 141, 143, 338–45. For the use of "work or fight" laws (or informal versions of them) against black women, see especially Tera W. Hunter, *To 'Joy My Freedom: Southern Black Women's Lives and Labors after the Civil War* (Cambridge, Mass., 1997), 227–32.

57. *VEP,* 18, 19, and 26 September 1918; draft report on Greenville, in "Migration Study," NUL; Walter F. White to Rev. A. D. Williams, 21 August 1918, Walter F. White to Dr. F. R. Belcher, 22 August 1918, NAACP 10, reel 23, frames 141, 143.

58. Vardaman quoted in Jean Lang Scheiber and Harry N. Scheiber, "The Wilson Administration and the Wartime Mobilization of Black Americans, 1917–18," *Labor History* 10 (1969), 441; Vicksburg *Herald,* no date, quoted (p. 5) in Moorfield Story, *The Negro Question,* an address published as a pamphlet by the NAACP in 1918 and saved in records of the Bureau of Investigation of the Justice Department; see Theodore Kornweibel Jr., *Federal Surveillance of Afro-Americans (1917–1925): The First World War, the Red Scare, and the Garvey Movement* (Frederick, Md., n.d.), reel 9, frame 128 ff.

59. McMillen, *Dark Journey,* 302–7; John A. Miller to Walter White, 3 September 1918, NAACP 7A, reel 14, frame 36 ff. While it has often been noted that the war led to an upsurge in lynchings, this did not really occur until the war was over. In the South as a whole, there were twenty-six lynchings of blacks in 1917, the lowest number recorded since systematic records began to be kept in 1882. This increased to thirty-eight in 1918, still well below average for the years 1910 to 1916. The number shot up to sixty in 1919, the highest recorded since 1908. In the Delta, Piedmont, and coastal areas analyzed here, there were no lynchings in 1917, one in 1918, and ten in 1919. Data from Stewart E. Tolnay and E. M. Beck, *A Festival of Violence: An Analysis of Southern Lynchings, 1882–1930* (Urbana, Ill., 1995), table C-3, and from data kindly supplied to the author by Tolnay and Beck.

60. See *VEP,* 1 April 1918, as well as reports on "Church of God in Christ, Reverend Charles H. Mason, 1917–1919," in Miscellaneous Files, War Department: General and Special Staffs—Military Intelligence Division, Record Group 165, National Archives and Records Service, in Kornweibel, ed., *Federal Surveillance of Afro-Americans,* reel 22, frames 1–61; *VEP,* 8 and 17 July 1918. For other stories about black participation in the war, see *VEP,* 6 June 1917, 8 April 1918, 22 June 1918, 13 February 1919. For a gen-

eral treatment of wartime mobilization of blacks, see Scheiber and Scheiber, "Wilson Administration."

61. *GHJ,* 10 August 1917, 24 August, 14 September, 12 October 1917, 22 February 1918.

62. See William Jordan, "The 'Damnable Dilemma': African American Accommodation and Protest during World War One," *JAH* 81 (1995), 1562-83.

63. Mrs. Edward McGehee to Mrs. Joseph Lamar, 15 July 1918, "Mississippi" file for 1918, box 509, CWDW; A. C. Griggs, "Lucy Craft Laney," *Journal of Negro History* 19 (1934), 96-102; Savannah *Morning News,* 15 May, 11 June, 22 October 1917, 4 May and 9 May 1918.

64. McMillen, *Dark Journey,* 314-16; Dittmer, *Black Georgia,* 205-7; Steven A. Reich, "Soldiers of Democracy: Black Texans and the Fight for Citizenship, 1917-1921," *JAH* 82 (1996), 1478-1504.

65. Social Circle: Charter Application, 17 November 1921; Mound Bayou: Charter Application, 9 March 1919, NAACP Branch Files. Social Circle was further west, toward Atlanta, than the "eastern Piedmont" of this study.

66. Brunswick: Charter Application, 9 September 1918; Savannah: James Garfield Lemon to Roy Nash, February [n.d.] 1917; A. B. Singfield to Roy Nash, 7 June 1917; Lemon to James Weldon Johnson, 30 August 1917; Lemon report to NAACP, 30 January 1918, all in NAACP Branch Files.

67. Charter Application, Augusta, Georgia, 9 February 1917; Wilson Jefferson to Roy Nash, 7 March 1917; Jefferson to Nash, 11 April 1917 ["manhood bartered away"]; Jefferson to James Weldon Johnson, 3 May 1917, all in NAACP Branch Files.

68. T. G. Ewing Jr., to NAACP, 9 May 1918, and Charter Application, Vicksburg, Miss., NAACP Branch Files.

69. *VDH,* 24 July 1918; *VEP,* 24 July 1918; Harris, "Etiquette, Lynching, and Racial Boundaries," 397. Sketchy biographical information on Miller is available in *Who's Who in Colored America, 1928-29,* p. 266, and in Williams College *Reunion Book, 1933,* pp. 21-22. I am grateful to Lynne K. Fonteneau of the Williams College Archives and Special Collections for the latter reference. See also Mollison, *The Leading Afro-Americans of Vicksburg.*

70. The quotation is from a typescript letter to Brunini titled "Vicksburg, Miss. July 11-16," series 6, box 86, NUL. The writer of the letter is not identified, but the topic and date (identical to that on the affidavit mentioned) clearly identifies it as connected with the teacher controversy. Some of Vicksburg's African Americans later told an investigator that discontent over the "immorality of school teachers" whose jobs were "in the hands of white trustees" was a contributing cause of black out-migration from the city; see folder "Migration Study. Negro Migrants, Letters From 1916-17," and "Vicksburg," in folder "Migration Study Mississippi Summary," both in NUL.

71. *VEP,* 26 June 1918, 25 June 1918, 27 June 1918.

72. John A. Miller to Walter White, 3 September 1918, NAACP 7A, reel 14.

73. Miller to John Shillady, 29 October 1918, NAACP 7A, reel 14. This white informant was Joseph Short, the clerk of the U.S. court in the city. Miller later claimed that he did finally agree to take $150 worth of bonds

74. *VEP,* 24, 25, 26, 27 July 1919; *VDH,* 25, 26, 27 and 31 July 1919; Miller to John

Shillady, 8 August 1918, NAACP, reel 14. The change in tone in the news reports is notable; the original report of the attack on Miller and Clay had referred to the "patriotic" members of the crowd; the women's attackers were simply "mob leaders." The signers of the appeal on the day after the attack included two judges, the secretary of the board of trade, two bank presidents, and five other prominent businessmen. Identifications were made from the Vicksburg city directory for 1918.

75. Whitecappers had operated in areas in which whites and blacks competed for good land to rent and often were intent on driving away African Americans completely. Their activities were anathema to white planters and planter-merchants who depended upon black labor. William F. Holmes, "Whitecapping: Agrarian Violence in Mississippi, 1902–1906," *JSH* 35 (1969), 165–85; W. Fitzhugh Brundage, *Lynching in the New South: Georgia and Virginia, 1880–1930* (Urbana, Ill., 1993), 19–28.

76. *VEP,* 26 July 1918; *VDH,* 27 July 1918. While Wilson's statement did not touch on race as an issue, in fact it was partly a response to intense pressure brought to bear on Wilson from black leaders in the North and even members of his own administration to condemn racial violence; see Scheiber and Scheiber, "Wilson Administration," 456–57. Almost immediately after that attack on the women, the police chief and mayor claimed that the incident was separate from the earlier attacks on Miller and Cook; in fact the evidence strongly suggests the same men were instigators in both events. Miller told the NAACP that he had been taken to city hall by, among others "public auto driver Patterson," almost certainly the same Frank Patterson prosecuted for the attack on the women. The only other attacker mentioned by name in Miller's correspondence was "Eades," who he identified as a Vicksburg policeman. Eades was not prosecuted for the later attack on the women. Miller to John Shillady, 19 August 1918, NAACP, reel 14; *VEP,* 26 July 1918.

77. Alice Dunbar Nelson to Hannah Jane Patterson, 23 August 1918, folder 131, box 512, CWDW.

Chapter 7   Twilight in Cotton's Kingdom

1. Ledger 67, "Annual Reports Empire Plantation Co. 1913–1925," box L5, DPL; "D&PL Annual Statements and President's Reports, 1921," box 1, DPL. Both these planting enterprises were owned by the British investors, although it is not clear from the records whether they had identical or merely overlapping shareholders. They were later merged into one operation. The D&PL reports for each year include a detailed summary of expenses and income for each of the more than a dozen individual plantations that made up the company, as well as an overall summary statement of earnings. The Empire Plantation Company reports concern that separate operation only and are somewhat less detailed.

2. Ledger 67, "Empire Plantation," DPL.

3. Ledger 67, "Empire Plantation," DPL, report for 1917. These plantations produced high-quality cotton that typically earned a premium over the average cotton price. The reports do not indicate how many tenants were on the Empire Plantation, but based on data for D&PL for 1925, its 2,800-plus acres probably were worked by about 150 tenant families. Thus in 1917 these families would have earned about $900 each for their cotton, plus, in most cases, additional wage payments for extra labor. Tenants were well aware that planters in 1917 made out handsomely because of the difference in price between the

purchase from the tenant and the sale in the market. See, for example, the report on "Mound Bayou and Bolivar Co." in "Migration Study, Mississippi," box 86, NUL. For the folk tale, see James C. Cobb, *The Most Southern Place on Earth: The Mississippi Delta and the Roots of Regional Identity* (New York, 1992), 155.

4. Ledger 67, "Empire Plantation," DPL, reports for 1918, 1919. The figures for dividends and capital returns are noted in the report for 1920.

5. Ibid., report for 1920.

6. Ibid., reports for 1921–24, and "D&PL Annual Statements and President's Reports," both in DPL. The 1924 report is the last in the files for Empire Plantation. The D&PL annual statements for 1923 and 1924 are missing, although information for the crop year 1923 is contained in the report for 1925 (the reports, issued in January, refer to the previous year's operations).

7. Ledger 67, "Empire Plantation," annual statements for 1916, 1917, DPL.

8. Ledger 67, "Empire Plantation," annual statements for 1920, 1923, and "D&PL Annual Statements and President's Reports," 1921, both DPL.

9. Financial Records: Minutes: Managers' Meeting, 20 January 1925, DPL.

10. "DPL Annual Statements," 1921; Financial Records, Minutes: Managers' Meeting, 21 October 1921, both DPL.

11. Minutes: Managers' Meeting, 21 October 1921 and December 2, 1921, both DPL.

12. Ruby Sheppeard Hicks, *The Song of the Delta* (Jackson, Miss., 1976), 65; Sunflower *Tocsin*, 22 March 1917.

13. Ledger 67, "Empire Plantation," annual statement for 1923; Oscar Johnston to James R. Leavell (vice president of the Continental & Commercial Bank, Chicago), 23 December 1926; Oscar Johnston to Edoardo Giannini [Rome, Italy], 28 December 1926; D. A. Davidson, USDA Bureau of Animal Husbandry [New Braunfels, Texas], to Oscar Johnston, 20 March 1927, in Oscar Johnston Correspondence, all in DPL.

14. For trends in cotton production and numbers of black tenants, see Charts 5 and 15, Appendix.

15. Annual Report, 1928, DPL. For the flood, see John M. Barry, *Rising Tide: The Great Mississippi Flood of 1927 and How It Changed America* (New York, 1997); Pete Daniel, *Deep'n As It Come: The 1927 Mississippi River Flood* (New York, 1977).

16. Barry, *Rising Tide*, 13–17; Daniel, *Deep'n As It Come*, 4–11. A mile of standard levee contained 13.5 times the cubic yardage of earth as the standard mile in 1882.

17. Barry, *Rising Tide*, 192–200.

18. Ibid. (quotations from Ogden, Jones, Sanders, and Mason, pp. 199–201); Daniel, *Deep'n As It Come*, 14–15 (including second quotation from Sanders; quotation from Williams).

19. Barry, *Rising Tide*, 202–9; Daniel, *Deep'n As It Come*, 16–23.

20. Daniel, *Deep'n As It Come*, 52–62, 69; Barry, *Rising Tide*, 272–81; Joe Rice Dockery Oral History, MDAH. The Moore story, though recorded by Pete Daniel, appears in Barry, p. 276.

21. Barry, *Rising Tide*, 303–17; Daniel, *Deep'n As It Come*, 154–55 (including quotation from a letter from Walter White to NAACP headquarters, 16 May 1927), 158 (quoting an unpublished report to the Red Cross by the Colored Advisory Committee); Oscar Johnston to Harry M. Bryan, 4 May 1927, Oscar Johnston Correspondence, DPL.

22. Barry, *Rising Tide,* 324–27, 332–34; W. A. Percy, *Lanterns on the Levee: Recollections of a Planter's Son* (New York, 1941; reprint, Baton Rouge, La., 1973), 267–68.

23. Lyrics from Patton's "High Water Everywhere" (I), in Eric Sackheim, ed., *The Blues Line: A Collection of Blues Lyrics* (New York, 1975), 193. Patton also recorded a second version of "High Water Everywhere."

24. Annual statements, 1927, 1928, 1929, DPL (quotation from 1928). See Charts 5 and 15 for trends in cotton production and numbers of tenants in the Delta.

25. *GHJ,* 15 December 1916. The land value of up to $200 is from Arthur F. Raper, *Preface to Peasantry: A Tale of Two Black Belt Counties* (Chapel Hills, N.C., 1936; reprint, New York, 1968), 204.

26. Raper, *Preface to Peasantry,* 208; Atlanta *Constitution,* 26 September 1920. Greene's black population was 11,974 in 1880, 11,636 in 1910, and 11,200 in 1920. Meanwhile the white population grew from 6,875 to 7,771 between 1910 and 1920. On the sources of white migrants, see Raper, *Preface to Peasantry,* 187.

27. Charley Patton, "Mississippi Bo' Weavil Blues," in "The Complete Paramount Recordings of Charley Patton" (Black Swan HCD-21); *GHJ,* 6 October 1916.

28. *GHJ,* 30 May and 12 October 1919, 11 February 1921; Raper, *Preface to Peasantry,* 201–5. For cotton production in the county, see data in Raper, 202. (Note that Raper's data is based on cotton ginned in Greene County. The census figure for 1919 of 22,343 bales is actual production in the county.)

29. Lyrics quoted from Paul Oliver, "Blues Fell this Morning: Meaning in the Blues" (2d ed.; New York, 1990), 16–18. Blues historians have given somewhat conflicting accounts of Arnold's birthplace; according to William Barlow he was from a "small town just south of Atlanta." (Barlow, *"Looking Up at Down": The Emergence of Blues Culture* (Philadelphia, 1989), 308. The song was recorded in Chicago in 1935.

30. Raper, *Preface to Peasantry,* 115, 111, 103, 205–7.

31. Population figures are summarized in Chart 2, Appendix. For destinations of out-migrants, see Raper, *Preface to Peasantry,* 195–99. Raper's data are from Greene County (as well as Macon County in another part of the state). Only one-sixth of the migrants went directly to the North. One-third went to Atlanta, by far the most common destination. Fewer than one in twenty went to neighboring counties.

32. *GHJ,* 24 May 1929. Summary production figures are taken from U.S. Censuses of Agriculture in 1920 and 1925.

33. Raper, *Preface to Peasantry,* 38, 162, 176–77, 173.

34. The Dents' financial dealings in the 1920s can be traced in part 5, HBP. On Ford, see "Henry Ford at Richmond Hill: A Venture in Private Enterprise," in George A. Rogers and R. Frank Saunders, *Swamp Water and Wiregrass: Sketches of Coastal Georgia* (Macon, Ga., 1984), 205–17.

35. *Southeast Georgian* [St. Marys, then Kingsland], 6 February 1920. Number of manufacturing workers is reported in the U.S. Bureau of the Census, *Fifteenth Census, 1930, Census of Occupations.*

36. *Official Program of Opening Exercises and Historical Pageant. Presented in Connection with the Opening of the Brunswick–St. Simons Highway, July 11, 1924,* pamphlet in Brunswick Regional Library; Brunswick *News,* 1 July, 5 July 1929. On 4 July 1929 a record 1,992 cars with 6,507 passengers crossed on the causeway.

37. Brunswick *News*, 4, 26, 27, 30 December 1928; William S. McFeely, *Sapelo's People: A Long Walk into Freedom* (New York, 1994), 146–48; Burnette Vanstory, *Georgia's Land of the Golden Isles* (reprint, Athens, Ga., 1981), 63–68; Harold H. Martin, *This Happy Isle: The Story of Sea Island and the Cloister* (Sea Island, Ga., 1978).

38. The most complete account is in Martin, *This Happy Isle*.

39. Martin, *This Happy Isle*; Lydia Parrish, *Slave Songs of the Georgia Sea Islands* (1942; reprint Athens, Ga., 1992), 17. For population trends, see Chart 1, Appendix. Mean acreage harvested or black-owned and -operated farms, as reported in the 1930 Census of Agriculture, was 9.5 on the coast, 30.0 in the Piedmont, and 21.0 in the Delta.

40. Oscar Johnston to American Red Cross headquarters, 9 May 1927, Oscar Johnston Correspondence, DPL.

41. Dorothy Dickins, *A Nutrition Investigation of Negro Tenants in the Yazoo-Mississippi Delta*, Bulletin 254, Mississippi Agricultural Experiment Station (August 1928) (quotations pp. 10, 11). The counties were Bolivar, Coahoma, Quitman, and Sharkey. All the families (seventy-seven sharecroppers and two cash tenants) had at least one member who could read and write. The study was completed in February and March 1927.

42. Ibid., 40–41, 6, 37.

43. Ibid., 17, 38, 44, 47.

44. Donald Dewey Scarborough, *An Economic Study of Negro Farmers as Owners, Tenants, and Croppers*, Phelps-Stokes Fellowship Studies, no. 7 (*Bulletin of the University of Georgia*, vol. 25, September 1924), income and expenditures at 26, 31; Raper, *Preface to Peasantry*, 52–53, 55. The counties studied by Scarborough include Wilkes, Clarke, Oconee, and Cobb. Wilkes is part of the "eastern Piedmont" as defined for this book; Clarke and Oconee are just to the north, Cobb somewhat further to the northwest. The data are not reported by county.

45. Scarborough, *Economic Study*, 29; Raper, *Preface to Peasantry*, 55, 63–65.

46. Raper, *Preface to Peasantry*, 22.

47. Scarborough, *Economic Study*, 8; Raper, *Preface to Peasantry*, 85–87. The figure for automobiles on the D&PL properties comes from a census of the plantations taken in 1925, in DPL. The census includes figures for each plantation (plus the sawmill and group "quarters"), most of which include figures for workers, families, stock, cotton production, and other information. For some plantations some data are missing, and the totals given for the company as a whole do not always agree with the sum of the individual numbers, so the number of families and automobiles given here is approximate, though certainly close to the true number.

48. Raper, *Preface to Peasantry*, 21–22, 99.

49. Ibid., 107–8, 157, 55. Annual incomes (cash plus provisions) by race in Greene County in 1934 were: white owners, $648; black owners, $502; white renters, $551; black renters, $417; white sharecroppers, $385; black sharecroppers, $282; white wage hands, $217; black wage hands, $112.

50. Annual reports for 1929 and 1930, DPL. The reports cover operations of the previous calendar year.

51. Annual reports for 1931, 1932, and 1933, DPL. The actual prices received or paid by the company mirror, but do not match exactly, the "season average" price of cotton reported in *Hist. Stat.* For example, the company actually sold its 1931 crop for an average

of 6.41 cents per pound, while the national season average was 5.66 cents per pound. *Hist. Stat.,* 517. On the effects of the drought, see Nan Woodruff, *As Rare as Rain: Federal Relief in the Great Southern Drought of 1930–31* (Urbana, Ill., 1985), 3–38. Text of "Dry Spell Blues" is from Jeff Todd Titon, *Early Downhome Blues: A Musical and Cultural Analysis* (Urbana, Ill., 1977; 2d ed., Chapel Hill, N.C., 1994), 119.

52. *GHJ,* 6 and 13 December 1929, 11 April 1930.

53. Raper, *Preface to Peasantry,* 111, 35, 55. Average gross income for all black farm families was $390 in 1927, $321 in 1934.

54. Martin, *This Happy Isle,* 62–70; William Barton McCash and June Hall McCash, *The Jekyll Island Club: Southern Haven for America's Millionaires* (Athens, Ga., 1989), 179–92.

Chapter 8   "Discord, dissension, and hatred"

1. John Dittmer, *Black Georgia in the Progressive Era, 1900–1920* (Urbana, Ill., 1977), 204; *VEP* 22 March, 12 April 1919.

2. *VEP,* 19, 23, 24 April, 7, 8, 9 and 14 May 1919.

3. Ibid., 15 May 1919. Unless otherwise noted, the detailed description of the events below comes from this source. This day's edition and other documents related to the lynching can be found in reel 14, frames 261 ff, NAACP 7A.

4. *VEP,* 16 May 1919; *VDH,* 18 May 1919; see also Neil R. McMillen, *Dark Journey: Black Mississippians in the Age of Jim Crow* (Urbana, Ill., 1989),241.

5. *VEP,* 16 April, 15 and 17 May 1919; *VDH,* 22 May 1919.

6. Letter from "G.A.S.," *VDH,* 22 May 1919.

7. The occupations of petition signers were identified from the Vicksburg *City Directory* for 1918, or, in some instances, for 1912. As far as can be determined, the petition was signed by white men only.

8. *VEP,* 7 and 12 July 1919. Occupations of grand jury members were found in the city directories or the 1910 manuscript U.S. Census of Population.

9. J. W. McRaven to Will Henry and Lucile, 29 March, 6 April, 11 April, and 6 December 1922, 2 February 1923, J. W. McRaven Letters, MDAH. These letters are typescripts prepared by McRaven's son, William Henry McRaven.

10. J. W. McRaven to Will Henry, 24 March 1924, 7 June 1923, 9 September 1923, McRaven to Will Henry and Lucile, 26 September 1922, "Flying Squadron," McRaven Letters, MDAH.

11. J. W. McRaven to Will Henry, 9 January 1924 and 7 June 1923; to Will Henry and Lucile, 26 January 1929, MDAH.

12. *The Woman Voter* [Clarksdale, Miss.], 3 and 17 August, 30 November 1922, 16 March 1923.

13. *GHJ,* 15 August 1919, 24 January 1919, 1 August 1919; *Southeast Georgian* [St. Marys, then Kingsland], 2 March 1922; *VEP,* 16 July 1919.

14. *VEP,* 19 February, 25, 21, and 26 April 1919; *VDH,* 15 April 1919; *The Woman Voter* [Clarksdale], 23 November 1922.

15. Richard C. Cortner, *A Mob Intent on Death: The NAACP and the Arkansas Riot*

Cases (Middletown, Conn., 1988), chap. 1; *VEP*, 7 February 1919, 28 March 1919, 9 April 1919 (story reprinted from the London *Daily Express*).

16. *VEP*, 17 April 1919.

17. The only lynching along the coast between 1918 and 1930 involved two men accused of rape in the interior town of Jesup, Georgia, who were taken from a train by outsiders and killed in Liberty County while en route to the supposed safety of the Savannah jails.

18. Cremer: Atlanta *Constitution*, 26 September 1920; *GHJ*, 1 October 1920 (which calls the victim Felix Cooper). Smalley: Atlanta *Constitution*, 17 August 1921 (Fitzhugh Brundage omits this incident from his analyses of Georgia lynchings in *Lynching in the New South: Georgia and Virginia, 1880–1930* [Urbana, Ill., 1993], on the grounds that a killing by police during such a shootout deserves a different classification).

19. Green: Memphis *Commercial-Appeal*, 5 March 1919, clipping, along with related material in reel 13, frames 454–84, NAACP 7A; Lincoln County: New York *Times*, 7 October 1919, and New York *Call*, 7 October 1919, clippings in reel 10, frame 820 ff, NAACP 7A; Atlanta *Constitution*, 7 October 1919. The *Call* reported that Martin was killed after being taken as a hostage until Gordon was turned over; the *Constitution* that he was killed for praising Gordon's deeds.

20. *VEP* 16 May 1919; Atlanta *Constitution*, 11 September 1919; New York *Herald*, 11 September 1919. See also clippings in reel 10, frame 405 ff, NAACP 7A. Truett's lynching is listed in the database of Stewart Tolnay and E. M. Beck.

21. Minnifield: New York *Times*, 30 July 1923, clipping in reel 14, frame 336, NAACP 7A; Smalley: Augusta *Herald*, 17 August 1921, clipping, reel 10, frame 505, idem; Richards: clippings reel 11, frame 116, idem.

22. Washington, Ga., *News-Reporter*, 2 July 1920, in reel 2, frame 749, NAACP 7A; letter from H. J. Rowe, editor of the Athens *Banner*, to New York *World*, 29 September 1919, reel 10, frame 413, NAACP 7A.

23. Hortense Powdermaker, *After Freedom: A Cultural Study in the Deep South* (New York, 1939; reprint, Madison, Wis., 1993), 18; *GHJ*, 9 November 1917, 27 June, 24 October 1919.

24. Clement C. Mosely, "Invisible Empire: The History of the Ku Klux Klan in Twentieth Century Georgia" (Ph.D. diss., University of Georgia, 1968); Nancy K. MacLean, *Behind the Mask of Chivalry: The Making of the Second Ku Klux Klan* (New York, 1994), chap. 1.

25. MacLean, *Behind the Mask*, 55–56; Roger K. Hux, "The Ku Klux Klan in Macon, 1919–1925," *GHQ* 62 (1978), 155–68.

26. *GHJ*, 4 February 1921 (excerpt in Raper Papers, SHC, folder 974); Sunflower *Tocsin*, 14 June 1923; reel 13, frames 664–72, NAACP 7A.

27. Leland *Enterprise*, 18 March 1922, clipping in Percy Papers, MDAH. On the moral crusading of the Klan, see also MacLean, *Behind the Mask*, 98–124.

28. *The Woman Voter* [Clarksdale, Miss.], 3 August 1922, 29 June, 25 January, 4 May 1923.

29. See clippings for 1924 from the Memphis *Commercial-Appeal* and the Jackson *Clarion Ledger* in Scrapbook, vol. 8, Somerville-Nugent Papers, Schlesinger Library, Har-

vard University. For Percy's purchases of whiskey, see, for example, Percy to Jake L. Strickland, 25 October and 31 December 1924, Percy Papers. In addition to other sources cited, the account below of LeRoy Percy's fight against the Klan in Washington County is based on Lewis Baker, *The Percys of Mississippi: Politics and Literature in the New South* (Baton Rouge, La., 1983), 95–112; Bertram Wyatt-Brown, *The House of Percy: Honor, Melancholy, and Imagination in a Southern Family* (New York, 1994), 226–38; and John M. Barry, *Rising Tide: The Great Mississippi Flood of 1927 and How It Changed America* (New York, 1997), 143–55.

30. Percy's speech is reprinted in a pamphlet, *The Face at Your Window*, in the Percy Papers (quotations pp. 4, 9, 12, 11).

31. Dick Cox to LeRoy Percy, 5 March 1922; *Speech of Ex-United States Senator LeRoy Percy*, 23 April 1923, p. 4; Percy, *Face at Your Window*, 14, all in Percy Papers.

32. William Alexander Percy, *Lanterns on the Levee: Recollections of a Planter's Son* (New York, 1941; reprint, Baton Rouge, La., 1973), 236.

33. *GHJ*, 17 October 1924.

34. Dittmer, *Black Georgia*, 203, 206, 208–9; *VEP*, 19 April 1919; McMillen, *Dark Journey*, 275–79.

35. Cortner, *A Mob Intent on Death*, 5–23. For Mississippi commentary on the "insurrection," see *VEP*, 4, 6, 11 October 1919. As Cortner's book recounts, the death sentences and convictions of the black "rioters" were eventually overturned by the U.S. Supreme Court. The branch files records of the NAACP for the 1920s show very little activity in either cities or towns in the Delta, Piedmont, or Georgia coast.

36. Arthur F. Raper, *Preface to Peasantry: A Tale of Two Black Belt Counties* (Chapel Hill, N.C., 1936; reprint, New York, 1968), 359–72.

37. Powdermaker, *After Freedom*, 232–52, 274–85 (quotation p. 276); see also Raper, *Preface to Peasantry*, 391.

38. Powdermaker, *After Freedom*, 285; Raper, *Preface to Peasantry*, 122, 138–39.

39. Raper, *Preface to Peasantry*, 373–83; Powdermaker, *After Freedom*, 122.

40. On "shouts," see Chapter 5, and Art Rosenbaum, *Shout Because You're Free: The African American Ring Shout Tradition in Coastal Georgia* (Athens, Ga., 1998).

41. Peter D. Goldsmith, *When I Rise Cryin' Holy: African-American Denominationalism on the Georgia Coast* (New York, 1989), quotation p. 187.

42. Raper, *Preface to Peasantry*, 390. Only one major blues singer of the era, Georgia's Blind Blake, is thought to have possibly come from the Sea Island region. Blake's reputation, though, was made in the Piedmont. See Bruce Bastin, *Red River Blues* (Urbana, Ill., 1986), 84–87.

43. Dorothy Dickins, *A Nutrition Investigation of Negro Tenants in the Yazoo-Mississippi Delta*, Bulletin 254, Mississippi Agricultural Experiment Station (August 1928), 10; Raper, *Preface to Peasantry*, 66. Raper's figures are combined for Greene County and for Macon County in middle Georgia.

44. Jeff Todd Titon, *Early Downhome Blues: A Musical and Cultural Analysis* (Urbana, Ill., 1977; 2d ed., Chapel Hill, N.C., 1994), 193–217; Robert Palmer, *Deep Blues* (New York, 1981), 77.

45. Bastin, *Red River Blues*, 97–105, 118, 125–40.

46. Palmer, *Deep Blues*, 79–81.

47. Palmer, *Deep Blues,* 111–14 (quotation p. 113); Peter Guralnick, *Searching for Robert Johnson* (New York, 1989).

48. Guralnick, *Searching for Robert Johnson,* 20–23, 37, 59 (quoting Shines); Palmer, *Deep Blues,* 124–25; lyric from notes accompanying *Robert Johnson: The Complete Recordings* (Columbia C2K 47222).

49. Palmer, *Deep Blues,* 123–28.

50. Telegram from L. J. Folz to Judge W. A. Alcorn, in reel 13, frame 670, NAACP 7A.

51. Morton Sosna, *In Search of the Silent South: Southern Liberals and the Race Issue* (New York, 1977), chap. 2; Wilma Dykeman and James Stokely, *Seeds of Southern Change: The Life of Will Alexander* (New York, 1962), 58–76; Brundage, *Lynching in the New South,* 234–35 (quotation p. 234).

52. Brundage, *Lynching in the New South,* 362, n. 84.

53. Dykeman and Stokely, *Seeds of Southern Change,* 112–17; Jacquelyn Dowd Hall, *Revolt against Chivalry: Jessie Daniel Ames and the Women's Campaign against Lynching* (New York, 1979).

54. Daniel Joseph Singal, *The War Within: From Victorian to Modernist Thought in the South, 1919–1945* (Chapel Hill, N.C., 1982), 328–38.

55. *GHJ,* 6 April 1928; Raper, *Preface to Peasantry,* 170–71.

56. Brundage, *Lynching in the New South,* 232–33; Atlanta *Constitution,* 2 July 1922.

57. Brundage, *Lynching in the New South,* 239, 235–36.

58. Angeline Coleman to Walter White, 4 October 1927, and newspaper clippings, reel 13, frames 664–72, NAACP 7A.

59. Powdermaker, *After Freedom,* appendix A, 381–91.

60. Powdermaker's respondents included 159 junior college students and 97 "adults"; 129 were male, 120 female, and 7 did not indicate sex. Powdermaker was in Indianola between 1932 and 1934.

61. David M. Oshinsky, *"Worse Than Slavery": Parchman Farm and the Ordeal of Jim Crow Justice* (New York, 1996), 139–42.

62. The case is documented in clippings in reel 13, frame 740 ff, NAACP 7A. Most of the detail comes from a clipping from the Jackson *Daily News,* 1 January 1929. "By causes unknown" and the estimate of a three-mile line of cars is from the Clarksdale *Press Register,* 1 January 1929.

Chapter 9   "Uncle Sam is my shepherd"

1. *You Are a Citizen!,* in "Augusta, Georgia" folders, box 43, NAACP Branch Files.

2. Rev. William Merriwether to R. W. Bagnall, 13 August 1931; Sam B. Wallace to R. W. Bagnall, 23 August and 22 October 1931, "Augusta, Georgia" folders, box 43, NAACP Branch Files.

3. Ralph J. Bunche, *The Political Status of the Negro in the Age of FDR,* edited and with an introduction by Dewey W. Grantham (Chicago, 1973), 301, 403, 126–28, 435, 404–5, 412–13; report on Darien, Georgia, in "Wilhemina Jackson Memos and Notes," box 82, Bunche Papers.

4. Bunche, *Political Status of the Negro,* 412–13.

5. Ibid., 124–28, 138–39, 234, 370 (quotation); David L. Cohn, *Where I Was Born*

and Raised (Boston, 1948; part 1 first published as *God Shakes Creation,* 1935), 198; John Dollard, *Caste and Class in a Southern Town* (New Haven, Conn., 1937; reprint, Madison, Wis., 1988), 218.

6. *GHJ,* 19 September 1919, 20 January 1920, 29 August 1930; *Southeast Georgian* [St. Marys, then Kingsland], 19 June 1924; 4 September 1924, 22 July, 9 September 1926.

7. *Southeast Georgian* [St. Marys, then Kingsland], 6 May, 27 May 1920, 3 June, 29 July, 5 August, 2 September, 9 September 1920.

8. J. W. McRaven to Will Henry, Lucile, and "The Kid" [Annette] [n.d.]; to Will Henry and Lucile, 19 October 1928, McRaven Letters, MDAH. Vote totals are taken from *The World Almanac and Book of Facts 1929* (New York, 1929) — though note that the columns for Mississippi are mislabeled that year.

9. *GHJ,* 28 September, 26 October, 2 November 1928. Smith easily carried Greene County with 627 votes to Hoover's 70, with another 175 votes going to an "Anti-Smith" slate.

10. Votes from *World Almanac.*

11. *GHJ,* 27 January 1928; John M. Barry, *Rising Tide: The Great Mississippi Flood of 1927 and How It Changed America* (New York, 1997), 399–407.

12. These programs included agricultural credit corporations and credit banks as well as emergency loans for seed and fertilizers. For the effects in Greene County, see Arthur F. Raper, *Preface to Peasantry: A Tale of Two Black Belt Counties* (1936; reprint, New York, 1968), 228–30 (quotation p. 229).

13. *GHJ,* 28 October 1932 and 9 October 1931 (reprinted from the Albany *Herald*).

14. *GHJ,* 25 September, 2, 9, 16 October 1931.

15. Arthur Raper, "The Black Belt Farmers of Alabama and Georgia," MSS in folder 34, Raper Papers; letter to Governor M. S. Connor, 23 August 1933, quoted in "LeFlore County, Mississippi," RPA, BAE, 47–48. This letter is in the actual draft report, a copy of which is in BAE files, rather than the summary which can also be found in the files. The author of the letter was not identified and the letter itself was not included in a summary of the report to be sent to the state administrator, as otherwise "the Welfare Workers would most likely be forced to resign by the Board of Supervisors" (p. 50).

16. Morgan County, Georgia, 23 November 1934, 1, RPA; Greene County, Georgia, 29 November 1935, RRR; McDuffie County, Georgia, 16 October 1935, RRR; "LeFlore County, Mississippi," 9 November 1934, RPA; McIntosh County, Georgia, 29 October 1935, 2, 4, 6–8, 12, RRR. For an account of the relief efforts in Georgia, see Michael S. Holmes, *The New Deal in Georgia: An Administrative History* (Westport, Conn., 1975). As Holmes shows, the bureaucratic personnel at the state level for the FERA, the CWA, and the WPA were largely the same people.

17. Greene County, Georgia, 6, McDuffie County, Georgia, 1, 6–7, 12, both RRR.

18. "LeFlore County, Mississippi," RPA, 48; Morgan County, Georgia, RPA, 50; Greene County, Georgia, RRR, 14; "LeFlore County, Mississippi" summary, RPA, 5.

19. "Monied pressure" from "LeFlore County, Mississippi," 49, RPA; "peonage" quotation and LeFlore numbers from "LeFlore County, Mississippi [summary]," 1, RPA; numbers for Eastern Piedmont from manuscript tables compiled for Georgia counties in folder 41, Raper Papers, SHC.

20. "LeFlore County, Mississippi," 49, 68, RPA; Washington County, Mississippi, 2, RRR.

21. MSS Table, "Federal Relief in Georgia August 1933–March 1934," folder 41, Raper Papers; "Morgan County, Georgia," 46, RPA.

22. "LeFlore County, Mississippi," xxix, RPA; MSS Tables, "Federal Relief in Georgia August 1933–March 1934," folder 41, and "CWA Payroll for Greene County, Georgia, 1933–1934," folder 984, Raper Papers, SHC; Raper, *Preface to Peasantry*, 264.

23. Raper, *Preface to Peasantry*, 243–45; George B. Tindall, *The Emergence of the New South, 1913–1945* (Baton Rouge, La., 1967), 393–95.

24. Raper, *Preface to Peasantry*, 245–47; Tindall, *Emergence of the New South*, 395–96. The quota system had some flexibility in that farmers who failed to grow enough to meet their quotas could sell their excess "tax-free" certificates to others.

25. These numbers are based on the annual reports in DPL. The company in most years continued to show net losses because it was making large interest and mortgage payments, but these latter payments also went largely to the shareholders.

26. Raper, *Preface to Peasantry*, 243–53, describes instances of landlords' abuse and provides the incomes for Greene County. For general discussion see Donald H. Grubbs, *Cry from the Cotton: The Southern Tenant Farmers' Union and the New Deal* (Chapel Hill, N.C., 1971); David Eugene Conrad, *The Forgotten Farmers: The Story of Sharecroppers in the New Deal* (Urbana, Ill., 1965). The precise rules for division of federal payments (in both 1933 and later years), and the results in terms of farmer income, are outlined in Warren C. Whatley, "Labor for the Picking: The New Deal in the South," *JEH* 43 (1983), 905–29.

27. On the STFU, see Grubbs, *Cry from the Cotton;* on the SCU in Alabama, see Robin D. G. Kelley, *Hammer and Hoe: Alabama Communists during the Great Depression* (Chapel Hill, N.C., 1990). On the controversies over policy see, in addition to sources cited above, Lawrence J. Nelson, "The Art of the Possible: Another Look at the 'Purge' of the AAA Liberals in 1935," *AH* 57 (1983), 416–35; Lawrence J. Nelson, "Oscar Johnston, the New Deal, and the Cotton Subsidy Payments Controversy, 1936–37," *JSH* 40 (1974), 399–416.

28. On the "purge" of liberals from the AAA, see Conrad, *Forgotten Farmers*, chap. 8; Nelson, "The Art of the Possible."

29. Johnston to Henry Wallace, 6 February 1935, quoted in Nelson, "Art of the Possible," 428.

30. Johnston to William Alexander Percy, 10 November 1938, Oscar Johnston General Correspondence, DPL; Buck Jones to William Amberson, 10, 11, 12, 14 April 1934, William Ruthrauff Amberson Papers, SHC. Michael Holmes found little evidence of outright cheating in the records of AAA investigations: Holmes, *New Deal in Georgia*, 253–64.

31. "Morgan County," 22; "Greene County," 8, both RRR; Regulations quoted in Nelson, "Art of the Possible," 420; Frank J. Welch, *The Plantation Land Tenure System in Mississippi*, Bulletin 385, Mississippi Agricultural Experiment Station (1943), 38–41, 45–49 (quotation p. 38).

32. Gavin Wright, *Old South, New South: Revolutions in the Southern Economy Since the Civil War* (New York, 1986), 226–35; Whatley, "Labor for the Picking"; Welch, *Plantation Land Tenure System*, 28, 35.

33. As Warren Whatley has demonstrated, the changes are even more obvious when measured in terms of acres of crops harvested: Whatley, "Labor for the Picking." The numbers, from the censuses of agriculture in 1930 and 1940, are given in Table 25, Appendix.

34. This and the following paragraphs are based on a document in folder 43, Raper Papers, SHC: "Putnam County, Georgia — Middle 1930's (Raper's Field Notes)," marked, in pencil, "Oct. 1–4 1934." The interviewers would also survey about twenty-five families for a different project in Morgan County.

35. Taylor C. Miller to Dr. W. A. Hartman of Alabama's emergency relief administration, 9 October 1934, copy in Raper Papers.

36. The Raper quotation here arose from a similar incident in Greene County itself, when Raper was investigated by the grand jury to find out whether he belonged to any organizations that planned to overthrow the government. The investigation, it turned out, arose from reports (correct ones) that Raper was using "Mr." and "Mrs." in introducing black staff investigators. Folder 96, Raper Papers, SHC.

37. Augusta: correspondence in folders for Augusta, in box G-45; Savannah: membership report, 23 February 1932, box G-46; Vicksburg: Cleve Johnson to Moorefield Story, 11 August 1933; charter application, 18 January 1935, box G-106, all in NAACP Branch Files.

38. Savannah: interview with John Cabell, Collector of Taxes, Savannah, in "R. T. Bunche Field Notes, Bk. I," 52–53, box 85, Bunche Papers; interview with George Fuller, ibid., 54–55; interview with T. J. Hopkins, Savannah, ibid., 57. Augusta: copy of document "Committee on Negro Franchise," in folder "Wilhelmina Jackson Memos and Notes," box 82, Bunche Papers; Vicksburg: "Vicksburg, Mississippi," in folder "James Jackson Field Notes and Interviews," 19, ibid; Guido Van Rijn, *Roosevelt's Blues: African-American Blues and Gospel Songs on FDR* (Jackson, Miss., 1997), 96–99; Arthur Raper, *Tenants of the Almighty* (New York, 1943), 376. On voting drives see also Bunche, *Political Status of the Negro,* 301, 326, and on NAACP organizing in Georgia, Patricia Sullivan, *Days of Hope: Race and Democracy in the New Deal Era* (Chapel Hill, N.C., 1996), 143–44.

39. Raper, "Putnam County, Georgia — Middle 1930s," 7–8, Raper Papers, SHC; anonymous letter quoted in "LeFlore County, Mississippi," 49, RPA.

40. Raper, *Preface to Peasantry,* quotations (in order) on 4, 3, 5, 4; Wallace statement from Russel Lord, *The Wallaces of Iowa* (New York, 1947), quoted in Sullivan, *Days of Hope,* 2.

41. John Dollard, *Caste and Class in a Southern Town* (New Haven, Conn., 1937; reprint, Madison, Wis., 1988); Hortense Powdermaker, *After Freedom: A Cultural Study in the Deep South* (New York, 1939; reprint, Madison, Wis., 1993).

42. On Powdermaker, see the illuminating introduction to the 1993 reprint of *After Freedom* by Brackette F. Williams and Drexel G. Woodson. African American scholars such as W. E. B. Du Bois had, of course, long written about southern racialist culture.

43. Powdermaker, *After Freedom,* 19–30, 50–71 (quotation p. 19); Dollard, *Caste and Class,* 61–96 (quotation p. 62).

44. On poor whites and race, see Powdermaker, *After Freedom,* 29; Dollard, *Caste and Class,* 58; on titles, Powdermaker, 45, Dollard, 179–81, 349–50; on violence, Powdermaker, 52–55, Dollard, 331 (quotation), 359–61; on vigilance, Dollard, 48, 166.

45. Dollard, *Caste and Class,* 384, 440; Powdermaker, *After Freedom,* 373.

46. Dan B. Miller, *Erskine Caldwell: The Journey from Tobacco Road: A Biography* (New York, 1995), chaps. 1, 2.

47. Erskine Caldwell, *Tobacco Road* (1932; reprint, New York, 1940), 105, 111, 112.

48. J. H. Marion Jr., writing in *Christian Century* 55 (1938), reprinted in *Critical Essays on Erskine Caldwell*, ed. Scott MacDonald (Boston, 1981), 178.

49. J. Raiford Watkins, "Caldwell's Novel Is of Georgians," Augusta *Chronicle*, 14 February 1932; "Library Admits Caldwell Novel," ibid., 9 March 1932, both in *Critical Essays on Caldwell*, ed. MacDonald, 11–13, 15–16. Caldwell's four articles are also reprinted in ibid., 97–107; James Barlow Jr. to the New York *Post*, 6 March 1935, in ibid., 111; Thomas J. Hamilton, editor of the *Augusta Chronicle*, in ibid., 113.

50. The *Chronicle's* series ran 10–14 March 1935, and is reprinted in *Critical Essays on Caldwell*, ed. MacDonald, 117–31 (quotations pp. 120, 121, 118).

51. Jerry W. Dallas, "The Delta and Providence Farms," *Mississippi Quarterly* 40 (1987), 283–308 (quotation p. 297).

52. Sullivan, *Days of Hope*, 41–67 (quotation p. 48).

53. On the FSA see Sidney Baldwin, *Poverty and Politics: The Rise and Decline of the Farm Security Administration* (Chapel Hill, N.C., 1968); Paul E. Mertz, *New Deal Policy and Southern Rural Poverty* (Baton Rouge, La., 1978).

54. *Report on Economic Conditions of the South*, reprinted in *Confronting Southern Poverty in the Great Depression: The Report on Economic Conditions of the South with Related Documents* (New York, 1996), ed. David L. Carlton and Peter A. Coclanis, 39–80, quotation p. 63; Franklin D. Roosevelt speech at Barnesville, Georgia, 11 August 1938, in ibid., 130, 131–32.

55. William Rhea Blake to Oscar Johnston, 15 July and 2 August 1937, and "Recommendations of the Delta Chamber of Commerce to the National Tenancy Commission," in "OJ—Delta Chamber of Commerce," 2, 4–5, Oscar Johnston Correspondence, DPL; Bunche, *Political Status of the Negro*, 203–4, quoting Jackson (Miss.) *Daily News*. See also Tindall, *Emergence of the New South*, 533–37, and Lee J. Alston and Joseph P. Ferrie, *Southern Paternalism and the American Welfare State: Economics, Politics, and Institutions in the South, 1865–1965* (Cambridge, 1999), 49–98.

56. William Anderson, *The Wild Man from Sugar Creek: The Political Career of Eugene Talmadge* (Baton Rouge, La., 1975), quotations pp. 103, 110; Holmes, *New Deal in Georgia*, 23–33, 80–85.

57. Franklin D. Roosevelt, "Speech at Barnesville, Georgia, August 11, 1938," in *Confronting Southern Poverty*, ed. Carlton and Coclanis, 129–35 (quotations pp. 131–32, 134).

58. *GHJ*, 1, 14, 21, 28 September 1934. The *Herald-Journal* failed to mention the name of a worker or union organizer. On the strike in the South, see Jacqueline Dowd Hall, James LeLoudis, Robert Korstad, Mary Murphy, Lu Ann Jones, and Christopher B. Daly, *Like a Family: The Making of a Southern Cotton Mill World* (Chapel Hill, N.C., 1987), 328–54.

59. *GHJ*, 19 August, 2 September 1938.

60. Party officer quoted in Bunche, *Political Status of the Negro*, 206. Greene County precinct returns are from *GHJ*, 16 September 1938. The number of eligible voters in the county in 1930, as reported by the U.S. *Census of Population*, was 3,105 blacks and 3,198 whites. Total vote in Greene was George, 529, Talmadge, 514, and Camp, 385. In the eastern Piedmont as a whole George received 14,837 votes, Talmadge 8,296, and Camp 4,510. Talmadge did carry seven of the fifteen counties included here; the large margin for

George in the popular vote came mainly from urban Richmond County. In the state as a whole George received 44 percent of the vote, Talmadge 32 percent, and Camp 24 percent. County and state totals are from Alexander Heard and Donald S. Strong, *Southern Primaries and Elections 1920–1949* ([Tuscaloosa, Ala.], 1950), 64–65.

61. Raper, *Tenants of the Almighty,* 203–334 (quotation p. 270).

62. Ibid., 243; Baldwin, *Poverty and Politics,* 383–94; Holmes, *New Deal in Georgia,* 344.

63. Welch, *Plantation Land Tenure System,* 32–34, 42. For overviews of the "Southern enclosure," see especially Jack Temple Kirby, *Rural Worlds Lost: The American South, 1920–1960* (Baton Rouge, La., 1987), 51–79; Pete Daniel, *Breaking the Land: The Transformation of Cotton, Tobacco, and Rice Cultures since 1880* (Urbana, Ill., 1985).

64. "McIntosh County, Georgia," RRR; "Impressionistic Notes on the Burroughs Community Chatham County, Georgia," 1934, folder 43, Raper Papers.

65. Ownership and acreage data from U.S. *Census of Agriculture, 1935.*

Conclusion

1. Gunnar Myrdal, *An American Dilemma: The Negro Problem and Modern Democracy* (New York, 1944). On Myrdal's project, see Walter A. Jackson, *Gunnar Myrdal and America's Social Conscience: Social Engineering and Racial Liberalism, 1838–1987* (Chapel Hill, N.C., 1990), esp. 117–34.

2. "W. Jackson's Field Notes — Memorandum — Personal Experiences for Negro Field Workers," box 85, Bunche Papers.

3. Memorandum on Darien, Georgia, "Wilhelmina Jackson Memos and Notes," box 82, "Robb Lewis," in "R. T. Bunche Field Notes, Southern Trip-Book III," p. 40, typescript, box 85, "Vicksburg Mississippi," p. 9, typescript in "James Jackson Field & Interview Notes," box 82, all in Bunche Papers.

4. David C. Barrow Jr., "A Georgia Plantation," *Scribners Monthly* 21 (1881), 830–36, quotation p. 830; Charles S. Aiken, *The Cotton Plantation South since the Civil War* (Baltimore, Md., 1998), 88–91.

5. Arthur F. Raper and Ira De A. Reid, *Sharecroppers All* (Chapel Hill, N.C., 1941), 3–17; "Robb Lewis," in "R. T. Bunche Field Notes, Southern Trip-Book III," p. 41, typescript, in box 85, Bunche Papers.

6. Lawrence J. Nelson, "Welfare Capitalism on a Mississippi Plantation in the Great Depression," *JSH* 50 (1984), 225–50; "Biggest Cotton Plantation," *Fortune* 15 (1937), 125–32, 156, 158, 160; photographs of the Hopson plantation by Marion Post Wolcott, Farm Security Administration Photography Collection, Library of Congress.

7. Memorandum on Darien, Georgia, and copy of *You Are a Citizen!,* in "Wilhelmina Jackson Memos and Notes," and "Vicksburg Mississippi," typescript in "James Jackson Field & Interview Notes," p. 15, in box 82, Bunche Papers.

8. "Vicksburg Mississippi," typescript in "James Jackson Field & Interview Notes," pp. 1–4, in box 82, Bunche Papers.

9. William Faulkner, *Go Down, Moses,* in *Novels, 1942–1954* (New York, 1994), 130, 269; William Alexander Percy, *Lanterns on the Levee: Recollections of a Planter's Son*

(New York, 1941; reprint, Baton Rouge, La., 1973), 74; Arthur Raper, *Tenants of the Almighty* (New York, 1943).

Coda

1. Bertram Wyatt-Brown, *The House of Percy: Honor, Melancholy, and Imagination in a Southern Family* (New York, 1994), 3-4, 254-56; unidentified clipping, Percy Papers, MDAH; LeRoy Percy to Alice D. Jenkins, 21 July 1922, quoted in Wyatt-Brown, 236.

2. Peter Guralnick, *Searching for Robert Johnson* (New York, 1989), 50-52; Stephen C. LeVere, notes accompanying *Robert Johnson, The Complete Recordings* (Columbia 46222), 16-18. Later Delta bluesmen, like Muddy Waters (born McKinley Morganfield) from Rolling Fork and B. B. King from Indianola, made their reputations with electrified bands in the urban North.

No gravestone marked Johnson's grave until 1991, when a worshipful rock band set a tombstone where they thought Johnson lay. The band thereby trumped Columbia Records, which had planned a big ceremony to place their own tombstone at the grave, to celebrate the success of their reissue of Johnson's recordings the year before. When a church deacon refused to accept a second tombstone, the company found a more accommodating church nearby, placed their marker, and created a competing site for tourists to visit. If Johnson's spirit had missed that Greyhound and hung around, he must have enjoyed the show; see Jeff Todd Titon, *Early Downhome Blues: A Musical and Cultural Analysis* (Urbana, Ill., 1977; 2d ed., Chapel Hill, N.C., 1994), 277.

3. Augusta *Chronicle*, 24 and 29 October, 5 and 12 November 1933.

4. C. Vann Woodward, *Tom Watson: Agrarian Rebel* (New York, 1938; reprint, New York, 1970), 470-86 (quotations pp. 471, 473). In the eastern Piedmont Watson won 10,627 votes to a combined 9,731 for his two opponents.

5. Harold H. Martin, *This Happy Isle: The Story of Sea Island and the Cloister* (Sea Island, Ga., 1978), 62-73; Frances Butler Leigh, *Ten Years on a Georgia Plantation since the War* (London, 1883; reprint, New York, 1969), 46; Burnette Vanstory, *Georgia's Land of the Golden Isles* (1956; reprint, Athens, Ga., 1981), 146-47.

6. Lydia Parrish, *Slave Songs of the Georgia Sea Islands* (1942; reprint, Athens, Ga., 1992), 31, 174-75, 192; Georgia Writers' Project, *Drums and Shadows: Survival Studies among the Georgia Coastal Negroes* (1940; reprint Athens, Ga., 1986), 113, 127 (quotation), 130, 141, 147, 77, 174. On the alignment of graves, witnessed by an anthropologist in the South Carolina Sea Islands in the 1920s, see Margaret Washington Creel, *"A Peculiar People": Slave Religion and Community Culture among the Gullahs* (New York, 1988), 317, 320.

7. Martin, *This Happy Isle*, 72-73.

ESSAY ON SOURCES

The purpose of this essay is to draw attention to the most important primary and secondary sources on which *Deep Souths* is based and to note secondary works whose importance may not be reflected in the notes. It is not intended to provide a complete bibliographical reference, something for which the notes are the best guide. With a few exceptions as noted, I used as primary sources only material that originated in or reported information on one of the three areas I have compared. Census and tax records, the sources for the charts and tables, are discussed briefly in a separate note in the Appendix.

Primary Sources

Unpublished plantation and other manuscript records. Among the most useful sources for this study were records of plantation owners and managers. Far too many generalizations about the rural economy in the post–Civil War South have been made without consulting such records. The Manigault Family Papers cover the history of Gowrie Plantation on the Savannah River. Major parts of the family's papers are at the Southern Historical Collection at the University of North Carolina (SHC) and at the Georgia Historical Society in Savannah (GHS), which includes typescripts of much of the material at SHC. Also at the GHS are the Spalding Family Papers, much of which relate to the attempts of the Spalding heirs to keep up production on Sapelo Island, and records related to several Savannah River plantations compiled by employees of the Federal Writers' Project in the 1930s. The Hofwyl-Broadfield Papers contain the records of one of the last surviving Georgia rice plantations. The originals are at the Hofwyl Plantation State Park near Darien; I used a microfilm copy at the Brunswick Public Library. For the Piedmont region, a valuable set of postwar plantation records are included in the David C. Barrow Papers at the University of Georgia Library. The Benton Miller Journal, at the Georgia Department of Archives and History (GDAH), is a rare record left by a small Piedmont farmer. For the Delta, informative letters from planter George Collins for the 1870s and 1880s are in the Anne (Cameron) Collins Papers at SHC. Also at SHC are useful plantation journals on microfilm, the Clive Metcalf Diary and the Newstead Plantation Records. The

Percy Family Papers at the Mississippi Department of Archives and History (MDAH) have a great deal of material related to one of the most important families in the Delta's history. The Percys owned and operated plantations, advised others who were doing so, and played a major role in the Delta's politics. The Mitchell Memorial Library, Mississippi State University, has the records of the Delta & Pine Land Company, the combined operations of which made it the world's biggest cotton plantation. The British owners of the company required a high level of detailed record keeping and reporting, and, as a result, the records offer an unparalleled inside view of a large plantation for the period after 1910. The Walter Sillers Papers at Delta State University have the voluminous files of a Delta planter, lawyer, and politician.

In addition to the plantation records, several manuscript collections provided important material on the economic, cultural, and social life of the three regions. The GHS has the papers of Walter Wray, a small Piedmont planter and Populist Party activist, and the Hilton Papers, left by a family of coastal lumber entrepreneurs, include the memoir of Thomas Hilton, "High Water on the Bar." The GDAH has the papers of the Thomas Carnegie family, who bought most of Cumberland Island and lived there for many years. The McRaven Letters at MDAH offer a portrait of a family from a small Mississippi city in the 1920s. The Dun & Bradstreet Collection at Baker Library, Harvard Business School, includes the R. G. Dun & Co. Credit Ledgers, with reports on merchants in every county in the United States. The Robert Preston Brooks Papers at the University of Georgia have material used by Brooks in his research on Georgia farmers in the Piedmont. The extensive Arthur Franklin Raper Papers at SHC have much material related to Raper's research in Greene County, Georgia, in the 1920s and 1930s. The Thomas E. Watson Papers at SHC are disappointingly thin. The Ralph Bunche Papers at the UCLA Research Library have much unpublished material related to Bunche's participation in Gunnar Myrdal's research into African American life in the late 1930s.

Two sets of organizational records at the Library of Congress, those of the National Association for the Advancement of Colored People and of the National Urban League (NUL), provided much on African American life after 1910. The most helpful parts of the NAACP papers are Series G, the records of local branches, and two sections that have been microfilmed as part of *The Papers of the NAACP*, August Meier and John H. Bracey Jr., editorial advisors (Frederick, Md., 1981–): Part 7, Series A, "Anti-Lynching Investigative Files, 1912–1953," and Part 10, "Peonage, Labor, and the New Deal, 1913–1939." The NUL records have much unpublished material related to the organization's research into the causes of black migration to the North during World War I.

Photographs, music, oral histories. For photographic research in Georgia, the Vanishing Georgia Collection at the GDAH has rich material on many of Georgia's counties. For the 1930s, the photographs of the Farm Security Administration and related agencies are justifiably renowned. Most of the collection can now be viewed on the American Memory website of the Library of Congress (http://memory.loc.gov). Many excellent photographs made for the FSA by Jack Delano are in the Raper Collection at SHC, rather than at the Library of Congress.

Early field recordings of African American music, done by Alan Lomax, John Work, and their collaborators, and originally issued by the Library of Congress, have recently been reissued as compact disks. Included are *Afro-American Blues and Game Songs* (AFS L4; reissue Rounder CD 1513), which includes the 1941 recordings of Muddy Waters and several children's game songs recorded in the Delta, and *Negro Blues and Hollers* (AFS L59; reissue Rounder CD 1501), which has recordings of both blues singers and singing by church congregations in the Delta. A compilation from the Smithsonian Collection of Recordings that includes examples from the best-known early blues musicians who were recorded is *The Blues* (4 vols., Sony RD 101). All or most of the recorded work of the two towering giants of Delta blues is available on CD: *Robert Johnson: The Complete Recordings* (Columbia 46222), and *The Voice of the Delta: The Complete Paramount Recordings of Charley Patton* (Black Swan HCD-21 and HCD-22). Lawrence Gellert (collector) and Elie Siegmeister (arranger), *Negro Songs of Protest* (New York, 1936), includes protest songs collected by Gellert in the 1930s, mainly in the Piedmont areas. There are, as far I can determine, no recordings currently available.

Oral histories contain much insight on life in the rural South. Among the most useful for this book were the Oral History Collection at MDAH and the Oral History Collection at Mitchell Memorial Library at Mississippi State University. The latter includes a series of oral histories related to the Delta & Pine Land Company. Many oral histories collected by the 1930s Federal Writers' Project are available on the Library of Congress's American Memory website (see above).

Unpublished government records. The GDAH has many county-level records on microfilm, including court records and local education records. Among Georgia's state-level records, I drew especially on the Monthly Reports of the Misdemeanor Chain Gangs, 1898–1901. At MDAH, the Governors' Papers are dominated by material related to requests for pardon, some of which offer much insight into the criminal justice system of the state.

Among federal records in the National Archives and Records Service, those of the Bureau of Agricultural Economics of the U.S. Department of Agriculture (Record Group 83) have much unpublished material on the various research projects of the BAE, including many on Delta agriculture. Records of the Committee on Women's Defense Work, part of the First World War–era Council of National Defense (RG 62), have informative letters from Alice Dunbar Nelson, who was hired to help organize the work of African American women. Many of the records of the Justice Department related to investigations of peonage have been collected on microfilm under the editorship of Pete Daniel: *The Peonage Files of the U.S. Department of Justice, 1901–1945* (Frederick, Md., 1989).

Newspapers and contemporary magazines. Newspapers provide both information and insight into events at the local level that are hard to find elsewhere. Among
those I consulted were, for the Georgia Coast: the Savannah *Morning News,* Savannah *Tribune* (an African American paper), Darien *Timber Gazette,* Brunswick *Daily
News,* and *Southeast Georgian* (St. Marys, Ga.); for the Delta: the Sunflower *Tocsin*
and Indianola *Enterprise,* both published in Sunflower County, Vicksburg *Evening
Post* and Vicksburg *Daily Herald,* and *The Woman Voter,* published in the 1920s in
Clarksdale, Mississippi; for the Piedmont: the Augusta *Chronicle;* the Glascock *Banner* (Gibson, Ga.), and the *Wool Hat* (Gracewood, Ga.), both Populist Party support-
ers; the Sparta *Ishmaelite,* and, perhaps the most frequently used, the Greensboro
Herald-Journal.

Contemporary magazines were especially useful in two areas. In the first decades
after Reconstruction, general magazines such as *Scribners Monthly* and *Harper's
Monthly Magazine* carried accounts of the South's social and physical landscapes.
Around the turn of the century, journals of opinion and comment, especially the
Independent, carried discussions and commentary on race relations in the South,
including several pieces by residents of the Delta, Atlantic coast, or Piedmont.

Other published primary sources, including government documents. Valuable
published diaries and memoirs by people of the Deep Souths include Frances Butler
Leigh, *Ten Years on a Georgia Plantation since the War* (London, 1883), an account
of Leigh's and her husband's operation of the Butler plantations on the Altamaha and
on St. Simons Island; Ruby Sheppeard Hicks, *The Song of the Delta* (Jackson, Miss.,
1976), a memoir of a Delta childhood by a woman from a middling white farmer's
family; William Alexander Percy, *Lanterns on the Levee: Recollections of a Planter's
Son* (New York, 1941), the well-known memoir of the heir to the Percy plantations,
who offers a view from the inside of the Delta's planting class; Charles A. Le Guin, ed.,
A Home-Concealed Woman: The Diaries of Magnolia Wynn Le Guin, 1901–1913
(Athens, Ga., 1990), a revealing diary by the wife of a middle-class Piedmont farmer
and miller (Le Guin lived outside the boundaries of the Georgia eastern Piedmont as
defined here); Virginia Ingraham Burr, ed., *The Secret Eye: The Journal of Ella Gertrude Clanton Thomas, 1848–1889* (Chapel Hill, N.C., 1990), a fascinating diary of
a wealthy slave mistress who became a suffragist late in life; and James M. Clifton,
ed., *Life and Labor on Argyle Island* (Savannah, 1978), a volume of letters and papers
related to the Manigault family's Gowrie plantation on the Savannah. The Atlanta
University Studies, most edited by W. E. B. Du Bois, were annual volumes based on
conferences on various topics related to African American life; they contain much
useful information and are good sources for elite black opinion in this time period.
The Phelps-Stokes Fellowship Studies, published by the University of Georgia in the
1920s, include two with information on Piedmont counties: Donald Dewey Scarborough, *An Economic Study of Negro Farmers as Owners, Tenants, and Croppers*
(Athens, Ga.: *Bulletin of the University of Georgia,* 1924), and John William Fan-

ning, *Negro Migration* (Athens, Ga.: *Bulletin of the University of Georgia*, 1930). Alfred Stone, *Studies in the American Race Problem* (New York, 1908), collects papers by a thoughtful, conservative Delta planter who reflected the outlook of his class. L[ily] H. Hammond, *In Black and White: An Interpretation of Southern Life* (1914; reprint New York, 1972) is by a Progressive Era reformer from Augusta who had come to the realization that middle-class blacks had much in common with middle-class whites. *Tobacco Road* (New York, 1932) is Erskine Caldwell's famous caricature of poor white life, based on his memories of Jefferson County, Georgia, where he had spent his teenage years.

Among the many publications of the U.S. Census (my use of which is also briefly discussed in the Appendix), special mention should be made of the two-volume *Report on Cotton Production in the United States* by Eugene W. Hilgard, issued as part of the *Tenth Census, 1880*. It includes, for every region and county of the cotton South, a discussion of soil, rainfall patterns, and other physical characteristics, as well as labor conditions and related economic topics. Among the most useful of many publications from the U.S. Department of Agriculture was *A Study of the Tenant Systems of Farming in the Yazoo-Mississippi Delta*, by E. A. Boeger and E. A. Goldenweiser, Bulletin 337 (Washington, D.C., 1916). The Mississippi Agricultural Experiment Station produced useful publications, including *The Plantation Land Tenure System in Mississippi*, by Frank J. Welch, Bulletin 385 (Starkville, Miss., 1943), and *A Nutrition Investigation of Negro Tenants in the Yazoo-Mississippi Delta*, by Dorothy Dickins, Bulletin 254 (Starkville, Miss., 1928). U.S. Department of Labor, *The Negro Landholder of Georgia*, by W. E. B. Du Bois, Bulletin 35 (Washington, D.C., 1901), contains county-by-county information compiled from local tax records.

Several works of contemporary research straddle the division between primary and secondary sources. In early-twentieth-century Georgia, two economists analyzed Georgia's farm economy: Robert P. Brooks, *The Agrarian Revolution in Georgia, 1865–1912* (Madison, Wis., 1914), and E. M. Banks, *The Economics of Land Tenure in Georgia* (New York, 1905). Among Arthur Raper's many publications, his study of Macon and Greene Counties in Georgia, *Preface to Peasantry: A Tale of Two Black Belt Counties* (Chapel Hill, N.C., 1936) is the best and is deservedly considered a classic. The Georgia Writers' Project, *Drums and Shadows: Survival Studies among the Georgia Coastal Negroes* (1940; reprint, Athens, Ga., 1986), has much on African American folklore in the words of African Americans themselves. Lydia Parrish, *Slave Songs of the Georgia Sea Islands* (1942; reprinted with foreword by Art Rosenbaum, Athens, Ga., 1992), has lyrics and music from African Americans in the Sea Islands with lively commentary by Parrish. Two classic analyses of race and class in the Mississippi Delta were published in the 1930s by researchers who did their work in Indianola: Hortense Powdermaker, *After Freedom: A Cultural Study in the Deep South* (New York, 1939; reprint, Madison, Wis., 1993), and John Dollard, *Caste and Class in a Southern Town* (New Haven, Conn., 1937; reprint, Madison, Wis., 1988).

Secondary Sources

General works on the South. The place to begin for secondary literature on the South is John B. Boles and Evelyn Thomas Nolen, eds., *Interpreting Southern History: Historiographical Essays in Honor of Sanford W. Higginbotham* (Baton Rouge, La., 1987). Especially relevant for this book are the essays there by LaWanda Cox, "From Emancipation to Segregation: National Policy and Southern Blacks," 199–253; Harold D. Woodman, "Economic Reconstruction and the Rise of the New South, 1865–1900," 254–307; and Richard L. Watson Jr., "From Populism through the New Deal: Southern Political History," 308–89.

Among large-scale syntheses of southern history after the Reconstruction, none has been more influential than C. Vann Woodward, *Origins of the New South, 1877–1913* (Baton Rouge, La., 1951). At the center of Woodward's account is the struggle for political power and the ultimate triumph in that struggle of a new business class over ordinary farmers and blacks. Edward L. Ayers, *The Promise of the New South: Life after Reconstruction* (New York, 1992), covers most of the same ground, but pays more attention to culture and to the variety and complexity of southerners' experiences. The approach in *Deep Souths* is somewhat closer in spirit to Ayers's approach, but Woodward's treatment of the basic economic and political forces at work has influenced me a great deal, as it has virtually every historian of the New South. George B. Tindall, *The Emergence of the New South, 1913–1945* (Baton Rouge, La., 1967), almost encyclopedic in scope, opened many veins of research, some still largely unexploited. For the period of Reconstruction itself, the essential synthesis is Eric Foner, *Reconstruction: America's Unfinished Revolution* (New York, 1988).

Broad surveys and interpretations of specific topics in southern history. The treatment of the South's economy that has influenced my approach more than any other is Gavin Wright, *Old South, New South: Revolutions in the Southern Economy Since the Civil War* (New York, 1986). Wright argues that the South's economy was dominated by a low-wage labor market that set it apart from the rest of the United States. Gilbert Fite's *Cotton Fields No More: Southern Agriculture, 1865–1980* (Lexington, Ky., 1984), which emphasizes the basic problem of low productivity in southern agriculture, has also influenced my interpretation. An illuminating comparative approach to southern economic history is Pete Daniel, *Breaking the Land: The Transformation of Cotton, Tobacco, and Rice Cultures since 1880* (Urbana, Ill., 1985). Charles S. Aiken, *The Cotton Plantation South since the Civil War* (Baltimore, Md., 1998), is an outstanding analysis by a historical geographer. Robert Tracy McKenzie, *One South or Many? Plantation Belt and Upcountry in Civil War–Era Tennessee* (New York, 1994), approaches some of the same questions raised here with a detailed analysis of agriculture change in three Tennessee regions.

Anne Firor Scott, *The Southern Lady: From Pedestal to Politics, 1830–1930* (Chicago, 1970), is the place to begin for the study of the South's white women. Two works by Jacqueline Jones that cover, in significant part, the South's poor blacks and whites, have influenced my understanding of black and white families in the South: *Labor of Love, Labor of Sorrow: Black Women, Work, and the Family from Slavery to the Present* (New York, 1985), and *The Dispossessed: America's Underclass from the Civil War to the Present* (New York, 1992). Jack Temple Kirby subtly, and without sentimentality, analyzes black and white family and community culture before the "great enclosure" of the 1930s in *Rural Worlds Lost: The American South, 1920–1960* (Baton Rouge, La., 1987).

On race in the postwar South, three major interpretations stand out. C. Vann Woodward, *The Strange Career of Jim Crow* (New York, 1955, and subsequent editions), first showed that segregation had a history and a politics. Joel Williamson, *The Crucible of Race: Black-White Relations in the American South since Emancipation* (New York, 1984), emphasizes the emotional and psychological sources of white racism. Leon F. Litwack, *Trouble in Mind: Black Southerners in the Age of Jim Crow* (New York, 1998), is a recent work that chronicles the cost of white racism to African Americans. Litwack's book is deeply researched, beautifully written, and deserves to be read by anyone interested in southern (or indeed American) history. At the same time, Litwack's approach to his material is quite different from the one in *Deep Souths;* he treats all parts of the South as virtually interchangeable, and, though he emphasizes the importance of the 1890s as a moment when both black defiance and white oppression intensified, there is otherwise little sense of historical change in *Trouble in Mind* for the period from Reconstruction to the New Deal.

State, regional, and local studies. Kenneth Coleman, ed., *A History of Georgia* (Athens, Ga., 1977), is an excellent synthesis. Charles L. Flynn, *White Land, Black Labor: Caste and Class in Late-Nineteenth-Century Georgia* (Baton Rouge, La., 1983), addresses a number of themes related to the present work. For Mississippi's political history, see Bradley G. Bond, *Political Culture in the Nineteenth-Century South: Mississippi, 1830–1890* (Baton Rouge, La., 1995), and Albert D. Kirwan, *Revolt of the Rednecks: Mississippi Politics, 1876–1925* (Lexington, Ky., 1951). Barton C. Shaw, *The Wool-Hat Boys: Georgia's Populist Party* (Baton Rouge, La., 1984), is one of the best state-level studies of Populism. African American life in Georgia and Mississippi has been admirably interpreted in John Dittmer, *Black Georgia in the Progressive Era, 1900–1920* (Urbana, Ill., 1977), and Neil R. McMillen, *Dark Journey: Black Mississippians in the Age of Jim Crow* (Urbana, Ill., 1989). The agricultural background for Mississippi is covered in John Hebron Moore, *The Emergence of the Cotton Kingdom in the Old Southwest: Mississippi, 1770–1860* (Baton Rouge, La., 1988), and for Georgia in Willard Range, *A Century of Georgia Agriculture, 1850–1960* (Athens, Ga., 1954).

The Delta has been the subject of two superb works, Robert L. Brandfon, *Cotton Kingdom of the New South: A History of the Yazoo-Mississippi Delta from Reconstruction to the Twentieth Century* (Cambridge, Mass., 1967), and James C. Cobb,

The Most Southern Place on Earth: The Mississippi Delta and the Roots of Regional Identity (New York, 1992). Robert W. Harrison, *Alluvial Empire* (Little Rock, 1961), is an essential source for understanding the Delta's levee system. Christopher Morris, *Becoming Southern: Warren County and Vicksburg, Mississippi, 1760–1860* (New York, 1994), traces the rise of slave society in one county at the edge of the Delta. Christopher Waldrep, *The Roots of Disorder: Race and Criminal Justice in the American South, 1817–80* (Urbana, Ill., 1998), also a study of Warren County, analyzes the changes in the legal system brought about by emancipation. Sidney Nathans, " 'Gotta Mind to Move, a Mind to Settle Down': Afro-Americans and the Plantation Frontier," in *A Master's Due: Essays in Honor of David Herbert Donald,* ed. William J. Cooper Jr., Michael F. Holt, and John McCardell (Baton Rouge, La., 1985), is an outstanding portrait of the Cameron property in Tunica County. John Charles Willis, "On the New South Frontier: Life in the Yazoo-Mississippi Delta, 1865–1920" (Ph.D. diss., University of Virginia, 1991), like Nathans, emphasizes how the frontier quality of the early Delta affected life there and produced often surprising results. Valerie Grim, "Black Farm Families in the Yazoo-Mississippi Delta: A Study of the Brooks Farm Community, 1920–1970" (Ph.D. diss., Iowa State University, 1990), has much excellent material on Delta families based on oral histories, though it suggests a possibly too rosy view of African American family life.

Although focusing on South Carolina, much of the analysis in Peter Coclanis, *The Shadow of a Dream: Economic Life and Death in the South Carolina Low Country, 1670–1920* (New York, 1988), applies to the Georgia coast as well. For the specific Georgia background, see Julia Floyd Smith, *Slavery and Rice Culture in Low Country Georgia, 1750–1860* (Knoxville, Tenn., 1985). William Dusinberre, *Them Dark Days: Slavery in the American Rice Swamps* (New York, 1996), analyzes in rich detail three antebellum rice plantations, including Gowrie and Butler's Island on Georgia's rice coast. Mart A. Stewart, *"What Nature Suffers to Groe": Life, Labor, and Landscape on the Georgia Coast, 1680–1920* (Athens, Ga., 1996), is an excellent study by an environmental historian. William S. McFeely, *Sapelo's People: A Long Walk into Freedom* (New York, 1994), offers a thoughtful meditation on the history of Sapelo's black population. Buddy Sullivan, *Early Days on the Georgia Tidewater: The Story of McIntosh County and Sapelo* (Darien, Ga., 1990), is an unusually informative county history.

J. William Harris, *Plain Folk and Gentry in a Slave Society: White Liberty and Black Slavery in Augusta's Hinterlands* (Middletown, Conn., 1985), discusses the economy and society of Georgia's eastern Piedmont before emancipation. Jonathon M. Bryant, *How Curious a Land: Conflict and Change in Greene County, Georgia, 1850–1885* (Chapel Hill, N.C.,1996), is an excellent analysis of a crucial period of one Piedmont county's history. Greene County is also one of the case studies in Edward L. Ayers, *Vengeance and Justice: Crime and Punishment in the Nineteenth-Century American South* (New York, 1984). LeeAnn Whites, *The Civil War as a*

Crisis in Gender: Augusta, Georgia, 1860–1890 (Athens, Ga., 1995), suggestively treats gender relations among whites at the local level. Two dissertations are especially informative on the cultural and social relationships between city and countryside in Georgia's Piedmont: Randolph Dennis Werner, "Hegemony and Conflict: The Political Economy of a Southern Region, Augusta, Georgia, 1865–1895" (Ph.D. diss., University of Virginia, 1977), and Julia Mary Walsh, " 'Horny-Handed Sons of Toil': Workers, Politics, and Religion in Augusta, Georgia, 1880–1910" (Ph.D. diss., University of Illinois at Urbana-Champaign, 1999).

Biographies. Malcolm Bell Jr., *Major Butler's Legacy: Five Generations of a Slaveholding Family* (Athens, Ga., 1987), is a revealing study of the family that included Frances Butler Leigh. Russell Duncan, *Freedom's Shore: Tunis Campbell and the Georgia Freedmen* (Athens, Ga., 1986), traces the career of the leading black politician in McIntosh County. C. Vann Woodward, *Tom Watson: Agrarian Rebel* (New York, 1938), is a classic treatment of the leading Piedmont Populist. E. Merton Coulter, *James Monroe Smith, Georgia Planter, before Death and After* (Athens, Ga., 1961), is an admiring account of a planter who built his fortune from the labor of convicts. Dan B. Miller, *Erskine Caldwell: The Journey from Tobacco Road: A Biography* (New York, 1995), is excellent on the formative experiences of the most popular writer to emerge from the Piedmont in the 1930s. Kent Anderson Leslie, *Woman of Color, Daughter of Privilege: Amanda America Dickson, 1849–1893* (Athens, Ga., 1995), tells the story of Augusta's wealthiest African American resident. Also informative on Augusta's black elite is Glenn T. Eskew, "Black Elitism and the Failure of Paternalism in Postbellum Georgia: The Case of Bishop Lucius Henry Holsey," *Journal of Southern History* 58 (1992): 637–66. The Percy family of the Delta is the subject of two multigeneration treatments: Bertram Wyatt-Brown, *The House of Percy: Honor, Melancholy, and Imagination in a Southern Family* (New York, 1994), and Lewis Baker, *The Percys of Mississippi: Politics and Literature in the New South* (Baton Rouge, La., 1983). For most purposes, Wyatt-Brown's subtle treatment is better, but on some aspects of politics, Baker's is more informative. The life of Mississippi's most notoriously racist politician in the early twentieth century is covered well in William F. Holmes, *The White Chief: James Kimble Vardaman* (Baton Rouge, La., 1970). Lawrence J. Nelson, *King Cotton's Advocate: Oscar G. Johnston and the New Deal* (Knoxville, Tenn., 1999), is an excellent study of the man who directed the Delta & Pine Land Co. after 1927 and who had a major influence on the New Deal's cotton policies. The Delta's preeminent bluesmen are the subject of musically informed biographies: Stephen Calt and Gayle Wardlow's contentious *King of the Delta Blues: The Life and Music of Charlie Patton* (Newton, N.J., 1988), and Peter Guralnick's reflective *Searching for Robert Johnson* (New York, 1989).

The economics of the postwar rural South. The economic transformation of southern agriculture after the Civil War has been the subject of a large body of work by historians and economists, though agreement on basic issues has remained elusive.

Some of the important general interpretations have been mentioned above. Important treatments that have stressed the repressiveness of southern economic institutions and the bleak results for black farmers and laborers are Jay R. Mandle, *The Roots of Black Poverty: The Southern Plantation Economy after the Civil War* (Durham, N.C., 1978), revised as *Not Slave, Not Free: The African American Economic Experience since the Civil War* (Durham, N.C., 1992), and Roger Ransom and Richard Sutch, *One Kind of Freedom: The Economic Consequences of Emancipation* (New York, 1977). Ransom and Sutch's argument that local merchant monopolies contributed significantly to black poverty has been challenged by a number of contributors to Gary M. Walton and James F. Sheperds, eds., *Market Institutions and Economic Progress in the New South, 1865–1900: Essays Stimulated by One Kind of Freedom: The Economic Consequences of Emancipation* (New York, 1981). A survey and analysis with a more optimistic account of black economic progress is Robert Higgs, *Competition and Coercion: Blacks in the American Economy, 1865–1914* (New York, 1977). Higgs argues that market forces mitigated some of the effects of white racism.

Gerald David Jaynes, *Branches without Roots: Genesis of the Black Working Class in the American South, 1862–1882* (New York, 1986), is the best account of the forces at work in the rise of sharecropping, though, like many others, he places the completion of this process at too early a date. Two contributions to Thavolia Glymph and John J. Kushma, eds., *Essays on the Postbellum Southern Economy* (College Station, Tex., 1985), stress the revolutionary nature of the changes in rural society in the South after the Civil War: Barbara Jeanne Fields, "The Advent of Capitalist Agriculture: The New South in a Bourgeois World," 73–94, and Harold D. Woodman, "The Reconstruction of the Cotton Plantation in the New South," 95–119. The legal changes that accompanied the transition to free labor are traced in Harold D. Woodman, *New South, New Law* (Baton Rouge, La., 1995). William Cohen focuses on attempts — largely unsuccessful — to limit black mobility by law in *At Freedom's Edge: Black Mobility and the Southern White Quest for Racial Control, 1861–1915* (Baton Rouge, La., 1991). Pete Daniel analyzes extralegal methods of limiting mobility, and federal attempts to combat them, in *Shadow of Slavery: Peonage in the South, 1901–1969* (Urbana, Ill., 1972; 2nd ed., 1990). Nell Irvin Painter tells the story of the first popular movement by African Americans in the lower Mississippi Valley to leave the South in *The Exodusters: Black Migration to Kansas after Reconstruction* (New York, 1977). In an earlier analysis of peonage, I concluded that most historians have greatly exaggerated the degree to which genuine debt peonage existed in the New South: "The Question of Peonage in the History of the New South," in *Plain Folk of the South Revisited*, ed. Samuel C. Hyde Jr. (Baton Rouge, La., 1997), 100–125.

Race and segregation. In addition to the general works cited above, a number of important works focus on specific aspects of race and race relations. Among several recent analyses of lynching, the best are W. Fitzhugh Brundage, *Lynching in the New*

South: Georgia and Virginia, 1880–1930 (Urbana, Ill., 1993), which discusses both the causes of and the resistance to lynching in those two states, and Stewart E. Tolnay and E. M. Beck, *A Festival of Violence: An Analysis of Southern Lynchings, 1882–1930* (Urbana, Ill., 1995), a statistical analysis that stresses underlying economic factors as causes of lynching. J. Morgan Kousser, *The Shaping of Southern Politics: Suffrage Restriction and the Establishment of the One-Party South, 1880–1920* (New Haven, Conn., 1974), is a thorough analysis that argues that the political motives of conservative Democrats were the single most important impulse behind disfranchisement. Grace Elizabeth Hale, *Making Whiteness: The Culture of Segregation in the South, 1890–1940* (New York, 1998), is an innovative cultural study of the making of the age of segregation.

Populism and politics in the 1890s. Southern Populism remains a movement about which historians disagree. Robert C. McMath Jr., *American Populism: A Social History, 1877–1898* (New York, 1993), is an excellent synthesis of the facts and the interpretations. McMath is also the author of the indispensable work on the Populist forerunners, *The Populist Vanguard: A History of the Southern Farmers' Alliance* (Chapel Hill, N.C., 1975). Woodward's biography of Tom Watson, cited above, is the best example of an interpretation that sees the Populists as economic radicals and racial liberals. Richard Hofstadter, *The Age of Reform: From Bryan to FDR* (New York, 1955), sees the Populists as more reactionary. Barton Shaw's study of Georgia Populists, cited above, leans more toward Hofstadter's view than Woodward's; my interpretation in Chapter 3, above, is closer to Woodward than to Hofstadter. Lawrence Goodwyn, *Democratic Promise: The Populist Moment in America* (New York, 1976), like McMath, argues that the experience of the Farmers' Alliance is the key to understanding Populism, and Steven Hahn, in *The Roots of Southern Populism: Yeoman Farmers and the Transformation of the Georgia Upcountry, 1850–1890* (New York, 1983), sees local disputes over fence laws and similar issues as important Populist forerunners. Hahn's book focuses on a region that borders Georgia's eastern Piedmont to the north. Some of Hahn's key arguments have been disputed in Shawn Everett Kantor, *Politics and Property Rights: The Closing of the Open Range in the Postbellum South* (Chicago, 1998). Two incisive studies of the "Lost Cause" ideology and its social and cultural functions are Charles Reagan Wilson, *Baptized in Blood: The Religion of the Lost Cause, 1865–1920* (Athens, Ga., 1980), and Gaines M. Foster, *Ghosts of the Confederacy: Defeat, the Lost Cause, and the Emergence of the New South, 1865 to 1913* (New York, 1987).

The early twentieth century. The economic and social history of the early-twentieth-century South has not been much studied by historians; an exception is Jeannie Whayne, *A New Plantation South: Land, Labor, and Federal Favor in Twentieth-Century Arkansas* (Charlottesville, Va., 1996), a study of an Arkansas county much like parts of the Mississippi Delta. Melton Alonzo McLaurin includes treatment of workers and strikes in Augusta in *Paternalism and Protest: Southern*

Cotton Mill Workers and Organized Labor, 1875–1905 (Westport, Conn. 1971). The invasion of the Sea Islands by wealthy northerners is recounted in William Barton McCash and June Hall McCash, *The Jekyll Island Club: Southern Haven for America's Millionaires* (Athens, Ga., 1989), and Harold H. Martin, *This Happy Isle: The Story of Sea Island and the Cloister* (Sea Island, Ga., 1978), which includes an account of Howard Coffin's purchase of Sapelo Island.

Basic surveys of Progressivism in the South are Dewey W. Grantham, *Southern Progressivism: The Reconciliation of Progress and Tradition* (Knoxville, Tenn., 1983), and William A. Link, *The Paradox of Southern Progressivism, 1880–1930* (Chapel Hill, N.C., 1992). African American thought in the era is surveyed in August Meier, *Negro Thought in America, 1880–1915: Racial Ideologies in the Age of Booker T. Washington* (Ann Arbor, Mich., 1963). Jack Temple Kirby, *Darkness at the Dawning: Race and Reform in the Progressive South* (Philadelphia, 1972), explains why white progressives thought segregation itself was a "reform." David M. Oshinsky traces the transformation of Mississippi's penal system in the Progressive period in *"Worse Than Slavery": Parchman Farm and the Ordeal of Jim Crow Justice* (New York, 1996); Alex Lichtenstein does the same for Georgia in *Twice the Work of Free Labor: The Political Economy of Convict Labor in the New South* (London, 1996). Two superb works on black women in the Progressive Era that influenced my approach are Evelyn Brooks Higginbotham, *Righteous Discontent: The Women's Movement in the Black Baptist Church, 1880–1920* (Cambridge, Mass., 1993), and Glenda Elizabeth Gilmore, *Gender and Jim Crow: Women and the Politics of White Supremacy in North Carolina, 1896–1920* (Chapel Hill, N.C., 1996). Other helpful accounts of the work of activist black women can be found in Cynthia Neverdon-Morton, *Afro-American Women of the South and the Advancement of the Race, 1895–1925* (Knoxville, Tenn., 1989), and Dorothy Salem, *To Better Our World: Black Women in Organized Reform, 1890–1920*, vol. 11 in *Black Women in United States History*, ed. Darlene Clark Hine (Brooklyn, 1990). John Patrick McDowell, *The Social Gospel in the South: The Woman's Home Mission Movement in the Methodist Episcopal Church, South, 1886–1939* (Baton Rouge, La., 1982), treats an important institutional base for white women reformers. Marjorie Spruill Wheeler, *New Women of the New South: The Leaders of the Woman Suffrage Movement in the Southern States* (New York, 1993), explains the background and strategies of leading southern suffragists, including Nellie Nugent Somerville of Greenville, Mississippi.

Religion, family life, the black middle class. A fine survey of African American religion in the late nineteenth century is William E. Montgomery, *Under Their Own Vine and Fig Tree: The African-American Church in the South, 1865–1900* (Baton Rouge, La., 1993). The unique comparative approach in Paul Harvey, *Redeeming the South: Religious Cultures and Racial Identities among Southern Baptists* (Chapel Hill, N.C., 1997), which considers both black and white Baptists, makes it especially valuable. Margaret Washington Creel, *"A Peculiar People": Slave Religion and Com-*

munity Culture among the Gullahs (New York, 1988), provides background on the religious history of the Sea Island region, and Peter D. Goldsmith, *When I Rise Cryin' Holy: African-American Denominationalism on the Georgia Coast* (New York, 1989), analyzes the arrival of the Church of God in Christ on St. Simons Island.

The most complete analysis of family demography among rural southern blacks, and an excellent guide to the issues and extensive literature on this much-debated topic, is Stewart E. Tolnay, *The Bottom Rung: African American Family Life on Southern Farms* (Urbana, Ill., 1999). Loren Schweninger, *Black Property Owners in the South, 1790–1915* (Urbana, Ill., 1990), is the first comprehensive look at the accumulation of property by the South's African American middle class.

African American culture: the Sea Islands; the blues. Lawrence W. Levine, *Black Culture and Black Consciousness: Afro-American Folk Thought from Slavery to Freedom* (New York, 1977), is an outstanding survey and interpretation of a wide range of African American culture. Art Rosenbaum, *Shout Because You're Free: The African American Ring Shout Tradition in Coastal Georgia* (Athens, Ga., 1998), describes and analyzes the ring shout as practiced in perhaps the last living congregation that still performs it. Bessie Jones and Bess Lomax Hawes, *Step It Down: Games, Plays, Songs, and Stories from the Afro-American Heritage* (New York, 1972), explains children's games from the Sea Islands.

The blues has been the subject of a large and rich literature. Two surveys are William Barlow, *"Looking Up at Down": The Emergence of Blues Culture* (Philadelphia, 1989), more complete and scholarly, and Francis Davis, *The History of the Blues* (New York, 1995), a more impressionistic but still valuable account. Jeff Todd Titon, *Early Downhome Blues: A Musical and Cultural Analysis* (Urbana, Ill., 1977; 2d ed., Chapel Hill, N.C., 1994), is especially good on how the blues was a "song-producing system," and on the impact of recordings. The second edition includes a CD with recordings of several of the songs analyzed in the text. For blues in the Delta, in addition to the biographies cited above, I found most helpful David Evans, *Big Road Blues: Tradition and Creativity in the Folk Blues* (Berkeley, 1982), and Robert Palmer, *Deep Blues* (New York, 1982). Alan Lomax, *The Land Where the Blues Began* (New York, 1993), is a vivid account of Lomax's recording visits to the Delta, starting in the 1930s. As a firsthand record of musicians, musical performance, and the cultural milieu of the blues, it is irreplaceable, but it cannot always be trusted on matters of fact for anything that Lomax did not witness. Bruce Bastin, *Red River Blues* (Urbana, Ill., 1986), is a good survey of blues in the Piedmont.

World War I, the 1920s, and the New Deal. Peter Gottlieb, *Making Their Own Way: Southern Blacks' Migration to Pittsburgh, 1916–30* (Urbana, Ill., 1987), and James R. Grossman, *Land of Hope: Chicago, Black Southerners, and the Great Migration* (Chicago, 1989), are the best accounts of the great migration. Blaine Brownell, *The Urban Ethos in the South, 1920–1930* (Baton Rouge, La., 1975), is one of the few treatments of the South in the 1920s and the best on urbanization.

Morton Sosna, *In Search of the Silent South: Southern Liberals and the Race Issue* (New York, 1977), surveys the beginnings of racial liberalism in the South. The impact of the 1927 flood on the Delta is described in Pete Daniel, *Deep'n As It Come: The 1927 Mississippi River Flood* (New York, 1977), and John M. Barry, *Rising Tide: The Great Mississippi Flood of 1927 and How It Changed America* (New York, 1997), a wonderfully written account that is particularly informative on LeRoy and William Alexander Percy. Nancy MacLean, *Behind the Mask of Chivalry: The Making of the Second Ku Klux Klan* (New York, 1994), interprets the southern Klan in the 1920s based on a case study of Athens, Georgia, just north of the Piedmont region included here.

Harvard Sitkoff, *A New Deal for Blacks: The Emergence of Civil Rights as a National Issue* (New York, 1978), is an admirable synthesis that argues that the New Deal era had a significant impact on African American life and white racial attitudes. Patricia Sullivan, *Days of Hope: Race and Democracy in the New Deal Era* (Chapel Hill, N.C., 1996), makes a similar kind of argument, focusing on activists in the South itself. Ralph J. Bunche, *The Political Status of the Negro in the Age of FDR*, edited and introduced by Dewey W. Grantham (Chicago, 1973), contains Bunche's long memoranda to Gunnar Myrdal and includes much detailed information on local conditions for blacks throughout the South. Books covering the New Deal's agricultural programs and their effects on sharecroppers and poor farmers include Sidney Baldwin, *Poverty and Politics: The Rise and Decline of the Farm Security Administration* (Chapel Hill, N.C., 1968); David Eugene Conrad, *The Forgotten Farmers: The Story of Sharecroppers in the New Deal* (Urbana, Ill., 1965); Donald H. Grubbs, *Cry from the Cotton: The Southern Tenant Farmers' Union and the New Deal* (Chapel Hill, N.C., 1971); and Paul E. Mertz, *New Deal Policy and Southern Rural Poverty* (Baton Rouge, La., 1978).

INDEX

AAA. *See* Agricultural Adjustment Act of 1933

Africa, as source of black culture, 2, 183, 184, 185

African Americans: burial customs of, 334–35; as businessmen, 152–53, 178; citizenship and, 70–75, 198–202; community life of, 280–83; disfranchisement of, 106, 198–99; divorce among, 161–62; elitism among, 108, 152, 170, 179, 435; etiquette rules for, 76–77, 200, 308, 313, 326; family life of, 155–56, 396nn3,4, 397n7, 398n23, 438–39; as landowners, 4, 15–16, 22–23, 36, 47, 51, 53, 78, 103, 137, 158, 198, 282; living standards, 257–61, 310; middle class of, 4, 170, 177–83, 195, 198, 208–9, 282; mobility of, 61, 110, 137, 278; political activities of, 2, 3, 40, 103, 309; Populist attitude toward, 95–98, 107–12, 115; on race, 210–15; religion of, 166–67, 280–82, 438–39; as Republicans, 71–74, 103, 152, 326; as soldiers, 223, 227–28, 235, 264; as tenant farmers, 3, 25, 28, 29, 47, 53; as turpentine laborers, 143; as unequal citizens, 198–202, 306, 308; voting by, 56, 59, 71, 72–74, 75, 95–96, 97, 99, 100, 104, 105–6, 108, 114, 211; white murders by, 272–73; white perceptions of, 76–77, 202–9; WWI draft of, 223; as WWI veterans, 279, 326. *See also* education; Great Migration; segregation; sharecropping/sharecroppers; tenant farmers

African-American women, 143; birth rate of, 154; church work of, 281; as domestics, 158–59, 163, 398n26; education of, 180; as family heads, 160, 161; farm work of, 154–55, 161; lynching of, 208; marriages of, 161–62, 163, 164, 398n21; in middle class, 180–81, 209, 309, 311; as mistresses of white men, 163, 181, 197, 231; as NAACP members, 229, 230; as political activists, 309, 403n73; as reform activists, 180–83; sexual exploitation of, 163, 172; sociological study of, 161–62, 312; WWI work of, 224–25

African Methodist Episcopal Church, 222, 229, 402n64

African Methodist Episcopal Zion Church, 402n64

After Freedom (Powdermaker), 311–13

Agricultural Adjustment Act of 1933 (AAA), 302, 303, 305–6, 321, 322–23

Agricultural Adjustment Administration, 304

Alexander, Will, 286, 316, 320

Altamaha Rice Planters Association, 24

Altamaha River, 16, 23, 141–42; rice plantations along, 11, 21, 31, 101, 140

American Legion, 309, 334

Andrews, Frank, 222, 268

anti-enticement laws, 58, 61

Arlington plantation, 128, 130

Armistead, A. A., 201–2

Arnold, Kokomo, 251, 285, 414n29

Association of Southern Women for the Prevention of Lynching, 286

Athens, Ga., 137, 275

Atlantic coast. *See* Sea Island region

Augusta, 19, 168; black middle class in, 178, 179–80; black-white relations in, 402n65; elections in, 293, 294, 295; Jim Crow laws in, 211; lynching in, 176; manufacturing